Dictionary of Literary Biography

Dictionary of Literary Biography Documentary Series

1 *Sherwood Anderson, Willa Cather, John Dos Passos, Theodore Dreiser, F. Scott Fitzgerald, Ernest Hemingway, Sinclair Lewis,* edited by Margaret A. Van Antwerp (1982)

2 *James Gould Cozzens, James T. Farrell, William Faulkner, John O'Hara, John Steinbeck, Thomas Wolfe, Richard Wright,* edited by Margaret A. Van Antwerp (1982)

3 *Saul Bellow, Jack Kerouac, Norman Mailer, Vladimir Nabokov, John Updike, Kurt Vonnegut,* edited by Mary Bruccoli (1983)

4 *Tennessee Williams,* edited by Margaret A. Van Antwerp and Sally Johns (1984)

5 *American Transcendentalists,* edited by Joel Myerson (1988)

6 *Hardboiled Mystery Writers: Raymond Chandler, Dashiell Hammett, Ross Mac-* donald, edited by Matthew J. Bruccoli and Richard Layman (1989)

7 *Modern American Poets: James Dickey, Robert Frost, Marianne Moore,* edited by Karen L. Rood (1989)

8 *The Black Aesthetic Movement,* edited by Jeffrey Louis Decker (1991)

9 *American Writers of the Vietnam War: W. D. Ehrhart, Larry Heinemann, Tim O'Brien, Walter McDonald, John M. Del Vecchio,* edited by Ronald Baughman (1991)

10 *The Bloomsbury Group,* edited by Edward L. Bishop (1992)

11 *American Proletarian Culture: The Twenties and The Thirties,* edited by Jon Christian Suggs (1993)

12 *Southern Women Writers: Flannery O'Connor, Katherine Anne Porter, Eudora Welty,* edited by Mary Ann Wimsatt and Karen L. Rood (1994)

13 *The House of Scribner, 1846–1904,* edited by John Delaney (1996)

14 *Four Women Writers for Children, 1868–1918,* edited by Caroline C. Hunt (1996)

15 *American Expatriate Writers: Paris in the Twenties,* edited by Matthew J. Bruccoli and Robert W. Trogdon (1997)

16 *The House of Scribner, 1905–1930,* edited by John Delaney (1997)

17 *The House of Scribner, 1931–1984,* edited by John Delaney (1998)

18 *British Poets of The Great War: Sassoon, Graves, Owen,* edited by Patrick Quinn (1999)

19 *James Dickey,* edited by Judith S. Baughman (1999)

See also DLB 210, 216, 219, 222, 224, 229, 237, 247, 253, 254, 263, 269, 273, 274, 280, 284, 288, 291, 294, 298, 301, 304

Dictionary of Literary Biography Yearbooks

1980 edited by Karen L. Rood, Jean W. Ross, and Richard Ziegfeld (1981)

1981 edited by Karen L. Rood, Jean W. Ross, and Richard Ziegfeld (1982)

1982 edited by Richard Ziegfeld; associate editors: Jean W. Ross and Lynne C. Zeigler (1983)

1983 edited by Mary Bruccoli and Jean W. Ross; associate editor Richard Ziegfeld (1984)

1984 edited by Jean W. Ross (1985)

1985 edited by Jean W. Ross (1986)

1986 edited by J. M. Brook (1987)

1987 edited by J. M. Brook (1988)

1988 edited by J. M. Brook (1989)

1989 edited by J. M. Brook (1990)

1990 edited by James W. Hipp (1991)

1991 edited by James W. Hipp (1992)

1992 edited by James W. Hipp (1993)

1993 edited by James W. Hipp, contributing editor George Garrett (1994)

1994 edited by James W. Hipp, contributing editor George Garrett (1995)

1995 edited by James W. Hipp, contributing editor George Garrett (1996)

1996 edited by Samuel W. Bruce and L. Kay Webster, contributing editor George Garrett (1997)

1997 edited by Matthew J. Bruccoli and George Garrett, with the assistance of L. Kay Webster (1998)

1998 edited by Matthew J. Bruccoli, contributing editor George Garrett, with the assistance of D. W. Thomas (1999)

1999 edited by Matthew J. Bruccoli, contributing editor George Garrett, with the assistance of D. W. Thomas (2000)

2000 edited by Matthew J. Bruccoli, contributing editor George Garrett, with the assistance of George Parker Anderson (2001)

2001 edited by Matthew J. Bruccoli, contributing editor George Garrett, with the assistance of George Parker Anderson (2002)

2002 edited by Matthew J. Bruccoli and George Garrett; George Parker Anderson, Assistant Editor (2003)

Concise Series

Concise Dictionary of American Literary Biography, 7 volumes (1988–1999): *The New Consciousness, 1941–1968; Colonization to the American Renaissance, 1640–1865; Realism, Naturalism, and Local Color, 1865–1917; The Twenties, 1917–1929; The Age of Maturity, 1929–1941; Broadening Views, 1968–1988; Supplement: Modern Writers, 1900–1998.*

Concise Dictionary of British Literary Biography, 8 volumes (1991–1992): *Writers of the Middle Ages and Renaissance Before 1660; Writers of the Restoration and Eighteenth Century, 1660–1789; Writers of the Romantic Period, 1789–1832; Victorian Writers, 1832–1890; Late-Victorian and Edwardian Writers, 1890–1914; Modern Writers, 1914–1945; Writers After World War II, 1945–1960; Contemporary Writers, 1960 to Present.*

Concise Dictionary of World Literary Biography, 4 volumes (1999–2000): *Ancient Greek and Roman Writers; German Writers; African, Caribbean, and Latin American Writers; South Slavic and Eastern European Writers.*

Dictionary of Literary Biography® • Volume Three Hundred Four

Bram Stoker's *Dracula:*
A Documentary Volume

Dictionary of Literary Biography® • Volume Three Hundred Four

Bram Stoker's *Dracula:*
A Documentary Volume

Edited by
Elizabeth Miller
Memorial University of Newfoundland

A Bruccoli Clark Layman Book

Detroit • New York • San Francisco • San Diego • New Haven, Conn. • Waterville, Maine • London • Munich

Dictionary of Literary Biography
Volume 304: Bram Stoker's *Dracula:*
A Documentary Volume
Elizabeth Miller

Advisory Board
John Baker
William Cagle
Patrick O'Connor
George Garrett
Trudier Harris
Alvin Kernan

Editorial Directors
Matthew J. Bruccoli and Richard Layman

LIBRARY OF CONGRESS CATALOGING-IN-PUBLICATION DATA

Bram Stoker's Dracula: a documentary volume / edited by Elizabeth Miller.
      p. cm. — (Dictionary of literary biography ; v. 304)
"A Bruccoli Clark Layman Book."
Includes bibliographical references and index.
      ISBN 0-7876-6841-9 (hardcover : alk. paper)
      1. Stoker, Bram, 1847–1912. Dracula. 2. Horror tales, English—
      History and criticism. 3. Dracula, Count (Fictitious character) 4. Vampires
      in literature. I. Miller, Elizabeth, 1939– II. Series.

PR6037.T617D78 2005
823'.8—dc22   2004016783

Printed in the United States of America
10 9 8 7 6 5 4 3 2 1

Contents

Contents

Plan of the Series

The advisory board, the editors, and the publisher of the *Dictionary of Literary Biography* are joined in endorsing Mark Twain's declaration. The literature of a nation provides an inexhaustible resource of permanent worth. Our purpose is to make literature and its creators better understood and more accessible to students and the reading public, while satisfying the needs of teachers and researchers.

To meet these requirements, *literary biography* has been construed in terms of the author's achievement. The most important thing about a writer is his writing. Accordingly, the entries in *DLB* are career biographies, tracing the development of the author's canon and the evolution of his reputation.

The purpose of *DLB* is not only to provide reliable information in a usable format but also to place the figures in the larger perspective of literary history and to offer appraisals of their accomplishments by qualified scholars.

The publication plan for *DLB* resulted from two years of preparation. The project was proposed to Bruccoli Clark by Frederick G. Ruffner, president of the Gale Research Company, in November 1975. After specimen entries were prepared and typeset, an advisory board was formed to refine the entry format and develop the series rationale. In meetings held during 1976, the publisher, series editors, and advisory board approved the scheme for a comprehensive biographical dictionary of persons who contributed to literature. Editorial work on the first volume began in January 1977, and it was published in 1978. In order to make *DLB* more than a dictionary and to compile volumes that individually have claim to status as literary history, it was decided to organize volumes by topic, period, or

genre. Each of these freestanding volumes provides a biographical-bibliographical guide and overview for a particular area of literature. We are convinced that this organization—as opposed to a single alphabet method—constitutes a valuable innovation in the presentation of reference material. The volume plan necessarily requires many decisions for the placement and treatment of authors. Certain figures will be included in separate volumes, but with different entries emphasizing the aspect of his career appropriate to each volume. Ernest Hemingway, for example, is represented in *American Writers in Paris, 1920–1939* by an entry focusing on his expatriate apprenticeship; he is also in *American Novelists, 1910–1945* with an entry surveying his entire career, as well as in *American Short-Story Writers, 1910–1945, Second Series* with an entry concentrating on his short fiction. Each volume includes a cumulative index of the subject authors and articles.

Between 1981 and 2002 the series was augmented and updated by the *DLB Yearbooks*. There have also been nineteen *DLB Documentary Series* volumes, which provide illustrations, facsimiles, and biographical and critical source materials for figures, works, or groups judged to have particular interest for students. In 1999 the *Documentary Series* was incorporated into the *DLB* volume numbering system beginning with *DLB 210: Ernest Hemingway*.

We define literature as the *intellectual commerce of a nation:* not merely as belles lettres but as that ample and complex process by which ideas are generated, shaped, and transmitted. *DLB* entries are not limited to "creative writers" but extend to other figures who in their time and in their way influenced the mind of a people. Thus the series encompasses historians, journalists, publishers, book collectors, and screenwriters. By this means readers of *DLB* may be aided to perceive literature not as cult scripture in the keeping of intellectual high priests but firmly positioned at the center of a nation's life.

DLB includes the major writers appropriate to each volume and those standing in the ranks behind them. Scholarly and critical counsel has been sought in deciding which minor figures to include and how full their entries should be. Wherever possible, useful references are made to figures who do not warrant separate entries.

Each *DLB* volume has an expert volume editor responsible for planning the volume, selecting the figures for inclusion, and assigning the entries. Volume editors are also responsible for preparing, where appropriate, appendices surveying the major periodicals and literary and intellectual movements for their volumes, as well as lists of further readings. Work on the series as a whole is coordinated at the Bruccoli Clark Layman editorial center in Columbia, South Carolina, where the editorial staff is responsible for accuracy and utility of the published volumes.

One feature that distinguishes *DLB* is the illustration policy—its concern with the iconography of literature. Just as an author is influenced by his surroundings, so is the reader's understanding of the author enhanced by a knowledge of his environment. Therefore *DLB* volumes include not only drawings, paintings, and photographs of authors, often depicting them at various stages in their careers, but also illustrations of their families and places where they lived. Title pages are regularly reproduced in facsimile along with dust jackets for modern authors. The dust jackets are a special feature of *DLB* because they often document better than anything else the way in which an author's work was perceived in its own time. Specimens of the writers' manuscripts and letters are included when feasible.

Samuel Johnson rightly decreed that "The chief glory of every people arises from its authors." The purpose of the *Dictionary of Literary Biography* is to compile literary history in the surest way available to us—by accurate and comprehensive treatment of the lives and work of those who contributed to it.

The *DLB* Advisory Board

Introduction

While vampire lore predates Bram Stoker's *Dracula* (1897) by several hundred years, the Irish author's novel ensured the myth a permanent place in Western culture. The name "Dracula" evokes instant recognition, even among the many who have never read Stoker's book. While most people know Count Dracula from the movies rather than from the novel itself, the character has managed to insinuate himself into every aspect of contemporary culture, from Halloween costumes and comic books to chamber musicals and ballet productions.

Dracula was not, as is commonly believed, an instant success. When first published in 1897, the novel drew mixed reviews, several of which singled out such artistic flaws as mawkish sentiment, static characters, and protracted dialogue. The book had modest sales in the years that followed, its popularity not hitting full stride until well after Stoker's death in 1912, primarily as a result of the successful run of a stage adaptation on Broadway in the late 1920s, followed by the blockbuster movie version (starring Bela Lugosi as Count Dracula) released in 1931 by Universal Studios. In the academic community the book was virtually ignored, or at best dismissed as a second-rate horror story by a third-rate author. This situation changed in the 1970s. That *Dracula* began to draw serious attention from scholars was owing in large part to two factors: the postmodernist challenge to the traditional literary canon, accompanied by a reluctance to elevate one type of literature over another; and the popularity of psychoanalytic criticism.

Early scholars of Stoker's novel approached it cautiously. In his 1972 essay "*Dracula:* Bram Stoker's Spoiled Masterpiece" Royce MacGillivray wrote, "I think I can show that *Dracula* is substantial enough to deserve the attention of scholars." In 1983 Franco Moretti noted in *Signs Taken for Wonders: Essays in the Sociology of Literary Forms* that "Only a few years ago, to write about *Dracula* meant being taken for an eccentric loafer, and one's main worry was to prove that one's work was legitimate." That same year Oxford University Press published an edition of *Dracula* as the one hundredth title in the World's Classics series. In the introduction to the Oxford edition A. N. Wilson condescendingly remarks that *Dracula* "is patently not a great work of literature. The writing is of a powerful, workaday sensationalist kind. No one in their right mind would think of Stoker as a 'great writer.'" Given the inclusion of the novel in a series devoted to the "classics," Wilson begrudgingly concedes that *Dracula* is a "second-rate classic, for reasons which can be best discerned by looking at the vast sub-culture which the book has inspired."

Although one still encounters some reluctance to take the novel seriously, *Dracula* has been investigated since the 1970s by a wide range of researchers, scholars, and aficionados from disparate fields. Their works include biographies of Stoker, annotated editions of the novel (one of which boasts 3,500 annotations), analyses of the influences that shaped the text (biographical, historical, folkloric, and contextual), accounts of the far-reaching impact of the novel (especially on fiction and cinema), and a range of critical interpretations of the text itself. Scholarly interest has gone beyond *Dracula* into the area of the vampire legend, with several studies focusing on a disparate range of subjects from ancient vampire lore to the underground vampire community in contemporary America.

Given the plethora of books, articles, and documentaries about *Dracula,* one might well ask why a new volume is deemed necessary. One reason is that no existing study of the novel encompasses the entire range of its pretextual, textual, and posttextual stages. *DLB 304: Bram Stoker's* Dracula: *A Documentary Volume* brings together a comprehensive collection of primary and secondary materials on all three. This book has a second objective. Any scholar or researcher working on the novel is forced to navigate around the misconceptions and misinformation that have permeated every aspect of the subject, from biographies of Stoker to studies of *Dracula.* The popularity of the novel has had a negative consequence: the dissemination of an unsettling amount of unreliable information. The problem is pervasive; the perpetrators range from casual writers who seem interested only in capitalizing on a subject that "sells," to serious scholars whose works are considered authoritative texts. Conjectures and inaccuracies are accepted as facts, and the errors are rapidly compounded in subsequent studies. Consequently, misconceptions, contradictory findings, overstatements, fabricated "evidence" for literary theories, and the like have taken shape. To rectify this situation, this volume presents primary documents, many of which are not readily available to the researcher. A case in point is Stoker's working notes for *Dracula,* held by the Rosenbach Museum and Library in Philadelphia. As yet unpublished, these notes are a gold mine of information about the stages Stoker went through while preparing the book.

No novel exists in a vacuum. To begin with, *Dracula* has an author. Despite declarations by some literary scholars that the author has limited (or even no) significance, biographical information can often shed considerable light on the genesis of a novel. In the case of Stoker, the subject of the first chapter of this volume, he was, as the obituaries illustrate, far better known in his own day as Sir Henry Irving's theater manager than as a novelist. Even though there are significant gaps in the story of Stoker's life, certain aspects—notably, his Irish roots, his experiences with the theater, and the debate about the cause of his death—may have relevance for an understanding of *Dracula.*

Especially useful, given the extent to which "Dracula" has become synonymous with "vampire," is an overview of the vampire legend, provided in the second chapter. The vampire did not originate with Stoker's novel; indeed, by the time *Dracula* appeared, the vampire had firmly established itself as a literary trope. The story of this creature of the night originates in the folk legends of many cultures, although the primary influence on Stoker's conception came from central and eastern European lore. Interest in vampires came to the fore in the eighteenth century, the Age of Enlightenment, when a rash of "vampire sightings" throughout central and eastern Europe resulted in official inquiries as well as academic debates. It is hardly surprising that writers of Gothic fiction, first in Germany and later in England, gave the creature a permanent home in their imaginative works. The repulsive walking corpse of folk legend was gradually transformed into the aristocratic, Byronic seducer, primarily as a consequence of the seminal story "The Vampyre" (1819), by John William Polidori, George Gordon, Lord Byron's personal physician.

Appreciation of *Dracula* is enhanced through an awareness of its historical, literary, social, and cultural context. Chapter 3 begins with an exploration of the origins of the Gothic novel, of which *Dracula* is one of the best-known examples, followed by a consideration of the role possibly played in the shaping of *Dracula* by Irish supernatural lore and literature. Some of Stoker's other writings, both fiction and nonfiction, have con-

nections with his most famous work. But the most important biographical impact on the creation of *Dracula* resulted from Stoker's many years at London's Lyceum Theatre, working closely with the famous Shakespearean actor Irving. The influence of theater in general as well as of specific plays—notably, Johann Wolfgang von Goethe's *Faust* (1808, 1832) and several from the Shakespearean repertoire—cannot be overestimated. Then there is the wider social and cultural context. Written during the turbulent 1890s, *Dracula* can be seen to encode the fears and anxieties of late-Victorian England about such issues as atavism, criminality, the blurring of gender boundaries, and the challenges to Christian teaching posed by evolutionary theory.

In chapter 4 attention turns to the composition of *Dracula.* Pretextual stages include Stoker's working notes for the novel, a typescript (currently held by a private collector), the contract signed in 1897 with Constable of London, and a dramatic reading presented at the Lyceum Theatre just days before the publication of the novel. The most important resource is the collection of Stoker's working notes. They not only provide a unique insight into early conceptions of the plot, characters, and structure of *Dracula* but also offer a wealth of information about the sources that Stoker consulted and freely used. The notes answer many vital questions, including two that baffled scholars for some time: the source for the name "Dracula" and the inspiration for selecting Transylvania as the count's homeland.

The remarkable publication history of *Dracula* since the first Constable edition of 1897 is the subject of chapter 5. Stoker's novel has evidently never been out of print. Within fifteen years of its first appearance, it had been reprinted several times. It was published in the United States by Doubleday and McClure in 1899, abridged as a paperback in 1901, and translated into Icelandic that same year. More than two hundred subsequent editions have appeared, including several annotated texts, editions with extensive critical apparatus, and translations into dozens of foreign languages.* Abridged editions for children, graphic novels, and comic-book versions are widespread, as are prequels and sequels. The story of the infamous count from Transylvania has resurfaced in every conceivable art form.

The endurance and influence of *Dracula* is beyond dispute. Chapter 6 provides an overview of how the book has permeated modern culture. Beginning with various adaptations for stage and screen from the 1920s

---

*The quotations from *Dracula* cited throughout this volume are from the first Constable edition of 1897. Because of the many editions of the novel, quotations are identified by chapter, section title, and date, not by page number.

to the present, *Dracula* has spawned an entire subgenre of vampire literature and cinema. Dracula tourism flourishes in Romania, and Dracula societies have sprung up around the world. Critics now consider *Dracula* worthy of literary analysis, recognizing that it is a textually dense narrative that generates readings rather than closing them down. Its links with such a wide range of academic disciplines as anthropology, biology, history, law, literature, medicine, political science, psychology, religion, and sociology provide many paths for the scholar to follow. A novel once simplistically interpreted as just another morality tale about the supremacy of good over evil has been deconstructed by many as a text that challenges the dominant discourses of its time and blurs the boundaries between life and death, science and superstition, West and East, human and animal, and male and female. Chapter 6 concludes with a comprehensive survey of approaches to the novel, including biographical, narratological, psychoanalytical, Marxist, feminist, new historicist, and postcolonialist analyses.

The explosion of scholarly interest in *Dracula,* as evidenced in the checklist found at the end of this volume, is both a measure of the significant contribution of the novel to the bridging of the gap between popular and "serious" writing and an indication of the enduring power of the vampire myth that Stoker borrowed and reshaped, a legend that resonates in different ways for each generation, inviting them to confront their own fears, anxieties, and desires. *Dracula* has managed to implant itself in the collective consciousness and shows no sign of disappearing.

–Elizabeth Miller

Acknowledgments

This book was produced by Bruccoli Clark Layman, Inc. George Parker Anderson was the in-house editor.

Production manager is Philip B. Dematteis.

Administrative support was provided by Carol A. Cheschi.

Accountant is Ann-Marie Holland.

Copyediting supervisor is Sally R. Evans. The copyediting staff includes Phyllis A. Avant, Caryl Brown, Melissa D. Hinton, Philip I. Jones, Rebecca Mayo, Nadirah Rahimah Shabazz, Joshua Shaw, and Nancy E. Smith.

Pipeline manager is James F. Tidd Jr.

Editorial associate is Jessica R. Goudeau.

In-house prevetter is Catherine M. Polit.

Permissions editor is Amber L. Coker.

Layout and graphics supervisor is Janet E. Hill. The graphics staff includes Zoe R. Cook and Sydney E. Hammock.

Office manager is Kathy Lawler Merlette.

Photography editors are Mark J. McEwan and Walter W. Ross.

Digital photographic copy work was performed by Joseph M. Bruccoli.

Systems manager is Donald Kevin Starling.

Typesetting supervisor is Kathleen M. Flanagan. The typesetting staff includes Patricia Marie Flanagan and Pamela D. Norton.

Walter W. Ross is library researcher. He was assisted by the following librarians at the Thomas Cooper Library of the University of South Carolina: Jo Cottingham, interlibrary loan department; circulation department head Tucker Taylor; reference department head Virginia W. Weathers; reference department staff Laurel Baker, Marilee Birchfield, Kate Boyd, Paul Cammarata, Joshua Garris, Gary Geer, Tom Marcil, Rose Marshall, and Sharon Verba; interlibrary loan department head Marna Hostetler; and interlibrary loan staff Bill Fetty, Nelson Rivera, and Cedric Rose.

Permissions

Peter Beal / Sotheby's

Excerpts from Peter Beal, "The Original Publishing Contracts for 'Dracula'," item 100, Sotheby's catalogue, 10 July 2001. Reprinted with permission of the author.

Bedford / St. Martin's

John Paul Riquelme, "A Critical History of Dracula," in Stoker, *Dracula,* edited by Riquelme (Boston: Bedford/St. Martin's Press, 2002), pp. 409–433. Copyright © 2002 by Bedford/St. Martin's. Reprinted with permission of Bedford/St. Martin's.

Joseph S. Bierman

Excerpts from Joseph S. Bierman, "The Genesis and Dating of Dracula from Bram Stoker's Working Notes," *Notes and Queries,* 24 (1977): 39–41.

Ronald V. Borst / Hollywood Movie Posters

Illustrations on pages 298, 319, 322, 323, 325, 326, and 328; used with permission of Ronald V. Borst.

Bowling Green State University Press

Excerpt from Roxana Stuart, *Stage Blood: Vampires of the 19th Century Stage* (Bowling Green, Ohio: Bowling Green State University Press, 1994), p. 3. Reprinted with permission of the author.

Bram Stoker Estate

Excerpts from *Dracula; or, The Un-Dead: A Play in Prologue and Five Acts by Bram Stoker,* pp. 14–15, 106–107, 192–193.
  Stoker to William Gladstone, 24 May 1897, reprinted in *Journal of Dracula Studies,* 1 (1999): 48.
  Florence Stoker, foreword to first installment of *Dracula* in the June 1926 issue of *The Argosy: The World's Best Short Stories* (London).

Illustrations on pages 122, 250, and 275; used with permission of the Bram Stoker Estate.

Broadview Press

Glennis Byron, "The Degeneration of Society" and "Dracula, Science and Technology," in Stoker, *Dracula,* edited by Byron (Peterborough: Broadview, 1998), pp. 21–22, 22–23.

Stu Burns

Stu Burns, "A Short History of Vampire Folklore," published with permission of the author.

Margaret Carter

Margaret Carter, "Revamping of Dracula in Contemporary Fiction," *Journal of Dracula Studies,* 3 (2001): 15–19. Reprinted with permission of the author.

Cinema Bookshops, London

Illustrations on pages 320 and 330; used with permission.

Chris Coover

Excerpts from Chris Coover, *Bram Stoker's Dracula: The Original Typed Manuscript* (New York: Christie's, 2002), pp. 9, 15–17. Reprinted with permission of the author.

Corbis

Illustrations on pages 335, 339, and 347; used by permission of Corbis.

Richard Dalby

Excerpt from Richard Dalby, "Hall Caine," *Bram Stoker Society Journal,* 11 (1999): 24–25.
  Illustratons on pages 278 and 279; used by permission of Richard Dalby.

Cinema Bookshops, London

Illustrations on pages 320 and 330; used with permission.

Illustrations on pages 278 and 279; used by permission of Richard Dalby.

Bernard Davies

Bernard Davies, "Inspirations, Imitations, and In-Jokes in Stoker's Dracula," in *Dracula: The Shade and the Shadow,* edited by Elizabeth Miller (Westcliff-on-Sea, U.K.: Desert Island Books, 1998), pp. 131–137. Reprinted with permission of the author.

Noel Dobbs

Illustrations on pages 8, 11, and 18; used by permission of Noel Dobbs.

Duke University Press

Alexander Pope letter to Dr. William Oliver, February 1740, and Horace Walpole letter to Lady Ossory, 16 January 1786, quoted in James Twitchell, *The Living Dead: A Study of the Vampire in Romantic Literature* (Durham, N.C.: Duke University Press, 1981), pp. 8, 32.

Robert Eighteen-Bisang

Robert Eighteen-Bisang, "The First Dracula" and "Four Main Editions," revised from "Editions of Dracula," in Eighteen-Bisang and J. Gordon Melton, eds., *Dracula: A Century of Editions, Adaptations and Translations* (Santa Barbara: Transylvanian Society of Dracula, 1998). Published with permission of the author.

Illustrations on pages 257, 259, 270, 271, 272, 273, 281, 283, 285, and 287; used by permission of Robert Eighteen-Bisang.

Daniel Farson

Excerpt from Daniel Farson, *The Man Who Wrote Dracula: A Biography of Bram Stoker* (New York: St. Martin's Press, 1975), pp. 233–235.

Getty

Illustrations on pages 339 and 348; used by permission of Getty.

Peter Haining and Peter Tremayne

Excerpt from Peter Haining and Peter Tremayne, *The Un-Dead: The Legend of Bram Stoker and Dracula* (London: Constable, 1997), pp. 22–23.

Harry Ransom Humanities Research Center

Arthur Conan Doyle to Bram Stoker, 20 August 1897, Holograph. Harry Ransom Humanities Research Center, University of Texas at Austin.

Robert J. Havlik

Excerpt from Stoker, "Bram Stoker's Lecture on Abraham Lincoln," edited by Robert J. Havlik, *Irish Studies Review,* 10 (2002): 27.

Lokke Heiss

Lokke Heiss, "Madame Dracula: The Life of Emily Gerard" and "Discovery of a Hungarian *Drakula,*" published with permission of the author.

Illustration on page 183; used by permission of Lokke Heiss.

Lokke Heiss / Hungarian National Library

Illustration on page 297; used by permission of Lokke Heiss and the Hungarian National Library.

James Craig Holte

James Craig Holte, "Film Adaptations of Dracula," published with permission of the author.

William Hughes

Excerpt from William Hughes, "A Biography of Bram Stoker," in Hughes, *Bram Stoker (Abraham Stoker), 1847–1912: A Bibliography,* Victorian Fiction Research Guide, no. 25 (St. Lucia: University of Queensland, 1997), pp. 1–6. Reprinted with permission of the author.

Massimo Introvigne

Excerpt from Massimo Introvigne, "Antoine Faivre: Father of Contemporary Vampire Studies," in *Gnoses Ésotérisme & Imaginaire Symbolique: Mélanges offerts à Antoine Faivre,* edited by Richard Caron and others (Leuven: Peeters, 2001), pp. 601–602.

Irving Society

"A Brief Biography of Henry Irving," courtesy of The Irving Society, London.

Clive Leatherdale

Excerpts from Leatherdale, *Dracula, the Novel & the Legend: A Study of Bram Stoker's Gothic Masterpiece,* revised edition (Brighton, U.K.: Desert Island Books, 2001), pp. 80–82, 86–87. Reprinted with permission of the author.

Excerpt from "'Dracula's Guest' and Dracula," in *Dracula: The Shade and the Shadow,* edited by Elizabeth Miller (Westcliff-on-Sea, U.K.: Desert Island Books, 1998), pp. 143–146. Reprinted with permission of the author.

Clive Leatherdale / Desert Island Books

Illustration on page 202; used by permission of Clive Leatherdale.

Leeds University Library

Illustrations on pages 95 and 368; used by permission of the Brotherton Collection, Leeds University Library.

Jean Marigny

Report of Gerard Van Swieten to Empress Maria Theresa (1755), in Jean Marigny, ed., *Vampires: Restless Children of the Night* (New York: Harry Abrams, 1994), pp. 111–113.

Dennis McIntyre

Dennis McIntyre, "Clontarf and the Bram Stoker Heritage Centre," published with permission of the author.

Raymond McNally

Raymond McNally, "Hungarian Antidotes Against Vampires," in *A Clutch of Vampires* (New York: Warner Paperback Library, 1975), pp. 58–59.

J. Gordon Melton

Excerpts from J. Gordon Melton, "What Is a Vampire?," "Christianity and Vampires," and "Blood," in Melton, *The Vampire Book: The Encyclopedia of the Undead,* revised edition (Detroit: Visible Ink Press, 1999), pp. xx–xxi, 117–119, 53–56. Reprinted with permission of the author.

Diane Milburn

Excerpt from Diane Milburn, "'For the Dead Travel Fast': Dracula in Anglo-German Context," in Miller, *Dracula: The Shade and the Shadow,* edited by Elizabeth Miller (Westcliff-on-Sea, U.K.: Desert Island Books, 1998), pp. 43–44.

Elizabeth Miller

Elizabeth Miller, "Dracula and Shakespeare: The Count Meets the Bard," "The Icelandic Edition of Dracula," and "Shape-shifting Dracula: The Abridged Edition of 1901," revised from *Reflections on Dracula: Ten Essays* (White Rock, B.C.: Transylvania Press, 1997). Published with permission of the author.

Miller, "The Notes: An Overview," "A Dracula 'Who's Who,'" and "The Search for Castle Dracula," revised from *Dracula: Sense & Nonsense* (Westcliff-on-Sea, U.K.: Desert Island, 2000), pp. 17–21, 88–93, 156–170. Published with permission of the author.

Miller, "Filing for Divorce: Count Dracula vs Vlad the Impaler," revised from Miller, ed., *Dracula: The Shade and the Shadow,* edited by Miller (Westcliff-on-Sea, U.K.: Desert Island, 1998), pp. 165–179. Published with permission of the author.

Miller, "Typing Transylvania," "The Historical Dracula: A Brief Biography," "The Changed Ending," "Dracula: The Ever Widening Circle," "The Flaws of Dracula," and "Schizophrenic Dracula: Romania, the Media, and the World Dracula Congress," published with permission of the author.

Illustrations on pages 23, 204, 221, 223, 271, 289, 351, 353, 360, and 363; used by permission of Elizabeth Miller.

Goldie Morgentaler

Goldie Morgentaler, "Blood Transfusion in the Nineteenth Century," published with permission of the author.

Stephanie Moss

Stephanie Moss, "Bram Stoker, Henry Irving and the Late Victorian Theatre," published with permission of the author.

Munch Estate / National Gallery of Oslo

Illustration on page 29; © Munch-Museet / Munch-Ellingsen-Gruppen / BONO 2000.

Natural History

Paul Barber, "The Real Vampire: Forensic Pathology and the Lore of the Undead." With permission from *Natural History,* October 1990. Adaptation from book *Vampires, Burial, and Death: Folklore and Reality,* Yale University Press, by Paul Barber. Copyright © the American Museum of Natural History (1990).

Oscar Wilde Estate

Oscar Wilde to Florence Balcombe (five excerpted letters) and Wilde to Ellen Terry, 3 January 1881 (excerpt), in *The Letters of Oscar Wilde,* edited by Rupert Hart-Davis (New York: Harcourt, Brace & World, 1962), pp. 51, 54, 55, 74, 330–331.

   Illustration on page 17; used by permission of the Oscar Wilde Estate.

Douglas Paraschuk / Stratford Festival

Illustration on page 366; used by permission of Douglas Paraschuk.

PFD

Excerpt from Christopher Frayling, "Bram Stoker's Working Papers for Dracula." Reprinted with permission of The Peters Fraser & Dunlop Group on behalf of Christopher Frayling © Frayling, ed., *Vampyres: Lord Byron to Count Dracula* (London: Faber & Faber, 1992), pp. 303–316.

Albert Power

Excerpt from Albert Power, "Bram Stoker and the Tradition of Irish Supernatural Fiction," in *Dracula: Celebrating 100 Years,* edited by Leslie Shepard and Power (Dublin: Mentor Press, 1997), pp. 58–67. Reprinted with permission of the author.

Katherine Ramsland

Excerpt from Katherine Ramsland, *The Science of Vampires* (New York: Berkley, 2002), pp. 116–118.

Robert A. Freedman Dramatic Agency

Excerpts from *Dracula: The Vampire Play–Dracula: The Ultimate, Illustrated Edition of the World-Famous Vampire Play,* edited by David J. Skal (New York: St. Martin's Press, 1993).

Rosenbach Museum & Library, Philadelphia

Illustrations on pages 141, 170, 172, 174, 176, 178, 180, 190, 194, 198, 207, 219, and 220; used by permission of the Rosenbach Museum & Library.

Victor Sage

Victor Sage, "The Gothic Novel," in *The Handbook to Gothic Literature,* edited by Marie Mulvey-Roberts (New York: New York University Press, 1998), pp. 81–88. Reprinted with permission of the author.

Scarsborough Borough Council

Illustration on page 229; used by permission of the Scarsborough Borough Council.

Carol A. Senf

Carol A. Senf, "The Literary Vampire Before Dracula," published with permission of the author.

Leslie Shepard

Leslie Shepard, "A Note on the Death Certificate of Bram Stoker," in *Dracula: Celebrating 100 Years,* pp. 19–180. Reprinted with permission of the author.

   Shepard, "The Library of Bram Stoker," in *Bram Stoker's Dracula: Sucking Through the Century, 1897–1997,* edited by Carol M. Davison (Toronto: Dundurn, 1997), pp. 411–414. Reprinted with permission of the author.

   Illustrations on page 27 and 148; used by permission of Leslie Shepard.

David J. Skal

David J. Skal, "'His Hour upon the Stage': Theatrical Adaptations of Dracula," in Stoker, *Dracula,* edited by Nina Auerbach and Skal (New York: Norton, 1997), pp. 371–381. Reprinted with permission of the author.

   Illustrations on pages 20, 91, 269, 302, 316, and 354; used by permission of David J. Skal.

Spiderweb Art Gallery

Illustrations on page 293; used by permission of Spiderweb Art Gallery.

Sylvia Starshine

Excerpts from introduction to *Dracula; or, The Un-Dead: A Play in Prologue and Five Acts by Bram Stoker,* edited by Sylvia Starshine (Nottingham: Pumpkin, 1997), pp. xii–xiii, xx–xxi, xxv, xxvii–xxxiii, xxxiii–xxxiv. Reprinted with permission of the author.

The Times

"Immigrant's Fears of Vampires Led to Death," *The Times* (London), 9 January 1973, p. 4.

Transylvanian Journal

Excerpt from Massimo Introvigne, "Satanism Scares and Vampirism," *Transylvanian Journal,* 2 (Spring–Summer 1996): 39.

Jörg Waltje

Jörg Waltje, "Filming Dracula: Vampires, Genre, and Cinematography," *Journal of Dracula Studies,* 2 (2000): 24–33. Reprinted with permission of the author.

Jeanne Keyes Yongson

Excerpt from Jeanne Keyes Yongson, "Nosing Around Nosferatu," in *Dracula: Celebrating 100 Years,* edited by Leslie Shepard and Albert Power (Dublin: Mentor Press, 1997) pp. 120–125. Reprinted with permission of the author.

Illustrations on pages 9, 10, 12, 13, 20, 25, 131, 232, 252, 254, 300, 304, 318, and 356; used by permission of Jeanne Keyes Yongson.

Bram Stoker's *Dracula:*
A Documentary Volume

Dictionary of Literary Biography

Publications by Bram Stoker

See also the Stoker entries in *DLB 36: British Novelists, 1890–1929: Modernists; DLB 70: British Mystery Writers, 1860–1919;* and *DLB 178: British Fantasy and Science-Fiction Writers Before World War I.*

BOOKS: *The Necessity for Political Honesty,* University of Dublin, College Historical Society (Dublin: James Charles, 1872);

The Duties of Clerks of Petty Sessions in Ireland (Dublin: Printed for the author by J. Falconer, 1879);

Under the Sunset (London: Sampson Low, Marston, Searle & Rivington, 1882 [i.e., 1881])–comprises "Under the Sunset," "The Rose Prince," "The Invisible Giant," "The Shadow Builder," "How 7 Went Mad," "Lies and Lilies," "The Castle of the King," and "The Wondrous Child";

A Glimpse of America: A Lecture Given at the London Institution, 28th December, 1885 (London: Sampson Low, Marston, 1885);

The Snake's Pass (London: Sampson Low, Marston, Searle & Rivington, 1891); [i.e., 1890]; New York: Harper, 1891 [i.e., 1890]);

The Man from Shorrox' (New York: De Vinne, 1894);

Crooken Sands (New York: De Vinne, 1894);

The Watter's Mou' (New York: De Vinne, 1894; London: Constable, 1895);

The Shoulder of Shasta (London: Constable, 1895);

Dracula (London: Constable, 1897; New York: Doubleday, McClure, 1899);

Miss Betty (London: Pearson, 1898);

Sir Henry Irving and Miss Ellen Terry In Robespierre, Merchant of Venice, The Bells, Nance Oldfield, The Amber Heart, Waterloo, etc. (New York: Doubleday, McClure, 1899);

The Mystery of the Sea (New York: Doubleday, Page, 1902; London: Heinemann, 1902);

The Jewel of Seven Stars (London: Heinemann, 1903; New York: Harper, 1904);

The Man (London: Heinemann, 1905; New York: Century, 1905);

Personal Reminiscences of Henry Irving, 2 volumes (London: Heinemann, 1906; New York: Macmillan, 1906);

Lady Athlyne (London: Heinemann, 1908; New York: Reynolds, 1908);

Snowbound: The Record of a Theatrical Touring Party (London: Collier, 1908);

The Lady of the Shroud (London: Heinemann, 1909);

Famous Imposters (London: Sidgwick & Jackson, 1910; New York: Sturgis & Walton, 1910);

The Lair of the White Worm (London: Rider, 1911); republished as *The Garden of Evil* (New York: Paperback Library, 1966);

Dracula's Guest and Other Weird Stories (London: Routledge, 1914; New York: Hillman-Curl, 1937)–comprises "Dracula's Guest," "The Judge's House," "The Squaw," "The Secret of the Growing Gold," "A Gipsy Prophecy," "The Coming of Abel Behenna," "The Burial of the Rats," "A Dream of Red Hands," and "Crooken Sands";

Dracula: or The Un-Dead: A Play in Prologue and Five Acts, edited and annotated by Sylvia Starshine (Nottingham: Pumpkin Books, 1997).

Other Publications:

POEM

"One Thing Needful," in *A Volunteer Haversack* (Edinburgh: Printed for the Queen's Rifle Volunteer Brigade: The Royal Scots, 1902), pp. 173–174.

FICTION

"The Crystal Cup," *London Society,* 22 (1872): 228–235;

"The Primrose Path. A Serial in Ten Chapters," *The Shamrock,* 12 (1875): 289–293, 312–317, 330–334, 345–349, 360–365;

"Buried Treasures. A Serial in Four Chapters," *The Shamrock,* 12 (1875): 376–379, 403–406;

"The Chain of Destiny. A Serial in Ten Chapters," *The Shamrock,* 12 (1875): 446–449, 498–499, 514–516, 530–533, 546–548;

"Our New House," *The Theatre Annual for 1886,* pp. 71–78;

"The Dualitists; or, the Death Doom of the Double Born," *The Theatre Annual for 1887,* pp. 18–29;

"The Judge's House," *Illustrated Sporting and Dramatic News,* 2 December 1891, pp. 10–11;

"The Secret of the Growing Gold," *Black and White,* 3 (23 January 1892): 118–121;

"Lord Castleton Explains," *The Gentlewoman,* 4 (30 January 1892): 138–139;

"The Squaw," *Illustrated Sporting and Dramatic News,* 2 December 1893, pp. 24–25;

"A Dream of Red Hands," *The Sketch,* 6 (11 July 1894): 578–580;

"The Red Stockade: A Story Told by the Old Coastguard," *Cosmopolitan Magazine,* 17 (October 1894): 619–630;

"The 'Eroes of the Thames: The Story of a Frustrated Advertisement," *The Royal Magazine* (20 October 1908): 566–570;

"The Way of Peace," *Everybody's Story Magazine* (December 1909): 204–209;

"Greater Love," *The London Magazine,* 33 (1914–1915): 161–168.

NONFICTION

"The American Audience," *Fortnightly Review,* 37 (1885): 197–201;

"Actor-Managers," *The Nineteenth Century,* 27 (June 1890): 1040–1051;

"Dramatic Criticism," *The North American Review,* 158 (March 1894): 325–331;

"The Art of Ellen Terry," *Cosmopolitan,* 31 (July 1901): 241–250;

The Works of Hall Caine, 10 volumes, introductions by Stoker (London: Heinemann, 1905);

"Henry Irving's Fight for Fame," *Success Magazine* (February 1906): 87–88, 126;

"Fifty Years on the Stage. An Appreciation of Miss Ellen Terry by Bram Stoker," *Graphic,* 28 April 1906, p. 537;

"The Great White Fair in Dublin," *The World's Work,* 9 (May 1907): 570–576;

"The World's Greatest Ship-Building Yard. Impressions of a Visit to Messrs. Harland and Wolff's Ship-Building Yards at Belfast," *The World's Work,* 9 (May 1907): 647–650;

"Sir Arthur Conan Doyle Tells of His Career and Work, His Sentiments Towards America, and His Approaching Marriage," *The World* (28 July 1907);

"The Tendency of the Modern Stage. A Talk with Sir W. S. Gilbert on Things Theatrical," *Daily Chronicle,* 2 January 1908, p. 8;

"Mr. Winston Churchill Talks of His Hopes, His World, and His Ideals to Bram Stoker," *Daily Chronicle,* 15 January 1908, p. 8;

"How Mr. Pinero Writes Plays, told in an Interview by Bram Stoker," *Daily Chronicle,* 15 February 1908, p. 8;

"The Question of a National Theatre," *The Nineteenth Century,* 63 (May 1908): 734–742;

"Mr. DeMorgan's Habits of Work. The Career of a Man Who Began to Write After He Was Sixty-Four Years Old," *The World's Work,* 16 (July 1908): 10337–10342;

"The Censorship of Fiction," *The Nineteenth Century and After,* 64 (September 1908): 479–487;

"Americans as Actors," *Fortnightly Review,* 91 (February 1909): 243–252;

"Dead-Heads," *Fortnightly Review,* 92 (October 1909): 646–658;

"The American 'Tramp' Question and the Old English Vagrancy Laws," *North American Review,* 190 (1909): 605–614;

"The Censorship of Stage Plays," *The Nineteenth Century and After,* 66 (December 1909): 974–989;

"Irving and Stage Lighting," *The Nineteenth Century and After,* 69 (May 1911): 903–912;

"Bram Stoker's Lecture on Abraham Lincoln," edited by Robert J. Havlik, *Irish Studies Review,* 10 (2002): 5–27.

Bram Stoker: A Chronology

1847   Abraham "Bram" Stoker, the third of seven children, is born on 8 November in Clontarf, a seaside suburb of Dublin, Ireland, to Abraham Stoker, a Dublin civil servant, and Charlotte Thornley Stoker, a social activist from Sligo.

1860s   Attends Trinity College, Dublin. He excels in athletics and serves as president of the Philosophical Society; an active debater, he defends the poetry of Walt Whitman against fierce criticism.

1870   Graduates from Trinity College and is appointed to a civil-service post at Dublin Castle.

1871   Begins writing theater reviews for the *Dublin Mail.*

1872   Publication of first short story, "The Crystal Cup," in *London Society* magazine.

1876   Reviews Henry Irving's performance in a Dublin production of *Hamlet;* their lifelong close friendship begins. Stoker's father dies in Naples.

1877   Promoted to the office of inspector of petty sessions.

1878   Accepts Irving's offer of a position as acting manager of the Lyceum Theatre in London. In December, Stoker marries Florence Balcombe, a noted beauty who had been courted by Oscar Wilde, at St. Ann's Church, Dublin.

1879   Publication of first book, *The Duties of Clerks of Petty Sessions in Ireland,* which he later referred to as "dry as dust." The Stokers' only child, Irving Noel Thornley Stoker, is born in December; as an adult, Noel dropped the name "Irving" likely out of resentment of the actor's demands on his father's time.

1881   Publication of *Under the Sunset,* a collection of stories, some with gothic themes, dedicated to his son. Stoker receives the Bronze Medal of the Royal Humane Society for attempting to save the life of a suicide.

1883   Undertakes the first of several tours to North America with the Lyceum Theatre Company. During these visits, Stoker befriends Walt Whitman and Mark Twain.

1885   Irving plays Mephistopheles on the Lyceum stage, a role that likely helped shape Stoker's conception of Count Dracula.

1886   Publication of *A Glimpse of America,* praised by explorer Henry Stanley as containing "more information about America than any other book that has ever been written." Stoker later incorporates an American character (Quincey Morris) into *Dracula.*

1888   Jack the Ripper terrorizes London. In his preface to the Icelandic edition of *Dracula,* Stoker compares the vampire's crimes to the murders of Jack the Ripper.

1890   Called to the bar in London. On 8 March he begins making notes for the novel that becomes *Dracula;* spends summer in Whitby, Yorkshire, where he first encounters the name "Dracula" in a library book. Publication of Stoker's first novel, *The Snake's Pass,* an Irish romantic tale of bogs, superstitions, and buried treasure.

1892	Completes a chapter outline for the novel, setting the narrative in the following year. He hears Tennyson reading his poetry on a recorded cylinder, a device he later uses in *Dracula*.
1893	Spends the first of several summers in Cruden Bay, Scotland, where he does much of his writing, most likely including *Dracula*.
1894	Publication of three short novels: *The Man from Shorrox'*, *Crooken Sands*, and *The Watter's Mou'*.
1895	Publication of *The Shoulder of Shasta*, a novel set in America. Stoker's brother William Thornley Stoker, a distinguished physician, and Irving are both knighted by Queen Victoria.
1897	Publication of *Dracula* by Constable in London in late May; it is preceded by a dramatic reading of an abridged version, titled *Dracula: or The Un-Dead*, on 18 May.
1898	Publication of *Miss Betty*, a romance called by one reviewer "a pretty little tale of a woman's devotion."
1899	Publication of the first American edition of *Dracula* by Doubleday and McClure.
1901	Publication of first foreign edition of *Dracula* (abridged) in Icelandic, for which Stoker wrote the preface. Stoker's mother dies.
1902	Publication of *The Mystery of the Sea*, a novel set in Cruden Bay.
1903	Publication of *The Jewel of Seven Stars*, a novel based on Egyptology.
1905	Publication of *The Man*, a romance about a forthright woman. Irving dies.
1906	Suffers his first stroke. Publication of *Personal Reminiscences of Henry Irving*, the book for which he is best known among his contemporaries.
1908	Publication of *Lady Athlyne*, a romantic novel, and *Snowbound*, a volume of short stories about a traveling theater company.
1909	Publication of *The Lady of the Shroud*, a novel with elements of the supernatural and the occult.
1910	Suffers his second stroke. Publication of *Famous Imposters*.
1911	Publication of last novel, *The Lair of the White Worm*, a dark tale of a giant worm that terrorizes the countryside of Yorkshire.
1912	Dies in London on 20 April. Cremated, his ashes are interred at Golders Green.
1913	Stoker's books, presentation copies, and manuscripts are auctioned at Sotheby's in London. Included are the working papers for *Dracula*, now located at the Rosenbach Museum in Philadelphia.
1914	Publication by Florence Stoker of *Dracula's Guest and Other Weird Stories*.

I. Bram Stoker, the Man and the Writer

The Author of *Dracula*

Bram Stoker's life has been eclipsed by the fame of his fictional creation Count Dracula. The titles of all four full-length biographies of Stoker refer to his most famous work: Harry Ludlam's A Biography of *Dracula:* The Life Story of Bram Stoker *(1962), Daniel Farson's* The Man Who Wrote *Dracula:* A Biography of Bram Stoker *(1975), Barbara Belford's* Bram Stoker: A Biography of the Author of *Dracula (1996) and Paul Murray's* From the Shadow of *Dracula:* A Life of Bram Stoker *(2004). Although critics have recently begun to examine Stoker's lesser-known works,* Dracula *(1897) remains the focus of critical and scholarly interest.*

A review of what is known of Stoker's life provides a useful starting point for approaching the novel that has become a permanent part of Western culture.

A Biography of Bram Stoker
William Hughes

Abraham "Bram" Stoker was born at 15, The Crescent, Clontarf, County Dublin, on 8 November 1847. He was a sickly child, who, by his own admission, was not expected to live.[1] His father, Abraham senior, was a member of the British civil administration in Ireland, a clerk based in the Chief Secretary's Office of Dublin Castle. Mundane as this post may sound, he was confident enough to describe his profession as simply "Gentleman" when completing his son's baptismal certificate at the Anglican parish church of St. John the Baptist, Clontarf, on 3 December 1847.[2] Presumably because of his unspecified illness, Abraham junior was educated first at home, and subsequently at a small private day school. From this basic information, and from the cultural development of education in the period, it may be deduced that the author's pre-university experience was one which schooled him in the discourses and social graces which linked the Anglicised, Irish Gentleman to his English counterpart–Protestantism, the Classics, and the physical culture of a generation influenced by Carlyle and Muscular Christianity.[3] It is also worth noting that, despite the financial difficulties that frequently beset large families, Stoker's brothers followed their father into respectable professional careers: William, George and

Bram Stoker (Laurence Irving, Henry Irving, the Actor and His World, *1951; Thomas Cooper Library, University of South Carolina)*

Richard studied medicine; Tom joined the Indian Civil Service. Bram himself was called to the English Bar in 1890.

On 2 November 1864, at the age of sixteen, Stoker matriculated at Trinity College, Dublin. His college career does not appear to have been academically distinguished. Despite his later claim that he "had got Honours in pure Mathematics," his name does not appear amongst those who achieved the distinctions of Moderations or Respondency.[4] Stoker, still styled as Abraham, received the degree of Bachelor of Arts at the Spring Commencements on 1 March 1870, and was admitted to the degree of Master in Arts, as was customary at Trinity College, without further study on 9 February 1875.

Abraham and Charlotte Stoker, Bram's parents. Twenty years younger than her husband, Charlotte bore seven children and was a social crusader for the poor (courtesy of Noel Dobbs).

The author did, however, distinguish himself in other areas of College life, advancing these achievements as integral, rather than supplementary, to the more formal requirements of his scholarly environment. The influence of Carlyle and Kingsley is apparent in the rhetoric of Stoker's own assessment of his university career:

> In my College days I had been Auditor of the Historical Society–a post which corresponds to the Presidency of the Union in Oxford or Cambridge–and had got medals, or certificates, for History, Composition and Oratory. I had been President of the Philosophical Society; had got Honours in pure mathematics. I had won numerous silver cups for races of various kinds. I had played for years in the University football team, where I had received the honour of a "cap"! I was physically immensely strong. In fact I feel justified in saying I represented in my own person something of that aim of university education *mens sana in corpore sano*.[5]

This phase of Stoker's life has again been the subject of comparatively little critical attention. Where mod-

ern scholarship does touch upon the author's College career, it is normally in connection with his defence of the poetry of Walt Whitman in the debating chamber.[6] An investigation of Stoker's involvement in the two College debating societies prior to and following his graduation in 1870, however, provides both a fascinating insight into the student preoccupations of the period, and a reminder again of the homosocial, gentlemen's club-like tenor of College life in the nineteenth century.

Written minutes for the Dublin University Philosophical Society are extant only from the 1867–8 session. These record that "Mr A. Stoker" read a paper entitled "Sensationalism; in Fiction and Society" at a general meeting held on 7 May 1868. This paper, Stoker's first, with his subsequent addresses entitled "Shelley" and "The Means of Improvement in Composition" have not survived. The Philosophical Society did, however, authorize and fund the publication of "The Necessity for Political Honesty," delivered at the opening meeting of 1872. In the debating chamber of the rival Historical Society, the author's career is, again, well docu-

The house in Clontarf (Dublin) where Stoker was born (photograph by Jeanne Youngson)

Clontarf and the Bram Stoker
Heritage Centre

Clontarf is a seaside suburban area on the north eastern side of Dublin City, just three miles from the city centre. The name Clontarf is an ancient one and has been handed down in writing for over twelve hundred years. It derives from the original Gaelic name Cluain Tarbh–the meadow of the bull.

It is famous, historically, as the site of the epic Battle of Clontarf in 1014 when the Irish High King Brian Boru defeated the Vikings to end their political power in Ireland. Other major events in Irish history with a strong Clontarf connection include Daniel O'Connell and the Repeat Movement (1843), James Stephens and the I.R.B. (1866), the Howth Gun Running (1914), and the role of Clontarf Town Hall in the Irish Rebellion of Easter 1916. Among Clontarf's historical treasures are Clontarf Cemetery and Church

ruin (dating back to 550 A.D.), Clontarf Castle (dating from 1172), Lord Charlemont's Sicilian Casino (completed in 1773). More modern are St. Anne's Estate (former home of Guinness brewing family) and the Bull Island (a biosphere reserve). Clontarf has six churches, all worthy of a visit.

Today Clontarf is renowned as the birth place of Abraham (Bram) Stoker, the author of the international best-selling novel, the immortal gothic tale *Dracula*. An annual Bram Stoker International Summer School is held in Clontarf each year. Visitors to the area can now visit the splendid Bram Stoker Heritage Centre.

–Dennis McIntyre, Bram Stoker
Heritage Centre, Clontarf

Ruins of church in Clontarf where Bram Stoker was baptized (photograph by Jeanne Youngson)

mented. It appears that whatever his personal politics, he adopted a solidly conservative stance in debate, speaking against motions including "That Vote by Ballot is Desirable," "That the Social and Political Disabilities of Women Ought to be Removed," and "That England Should Prepare for an early Emancipation of Her Colonies." Significantly, given his later contributions to the London journal *The Nineteenth Century,* he is also listed as a speaker against a motion, "That the Novels of the Nineteenth Century are More Immoral in their Tendency than those of the Eighteenth." The College debating chamber thus appears to be the forum in which the author won his "medals, or certificates," gaining two silver medals from the Historical Society and a Certificate in Oratory from the Philosophical Society between 1869 and 1870.[7]

Stoker's career as a university athlete was equally distinguished. The author is listed as a mem-

ber of the Dublin University Football Club Second Fifteen for the 1867–8 and 1868–9 seasons. In the lists for the 1869–70 and 1870–1 seasons he is noted as a member of the First Fifteen. Caps were awarded for distinguished play in College Rugby Football from 1867, although all games were played within the College–against the Rowing Club or the Law School, for example–until the 1871–2 season. Stoker, it appears, never became the Dublin equivalent of an Oxbridge "Blue."[8] The "numerous silver cups" mentioned by the author in *Personal Reminiscences of Henry Irving* were awarded for his victories in the Dublin University Foot Races and Seven Mile Walking Race of 1866 and 1868 respectively, and for his success at weightlifting in the Dublin University Gymnasium in 1870.[9]

Bram Stoker, it appears, was a popular, willing and able participant in the physical and overwhelmingly masculine culture of Trinity College in the

Bram Stoker at age seven (courtesy of Noel Dobbs)

Childhood Illness

In my babyhood I used, I understand, to be often at the point of death. Certainly till I was about seven years old I never knew what it was to stand upright. I was naturally thoughtful and the leisure of long illness gave opportunity for many thoughts which were fruitful according to their kind in later years.

–Bram Stoker, *Personal Reminiscences of Henry Irving,*
volume 1 (New York & London:
Macmillan, 1906), p. 31

1860s and 1870s.[10] His experiences at Trinity, it may be argued, concretized the competitive and intellectual attitudes instilled into him during his youth. His graduation was thus another milestone in a process of acculturation which prepared the individual for acceptance within a society of gentlemen sharing similar aspirations and common standards of behavior. These standards, their relevance to the relative positions of the sexes in Western society and their apparent ability to transcend the boundaries of race and nationality, were to inform Stoker's writings from *A Glimpse of America* to *The Lair of the White Worm.*

The author's success in mobilizing the discourses of the Anglo-Irish ascendancy would appear to be affirmed by his appointment to a Civil Service post within Dublin Castle in 1870, and again by his subsequent promotion to the office of Inspector of Petty Sessions in 1877. In this latter position, Stoker was to research and complete his first published work, *Duties of Clerks of Petty Sessions in Ireland,* a reference book for civil servants working within the Irish legal system. It is during this period, also, that the author's political beliefs appear to have crystallized, leading him by 1880 to a belief in the principles of Irish Home Rule, and eventually to membership of the National Liberal Club in London.[11] There is no evidence to suggest that Stoker ever viewed himself as part of a political or cultural consciousness beyond that possible within an integrated United Kingdom. This apparent lack of an explicit commitment to anything beyond a Liberal conception of Home Rule, coupled with a presumed literary alignment with what W. J. McCormack calls "the London exiles . . . as against the home-based revivalists,"[12] has ensured Stoker's exclusion from the heavily-politicized Irish canon of modern criticism. The perception of the author upon which this exclusion is based, however, points again to the nature of Stoker's education and social training—both of which, it may be argued, minimized the disruption of his transition from Dublin society to that of London.

During the early years of his service within Dublin Castle Stoker began to draft a series of short stories, though with little immediate success. Though he published a fantasy, "The Crystal Cup," in a London-based periodical in 1872, a letter by the author dated 6 October 1874 reveals that another short story, "Jack Hammon's Vote," (now lost) was refused in turn by *The Cornhill Magazine, Macmillan's Magazine, Temple Bar* and *Blackwood's.* The author was, however, to successfully place three serial

Dublin Castle, where Stoker worked from 1870 to 1878 as a clerk in the civil service, before he met Henry Irving and became his business manager (photograph by Jeanne Youngson)

pieces with *The Shamrock,* a Dublin weekly, in 1875. Stoker met with a more favorable reception as the anonymous (and, for the most part, unpaid) dramatic critic for the *Dublin Mail,* from 1871.[13] His experiences as a critic, with the social and political contacts made through his continuing membership in the Philosophical and Historical Societies, appear to have served as the qualifications which obtained for him the editorship of a short-lived evening periodical, *The Irish Echo,* first published on 6 November 1873.[14] He was to resign his editorship four months later, as the periodical, by then renamed *The Halfpenny Press,* ran into financial difficulties. Stoker was, though, to return to commercial periodical writing. He was an occasional contributor to the London *Daily Telegraph,* specializing in the public activities of well-known theatrical personalities, although his motives here appear to have been linked to publicity and to his social connection with the editor, rather than pecuniary gain. He supplied articles on the theatre and literature to the London monthly *The Nineteenth Century* between 1890 and 1911—again, it might appear, partly as a consequence of his friendship with the journal's editor, James Knowles. With the publisher William Heinemann he was a partner in the latter's venture into English-language publishing for the Continental Market, a rival to the Tauchnitz series marketed under the imprint of Heinemann and Balestier.[15] Finally, during his later years, when his finances were at a low ebb, he supplied a series of illustrated interviews, again with old associates, for a popular London newspaper, *The Daily Chronicle.*

Stoker's residence on Kildare Street, Dublin, with a commemorative plaque. This was his first bachelor residence after his parents moved to France in 1872, following his father's retirement (photograph by Jeanne Youngson).

Much of Stoker's non-fictional writing, as has been noted, concerned the theatre. The central figure in his theatrical cosmology was the Victorian actor-manager, Henry (later, Sir Henry) Irving. Stoker's description of his first protracted encounter with the man who was to become his professional and social associate is frequently quoted but bears repeating. At an after-dinner gathering of a dozen men, Irving recited Thomas Hood's dramatic narrative poem *The Dream of Eugene Aram,* physically collapsing at its climax. Stoker confides:

> As to its effect, I had no adequate words. I can only say that after a few seconds of stony silence following his collapse I burst out into something like a violent fit of hysterics. . . . In those moments of our mutual emotion he too had found a friend and knew it. Soul had looked into soul! From that hour began a friendship as profound, as close, as lasting as can be between two men.[16]

It has been argued that Stoker's perception of his relationship with Irving differed markedly from that perceived by the actor.[17] The author's insistence upon the strongly homosocial bond which, he argued, persisted between himself and Irving is, however, mirrored in at least two of the obituaries that followed Stoker's death. One in *The New York Times* noted that:

> As the *fidus Achates* of Henry Irving, and later as his Boswell, Bram Stoker, who has just died in London, gained international fame. . . . Irving placed implicit confidence in Stoker's judgement and business sense, while Stoker looked upon Irving as the only supremely great man in the world.[18]

Elsewhere, the Manx novelist, Hall Caine, a close friend of both men, argued in favor of the author's version of the relationship:

Sir Thornley Stoker, Bram's oldest brother. He was knighted in 1895
for his distinguished service in medicine, a profession two of
his brothers also practiced (Illustrograph *[Dublin],*
Midsummer 1895; Barbara Belford, Bram Stoker:
A Biography of the Author of Dracula,
1996; Elizabeth Miller Collection).

Much has been said of his relation to Henry Irving, but I
wonder how many were really aware of the whole depth
and significance of that association. Bram seemed to give
up his life to it. . . . I say without any hesitation that never
have I seen, never do I expect to see, such absorption of
one man's life in the life of another.[19]

It would seem, therefore, that the public viewed
Stoker largely as an appendage of Irving, or of the
Lyceum Theatre, rather than as an individual in his
own right.[20] A report of Stoker's attempt to rescue a
Thames suicide, for example, describes the author as
Irving's "faithful Bram."[21] Stoker appears to have
fostered this impression so that, as Ellen Terry con-
cludes, the author in his *Personal Reminiscences of Henry
Irving* "described everyone connected with the
Lyceum except himself."[22]

Irving invited Stoker to become his Acting
Manager following a visit to Dublin towards the
close of 1878. Stoker's acceptance of Irving's offer

caused him to bring forward the date of his marriage
to Florence Balcombe, who numbered Oscar Wilde
among her former suitors.[23] The author was to retain
his position, which made him Irving's accountant,
secretary, and public spokesman for twenty-seven
years, until the actor's death in 1905. There is evidence to suggest that Stoker wrote at least some of
the speeches delivered by the actor between 1878 and
1905. A letter written by L. F. Austin, Irving's private secretary, dated simply March 1885 reveals further that Stoker was the author of an article
published that year under Irving's name in *The Fortnightly Review*.[24] Stoker was the major practical organizer of the Lyceum Company's provincial seasons,
and of eight tours made in the United States. Eight of
the author's novels, including *Dracula,* were therefore
completed on a part-time basis during Stoker's working lifetime. Irving's death, which came at the end of
a long period of physical debilitation and financial
hardship, signaled the beginning of what may be
read as a consequent decline in Stoker's personal fortunes. Quite simply, the author had made little professional or financial provision for a life outside of
the theatre. Stoker's health, also, was by this time in
visible decline. It has been stated that he was a sufferer from Bright's Disease (nephritis) as early as
1897.[25] At the beginning of 1906 the author also
experienced a paralytic stroke which prostrated him
for some months, and left him with disturbed vision.
He appears to have experienced a further collapse,
which he explains as the consequence of overwork,
in 1909 or 1910.[26]

It was during the forced convalescence following his stroke that Stoker researched and wrote *Personal Reminiscences of Henry Irving,* the biography for
which the author's contemporaries believed he
would be chiefly remembered. Though this work,
which was republished within twelve months in a
cheaper edition, was on the whole a commercial success, it could in no way be considered as the financial
foundation of a second career in the wake of Irving's
demise. The paperback volume of theatrical short
stories, *Snowbound,* and the romantic novel, *Lady Athlyne,* both published in 1908, appear to have brought
the author little financial reward, neither reaching a
second edition. Stoker, therefore, embarked upon a
succession of new ventures, each of which taxed his
waning energy whilst bringing him limited remunera-
tion. He became the business manager to a West End
musical production of *The Vicar of Wakefield,* scripted
by Laurence Housman and produced by the American opera singer, David Bispham. The production
closed after two months. He then undertook a lecture
tour in the English provinces which terminated,

"The Jewel of the Strand"

The Lyceum Theatre, under the artistic direction of Henry Irving, became the unofficial national theater of England during the last quarter of the nineteenth century. The building, designed by Samuel Beazley in 1830 after a previous incarnation had burned down, occupied a site that had been associated with entertainment since the Society of Arts founded "a Room for Exhibitions and Concerts" near there in 1772. The theater did not achieve greatness until Irving signed the lease in 1878.

Irving and the popular actress Ellen Terry, who became known as the "Lord and Lady of the Lyceum," were able to draw enthusiastic audiences to productions of the works of Shakespeare as well as to contemporary plays and through their performances were able to raise the appreciation of acting as an art. A contemporary critic, H. Booth, wrote that "it soon became almost a religion to attend the Lyceum."

As Irving's admirer and friend, Stoker was associated with the Lyceum for most of his professional life. His position as business manager brought him into contact with many of the leading figures of his day. Stoker was associated with the Lyceum until Irving took his final bow there in 1902. Irving's company, accompanied by Stoker, continued touring until the actor's death in 1905.

apparently at short notice, in Sheffield. Finally, he gained a short appointment as organizer of the British section of the 1908 Paris Theatrical Exhibition. At the same time, he was active in commercial journalism, publishing a number of nonfictional articles in the United Kingdom and the United States, and a series of interviews in the London press. This was, indeed, his most productive phase as a writer of fiction: just under half of his fictional publications came to fruition within a period of seven years. But the financial rewards were, again, light compared to the output.

By 1911 Stoker faced an acute financial crisis. As his application for a grant from the Royal Literary Fund reveals, his income was now significantly dependent upon his work as an author. Stoker's income for 1910, according to his application, totalled £409 from investments, and just over £166 from literary work, including, presumably, the advance for his final novel, *The Lair of the White Worm*. The Committee of the Royal Literary Fund, after considering Stoker's application and the letters of reference supplied by Anne Ritchie, Henry F. Dickens and W. S. Gilbert, awarded the author a grant of £100 on 9 March 1911. He was, however, by this time terminally ill. He died at his home in Pimlico, London, on 20 April 1912, leaving his whole estate, which had a net value of just over £4,664, to his wife. Although one biographer has argued that the author was a victim of tertiary syphilis, the death cer-

The Lyceum Theatre in London, circa 1895. Stoker was the business manager of the theater from 1878 to 1902 (Barbara Belford, Bram Stoker: A Biography of the Author of Dracula, 1996; Elizabeth Miller Collection).

tificate, with its enigmatic coda, "exhaustion," is far from conclusive.[27] Stoker was cremated following a quiet service at Golders Green, London, which was attended by Hall Caine, Genevieve Ward, Ford Madox Hueffer and Laurence Irving, the actor's second son.

—revised with the approval of the author
from his *Bram Stoker: A Bibliography*,
Victorian Fiction Research Guide 25
(University of Queensland,
1997), pp. 1–6

1. Bram Stoker, *Personal Reminiscences of Henry Irving*, 2 vols. (London: Heinemann, 1906), vol. 1, p. 31.
2. Entry number 62 in the Parish Register of the church of St. John the Baptist, Clontarf, Dublin.
3. For an account of the culture of formal education in this period see: M. Girouard, *The Return to Camelot: Chivalry and the English Gentleman* (London: Yale University Press, 1981), pp. 164–176; J. R. de S. Honey, *Tom Brown's Universe: The Development of the Public School in the Nineteenth Century* (London: Millington, 1977), passim.

Stoker as a Poet

Among Stoker's more obscure works is the following poem, believed to be the only verse he ever published.

One Thing Needful

In Martha's house the weary Master lay,
Spent with His faring through the burning day.
  The busy hostess bustled through the room
On household cares intent, and at His feet
The gentle Mary took her wonted seat.
  Soft came His words in music through the gloom.

Cumbered about much serving Martha wrought–
Her sister listening as the Master taught–
  Till, something fretful, an appeal she made:
'Doth it not matter that on me doth fall
The burden? Mary helpeth not at all.
  Master! command her that she give me aid!'

'Ah! Martha, Martha, thou art full of care,
And many things thy needless trouble share!'
  Thus, with the love that chides, the Master spake.
'One thing alone is needful! That good part
Hath Mary chosen from her loving heart;
  And that part from her I shall never take!'

. . . .

One thing alone we lack! Our souls indeed
Have fiercer hunger than the body's need.
  Ah! Happy they that look in loving eyes!
The harsh world round them fades; the Master's voice
In sweetest music bids their souls rejoice,
  And wakes an echo there that never dies.

–A Volunteer Haversack (Edinburgh: Printed for the
Queen's Rifle Volunteer Brigade: the
Royal Scots, 1902), pp. 173–174

College Historical Society Address, 1872, Appendix, pp. 40–41, 51.

8. *Dublin University Football Club 1854–1954* (Dublin: Mountford, 1954), pp. 50–52, 65.

9. Daniel Farson, *The Man Who Wrote Dracula* (London: Joseph, 1975), p. 18.

10. C. Sweeting, "Bram Stoker," *University Philosophical Society, Trinity College Dublin, Centenary Review,* ed. J. P. Cinnamond (Dublin: The Centenary Committee of the Philosophical Society, 1953), p. 52.

11. Stoker, *Reminiscences,* vol. 1, p. 343. See also *Who Was Who* (London: A. & C. Black, 1935), p. 680.

12. W. J. McCormack, "Irish Gothic and After (1820–1945)," *The Field Day Anthology of Irish Writing,* ed. S. Deane (Londonderry: Field Day, 1991), vol. 2, p. 845.

13. Stoker's early theatre criticism is almost impossible to trace with accuracy due to the modern-day scarcity of the periodicals to which he was a contributor. A few extracts are, however, reprinted in *Personal Reminiscences of Henry Irving.* The volume also includes his *Dublin Mail* account of the University Night held in honor of Irving at the Theatre Royal Dublin on 11 December 1876: see vol. 1, p. 22, pp. 26–27, pp. 37–40.

14. Harry Ludlam, *A Biography of Dracula: The Life Story of Bram Stoker* (London: Foulsham, 1962), pp. 33–34.

15. John St. John, *William Heinemann, A Century of Publishing 1890–1990* (London: Heinemann, 1990), p. 20.

16. Stoker, *Reminiscences,* vol. 1, p. 31–33.

17. For example, see Laurence Irving, *Henry Irving: The Actor and His World* (London: Columbus Books, 1989), p. 453, cf. 444; and Ellen Terry, "First Years at the Lyceum: The Story of What Henry Irving Did for the English Stage," *McClure's Magazine,* 30 (1908): 374.

18. *The New York Times,* 23 April 1912, p. 12.

19. Hall Caine, "Bram Stoker: The Story of a Great Friendship," *The Daily Telegraph,* 24 April 1912, p. 16. In this obituary, Caine also notes that he, as "Hommy Beg," was the dedicatee of *Dracula.*

20. Witness the title of Stoker's obituary: "Death of Mr. Bram Stoker: Sir H. Irving's Manager," *The Daily Telegraph,* 22 April 1912, p. 6.

21. *The Entr'acte,* 23 September 1882, p. 4; cf. Caine, "Bram Stoker," p. 16.

22. Terry 1908, p. 374.

23. The Stokers were married at St. Ann's Church, Dublin, on 4 December 1878 [entry number 120 in the Church Register]. For correspondence connected with the relationship between Oscar Wilde and Florence Balcombe see Farson, *Dracula,* pp. 41–42, pp. 60–61.

24. L. Irving, "Henry Irving," pp. 452–453. The article in question is "The American Audience," *Fortnightly Review,* 37 (1885): 197–201.

25. Farson, *Dracula,* p. 232.

26. See Stoker's letter to the Committee of the Royal Literary Fund, dated 25 February 1911, held at the British Library, London: British Library M1077/117 [Correspondence of the Royal Literary Fund, File 2841].

27. Farson, *Dracula,* pp. 233–235.

4. Under the regulations of the University of Dublin, candidates deemed to have passed their degree with Honours were termed "Moderators." Candidates for ordinary degrees who had passed with special merit were awarded "Respondency." A search of the Muniment Records of the University of Dublin, dated between 1864 and 1880, reveals that Stoker was not awarded either distinction.

5. Stoker, *Reminiscences,* vol. 1, p. 32.

6. For example, D. R. Perry, "Whitman's Influence on Stoker's *Dracula,*" *Walt Whitman Quarterly Review,* 3 (1986): 29–35.

7. *Undergraduate Philosophical Society Minute Book, 1861–67,* entries dated 7 May 1868 and 25 November 1869;

* * *

The Courtship of Florence Balcombe

Florence Ann Lemon Balcombe (Florrie) was born in Falmouth in 1858. At the age of seventeen she met Oscar Wilde in Clontarf, where her family then resided, and was courted by him for the next two years. Some time in the middle of 1878, however, Florence accepted a proposal of marriage from Bram Stoker. Possibly Florence viewed Stoker, a successful civil servant, as a better prospect; or she may have considered his connections with the theater scene as a stepping-stone to the fulfillment of her own desire to become an actress.

In the months that followed Florence's engagement, there was a flurry of correspondence between her and her former suitor. Even after the Stokers were married, Wilde kept in touch. He sent her inscribed copies of two of his books: The Happy Prince and Other Tales *(1888) and* Salome *(1893). Both inscriptions included the words "With kind regards to Bram."*

Stoker knew the Wilde family well and was a frequent visitor at the Dublin home of Oscar's parents. Little is known of his relationship with Oscar, who had entered Trinity College the year Stoker left the school. There is no record of how Stoker responded when Wilde faced public scandal, trial, and imprisonment during the 1890s. Curiously, though, Stoker fails to mention his earlier rival in Personal Reminiscences of Henry Irving, *which includes several pages of names of individuals that frequented the Lyceum Theatre.*

Oscar Wilde in 1876 (William Andrews Clark Memorial Library, University of California, Los Angeles)

Wilde wrote this letter from Bournemouth.

Oscar Wilde to Florence Balcombe, April 1878

My dear Florrie, I send you a line to wish you a pleasant Easter. A year ago I was in Athens and you sent me I remember a little Easter card—over so many miles of land and sea—to show me you had not forgotten me.

I have been greatly disappointed in not being able to come over, but I could only spare four days and as I was not feeling well came down here to try and get some ozone. The weather is delightful and if I had not a good memory of the past I would be very happy.

OSCAR WILDE

—The Letters of Oscar Wilde, *edited by Rupert Hart-Davies (New York: Harcourt, Brace & World, 1962), p. 51*

* * *

A pencil sketch of Florence Balcombe by Oscar Wilde. Florence, reported to have been one of the most beautiful women in Dublin, was courted by Wilde before she accepted Stoker's proposal of marriage in 1878 (Harry Ransom Humanities Research Center, University of Texas at Austin).

Florence Stoker and son Noel (courtesy of Noel Dobbs)

Florence and Bram Stoker

Florence and Bram were married at St. Ann's Church in Dublin on 4 December 1878. Five days later they left for London, where Bram began his employment with the Lyceum Theatre. A year later, their only child, Noel, was born in London. In the absence of clear documentation, it is difficult to assess the nature of their relationship. Stoker spent long hours at the theater and many months on tour, leaving his wife and son at home. According to family lore, Florence was frigid, possibly leading her husband to seek solace elsewhere.

After Stoker's death, Florence remained in London. In 1913 she auctioned off many of his books and manuscripts, including the working notes for Dracula. *The next year she permitted the publication of a collection of his stories,* Dracula's Guest and Other Weird Tales *(1914). She also is remembered for her legal battle with the German movie company that in 1922 released* Nosferatu, *a work clearly based on* Dracula, *without seeking her permission. The three-year battle ended in her favor.*

Florence Stoker died in 1937 at the age of 78.

By late 1878, Florence had agreed to marry Bram Stoker. Wilde wrote from Dublin.

Wilde to Balcombe, late 1878

Dear Florrie, As I shall be going back to England, probably for good, in a few days, I should like to bring with me the little gold cross I gave you one Christmas morning long ago.

I need hardly say that I would not ask it from you if it was anything you valued, but worthless though the trinket be, to me it serves as a memory of two sweet years—the sweetest of all the years of my youth—and I should like to have it always with me. If you would care to give it to me yourself I could meet you any time on Wednesday, or you might hand it to Phil, whom I am going to meet that afternoon.

Though you have not thought it worth while to let me know of your marriage, still I cannot leave Ireland without sending you my wishes that you may be happy; whatever happens I at least cannot be indifferent to your welfare: the currents of our lives flowed too long beside one another for that.

We stand apart now, but the little cross will serve to remind me of the bygone days, and though we shall never meet again, after I leave Ireland, still I shall always remember you at prayer. Adieu and God bless you.

OSCAR WILDE

—*The Letters of Oscar Wilde,* p. 54

* * *

Wilde to Balcombe, late 1878

Dear Florence, I could not come to Harcourt Street: it would be painful for both of us: but if you would care to see me for the last time I will go out to the Crescent on Friday at two o'clock. Perhaps it would be better for us both if we saw one another once more.

Send me a line and I will be there. Very truly yours

OSCAR WILDE

I will send you back your letters when I go to Oxford. The enclosed scrap I used to carry with me: it was written eighteen months ago: how strange and out of tune it all reads now.

—*The Letters of Oscar Wilde,* p. 55

* * *

Wilde to Balcombe, late 1878

Dear Florence, As you expressed a wish to see me I thought that *your mother's house* would be the only suitable place, and that we should part where we first met.

*Drawing of the Stoker family by George du Maurier (*Punch, *11 September 1886; Barbara Belford,* Bram Stoker: *A Biography of the Author of* Dracula, *1996; Elizabeth Miller Collection)*

As for my calling at Harcourt Street, you know, my dear Florence, that such a thing is quite out of the question: it would have been unfair to you, and me, and to the man you are going to marry, had we met anywhere else but under your mother's roof, and with your mother's sanction. I am sure that you will see this yourself on reflection; as a man of honour I could not have met you except with the full sanction of your parents and in their house.

As regards the cross, there is nothing "exceptional" in the trinket except the fact of my name being on it, which of course would have prevented you from wearing it ever, and I am not foolish enough to imagine that you care now for any memento of me. It would have been impossible for you to keep it.

I am sorry that you should appear to think, from your postscript, that I desired any clandestine "*meeting:*" after all, I find you know me very little.

Goodbye, and believe me yours very truly

OSCAR WILDE

–The Letters of Oscar Wilde, p. 55

* * *

Using the Lyceum's leading lady, Ellen Terry, as his go-between, Wilde sent flowers to Florence Stoker when she made her acting debut as one of one hundred vestal virgins in a performance of Tennyson's The Cup *(1881).*

Wilde to Ellen Terry, 3 January 1881

I send you some flowers–two crowns. Will you accept one of them, whichever you think will suit you best. The other–don't think me treacherous, Nellie–but the other please give to Florrie *from yourself.* I should like to think that she was wearing something of mine the first night she comes on the stage, that anything of mine should touch her. Of course if you think–but you won't think she will suspect? How could she? She thinks I never loved her, thinks I forget. My God how could I!

–The Letters of Oscar Wilde, p. 74

* * *

Wilde to Balcombe, 21 February 1893

My dear Florence, Will you accept a copy of *Salome–* my strange venture in a tongue that is not my own, but that I love as one loves an instrument of music on which one has not played before. You will get it, I hope, tomorrow, and I hope you will like it. With kind regards to Bram, believe me, always your sincere friend

OSCAR WILDE

–The Letters of Oscar Wilde, pp. 330–331

The Stoker residence on St. Leonard's Terrace, Chelsea, London, and the commemorative plaque that was dedicated in 1977.
The family lived there for several years, including 1897, the year Dracula *was published*
(photographs by Jeanne Youngson and David J. Skal).

Stoker's Reading

Although many of Stoker's books were likely sold before his death, the Sotheby sale of his library in 1913 suggests something of his wide-ranging interests.

The Library of Bram Stoker
Leslie Shepard

We may never know the full extent of Bram Stoker's personal library, but it is possible to form a general idea of its scope and subject matter, as distinct from the books which he studied in reference libraries for background information for his own books. The discovery of his research notes for *Dracula* (now in the Rosenbach Museum & Library, Philadelphia) threw a flood of light on the meticulous detail of his research, and Clive Leatherdale's study *The Origins of Dracula* (1987) lists over thirty such titles and examines in detail seventeen of them. These do not appear, however, to be books from Stoker's personal library.

However, Harry Ludlam's book *A Biography of Dracula: the Life Story of Bram Stoker* (1962) mentions that in 1910, two years before Stoker's death, Bram and his wife Florence moved from their house in Durham Place, Chelsea, to a smaller house in nearby St. George's Square, and discarded hundreds of books collected over many years. These included authors like Kipling, Mark Twain, and Stevenson, volumes of Egyptology, a history of the Ku Klux Klan, and sets of ordnance maps for the British Isles.

In the year following Stoker's death, the rest of his library was sold up, probably by his widow Florence, and the printed catalogue of Sotheby, Wilkinson, and Hodge in 1913 listed the remainder of the library. This was disposed of on Monday, 7th July, and ran to 317 items. The catalogue makes fascinating reading, and indicates the wide range of Stoker's interests and associations.

Travel and history were represented by books on Egypt, Asia, Canada, and America, which had survived the sale in 1910. Predictably, a number of other books were concerned with the theatre and theatrical history, including biographical studies of Stoker's idol Henry Irving. In addition to the works of Shakespeare and other items of Shakespeare interest, there were books on the Bacon cipher controversy. Books of poetry included such authors as Shelley, Browning, Tennyson, Eugene Field, James Whitcombe Riley, and Walt Whitman. Field and Riley were personal friends of Stoker, and Riley ("the Hoosier Poet") was also a favorite of Irving. Stoker had been captivated by Whitman's poems from the time that he first read *Leaves of Grass* when a student at Trinity College, Dublin. Stoker later became a great friend of that poet.

The Sotheby sale included seventeen Whitman items, mostly association copies inscribed "Bram Stoker, from his friend, the Author." Item 136 was a unique collection of fragments of Whitman's writings in his own hand on scraps of paper, mounted in an album. There was also an interesting autographed letter from Stoker describing how, with Edward Dowden, he had defended the poet from violent criticism in a discussion at the Fortnightly Club, Dublin. Whitman wrote: "My physique is entirely shatter'd, doubtless permanently from paralysis and other ailments. But I am up & dress'd & get out every day a little—live here quite lonesome but hearty & good spirits. Write to me again."

There were few works of fiction in the catalogue, but presumably these would have been sold off in 1910 when Stoker moved house. Remaining fiction books included the works of Stevenson, tales by H. Rider Haggard and Rudyard Kipling, Mary Shelley's *Frankenstein,* E.T.W. Hoffman's *Weird Tales,* and a volume of stories by J. Sheridan Le Fanu. Other books of folklore and occult interest included W. Silkes, *British Goblins,* Elliott O'Donnell, *Byways of Ghost-Land,* D. MacRitchie, *Fians, Fairies and Picts,* J.G. Campbell, *Superstitions and Witchcraft and Second Sight in the Highlands and Islands of Scotland,* and a volume of *Anancy Stories* of the West Indies by Pamela Colman Smith, with an autographed letter from her. There were also copies of the magazine *The Green Sheaf* edited by Smith, with her hand-coloured illustrations.

A large part of the collection was taken up by over sixty presentation copies of books to Stoker and his wife. Notable individuals who inscribed their books to Stoker included S.L. Clemens (Mark Twain), Bret Harte, Winston Churchill, W.B. Yeats, and Hall Caine. Caine was a special friend of Stoker, and the presentation copy of Caine's *My Story* (1908) reads "To my dear Bram, to whom this book owes much." It will be recalled that in turn, Stoker had dedicated *Dracula* to "my dear friend, Hommy-Beg" (a nickname for Caine).

One unique item in the catalogue was No. 143, a Death Mask and Hands, closed, of President Abraham Lincoln. These were cast by the sculptor Augustus St. Audens in 1886 from original moulds made by Leonard Wells Volk before Lincoln went to Washington for his first presidency. The moulds were found by Volk's son twenty-five years later, and twenty men subscribed to purchase the moulds and present them to the American nation. Each of the twenty received bronze casts of the face and hands with his name in each case, cast in bronze, and two of the men were Henry Irving and Bram Stoker. Item 144 was the original manuscript of Stoker's lecture on Lincoln.

Browsing through the Sotheby catalogue one discovers a great variety of subjects which must have had special interest for Stoker, such as: H. Ward, *Five Years with the Congo Cannibals* (1891), Robert Benson, *Sketches of Corsica* (1825), J. Baker, *Imperial Guide, with Picturesque Plans of the Great Post Roads* (1802), W. Morton (translator), *Collection of*

First Day _____ 18 _____ QUARTO

2 2 .   171   Whistler (J. M.) Memorial Exhibition, Catalogue of Paintings, Drawings, Etchings and Lithographs, EDITION DE LUXE, *portrait and illustrations, uncut, t. e. g.*   1905   *Drake*

10   172   Whistler (J. M.) Catalogue of Paintings, etc. 1905—Page (The), vol. I, in 12 parts as issued (*wanting nos. VIII, IX and X*), *portraits, woodcuts, etc.* only 140 copies printed, 1898   (10)   *Maggs*

6   173   Febure (Nic. de) Compleat Body of Chymistry, rendred into English by P. D. C. *plates, covers gone,* 1670—Temple (Sir J.) The Irish Rebellion, FIRST EDITION, *old calf,* 1646   (2)   *Holland*

9   174   [Mathews (C. J.)] Catalogue Raisonnée of Mr. Mathews's Gallery of Theatrical Portraits, *calf, presentation copy with autograph inscription,* "*John Pritt Harley Esq. from his great Admirer and Friend Anne Mathews, Saturday September 16, 1848*"   1833   *Stevens Bo*

5 17 6   175   Dryden (John) An Evening's Love, or the Mock-Astrologer, 1671 ; The Rival Ladies, a Tragi-Comedy, 1675 ; The Assignation : or Love in a Nunnery, 1678 ; Secret Love, or the Maiden Queen, 1679 ; Marriage a-la-Mode, a Comedy, 1684 ; The Wild Gallant, a Comedy, 1684 ; The Indian Emperor, or the Conquest of Mexico, 1686 ; The Conquest of Granada, 1687 ; The Spanish Fryar, 1690 ; The Kind Keeper, or Mr. Limberham, A Comedy, 1690 ; Amphitryon, or the Two Sosias, 1691 : and others by the same Author, some FIRST EDITIONS, in 1 vol. *old calf*   1671-91   *Maggs*

1 1 .   176   Play-Bills. Collection of Play-Bills of the Theatre-Royal, Edinburgh, ranging from Nov. 25, 1820, to Aug. 17, 1824, in 1 vol.   1820-24   *Edwards*

The following Six Manuscripts are mainly in the autograph of the Author, but some passages appear to be in the handwriting of an Amanuensis. They are all sold subject to the copyright being reserved.

4 15 .   177   STOKER (BRAM) Personal Reminiscences of Henry Irving, "THE ORIGINAL MANUSCRIPT"   1906   *Holland*

1 1   178   Stoker (B.) Lady of the Shroud, "THE ORIGINAL MANUSCRIPT," with the outline of the Story   1908   *Maggs*

5   179   Stoker (B.) Snowbound, the Record of a Theatrical Touring Party (the last four chapters only), "THE ORIGINAL MANUSCRIPT" 1908   *Burton*

14   180   Stoker (B.) Under the Sunset, "THE ORIGINAL MANUSCRIPT" 1882   *Maggs*

1 15   181   Stoker (B.) Lair of the White Worm (the last Book written by the Author), "THE ORIGINAL MANUSCRIPT"   1911   *Edwards*

2 2 .   182   Stoker (B.) Original Notes and Data for his "Dracula," *in a solander case*   (1)   *Drake*

FOLIO.

12 .   183   Harris (John) Complete Collection of Voyages and Travels in Europe, Asia, Africa and America, 2 vol. *maps and plates, calf*   1744   *O Neill*

184   Norden (F. L.) Travels in Egypt and Nubia, enlarged by P. Templeman, 2 vol. *plates, old calf*   1757   *wiklot 185*

Page from Sotheby's auction catalogue (1913), listing Stoker's Notes for Dracula *(item 182). The Notes were first bought by the American dealer James F. Drake for £2 2s.; they were eventually acquired by the Rosenbach Museum & Library in Philadelphia (Raymond McNally and Radu Florescu, eds.,* The Essential Dracula, *1979; Elizabeth Miller Collection).*

Proverbs, Bengali and Sanscrit (1832), J.C. Lavater, *Essays on Physiognomy* (5 vols., 1789), A. Balfour, *Second, Third and Fourth Reports of the Wellcome Research Laboratories at the Gordon Memorial College, Khartoum* (3 vols., 1906–11), J.W. Powell, *First and Second Annual Reports of the Bureau of Ethnology, 1880–1,* Nic. De Febure, *Compleat Body of Chymistry* (1670), *The Lightning Sea-Column or Sea-Mirrour, discovering all the Coasts and Islands of Europe, Africa, America and Asia* (1689), Sir W. Hamilton, *Collection of Vases, mostly of Pure Greek Workmanship, discovered in Sepulchres in the Kingdoms of the two Sicilies* (3 vols., 1791–95), *Statutes made and established from the time of Kyng Henry the thirde, unto the fyrste yere of the reigne of Henry the VIII* (1543), Wm. Rastall, *Collection of Statutes now in force from Magna Charta, untill the reigne of Queene Elizabeth* (1588), Geoffrey Chaucer, *Works* (1721), M. Sadeler, *Vestigi della Antichita di Roma* (n.d.), Wm. Stirling, *Some Apostles of Physiology, Account of their Lives and Labours* (privately printed, 1902), F. Harvey, *List of Portraits, Views, Autograph Letters, and Documents contained in an Illustrated Copy of the Princess Marie Liechtenstein's History of Holland House* (only 25 copies printed, n.d.)

Of special interest was an album of Original Pencil Sketches by William Fitzgerald, who was one of the illustrators for Stoker's book *Under the Sunset* (1882). Fitzgerald was responsible for the picture of the gloomy castle of the King of Death, which seems like a precursor of Stoker's Castle Dracula.

The Sotheby Catalogue also listed six autographed manuscripts of Stoker:

177   *Personal Reminiscences of Henry Irving*
178   *Lady of the Shroud (with the outline of the story).*
179   *Snowbound, the Record of a Theatrical Touring Party* (last four chapters only).
180   *Under the Sunset.*
181   *Lair of the White Worm.*
182   Original Notes and Data for *Dracula.*

Presumably this last item is the important acquisition by the Rosenbach Museum & Library, Philadelphia.

Looking through this fascinating Sotheby Catalogue it is sad to reflect that so many important items were dispersed and a number have been lost sight of for nearly eighty years. It is particularly unfortunate that the original manuscript items are not all in one collection for study. Meanwhile the Sotheby Catalogue reminds us of the wide ranging capacity of Stoker's enquiring mind, as well as the wide circle of his friendships.

–*Bram Stoker's Dracula: Sucking Through the Century, 1897–1997,* edited by Carol M. Davison (Toronto: Dundurn, 1997), pp. 411–414

Sir Henry Irving, knighted by Queen Victoria in 1895, was among the most celebrated actors of the late nineteenth century (Elizabeth Miller Collection).

The Passing of a Devoted Friend

At his death, Stoker was remembered far more for his devotion to Sir Henry Irving and for his personal qualities than for having written Dracula.

Obituary
The Times (London), 22 April 1912

The death took place at 26, St. George's Square, S.W., after a long illness, of Mr. Bram Stoker, who for nearly 30 years was the intimate friend of Sir Henry Irving. Mr. Stoker had been ill since 1906.

Bram, or baptismally Abraham Stoker, was born in Dublin in 1847, his father Abraham being one of the officials in the Chief Secretary's Department at the Castle. He was educated at Trinity College, where he won honours in science, mathematics, oratory, history, and composition, besides distinguishing himself as a sportsman and debater. He was for some time in the Irish Civil Service as Inspector of Petty Sessions, and was engaged in journalism as well, being editor of an evening paper and as a dramatic critic. How long he would have been content to play these humble though miscellaneous parts it is impossible to tell; but in 1876 or thereabouts he first came into contact with Henry Irving, and two years later he had permanently thrown in his lot with him as his manager and confidential secretary, and he remained with him until the end. Few men have played their part of *fidus achates* to a great personality with more gusto. Mr. Stoker must have found his new life thoroughly congenial. He shared Irving's counsels in all his enterprises; went about with him in the closest relationship as confidential secretary and right-hand man; assisted in many brilliant entertainments which his chief gave during the heyday of the Lyceum; met and was cordially treated by people of all sorts and conditions; and knew thoroughly the ins and outs of the financial side of the riskiest of all professions. From 1878, the year in which Irving became lessee and manager of the Lyceum, to 1905, when he died, the takings, as Stoker tells us, exceeded two millions. When the crash came, Stoker remained loyally at his friend's side, during the years which would have been fatal to less enduring spirits. After Irving's death, it was not unnatural that Stoker should write his biography, and this task Mr. Stoker presented with his customary enthusiasm. A fluent and flamboyant writer, with a manner and mannerisms which faithfully reflected the mind which moved the pen, Stoker managed to find time amid much arduous and distracting work, to write a good deal. He was a master of a particularly florid and creepy kind of fiction, represented by "Dracula" and other novels. He had also essayed musical comedy, and had of late years resumed his old connection with journalism. But his chief literary memorial with all its extravagances and shortcomings–Mr. Stoker was no very acute critic of his chief as an actor–cannot but remain a valuable record of the workings of genius as they appeared to his devoted associate and admirer.

Mr. Bram Stoker married Florence Anne Lemon, daughter of the late Lieutenant-Colonel Balcombe, who survives him with one son, Noel Thornley.

The funeral is to take place quietly at Golder's Green.

* * *

Funeral Notice

The funeral of Mr. Bram Stoker took place yesterday at the Golder's Green Crematorium. A service was held in the chapel by the Rev. Herbert Trundle. Among those present were Mr. Lawrence [sic] Irving, Mr. Hall Caine, Mr. Ford Maddox Hueffer and Miss Genevive Ward. Wreaths were sent by Miss Ellen Terry, Sir Athur Pinero, Mrs. Maxwell, and Mr. and Mrs. Frederick Watson.

–*The Times* (London), 25 April 1912

The most extensive tribute to Bram Stoker following his death was written by his closest friend, Thomas Hall Caine (1853–1931), one of the best-selling authors of the Victorian era. Stoker had dedicated Dracula *to Caine.*

Bram Stoker: The Story of a Great Friendship
Hall Caine

Bram Stoker is to be buried to-day. The remains will be cremated at Golder's-green Crematorium. Only the friends (and they are many) who knew and loved him will be there when the last offices are done, and that will be enough. He could have desired no more and no better. The big, breathless, impetuous hurricane of a man who was Bram Stoker had no love of the limelight.

A few days ago I stood, for the twentieth time or more, at the foot of that sloping stone, under the shadow of the pyramid of Caius Cestius, which bears Leigh Hunt's simple but great inscription "Cor Cordium." Nothing else was needed to tell the world the place of the great brother-poet's rest. And nothing else, and nothing less, will be necessary to tell the few friends who really and truly knew Bram Stoker (fully conscious that he had no other claim to greatness) that all that was mortal of his big heart has been committed to the dust.

In one thing our poor Bram, who had many limitations, was truly great. His was indeed the genius of friendship. I speak as perhaps the oldest of his surviving associates, outside the immediate circle of his family, when I say that never in any other man have I seen such capacity for devotion to a friend.

Much has been said of his relation to Henry Irving, but I wonder how many were really aware of the whole depth and significance of that association. Bram seemed to give up his life to it. It was not only his time and his services that he gave to Irving–it was his heart, which never failed for one moment in loyalty, in enthusiasm, in affection, in the strongest love that man may feel for man. I remember what all this was in those far-off first days of their relation, when Irving said one night in Liverpool, "Bram is going to join me"; I follow on in memory through the triumphant times of dazzling success, and the dark days of sickness, failing powers, and financial misfortune, down to the last great but tragic hour (and after it), and I say without any hesitation that never have I seen, never do I expect to see, such absorption of one man's life in the life of another.

IRVING AND HIS ALLY.

If Bram's body had its rightful resting-place it would be at Irving's feet; and yet he was a man of him-

Stoker's burial urn at Golders Green Crematorium (courtesy of Jeanne Youngson)

self, a strong and stalwart separate being who in his best days might have stood alone.

Never, I am certain, had he any thought of sacrifice, but while always rewarded with the gratitude of that other great heart, what a price he paid for his devotion to his chief! We who were very close to him realised this fact when the time of the asundering came, and we saw that with Irving's life poor Bram's had really ended. It was too late to begin afresh. The threads that had been broken thirty years before could not be pieced together. There could be no second flowing of the tide. It was the ebb, and though Bram made a brave fight for a new life, he knew well, and we knew well, that his chances were over.

I am partly conscious that in the world of the theatre there were those (and perhaps they were not a few) who attributed to Bram every misfortune that overtook them in their connection with his principal; but I wonder if they gave a thought to the inevitable difficulties of the place he filled. Into the life of nearly all great men (especially such a man as Irving was) there come moments when it is necessary to do disagreeable things, and yet not to seem to do them. Someone must then stand between, assuming the responsibility, taking the blame, accepting the blow. It would not be a gracious thing to say how

often during a score of years I saw Bram in that position. It is sweeter to remember that Irving himself always knew and never forgot.

Thinking of this reminds me how miserably mistaken was the estimate of Bram's personal character which prevailed at that period. He had to steel himself to say "No," and to shirk no painful duty, but his real nature was of the tenderest. When I think how tender it was there come crowding upon me incident after incident in which his humanity shone out as a bright light, though the scene of it was only the front of a box-office, the door to the gallery, the passageway to the pit. But it was not there that his best qualities appeared. Bram was a man of the theatre only by the accident of his great love for its leader, and his true self was something quite unlike the personality which was seen in that environment. Those who knew him there only hardly knew him at all.

Some hint of this would occasionally reveal itself among the scarcely favourable conditions of a public dinner, when, as a speaker (always capable of the racy humour which is considered necessary to that rather artificial atmosphere), he would strike, in the soft roll of his rich Irish tongue, a deep and almost startling emotion that would obliterate the facile witticisms of more important persons.

LITERARY WORK.

I cannot truly say that this deeper side of the man ever expressed itself in his writings. He took no vain view of his efforts as an author. Frankly, he wrote his books to sell, and except in the case of one of them (his book on Irving), he had no higher aims. But higher aims were there, and the power of realising them had not been denied to him.

When I think of his literary output I regret the loss of the one book with which he might have enriched the literature of autobiography. The multitude of interesting persons with whom his position brought him into contact—Tennyson, Disraeli, Gladstone, Randolph Churchill, Archbishop Benson, Henry Ward Beecher, President Cleveland, Walt Whitman, Rénan—had left him with a vast store of memories which the public would have welcomed if he had written them down. He never did write them, and the world is the poorer for want of his glimpses, however brief and casual, of some of its great souls in their happiest hours.

In concluding this little and imperfect tribute to the memory of a massive and muscular and almost volcanic personality that must have been familiar by sight to many thousands in Great Britain and America, I could wish to end where I began with the warmest and most affectionate recognition of his genius for friendship. No one knows better than the friend to whom, under various disguises (impenetrable to all except themselves), he dedicated in words of love some of his best-known works ("Dracula" in particular), how large was the heart that was not entirely exhausted even by its devotion to the great man with whom his name is generally associated. There were moments during the past twenty-odd years when I felt ashamed that anybody should give me his time, his energy, and his enthusiasm as Bram gave them, and the only way in which I could reconcile myself to his splendid self-sacrifice was to remember that he loved to make it. I can think of nothing—absolutely nothing—that I could have asked Bram Stoker to do for me that he would not have done. It is only once in a man's life that such a friendship comes to him, and when the grave is closed on the big heart which we are to bury to-day, I shall feel that I have lost it.

Of the devotion of his wife during these last dark days, in which the whirlwind of his spirit had nothing left to it but the broken wreck of a strong man, I cannot trust myself to speak. That must always be a sacred memory to those who know what it was. If his was the genius of friendship, hers must have been the genius of love.

—The Daily Telegraph (London), 24 April 1912, p. 16

The Debate about Stoker's Death

Given the widely held supposition that Stoker died of syphilis and the application of this "fact" to interpretations of Dracula, *it is worth examining both sides of the debate. The theory was first put forth by Stoker's great-nephew, Daniel Farson, and later vehemently repudiated by Irish antiquarian and Stoker scholar Leslie Shepard.*

Death from Syphilis
Daniel Farson

It has been stated and repeated that Bram died from "exhaustion." It is a gratifying epitaph, with the implication that he wore himself out through overwork on behalf of others. But this is not the whole truth.

"Exhaustion" struck me as a curious expression for a death certificate, but when I received a copy I was no wiser from the other words I found there, until I showed them to my doctor. Bram died of tertiary syphilis. The medical terminology on his death certificate reads in full: "Locomotor Ataxy 6 months Granular Contracted Kidney. Exhaustion. Certified by James Browne M.D."

My doctor was astonished that Dr Browne had not used a customary subterfuge, such as "specific disease." "Locomotor ataxia" is the equivalent of *Tabes Dorsalis* and *General Paresis,* better known as GPI—General Paralysis of the Insane. Various stages of the disease have been recorded in older medical books, which were more extensive.

> Preliminary stage: a change in character, marked by acts which may astonish the friends and relatives . . . unaccountable fatigue . . . mental restlessness . . . the patient may launch into extravagances and speculation of the wildest character. A common feature at this stage is the display of an unbounded egoism.
>
> *Second stage:* The intensity of the excitement is often extreme, acute maniacal stages are frequent; incessant restlessness, obstinate sleeplessness, noisy, boisterous excitement, and blind, uncalculating violence especially characterises such states.
>
> The patient becomes bedridden, death occurs from exhaustion.

I hesitated to include this until I was convinced that by revealing it, I would show Bram Stoker in a clearer light. It explains so much. The failing eyesight, for example, following his "stroke," after Irving's death: Mott states that about 50 per cent of his asylum cases of tabo. paralysis had preceding optic atrophy. Its occurrence therefore is of grave significance. The mental symptoms may be delayed for several years.

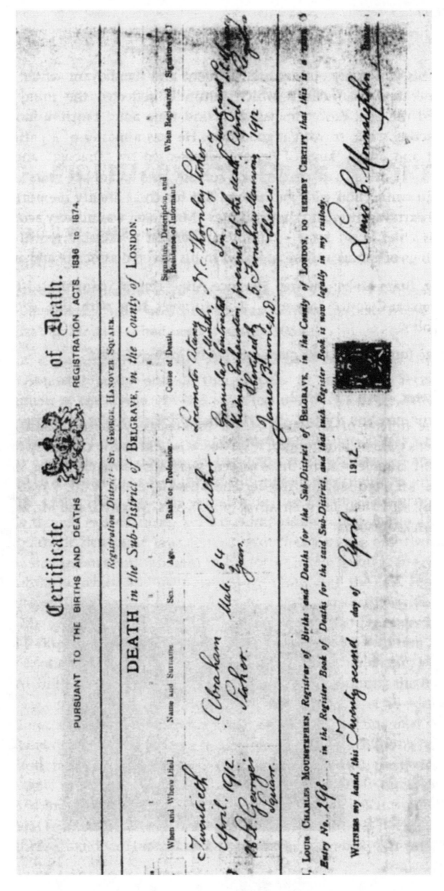

Stoker's death certificate (Leslie Shepard Collection)

When his wife's frigidity drove him to other women, probably prostitutes among them, Bram's writing showed signs of guilt and sexual frustration. At a later stage, when the disease had taken possession, there was the revulsion from Lady Arabella's "snake hole," and his statement that "the only emotions which in the long run harm, are those arising from the sex impulse."

He probably caught syphilis around the turn of the century, possibly as early as the year of *Dracula*, 1897. (It usually takes ten to fifteen years before it kills.) By 1897 it seems that he had been celibate for more than twenty years, as far as Florence was concerned. This would explain Bram's reputation as a "womaniser." Possibly the disease was contracted in Paris, where so many "faithful" husbands, such as Charles Dickens and Wilkie Collins, had gone for discreet pleasure before him.

—*The Man Who Wrote Dracula: A Biography of Bram Stoker*
(New York: St. Martin's Press, 1975), pp. 233–235

* * *

A Note on the Death Certificate of Bram Stoker
Leslie Shepard

In the last few years, a reckless mythology alleges that Bram Stoker died of syphilis. There are two sources for this story. The main source is Daniel Farson, great-nephew of Stoker, in his book *The Man Who Wrote Dracula* (1975). A secondary source is a family tradition of Senator David Norris, a connection of the Dublin city branch of the Stoker family. Farson's claim rests on the interpretation of the Death Certificate of Stoker, which reads: "Locomotor Ataxy 6 months, Granular Contracted Kidney, Exhaustion." Farson asserts that "Locomotor Ataxy" is a euphemism for *Tabes Dorsalis* or General Paralysis of the Insane, the final stages of syphilis. Senator Norris was under the impression that Stoker "died of the pox," but this belief may derive from the Death Certificate as well as gossip amongst ancestors scandalised by the sensationalism of Stoker's novel *Dracula*. Dublin gossip is often hurtful and scandalous, as well as witty. Since Bram Stoker died in London, the Death Certificate could well have been the source of this gossip. Farson's surprisingly emphatic interpretation of the Death Certificate of his relative rests on the common medical identification of

"Locomotor Ataxy" with the final stage of syphilis, but this is by no means invariable. I consulted a medical lecturer at the Wellcome Institute for the History of Medicine, who stated as follows:

> 'As for 'Locomotor Ataxy,' it usually, (one can never put it more strongly than that) refers to the consequences of cerebellum disease due to tertiary syphilis. There is therefore a definite indication that syphilis is related to cause of death, but one can not be certain.'

This cautious statement confirms that there is no definite justification for assuming syphilis, and the circumstances surrounding Stoker's later years would seem to militate against the possibility. *Tabes Dorsalis* is usually the culmination of several years physical deterioration and brain damage, expressed in disturbances of vision, palsy, disorientation in walking, accompanied by mental degeneration. In the case of Stoker, he did not exhibit the mental deterioration that might be characteristic of General Paralysis of the Insane, since he was mentally alert and active with literary work almost up to his death in 1912. The fact that he had some muscular disorientation described as "locomotor ataxy" is hardly surprising, since nine years earlier he had suffered a severe stroke after the death of his friend and idol Henry Irving. As Stoker's biographer Harry Ludlam wrote: "He suffered a stroke which laid him unconscious for twenty-four hours, and which began a painful illness that dragged on for weeks, robbing his robust frame of much of its boundless vitality and leaving his eyesight impaired." In the following years, however, Stoker revised his novel *The Man,* corrected proofs of his biography of Irving, and published five other books: *Lady Athlyne* (1908), *Snowbound* (1908), *The Lady of the Shroud* (1909), *Famous Impostors* (1910), *The Lair of the White Worm* (1911), as well as a number of articles in periodicals. None of this is characteristic of a man in the final stages of syphilis! Some physical difficulties were inevitable. He had struggled for years with overwork. The aftermath of the stroke in late life, coupled with earlier suffering from Bright's Disease and gout, could be expected to result in a condition of *paralysis agitans* or palsy, affecting his gait. The really significant cause of death is surely the single word "Exhaustion."

—*Dracula: Celebrating 100 Years,* edited by Leslie Shepard and Albert Power (Dublin: Mentor Press, 1997), pp. 179–180

II. The Vampire before *Dracula*

The Roots of the Vampire Legend

Though the name "Dracula" has become synonymous with "vampire," Bram Stoker certainly did not invent the idea of the vampire, which has its origins in the folk legends of many countries, most specifically in central and eastern Europe. Most folklorists agree that the word "vampire" has Slavic roots, first appearing as a proper name (Upir) in a Russian manuscript of the eleventh century and as a generic term in a Serbian manuscript two hundred years later. Vampire-like creatures have been identified in the myth and lore of many cultures. Those who have attempted to explain the roots of the vampire myth have explored not only folklore but also religion and unexplained pathologies.

A folklorist and contributing editor to the American Bibliography of Slavic and East European Studies, *Stu Burns wrote the following essay for this volume.*

A Short History of Vampire Folklore
Stu Burns

The Vampire, *a painting by Edvard Munch. The vampire myth inspired many writers and artists before Bram Stoker. This 1895 painting was finished two years before* Dracula *was published (National Gallery, Oslo).*

The vampire, generally defined in folklore as a corpse that returns from the grave to suck the blood of the living, is commonly associated with eastern Europe. Its basic characteristics, however, can be found in different forms of the motif in a variety of cultures separated from one another by both time and space. For example, given that death is frequently a taboo, fear of the dead is central to vampire belief. Likewise, many cultures fetishize blood as a symbol of life and prohibit its ingestion or use. Further, there is the tendency among humans to seek out scapegoats, blaming them for misfortune and attacking them in hopes of removing negative influences. Given these common characteristics, it is not difficult to explain the recurrent folk motif of the malevolent corpse that must be destroyed to restore health and well-being to the community.

Ancient literature includes a few characters who share certain attributes with the traditional vampire. Babylonian cuneiform poems, for example, refer to "ghosts that break through all the houses" as they "spill their blood like rain." Also, the Babylonian *Epic of Gilgamesh* refers to a female demon named Lillu who was later appropriated by Hebrew belief as Lilith, the myth-ological first wife of Adam who both preys on young children by sucking their blood and saps men of their virility by having sex with them as they sleep. In ancient Greece, Philostratus included a vampire-like account in his *Life of Apollonius of Tyana*. In this case, Apollonius rescues his student Menippus from marrying a *lamia,* a creature that feeds on the blood of strong young men. Both the great Roman poet Ovid and the church father St. Augustine write about *lemures,* evil ghosts who are given food during a spring festival to keep them from draining the household's vitality.[1] Even Homer's *Odyssey* invokes vampiric motifs; to get information from the underworld, Odysseus must feed the dead spirits blood, which they fight over ravenously. These ancient allusions may not satisfy all the proper criteria for vampire stories, but one can recognize the familiar tropes of the malevolent dead and the equation of blood with life.

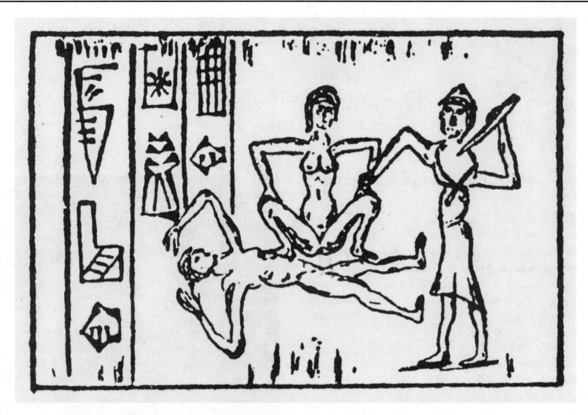

Babylonian depiction of vampire-like creatures (Peter Haining, The Dracula Scrapbook, *1976, Thomas Cooper Library, University of South Carolina)*

Apparitions similar to the vampire are evident in non-Western folklore as well. In Malaysian folk belief, there is the terrible *langsuyar,* a woman who dies in childbirth (or in the forty days after). Like Lilith, the morbidly beautiful langsuyar returns from the dead to suck the blood of infants; her stillborn child returns as a supernatural night owl, the *pontianak*.[2] In another odd twist, the Javanese version of this langsuyar/pontianak legend switches the two signifiers, calling the mother pontianak and the child langsuyar. A similar circumstance is evident in Serbian belief, where the vampire and the werewolf share the same name: *vukodlak*.[3] In addition, the trope of the supernatural creature who sucks the blood of infants is echoed in the Mexican region of Tlazcala, where mothers guard against the demonic (but not obviously undead) *tlahuelpuchi,* a female being which is very similar to Lilith or the langsuyar.[4]

Along more ritualistic lines, there is (or at least was into the 1970s) a traditional Bantu belief in northern Zimbabwe that dead ancestors must be fed animal blood in a ritual sacrifice. The consequence for not making this offering is that the spirit of the dead forerunner may rise to bring illness or death. Likewise, some Hindu sects venerated a fanged goddess, Kali, whose myth includes epic blood drinking, unbridled sexuality, and killing on a grand scale. Though Kali is divine and not undead, her representations certainly square with the popular image of the vampire—with the exception of two supplemental arms in the Hindu tradition. South Asia is also home to the legend of the *rakshasha,* a fanged nocturnal creature who lives in graveyards and devours the innocent, including women and children. The rakshasha is not an explicit blood-drinker, though it fits the vampire motif in other ways. Much closer to the classic vampire motif are English legends recounted by medieval chronicler William of Newburgh in 1196. William's tales feature dead men who return from the grave to harass their wives and other living acquaintances. These revenants are blamed for the plague, and are dealt with by exhuming their bodies (which, as we will see later in Slavic examples, are filled with warm, liquid blood unlike the coagulated blood of corpses) and cremating them.[5]

Although there are many creatures in world folklore that fit parts of the vampire motif, the largest and most coherent body of vampire lore still comes from eastern Europe. Apart from the aforementioned Serbian *vukodlak,* there are numerous vampire-like creatures in the folklore of almost every Slavic nation; in addition similar themes also occur in the folk literatures of other Eastern Orthodox regions such as Romania and Greece. The Greek creatures are called *vrykolakas;* Romanians fear the *strigoi;* and Croatians stage ritual killings of the *kudlak.* In northern Russia and Siberia, the bloodsucking revenant is the *eretik,* while the creature goes by *doppelsauger* among the German Slavs. The term "vampire" itself is probably a Western coinage derived from the Polish *upier* or the Bulgarian *upir,* with the Bulgarian term being the most common synonym for "vampire" in most Slavic languages.[6] To say that any one of these folk traditions represents the "real" vampire would be ludicrous. It is best to acknowledge that each version, though it may be unique, stays very close to the central motif, and thus each legend is part of an interconnected theme in eastern European folklore.

Further, it is important to note that folklife and cultural performance are essential components of vampire folklore. The vampire is a creature to be hunted, not endured, and most vampire legends end with a "successful" hunt, signified by the disinterment of one or more corpses and their subsequent destruction. Although bloodsucking may be sublimated by other evil acts in many vampire legends, one thing that is common throughout Slavic folklore is that the vampire itself, no matter what language or region, is almost always a corpse. Several scholars have proposed "explanations" for the vampire motif in some medical or psychological condition that causes people to act in a vampiric manner. Such proposals have included schizophrenia, rabies, and a rare form of anemia called *porphyria.*[7] While these explanations would be somewhat plausible if folkloric vampires looked and acted like their counterparts in literature and film, in simple fact they do not. The typical Slavic vampire has very little personality. Firsthand reports of vampire hunts rarely mention any conversations with the quarry, nor do they detail what happens between vampire and victim. Most often, people simply begin getting sick and wasting away, and a recently dead person is cast as a supernatural scapegoat. Though some stories do make characters out of the vampire, these are usually embellishments that do not show up until the tale has been told many times and the immediate threat has passed. In any event, almost all vampires are dead people, and interpretations that cast vampires as living people run counter to actual accounts. Instead of looking at the vampire itself for explanations, we should look at its context for interpretations.

The vampire's malevolent activities vary from one account to another. In some stories, the deceased person wanders the village spreading disease with the dreadful stench of death. Other times, the vampire might be blamed for crop failure or even attacks of diarrhea. However, the vampire's most common harmful act is to spread a plague of sudden deaths that the community attributes to the creature's blood-drinking habits (though the vampire's tell-tale bite marks on the neck are a creation of fiction, not of folklore). In his excellent study, Paul Barber sensibly attributes such deaths to sudden onsets of epidemics, and he explains the blood connection by pointing out that exhumed vampires were bloated, as if from heavy feasting, and often had blood coming from their mouths and noses. These are both natural parts of the decomposition process, though this would not have been clear before the advent of modern forensic pathology.[8] Barber certainly has a point here. To attribute the vampire's association with blood to strictly physical phenomena, however, is to ignore the immense cultural resonance that blood carries, and it is important to keep the importance of blood as a cultural signifier in mind when examining the vampire. After all, in the Christian Scripture "the blood is the life" (Deut. 12:23), and its full meaning goes beyond tell-tale manifestations on corpses. As we have seen in other cultures, drinking blood is a sign of absolute metaphysical degeneracy, a violation of the most dearly held taboos. Losing blood is losing life in its most direct form, and the vampire who takes blood is the most corrupt creature of all.

The vampire's supernatural powers vary between regions. In Russian tales, the vampire is often a master of sorcery with shape-shifting abilities and any number of other magical aptitudes, including putting entire gatherings to sleep with a wave of its hand. Other stories cast the vampire as a relative weakling easily driven off by a gathering of a few people. One ability that all vampires share, at least hypothetically, is the power to escape the grave without disturbing the earth, though in some cases a vampire's grave is indicated by small holes in the surface through which the vampire emerges in a misty form. A vampiric power that does not appear in Slavic folklore is transformation into a bat. The vampire bats of Latin America were unknown to the pre-industrial Slavs, and this picturesque addition to the motif would have to wait until the publication of *Dracula* in 1897. In traditional folklore outside of Russia, if a vampire transformed into anything, it would take the form of a wolf or a butterfly.

Understanding how bodies are selected as vampires is essential to comprehending their role as supernatural scapegoats. Sometimes the designation is applied innocently; the first person to die in an outbreak, for example, may end up taking blame for subsequent deaths. Disruption of funerary customs, like stepping over the body or allowing an animal to do so, may be perceived as disrupting the soul's ascent to heaven, thus trapping it in an unnatural state. Mistakes of birth, such as being born between Christmas and January 6 (Epiphany), being born with a membrane (caul) around the head, or being nursed after weaning (as in the German *doppelsauger*) may destine a baby for vampirism. Most popularly, being a vampire's victim is enough to become a vampire after death. Most vampires, however, are not innocent victims; even those who died by a vampire's bite usually had some moral failing that separated them from the community. Excommunicants often became vampires, as did heretics and unbaptized people. Criminals, suicides, and antisocial people were also popular targets; even priests who became vampires were usually classified as "quarrelsome" in life.[9] Thus, vampirism seems to function as a means of social control, as well as a mechanism to sanction "others" in the community.

In addition to signifying the "other," vampire folklore is also a reflection of gender roles. Most vampires are male, and they prey indiscriminately. They are also highly sexual, often returning to sleep with their widows, especially if they are "young and pretty"; in Serb folklore, children of such couplings are remarkable for being born without bones. Female vampires are uncommon in eastern Europe. When they do appear, however, their activities are highly gendered. They are almost never blamed for the deaths of adults; rather, their prey tends to be babies or small children. In a parallel with the Lilith and langsuyar legends, it is not uncommon for a woman who has died in childbirth to return as a vampire and feed on her own baby. Presumably this is a reflection of the woman's sphere of influence in life. Since the typical gender paradigms assign childrearing duties to women, it would follow that this control would extend to the vampire motif as well, especially in rigidly patriarchal cultures where men typically do not fear violence from women.

Warding off the undead is a key performance in vampire folklore. Religion is certainly invoked to this end, although the crucifix and the Eucharist that Van Helsing employs in *Dracula* are not typically used. In Serbia, doors were commonly painted with tar crosses during a vampire scare, and "suspicious" corpses were often buried with icons. More often, though, a number of pseudo-pagan practices are employed to keep the vampire at bay, some of which seem to assume that vampires are afflicted with obsessive-compulsive disorder. For example, mustard seeds were often scattered in coffins of suspected vampires in the belief that the vampire would have to count each seed before leaving the grave. Likewise, Balkan peasant homes would often sport heavily knotted ropes over their windows, as the vampire would have to untie each knot before it could enter; such ropes were often placed in coffins as well. The fictional use of garlic to ward off vampires does

---

Staving Off Vampires in Romania

Because of Bram Stoker's novel, vampires are primarily associated with the Transylvania region of Romania. While the word "vampire" is certainly not Romanian, the Romanian "strigoi" does share some of the characteristics of the vampire. In "The Romanian Folkloric Vampire," an essay included in Alan Dundes's The Vampire: A Casebook *(1998), Jan Perkowski describes cases of strigoi, who appear "ruddy and bloated in grave," who leave a "human victim drained of blood," and who are seen to have "blood on lips" (pp. 42–43).*

The precautions against visits from vampires are taken more especially before St. Andrew's Day and St. George's Day, but also before Easter Sunday and on the last day of the year. Garlic keeps off vampires, wolves, and evil spirits, and millet has a similar action. On St. Andrew's Eve and St. George's Eve, and before Easter and the New Year, windows should be anointed with garlic in the form of a cross, garlic put on the door and everything in the house, and all the cows in the cowshed should be rubbed with garlic. When vampires do enter, they enter by the chimney or by the keyhole, so these orifices call for special attention when garlic is being rubbed in. Even though the window is anointed with garlic, it is wisest to keep it shut. Especially on St. Andrew's Eve, all lamps may be put out and everything in the house turned upside down, so that if a vampire does come, it will not be able to ask any of the objects in the house to open the door. It is just as well for people not to sleep at all, but to tell stories right up to cockcrow. If you are telling stories, vampires cannot approach. Women should keep on saying their prayers. They may also beat on the hemp brakes to keep the vampires away. It is unwise to leave hemp brakes or shovels where vampires can get hold of them, for they like to ride on them. Vampires also like to take the tongues of hemp brakes as weapons and fight with them, till the sparks fly; hence the tongues should never be left fixed in the hemp brakes. Especially on St. George's Eve, it is a wise precaution to put on your shirt inside out, and to put a knife or scythe under your head when you sleep, turning the cutting edge outwards. It may also be as well to sleep with the feet where the head usually is, so that, if a vampire does enter, it will not find you.

–Agnes Murgoci, "The Vampire in Roumania,"
Folklore, 37 (1926): 333–334

---

have roots in folklore, but incense was actually more popular. Pre-emptive corpse mutilation was also practiced; bodies at risk often had their leg tendons severed, their mouths sewn shut, or were at least buried facedown in hopes that they would not be able to find their way back up. In many Balkan cases, a sickle was buried with the body to keep it from walking, though the cultural context of this act is not immediately apparent.[10]

Kali, a fanged Hindu goddess who drinks blood
(©Ajanta Art Co., Calcutta, India)

Though protection against vampires is an important part of the scapegoating mechanism which is at work here, the destruction of the creatures in communal vampire hunts holds even deeper resonance. When the community suspects a vampire, it may resort to rituals that do not involve the corpse, such as asking the local priest to grant the deceased sinner absolution or, in another pseudo-pagan twist, hiring the supposed son of a vampire, called a *dhampir* or a *krinsk* by the Roma and Croats, respectively, to "wrestle" with the vampire until victory is declared.[11] Pagan and Christian traditions may also be combined, as in the Bulgarian ritual of luring a mist-bodied vampire into a bottle with blood and food, then sealing the container with a piece of an icon and throwing the lot into a fire. More often, however, vampire hunters attacked the body itself. They would exhume the suspected corpse (or corpses) and see if it had decayed properly or was still intact and thus a vampire. This judgment was usually quite arbitrary. If the hunters had "found a vampire," they would attack the body in any number of ways, including pinning it in its grave with a wooden stake usually made of hawthorn, which legend held was the material of Jesus's cross. The hunters might also remove the heart and burn it, or cremate the body, though this was usually reserved for cases when the stake had "failed to work" as the necessary wood was prohibitively expensive. Lacking any further means of attacking the body, hunters would turn to new vampires until the mania subsided or the mysterious deaths ceased.[12]

It must be emphasized here that almost all vampires were peasants, not nobles as in the literary tradition, and the peasants themselves always performed the hunts, usually without permission or assistance from higher authority. The vampire hunt was always a local activity, whether the tightly knit communities were Balkan *zadruge* or Russian *miri,* and communal responsibility for group welfare was a major objective. When governments did become involved, it was usually to stop the hunts, which the ruling class typically viewed as nonsensical. One of the earliest recorded references to the Slavic vampire comes from just such a prohibition, as Tsar Stephan Dušan prohibited exhuming and cremating bodies "for magical means" in his 1349 codification of Serbian law. The Sorbonne's religious faculty echoed this sentiment in 1691 when it forbade a priest to participate in a Polish vampire hunt. Habsburg Empress Maria Theresa banned the hunts in 1755 and 1756, and Serbian Prince Miloš Obrenovic tried to halt the hunts as an autonomous Serbia emerged from 1815 to 1839.[13] As is the case with most attempts to change ingrained rituals, these attempts were not exceptionally successful.

The vampire was introduced to the West in the eighteenth century. This transmission was precipitated by the growth of the popular press, as well as Austrian and Venetian incursions into the Balkans as the Ottoman Empire began its decline. In 1732, 165 years before Bram Stoker published *Dracula,* Arnold Paole [Arnold Paul] became the first "media" vampire. Austrian military surgeon Johannes Fluckinger wrote an official account of a vampire hunt he had witnessed in Medvegia, a Serb village near Belgrade. Paole, a Serbian *hajduk* (bandit), had died in 1727. His passing was followed by a plague, and the peasants concluded that he was a vampire, especially since he had reportedly fought with a vampire in his army days. There were also reports that Paole had been seen prowling around the village after dark, though these were probably fabricated in the five years between the events and the record. In any event, Paole and four of his "victims" were exhumed, pronounced vampires, and cremated. By the time Fluckinger came on the scene, the plague had returned, and the vampire hunt resumed. This time, sixteen bodies were exhumed, and eleven (including six more hajduks) were pronounced vampires and cremated.[14]

Examined critically, the Medvegia case is a startling example of how a vampire hunt worked. Of the sixteen bodies exhumed in 1732, twelve were either hajduks or from hajduk families, and all six hajduks exhumed were declared vampires; the identities of the four men cremated with Paole in 1727 are not known. Taken in historical context, it seems that this vampire hunt was a gruesome effigy-burning against the hajduks, who were by and large working for the Habsburg occupying force that had turned the Serbian capital, Belgrade, into a German city only a few years earlier. Such nuances were lost when Fluckinger's account was published, however. His article spread like wildfire, even appearing in the

French *Mercure Galant* and several English gazettes. To the general public, the overly credulous Fluckinger seemed like a respectable witness; he was a rational physician, and his account was witnessed by two other medical officers. Further, the vampire was a terrifying, exciting creature whose attacks could seemingly come without reason or cause. By the end of 1732, at least thirteen books on vampires had been published; and the vampire was a popular phenomenon in western Europe.

By 1740, the vampire was part of the popular vernacular, with Alexander Pope confiding in a letter that he felt like "one of those vampires in Germany" when he ventured out at night to inspect his grotto.[15] In 1746, noted biblical scholar and Benedictine abbot Dom Augustin Calmet published the century's most comprehensive survey of vampire belief: *Dissertations sur les Apparitions des Anges des Démons et des Esprits, et sur les revenants, et Vampires du Hungrie, de Boheme, de Moravie, et de Silésie.* Drawing on earlier accounts, including the pre-1732 work of fellow biblical literalist Henry More and noted botanist and Near East ethnographer Pitton de Tournefort, Calmet produced a book in the scholastic tradition carrying the Roman Church's *imprimateur.* Though he approached the work with some logic and a respect for Tournefort's skepticism (the botanist had vividly recounted a vampire hunt on the Greek island of Mykonos that included a corpse being exhumed dozens of times for new creative heights of mutilation), Calmet nonetheless sided with More, at least temporarily, concluding that vampires were real.[16]

Naturally, Calmet's seemingly irrational work produced a backlash through the Enlightenment salon culture. The general reaction was that the frighteningly widespread belief in vampires was an aberration in the "age of reason," and Calmet became a laughingstock in intellectual circles. Already vilified by Voltaire as a simplistic biblical literalist, Calmet found himself on the satirist's agenda again in 1764 when Voltaire likened vampires to Jesuits and demoniacs in his *Dictionnaire Philosophique.*[17] Jean-Jacques Rousseau phrased this European fascination with the undead and its anti-irrational backlash poetically in his *Lettre à Christophe de Beaumont, Archevêque de Paris:* "If there ever is a well-attested history in the world, it is that of the vampires. Nothing is missing from it: interrogations, certifications by Notables, Surgeons, Parish Priests, Magistrates. The judicial proof is one of the most complete and with all that, who believes in vampires?"[18] This is the great paradox: in the era when Europe most fondly embraced rationalism, she also embraced the most irrational manifestation of peasant fear imaginable from the backwaters of the Continent. Thus was born the Enlightenment vampire.

The vampire is a motif that tugs at the soul of many civilizations in a myriad of ways. The vampire is fear of crib death in traditional Malaysia, fear of the seductress in ancient Rome, fear of disease (as well as a means of attacking transgressors) in peasant eastern Europe, and a call to visceral romance in Enlightenment western Europe. This was the creature that would inspire new genres of fiction, poetry, and lifestyle in the centuries to come. This was the vampire.

1. See: Brian Frost, *The Monster with a Thousand Faces: Guises of the Vampire in Myth and Literature* (Bowling Green: Bowling Green State University Popular Press, 1989), pp. 4–6; J. Gordon Melton, *The Vampire Book: The Encyclopedia of the Undead* (Detroit: Visible Ink Press, 1999), pp. 421–422; and Montague Summers, *The Vampire in Europe* (1929; repr. New York: Grammercy Books, 1996), pp. 3–5, 24–25.

2. It is worth pointing out that Lilith is also sometimes translated as "screech owl." This correlation may point to a deeper significance, and additional research is needed to begin to understand the meanings that can be elucidated by comparing the two legends.

3. Melton, *Vampire Book*, pp. 441–442.

4. See Hugo G. Nutini and John M. Roberts, *Bloodsucking Witchcraft: An Epistemological Study of Anthropomorphic Supernaturalism in Rural Tlaxcala* (Tucson: University of Arizona Press, 1993).

5. For details see the following: Anthony Masters, *The Natural History of the Vampire* (New York: Putnam's, 1972); Melton, *Vampire Book*, pp. 393–394, 362; and Donald Glut, *True Vampires of History* (New York: H. C. Publishers, 1971).

6. For an analysis of the etymology of "vampire," see Katharina Wilson, "The History of the Word 'Vampire'," *Journal of the History of Ideas*, 45 (1985): 577–583.

7. See, for example: Lawrence Kayton, "The Relationship of the Vampire Legend to Schizophrenia," *Journal of Youth and Adolescence*, 1 (December 1972): 303–314; and Juan Gomez-Alonso, "Rabies: A Possible Explanation for the Vampire Legend," *Neurology*, 51 (1998): 856–859. As for vampirism and porphyria, that "connection" is outlined and challenged by Norine Dresser in *American Vampires* (New York: Norton, 1989), pp. 171–179.

8. For a detailed exploration of these and other related phenomena, see Paul Barber, *Vampires, Burial, and Death* (New Haven: Yale University Press, 1988).

9. Felix J. Oinas, *Essays on Russian Folklore and Mythology* (Columbus: Slavica, 1985), pp. 111–112, 121–122.

10. Barber, *Vampires*, pp. 46–56.

11. Jan Perkowski, *The Darkling: A Treatise on Slavic Vampirism* (Columbus: Slavica, 1989), p. 31.

12. See Paul Barber, *Vampires*, pp. 57–65.

13. See T. P. Vukanavic, "The Vampire," *Journal of the Gypsie Lore Society*, 36 (1957): 125–133; 37 (1958): 21–31, 111–119; and 38 (1959): 44–55. Also see John V. A. Fine Jr., "In Defense of Vampires," *East European Quarterly*, 21 (1987): 15–23.

14. Barber, *Vampires*, pp. 15–18.

15. M. R. Brownwell, "Pope and the Vampires in Germany," *Eighteenth-Century Life*, 2 (June 1976): 96–97.

16. Calmet did, however, express more skepticism in his revised edition of 1751, in which he suggests a lack of belief in vampirism in the usual sense of the word. For a discussion of Calmet's views, see Massimo Introvigne, "Satanism Scares and Vampirism from the Eighteenth Century to the Contemporary Anti-Cult Movement," *Transylvanian Journal*, 2 (Summer 1996): 38–40.

17. See Arnold Ages, "Voltaire, Calmet and the Old Testament," *Studies on Voltaire and the Eighteenth Century*, 41 (1966): 87–187.

18. Jean-Jacques Rousseau, *Letter to Beaumont, Letters Written from the Mountain, and Related Writings*, ed. Christopher Kelly and Eve Grace (Hanover, N.H.: Dartmouth University Press, 2001), p. 68.

* * *

In these excerpts from The Vampire Book: The Encyclopedia of the Undead *(1999), religious-studies scholar J. Gordon Melton discusses some of the powerful ideas that influenced the development of the vampire myth.*

Some Observations on Vampires, Blood, and Christianity

J. Gordon Melton

The common dictionary definition of a vampire serves as a starting point for inquiry: A vampire is a reanimated corpse that rises from the grave to suck the blood of living people and thus retain a semblance of life. That description certainly fits Dracula, the most famous vampire, but it is only a starting point and quickly proves inadequate in approaching the realm of vampire folklore. By no means do all vampires conform to that definition.

For example, while the subject of vampires almost always leads to a discussion of death, all vampires are not resuscitated corpses. Numerous vampires are disembodied demonic spirits. In this vein are the numerous vampires and vampirelike demons of Indian mythology and the *lamiai* of Greece. Vampires can also appear as the disembodied spirit of a dead person that retains a substantial existence; like many reported ghosts, these vampires can be mistaken for a fully embodied living corpse. Likewise, in the modern secular literary context, vampires sometimes emerge as a different species of intelligent life (possibly from outer space or the product of genetic mutation) or as otherwise normal human beings who have an unusual habit (such as blood-drinking) or an odd power (such as the ability to drain people emotionally). Vampire animals, from the traditional bat to the delightful children's characters Bunnicula and Count Duckula, are by no means absent from the literature. Thus vampires exist in a number of forms, although by far the majority of them are the risen dead.

As commonly understood, the characteristic shared by all of these different vampire entities is their need for blood, which they take from living human beings and animals. A multitude of creatures from the world's mythology have been vampires in the popular literature simply because periodic blood sucking was among their many attributes. When the entire spectrum of vampires is considered, however, that seemingly common definition falls by the way-side, or at the very least must be considerably supplemented. Some vampires do not take blood, rather they steal what is thought of as the life force from their victim. A person attacked by a traditional vampire suffers from the loss of blood, which causes a variety of symptoms; fatigue, loss of color in the face, listlessness, depleted motivation, and weakness. Various conditions that involve no loss of blood share those symptoms. For example, left unchecked, tuberculosis is a wasting disease that is similar to the traditional descriptions of the results of a vampire's attack.

Nineteenth-century romantic novelists and occultists suggested that real vampirism involved the loss of psychic energy to the vampire and wrote of vampiric relationships that had little to do with the exchange of blood. In *Dracula*, Renfield quoted the Bible in noting that "the blood is the life." Thus it is not necessarily the blood itself that the vampire seeks, but the psychic energy or "life force" believed to be carried by it. The metaphor of psychic vampirism can easily be extended to cover various relationships in which one party steals essential life elements from the other, such as when rulers sap the strength of the people they dominate.

On the other extreme, some modern "vampires" are simply blood drinkers. They do not attack and drain victims, but obtain blood in a variety of legal manners (such as locating a willing donor or a source at a blood bank). In such cases, the consumption of the blood has little to do with any ongoing relationship to the source of the blood. It, like food, is merely consumed. Often times, modern vampires even report getting a psychological or sexual high from drinking blood.

–pp. xx–xxi

. . . .

The Significance of Blood

Since ancient times, humans have seen the link between blood and life. Women made the connection between birth and their menstrual flow. Hunters observed the relationship between the spilling of blood and the subsequent loss of consciousness, the ceasing of

Models of Malayan vampires (Peter Haining, The Dracula Scrapbook, *1976; Thomas Cooper Library, University of South Carolina)*

breath, and the eventual death of the animals they sought. And if an animal died of some cause with no outward wound, when cut, the blood often did not flow. Blood was identified with life, and thinkers through the ages produced endless speculations about that connection. People assigned various sacred and magical qualities to blood and used it in a variety of rituals. People drank it, rubbed it on their bodies, and manipulated it in ceremonies.

Some believed that by drinking the blood of a victim the conqueror absorbed the additional strength of the conquered. By drinking the blood of an animal one took on its qualities. As late as the seventeenth century, the women of the Yorkshire area of England were reported to believe that by drinking the blood of their enemies they could increase their fecundity.

Among blood's more noticeable qualities was its red color as it flowed out of the body, and as a result redness came to be seen as an essential characteristic of blood, the vehicle of its power. Red objects were often endowed with the same potency as blood. In particular, red wine was identified with blood, and in ancient

Greece, for example, red wine was drunk by the devotees of the god Dionysus in a symbolic ritual drinking of his blood.

Blood was (and continues to be) seen as somehow related to the qualities possessed by an individual, and beliefs carried references to admirable people as having "good" blood or evil persons as possessing "bad" blood. The blood of the mother was passed to the child, and with it the virtues and defects of the parents were passed to any offspring. Thus blood, in a somewhat literal sense, carried the essential characteristics of the larger collectives—families, clans, national/ethnic groups, even whole races. Such beliefs underlie the modern myth which permitted the Nazi purge of Jews and other supposed lesser races and the practices in American blood banks until recent decades to separate "negro" blood from that of "white" people.

To a lesser extent, blood was identified with other body fluids, most notably semen. In the process of creating a baby, men do not supply blood, only their seed. Thus it was through the semen that male characteristics were passed to the child. In the mythology of race, each of the body fluids—semen, the blood that flowed when the hymen was broken, and menstrual blood—were associated together as part of the sexual life and ascribed magical properties. This association was quite explicit in the sexual teaching of modern ritual magic.

Blood in the Biblical Tradition

The ancient Jewish leaders made the same identification of blood and life. In the book of Genesis, God tells Noah,

> But you must not eat the flesh with the life, which is the blood, still in it. And further, for your life-blood I will demand satisfaction; from every animal will I require it, and from a man also will require satisfaction for the death of his fellow-man.
>
> He that shed the blood of a man, for that man his blood shall be shed; for in the image of God has God made man.

Israel instituted a system of blood sacrifice in which animal blood was shed as an offering to God for the sins of the people. The book of Leviticus included detailed rules for such offerings with special attention given to the proper priestly actions to be taken with the blood. The very first chapter stated the simple rules for offering a bull. It was to be slaughtered before the Tent of the Presence, and the priest was to present the blood and then fling it against the altar. The mysterious sacredness of the blood was emphasized in that God reserved it to himself. The remaining blood was spilled before the altar, and strictures were announced against

the people eating the blood. "Every person who eats the blood shall be cut off from his father's kin" (Lev. 7:27).

Special rules were also established for women concerning their menstrual flow and the flow of blood that accompanied childbirth. Both made a woman ritually impure, and purification rituals had to be performed before she could again enter a sanctuary. In like measure, the discharge of semen caused a man to be ritually impure.

The most stringent rules concerning blood were in that section of Leviticus called the Holiness Code, a special set of rules stressing the role of the people, as opposed to the priest, in being holy before God. Very early in the code, the people are told:

> If any Israelite or alien settled in Israel eats blood, I will set my face against the eater; and cut him off from his people, because the life of a creature is the blood, and I appoint it to make expiation on the altar for yourselves; for the blood is the life that makes expiation. Therefore I have told the Israelites that neither you, nor any alien settled among you, shall eat blood.

Indeed, "For the blood is the life" has been the most quoted Biblical phrase in the vampire literature.

Christianity took Jewish belief and practice to its extreme and logical conclusion. Following his death and (as Christians believe) his resurrection, Jesus, its founder, was worshiped as an incarnation of God who died at the hands of Roman executioners. Christians depicted his death as a human sacrifice, analogous, yet far more powerful, than the Jewish animal sacrifices. As the accounts of his last days were assembled Jesus instituted the Lord's Supper during which he took a cup of wine and told his disciples, "Drink from it, all of you. For this is my blood, the blood of the covenant, shed for many for the forgiveness of sins" (Matthew 26:27). Following his sentencing of Jesus, the Roman governor Pilate washed his hands and told the crowd who had demanded Jesus' death, "My hands are clean of this man's blood." The crowd replied, "His blood be upon us, and on our children" (Matthew 27:24–26). As he hung on the cross, a soldier pierced his side with a lance, and his blood flowed from the wound.

Early Christian thought on the significance of Christ's death was clearly presented in the Apocalypse (The Book of Revelation) in which John spoke of Jesus as the one who "freed us from our sins with his life's blood" (Revelation 1:5). He admonished those suffering persecution by picturing their glory in heaven as the martyrs for the faith. They wore a white robe which had been washed in the blood of the Lamb.

In Christian lands, to the common wisdom concerning life and blood, theological reflection added a special importance to blood. The blood of Christ, in the

One form of a Japanese vampire is a huge cat that usually preys on females in their sleep (Peter Haining,
The Dracula Scrapbook, *1976; Thomas Cooper Library, University of South Carolina).*

form of the red wine of the Eucharist, became the most sacred of objects. So holy had the wine become that during the Middle Ages a great controversy arose over allowing the laity to have the cup. Because of possible carelessness with the wine, the Roman Catholic Church denied the cup, a practice which added more fuel to the fire of the Protestant Reformation of the sixteenth century.

In the light of the special sacredness of Christ's blood, the vampire, at least in its European appearances, took on added significance. The vampire drank blood in direct defiance of the biblical command. It defiled the holy and stole that which was reserved for God alone.

–pp. 53–56

. . . .

Christianity and Vampires

The belief in vampires preceded the introduction of Christianity into southern and eastern Europe. It seems to have originated independently as a response to unexplained phenomena common to most cultures.

Ancient Greek writings tell of the *lamiai,* the *mormolykiai,* and other vampire-like creatures. Independent accounts of vampires emerged and spread among the Slavic people and were passed to their non-Slavic neighbors. Possibly the Gypsies brought some belief in vampires from India that contributed to the development of the myth. As Christianity spread through the lands of the Mediterranean Basin and then northward across Europe, it encountered these vampire beliefs that had already arisen among the many Pagan peoples. However, vampirism was never high on the Christian agenda and was thus rarely mentioned. Its continued presence was indicated by occasional documents such as an eleventh-century law promulgated by Charlemagne as emperor of the new Holy Roman Empire. The law condemned anyone who promoted the belief in the witch/vampire (specifically in its form as a *strix*), and who on account of that belief caused a person thought to be a vampire to be attacked and killed.

By the end of the first Christian millennium, the Christian Church was still organizationally united and in agreement upon the basic Christian affirmation (as contained in the Nicene Creed) but had already begun to differentiate itself into its primarily Greek (Eastern Orthodox) and Latin (Roman Catholic) branches. The Church formally broke in the year 1054 with each side excommunicating the other.

During the second Christian millennium, the two churches completed their conquests through the remaining parts of Europe, especially eastern Europe. Meanwhile, quite apart from the major doctrinal issues which had separated them in the eleventh century, the theology in the two churches began to develop numerous lesser differences. These would become important especially in those areas where the boundaries of the two churches met and wars brought people of one church under the control of political leaders of the other. Such a situation arose, for example, in the twelfth century when the predominantly Roman Catholic Hungarians conquered Transylvania, then populated by Romanians, the majority of whom were Eastern Orthodox. Slavic but Roman Catholic Poland was bounded on the east by Orthodox Russian states. In the Balkans, Roman Catholic Croatia existed beside predominantly Orthodox Serbia.

One divergence between the two churches frequently noted in the vampire literature was their different understanding of the noncorruptibility of dead bodies. In the East, if the soft tissue of a body did not decay quickly once placed in the ground, it was generally considered a sign of evil. That the body refused to disintegrate meant that the earth would, for some reason, not receive it. A noncorrupting body became a candidate for vampirism. In the West, quite the opposite was true. The body of a dead saint often did not experience corruption like that of an ordinary body. Not only did it not decay, but it frequently emitted a pleasant odor. It did not stink of putrefaction. These differing understandings of incorruptibility explain in large part the demise of belief in vampires in the Catholic West, and the parallel survival of belief in Orthodox lands, even though the Greek Church officially tried to suppress the belief.

Vampires and Satan

Admittedly, vampires were not a priority issue on the agenda of Christian theologians and thinkers of either church. However, by 1645 when Leo Allatius (1586–1669) wrote the first book to treat the subject of vampires systematically, it was obvious that much thought, especially at the parish level, had been devoted to the subject. The vampire had been part of the efforts of the church to eliminate Paganism by treating it as a false religion. The deities of the Pagans were considered unreal, nonexistent. In like measure, the demons of Pagan lore were unreal.

Through the thirteenth and fourteenth centuries, as the Inquisition became a force in the Roman Catholic Church, a noticeable change took place in theological perspectives. A shift occurred in viewing Paganism (or witchcraft). It was no longer considered merely a product of the unenlightened imagination, it was the work of the devil. Witchcraft was transformed in the popular mind into Satanism. The change of opinion on Satanism also provided an opening for a reconsideration of, for example, the incubus/succubus and the vampire as also somehow the work of the devil. By the time Allatius wrote his treatise on the vampire, this changing climate had overtaken the church. Allatius was Greek, but he was also a Roman Catholic rather than an Orthodox believer. He possessed a broad knowledge of both churches. In his *De Graecorum hodie quirundam opinationibus,* the vampire toward which he primarily turned his attention was the *vrykolakas,* the Greek vampire.

Allatius noted that among the Eastern Orthodox Greeks a *noncanon,* that is, an ordinance of uncertain authorship and date, was operative in the sixteenth century. It defined a *vrykolakas* as a dead man who remained whole and incorrupt, who did not follow the normal pattern of disintegration which usually occurred very quickly in a time before embalming. Occasionally, such a *vrykolakas* was found, and it was believed to be the work of the devil. When a person discovered a *vrykolakas,* the local priest was to be summoned. The priest chanted an invocation to the Mother of God and again repeated the services of the dead. The earlier noncanon, however, originated in the period when the church was attacking the belief in vampires as superstition and was designed to reverse some centuries-old beliefs about vampires. It ascribed incidents involving *vrykolakas* to someone seeing a dead person, usually at night, frequently in dreams. Such dreams were the work of the devil. The devil had not caused the dead to rise and attack its victims, but deluded the individual with a false dream.

Allatius himself promoted the belief that was gaining dominance in the West through the sixteenth century: Vampires were real and were themselves the work of the devil. Just as the Inquisition in the previous century had championed the idea that witchcraft was real and that witches actually communed with the devil, so vampires were actually walking around the towns and villages of Europe. They were not the dead returned, they were bodies reanimated by the devil and his minions. Allatius even quoted the witchfinders bible, the *Malleus Maleficarum* (*The Witch's Hammer*), which noted the three conditions necessary for witchcraft to exist: the devil, a witch, and the permission of God. In like measure, Allatius asserted that for vam-

---

Immigrant's Fears of Vampires Led to Death

From Our Correspondent
Stoke on Trent, Jan 8

Precautions taken by a Polish immigrant against vampires killed him, it was stated at an inquest here today. For years, Mr Demitrious Myiciura, aged 68, surrounded himself with objects to ward off vampires, even putting garlic in the keyhole of his lodgings at The Villas, Stoke, a house described by a police officer as "like a real Dracula's castle."

Mr. Myiciura, a retired pottery worker who came to England 25 years ago, died by choking on a piece of garlic which he had placed in his mouth before going to sleep.

What Police Constable John Pye, aged 22, found when he broke into the room led him to read the *Natural History of the Vampire* by Anthony Masters.

PC Pye told the inquest: "In the room was a ritual distribution of objects as antidotes to vampires." There was a bag of salt to the left of the dead man's face, one between his legs and other containers scattered around the room.

"Salt was also sprinkled on his blankets. There was a strong smell of garlic in the room. Outside his window was a washing-up bowl containing cloves of garlic. From the book I found that these things were some of the methods used as a precaution against vampires. Apparently it was a Bulgarian custom but there was no evidence that this man had been attacked."

The dead man's landlady, Mrs. Eugizig Rodaziehwicz, said: "He thought vampires were everywhere. He used salt, pepper and garlic to keep them away."

Mr. Frederic Hails, city coroner, said: "This is a strange case. This man took precautions against vampires he thought were in the neighbourhood. He had a superstitious fear of vampires and choked on a clove of garlic used to ward them off."

A verdict of accidental death was recorded.

– *The Times* (London), 9 January 1973, p. 4

---

pires to exist all that was needed was the devil, a dead body, and the permission of God.

The tying of vampirism to the devil by Allatius and his colleagues brought Satan into the vampire equation. Vampirism became another form of Satanism and the vampire the instrument of the devil. Also, his victims were tainted by evil. Like the demons, vampires were alienated from the things of God. They could not exist in the realms of the sacred and would flee from the effective symbols of the true God, such as the crucifix, or from holy things, such as holy water and the eucharistic wafer, which both Orthodox and Roman Catholics believed to be the very body of Christ. In like measure, the offices of the church through the priest were an effective means of stopping the vampire. In the Eastern Orthodox church, the people always invited the priest to participate in their antivampire efforts. In its attempt to counter the superstitious belief in vampires, the Orthodox church ordered its priests not to participate in such activities, even threatening excommunication.

– *The Vampire Book: The Encyclopedia of the Undead*
(Detroit: Visible Ink Press, 1999), pp. 117–119

Eighteenth-Century Vampire Sightings

The word "vampyre" appeared in an English periodical in 1732, occasioned by a rash of vampire sightings documented in several parts of central and eastern Europe, the best known of which was the case of Arnold Paul. The sightings were so widespread that in some countries government officials became directly involved. For example, Austria's Empress Maria Theresa intervened after a new outbreak of vampirism had been reported in Silesia. In 1755 she sent her chief physician, Gerard Van Swieten, to investigate. His declaration that the claim was false led the empress to pass decrees aimed at stopping the spread of vampire hysteria and to ensure that all investigations were thenceforth conducted by civil rather than religious authorities. The many reports of sightings triggered a variety of discussion and analysis, ranging from detailed reports of apparent sightings collected and published in 1746 by French biblical scholar Dom Augustin Calmet to satirical commentary by the Enlightenment philosopher Voltaire.

In this excerpt from his article on the influential scholar Antoine Faivre, professor of religious studies at the Sorbonne, Massimo Introvigne discusses the sightings that attracted attention.

The Medwegya Scare and Its Consequences

Massimo Introvigne

The vampire scare in Medwegya [Medvegia, Madreiga], Serbia, between 1727–32 was the catalyst for the explosion of European interest in vampires generally. In 1734 [Michael] Ranft wrote in the German translation of his book on the *nachzehrer*—which . . . included a section on vampires—that "at the last Easter fair in Leipzig it was impossible to enter a bookstore without seeing something about bloodsuckers."[1] In fact, there were two different Medwegya scares. The first took place in 1727, after the death the previous year of a local soldier, Arnold Paole. The soldier had told his fellow villagers that he had been bitten by a vampire, but did not expect to become one since he had taken the precaution of eating earth taken from the grave of another vampire and anointing himself with vampire blood. The precautions were not really effective, however, and according to the villagers, Paole turned into an "arch-vampire" very soon after his death. He sucked the blood of four Medwegya peasants in 1727 before a stake was driven through his heart. Outside Serbia, the original 1727 incident remained unknown. However, in 1731 villagers again complained that vampires were running loose in Medwegya. It was suspected that they were people, recently dead, who in life had been bitten by Paole. This time, the villagers called in the Austrian authorities, who first dispatched a Vienna doctor called Glaser to investigate the matter. Glaser arrived in Medwegya on December 12, 1731, and subsequently wrote a short report for the Marquis Botta d'Adorno, the Austrian administrator of Serbia. The Marquis became concerned and appointed a full commission to investigate further. The commission, headed by a military surgeon, Johann Flückinger, and including two additional military doctors, J.H. Siegel and Johann Friedrich Baumgarten, arrived in Medwegya on January 7, 1732. By 20th century standards, the Austrian bureaucrats worked surprisingly fast. The report of the Flückinger commission—under the title *Visum et Repertum* ("Seen and Reported")—was filed in Belgrade on January 26, 1732 and published in Nuremberg a few months later.[2] The report concluded that vampires were a reality, although Flückinger and his colleagues had not themselves witnessed any bloodsucking incident. They had, however, examined fifteen corpses, and concluded that eleven of them must have been vampires, because they were still "full of fresh blood." *Visum et Repertum* became a bestseller in Germany, and was largely quoted not only by the press in Germany but in England (*London Journal*), Holland (*Le Glaneur historique*), and France (*Mercure de France*)[3] as well. It is in this context that the words

---

Seen and Discovered

In this excerpt from his report to Emperor Charles VI, Regimental Field Surgeon Johannes Flückinger describes the disinterment of the man believed to be the cause of the outbreak of vampirism in the area.

In 20 or 30 days after his death some people complained that they were being bothered by this same Arnod Paole; and in fact four people were killed by him. In order to end this evil, they dug up this Arnod Paole 40 days after his death—this on the advice of a soldier, who had been present at such events before; and they found that he was quite complete and undecayed, and that fresh blood had flowed from his eyes, nose, mouth, and ears; that the shirt, the covering, and the coffin were completely bloody; that the old nails on his hands and feet, along with the skin, had fallen off, and that new ones had grown; and since they saw from this that he was a true vampire, they drove a stake through his heart, according to their custom, whereby he gave an audible groan and bled copiously. Thereupon they burned the body the same day to ashes and threw these into the grave. These people say further that all those who were tormented and killed by the vampire must themselves become vampires.

Therefore they disinterred the above-mentioned four people in the same way. Then they also add that this Arnod Paole attacked not only the people but also the cattle, and sucked out their blood. And since the people used the flesh of such cattle, it appears that some vampires are again present here, inasmuch as, in a period of three months, 17 young and old people died, among them some who, with no previous illness, died in two or at the most three days.

—translated from *Visum et Repertum*
(Nuremberg, 1732)

"vampyre (wampire)" and "wampyre" were first used in French and English. Politicians also began to take a worried interest in vampires. French and Prussian ambassadors in Vienna informed their governments of the Medwegya incidents, whilst in Prussia King Frederick Wilhelm I personally asked the Royal Society of Science to investigate. Within one month, Count Otto zum Stein, on behalf of the Society, was able to inform the King that vampires were merely figments of the popular imagination and he need not worry.[4] Kings might not worry, but scholars did, and a widespread European debate was opened in the year 1732. Within a year (1732–33), as Faivre has been the first to document, no less than twenty books and articles on vampires had been published in Germany.

—Massimo Introvigne, "Antoine Faivre: Father of Contemporary Vampire Studies," in *Gnoses Ésotérisme & Imaginaire Symbolique: Mélanges offerts à Antoine Faivre,* edited by Richard Caron and others (Leuven: Peeters, 2001), pp. 601–602

1. Michael Ranft, *Tractat von dem Kauen und Schmatzen der Todten in Gräber* (Leipzig, 1734), p. 178.
2. *Visum et Repertum* (Nuremberg, 1732); French trans. Antoine Faivre, *Les Vampires: Essai historique, critique et littéraire* (Paris, 1962).
3. For a full bibliography, see Antoine Faivre, "Du Vampire villageois aux discours des clercs," *in Les Vampires: Actes du Colloque de Cerosy-la-Salle 4–11 août 1992,* ed. Antoine Faivre and Jean Marigny (Paris, 1993), pp. 45–74.
4. See Faivre, "Du Vampire villageois," pp. 64–65.

* * *

Caleb D'Anvers was the pseudonym of the English poet and political writer Nicholas Amhurst. The Craftsman, a weekly newspaper, was founded by Amhurst in 1726. Here Amhurst employs the metaphorical potential of the vampire to political advantage. These are apparently the first occurrences of the word "vampyre" in print in English.

Political Vampyres
Caleb D'Anvers

One Evening last Week I call'd to see a Friend and met a Company of Gentleman and Ladies, engaged in a Dispute about *Prodigies,* occasioned by a very remarkable Event, which hath lately happen'd in *Hungary.* The Account of this Affair, as it is given us in the *London Journal* of *March* the 11th, is of so extraordinary a Nature, that it will be difficult to give my Readers any just Conception of it, without quoting it at large.

. . . .

After quoting from the report of the Arnold Paul case in Medwegya, Amhurst returns to his story.

I shall now proceed to give my Readers the Substance of our Conversation upon this extraordinary Narrative.

The Brunt of the Dispute, upon my entering the Room, lay between a grave *Doctor of Physick* and a *beautiful young Lady,* who was a great Admirer of *strange* and *wonderful Occurrences.* The *Doctor* endeavoured to ridicule such *romantick Stories,* by treating them as the common Artifices of *News-writers* to fill up their Papers, at a dead Season, for want of other Intelligence. The *young Lady* confess'd, with a good deal of Modesty and Candour, that she believed such Things were frequently done; but still insisted on the Truth of this Relation, which stood attested by such *unexceptionable Witnesses.* She observed that the *Time,* the *Place* and the *Names* of the Persons concerned in this Affair were particularly mentioned; that an authentick Account of it appears to have

been transmitted to the Court of *Vienna,* sign'd by no less than six Persons; four of whom were *Surgeons* and the other two *Officers of the Army;* that such Gentlemen must i.e. suppos'd to have too much Skill to be impos'd upon Themselves in such a Matter, and too much Honour to impose upon others. To This the *Doctor* reply'd, with some Disdain, that all the *Surgeons* and *Soldiers* in the Universe should never make Him believe that a *dead Body,* whose animal Powers were totally extinguish'd, could torment the living, by *sucking their Blood,* or performing any other *active and operative Functions.* He added, that it was contrary to all the Principles of Philosophy, as well as the Laws of Nature; and, in my Opinion, urged the Point somewhat too far against a *young, female Opponent;* who, by the Colour in her Cheeks, appeared to be a little nettled and, with a scornful Smile, return'd; *well, well,* Doctor, *you may say what you please; but as wise as you pretend to be now, it is not long ago that you endeavoured to make us believe a Fact, equally ridiculous and absurd. Surely,* Doctor, *said she, you cannot have forgot the famous* Rabbit-Woman *of* Godalmin.—The Smartness of this Reply produced an hearty Laugh on the *Lady's* Side, and put the *Doctor* somewhat out of Countenance. Then turning to me, with an Air of Triumph and Satisfaction, *I am sure, said she, Mr.* D'Anvers, *that you are of my Opinion and believe there may be such Things as* VAMPYRES—A Man, who hath any Degree of Complaisance, is loth to contradict a *pretty Girl,* who forestalls his Judgment in so agreeable a Manner. I desired therefore to read over the Account very attentively before I gave my Opinion upon it, and, clapping on my *political Spectacles,* I soon discovered a secret Meaning in it, which I was in Hopes would moderate the Dispute. I perceived the whole Company waited with Impatience for my Answer; so that having unsaddled my Nose, and composed my Muscles into a becoming Gravity for such an Occasion, I delivered my self to them in the following Manner.

Gentlemen and Ladies,
I think this Dispute may be easily compromis'd, without any Reproach, or Disgrace to either Side. I must agree with the *learned Doctor* that an *inanimated Corpse* cannot possibly perform any *vital Functions;* and yet I am firmly persuaded, with the *young Lady,* that there are *Vampyres,* or *dead Bodies,* which afflict and torment the *Living.* In order to explain my self the more clearly on this Head, I must desire you to reflect that the Account, now before us, comes from the Eastern Part of the World, which hath been always remarkable for writing in the *allegorical Style.* Besides, it deserves our Consideration that the States of *Hungary* are, at present, under the Subjection of the *Turks,* or the *Germans,* and

governed by Them with a pretty hard Rein; which obliges Them to couch all their Complaints under *Types, Figures* and *Parables.* I believe you will make no Doubt that this Relation of the *Vampyres* is a Piece of that Kind and contains a secret Satire upon the Administration of *those Countries,* when you consider the following Particulars.

You see that the Method, by which these *Vampyres* are said to torment and kill the *Living,* is by *sucking out all their Blood;* and what, I pray, is a more common Phrase for a *ravenous Minister,* even in this Part of the World, than a *Leech,* or *Blood sucker,* who preys upon human Gore, and fattens Himself upon the Vitals of his Country?

Now, if you admit of this Interpretation, which I think far from being strain'd, the whole Mystery of the *Vampyres* will unfold it self of Course; for a *plundering Minister* carries his Oppressions beyond the Grave and continues to torment Those, whom He leaves behind Him, by anticipating the *publick Revenues* and entailing a Perpetuity of *Taxes* and *Gabels* upon the People, which must drain the Body politick by Degrees of all its Blood and Spirits.

It is farther said, in the Narrative, *that all such as have been tormented, or kill'd by the* Vampyres, *become* Vampyres, *when They are dead.*—This likewise is perfectly agreeable to my System; for those Persons, who groan under the Burthens of *such a Minister,* are often obliged to sell, or mortgage their Estates, and therefore may be Said, in a proper Sense, to torment *their unhappy Posterity* in the same Manner.

Whether this *Arnold Paul,* or *Paul Arnold,* mentioned in the Narrative, was a Person in any Office, or Employment in the Administration, which gave Him a Power of oppressing the People, either as a *Tax-layer,* or a *Tax-gatherer,* I am not able to determine, without farther Enquiry. He is said, indeed, to have been an *Hoyduke,* which I take to be a Character of some Consequence in those Countries; but, perhaps, He might have been employ'd only as a *ministerial Tool,* or *Instrument of Oppression,* under some *great Blood sucker of State.* For my own Part, I am inclined to this Opinion; because it is said that He had kill'd only *four Persons;* whereas, if He had been a *Vampyre* of any considerable Rank, We should in all Probability have heard of his *Thousands and his ten Thousands.*

I confess there is a Circumstance or two in the Account of *this Man,* which may seem, at first Sight, to clear Him from any such Aspersions, and even to contradict my Explanation of the *Vampyres.* I mean that Passage, where it is said, *that when his Body was taken up,* forty Days *after He had been dead, They found it to be fresh and free from any Manner of* CORRUPTION; but I think even this Difficulty will admit of a rational Solution; for

Hungarian Antidote Against Vampires

The following is excerpted from a letter written in 1732 by an officer of the Austrian Imperial Army, who was stationed in Hungary. It was published in Les Lettres Juives *(1732).*

As for these Hungarian specters, the thing generally happens in this manner: a man finds himself fallen into a languid state, loses his appetite, decreases visibly in bulk and, at eight or ten days' end, dies without a fever or any other symptom of illness save anemia and loss of flesh and a dried, withered body.

In Hungary they say that a vampire has attacked him and sucked his blood. Many of those who fall ill in this way declare that a white spectre is following them and sticks to them as close as their own shadow. When we were in our Kalocsa-Bács quarters, in the country of Temesvár, two officers of the regiment in which I was a cornet died from this languor, and several more were attacked and would have perished had not a corporal of our regiment put an end to these maladies by resorting to the remedial ceremonies which are practiced by local people. These are very unusual, and although they are considered an infallible cure I cannot remember ever having seen these in any ritual.

They select a young lad who is innocent of girls, that is to say who has never performed the sexual act. He is placed upon a young stallion who has not yet mounted a mare, who has never stumbled, and who must be pitch-black without a speck of white. The stud is ridden into the cemetery to and fro among the graves, and the grave over which the horse refuses to pass, in spite of blows liberally administered to him, is where the vampire lies.

The tomb is opened and they find a sleek, fat corpse, as healthily colored as though the man were quietly and happily sleeping in calm repose. With one single blow from a sharp spade they cut off the head, whereupon there gushes forth a *warm* stream of blood of rich red color, filling the whole grave. It could easily be surmised that they had just decapitated a big brawny fellow of most sanguine habit and complexion.

When this business is done, they refill the grave with earth and then the ravages of the disease immediately cease, whilst those suffering from this malady gradually recover their strength, just as convalescents recuperate after a long illness.

This is exactly what occurred in the case of our young officers who had sickened. As the colonel of the regiment, the captain, and the lieutenant were absent, I happened to be in command just then and I was very angry to find that the corporal had arranged the affair without my knowledge.

—translated by Raymond T. McNally in his
A Clutch of Vampires (New York:
Warner, 1975), pp. 58–59

An English Gentleman's Report

The following excerpt–from a manuscript titled "The Travels of three English Gentlemen, from Venice to Hamburgh, being the grand Tour of Germany, in the Year 1734"–was evidently written in the 1730s but did not appear in print until it was published in The Harleian Miscellany: A Collection of Scarce, Curious, and Entertaining Pamphlets and Tracts, as well in Manuscript as in Print *in 1809.*

The editor for The Harleian Miscellany *described the writer as "a person of curiosity" and "a member of the Royal Society, and of the University of Oxford."*

We must not omit observing here, that our landlord seemed to pay some regard to what Baron Valvasor has related of the Vampyres, said to infest some parts of this country. These Vampyres are supposed to be the bodies of deceased persons, animated by evil spirits, which come out of the graves, in the night-time, suck the blood of many of the living, and thereby destroy them. Such a notion will, probably, be looked upon as fabulous and exploded, by many people in England; however, it is not only countenanced by Baron Valvasor, and many Carnioleze noblemen, gentlemen, etc. as we were informed; but likewise actually embraced by some writers of good authority. M. Jo. Henr. Zopfius, director of the *gymnasium* of Essen, a person of great erudition, has published a dissertation upon them, which is extremely learned and curious, from whence we shall beg leave to transcribe the following paragraph: "The Vampyres, which come out of the graves in the night-time, rush upon people sleeping in their beds, suck out all their blood, and destroy them. They attack men, women, and children; sparing neither age nor sex. The people, attacked by them, complain of suffocation, and a great interception of spirits; after which, they soon expire. Some of them, being asked, at the point of death, what is the matter with them? say they suffer in the manner just related from people lately dead, or rather the spectres of those people; upon which, their bodies (from the description given of them, by the sick person), being dug out of the graves, appear in all parts, as the nostrils, cheeks, breast, mouth, &c. turgid and full of blood. Their countenances are fresh and ruddy; and their nails, as well as hair, very much grown. And, though they have been much longer dead than many other bodies, which are perfectly putrified, not the least mark of corruption is visible upon them. Those who are destroyed by them, after their death, become Vampyres; so that, to prevent so spreading an evil, it is found requisite to drive a stake through the dead body, from whence, on this occasion, the blood flows as if the person was alive. Sometimes the body is dug out of the grave, and burnt to ashes; upon which, all disturbances cease. The Hungarians call these spectres *Pamgri,* and the Servians *Vampyres;* but the etymon, or reason of these names is not known."

. . . .

These spectres are reported to have infested several districts of Servia, and the bannat of Temeswaer, in the year 1725, and for seven or eight years afterwards; particularly those of Mevadia, or Meadia, and Parakin, near the Morava. In 1732, we had a relation of some of their feats in the neighborhood of Cassovia; and the public prints took notice of the tragedies they acted in the bannat of Temeswaer, in the year 1738. Father Gabriel Rzaczynski, in his Natural History of the kingdom of Poland, and the great duchy of Lithuania, published at Sendomir, in 1721, affirms, that in Russia, Poland, and the great duchy of Lithuania, dead bodies, actuated by infernal spirits, sometimes enter people's houses in the night, fall upon men, women, and children, and attempt to suffocate them; and that of such diabolical facts his countrymen have several very authentic relations. The Poles call a man's body thus informed, Upier, and that of a woman, Upierzyca, i.e. a 'winged or feathered creature;' which name seems to be deduced from the surprizing lightness and activity of these incarnate demons. If we remember right, an account of them also, from Poland, is to be met with in some of the news-papers for 1693; perfectly agreeing with those of the Servian Vampyres given us by M. Zopfius. In fine, the notion of such pestiferous beings has prevailed from time immemorial over a great part of Hungary, Servia, Carniola, Poland, &c. as is evinced by several authors in conjunction with the aforesaid M. Zopfius.

–The Harleian Miscellany, volume 4 (London: Printed for White and Co., and others, 1809), pp. 375–376

it is the *Mind,* not the *Body,* which is the Author of all Wickedness; and a Man can no more carry his *bad Qualities,* than his *Riches* with Him into the Grave. He leaves his *Corruption,* as well as the *Fruits* of it, in this World, to stink in the Nostrils of his Posterity.

Another Article in this Account, which may be thought an Objection to *my Scheme,* is the Method of destroying these *posthumous Tyrants;* for it is said *that, as They observ'd, from all these Circumstances, that this Arnold was a* Vampyre, *they drove a Stake through his Heart, according to Custom; at which He gave an horrid Groan and lost a great deal of Blood. Afterwards, they burnt his Body to Ashes, the same Day, and threw them into his Grave.*

From hence, perhaps, it may be argued that there must be somewhat more than an *Allegory* in this Affair; for otherwise of what Advantage could it be to destroy his *Body* with so much Ceremony? But I think this Objection is so far from being of any Weight, that I apprehend it to be rather a Corroboration of my Hypothesis.–Nay, it seems to be an Argument that the whole Story is only a *Fable,* or *Fiction,* made use of to convey a satirical Invective against some *living Oppressor;* for as a *dead Corpse* cannot perform any *vital Functions* (according to the judicious Observation of my *learned Friend* there) so neither can it be sensible of any *Pain,* or express it by any *Sounds,* tho' a thousand stakes should be driven through it. But, is it not probable that *this Ceremony* was designed only as a Mark of Ignominy, to deter others from the same Practices, just as We drive a Stake though the Body of a *Self-murderer;* or, might it not be a superstitious Usage, of great Credit amongst the Vulgar, like our *laying of Spirits in the* Red Sea?

As to the *Blood,* which *Arnold* is said to have lost, when the Stake was driven through his Heart, nothing can be understood by it but making Him refund the *corrupt Wages,* which he had suck'd out of the Veins of his Countrymen.

I think I have said enough to convince you that We are not to understand this Account according to the *Letter;* in which Seane it appears *ridiculous* and *impossible,* to use the Words of the *admirable News Paper* now before us; whereas in the *other figurative Sense,* which I have put upon it, nothing can be more rational, obvious and intelligible. The Histories of all Countries, and especially our own, supply us with so many Instances of *Vampyres,* in this Sense, that it would fill up Volumes only to enumerate them. In former Times, the *Gavestons, Spencers* and *De la Poles, Empson* and *Dudley, Wolsey, Buckingham* and an Hundred more were *Vampyres* of the first Magnitude, and spread their Cruelties far and wide through this Island; nor shall We be at a Loss for Instances of the same Kinds in these latter Ages, if We please to consult our Annals, or our Memories a little backwards.

Give me Leave to observe, in this Place, that *private Persons* may be *Vampyres,* in some Degree, as well as Those in *publick Employments.* I look upon all *Sharpers, Usurers* and *Stockjobbers* in this Light, as well as *fraudulent Guardians, unjust Stewards,* and the *dry Nurses of great Estates.* I make no Doubt that a *noble Colonel,* lately deceased, hath already convinced several Families that He is a *Vampyre;* and I could mention several *other Gentlemen,* in great Favour at present, who have intitled Themselves to the same Denomination.

It will not, I suppose, be denied that many of the *late Southsea Directors* were Tormentors of this Sort; and I heartily wish that the *present Managers of that Company* may not furnish us with some Influences of the same Nature.

The *Charitable Corporation* hath produced a plentiful Crop of these *Blood-suckers,* whose Depredations have already ruined a Multitude of People, and I am afraid will torment others, even yet unborn, notwithstanding all the glorious and indefatigable Pains, which the *Gentlemen of the Committee* have taken to unravel this Scene of Iniquity, as well as the wise Provisions, which the *Parliament* hath made for the Relief of the *unhappy Sufferers.*

It must be confess'd that *these virtuous and industrious Gentlemen* have display'd their Abilities for Mischief, as far as a poor Capital of *five or six hundred thousand Pounds* would give them Room; but what a glorious, extended Ruin might We have expected from Them, if they had moved in an higher Sphere, and had been trusted with the Riches of a whole nation? Nothing but the Power of a *TR––––y* can raise up a *compleat Vampyre;* and *England* hath seen many such within a Century, or two.

It is somewhere observ'd that *Cecil,* Earl of *Salisbury* was the *last good Treasurer* and the *first bad one,* since Queen *Elizabeth's* Reign; but, perhaps, this Reflection may be a little too severe; for We are told that Bishop *Juxon* accounted with the utmost Exactness, when He laid down the Staff; and notwithstanding the Censures, which different Parties have past on the Earl of *Godolphin* and *Oxford,* on other Accounts, they both went out of their Office with *clean Hands* and dyed *poor.*

Mezeray gives us a very extraordinary Instance of a Treasurer in *France,* (one *Girard de Possi*) who was seiz'd with a Remorse of Conscience for having robb'd his Master of a very great Sum of Money, and refunded it into the *Exchequer* of his own Accord; but the Historian adds *that He believes* this Example *will always remain singular, and that We shall never see* another Financier, *who will follow such a Precedent; for whatever Corruption* these Gentlemen *are guilty of, They commonly chuse to go to the* Gallows, *rather than make any* Restitution.

Since therefore this appears to be the Case, We can never be too much upon our Guard against Persons in *such Stations,* and I leave it to be considered whether instead of driving a Stake through the Body of a *corrupt Treasurer,* when He is dead, it would not be more adviseable to administer a *certain, Parliamentary Emetick,* which will make Him disgorge all his ill-gotten Wealth, whilst He is alive. I look upon This as the most effectual Method to destroy a *great, overgrown Vampyre,* and secure our Posterity from his tormenting Oppressions, when an End is put to his natural Life, and his Carcass is rotten in the Ground.

Having finished my Speech, which was honoured with the strictest Attention, I was very much pleased to find it produce the desired Effect, by putting an End to the Dispute, which occasioned it. The *Doctor* only nodded his Head and told me with a Smile, *that I had a political Turn for every Thing.* The *young Lady* express'd her Satisfaction in the most obliging Terms, and was pleas'd to say that my Solution of *this Prodigy* would make a very good *Craftsman*. She was immediately seconded by the whole Company, who press'd me with so much Importunity to print it in my next Paper, that I could not in good Manners refuse their Request, and I hope my loving Readers will excuse me, on that Account, for troubling Them this Week with a loose, unpremeditated Piece of Conversation.

—The Country Journal: or, The Craftsman,
no. 307 (20 May 1732)

* * *

By far the most influential writings about the eighteenth-century vampire sightings came from a French biblical scholar, Dom Augustin Calmet. His two-volume dissertation was first published in 1746 and revised as Traité sur les apparitions des esprits et sur les vampires *(1751; translated as* The Phantom World, *1850). In his "Advertisement" for his work, Calmet explains his purpose:*

> Every body talks of apparitions of angel and demons, and of souls separated from the body. The reality of these apparitions is considered as certain by many persons, while others deride them and treat them as altogether visionary.
>
> I have determined to examine this matter, just to see what certitude there can be on this point. . . .

Dom Augustin Calmet on Vampires

The following excerpt is from Calmet's preface to the second volume of his work, in which he treats vampires.

. . . In this age, a new scene presents itself to our eyes, and has done for about sixty years in Hungary, Moravia, Silesia, and Poland; men, it is said, who have been dead for several months, come back to earth, talk, walk, infest villages, ill use both men and beasts, suck the blood of their near relations, destroy their health, and finally cause their death; so that people can only save themselves from their dangerous visits and their hauntings, by exhuming them, impaling them, cutting off their heads, tearing out their hearts, or burning them. These are called by the name of oupires or vampires, that is to say, leeches; and such particulars are related of them, so singular, so detailed, and attended by such probable circumstances, and such judicial information, that one can hardly refuse to credit the belief which is held in those countries, that they come out of their tombs, and produce those effects which are proclaimed of them.

—p. 2

. . . .

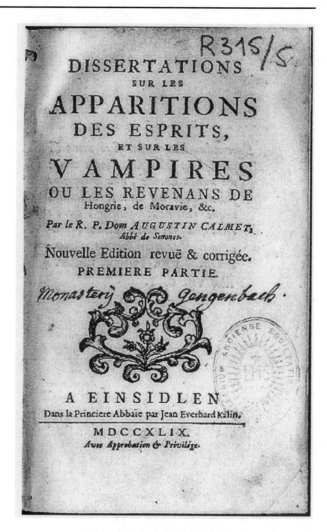

Title page for the 1749 edition of Calmet's controversial work (Library of Congress)

Calmet titles his second volume "Dissertation on Those Persons Who Return to Earth Bodily, the Excommunicated, the Oupires or Vampires, Vroucolacas, Etc."

The *revenans* of Hungary, or vampires, which form the principal object of this dissertation, are men who have been dead a considerable time, sometimes more, sometimes less; who leave their tombs, and come and disturb the living, sucking their blood, appearing to them, making a noise at their doors and in their houses, and lastly, often causing their death. They are named vampires, or oupires, which signifies, they say, in Sclavonic, a leech. The only way to be delivered from their haunting, is to disinter them, cut off their head, impale them, burn them, or pierce their heart.

Several systems have been propounded to explain the return and apparition of the vampires.

Voltaire on Vampires

Voltaire (engraving by D. Kimberly; frontispiece for A Philosophical
Dictionary, *1874; Thomas Cooper Library,
University of South Carolina)*

*François-Marie Arouet Voltaire, the great Enlightenment
thinker, ridiculed the idea of vampires in his* Dictionnaire
philosophique *(1764).*

What! is it in our eighteenth century that vampires
exist? Is it after the reigns of Locke, Shaftsbury, Tren-
chard, and Collins? Is it under those of D'Alembert,
Diderot, St. Lambert, and Duclos, that we believe in
vampires, and that the reverend father Dom Calmet,
benedictine priest of the congregation of St. Vannes and
St. Hidulphe, abbé of Senon,—an abbey of a hundred
thousand livres a year, in the neighbourhood of two
other abbeys of the same revenue,—has printed and
reprinted the history of vampires, with the approbation
of the Sorbonne, signed Marcilli?

These vampires were corpses, who went out of their
graves at night to suck the blood of the living, either at
their throats or stomachs, after which they returned to
their cemeteries. The persons so sucked waned, grew
pale, and fell into consumptions; while the sucking
corpses grew fat, got rosy, and enjoyed an excellent
appetite. It was in Poland, Hungary, Silesia, Moravia,
Austria, and Lorraine, that the dead made this good
cheer. We never heard speak of vampires in London,
nor even at Paris. I confess, that in both these cities
there were stock-jobbers, brokers, and men of business,
who sucked the blood of the people in broad day-light;
but they were not dead, though corrupted. These true
suckers lived not in cemeteries, but in very agreeable
palaces.

Who would believe, that we derive the idea of vampires from Greece? Not from the Greece of Alexander,
Aristotle, Plato, Epicurus and Demosthenes; but from
christian Greece, unfortunately schismatic.

. . . .

But all these stories, however true they might be, had
nothing in common with the vampires who rose to suck
the blood of their neighbors, and afterwards replaced
themselves in their coffins. They looked if they could
not find in the Old Testament, or in the mythology,
some vampire whom they could quote as an example;
but they found none. It was proved, however, that the
dead drank and ate, since in so many ancient nations
food was placed on their tombs.

The difficulty was to know whether it was the soul or
the body of the dead which ate. It was decided that it
was both. Delicate and unsubstantial things, as sweet-
meats, whipped cream, and melting fruits, were for the
soul, and roast beef and the like were for the body.

The kings of Persia were, said they, the first who
caused themselves to be served with viands after their
death. Almost all the kings of the present day imitate
them, but they are the monks who eat their dinner and
supper, and drink their wine. Thus, properly speaking,
kings are not vampires: the true vampires are the monks,
who eat at the expense of both kings and people.

It is very true that St. Stanislaus, who had bought a
considerable estate from a Polish gentleman, and not
paid him for it, being brought before king Boleslas by
his heirs, raised up the gentleman; but this was solely to
get quittance. It is not said that he gave a single glass of
wine to the seller, who returned to the other world without having eaten or drunk. They afterwards treated of
the grand question, whether a vampire could be
absolved who died excommunicated, which comes
more to the point.

I am not profound enough in theology to give my
opinion on this subject, but I would willingly be for
absolution, because in all doubtful affairs we should
take the mildest part.

Odia restringenda, favores ampliandi.

The result of all this is, that a great part of Europe
has been infested with vampires for five or six years,
and that there are now no more; that we have had con-
vulsionaries in France for twenty years, that we have
them no longer; that we have had demoniacs for seventeen hundred years, but have them no longer; that the
dead have been raised ever since the days of Hippoly-
tus, but that they are raised no longer; and lastly, that
we have had jesuits in Spain, Portugal, France, and the
two Sicilies, but that we have them no longer.

*–A Philosophical Dictionary; from the French
of M. de Voltaire,* volume 2 (Boston:
J. P. Mendum 1874), pp. 371–372

Some persons have denied and rejected them as chimerical, and as an effect of the prepossession and ignorance of the people of these countries, where they are said to return.

Others have thought that these people were not really dead, but that they had been interred alive, and returned naturally out of their tombs.

Others believe that these people are truly dead, but that God, by a particular permission or command, permits or commands them to come back to earth, and resume for a time their own body; for when they are exhumed, their bodies are found entire, their blood red and fluid, and their limbs supple and pliable.

Others maintain that it is the demon who causes these *revenans* to appear, and by their means does all the harm he can both to men and animals.

–Chapter I, pp. 5–6

. . . .

Calmet evidently accepts the report of Johannes Flückinger in Visum et Repertum *as wholly reliable. He writes, "we cannot refuse to believe that to be true which is juridically attested, and by persons of probity. We will here give a copy of what happened in 1732, and which is inserted in the* Glaneur, *No. XVIII" (p. 36).*

CHAPTER X.

OTHER INSTANCES OF GHOSTS— CONTINUATION OF THE GLEANER.

In a certain canton of Hungary, named in Latin *Oppida Heidanum,* beyond the Tibisk, *vulgo* Teiss, that is to say, between that river which waters the fortunate territory of Tokay and Transylvania, the people known by the name of *Heyducqs* believe that certain dead persons, whom they call vampires, suck all the blood from the living, so that these become visibly attenuated, whilst the corpses, like leeches, fill themselves with blood in such abundance that it is seen to come from them by the conduits, and even oozing through the pores. This opinion has just been confirmed by several facts which cannot be doubted, from the rank of the witnesses who have certified them. We will here relate some of the most remarkable.

About five years ago, a certain Heyducq, inhabitant of Madreiga, named Arnald Paul, was crushed to death by the fall of a wagon-load of hay. Thirty days after his death four persons died suddenly, and in the same manner in which, according to the tradition of the country, those die who are molested by vampires. They then remembered that this Arnald Paul had often related that in the environs of Cassovia, and on the frontiers of Turkish Servia, he had often been tormented by a Turkish vampire; for they believe also that those who have been passive vampires during life become active ones after their death, that is to say, that those who have been sucked, suck also in their turn; but that he had found means to cure himself by eating earth from the grave of the vampire, and smearing himself with his blood; a precaution which, however, did not prevent him from becoming so after his death, since, on being exhumed forty days after his interment, they found on his corpse all the indications of an arch-vampire. His body was red, his hair, nails, and beard had all grown again, and his veins were replete with fluid blood, which flowed from all parts of his body upon the winding-sheet which encompassed him. The Hadnagi, or bailli of the village, in whose presence the exhumation took place, and who was skilled in vampirism, had, according to custom, a very sharp stake driven into the heart of the defunct Arnald Paul, and which pierced his body through and through, which made him, as they say, utter a frightful shriek, as if he had been alive: that done, they cut off his head, and burnt the whole body. After that they performed the same on the corpses of the four other persons who died of vampirism, fearing that they in their turn might cause the death of others.

All these performances, however, could not prevent the recommencement of similar fatal prodigies towards the end of last year, (1732), that is to say, five years after, when several inhabitants of the same village perished miserably. In the space of three months seventeen persons of different sexes and different ages died of vampirism; some without being ill, and others after languishing two or three days. It is reported, amongst other things, that a girl named Stanoska, daughter of the Heyducq Jotiützo, who went to bed in perfect health, awoke in the middle of the night all in a tremble, uttering terrible shrieks, and saying that the son of the Heyducq Millo, who had been dead nine weeks, had nearly strangled her in her sleep. She fell into a languid state from that moment, and at the end of three days she died. What this girl had said of Millo's son made him known at once for a vampire: he was exhumed, and found to be such. The principal people of the place, with the doctors and surgeons, examined how vampirism could have sprung up again after the precautions they had taken some years before.

They discovered at last, after much search, that the defunct Arnald Paul had killed not only the four persons of whom we have spoken, but also several oxen, of which the new vampires had eaten, and amongst others the son of Millo. Upon these indications they resolved to disinter all those who had died within a certain time, &c. Amongst forty, seventeen were found with all the most evident signs of vampirism; so they transfixed their hearts and cut off their heads also, and then cast their ashes into the river.

All the informations and executions we have just mentioned were made juridically, in proper form, and attested by several officers who were garrisoned in the country, by the chief surgeons of the regiments, and by the principal inhabitants of the place. The verbal process of it was sent towards the end of last January to the Imperial Council of War at Vienna, which had established a military commission to examine into the truth of all these circumstances.

Such was the declaration of the Hadnagi Barriarar and the ancient Heyducqs, and it was signed by Battuer, first lieutenant of the regiment of Alexander of Wurtemburg, Clickstenger, surgeon-in-chief of the regiment of Frustemburch, three other surgeons of the company, and Guoichitz, captain at Stallach.

–pp. 37–40

. . . .

CHAPTER XIII.

NARRATION EXTRACTED FROM THE "MERCURE GALENT" OF 1693 AND 1694, CONCERNING GHOSTS.

The public memorials of the years 1693 and 1694 speak of *oupires,* vampires or ghosts, which are seen in Poland, and above all in Russia. They make their appearance from noon to midnight, and come and suck the blood of living men or animals in such abundance that sometimes it flows from them at the nose, and principally at the ears, and sometimes the corpse swims in its own blood oozed out in its coffin. It is said that the vampire has a sort of hunger, which

makes him eat the linen which envelops him. This reviving being, or *oupire,* comes out of his grave, or a demon in his likeness, goes by night to embrace and hug violently his near relations or his friends, and sucks their blood so much as to weaken and attenuate them, and at last cause their death. This persecution does not stop at one single person; it extends to the last person of the family, if the course be not interrupted by cutting off the head or opening the heart of the ghost, whose corpse is found in his coffin, yielding, flexible, swollen, and rubicund, although he may have been dead some time. There proceeds from his body a great quantity of blood, which some mix up with flour to make bread of; and that bread eaten in the usual manner protects them from being tormented by the spirit, which returns no more.

–pp. 52–53

. . . .

For this story Calmet cites the German author Michael Rauff, who "has composed a work, entitled De Masticatione Mortuorum in Tumulis– 'Of the Dead who masticate in their Graves'" *(p. 177).*

CHAPTER XLVI.

SINGULAR INSTANCE OF A HUNGARIAN GHOST.

The most remarkable instance cited by Rauff is that of one Peter Plogojovitz, who had been buried ten weeks in a village of Hungary, called Kisolova. This man appeared by night to some of the inhabitants of the village while they were asleep, and grasped their throat so tightly that in four-and-twenty hours it caused their death. Nine persons, young and old, perished thus in the course of eight days.

The widow of the same Plogojovitz declared that her husband since his death had come and asked her for his shoes, which frightened her so much that she left Kisolova to retire to some other spot.

From these circumstances the inhabitants of the village determined upon disinterring the body of Plogojovitz and burning it, to deliver themselves from these visitations. They applied to the Emperor's officer, who commanded in the territory of Gradiska in Hungary, and even to the Curé of the same place, for permission to exhume the body of Peter Plogojovitz. The officer and the Curé made much demur in granting it, but the peasants declared that if they were refused permission to disinter the body of this man, whom they had no doubt was a true vampire, (for so they called these revived corpses,) they should be obliged to forsake the village, and go where they could.

The Emperor's officer, who wrote this account, seeing he could hinder them neither by threats nor promises, went with the Curé of Gradiska to the village of Kisolova, and having caused Peter Plogojovitz to be exhumed, they found that his body exhaled no bad smell; that he looked as when alive, except the tip of the nose; that his hair and beard had grown, and instead of his nails which had fallen off, new ones had come; that under his cuticle, which appeared whitish, there was a new skin, which looked healthy, and of a natural colour; his feet and hands were as whole as could be desired in a living man. They remarked also in his mouth some fresh blood, which these people believed that this vampire had sucked from the men whose death he had occasioned.

The Emperor's officer and the Curé having diligently examined all these things, and the people who were present feeling their indignation awakened anew, and being more fully persuaded that he was the true cause of the death of their compatriots, ran directly for a sharp pointed stake, which they thrust into his breast, whence there issued a quantity of fresh and crimson blood, and also from the nose and mouth. After this the peasants placed the body on a pile of wood, and saw it reduced to ashes.

M. Rauff, from whom we have these particulars, cites several authors who have written on the same subject, and have related instances of dead people who have eaten in their tombs. He cites particularly Gabril Rzaczincki in his history of the Natural Curiosities of the Kingdom of Poland, printed at Sandomir in 1721.

–The Phantom World: or The Philosophy of Spirits, Apparitions, &c., 2 volumes, translated by Henry Christmas (London: Richard Bentley, 1850), pp. 180–182

* * *

Did Calmet Believe in Vampires?

Italian scholar Massimo Introvigne has challenged the widely held view that Calmet was himself a believer in vampires. The following is excerpted from his article "Satanism Scares and Vampirism."

It is commonly argued that belief in the reality of vampires in the 18th century was supported by the famous *Dissertation* by Benedictine scholar Dom Augustin Calmet (1672–1757). Most of those criticizing Calmet–including some of his contemporaries–probably did not read carefully his book and trusted the ironical remarks of Voltaire, who–on the other hand–had been the guest of Calmet in his abbey of Senones and held the Benedictine in some regard for his prodigious erudition in historical and theological matters. It is true that Calmet, in his 1746 book, amassed in an apparently uncritical way reports of vampire incidents from all over Eastern Europe and became the source of all modern vampirology. On the other hand, recent scholarship tends to regard Calmet, based on his correspondence with a number of fellow Catholic scholars and priests, as much more skeptical than it is usually believed. Since a number of passages in his 1746 book were ambiguous, they were corrected in the second edition, of 1751, where Calmet concludes that he does believe that some corpses may be "conserved" (perhaps because they were buried when the subject was only apparently dead) but he does not believe in vampirism in the usual sense of the term. As we shall see, in the 19th century Calmet would be accused by Catholic demonologists of being a skeptical Enlightenment philosopher in disguise. Italian scholar Nadia Minerva–in a study of the Satanism scares in the 18th century–has concluded that Calmet was neither a skeptic in disguise (if he did not believe in vampires, he did believe firmly in a number of other diabolical manifestations), nor the gullible true believer depicted by Voltaire. He tried a "middle way" that he called the "voie raisonnable" ("reasonable way,") arguing that some phenomena were perhaps true but most were not. His peculiar literary style of repeating first all the vampire stories as if they were actually true, then criticizing them, in later chapters of the book, maintained however an ambiguity to the whole exercise.

–Transylvanian Journal, 2 (Spring/Summer 1996): 39

*Gérard Van Swieten (print by R. Vinkeles; Rijksmuseum voor de Geschiedenis der Natuurwetenschappen, Leiden)
and Empress Maria Theresa (portrait by Jean Etienne Liotard; Rijksmuseum, Amsterdam)*

Gérard Van Swieten was commissioned by Austrian empress Maria Theresa to investigate the vampire phenomena. As a result of his report (January 1755), which dismissed belief in vampires as mere superstition, the empress issued a decree on 1 March of the same year declaring that, as vampires do not exist, it would be a criminal offense to take bodies out of their graves in order to deal with them as "vampires."

Report of Gérard Van Swieten to Empress Maria Theresa

An English Vampire

Some months ago I read a small English treatise printed in London, in 1751, in which one could read of a notable and well-proven fact. In the month of February 1750, the tomb of an old family in the county of Devonshire in England was opened: among many bones and numerous rotting caskets was found an intact wooden box: it was opened out of curiosity; within was found the whole body of a man: the flesh yet retained its natural firmness; the joints of the shoulders, neck, and fingers were completely supple: when the face was pressed, it gave under the finger but

regained its shape as soon as the pressure lifted: the same thing was tried on the entire body; the beard was black and four inches long. The cadaver had not been embalmed, as no sign of incision was spotted. There you have an English vampire, which for 80 years had rested peacefully in its tomb, bothering no one.

Superstition, Daughter of Ignorance

Let us examine the alleged facts offered as proof of vampirism. Rosina Iolackin, died 22 December 1754, was dug up on 19 January 1755 and declared a vampire fit for the fire, because she was found intact in her tomb. In the winter, anatomists keep cadavers in the open air for six weeks and even two months without putrefaction. And it is worth noting that this winter has been particularly harsh.

Most of the bodies of all the other unearthed cadavers had already decomposed: but it sufficed that they were not completely putrefied, so, quick, into the fire! What ignorance! . . . Two sterilization specialists, "surgeons" who had never seen a dried-up cadaver, who knew nothing of the structure of the human body, as they themselves confessed to the commissioners, were the witnesses who were to establish the sentence of fire. . . .

It is on bases of this sort that this entire story has been concocted, that sacrileges are being committed, and that the sanctuary of tombs is being violated; discredit has been heaped on the reputation of the dead and their families, who have only the same sort of treatment to look forward to, if such abuses do not gradually disappear: to the hands of the executioners are thrown the bodies of children expired in innocence; men whose manner of life gave not the least suspicion of having the misfortune to be dug up, simply because a supposed witch had been placed in the earth.

They are declared witches; not only are their bodies given over to the executioner, so that they will be reduced to ashes, but their sentence emphasizes that they will have been much more severely punished than if they were still alive; and that their bodies be burned with infamy, to set an example for their accomplices.

Where are the laws that authorize such judgments? It is admitted that they do not exist, but it is coldly asserted that custom demands them. What a shower of disasters! Such things upset me and put me in such a fury that I must here end my account before I overstep the bounds of decency.

–Jean Marigny, *Vampires: Restless Children of the Night,* translated by Lory Frankel (New York: Harry Abrams, 1994), pp. 111–113

. . .

* * *

Anthropologist Paul Barber in this 1990 essay for Natural History *provides sound explanations as to what may have led to the widespread belief in vampires during the eighteenth century.*

The Real Vampire
Paul Barber

I saw the count lying within the box upon the earth, some of which the rude falling from the cart had scattered over him. He was deathly pale, just like a waxen image, and the red eyes glared with the horrible vindictive look which I knew too well. . . .

The eyes saw the sinking sun, and the look of hate in them turned to triumph.

But on the instant, came the sweep and flash of Jonathan's great knife. I shrieked as I saw it shear through the throat; whilst at the same moment Mr. Morris's bowie knife plunged into the heart.

It was like a miracle; but before our very eyes, and almost in the drawing of a breath, the whole body crumbled into dust and passed from our sight.

–Bram Stoker, *Dracula*

If a typical vampire of folklore were to come to your house this Halloween, you might open the door to encounter a plump Slavic fellow with long fingernails and a stubbly beard, his mouth and left eye open, his face ruddy and swollen. He would wear informal attire–a linen shroud–and he would look for all the world like a dishevelled peasant.

If you did not recognize him, it would be because you expected to see–as would most people today–a tall, elegant gentleman in a black cloak. But that would be a vampire of fiction–the count, the villain of Bram Stoker's novel and countless modern movies, based more or less on Vlad Tepes, a figure in Romanian history who was a prince, not a count; ruled in Walachia, not Transylvania; and was never viewed by the local populace as a vampire. Nor would he be recognized as one, bearing so little resemblance to the original Slavic revenant (one who returns from the dead)–the one actually called *upir* or *vampir*. But in folklore, the undead are seemingly everywhere in the world, in a variety of disparate cultures. They are people who, having died before their time, are believed to return to life to bring death to their friends and neighbors.

We know the European version of the vampire best and have a number of eyewitness accounts telling of the "killing" of bodies believed to be vampires. When we read the reports carefully and compare their findings with what is now known about forensic pathology, we can see why people believed that corpses came to life and returned to wreak havoc on the local population.

Europeans of the early 1700s showed a great deal of interest in the subject of the vampire. According to the *Oxford English Dictionary,* the word itself entered the English language in 1734, at a time when many books were being written on the subject, especially in Germany.

One reason for all the excitement was the Treaty of Passarowitz (1718), by which parts of Serbia and Walachia were turned over to Austria. The occupying forces, which remained there until 1739, began to notice, and file reports on, a peculiar local practice: exhuming bodies and "killing" them. Literate outsiders began to attend such exhumations. The vampire craze was an early "media event," in which educated Europeans became aware of practices that were by no means of recent origin.

In the early 1730s, a group of Austrian medical officers were sent to the Serbian village of Medvegia to investigate some very strange accounts. A number of people in the village had died recently, and the villagers blamed the deaths on vampires. The first of these vampires, they said, had been a man named Arnold Paole, who had died some years before (by falling off a hay wagon) and had come back to haunt the living.

To the villagers, Paole's vampirism was clear: When they dug up his corpse, "they found that he was quite complete and undecayed, and that fresh blood had flowed from his eyes, nose, mouth, and ears; that the shirt, the covering, and the coffin were completely bloody; that the old nails on his hands and feet, along with the skin, had fallen off, and that new ones had grown; and since they saw from this that he was a true vampire, they drove a stake through his heart, according to their custom, whereby he gave an audible groan and bled copiously."

This new offensive by the vampires–the one that drew the medical officers to Medvegia–included an attack on a woman named Stanacka, who "lay down to sleep fifteen days ago, fresh and healthy, but at midnight she started up out of her sleep with a terrible cry, fearful and trembling, and complained that she had been throttled by the son of a Haiduk by the name of Milloe, who had died nine weeks earlier, whereupon she had experienced a great pain in the chest and became worse hour by hour, until finally she died on the third day."

In their report, *Visum et Repertum* (Seen and Discovered), the officers told not only what they had heard from the villagers but also, in admirable clinical detail, what they themselves had seen when they exhumed and dissected the bodies of the supposed victims of the vampire. Of one corpse, the authors observed, "After the opening of the body there was found in the *cavitate pectoris* a quantity of fresh extravascular blood. The *vasa* [vessels] of the *arteriae* and *venae,* like the *ventriculis cordis,* were not, as is usual, filled with coagulated blood, and the whole *viscera,* that is, the *pulmo* [lung], *hepar* [liver], *stomachus, lien* [spleen], *et intestina* were quite fresh as they would be in a healthy person." But while baffled by the events, the medical officers did not venture opinions as to their meaning.

Modern scholars generally disregard such accounts–and we have many of them–because they invariably contain "facts" that are not believable, such as the claim that the dead Arnold Paole, exhumed forty days after his burial, groaned when a stake was driven into him. If that is untrue–and it surely seems self-evident that it must be untrue–then the rest of the account seems suspect.

Yet these stories invariably contain details that could only be known by someone who had exhumed a decomposing body. The flaking away of skin described in the account of Arnold Paole is a phenomenon that forensic pathologists refer to as "skin slippage." Also, pathologists say that it is no surprise that Paole's "nails had fallen away," for that too is a normal event. (The Egyptians knew this and dealt with it either by tying the nails onto the mummified corpse or by attaching them

with little golden thimbles.) The reference to "new nails" is presumably the interpretation of the glossy nail bed underneath the old nails.

Such observations are inconvenient if the vampire lore is considered as something made up out of whole cloth. But since the exhumations actually took place, then the question must be, how did our sources come to the conclusions they came to? That issue is obscured by two centuries of fictional vampires, who are much better known than the folkloric variety. A few distinctions are in order.

The folklore of the vampire comes from peasant cultures across most of Europe. As it happens, the best evidence of actual exhumations is from Eastern Europe, where the Eastern Orthodox church showed a greater tolerance for pagan traditions than the Catholic church in Western Europe.

The fictional vampire, owing to the massive influence of Bram Stoker's *Dracula,* moved away from its humble origin. (Imagine Count Dracula–in formal evening wear–undergoing his first death by falling off a hay wagon.)

Most fiction shows only one means of achieving the state of vampirism: people become vampires by being bitten by one. Typically, the vampire looms over the victim dramatically, then bites into the neck to suck blood. When vampires and revenants in European folklore suck blood–and many do not–they bite their victims somewhere on the thorax. Among the Kashubes, a Slavic people of northern Europe, vampires chose the area of the left breast; among the Russians, they left a small wound in the area of the heart; and in Danzig (now Gdansk), they bit the victim's nipples.

People commonly believed that those who were different, unpopular, or great sinners returned from the dead. Accounts from Russia tell of people who were unearthed merely because while alive they were alcoholics. A more universal category is the suicide. Partly because of their potential for returning from the dead or for drawing their nearest and dearest into the grave after them, suicides were refused burial in churchyards.

One author lists the categories of revenants by disposition as "the godless [people of different faiths are included], evildoers, suicides, sorcerers, witches, and werewolves; among the Bulgarians the group is expanded by robbers, highwaymen, arsonists, prostitutes, deceitful and treacherous barmaids and other dishonourable people."

A very common belief, reported not only from Eastern Europe but also from China, holds that a person may become a revenant when an animal jumps over him. In Romania there is a belief that a bat can transform a corpse into a vampire by flying over it. This circumstance deserves remark if only because of its rarity, for as important as bats are in the fiction of vampires, they are generally unimportant in the folklore. Bats came into vampire fiction by a circuitous route: the vampire bat of Central and South America was named after the vampire of folklore, because it sucks (or rather laps up) blood after biting its victim. The bat was then assimilated into the fiction: the modern (fictional) vampire is apt to transform himself into a bat and fly off to seek his victims.

Potential revenants could often be identified at birth, usually by some defect, as when (among the Poles of Upper Silesia and the Kashubes) a child was born with teeth or a split lower lip or features viewed as somehow bestial—for example, hair or a taillike extension of the spine. A child born with a red caul, or amniotic membrane, covering its head was regarded as a potential vampire.

The color red is related to the undead. Decomposing corpses often acquire a ruddy color, and this was generally taken for evidence of vampirism. Thus, the folkloric vampire is never pale, as one would expect

of a corpse; his face is commonly described as florid or of a healthy color or dark, and this may be attributed to his habit of drinking blood. (The Serbians, referring to a red-faced, hard-drinking man, assert that he is "blood red as a vampire.")

In various parts of Europe, vampires, or revenants, were held responsible for any number of untoward events. They tipped over Gypsy caravans in Serbia, made loud noises on the frozen sod roofs of houses in Iceland (supposedly by beating their heels against them), caused epidemics, cast spells on crops, brought on rain and hail, and made cows go dry. All these activities attributed to vampires do occur: storms and scourges come and go, crops don't always thrive, cows do go dry. Indeed, the vampire's crimes are persistently "real-life" events. The issue often is not whether an event occurred but why it was attributed to the machinations of the vampire, an often invisible villain.

Bodies continue to be active long after death, but we moderns distinguish between two types of activity: that

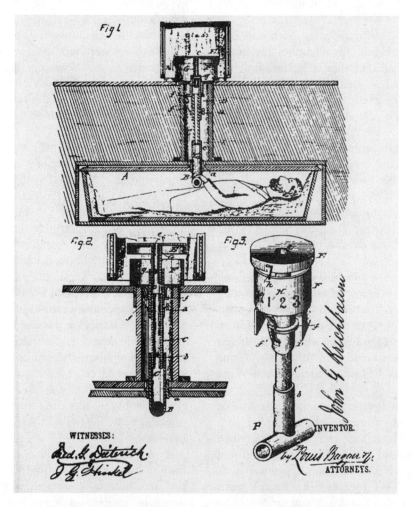

Krichbaum's device for determining life in buried persons, patent sketch (1882; Leonard Wolf, Dracula: The Connoisseur's Guide, *1997; Elizabeth Miller Collection)*

which we bring about by our will (in life) and that which is caused by other entities, such as microorganisms (in death). Because we regard only the former as "our" activity, the body's posthumous movements, changes in dimension, or the like are not real for us, since we do not will them. For the most part, however, our ancestors made no such distinction. To them, if after death the body changed in color, moved, bled, and so on (as it does), then it continued to experience a kind of life. Our view of death has made it difficult for us to understand earlier views, which are often quite pragmatic.

Much of what a corpse "does" results from misunderstood processes of decomposition. Only in detective novels does this process proceed at a predictable rate. So when a body that had seemingly failed to decompose came to the attention of the populace, theories explaining the apparent anomaly were likely to spring into being. (Note that when a saint's body failed to decompose it was a miracle, but when the body of an unpopular person failed to decompose it was because he was a vampire.) But while those who exhumed the bodies of suspected vampires invariably noted what they believed was the lack of decomposition, they almost always presented evidence that the body really was decomposing. In the literature, I have so far found only two instances of exhumations that failed to yield a "vampire." (With so many options, the body almost certainly will do something unexpected, hence scary, such as showing blood at the lips.) Our natural bias, then as now, is for the dramatic and the exotic, so that an exhumation that did not yield a vampire could be expected to be an early dropout from the folklore and hence the literature.

But however mythical the vampire was, the corpses that were taken for vampires were very real. And many of the mysteries of vampire lore clear up when we examine the legal and medical evidence surrounding these exhumations. "Not without astonishment," says an observer at the exhumation of a Serbian vampire in 1725, "I saw some fresh blood in his mouth, which, according to the common observation, he had sucked from the people killed by him." Similarly, in *Visum et Repertum,* we are told that the people exhuming one body were surprised by a "plumpness" they asserted had come to the corpse in the grave. Our sources deduced a cause-and-effect relationship from these two observations. The vampire was larger than he was because he was full to bursting with the fresh blood of his victims.

The observations are clinically accurate: as a corpse decomposes, it normally bloats (from the gases given off by decomposition), while the pressure from the bloating causes blood from the lungs to emerge at the mouth. The blood is real, it just didn't come from "victims" of the deceased.

But how was it that Arnold Paole, exhumed forty days after his death, groaned when his exhumers drove a stake into him? The peasants of Medvegia assumed that if the corpse groaned, it must still be alive. But a corpse does emit sounds, even when it is only moved, let alone if a stake were driven into it. This is because the compression of the chest cavity forces air past the glottis, causing a sound similar in quality and origin to the groan or cry of a living person. Pathologists shown such accounts point out that a corpse that did not emit such sounds when a stake was driven into it would be unusual.

To vampire killers who are digging up a corpse, anything unexpected is taken for evidence of vampirism. Calmet, an eighteenth-century French ecclesiastic, described people digging up corpses "to see if they can find any of the usual marks which leads them to conjecture that they are the parties who molest the living, as the mobility and suppleness of the limbs, the fluidity of the blood, and the flesh remaining uncorrupted." A vampire, in other words, is a corpse that lacks rigor mortis, has fluid blood, and has not decomposed. As it happens, these distinctions do not narrow the field very much: Rigor mortis is a temporary condition, liquid blood is not at all unusual in a corpse (hence the "copious bleeding" mentioned in the account of Arnold Paole), and burial slows down decomposition drastically (by a factor of eight, according to a standard textbook on forensic pathology). This being the case, exhumations often yielded a corpse that nicely fit the local model of what a vampire was.

None of this explains yet another phenomenon of the vampire lore–the attack itself. To get to his victim, the vampire is often said to emerge at night from a tiny hole in the grave, in a form that is invisible to most people (sorcerers have made a good living tracking down and killing such vampires). The modern reader may reject out of hand the hypothesis that a dead man, visible or not, crawled out of his grave and attacked the young woman Stanacka as related in *Visum et Repertum.* Yet in other respects, these accounts have been quite accurate.

Note the sequence of events: Stanacka is asleep, the attack takes place, and she wakes up. Since Stanacka was asleep during the attack, we can only conclude that we are looking at a culturally conditioned interpretation of a nightmare–a real event with a fanciful interpretation.

The vampire does have two forms: one of them the body in the grave; the other–and this is the mobile one–the image, or "double," which here appears as a dream. While we interpret this as an event that takes place within the mind of the dreamer, in nonliterate cultures the dream is more commonly viewed as either an invasion by the spirits of whatever is dreamed about (and these can include the dead) or evidence that the dreamer's soul is taking a nocturnal journey.

In many cultures, the soul is only rather casually attached to its body, as is demonstrated by its habit of leaving the body entirely during sleep or unconsciousness or death. The changes that occur during such conditions—the lack of responsiveness, the cessation or slowing of breathing and pulse—are attributed to the soul's departure. When the soul is identified with the image of the body, it may make periodic forays into the minds of others when they dream. The image is the essence of the person, and its presence in the mind of another is evidence that body and soul are separated. Thus, one reason that the dead are believed to live on is that their image can appear in people's dreams and memories even after death. For this reason some cultures consider it unwise to awaken someone suddenly: he may be dreaming, and his soul may not have a chance to return before he awakens, in which case he will die. In European folklore, the dream was viewed as a visit from the person dreamed about. (The vampire is not the only personification of the dream: the Slavic *mora* is a living being whose soul goes out of the body at night, leaving it as if dead. The *mora* first puts men to sleep, and then frightens them with dreams, chokes them, and sucks their blood. Etymologically, *mora* is cognate with the *mare* of nightmare, with German *Mahr,* and with the second syllable of the French *cauchemar.*)

When Stanacka claimed she was attacked by Milloe, she was neither lying nor even making an especially startling accusation. Her subsequent death (probably from some form of epidemic disease: others in the village were dying too) was sufficient proof to her friends and relatives that she had in fact been attacked by a dead man, just as she had said.

This is why our sources tell us seemingly contradictory facts about the vampire. His body does not have to leave the grave to attack the living, yet the evidence of the attack—the blood he has sucked from his victims—is to be seen on the body. At one and the same time he can be both in the grave in his physical form and out of it in his spirit form. Like the fictional vampire, the vampire of folklore must remain in his grave part of the time—during the day—but with few exceptions, folkloric vampires do not travel far from their home towns.

And while the fictional vampire disintegrates once staked, the folkloric vampire can prove much more troublesome. One account tells that "in order to free themselves from this plague, the people dug the body up, drove a consecrated nail into its head and a stake through its heart. Nonetheless, that did not help: the murdered man came back each night." In many of these cases, vampires were cremated as well as staked.

In Eastern Europe the fear of being killed by a vampire was quite real, and the people devised ways to protect themselves from attacks. One of the sources of protection was the blood of the supposed vampire, which was baked in bread, painted on the potential victim, or even mixed with brandy and drunk. (According to *Visum et Repertum,* Arnold Paole had once smeared himself with the blood of a vampire—that is, a corpse—for protection.) The rationale behind this is a common one in folklore, expressed in the saying "similia similiis curantur" (similar things are cured by similar things). Even so, it is a bit of a shock to find that our best evidence suggests that it was the human beings who drank the blood of the "vampires," and not the other way around.

Perhaps foremost among the reasons for the urgency with which vampires were sought—and found—was sheer terror. To understand its intensity we need only recall the realities that faced our informants. Around them people were dying in clusters, by agencies that they did not understand. As they were well aware, death could be extremely contagious: if a neighbor died, they might be next. They were afraid of nothing less than death itself. For among many cultures it was death that was thought to be passed around, not viruses and bacteria. Contagion was meaningful and deliberate, and its patterns were based on values and vendettas, not on genetic predisposition or the domestic accommodations of the plague-spreading rat fleas. Death came from the dead who, through jealousy, anger, or longing, sought to bring the living into their realm. And to prevent this, the living attempted to neutralize or propitiate the dead until the dead became powerless—not only when they stopped entering dreams but also when their bodies stopped changing and were reduced to inert bones. This whole phenomenon is hard for us to understand because although death is as inescapable today as it was then, we no longer personify its causes.

In recent history, the closest parallel to this situation may be seen in the AIDS epidemic, which has caused a great deal of fear, even panic, among people who, for the time being at least, know little about the nature of the disease. In California, for instance, there was an attempt to pass a law requiring the quarantine of AIDS victims. Doubtless the fear will die down if we gain control over the disease—but what would it be like to live in a civilization in which all diseases were just as mysterious? Presumably one would learn—as was done in Europe in past centuries—to shun the dead as potential bearers of death.

–Barber, "The Real Vampire: Forensic Pathology and the Lore of the Undead," *Natural History* (October 1990): 74–82

The Vampire Comes to England

The vampires of eastern European folklore (and certainly those described in Calmet's book) are only distantly related to the romantic, seductive members of the "undead" to which we have become accustomed in popular culture today. That image of the vampire has its origins in literature. The reports about vampire sightings coincided with—and perhaps contributed to—a rising interest in Gothic literature, first in Germany and later, during the last decades of the eighteenth century, in England. The Gothic movement was part of the broader period of Romanticism, with its challenge to rationalism and its shift of philosophical emphasis to subjectivity, emotion, intuition, and imagination. The adoption of the figure of the vampire by Gothic writers was inevitable. The bloodsucking revenant made its initial appearance in German poetry, notably in works by Heinrich August Ossenfelder, and Johann Wolfgang von Goethe. From there the fictional vampire made its way to England, to be embraced by Romantic poets and changed forever by John William Polidori, an obscure physician better known for his associations with George Gordon, Lord Byron, than for his literary works.

The earliest known poem concerning a vampire, "Der Vampir," was written by the German poet Heinrich August Ossenfelder in 1748.

The Vampire

My dear young maiden clingeth
Unbending, fast and firm
To all the long-held teaching
Of a mother ever true;
As in vampires unmortal
Folk on the Theyse's portal
Heyduck-like do believe.
But my Christian thou dost dally,
And wilt my loving parry
Till I myself avenging
To a vampire's health a-drinking
Him toast in pale tockay.

And as softly thou art sleeping
To thee shall I come creeping
And thy life's blood drain away.
And so shalt thou be trembling
For thus shall I be kissing
And death's threshold thou'lt be crossing
With fear, in my cold arms.
And last shall I thee question
Compared to such instruction
What are a mother's charms?

—translated by Aloysius Gibson in The Vampire in
Verse: An Anthology, *edited by Steven Moore
(New York: Dracula Press, 1985), p. 12*

* * *

Pre-Romantic Vampires

Occasional references to the vampire, usually metaphorical, appeared in English prior to the Romantic period.

Alexander Pope joked about his ill health making him a vampire in this letter.

Since his burial (at Twitnam) he has seen some times in Mines and Caverns & been very troublesome to those who dig Marbles & Minerals. If ever he has walk'd above ground, He has been (like the Vampires in Germany) such a terror to all sober & innocent people, that many wish a stake were drove thro' him to keep him quiet in his Grave.

—Pope to Dr. William Oliver, February 1740

Charles Forman's employment of the word "vampire" in a work that was written in 1688, though not printed until 1741, is an indication of its common usage.

Our Merchants, indeed, bring money into their country, but it is said, there is another Set of Men amongst us who have as great an Address in sending out again to foreign Countries without any Returns for it, which defeats the Industry of the Merchant. These are the Vampires of the Publick, and Riflers of the Kingdom.

*—Some Queries and Observations upon the Revolution
in 1688 (London: Printed and sold
by Olive Payne . . ., 1741)*

Horace Walpole commented on the beliefs of King George II in this letter.

I know that our late King, though not apt to believe more than his neighbours, had no doubt of the existence of vampires and their banquets on the dead.

—Walpole to Lady Ossory, 16 January 1786

Johann Wolfgang von Goethe (Peter Haining, The Dracula Scrapbook, *1976; Thomas Cooper Library, University of South Carolina)*

This excerpt is from Johann Wolfgang von Goethe's ballad "Die Braut von Korinth," which he wrote in 1797. In his letters Goethe indicates that the poem was written in a few hours but that he had been thinking of it for years. In the poem a beautiful Corinthian maiden, who died after her newly baptized Christian mother promised her to God's service, comes to the pagan Athenian youth to whom she once had been pledged in marriage.

From "The Bride of Corinth"

In her care to see that nought went wrong,
Now the mother happen'd to draw near;
At the door long hearkens she, full long,
Wond'ring at the sounds that great her ear.
Tones of joy and sadness,
And loves blissful madness,
As of bride and bridegroom they appear.

From the door she will not now remove,
'Till she gains full certainty of this;
And with anger hears she vows of love,
Soft caressing words of mutual bliss,
"Hush! the cock's loud strain!
But thou'lt come again,
When the night returns!"—then kiss on kiss.

Then her wrath the mother cannot hold,
But unfastens straight the lock with ease:—
"In this house are girls become so bold,
As to seek e'en strangers' lusts to please?"
By her lamp's clear glow
Looks she in,—and oh!
Sight of horror!—'tis her child she sees.

Fain the youth would, in his first alarm,
With the veil that o'er her had been spread,
With the carpet, shield his love from harm;
But she casts them from her, void of dread,
And with the spirit's strength,
In its spectre length,
Lifts her figure slowly from the bed.

"Mother! mother!"—Thus her wan lips say:
"May not I one night of rapture share?
From the warm couch am I chased away?
Do I waken only to despair?
It contents not thee
To have driven me
An untimely shroud of death to wear?"

"But from out my coffin's prison-bounds
By a wond'rous fate I'm forced to rove,
While the blessings and the chaunting sounds
That your priests delight in, useless prove.
Water, salt, are vain
Fervent youth to chain,
Ah, e'en earth can never cool down love!"

"When the infant vow of love was spoken,
Venus' radiant temple smiled on both.
Mother! thou that promise since has broken,
Fetter'd by a strange, deceitful oath.
Gods, though, hearken ne'er,
Should a mother swear
To deny her daughter's plighted troth."

"From my grave to wander I am forc'd,
Still to seek The God's long-sever'd link,
Still to love the bridegroom I have lost,
And the life-blood of his heart to drink;
When his race is run,
I must hasten on,
And the young must 'neath my vengeance sink.

"Beauteous youth! no longer mayst thou live;
Here must shrivel up thy form so fair;
Did not I to thee a token give.
Taking in return this lock of hair?
View it to thy sorrow!
Grey thou'lt be to-morrow,
Only to grow brown again when *there*."

"Mother, to this final prayer give ear!
Let a funeral pile be straightway dress'd;
Open then my cell so sad and drear,
That the flames my give the lovers rest!
When ascends the fire
From the glowing pyre,
To the gods of old we'll hasten, blest."

—*Poems of Goethe,* translated by Edgar Alfred Bowring, second edition (New York: Hurst, 1874), p. 149–151

* * *

Robert Southey (J. Gordon Melton, The Vampire Book, *1999; Richland County Public Library)*

In this passage from book 8, stanzas 8–11, of Robert Southey's epic poem Thalaba the Destroyer, *the protagonist, Thalaba, and his father-in-law, Moath, confront Oneiza, who died on her wedding day.*

Excerpt from *Thalaba, the Destroyer*
Robert Southey

In silence on Oneiza's grave
The Father and the Husband sate.

The Cryer from the minaret
Proclaimed the midnight hour;
"Now! now!" cried Thalaba,
And o'er the chamber of the tomb
There spread a lurid gleam
Like the reflection of a sulphur fire,
And in that hideous light
Oneiza stood before them. it was She,
Her very lineaments, and such as death
Had changed them, livid cheeks, and lips of blue.
But in her eyes there dwelt
Brightness more terrible
Than all the loathsomeness of death.
"Still art thou living, wretch?"
In hollow tones she cried to Thalaba,
"And must I nightly leave my grave
"To tell thee, still in vain,
"God has abandoned thee?"

"This is not she!" the Old Man exclaimed,
"A Fiend! a manifest Fiend!"
And to the youth he held his lance,
"Strike and deliver thyself!"
"Strike HER!" cried Thalaba,

And palsied of all powers
Gazed fixedly upon the dreadful form.
"Yea! strike her!" cried a voice whose tones
Flowed with such a sudden healing thro' his soul,
As when the desert shower
From death delivered him.
But unobedient to that well-known voice
His eye was seeking it,
When Moath firm of heart,
Performed the bidding; thro' the vampire corpse
He thrust his lance; it fell,
And howling with the wound
Its demon tenant fled.
A sapphire light fell on them,
And garmented with glory, in their sight
Oneiza's spirit stood.

–Robert Southey, *Thalaba the Destroyer*
(London: Printed for T. N. Longman
and O. Rees, 1801), pp. 101–105

* * *

John Stagg, a minor Romantic poet, provides a prose introduction to his poem in which he discusses the story of the vampire, "founded on an opinion or report which prevailed in Hungary, and several parts of Germany, towards the beginning of the last century." In the preceding verses of the poem, Gertrude's dying husband, Herman, has explained how his once cherished friend, Sigismund, has turned into a goblin who drinks his "vital blood."

From "The Vampyre"

The live-long night poor Gertrude sate,
Watch'd by her sleeping, dying lord;
The live-long night she mourn'd his fate,
The object whom her soul ador'd.

Then at what time the vesper-bell
Of yonder convent sadly toll'd,
The, then was peal'd his passing knell,
The hapless Herman he was cold!

Just at that moment Gertrude drew
From 'neath her cloak the hidden light;
When, dreadful! She beheld in view
The shade of Sigismund!–sad sight!

Indignant roll'd his ireful eyes,
That gleam'd with wild horrific stare;
And fix'd a moment with surprise,
Beheld aghast th'enlight'ning glare.

His jaws cadaverous were besmear'd
With clott'd carnage o'er and o'er,
And all his horrid whole appear'd
Distent, and fill'd with human gore!

With hideous scowl the spectre fled;
She shriek'd aloud;–then swoon'd away!
The hapless Herman in his bed,
All pale, a lifeless body lay!

Next day in council 'twas decree,
(Urg'd at the instance of the state,)
That shudd'ring nature should be freed
From pests like these ere 'twas too late.

The choir then burst the fun'ral dome
Where Sigismund was lately laid,
And found him, tho' within the tomb,
Still warm as life, and undecay'd.

With blood his visage was distain'd,
Ensanguin'd were his frightful eyes,
Each sign of former life remain'd,
Save that all motionless he lies.

The corpse of Herman they contrive
To the same sepulchre to take,
And thro' both carcases they drive,
Deep in the earth, a sharpen'd stake!

By this was finish'd their career,
Thro' this no longer they can roam;
From them their friends have nought to fear,
Both quiet keep the slumb'ring tomb.

–John Stagg, *The Minstrel of the North: or,*
Cumbrian Legends (London: Printed by
Hamblin and Seyfang, 1810)

The Byronic Hero and the Vampire

While the literary vampire was an adaptation of the Gothic villains of novelists such as Matthew Lewis and Ann Radcliffe, much of the appeal of the character came from its echoes of the emerging (and very popular) Byronic Hero–a complex, aloof aristocrat whose past is shrouded in secrecy; who, driven by some inner force, travels far and wide in search of oblivion; who leads women into disastrous, even diabolical affairs. Byron began the development of the character in his work in 1812 on Childe Harold *(1812, 1816, 1818) and brought the type to maturity in* Lara *(1814) and the poetic drama* Manfred *(1817).*

Polidori's Vampire

The most significant early contribution to the development of the literary vampire in English literature came from an unlikely source, Lord Byron's personal physician, John William Polidori. His story "The Vampyre" (1819) can be traced to a famous literary gathering on the shores of Lake Geneva in the summer of 1816. He and Byron, who had just left England amid scandal, were residing at the Villa Diodati where they were visited by Percy Bysshe Shelley, Mary Godwin (who soon became Mary Shelley), and Mary's stepsister Claire Clairmont. One evening, after a collective reading of ghost stories, Byron suggested that each member of the party write a story of his or her own. The best-known result of this challenge was Mary Shelley's Frankenstein *(1818). Byron wrote a fragment of a story about a mysterious nobleman, but soon discarded it. Later, Polidori used his employer's unfinished work as the basis of a story of his own, "The Vampyre," which became the prototype for most subsequent fictional vampires throughout the nineteenth century.*

Lord Byron, the model for the first vampire in English fiction (Peter Haining, The Dracula Scrapbook, *1976; Thomas Cooper Library, University of South Carolina)*

Although written in 1816, the following fragment, which Byron included in the volume titled Mazeppa, A Poem *(1819), was not published until after Polidori's story appeared in the 1 April 1919 issue of* The New Monthly Magazine, *and Universal Register. On 26 April 1819 Byron had written about "The Vampire," which mistakenly had been attributed to him, in a letter to the editor of* Galigani's Messenger, *a Paris-based newspaper that had a wide circulation among English readers:*

> In various numbers of your Journal–I have seen mentioned a work entitled 'The Vampire' with the addition of my name as that of the Author.–I am not the author and never heard of the work in question until now. . . . I have besides a personal dislike to 'Vampires' and the little acquaintance I have with them would by no means induce me to divulge their secrets.

Although the parallels that can be drawn from Byron's fragment and Polidori's story show the connection between the two pieces, there is no mention of a vampire in Byron's fragment. It is possible, though, that he revised his fragment before its publication.

A Fragment
George Gordon, Lord Byron

June 17, 1816.

In the year 17–, having for some time determined on a journey through countries not hitherto much frequented by travellers, I set out, accompanied by a friend, whom I shall designate by the name of Augustus Darvell. He was a few years my elder, and a man of considerable fortune and ancient family–advantages which an extensive capacity prevented him alike from undervaluing or overrating. Some peculiar circumstances in his private history had rendered him to me an object of attention, of interest, and even of regard, which neither the reserve of his manners, nor occasional indications of an inquietude at times nearly approaching to alienation of mind, could extinguish.

I was yet young in life, which I had begun early; but my intimacy with him was of a recent date: we had been educated at the same schools and university; but his progress through these had preceded mine, and he had been deeply initiated into what is called the world, while I was yet in my noviciate. While thus engaged, I heard much both of his past and present life; and although in these accounts there were many and irreconcileable contradictions, I could still gather from the whole that he was a being of no common order, and one who, whatever pains he might take to avoid remark, would still be remarkable. I had cultivated his acquaintance subsequently, and endeavoured to obtain his friendship, but this last appeared to be unattainable;

whatever affections he might have possessed seemed now, some to have been extinguished, and others to be concentred: that his feelings were acute, I had sufficient opportunities of observing; for, although he could control, he could not altogether disguise them: still he had a power of giving to one passion the appearance of another in such a manner that it was difficult to define the nature of what was working within him; and the expressions of his features would vary so rapidly, though slightly, that it was useless to trace them to their sources. It was evident that he was a prey to some cureless disquiet; but whether it arose from ambition, love, remorse, grief, from one or all of these, or merely from a morbid temperament akin to disease, I could not discover: there were circumstances alleged, which might have justified the application to each of these causes; but, as I have before said, these were so contradictory and contradicted, that none could be fixed upon with accuracy. Where there is mystery, it is generally supposed that there must also be evil: I know not how this may be, but in him there certainly was the one, though I could not ascertain the extent of the other–and felt loth, as far as regarded himself, to believe in its existence. My advances were received with sufficient coldness; but I was young, and not easily discouraged, and at length succeeded in obtaining, to a certain degree, that common-place intercourse and moderate confidence of common and every day concerns, created and cemented by similarity of pursuit and frequency of meeting, which is called intimacy, or friendship, accord-

---

Harriet Westbrook Shelley on Her Husband

Percy Bysshe Shelley abandoned his first wife, Harriet Westbrook Shelley, to be with Mary Godwin. Shortly before the birth of Shelley's second child, Harriet Westbrook Shelley wrote to a friend about her husband.

Your fears are verified. Mr. Shelley has become profligate and sensual. . . . and here I am, my dear friend, waiting to bring another infant into this woful world. Next month I shall be confined. He will not be near me. No, he cares not for me now. He never asks after me or sends me word how he is going on. In short, the man I once loved is dead. This is a vampire.

–Harriet Shelley to Catherine Nugent,
20 November 1814

After Harriet Shelley committed suicide by drowning in December 1816, Shelley married Mary Godwin, who as Mary Wollstonecraft Shelley became the author of Frankenstein; or, the Modern Prometheus *(1818).*

ing to the ideas of him who uses those words to express them.

Darvell had already travelled extensively; and to him I had applied for information with regard to the conduct of my intended journey. It was my secret wish that he might be prevailed on to accompany me: it was also a probable hope, founded upon the shadowy restlessness which I observed in him, and to which the animation which he appeared to feel on such subjects, and his apparent indifference to all by which he was more immediately surrounded, gave fresh strength. This wish I first hinted, and then expressed: his answer, though I had partly expected it, gave me all the pleasure of surprise—he consented; and, after the requisite arrangements, we commenced our voyages. After journeying through various countries of the south of Europe, our attention was turned towards the East, according to our original destination; and it was in my progress through these regions that the incident occurred upon which will turn what I may have to relate.

The constitution of Darvell, which must from his appearance have been in early life more than usually robust, had been for some time gradually giving way, without the intervention of any apparent disease: he had neither cough nor hectic, yet he became daily more enfeebled: his habits were temperate, and he neither declined nor complained of fatigue, yet he was evidently wasting away: he became more and more silent and sleepless, and at length so seriously altered, that my alarm grew proportionate to what I conceived to be his danger.

We had determined, on our arrival at Smyrna, on an excursion to the ruins of Ephesus and Sardis, from which I endeavoured to dissuade him in his present state of indisposition—but in vain: there appeared to be an oppression on his mind, and a solemnity in his manner, which ill corresponded with his eagerness to proceed on what I regarded as a mere party of pleasure, little suited to a valetudinarian; but I opposed him no longer—and in a few days we set off together, accompanied only by a serrugee and a single janizary.

We had passed halfway towards the remains of Ephesus, leaving behind us the more fertile environs of Smyrna, and were entering upon that wild and tenantless track through the marshes and defiles which lead to the few huts yet lingering over the broken columns of Diana—the roofless walls of expelled Christianity, and the still more recent but complete desolation of abandoned mosques—when the sudden and rapid illness of my companion obliged us to halt at a Turkish cemetery, the turbaned tombstones of which were the sole indication that human life had ever been a sojourner in this wilderness. The only caravansera we had seen was

left some hours behind us, not a vestige of a town or even cottage was within sight or hope, and this "city of the dead" appeared to be the sole refuge of my unfortunate friend, who seemed on the verge of becoming the last of its inhabitants.

In this situation, I looked round for a place where he might most conveniently repose:—contrary to the usual aspect of Mahometan burial-grounds, the cypresses were in this few in number, and these thinly scattered over its extent: the tombstones were mostly fallen, and worn with age:—upon one of the most considerable of these, and beneath one of the most spreading trees, Darvell supported himself, in a half-reclining posture, with great difficulty. He asked for water. I had some doubts of our being able to find any, and prepared to go in search of it with hesitating despondency—but he desired me to remain; and turning to Suleiman, our janizary, who stood by us smoking with great tranquillity, he said, "Suleiman, verbana su," (i.e. bring some water,) and went on describing the spot where it was to be found with great minuteness, at a small well for camels, a few hundred yards to the right: the janizary obeyed. I said to Darvell, "How did you know this?"—He replied, "From our situation; you must perceive that this place was once inhabited, and could not have been so without springs: I have also been here before."

"You have been here before!—How came you never to mention this to me? and what could you be doing in a place where no one would remain a moment longer than they could help it?'"

To this question I received no answer. In the mean time Suleiman returned with the water, leaving the serrugee and the horses at the fountain. The quenching of his thirst had the appearance of reviving him for a moment; and I conceived hopes of his being able to proceed, or at least to return, and I urged the attempt. He was silent—and appeared to be collecting his spirits for an effort to speak. He began.

"This is the end of my journey, and of my life—I came here to die: but I have a request to make, a command—for such my last words must be—You will observe it?"

"Most certainly; but have better hopes."

"I have no hopes, nor wishes, but this—conceal my death from every human being."

"I hope there will be no occasion; that you will recover, and—"

"Peace!—it must be so: promise this."

"I do."

"Swear it, by all that" —He here dictated an oath of great solemnity.

"There is no occasion for this—I will observe your request; and to doubt me is—"

Mary Shelley (portrait by S. J. Stump, National Portrait Gallery, London) and the frontispiece for the first illustrated edition of
Frankenstein, *1831 (Judith Wilt,* Ghosts of the Gothic, *1980; Thomas Cooper Library, University of South Carolina)*

My Own Vampire

In Frankenstein; or, the Modern Prometheus, *Victor Frankenstein reflects on his creation after realizing that it murdered his young brother, William.*

. . . I considered the being whom I had cast among mankind, and endowed with the will and power to effect purposes of horror, such as the deed which he had now done, nearly in the light of my own vampire, my own spirit let loose from the grave, and forced to destroy all that was dear to me.

–Mary Shelley, *Frankenstein,* revised edition (London: Henry Colburn & Richard Bentley, 1831), p. 62

"It cannot be helped,–you must swear."

I took the oath: it appeared to relieve him. He removed a seal ring from his finger, on which were some Arabic characters, and presented it to me. He proceeded–

"On the ninth day of the month, at noon precisely (what month you please, but this must be the day), you must fling this ring into the salt springs which run into the Bay of Eleusis: the day after, at the same hour, you must repair to the ruins of the temple of Ceres, and wait one hour."

"Why?"

"You will see."

"The ninth day of the month, you say?"

"The ninth."

As I observed that the present was the ninth day of the month, his countenance changed, and he paused. As he sate, evidently becoming more feeble, a stork, with a snake in her beak, perched upon a tombstone near us; and, without devouring her prey, appeared to be stedfastly regarding us. I know not what impelled me to drive it away, but the attempt was useless; she made a few circles in the air, and returned exactly to the same spot. Darvell pointed to it, and smiled: he spoke–I know not whether to himself or to me–but the words were only, "'Tis well!"

"What is well? what do you mean?"

"No matter: you must bury me here this evening, and exactly where that bird is now perched. You know the rest of my injunctions."

He then proceeded to give me several directions as to the manner in which his death might be best concealed. After these were finished, he exclaimed, "You perceive that bird?"

"Certainly."

"And the serpent writhing in her beak?"

"Doubtless: there is nothing uncommon in it; it is her natural prey. But it is odd that she does not devour it."

He smiled in a ghastly manner, and said, faintly, "It is not yet time!" As he spoke, the stork flew away. My eyes followed it for a moment, it could hardly be longer than ten might be counted. I felt Darvell's weight, as it were, increase upon my shoulder, and, turning to look upon his face, perceived that he was dead!

I was shocked with the sudden certainty which could not be mistaken—his countenance in a few minutes became nearly black. I should have attributed so rapid a change to poison, had I not been aware that he had no opportunity of receiving it unperceived. The day was declining, the body was rapidly altering, and nothing remained but to fulfil his request. With the aid of Suleiman's ataghan and my own sabre, we scooped a shallow grave upon the spot which Darvell had indicated: the earth easily gave way, having already received some Mahometan tenant. We dug as deeply as the time permitted us, and throwing the dry earth upon all that remained of the singular being so lately departed, we cut a few sods of greener turf from the less withered soil around us, and laid them upon his sepulchre.

Between astonishment and grief, I was tearless.

—*Mazeppa, A Poem* (London: Murray, 1819), pp. 59–69

* * *

As originally published in the 1 April 1819 issue of The New Monthly Magazine, and Universal Register, *Polidori's tale was mistakenly attributed to Lord Byron. In a long preface to the story, printed in brackets, the editor gives background for the vampire myth and even quotes a passage from Byron's epic poem,* The Giaour *(1813), which takes its title from a scornful Muslim term for a Christian.*

The reason for the attribution of Polidori's story to Byron is unknown. Doubtless, the story became popular and influential, in large part because the author was thought to be Lord Byron.

The Vampyre; a Tale by Lord Bryon
[John William Polidori]

[The superstition upon which this tale is founded is very general in the East. Among the Arabians it appears to be common: it did not, however, extend itself to the Greeks until after the establishment of Christianity; and it has only assumed its present form since the division of the Latin and Greek churches; at which time, the idea becoming prevalent, that a Latin

body could not corrupt if buried in their territory, it gradually increased, and formed the subject of many wonderful stories, still extant, of the dead rising from their graves, and feeding upon the blood of the young and beautiful. In the West it spread, with some slight variation, all over Hungary, Poland, Austria, and Lorraine, where the belief existed, that vampyres nightly imbibed a certain portion of the blood of their victims, who became emaciated, lost their strength, and speedily died of consumptions; whilst these human bloodsuckers fattened—and their veins became distended to such a state of repletion as to cause the blood to flow from all the passages of their bodies, and even from the very pores of their skins.

In the London Journal of March, 1732, is a curious, and of course *credible* account of a particular case of vampyrism, which is stated to have occurred at Madreyga, in Hungary. It appears, that upon an examination of the commander in chief and magistrates of the place, they positively and unanimously affirmed that, about five years before, a certain Heyduke, named Arnold Paul, had been heard to say, that, at Cassovia, on the frontiers of the Turkish Servia, he had been tormented by a vampyre, but had found a way to rid himself of the evil, by eating some of the earth out of the vampyre's grave, and rubbing himself with his blood. This precaution, however, did not prevent him from becoming a vampyre* himself; for, about twenty or thirty days after his death and burial, many persons complained of having been tormented by him, and a deposition was made, that four persons had been deprived of life by his attacks. To prevent further mischief, the inhabitants having consulted their Hadagni**, took up the body, and found it (as is supposed to be usual in cases of vampyrism) fresh, and entirely free from corruption, and emitting at the mouth, nose, and ears, pure and florid blood. Proof having been thus obtained, they resorted to the accustomed remedy. A stake was driven entirely through the heart and body of Arnold Paul, at which he is reported to have cried out as dreadfully as if he had been alive. This done, they cut off his head, burned his body, and threw the ashes into his grave. The same measures were adopted with the corses of those persons who had previously died from vampyrism, lest they should, in their turn, become agents upon others who survived them.

We have related this monstrous rodomontade, because it seems better adapted to illustrate the subject of the present observations than any other instance we could adduce. In many parts of Greece it is considered

---

*The universal belief is, that a person sucked by a vampyre becomes a vampyre himself, and sucks in his turn.

** Chief bailiff

as a sort of punishment after death, for some heinous crime committed whilst in existence, that the deceased is doomed to vampyrise, but be compelled to confine his infernal visitations solely to those beings he loved most while upon earth–those to whom he was bound by ties of kindred and affection. This supposition is, we imagine, alluded to in the following fearfully sublime and prophetic curse from the "Giaour."

But first on earth, as Vampyre sent,
Thy corse shall from its tomb be rent;
Then ghastly haunt thy native place,
And suck the blood of all thy race;
There from thy *daughter, sister, wife,*
At midnight drain the stream of life;
Yet loathe the banquet, which perforce
Must feed thy livid living corse.
Thy victims, ere they yet expire,
Shall know the demon for their sire;
As cursing thee, thou cursing them,
Thy flowers are withered on the stem.
But one that for *thy crime* must fall,
The youngest, best beloved of all,
Shall bless thee with a *father's* name–
That word shall wrap thy heart in flame!
Yet thou must end thy task and mark
Her cheek's last tinge–her eye's last spark,
And the last glassy glance must view
Which freezes o'er its lifeless blue;
Then with unhallowed hand shall tear
The tresses of her yellow hair,
Of which, in life a lock when shorn
Affection's fondest pledge was worn–
But now is borne away by thee
Memorial of thine agony!
Yet with thine own best blood shall drip
Thy gnashing tooth, and haggard lip;
Then stalking to thy sullen grave,
Go–and with Gouls and Afrits rave,
Till these in horror shrink away
From spectre more accursed than they.

Mr. Southey has also introduced in his wild but beautiful poem of "Thalaba," the vampyre corse of the Arabian maid Oneiza, who is represented as having returned from the grave for the purpose of tormenting him she best loved whilst in existence. But this cannot be supposed to have resulted from the sinfulness of her life, she being pourtrayed throughout the whole of the tale as a complete type of purity and innocence. The veracious Tournefort gives a long account in his travels of several astonishing cases of vampyrism, to which he pretends to have been an eye-witness; and Calmet, in his great work upon this subject, besides a variety of anecdotes, and traditionary narratives illustrative of its effects, has put forth some learned dissertations, tending to prove it to be a classical, as well as barbarian error.

We could add many curious and interesting notices on this singularly horrible superstition, and we may, perhaps, resume our observations upon it at some future opportunity; for the present, we feel that we have very far exceeded the limits of a note, necessarily devoted to the explanation of the strange production to which we now invite the attention of our readers; and we shall therefore conclude by merely remarking, that though the term Vampyre is the one in most general acceptation, there are several others synonimous with it, which are made use of in various parts of the world, namely, Vroucolocha, Vardoulacha, Goul, Broucoloka, &c.–ED.]

It happened that in the midst of the dissipations attendant upon a London winter, there appeared at the various parties of the leaders of the *ton* a nobleman, more remarkable for his singularities, than his rank. He gazed upon the mirth around him, as if he could not participate therein. Apparently, the light laughter of the fair only attracted his attention, that he might by a look quell it, and throw fear into those breasts where thoughtlessness reigned. Those who felt this sensation of awe, could not explain whence it arose: some attributed it to the dead grey eye, which, fixing upon the object's face, did not seem to penetrate, and at one glance to pierce through to the inward workings of the heart; but fell upon the cheek with a leaden ray that weighed upon the skin it could not pass. His peculiarities caused him to be invited to every house; all wished to see him, and those who had been accustomed to violent excitement, and now felt the weight of *ennui,* were pleased at having something in their presence capable of engaging their attention. In spite of the deadly hue of his face, which never gained a warmer tint, either from the blush of modesty, or from the strong emotion of passion, though its form and outline were beautiful, many of the female hunters after notoriety attempted to win his attentions, and gain, at least, some marks of what they might term affection: Lady Mercer, who had been the mockery of every monster shewn in drawing rooms since her marriage, threw herself in his way, and did all but put on the dress of a mountebank, to attract his notice;–though in vain:–when she stood before him, though his eyes were apparently fixed upon hers, still it seemed as if they were unperceived–even her unappalled impudence was baffled, and she left the field. But though the common adulteress could not influence even the guidance of his eyes, it was not that the female sex was indifferent to him: yet such was the apparent caution with which he spoke to the virtuous wife and innocent daughter, that few knew he ever addressed himself to females. He had, however, the reputation of a winning tongue; and whether it was that

John Polidori, whose tale about the vampire Lord Ruthven began a vampire craze in London and Paris (portrait by Philip J. Riley; David J. Skal, Hollywood Gothic, *1990, Bruccoli Clark Layman Archives)*

it even overcame the dread of his singular character, or that they were moved by his apparent hatred of vice, he was as often among those females who form the boast of their sex from their domestic virtues, as among those who sully it by their vices.

About the same time, there came to London a young gentleman of the name of Aubrey: he was an orphan left with an only sister in the possession of great wealth, by parents who died while he was yet in childhood. Left also to himself by guardians, who thought it their duty merely to take care of his fortune, while they relinquished the more important charge of his mind to the care of mercenary subalterns, he cultivated more his imagination than his judgment. He had, hence, that high romantic feeling of honour and candour, which daily ruins so many milliners' apprentices. He believed all to sympathise with virtue, and thought that vice was thrown in by Providence merely for the picturesque effect of the scene, as we see in romances; he thought that the misery of a cottage merely consisted in the vesting of clothes, which were as warm, but which were better adapted to the painter's eye by their irregular folds and various coloured patches. He thought, in fine, that the dreams of poets were the realities of life. He was handsome, frank, and rich: for these reasons, upon his entering into the gay circles, many mothers surrounded him, striving which should describe with least truth their languishing or romping favourites: the daughters at the same time, by their brightening countenances when he approached, and by their sparkling eyes, when he opened his lips, soon led him into false notions of his talents and his merit. Attached as he was to the romance of his solitary hours, he was startled at finding that except in the tallow and wax candles, that flickered not from the presence of a ghost, but from want of snuffing, there was no foundation in real life for any of that congeries of pleasing pictures and descriptions contained in those volumes, from which he had formed his study. Finding, however, some compensation in his gratified vanity, he was about to relinquish his dreams, when the extraordinary being we have above described, crossed him in his career.

He watched him; and the very impossibility of forming an idea of the character of a man entirely absorbed in himself, who gave few other signs of his observation of external objects, than the tacit assent to their existence, implied by the avoidance of their contact: allowing his imagination to picture every thing that flattered its propensity to extravagant ideas, he soon formed this object into the hero of a romance, and determined to observe the offspring of his fancy, rather than the person before him. He became acquainted with him, paid him attentions, and so far advanced upon his notice, that his presence was always recognized. He gradually learnt that Lord Ruthven's affairs were embarrassed, and soon found, from the notes of preparation in ——— Street, that he was about to travel. Desirous of gaining some information respecting this singular character, who, till now, had only whetted his curiosity, he hinted to his guardians, that it was time for him to perform the tour, which for many generations has been thought necessary to enable the young to take some rapid steps in the career of vice, towards putting themselves upon an equality with the aged, and not allowing them to appear as if fallen from the skies, whenever scandalous intrigues are mentioned as the subjects of pleasantry or of praise, according to the degree of skill shewn in carrying them on. They consented: and Aubrey immediately mentioning his intentions to Lord Ruthven, was surprised to receive from him a proposal to join him. Flattered by such a mark of esteem from him, who, apparently, had nothing in common with other men, he gladly accepted it, and in a few days they had passed the circling waters.

Hitherto, Aubrey had had no opportunity of studying Lord Ruthven's character, and now he found, that, though many more of his actions were exposed to his view, the results offered different conclusions from the apparent motives to his conduct. His companion was profuse in his liberality;—the idle, the vagabond, and the beggar, received from his hand more than enough to relieve their immediate wants. But Aubrey could not avoid remarking, that it was not upon the virtuous, reduced to indigence by the misfortunes attendant even upon virtue, that he bestowed his alms;— these were sent from the door with hardly suppressed sneers; but when the profligate came to ask something, not to relieve his wants, but to allow him to wallow in his lust, or to sink him still deeper in his iniquity, he was sent away with rich charity. This was, however, attributed by him to the greater importunity of the vicious, which generally prevails over the retiring bashfulness of the virtuous indigent. There was one circumstance about the charity of his Lordship, which was still more impressed upon his mind: all those upon whom it was bestowed, inevitably found that there was a curse upon it, for they all were either led to the scaffold, or sunk to the lowest and the most abject misery. At Brussels and other towns through which they passed, Aubrey was surprized at the apparent eagerness with which his companion sought for the centres of all fashionable vice; there he entered into all the spirit of the faro table: he betted, and always gambled with success, except where the known sharper was his antagonist, and then he lost even more than he gained; but it was always with the same unchanging face, with which he generally watched the society around: it was not, however, so when he encountered the rash youthful novice, or the luckless father of a numerous family; then his very wish seemed fortune's law—this apparent abstractedness of mind was laid aside, and his eyes sparkled with more fire than that of the cat whilst dallying with the half dead mouse. In every town, he left the formerly affluent youth, torn from the circle he adorned, cursing, in the solitude of a dungeon, the fate that had drawn him within the reach of this fiend; whilst many a father sat frantic, amidst the speaking looks of mute hungry children, without a single farthing of his late immense wealth, wherewith to buy even sufficient to satisfy their present craving. Yet he took no money from the gambling table; but immediately lost, to the ruiner of many, the last gilder he had just snatched from the convulsive grasp of the innocent: this might but be the result of a certain degree of knowledge, which was not, however, capable of combating the cunning of the more experienced. Aubrey often wished to represent this to his friend, and beg him to resign that charity and pleasure which proved the ruin of all, and did not tend to his

own profit;—but he delayed it—for each day he hoped his friend would give him some opportunity of speaking frankly and openly to him; however, this never occurred. Lord Ruthven in his carriage, and amidst the various wild and rich scenes of nature, was always the same: his eye spoke less than his lip; and though Aubrey was near the object of his curiosity, he obtained no greater gratification from it than the constant excitement of vainly wishing to break that mystery, which to his exalted imagination began to assume the appearance of something supernatural.

They soon arrived at Rome, and Aubrey for a time lost sight of his companion; he left him in daily attendance upon the morning circle of an Italian countess, whilst he went in search of the memorials of another almost deserted city. Whilst he was thus engaged, letters arrived from England, which he opened with eager impatience; the first was from his sister, breathing nothing but affection; the others were from his guardians, the latter astonished him; if it had before entered into his imagination that there was an evil power resident in his companion, these seemed to give him almost sufficient reason for the belief. His guardians insisted upon his immediately leaving his friend, and urged, that his character was dreadfully vicious, for that the possession of irresistible powers of seduction, rendered his licentious habits more dangerous to society. It had been discovered, that his contempt for the adultress had not originated in hatred of her character; but that he had required, to enhance his gratification, that his victim, the partner of his guilt, should be hurled from the pinnacle of unsullied virtue, down to the lowest abyss of infamy and degradation: in fine, that all those females whom he had sought, apparently on account of their virtue, had, since his departure, thrown even the mask aside, and had not scrupled to expose the whole deformity of their vices to the public gaze.

Aubrey determined upon leaving one, whose character had not yet shown a single bright point on which to rest the eye. He resolved to invent some plausible pretext for abandoning him altogether, purposing, in the mean while, to watch him more closely, and to let no slight circumstances pass by unnoticed. He entered into the same circle, and soon perceived, that his Lordship was endeavouring to work upon the inexperience of the daughter of the lady at whose house he chiefly frequented. In Italy, it is seldom that an unmarried female is met with in society; he was therefore obliged to carry on his plans in secret; but Aubrey's eye followed him in all his windings, and soon discovered that an assignation had been appointed, which would most likely end in the ruin of an innocent, though thoughtless girl. Losing no time, he entered the apartment of Lord Ruthven, and abruptly asked him his intentions with respect to the lady, informing him at the same time that he was aware of his being about to meet her that very night. Lord Ruthven answered, that his intentions were such as he supposed all would have upon such an occasion; and upon being pressed whether he intended to marry her, merely laughed. Aubrey retired; and, immediately writing a note, to say, that from that moment he must decline accompanying his Lordship in the remainder of their proposed tour, he ordered his servant to seek other apartments, and calling upon the mother of the lady, informed her of all he knew, not only with regard to her daughter, but also concerning the character of his Lordship. The assignation was prevented. Lord Ruthven next day merely sent his servant to notify his complete assent to a separation; but did not hint any suspicion of his plans having been foiled by Aubrey's interposition.

Having left Rome, Aubrey directed his steps towards Greece, and, crossing the Peninsula, soon found himself at Athens. He then fixed his residence in the house of a Greek; and soon occupied himself in tracing the faded records of ancient glory upon monuments that apparently, ashamed of chronicling the deeds of freemen only before slaves, had hidden themselves beneath the sheltering soil or many coloured lichen. Under the same roof as himself, existed a being, so beautiful and delicate, that she might have formed the model for a painter, wishing to pourtray on canvass the promised hope of the faithful in Mahomet's paradise, save that her eyes spoke too much mind for any one to think she could belong to those who had no souls. As she danced upon the plain, or tripped along the mountain's side, one would have thought the gazelle a poor type of her beauties, for who would have exchanged her eye, apparently the eye of animated nature, for that sleepy luxurious look of the animal suited but to the taste of an epicure. The light step of Ianthe often accompanied Aubrey in his search after antiquities, and often would the unconscious girl, engaged in the pursuit of a Kashmere butterfly, show the whole beauty of her form, floating as it were upon the wind, to the eager gaze of him, who forgot the letters he had just decyphered upon an almost effaced tablet, in the contemplation of her sylph-like figure. Often would her tresses falling, as she flitted around, show in the sun's ray such delicately brilliant and swiftly fading hues, as might well excuse the forgetfulness of the antiquary, who let escape from his mind the very object he had before thought of vital importance to the proper interpretation of a passage in Pausanias. But why attempt to describe charms which all feel, but none can appreciate?—It was innocence, youth, and beauty, unaffected by crowded drawing rooms, and stifling balls. Whilst he drew those remains of which he wished to preserve a memorial for his future hours, she would stand by, and watch the magic effects of his pencil, in tracing the scenes of her native place; she would then describe to him the circling dance upon the open plain, would paint to him in all the glowing colours of youthful memory, the marriage pomp she remembered viewing in her infancy; and then, turning to subjects that had evidently made a greater impression upon her mind, would tell him all the supernatural tales of her nurse. Her earnestness and apparent belief of what she narrated, excited the interest even of Aubrey; and often, as she told him the tale of the living vampyre, who had passed years amidst his friends, and dearest ties, forced every year, by feeding upon the life of a lovely female to prolong his existence for the ensuing months, his blood would run cold, whilst he attempted to laugh her out of such idle and horrible fantasies; but Ianthe cited to him the names of old men, who had at last detected one living among themselves, after several of their near relatives and children had been found marked with the stamp of the fiend's appetite; and when she found him so incredulous, she begged of him to believe her, for it had been remarked, that those who had dared to question their existence, always had some proof given, which obliged them, with grief and heartbreaking, to confess it was true. She detailed to him the traditional appearance of these monsters, and his horror was increased, by hearing a pretty accurate description of Lord Ruthven; he, however, still persisted in persuading her, that there could be no truth in her fears, though at the same time he wondered at the many coincidences which had all tended to excite a belief in the supernatural power of Lord Ruthven.

Aubrey began to attach himself more and more to Ianthe, her innocence, so contrasted with all the affected virtues of the women among whom he had sought for his vision of romance, won his heart; and while he ridiculed the idea of a young man of English habits, marrying an uneducated Greek girl, still he found himself more and more attached to the almost fairy form before him. He would tear himself at times from her, and, forming a plan for some antiquarian research, he would depart, determined not to return until his object was attained; but he always found it impossible to fix his attention upon the ruins around him, whilst in his mind he retained an image that seemed alone the rightful possessor of his thoughts. Ianthe was unconscious of his love, and was ever the same frank infantile being he had first known. She always seemed to part from him with reluctance; but it was because she had no longer any one with whom she could visit her favourite haunts, whilst her guardian was occupied in sketching or uncovering some fragment which had yet escaped the destructive hand of time. She had appealed to her parents on the subject of Vampyres, and they both, with several present, affirmed their existence, pale with horror at the very name. Soon after, Aubrey determined to proceed upon one of his excursions, which was to detain him for a few hours; when they heard the name of the place, they all at once begged of him not to return at night, as he must necessarily pass through a wood, where no Greek would ever remain after the day had closed, upon any consideration. They described it as the resort of the vampyres in their nocturnal orgies, and denounced the most heavy evils as impending upon him who dared to cross their path. Aubrey made light of their representations, and tried to laugh them out of the idea; but when he saw them shudder at his daring thus to mock a superior, infernal power, the very name of which apparently made their blood freeze, he was silent.

Next morning Aubrey set off upon his excursion unattended; he was surprised to observe the melancholy face of his host, and was concerned to find that his words, mocking the belief of those horrible fiends, had inspired them with such terror.–When he was about to depart, Ianthe came to the side of his horse and earnestly begged of him to return, ere night allowed the power of these beings to be put in action–he promised. He was, however, so occupied in his research, that he did not perceive that day-light would soon end, and that in the horizon there was one of those specks which in the warmer climates so rapidly gather into a tremendous mass and pour all their rage upon the devoted country.–He at last, however, mounted his horse, determined to make up by speed for his delay: but it was too late. Twilight in these southern climates is almost unknown; immediately the sun sets, night begins; and ere he had advanced far, the power of the storm was above–its echoing thunders had scarcely an interval of rest–its thick heavy rain forced its way through the canopying foliage, whilst the blue forked lightning seemed to fall and radiate at his very feet. Suddenly his horse took fright, and he was carried with dreadful rapidity through the entangled forest. The animal at last, through fatigue, stopped, and he found, by the glare of lightning, that he was in the neighbourhood of a hovel that hardly lifted itself up from the masses of dead leaves and brushwood which surrounded it. Dismounting, he approached, hoping to find some one to guide him to the town, or at least trusting to obtain shelter from the pelting of the storm. As he approached, the thunders, for a moment silent, allowed him to hear the dreadful shrieks of a woman mingling with the stifled exultant mockery of a laugh, continued in one almost unbroken sound; he was startled: but, roused by the thunder which again rolled over his head, he with a sudden effort forced open the door of the hut. He found himself in utter darkness; the sound, however, guided him. He was apparently unperceived; for though he called, still the sounds continued, and no notice was

taken of him. He found himself in contact with some one, whom he immediately seized, when a voice cried "again baffled," to which a loud laugh succeeded, and he felt himself grappled by one whose strength seemed superhuman: determined to sell his life as dearly as he could, he struggled; but it was in vain: he was lifted from his feet and hurled with enormous force against the ground:–his enemy threw himself upon him, and kneeling upon his breast, had placed his hands upon his throat, when the glare of many torches penetrating through the hole that gave light in the day, disturbed him–he instantly rose and, leaving his prey, rushed through the door, and in a moment the crashing of the branches, as he broke through the wood, was no longer heard.–The storm was now still; and Aubrey, incapable of moving, was soon heard by those without.–They entered; the light of their torches fell upon the mud walls, and the thatch loaded on every individual straw with heavy flakes of soot. At the desire of Aubrey they searched for her who had attracted him by her cries; he was again left in darkness; but what was his horror, when the light of the torches once more burst upon him, to perceive the airy form of his fair conductress brought in a lifeless corse. He shut his eyes, hoping that it was but a vision arising from his disturbed imagination; but he again saw the same form, when he unclosed them, stretched by his side. There was no colour upon her cheek, not even upon her lip; yet there was a stillness about her face that seemed almost as attaching as the life that once dwelt there:–upon her neck and breast was blood, and upon her throat were the marks of teeth having opened the vein:–to this the men pointed, crying, simultaneously struck with horror, "a Vampyre, a Vampyre!" A litter was quickly formed, and Aubrey was laid by the side of her who had lately been to him the object of so many bright and fairy visions, now fallen with the flower of life that had died within her. He knew not what his thoughts were–his mind was benumbed and seemed to shun reflection and take refuge in vacancy–he held almost unconsciously in his hand a naked dagger of a particular construction, which had been found in the hut.–They were soon met by different parties who had been engaged in the search of her whom a mother had soon missed.–Their lamentable cries, as they approached the city, forewarned the parents of some dreadful catastrophe.–To describe their grief would be impossible; but when they ascertained the cause of their child's death they looked at Aubrey and pointed to the corpse.–They were inconsolable; both died broken-hearted.

Aubrey being put to bed was seized with a most violent fever, and was often delirious; in these intervals he would call upon Lord Ruthven and upon Ianthe–by some unaccountable combination he seemed to beg of his former companion to spare the being he loved.—At other times he would imprecate maledictions upon his head, and curse him as her destroyer. Lord Ruthven chanced at this time to arrive at Athens, and, from whatever motive, upon hearing of the state of Aubrey, immediately placed himself in the same house and became his constant attendant. When the latter recovered from his delirium he was horrified and startled at the sight of him whose image he had now combined with that of a Vampyre; but Lord Ruthven by his kind words, implying almost repentance for the fault that had caused their separation, and still more by the attention, anxiety, and care which he showed, soon reconciled him to his presence. His Lordship seemed quite changed; he no longer appeared that apathetic being who had so astonished Aubrey; but as soon as his convalescence began to be rapid, he again gradually retired into the same state, of mind, and Aubrey perceived no difference from the former man, except, that at times he was surprised to meet his gaze fixed intently upon him with a smile of malicious exultation playing upon his lips: he knew not why, but this smile haunted him. During the last stage of the invalid's recovery, Lord Ruthven was apparently engaged in watching the tideless waves raised by the cooling breeze, or in marking the progress of those orbs, circling, like our world, the moveless sun; indeed he appeared to wish to avoid the eyes of all.

Aubrey's mind, by this shock, was much weakened, and that elasticity of spirit which had once so distinguished him now seemed to have fled for ever.—He was now as much a lover of solitude and silence as Lord Ruthven; but much as he wished for solitude, his mind could not find it in the neighbourhood of Athens; if he sought it amidst the ruins he had formerly frequented, Ianthe's form stood by his side—if he sought it in the woods, her light step would appear wandering amidst the underwood, in quest of the modest violet; then suddenly turning round would show, to his wild imagination, her pale face and wounded throat with a meek smile upon her lips. He determined to fly scenes, every feature of which created such bitter associations in his mind. He proposed to Lord Ruthven, to whom he held himself bound by the tender care he had taken of him during his illness, that they should visit those parts of Greece neither had yet seen. They travelled in every direction, and sought every spot to which a recollection could be attached; but though they thus hastened from place to place yet they seemed not to heed what they gazed upon.—They heard much of robbers, but they gradually began to slight these reports, which they imagined were only the invention of individuals, whose interest it was to excite the generosity of those whom they defended from pretended dangers. In consequence of thus neglecting the advice of the inhabitants, on one occasion they travelled with only a few guards, more to serve as guides

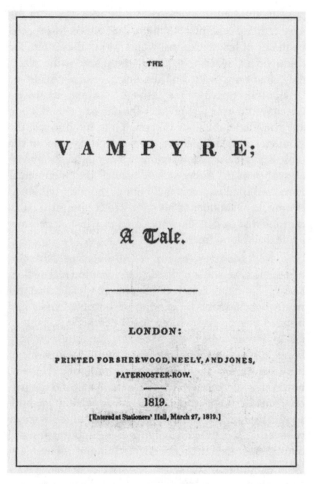

Title page for the pamphlet version of Polidori's tale. Although the attribution to Lord Byron had been removed and was denied in print, the story was still widely regarded as the work of the poet (David J. Skal, Vampires: Encounters with the Undead, *2001; Elizabeth Miller Collection).*

than as a defence.—Upon entering, however, a narrow defile, at the bottom of which was the bed of a torrent, with large masses of rock brought down from the neighbouring precipices, they had reason to repent their negligence;—for, scarcely were the whole of the party engaged in the narrow pass, when they were startled by the whistling of bullets close to their heads, and by the echoed report of several guns. In an instant their guards had left them, and placing themselves behind rocks had begun to fire in the direction whence the report came. Lord Ruthven and Aubrey, imitating their example, retired for a moment behind the sheltering turn of the defile; but ashamed of being thus detained by a foe, who with insulting shouts bade them advance, and being exposed to unresisting slaughter, if any of the robbers should climb above and take them in the rear, they determined at once to rush forward in search of the enemy.—Hardly had they lost the shelter of the rock, when Lord Ruthven received a shot in the shoulder that brought him to the ground.—Aubrey hastened to his assistance, and no longer heeding the contest or his own peril, was soon surprised by seeing the robbers' faces around him; his guards having, upon Lord Ruthven's being wounded, immediately thrown up their arms and surrendered.

By promises of great reward, Aubrey soon induced them to convey his wounded friend to a neighbouring cabin, and having agreed upon a ransom he was no more disturbed by their presence, they being content to merely guard the entrance till their comrade should return with the promised sum for which he had an order.–Lord Ruthven's strength rapidly decreased, in two days mortification ensued, and death seemed advancing with hasty steps.– His conduct and appearance had not changed; he seemed as unconscious of pain as he had been of the objects about him; but towards the close of the last evening his mind became apparently uneasy, and his eye often fixed upon Aubrey, who was induced to offer his assistance with more than usual earnestness–"Assist me! you may save me–you may do more than that–I mean not my life, I heed the death of my existence as little as that of the passing day; but you may save my honour, your friend's honour."–"How, tell me how; I would do any thing," replied Aubrey, "I need but little–my life ebbs apace–I cannot explain the whole–but if you would conceal all you know of me, my honour were free from stain in the world's mouth–and if my death were unknown for some time in England–I–I–but life."–"It shall not be known,"– "Swear!" cried the dying man, raising himself with exultant violence, "Swear by all your soul reveres, by all your nature fears, swear that for a year and a day you will not impart your knowledge of my crimes or death to any living being in any way, whatever may happen, or whatever you may see."–His eyes seemed bursting from their sockets: "I swear!" said Aubrey; he sunk laughing upon his pillow and breathed no more.

Aubrey retired to rest, but did not sleep, the many circumstances attending his acquaintance with this man rose upon his mind, and he knew not why; when he remembered his oath a cold shivering came over him, as if from the presentiment of something horrible awaiting him. Rising early in the morning he was about to enter the hovel in which he had left the corpse, when a robber met him, and informed him that it was no longer there, having been conveyed by himself and comrades, upon his retiring, to the pinnacle of a neighbouring mount, according to a promise they had given his lordship, that it should be exposed to the first cold ray of the moon that rose after his death. Aubrey astonished, and taking several of the men, determined to go and bury it upon the spot where it lay. But, when he had mounted to the summit he found no trace of either the corpse or the clothes, though the robbers swore they pointed out the identical rock on which they had laid the body. For a time his mind was bewil-

dered in conjectures, but he at last returned, convinced that they had buried the corpse for the sake of the clothes.

Weary of a country in which he had met with such terrible misfortunes, and in which all apparently conspired to heighten that superstitious melancholy that had seized upon his mind, he resolved to leave it, and soon arrived at Smyrna. While waiting for a vessel to convey him to Otranto, or to Naples, he occupied himself in arranging those effects he had with him belonging to Lord Ruthven. Amongst other things there was a case containing several weapons of offence, more or less adapted to ensure the death of the victim. There were several daggers and ataghans. Whilst turning them over, and examining their curious forms, what was his surprise at finding a sheath apparently ornamented in the same style as the dagger discovered in the fatal hut; he shuddered; hastening to gain further proof, he found the weapon, and his horror may be imagined when he discovered that it fitted, though peculiarly shaped, the sheath he held in his hand. His eyes seemed to need no further certainty–they seemed gazing to be bound to the dagger; yet still he wished to disbelieve; but the particular form, the same varying tints upon the haft and sheath were alike in splendour on both, and left no room for doubt; there were also drops of blood on each.

He left Smyrna, and on his way home, at Rome, his first inquiries were concerning the lady he had attempted to snatch from Lord Ruthven's seductive arts. Her parents were in distress, their fortune ruined, and she had not been heard of since the departure of his lordship. Aubrey's mind became almost broken under so many repeated horrors; he was afraid that this lady had fallen a victim to the destroyer of Ianthe. He became morose and silent, and his only occupation consisted in urging the speed of the postilions, as if he were going to save the life of some one he held dear. He arrived at Calais; a breeze, which seemed obedient to his will, soon wafted him to the English shores; and he hastened to the mansion of his fathers, and there, for a moment, appeared to lose, in the embraces and caresses of his sister, all memory of the past. If she before, by her infantine caresses, had gained his affection, now that the woman began to appear, she was still more attaching as a companion.

Miss Aubrey had not that winning grace which gains the gaze and applause of the drawing-room assemblies. There was none of that light brilliancy which only exists in the heated atmosphere of a crowded apartment. Her blue eye was never lit up by the levity of the mind beneath. There was a melancholy charm about it which did not seem to arise from misfortune, but from some feeling within, that appeared to indicate a soul conscious of a brighter realm. Her step was not that light footing, which strays where'er a butterfly or a colour may attract–it was sedate and pensive. When alone, her face was never brightened by the smile of joy; but when her brother breathed to her his affection, and would in her presence forget those griefs she knew destroyed his rest, who would have exchanged her smile for that of the voluptuary? It seemed as if those eyes,—that face were then playing in the light of their own native sphere. She was yet only eighteen, and had not been presented to the world; it having been thought by her guardians more fit that her presentation should be delayed until her brother's return from the continent, when he might be her protector. It was now, therefore, resolved that the next drawing room, which was fast approaching, should be the epoch of her entry into the "busy scene." Aubrey would rather have remained in the mansion of his fathers, and fed upon the melancholy which overpowered him. He could not feel interest about the frivolities of fashionable strangers, when his mind had been so torn by the events he had witnessed; but he determined to sacrifice his own comfort to the protection of his sister. They soon arrived in town, and prepared for the next day, which had been announced as a drawing-room.

The crowd was excessive—a drawing room had not been held for a long time, and all who were anxious to bask in the smile of royalty, hastened thither. Aubrey was there with his sister. While he was standing in a corner by himself, heedless of all around him, engaged in the remembrance that the first time he had seen Lord Ruthven was in that very place—he felt himself suddenly seized by the arm, and a voice he recognized too well, sounded in his ear—"Remember your oath." He had hardly courage to turn, fearful of seeing a spectre that would blast him, when he perceived, at a little distance, the same figure which had attracted his notice on this spot upon his first entry into society. He gazed till his limbs almost refusing to bear their weight, he was obliged to take the arm of a friend, and forcing a passage through the crowd, he threw himself into his carriage, and was driven home. He paced the room with hurried steps, and fixed his hands upon his head, as if he were afraid his thoughts were bursting from his brain. Lord Ruthven again before him—circumstances started up in dreadful array—the dagger—his oath.—He roused himself, he could not believe it possible—the dead rise again!—He thought his imagination had conjured up the image his mind was resting upon. It was impossible that it could be real—he determined, therefore, to go again into society; for though he attempted to ask concerning Lord Ruthven, the name hung upon his lips, and he could not succeed in gaining information. He went a few nights after with his sister to the assembly of a near relation. Leaving her under the protection of a matron, he retired into a recess, and there gave himself up to his own devouring thoughts. Perceiving, at last, that many were leaving, he roused himself, and entering another room, found his sister surrounded by several, apparently in earnest conversation; he attempted to pass and get near her, when one, whom he requested to move, turned round, and revealed to him those features he most abhorred. He sprung forward, seized his sister's arm, and, with hurried step, forced her towards the street: at the door he found himself impeded by the crowds of servants who were waiting for their lords; and while he was engaged in passing them, he again heard that voice whisper close to him—"Remember your oath!"—He did not dare to turn, but, hurrying his sister, soon reached home.

Aubrey became almost distracted. If before his mind had been absorbed by one subject, how much more completely was it engrossed, now that the certainty of the monster's living again pressed upon his thoughts. His sister's attentions were now unheeded, and it was in vain that she intreated him to explain to her what had caused his abrupt conduct. He only uttered a few words, and those terrified her. The more he thought, the more he was bewildered. His oath startled him;—was he then to allow this monster to roam, bearing ruin upon his breath, amidst all he held dear, and not avert its progress? His very sister might have been touched by him. But even if he were to break his oath, and disclose his suspicions, who would believe him? He thought of employing his own hand to free the world from such a wretch; but death, he remembered, had been already mocked. For days he remained in this state, shut up in his room, he saw no one, and ate only when his sister came, who, with eyes streaming with tears, besought him, for her sake, to support nature. At last, no longer capable of bearing stillness and solitude, he left his house, roamed from street to street, anxious to fly that image which haunted him. His dress became neglected, and he wandered, as often exposed to the noon-day sun as to the midnight damps. He was no longer to be recognized; at first he returned with the evening to the house; but at last he laid him down to rest wherever fatigue overtook him. His sister, anxious for his safety, employed people to follow him; but they were soon distanced by him who fled from a pursuer swifter than any—from thought. His conduct, however, suddenly changed. Struck with the idea that he left by his absence the whole of his friends, with a fiend amongst them, of whose presence they were unconscious, he determined to enter again into society, and watch him closely, anxious to forewarn, in spite of his oath, all whom Lord Ruthven approached with intimacy. But when he entered into a room, his haggard and suspicious looks were so striking, his inward shudderings so visible, that his sister was at last obliged to beg of him to abstain from seeking, for her sake, a society which affected him so strongly. When, however, remonstrance proved unavailing, the guardians thought proper to interpose, and, fearing that his mind was becoming alienated, they thought it high time to resume again that trust which had been before imposed upon them by Aubrey's parents.

Lord Ruthven and His Clan

An illustration from an undated edition of Polidori's tale, early 1850s (Christopher Frayling, Vampires: Lord Byron
to Count Dracula, 1991; Thomas Cooper Library, University of South Carolina)

Desirous of saving him from the injuries and sufferings he had daily encountered in his wanderings, and of preventing him from exposing to the general eye those marks of what they considered folly, they engaged a physician to reside in the house, and take constant care of him. He hardly appeared to notice it, so completely was his mind absorbed by one terrible subject. His incoherence became at last so great, that he was confined to his chamber. There he would often lie for days, incapable of being roused. He had become emaciated, his eyes had attained a glassy lustre;—the only sign of affection and recollection remaining displayed itself upon the entry of his sister: then he would sometimes start, and, seizing her hands, with looks that severely afflicted her, he would desire her not to touch him. "Oh, do not touch him—if your love for me is aught, do not go near him!" When, however, she inquired to whom he referred, his only answer was—"True! true!" and again he sank into a state, whence not even she could rouse him. This lasted many months: gradually, however, as the year was passing, his incoherences became less frequent, and his mind threw off a portion of its gloom, whilst his guardians observed, that several times in the day he would count upon his fingers a definite number, and then smile.

The time had nearly elapsed, when, upon the last day of the year, one of his guardians entering his room, began to converse with his physician upon the melancholy circumstance of Aubrey's being in so awful a situation when his sister was going next day to be married. Instantly Aubrey's attention was attracted; he asked anxiously to whom. Glad of this mark of returning intellect, of which they feared he had been deprived, they mentioned the name of the Earl of Marsden. Thinking this was a young earl whom he had met with in society, Aubrey seemed pleased, and astonished them still more by his expressing his intention to be present at the nuptials, and desiring to see his sister. They answered not, but in a few minutes his sister was with him. He was apparently again capable of being affected by the influence of her lovely smile; for he pressed her to his breast, and kissed her cheek, wet with tears, flowing at the thought of her brother's being once more alive to the feelings of affection. He began to speak with all his wonted warmth, and to congratulate her upon her marriage with a person so distinguished for rank and every accomplishment; when he suddenly perceived a locket upon her breast; opening it, what was his surprise at beholding the features of the monster who had so long influenced his life. He seized the portrait in a paroxysm of rage, and trampled it under foot. Upon her asking him why he thus destroyed the resemblance of her future husband, he looked as if he did not understand her—then seizing her hands, and gazing on her with a frantic expression of countenance, he bade her swear that she would never wed this monster, for he—But he could not advance—it seemed as if that voice again bade him remember his oath—he turned suddenly round, thinking Lord Ruthven was near him, but saw no one. In the meantime the guardians and physician, who had heard the whole, and thought this was but a return of his disorder, entered, and forcing him from Miss Aubrey, desired her to leave him. He fell upon his knees to them, he implored, he begged of them to delay but for one day. They, attributing this to the insanity they imagined had taken possession of his mind, endeavoured to pacify him, and retired.

Lord Ruthven had called the morning after the drawing room, and had been refused with every one else. When he heard of Aubrey's ill health, he readily understood himself to be the cause of it: but when he learned that he was deemed insane, his exultation and pleasure could hardly be concealed from those among whom he had gained this information. He hastened to the house of his former companion, and, by constant attendance, and the pretence of great affection for the brother and interest in his fate, he gradually won the ear of Miss Aubrey. Who could resist his power? His tongue had dangers and toils to recount—could speak of himself as of an individual having no sympathy with any being on the crowded earth, save with her to whom he addressed himself;—could tell how, since he knew her, his existence had begun to seem worthy of preservation, if it were merely that he might listen to her soothing accents;—in fine, he knew so well how to use the serpent's art, or such was the will of fate, that he gained her affections. The title of the elder branch falling at length to him, he obtained an important embassy, which served as an excuse for hastening the marriage, (in spite of her brother's deranged state,) which was to take place the very day before his departure for the continent.

Aubrey, when he was left by the physician and his guardian, attempted to bribe the servants, but in vain. He asked for pen and paper; it was given him; he wrote a letter to his sister, conjuring her, as she valued her own happiness, her own honour, and the honour of those now in the grave, who once held her in their arms as their hope and the hope of their house, to delay but for a few hours, that marriage, on which he denounced the most heavy curses. The servants promised they would deliver it; but giving it to the physician, he thought it better not to harass any more the mind of Miss Aubrey by, what he considered, the ravings of a maniac. Night passed on

without rest to the busy inmates of the house; and Aubrey heard, with a horror that may more easily be conceived than described, the notes of busy preparation. Morning came, and the sound of carriages broke upon his ear. Aubrey grew almost frantic. The curiosity of the servants at last overcame their vigilance, they gradually stole away, leaving him in the custody of an helpless old woman. He seized the opportunity, with one bound was out of the room, and in a moment found himself in the apartment where all were nearly assembled. Lord Ruthven was the first to perceive him: he immediately approached, and, taking his arm by force, hurried him from the room, speechless with rage. When on the staircase, Lord Ruthven whispered in his ear—"Remember your oath, and know, if not my bride to day, your sister is dishonoured. Women are frail!" So saying, he pushed him towards his attendants, who, roused by the old woman, had come in search of him. Aubrey could no longer support himself; his rage not finding vent, had broken a blood-vessel, and he was conveyed to bed. This was not mentioned to his sister, who was not present when he entered, as the physician was afraid of agitating her. The marriage was solemnized, and the bride and bridegroom left London.

Aubrey's weakness increased; the effusion of blood produced symptoms of the near approach of death. He desired his sister's guardians might be called, and when the midnight hour had struck, he related composedly what the reader has perused—he died immediately after.

The guardians hastened to protect Miss Aubrey; but when they arrived, it was too late. Lord Ruthven had disappeared, and Aubrey's sister had glutted the thirst of a VAMPYRE!

—The New Monthly Magazine and Universal Register,
11 (1 April 1819): 195–206

From *Don Juan*

Byron uses "vampire" as a figure of speech in canto XI, stanza 62, of his satirical poem. Having brought his young hero back to England, Byron has his narrator berate much of the contemporary literary community of "live and dead pretenders."

This is the literary *lower* Empire,
　Where the Praetorian bands take up the matter;
A 'dreadful trade,' like his who 'gathers samphire,'
　The insolent soldiery to soothe and flatter,
With the same feelings as you'd coax a vampire.

—Don Juan. Cantos IX.—X.—and XI.
(London: Printed for John Hunt, 1823)

An Evolving Tradition

With the success of Polidori's tale, vampire fiction contin- ued almost unabated throughout the nineteenth century, so that by the time Bram Stoker started Dracula, *many of the literary con- ventions of the genre had already been well established.*

The two best-known vampire tales published between Poli- dori's "The Vampyre" and Dracula *are* Varney the Vampyre *(1847), a work now thought to be written by James Malcolm Rymer, and Joseph Sheridan Le Fanu's "Carmilla" (1872). As critic Carol A. Senf shows in this essay written for this volume, both stories include motifs and passages that have resonance for readers of Stoker's novel.*

The Literary Vampire Before *Dracula*
Carol A. Senf

John Polidori's "The Vampyre," one of the first appearances of the vampire in English litera- ture, gained notoriety in the nineteenth century because of its association with the Byron-Shelley cir- cle. Its title character, Lord Ruthven, originates in folklore. An anonymous introduction to the first appearance of the story, in the *New Monthly Magazine* for April 1819, notes that belief in vampires is "very general in the east," where it resulted in stories "of the dead rising from their graves, and feeding upon the blood of the young and beautiful."[1]

Polidori adds his own touches, including the fact that moonlight rejuvenates vampires, a talent that the author of *Varney the Vampyre* would later use repeatedly. Polidori is also the first to make the vam- pire an aristocrat; Lord Ruthven would be followed by Sir Frances Varney, Countess Mircalla, and Count Dracula. Finally, Polidori adds eroticism, not- ing that the vampire is "forced every year, by feed- ing upon the life of a lovely female to prolong his existence for the ensuing months."[2] Folkloric vam- pires are simply hungry corpses with no special pref- erences in victims, but Polidori establishes the erotic attachment between vampire and victim, having Lord Ruthven woo Aubrey's sister and marry her. Only later do their guardians discover that she "had glutted the thirst of a VAMPYRE!" (p. 24).

Polidori also creates a more complex and inter- esting character than the vampire in folklore. Ruth- ven destroys victims by drinking their blood, but he is also a moral parasite, "a man entirely absorbed in himself" (p. 8). In addition, Lord Ruthven ruins vic- tims financially and socially. In this respect, he resembles characters from popular literature—Love- lace, Squire B, and other eighteenth-century rakes as well as both Gothic villains and the Byronic hero. That Polidori was thinking specifically of Byron is

evident in his choice of name, for Lady Caroline Lamb had named a Byronic character Lord Ruthven in her roman à clef, *Glenarvon* (1816).

Establishing Ruthven as both vampire and rake, Polidori emphasizes moral failure rather than supernatural ability. Indeed, Polidori waits until the work is half over to reveal that Ruthven is a vam- pire, presenting him instead as a destroyer of the victim's reputation and will. Believing that Ruthven is attracted to virtuous women, Aubrey learns those "whom he had sought, apparently on account of their virtue, had . . . thrown even the mask aside, and had not scrupled to expose the whole deformity of their vices to the public gaze" (p. 11). Even Ruth- ven's money is tainted:

> When the profligate came to ask something . . . to allow him to wallow in his lust, or to sink him still deeper in his iniquity, he was sent away . . . with rich charity. . . . All those upon whom it was bestowed, inevitably found . . . a curse upon it, for they were all either led to the scaffold, or sunk to the lowest and most abject misery. (p. 9)

This contagion is common to rake and vampire: both "pass on their conditions (moral depravity in the former and vampirism in the latter) to their vic- tims."[3]

Influenced by folklore and popular literature, Polidori contributes to the development of the mod- ern vampire by creating a monster that thrives in civilized urban settings. Much of "The Vampyre" occurs in drawing rooms and Continental resorts; in fact, Polidori was responsible for the "emphasis on contemporary settings in horror tales, rather than shadowy backgrounds remote in time and space."[4] Indeed the horror of Polidori's tale occurs when the reader understands that unspeakable things happen in ordinary places to ordinary people.

Studying "The Vampyre" reveals how the brutish folkloric vampire was transformed into a complex and interesting literary character. For exam- ple, Polidori makes his human characters responsible for much of the death and destruction that occur, thus focusing on everyday horrors. Lord Ruthven is directly responsible only for the deaths of Ianthe and Miss Aubrey. The men he ruins at the gambling tables and the women whose reputations he destroys are largely responsible for their own fates. Although other writers will explore the part the victim plays in its relationship with the vampire, Polidori hints at the vampire as social metaphor when he provides glimpses of a corrupt society where the wealthy, plagued by ennui, seek to alleviate boredom by flirt-

ing with vice. The ultimate predator, the vampire is
a logical member of such a society.

   "The Vampyre" was an instant success, due in
large part to the misconception that it had been written by Lord Byron himself. In the decades following
its first appearance in 1819, it was adapted for
numerous French and English melodramas and two
operas.[5] Christopher Frayling has observed that
"identification of 'The Vampyre' with accepted
mythologies about Lord Byron . . . limited the possibilities of character development."[6] Perhaps its most
popular adaptation was as a stage play by J. R.
Planché entitled *The Vampire, or The Bride of the Isles*
(1820). Best known as the inventor of a new
trap-door for the stage (nicknamed "the vampire
trap"), Planché has also been acknowledged for
introducing realistic detail on stage. Having designed

*Title page for the first opera inspired by Polidori's vampire tale
(David J. Skal,* Vampires: Encounters with the
Undead, *2001; Elizabeth Miller Collection)*

Vampires on Stage

*The popularity of Polidori's tale soon led to the production of
vampire plays. Roxana Stuart estimates that some thirty-five such
plays were produced in the nineteenth century and notes that
"Many important figures of 19th-century English, French, and
American theatre were involved in the production of these plays."*

   In June of 1820 *Le Vampire,* by Charles Nodier,
Pierre Carmouche, and Achille Jouffrey, was produced
in Paris, based on a short story by John Polidori which
in turn was based on an unfinished work of Lord
Byron. Parodies of the play were written by Eugène
Scribe and Mélesville, and by Nicholas Brazier,
Auguste Rousseau, Marc Antoine Désaugiers, and others. Within two months James Robinson Planché had
adapted the play into English in London. The vampire
was played by Thomas Potter Cooke, who became the
leading English actor of melodrama in the mid-19th
century.

   The success of the play in England was such that a
rival version quickly appeared by W. T. Moncrieff,
and the interest in vampires inspired dramatizations of
Robert Southey's *Thalaba the Destroyer* in 1823 and Lud-
vig Tieck's short story "Wake Not the Dead," which
was the basis for George Blink's play, *The Vampire Bride*
(c. 1834). In 1828 an opera, *Der Vampyr* by Heinrich
Marschner had long runs in Leipzig and, with English
libretto by Planché, in London.

—Roxana Stuart, *Stage Blood: Vampires of the
19th-Century Stage* (Bowling Green, Ohio:
Bowling Green State University Press,
1994), p. 3

---

and supervised the costumes for John Kemble's
revival of *King John,* resulting in the first recorded
attempt at historical accuracy in a Shakespearean
play,[7] Planché was well aware that his new play
could not be accused of historical accuracy:

> Samuel James Arnold . . . had placed in my hands for
> adaptation a French melodrama . . . which was laid . . .
> in Scotland. . . . I vainly endeavored to induce Mr.
> Arnold to let me change it to some place in the east of
> Europe. He had set his heart on Scotch music and
> dresses—the latter, by the way, were in stock. . . . The
> melodrama had a long run, was often revived, and is to
> this day [1872] a stock piece in the country.[8]

In 1829, Planché treated the subject more realistically
according to his "own ideas of propriety," setting the
play in Hungary "where the superstition exists to this
day," and substituted for a Scottish chieftain a "Wallachian Boyard."[9]

6 Handbill for James Planchés' theatrical version of *The Vampyre*, performed at the height of the Lord Ruthven craze in autumn 1820. Note the kilt worn by Mr T. P. Cooke in the role of Lord Ruthven.

Engraving by J. Findlay from Planché's The Vampire, or The Bride of the Isles *(1820; Elizabeth Miller,* Dracula, *2000; Elizabeth Miller Collection)*

The next major work to focus on the blood-sucker is *Varney the Vampyre or, The Feast of Blood,* issued in serial form in the mid-1840s and reprinted in book form in 1847. The author is given variously as James Malcolm Rymer or Thomas Preckett Prest. While the latter is more frequently cited, E. F. Bleiler's stylistic analysis (published with the Dover edition)[10] presents a convincing argument for Rymer. *Varney* was written at breakneck speed for an audience more interested in fast pace and suspense than in coherent character development.

Despite its aesthetic flaws, however, it was extraordinarily popular and continued for 868 pages.

Naming a minor character Count Pollidori [sic], the writer reveals his literary debt. Varney, who is as interested in money as in blood, is prevented from marrying the wealthy Isabella by several officers, including her brother Count Pollidori. The narrative includes other connections to both folklore and to the literary tradition, including a preface (1847, reprinted in the Dover edition) that points to the authenticity of vampires:

A belief in the existence of Vampyres first took its rise in Norway and Sweden, from whence it rapidly spread . . . taking a firm hold of the imaginations of the more credulous portion of mankind.

The following romance is collected from seemingly the most authentic sources, and the Author must leave the question of credibility entirely to his readers.

Thus the writer bases Varney on superstition and simultaneously questions those beliefs. There is no question, however, that he had folklore in mind when he wrote the first chapter:

It [the face] is perfectly white—perfectly bloodless. The eyes look like polished tin; the lips are drawn back, and the principal feature next to those dreadful eyes is the teeth . . . projecting like those of some wild animal, hideously, glaringly white, and fang-like. It approaches the bed with a strange, gliding movement. (vol. 1, p. 3)

If Varney's bestial behavior stems from folklore, his lasciviousness (reinforced by an accompanying illustration of him with his teeth at his victim's throat and his hand on her breast) comes from literature:

With a sudden rush . . . the figure seized the long tresses of her hair, and . . . drags her head to the bed's edge. He forces it back by the long hair . . . he seizes her neck in his fang-like teeth—a gush of blood, and a hideous sucking noise follows. *The girl has swooned, and the vampyre is at his hideous repast!* (vol. 1, p. 4; author's italics)

Like Lord Ruthven with Ianthe, Varney attacks Flora and drinks her blood, behavior that combines the brutality of the folkloric vampire with the Gothic villain's sexuality.

While adapting existing material, *Varney* also adds to the popular concept of the vampire: it reinforces Polidori's notion that vampires are aristocrats; suggests that they represent the power of the past over the present; and emphasizes the erotic attraction vampires have over victims.

Like Lord Ruthven, Sir Francis Varney is an aristocrat; and the aristocratic connection continues throughout nineteenth-century literature. Although Polidori, Le Fanu, and Stoker have no consistent rationale for making vampires aristocrats, all three link the aristocrat's hereditary power to the vampire's power over humans. Varney, however, is simply one of many aristocratic villains in popular literature, his title having little to do with his evil nature or his power. A reference to Sir George Crofton, father of one of his victims and a man who briefly believes himself a vampire, suggests that the writer may have associated aristocratic

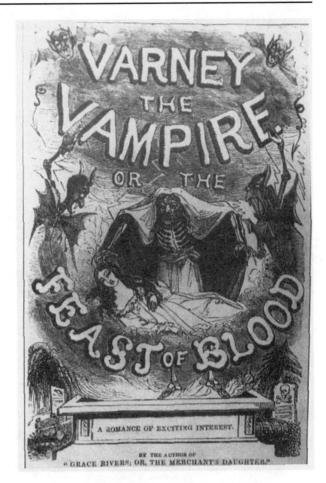

Cover illustration for the popular "penny dreadful" (David J. Skal, Hollywood Gothic, *1990; Bruccoli Clark Layman Archives)*

landlords with economic exploitation. Certainly the leader of a working class mob sees his class as economic victims: "Is we to be made into victims, or isn't we? What's Sir George Crofton and his family to us? To be sure he's the landlord of some of us, and a very good landlord he is, too, as long as we pay our rent" (vol. 2, p. 832).

More important than the economic relationship, however, is the fact that Varney comes from the past to influence the present. Thus, the author focuses on problems of inheritance. Later writers will use the vampire to reveal that past social values continue to influence the present. Even if he doesn't do more than suggest that Varney's swashbuckling behavior is the remnant of an earlier period, *Varney*'s author should be credited as the first to present the vampire specifically as a creature from the past.

Also developed in the narrative is the sexual attraction between vampire and victim. Merely suggested by Polidori, this erotic component will become even more explicit in later works. Here, Flora is fascinated by Varney:

> The glance of a serpent could not have produced a greater effect . . . than did the fixed gaze of those awful, metallic-looking eyes. . . . She drew her breath short and thick. Her bosom heaves, and her lips tremble, yet she cannot withdraw her eyes . . . He holds her with his glittering eyes. (vol. 1, pp. 3–4)

Despite her conscious fear, Flora becomes a sleepwalker, her unconscious desire taking her to Varney.

Because of the many inconsistencies in the story, the title character is difficult to classify. In several scenes, such as the first chapter in which he drinks Flora's blood and others in which he is identified as a supernatural being, Varney might come straight from folklore. Other scenes question whether Varney is a vampire. Bleiler's introduction to the Dover edition points out inconsistencies:

> Varney is identified . . . as a supernatural being who has lived since the days of Henry IV; as a turncoat from the days of the Commonwealth, sentenced to be a vampire because he had killed his son in a moment of rage; or as a modern criminal, not at all supernatural, who had been revived after being hanged. (p. xv)

Whether or not Varney is supernatural, the story focuses on human, not supernatural evil. The following passage, from one of the novel's many chase scenes, is a recognition that the vampire projects human cruelty: ". . . and as often was the miserable man [Varney] hunted from his place of refuge only to seek another, from which he was in like manner hunted by those who thirsted for his blood" (vol. 1, p. 375). The author does not develop this connection, but realistic nineteenth-century novelists and social writers will develop the metaphoric link between the vampire's behavior and reprehensible human behavior.

While *Varney the Vampyre* is read today as an example of mid-Victorian popular culture rather than for any intrinsic literary merit, Joseph Sheridan Le Fanu's "Carmilla" (published in 1872) is interesting in its own right. Conscious of an evolving literary tradition, Le Fanu adapts characteristics from both folklore and literature. Carmilla is an aristocrat, a sexual predator, and a creature from the past as well as a supernatural bloodsucker. Le Fanu's most original contribution is his break with the conception of the vampire as a Byronic male figure to create a femme fatale. Whereas folklore had presented the vampire as more bestial than human and even Varney, who is not without erotic appeal, is described as hideous, Carmilla is beautiful.

Thus she relies on seduction rather than on the male vampire's brutal direct attack. By day she woos Laura with words and actions, behavior that Laura describes as "like the ardor of a lover":

> [I]t embarrassed me; it was hateful and yet overpowering; and with gloating eyes she drew me to her, and her hot lips traveled along my cheek in kisses; and she would whisper, almost in sobs, "You are mine, you shall be mine, and you and I are one forever."[11]

Indeed, Carmilla's actions are consistently described as loving, not violent.

Carmilla, however, is definitely a vampire, not a human who resembles the supernatural creature; thus she is responsible for her victims' deaths, not just the destruction of their reputations or fortunes. Le Fanu's account of Carmilla's destruction could have come straight from folklore:

> The features, though a hundred and fifty years had passed since her funeral, were tinted with the warmth of life. . . . The body, therefore, in accordance with the ancient practice, was raised, and a sharp stake driven through the heart of the vampire, who uttered a piercing shriek. . . . Then the head was struck off, and a torrent of blood flowed from the severed neck. (p. 134)

Carmilla's death is gruesome and extraordinary, but Le Fanu generally stresses the ordinary rather than the exceptional. For example, although "Carmilla" is set in Styria, where the superstition had flourished in the eighteenth century, the author combines that exotic setting with realistic social details:

> A small income, in that part of the world, goes a great way. . . . Scantily enough ours would have answered among wealthy people at home. . . . But, in this lonely and primitive place, where everything is so marvelously cheap, I really don't see how ever so much more money would at all materially add to our comforts, or even luxuries. (p. 72)

The emphasis on financial security might come straight from Thackeray or Austen; and the castle, or schloss, which has none of the mysterious underground caverns familiar to readers of Radcliffe, Walpole, or Lewis, resembles the country houses of realistic fiction.

Besides using contemporary settings, Le Fanu creates a cast of characters who might have come from the pages of a realistic novel: Laura, the young narrator; two governesses; and her father, a retired diplomat. Even Carmilla initially appears only as an eccentric who likes to sleep late and wander at night. The plot is far from ordinary, of course, for Carmilla is centuries old. However, because Laura and her father refuse to

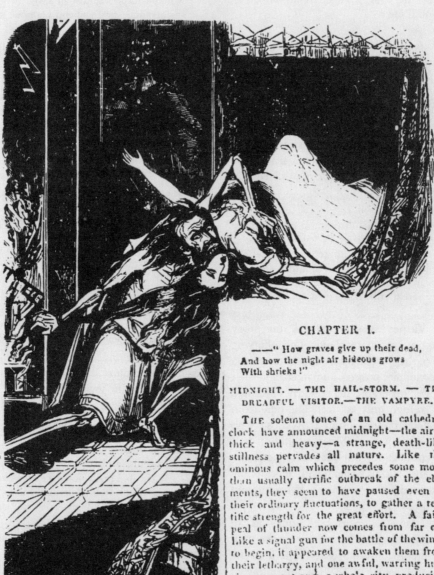

First page of the initial installment in 1847 of a horror serial that was told in 108 episodes totaling more than 800 pages
(Peter Haining, The Dracula Scrapbook, *1976; Thomas Cooper Library, University of South Carolina)*

*J. Sheridan Le Fanu (1814–1873). A fellow Dubliner, Stoker
may well have been influenced by Le Fanu's vampire tale,
"Carmilla" (David J. Skal, Vampires: Encounters
with the Undead, 2001; Elizabeth
Miller Collection).*

believe in the supernatural, the truth is not revealed until the end. Astute readers, recognizing that Carmilla is a vampire long before the characters do, become aware of other matters: the commonplace details that Laura observes, and the similarities between the vampire's traits and the evil in human nature.

Le Fanu, for example, links the vampire's predation to the treatment and occasional mistreatment of certain groups. Indifferent to people outside her circle, Laura describes the small "party who constitute the inhabitants of our castle" (p. 73) and admits she does not include servants. There is no indication that Laura harms these "invisible people," but the psychological distance from indifference to predation is not so far as it might seem initially. Hearing that a peasant woman had died from a wasting illness (probably caused by Carmilla or another vampire), Carmilla sneers: "'I don't trouble my head about peasants. I don't know who she is'" (p. 92). In fact, Laura and Carmilla often pretend that peasants do not exist even though they depend on them for food (quite literally in the case of Carmilla).

That Le Fanu establishes Laura as "every-woman" suggests that all women are potential victims. (Carmilla also alters the heterosexual behavior of Lord Ruthven and Varney by choosing women as victims.)

Nameless for the first part of the story, Laura never reveals her last name. Because she has been educated only for a social and sexual function, she has few interests except the subjects that were expected to be the centre of young women's lives—parties and the opportunities they present to meet eligible men. The only part of her life that makes Laura unique is her relationship with Carmilla.

The relationship begins when Laura is a child. Terrified by Carmilla's first visit, Laura becomes more frightened when her father laughs at her. The patronizing treatment continues. As Laura approaches womanhood she asks her father about her illness. He, however, chooses to conceal information that might have allowed her to protect herself. His refusal to divulge the doctor's suspicions about vampirism may stem from rationalism or a misguided desire to protect her. Like Van Helsing's plan to protect Mina, however, it leaves Laura vulnerable.

By constructing a genealogy of Laura's family that includes only the female line, Le Fanu suggests that other women have been similarly victimized. Laura's mother was from an old Hungarian family, and the picture of the Countess Mircalla (the name of which Carmilla is an anagram) came from her mother's family. In addition, Laura's mother may have been a victim also, for Laura dreams: "Your mother warns you to beware of the assassin" (p. 106) before she awakes to see a blood-drenched Carmilla. That Carmilla is an ancestor of Laura's mother suggests that Laura is the last in a line of victims.

By portraying the vampire as female, Le Fanu reveals that women, though considered weak and frail, may have more real power than men. Although the men use physical force to destroy Carmilla, this force is ultimately ineffectual. Laura's narrative concludes, not with the vampire's destruction, but with the acknowledgment that Carmilla still exists: "the memory of Carmilla returns to memory . . . and often from a reverie I have started, fancying I heard the light step of Carmilla at the drawing-room door" (p. 137). The preface, which reveals that Laura has died, also suggests that violence does not eliminate the vampire. It may also be Le Fanu's way of suggesting that a situation that has evolved over centuries can not be eradicated in an instant—perhaps not at all.

While Le Fanu builds on traditional notions of the vampire, which had originated in folklore and evolved in popular literature, he also creates a new kind of vampire in Carmilla, her "newness" a direct result of her gender. Beautiful and seductive rather than violent and aggressive, Carmilla manifests the sexuality at which Polidori and the creator of Varney had only hinted:

Illustration for Le Fanu's "Carmilla" in Dark Blue Magazine, *1872 (Leonard Wolf,* Dracula: The Connoisseur's Guide, *1997; Elizabeth Miller Collection)*

Sometimes it was as if warm lips kissed me, and longer and more lovingly as they reached my throat. . . . My heart beat faster, my breathing rose and fell rapidly and full drawn; a sobbing, that rose into a sense of strangulation, supervened, and turned into a dreadful convulsion, in which my senses left me, and I became unconscious. (pp. 105–106)

Carmilla's relationship to her victims suggests perverse sexuality that the family-respecting Victorians regarded as especially destructive as well as a power and autonomy rarely seen in women. Writing at a time when women were demanding more economic, social, political, and sexual power, Le Fanu modifies the vampire from folklore and earlier literature to create a powerful female figure that articulates these demands for female power and opens a new chapter in the tradition of the literary vampire.

1. Introduction to "The Vampyre," *New Monthly Magazine,* 1 April 1819; repr. in *The Vampyre and Ernestus Berchtold,* ed. D. L. Macdonald and Kathleen Scherf (Toronto: University of Toronto Press, 1994), p. 183.

2. John Polidori, "The Vampyre," in *The Penguin Book of Vampire Stories,* ed. Alan Ryan (New York: Penguin, 1987), p. 12. Subsequent quotations are from this anthology.

3. Carrol L. Fry, "Fictional Conventions and Sexuality in *Dracula,*" *Victorian Newsletter,* 42 (Fall 1972): 21.

4. Margaret L. Carter, *Shadow of a Shade: A Survey of Vampirism in Literature* (New York: Gordon, 1975), p. 26.

5. For a detailed examination of these adaptations, see Roxana Stuart, *Stage Blood: Vampires of the 19th-Century Stage* (Bowling Green, Ohio: Bowling Green State University Popular Press, 1994).

6. Christopher Frayling, ed., *The Vampire: Lord Ruthven to Count Dracula* (London: Victor Gollancz, 1978), p. 17.

7. Stephen Weschhusen, ed., *The Hour of One: Six Gothic Melodramas* (London: Gordon Fraser, 1975), pp. 9–10.

8. James Robinson Planché, *Recollections and Reflections: A Professional Autobiography* (London: Sampson Low, Marston, 1901), pp. 26–27.

9. Planché, *Recollections,* p. 104.

10. *Varney the Vampyre,* 2 vols. (New York: Dover, 1972), pp. xvii–xviii. Subsequent quotations are taken from this edition.

11. J. Sheridan Le Fanu, "Carmilla," 1872; repr. in *The Penguin Book of Vampire Stories,* p. 90. Subsequent quotations are from this anthology.

* * *

How to Destroy a Vampire

The blacksmith shuddered as he held the stake in an attitude to pierce the body, and even up to that moment it seemed to be a doubtful case, whether he would be able to accomplish his purpose or not; at length, when they all thought he was upon the point of abandoning his design, and casting the stake away, he thrust it with tremendous force through the body and the back of the coffin.

The eyes of the corpse opened wide—the hands were clenched, and a shrill, piercing shriek came from the lips—a shriek that was answered by as many as there were persons present, and then with pallid fear upon their countenances they rushed headlong from the spot.

–James Malcolm Rymer, *Varney, the Vampyre;*
or, The Feast of Blood (London:
E. Lloyd, 1847)

. . . The grave of the Countess Mircalla was opened; and the General and my father recognized each his perfidious and beautiful guest, in the face now disclosed to view. The features, though a hundred and fifty years had passed since her funeral, were tinted with the warmth of life. Her eyes were open; no cadaverous smell exhaled from the coffin. The two medical men, one officially present, the other on the part of the promoter of the inquiry, attested the marvellous fact, that there was a faint, but appreciable respiration, and a corresponding action of the heart. The limbs were perfectly flexible, the flesh elastic; and the leaden coffin floated with blood, in which to a depth of seven inches the body lay immersed. Here then, were all the admitted signs and proofs of vampirism. The body, therefore, in accordance with the ancient practice, was raised, and a sharp stake driven through the heart of the vampire, who uttered a piercing shriek at the moment, in all respects such as might escape from a living person in the last agony. Then the head was struck off, and a torrent of blood flowed from the severed neck.

–Joseph Sheridan Le Fanu, "Carmilla,"
in *In a Glass Darkly,* 3 volumes
(London: Bentley, 1872)

Arthur took the stake and hammer, and when once his mind was set on action his hands never trembled nor even quivered . . . . Arthur placed the point over the heart, and as I looked I could see its dint in the white flesh. Then he struck with all his might.

The Thing in the coffin writhed; and a hideous, blood-curdling screech came from the opened red lips. The body shook and quivered and twisted in wild contortions; the sharp white teeth champed together till the lips were cut, and the mouth was smeared with a crimson foam. But Arthur never faltered. He looked like a figure of Thor as his untrembling arm rose and fell, driving deeper and deeper the mercy-bearing stake, whilst the blood from the pierced heart welled and spurted up around it.

–*Dracula*, Chapter XVI, Dr. Seward's
Diary, 29 September

The most striking precursor to Dracula *is "The Mysterious Stranger," a German tale of unknown authorship that was translated into English in 1860. In this story one finds most of the attributes of the vampire that readers commonly associate with Stoker's Count: aristocratic heritage, pale complexion, and black clothing; two sharp fangs that leave distinctive marks on the victim's neck; supernatural strength; association with wolves and bats; the ability to both attract and repel; the power to shape-shift into mist; and the presence of an "expert" opponent who supplies information about the reality of vampires.*

From "The Mysterious Stranger"

"To die, to sleep,
To sleep, perchance to dream, ay, there's the rub . . . "
Hamlet.

Boreas, that fearful north-west wind, which in the spring and autumn stirs up the lowest depths of the wild Adriatic, and is then so dangerous to vessels, was howling through the woods, and tossing the branches of the old knotty oaks in the Carpathian Mountains, when a party of five riders, who surrounded a litter drawn by a pair of mules, turned into a forest-path, which offered some protection from the April weather, and allowed the travellers in some degree to recover their breath. It was already evening, and bitterly cold; the snow fell every now and then in large flakes. A tall old gentleman, of aristocratic appearance, rode at the head of the troop. This was the Knight of Fahnenberg, in Austria. He had inherited from a childless brother a considerable property, situated in the Carpathian Mountains; and he had set out to take possession of it, accompanied by his daughter Franziska, and a niece about twenty years of age, who had been brought up with her. Next to the knight rode a fine young man of some twenty and odd years–the Baron Franz von Kronstein . . .

. . . .

. . . Suddenly the old man stopped, he drew his horse sharply up, and remained in an attitude of attentive listening.

The Brontës' Vampires

In the novels published by Emily and Charlotte Brontë in 1847, the deeds of the past come to overshadow the present. In Emily Brontë's Wuthering Heights *(1847), the housekeeper Nelly wonders of her vengeful master Heathcliff, "Is he a ghoul or a vampire?"*

In this passage from Charlotte Brontë's Jane Eyre, *Jane, on the brink of marriage to Rochester, first sees the woman who is later identified as Rochester's mad Creole wife Bertha, whom he has long hidden.*

" . . . On waking, a gleam dazzled my eyes: I thought—oh, it is daylight! But I was mistaken: it was only candlelight. Sophie, I supposed, had come in. There was a light on the dressing-table, and the door of the closet, where, before going to bed, I had hung my wedding-dress and veil, stood open: I heard a rustling there. I asked, 'Sophie, what are you doing?' No one answered; but a form emerged from the closet: it took the light, held it aloft, and surveyed the garments pendent from the portmanteau. 'Sophie! Sophie!' I again cried: and still it was silent. I had risen up in bed; I bent forward: first, surprise, then bewilderment, came over me; and then my blood crept cold through my veins. Mr. Rochester, this was not Sophie, it was not Leah, it was not Mrs. Fairfax: it was not—no, I was sure of it, and am still—it was not even that strange woman, Grace Poole."

"It must have been one of them," interrupted my master.

"No, sir, I solemnly assure you to the contrary. The shape standing before me had never crossed my eyes within the precincts of Thornfield Hall before; the height, the contour, were new to me."

"Describe it, Jane."

"It seemed, sir, a woman, tall and large, with thick and dark hair hanging long down her back. I know not what dress she had on: it was white and straight: but whether gown, sheet, or shroud, I cannot tell."

"Did you see her face?"

"Not at first. But presently she took my veil from its place; she held it up, gazed at it long, and then she threw it over her own head, and turned to the mirror. At that moment I saw the reflection of the visage and features quite distinctly in the dark oblong glass."

"And how were they?"

"Fearful and ghastly to me—oh, sir, I never saw a face like it! It was a discoloured face—it was a savage face. I wish I could forget the roll of the red eyes and the fearful blackened inflation of the lineaments!"

"Ghosts are usually pale, Jane."

"This, sir, was purple: the lips were swelled and dark; the brow furrowed; the black eyebrows widely raised over the bloodshot eyes. Shall I tell you of what it reminded me?"

"You may."

"Of the foul German spectre—the Vampyre."

—Jane Eyre. *An Autobiography,* as Currer Bell, 3 volumes (London: Smith, Elder, 1847), chapter 24

"It appears to me we must be in the neighborhood of some village," said Franz von Kronstein; "for between the gusts of the storm I hear a dog howling."

"It is no dog, it is no dog!" said the old man uneasily, and urged his horse to a rapid pace. "For miles around there is no human dwelling; and except in the castle of Klatka, which indeed lies in the neighborhood, but has been deserted for more than a century, probably no one has lived here since the creation.—But there again," he continued; "well, if I wasn't sure of it from the first."

"That howling seems to bother you, old Kumpan," said the knight, listening to a long-drawn fierce sound, which appeared nearer than before, and seemed to be answered from a distance.

"That howling comes from no dogs," replied the old guide uneasily. "Those are reed-wolves; they may be on our track; and it would be as well if the gentlemen looked to their firearms."

"Reed-wolves? What do you mean?" inquired Franz in surprise.

"At the edge of this wood," said Kumpan, "there lies a lake about a mile long, whose banks are covered with reeds. In these a number of wolves have taken up their quarters, and feed on wild birds, fish and such like. They are shy in the summer-time, and a boy of twelve might scare them; but when the birds migrate, and the fish are frozen up, they prowl about at night, and then they are dangerous. They are worst, however, when the Boreas rages, for then it is just as if the fiend himself possessed them: they are so mad and fierce that man and beast become alike their victims; and a party of them have been known even to attack the ferocious bears of these mountains, and, what is more, to come off victorious." The howl was now again repeated more distinctly, and from two opposite directions. The riders in alarm felt for their pistols and the old man grasped the spear which hung at his saddle.

. . . .

"See, there is a light gleaming among the twigs; and there is another," cried Bertha. "There must be people close to us."

"No, no," cried the guide quickly. "Shut up the door, ladies. Keep close together, gentlemen. It is the eyes of wolves you see sparkling there." The gentlemen looked towards the thick underwood, in which every now and then little bright spots appeared, such as in summer would have been taken for glowworms; it was just the same greenish-yellow light, but less unsteady, and there were always two flames together. The horses began to be restive, they kicked and dragged at the rein, but the mules behaved tolerably well.

. . . .

Sir Richard Burton

Stoker first met the English explorer Sir Richard Burton (1821–1890) in August 1878 and was immediately impressed, as he told Irving: "I never saw any one like him. He is steel! He would go through you like a sword!" He was able to draw a fuller description of Burton when he met him at greater length the following year.

The Burtons remained in London till the end of February, in which month we met at supper several times. The first supper was at Irving's rooms in Grafton Street, on the night of Saturday, February 8, the other member of the party being Mr. Aubertin. The subdued light and the quietude gave me a better opportunity of studying Burton's face; in addition to the fact that this time I sat opposite to him and not beside him. The predominant characteristics were the darkness of the face–the desert burning; the strong mouth and nose, and jaw and fore-head–the latter somewhat bold–and the strong, deep, resonant voice. My first impression of the man as of

steel was consolidated and enhanced. He told us, amongst other things, of the work he had in hand. Three great books were partially done. The translation of the Arabian Nights, the metrical translation of Camoëns, and the Book of the Sword. These were all works of vast magnitude and requiring endless research. But he lived to complete them all.

. . . .

As he spoke the upper lip rose and his canine tooth showed its full length like the gleam of a dagger. Then he went on to say that such explorations as he had undertaken were not to be entered lightly if one had qualms as to taking life. That the explorer in savage places holds, day and night, his life in his hand; and if he is not prepared for every emergency, he should not attempt such adventures.

–*Personal Reminiscences,* volume 1, pp. 352, 359

Sir Richard Francis Burton (portrait by Sir Frederic Leighton, circa 1875; National Portrait Gallery, London)

Illustration from Burton's Vikram and the Vampire *(1870; Thomas Cooper Library, University of South Carolina)*

The party now found themselves some few hundred yards from the ruined castle of which Kumpan had spoken. It was, or seemed by moonlight to be, of some magnitude. Near the tolerably preserved principal building lay the ruins of a church which must have once been beautiful, placed on a little hillock dotted with single oak-trees and bramble-bushes. Both castle and church were still partially roofed in and a path led from the castle gate to an old oak-tree, where it joined at right angles the one along which the travellers were advancing.

The old guide seemed in much perplexity.

"We are in great danger, noble sir," said he. "The wolves will very soon make a general attack. There will then be only one way of escape: leaving the mules to their fate, and taking the young ladies on your horses."

"That would be all very well, if I had not thought of a better plan," replied the knight. "Here is the ruined castle; we can surely reach that, and then, blocking up the gates, we must just await the morning."

"Here? In the ruins of Klatka?—Not for all the wolves in the world!" cried the old man. "Even by daylight no one likes to approach the place, and, now, by night!—The castle, Sir Knight, has a bad name."

"On account of robbers?" asked Franz.

"No; it is haunted," replied the other.

"Stuff and nonsense!" said the baron. "Forward to the ruins; there is not a moment to be lost."

And this was indeed the case. The ferocious beasts were but a few steps behind the travellers. Every now and then they retired, and set up a ferocious howl. The party had just arrived at the old oak before mentioned and were about to turn into the path to the ruins, when the animals, as though perceiving the risk they ran of losing their prey, came so near that a lance could easily have struck them. The knight and Franz faced sharply about, spurring their horses amidst the advancing crowds, when suddenly, from the shadow of the oak stepped forth a man who in a few strides placed himself between the travellers and their pursuers. As far as one could see in the dusky light the stranger was a man of a tall and well-built frame; he wore a sword by his side and a broad-brimmed hat was on his head. If the party were astonished at his sudden appearance, they were still more so at what followed. As soon as the stranger appeared the wolves gave over their pursuit, tumbled over each other, and set up a fearful howl. The stranger now raised his hand, appeared to wave it, and the wild animals crawled back into the thickets like a pack of beaten hounds.

. . . .

The party were one day assembled in the old-fashioned hall, dinner had just been removed, and they were arranging in which direction they should ride. "I have it," cried Franziska suddenly, "I wonder we never thought before of going to view by day the spot where we fell in with our night-adventure with wolves and the Mysterious Stranger."

"You mean a visit to the ruins—what were they called?" said the knight.

"Castle Klatka," cried Franziska gaily. "Oh, we really must ride there! It will be so charming to go over again by daylight, and in safety, the ground where we had such a dreadful fright."

"Bring round the horses," said the knight to a servant; "and tell the steward to come to me immediately." The latter, an old man, soon after entered the room.

"We intend taking a ride to Klatka," said the knight: "we had an adventure there on our road—"

"So old Kumpan told me," interrupted the steward.

"And what do you say about it?" asked the knight.

"I really don't know what to say," replied the old man, shaking his head. "I was a youth of twenty when I first came to this castle, and now my hair is grey; half a century has elapsed during that time. Hundreds of times my duty has called me into the neighbourhood of those ruins, but never have I seen the Fiend of Klatka."

"What do you say? Whom do you call by that name?" inquired Franziska, whose love of adventure and romance was strongly awakened.

"Why, people call by that name the ghost or spirit who is supposed to haunt the ruins," replied the steward. "They say he only shows himself on moon-light nights—"

"That is quite natural," interrupted Franz smiling. "Ghosts can never bear the light of day; and if the moon did not shine, how could the ghost be seen, for it is not supposed that any one for a mere freak would visit the ruins by torch-light."

"There are some credulous people who pretend to have seen this ghost," continued the steward. "Huntsmen and woodcutters say they have met him by the large oak on the crosspath. That, noble sir, is supposed to be the spot he inclines most to haunt, for the tree was planted in remembrance of the man who fell there."

"And who was he?" asked Franziska with increasing curiosity.

"The last owner of the castle, which at that time was a sort of robbers' den, and the headquarters of all depredators in the neighbourhood," answered the old man. "They say this man was of superhuman strength, and was feared not only on account of his passionate

Vikram and the Vampire

Richard Burton translated eleven of the twenty-five tales of the Baital-Pachisi *as* Vikram and the Vampire; or, Tales of Hindu Devilry *in 1870. His wife, Isabel Burton, wrote a preface to the memorial edition published twenty-three years later.*

The Baital-Pachisi, or Twenty-five Tales of a Baital is the history of a huge Bat, Vampire, or Evil Spirit which inhabited and animated dead bodies. It is an old, and thoroughly Hindú, Legend composed in Sanskrit, and is the germ which culminated in the Arabian Nights, and which inspired the "Golden Ass" of Apuleius, Boccacio's "Decamerone," the "Pentamerone," and all that class of facetious fictitious literature.

The story turns chiefly on a great king named Vikram, the King Arthur of the East, who in pursuance of his promise to a Jogi or Magician, brings to him the Baital (Vampire), who is hanging on a tree. The difficulties King Vikram and his son have in bringing the Vampire into the presence of the Jogi are truly laughable; and on this thread is strung a series of Hindú fairy stories, which contain much interesting information on Indian customs and manners. It also alludes to that state, which induces Hindú devotees to allow themselves to be buried alive, and to appear dead for weeks or months, and then to return to life again; a curious state of mesmeric catalepsy, into which they work themselves by concentrating the mind and abstaining from food. . . .

–Isabel Burton, "Preface to The Memorial Edition," pp. xi–xii

The following excerpt is from the first framing section of the tales; the notes are those of Burton.

At length having passed over, somehow or other, a very difficult road, the Raja arrived at the smashana, or burning place pointed out by the jogi. Suddenly he sighted the tree where from root to top every branch and leaf was in a blaze of crimson flame. And when he, still dauntless, advanced towards it, a clamour continued to be raised, and voices kept crying, "Kill them! kill them! seize them! seize them! take care that they do not get away! let them scorch themselves to cinders! Let them suffer the pains of Patala."[1]

Far from being terrified by this state of things the valiant Raja increased in boldness, seeing a prospect of an end to his adventure. Approaching the tree he felt that the fire did not burn him, and so he sat there for a while to observe the body, which hung, head downwards, from a branch a little above him.

Its eyes, which were wide open, were of a greenish-brown, and never twinkled; its hair also was brown,[2] and brown was its face—three several shades which, notwithstanding, approached one another in an unpleasant way, as in an over-dried cocoa-nut. Its body was thin and was ribbed like a skeleton or a bamboo framework, and as it held on to a bough, like a flying fox,[3] by the toe-tips, its drawn muscles stood out as if they were ropes of coir. Blood it appeared to have none, or there would have been a decided determination of that curious juice to the head; and as the Raja handled its skin, it felt icy cold and clammy as might a snake. The only sign of life was the whisking of a ragged little tail much resembling a goat's.

Judging from these signs the brave king at once determined the creature to be a Baital—a Vampire. For a short time he was puzzled to reconcile the appearance with the words of the giant, who informed him that the anchorite had hung the oilman's son to a tree. But soon he explained to himself the difficulty, remembering the exceeding cunning of jogis and other reverend men, and determining that his enemy, the better to deceive him, had doubtless altered the shape and form of the young oilman's body.

With this idea, Vikram was pleased, saying, "My trouble has been productive of fruit." Remained the task of carrying the Vampire to Shanta-Shil the devotee. Having taken his sword, the Raja fearlessly climbed the tree, and ordering his son to stand away from below, clutched the Vampire's hair with one hand, and with the other struck such a blow of the sword, that the bough was cut and the thing fell heavily upon the ground. Immediately on falling it gnashed its teeth and began to utter a loud wailing cry like the screams of an infant in pain. Vikram having heard the sound of its lamentations, was pleased, and began to say to himself, "This devil must be alive." Then nimbly sliding down the trunk, he made a captive of the body, and asked "Who art thou?"

Scarcely, however, had the words passed the royal lips, when the Vampire slipped through the fingers like a worm, and uttering a loud shout of laughter, rose in the air with its legs uppermost, and as before suspended itself by its toes to another bough. And there it swung to and fro, moved by the violence of its cachinnation.

–Vikram and the Vampire
(London: Tylston & Edwards,
1893), pp. 35–37

---

1. The warm region below.
2. Hindus admire only glossy black hair; the "bonny brown hair" loved by our ballads is assigned by them to low-caste men, witches, and fiends.
3. A large kind of bat; a popular and silly Anglo-Indian name. It almost justified the irate Scotchman in calling "prodigious leears" those who told him in India that foxes flew and trees were tapped for toddy.

Vampire as a Figure of Speech

A wide variety of nineteenth-century authors found the vampire useful as a metaphor.

Thomas Carlyle in *The French Revolution: A History* (1837) comments: "And then the 'three thousand gaming-houses,' that are in Paris; cesspools for the scoundrelism of the world; sinks of iniquity and debauchery,—whereas without good morals Liberty is impossible! There, in these Dens of Satan, which one knows, and perseveringly denounces, do Sieur Motier's *mouchards* consort and colleague; battening vampyre-like on a People next-door to starvation. *'O Peuple!'* cries he ofttimes, with heart-rending accent. Treason, delusion, vampyrism, scoundrelism, from Dan to Beersheba!"

In Charles Dickens's *Bleak House* (1852–1853), the narrator says of Vholes: "So slow, so eager, so bloodless and gaunt, I felt as if . . . there were something of the Vampire in him."

In *Das Kapital* (1867; translated as *Capital*, 1887) Karl Marx found in the vampire an appropriate economic metaphor: "Capital is dead labour that, vampire-like, only lives by sucking living labour, and lives the more, the more labour it sucks." He later observed that "the prolongation of the working day quenches only in a slight degree the vampire thirst for the living blood of labour."

Walter Pater in *The Renaissance: Studies in Art and Poetry* (1873) writes of the Mona Lisa, "She is older than the rocks among which she sits; like the vampire, she has been dead many times, and learned the secrets of the grave. . . ."

temper, but of his treaties with the Turkish hordes. Any young woman, too, in the neighbourhood to whom he took a fancy, was carried off to his tower and never heard of more. When the measure of his iniquity was full, the whole neighbourhood rose in a mass, besieged his stronghold, and at length he was slain on the spot where the huge oak-tree now stands."

. . . .

The brilliantly lighted chamber gave a full view of the stranger. He was a man of about forty, tall, and extremely thin. His features could not be termed uninteresting—there lay in them something bold and daring—but the expression was on the whole anything but benevolent. There was contempt and sarcasm in the cold grey eyes, whose glance, however, was at times so piercing that no one could endure it long. His complexion was even more peculiar than the features: it could neither be called pale nor yellow; it was a sort of grey, or, so to speak, dirty white, like that of an Indian who has been suffering long from fever; and was rendered still more remarkable by the intense blackness of his beard and short cropped hair. The dress of the unknown was knightly, but old-fashioned and neglected; there were great spots of rust on the collar and breastplate of his armour; and his dagger and the hilt of his finely worked sword were marked in some places with mildew. As the party were just going to supper, it was only natural to invite the stranger to partake of it; he complied, however, only in so far that he seated himself at the table, for he ate no morsel. The knight, with some surprise, inquired the reason.

"For a long time past I have accustomed myself never to eat at night," he replied with a strange smile. "My digestion is quite unused to solids, and indeed would scarcely confront them. I live entirely on liquids."

"Oh, then we can empty a bumper of Rhine-wine together," cried the host.

"Thanks; but I neither drink wine nor any cold beverage," replied the other; and his tone was full of mockery. It appeared as if there was some amusing association connected with the idea.

"Then I will order you a cup of hippocras"—a warm drink composed of herbs—"it shall be ready immediately," said Franziska.

"Many thanks, fair lady; not at present," replied the other. "But if I refuse the beverage you offer me now, you may be assured that as soon as I require it—perhaps very soon—I will request that, or some other of you."

Bertha and Franz thought the man had something inexpressibly repulsive in his whole manner, and they had no inclination to engage him in conversation; but the baron, thinking that perhaps politeness required him to say something, turned towards the guest, and commenced in a friendly tone: "It is now many weeks since we first became acquainted with you; we then had to thank you for a singular service—"

"And I have not yet told you my name, although you would gladly know it," interrupted the other dryly. "I am called Azzo; and as"—this he said again with his ironical smile—"with the permission of the Knight of Fahnenberg, I live at the castle of Klatka, you can in future call me Azzo von Klatka."

"I only wonder you do not feel lonely and uncomfortable amongst those old walls," began Bertha. "I cannot understand—"

"What my business is there? Oh, about that I will willingly give you some information, since you and the young gentleman there take such a kindly interest in my person," replied the unknown in his tone of sarcasm.

Symons's Vampire

Arthur Symons wrote this poem in 1894.

The Vampire

Intolerable woman, where's the name
For your insane complexity of shame?
Vampire! white bloodless creature of the night,
Whose lust of blood has blanched her chill veins white,
Veins fed with moonlight over dead men's tombs;
Whose eyes remember many martyrdoms,
So that their depths, whose depth cannot be found,
Are shadowed pools in which a soul lies drowned;
Who would fain have pity, but she may not rest
Till she have sucked a man's heart from his breast,
And drained his life-blood from him, vein by vein,
And seen his eyes grow brighter for the pain,
And his lips sigh her name with his last breath,
As the man swoons ecstatically on death.

–Arthur Symons, *Lesbia and Other Poems*
(New York: Dutton, 1920), p. 1

Arthur Symons, 1891 (Karl Beckson, ed., The Memoirs of
Arthur Symons: Life and Art in the 1890s, *1977;
Thomas Cooper Library, University of South Carolina)*

Franz and Bertha both started, for he had revealed their thoughts as though he could read their souls. "You see, my lady," he continued, "there are a variety of strange whims in the world. As I have already said, I love what is peculiar and uncommon, at least what would appear so to you. It is wrong in the main to be astonished at anything, for, viewed in one light, all things are alike; even life and death, this side of the grave and the other, have more resemblance than you would imagine. You perhaps consider me rather touched a little in my mind, for taking up my abode with the bat and the owl; but if so, why not consider every hermit and recluse insane? You will tell me that those are holy men. I certainly have no pretension that way; but as they find pleasure in praying and singing psalms, so I amuse myself with hunting. Oh, away in the pale moonlight, on a horse that never tires, over hill and dale, through forest and woodland! I rush among the wolves, which fly at my approach, as you yourself perceived, as though they were puppies fearful of the lash."

. . . .

The following morning Franziska lay longer than usual in bed. When her friend went to her room, fearful lest she should be ill, she found her pale and exhausted. Franziska complained she had passed a very bad night; she thought the dispute with Franz about the stranger must have excited her greatly, for she felt quite feverish and exhausted, and a strange dream, too, had

worried her, which was evidently a consequence of the evening's conversation. Bertha, as usual, took the young man's part, and added that a common dispute about a man whom no one knew, and about whom anyone might form his own opinion, could not possibly have thrown her into her present state. "At least," she continued, "you can let me hear this wonderful dream."

To her surprise, Franziska for a length of time refused to do so.

"Come, tell me," inquired Bertha, "what can possibly prevent you from relating a dream–a mere dream? I might almost think it credible, if the idea were not too horrid, that poor Franz is not very far wrong when he says that the thin, corpse-like, dried-up, old-fashioned stranger has made a greater impression on you than you will allow."

"Did Franz say so?" asked Franziska. "Then you can tell him he is not mistaken. Yes, the thin, corpse-like, dried-up, whimsical stranger is far more interesting to me than the rosy-cheeked, well-dressed, polite, and prosy cousin."

"Strange," cried Bertha. "I cannot at all comprehend the almost magic influence which this man, so repulsive, exercises over you."

"Perhaps the very reason I take his part, may be that you are all so prejudiced against him," remarked Franziska pettishly. "Yes, it must be so; for that his appearance should please my eyes is what no one in his senses could imagine. But," she continued, smiling and holding out her hand to Bertha, "is it not laughable that I should get out of temper even with you about this stranger?–I can more easily understand it with Franz– and that this unknown should spoil my morning, as he has already spoiled my evening and my night's rest?"

"By that dream, you mean?" said Bertha, easily appeased, as she put her arm round her cousin's neck and kissed her. "Now, do tell it to me. You know how I delight in hearing anything of the kind."

"Well, I will, as a sort of compensation for my peevishness towards you," said the other, clasping her friend's hands. "Now, listen! I had walked up and down my room for a long time; I was excited–out of spirits–I do not know exactly what. It was almost midnight ere I lay down, but I could not sleep. I tossed about, and at length it was only from sheer exhaustion that I dropped off. But what a sleep it was! An inward fear ran through me perpetually. I saw a number of pictures before me, as I used to do in childish sicknesses. I do not know whether I was asleep or half awake. Then I dreamed, but as clearly as if I had been wide awake, that a sort of mist filled the room, and out of it stepped the knight Azzo. He gazed at me for a time, and then letting himself slowly down on one knee, imprinted a kiss on my throat. Long did his lips rest there; and I felt a slight pain, which always increased, until I could bear it no more. With all my strength I tried to force the vision from me, but succeeded only after a long struggle. No doubt I uttered a scream, for that awoke me from my trance. When I came a little to my senses I felt a sort of superstitious fear creeping over me–how great you may imagine when I tell you that, with my eyes open and awake, it appeared to me as if Azzo's figure were still by my bed, and then disappearing gradually into the mist, vanished at the door!"

"You must have dreamed very heavily, my poor friend," began Bertha, but suddenly paused. She gazed with surprise at Franziska's throat. "Why, what is that?" she cried. "Just look: how extraordinary–a red streak on your throat!"

Franziska raised herself, and went to a little glass that stood in the window. She really saw a small red line about an inch long on her neck, which began to smart when she touched it with her finger.

"I must have hurt myself by some means in my sleep," she said after a pause; "and that in some measure will account for my dream."

. . . .

The knight Azzo repeated his visits every now and then. He always came in the evening, and when the moon shone brightly. His manner was always the same. He spoke in monosyllables, and was coldly polite to the knight; to Franz and Bertha, particularly to the former,

contemptuous and haughty; but to Franziska, friendliness itself. Often when, after a short visit, he again left the house, his peculiarities became the subject of conversation. Besides his odd way of speaking, in which Bertha said there lay a deep hatred, a cold detestation of all mankind with the exception of Franziska, two other singularities were observable. During none of his visits, which often took place at supper-time, had he been prevailed upon to eat or drink anything, and that without giving any good reason for his abstinence. A remarkable alteration, too, had taken place in his appearance: he seemed an entirely different creature. The skin, before so shrivelled and stretched, seemed smooth and soft, while a slight tinge of red appeared in his cheeks, which began to look round and plump. Bertha, who could not at all conceal her ill-will towards him, said often, that much as she hated his face before, when it was more like a death's-head than a human being's, it was now more than ever repulsive; she always felt a shudder run through her veins whenever his sharp piercing eyes rested on her.

. . . .

It was on the morning of the following day; the sun had not risen above an hour, and the dew still lay like a veil of pearls on the grass or dripped from the petals of the flowers swaying in the early breeze, when the knight Woislaw hastened over the fields towards the forest, and turned into a gloomy path, which by the direction one could perceive led towards the towers of Klatka. When he arrived at the old oak-tree we have before had occasion to mention, he sought carefully along the road for traces of human footsteps, but only a deer had passed that way. Seemingly satisfied with his search, he proceeded on his way, though not before he had half drawn his dagger from its sheath, as though to assure himself that it was ready for service in time of need.

Slowly he ascended the path; it was evident he carried something beneath his cloak. Arrived in the court, he left the ruins of the castle to the left, and entered the old chapel. In the chancel he looked eagerly and earnestly around. A deathlike stillness reigned in the deserted sanctuary, only broken by the whispering of the wind in an old thorn-tree which grew outside. Woislaw had looked round him ere he perceived the door leading down to the vault; he hurried towards it and descended. The sun's position enabled its rays to penetrate the crevices, and made the subterranean chamber so light that one could read easily the inscriptions at the head and feet of the coffins. The knight first laid on the ground the packet he had hitherto carried under his cloak, and then going from coffin to coffin, at last remained stationary before the oldest of them. He

Mrs. Patrick Campbell and Philip Burne-Jones's painting "The Vampire." The actress was the model for the painting, which was presented to the public in the same year that Bram Stoker's Dracula *was published (courtesy of David J. Skal).*

read the inscription carefully, drew his dagger thoughtfully from its case, and endeavoured to raise the lid with its point. This was no difficult matter, for the rusty iron nails kept but a slight hold of the rotten wood. On looking in, only a heap of ashes, some remnants of dress, and a skull were the contents. He quickly closed it again, and went on to the next, passing over those of a woman and two children. Here things had much the same appearance, except that the corpse held together till the lid was raised, and then fell into dust, a few linen rags and bones being alone perceptible. In the third, fourth, and nearly the next half-dozen, the bodies were in better preservation: in some, they looked a sort of yellow-brown mummy; whilst in others a skinless skull covered with hair grinned from the coverings of velvet, silk, or mildewed embroideries; all, however, were touched with the loathsome marks of decay. Only one more coffin now remained to be inspected; Woislaw approached it, and read the inscription. It was the same that had before attracted the Knight of Fahnenberg: Ezzelin von Klatka, the last possessor of the tower, was described as lying therein. Woislaw found it more difficult to raise the lid here; and it was only by the exertion of much strength he at length succeeded in extracting

the nails. He did all, however, as quietly as if afraid of rousing some sleeper within; he then raised the cover, and cast a glance on the corpse. An involuntary "Ha!" burst from his lips as he stepped back a pace. If he had less expected the sight that met his eyes, he would have been far more overcome. In the coffin lay Azzo as he lived and breathed, and as Woislaw had seen him at the supper-table only the evening before. His appearance, dress, and all were the same; besides, he had more the semblance of sleep than of death—no trace of decay was visible—there was even a rosy tint on his cheeks. Only the circumstance that the breast did not heave distinguished him from one who slept. For a few moments Woislaw did not move; he could only stare into the coffin. With a hastiness in his movements not usual with him, he suddenly seized the lid, which had fallen from his hands, and laying it on the coffin, knocked the nails into their places. As soon as he had completed this work, he fetched the packet he had left at the entrance, and laying it on the top of the coffin, hastily ascended the steps, and quitted the church and the ruins.

. . . .

"The moment has arrived! The sun sinks, and before the moon rises, all must be over," said Woislaw quickly.

"What am I to do?" asked Franziska cheerfully.

"You see there that open vault!" replied the knight Woislaw, pointing to the door and flight of steps; "You must descend. You must go alone; I may not accompany you. When you have reached the vault you will find, close to the entrance, a coffin, on which is placed a small packet. Open this packet, and you will find three long iron nails and a hammer. Then pause for a moment; but when I begin to repeat the *Credo* in a loud voice, knock with all your might, first one nail, then a second, and then a third, into the lid of the coffin, right up to their heads."

Franziska stood thunderstruck; her whole body trembled, and she could not utter a word. Woislaw perceived it.

"Take courage, dear lady!" said he. "Think that you are in the hands of Heaven, and that, without the will of your Creator, not a hair can fall from your head. Besides, I repeat, there is no danger."

"Well, then, I will do it," cried Franziska, in some measure regaining courage.

"Whatever you may hear, whatever takes place inside the coffin," continued Woislaw, "must have no effect upon you. Drive the nails well in, without flinching: your work must be finished before my prayer comes to an end."

Franziska shuddered, but again recovered herself. "I will do it; Heaven will send me strength," she murmured softly.

"There is one thing more," said Woislaw hesitatingly; "perhaps it is the hardest of all I have proposed, but without it your cure will not be complete. When you have done as I have told you, a sort of"–he hesitated–"a sort of liquid will flow from the coffin; in this dip your finger, and besmear the scratch on your throat."

"Horrible!" cried Franziska. "This liquid is blood. A human being lies in the coffin."

"An *unearthly one* lies therein! That blood is your own, but it flows in other veins," said Woislaw gloomily. "Ask no more; the sand is running out."

Franziska summoned up all her powers of mind and body, went towards the steps which led to the vault, and Woislaw sank on his knees before the altar in quiet prayer. When the lady had descended, she found herself before the coffin on which lay the packet before mentioned. A sort of twilight reigned in the vault, and everything around was so still and peaceful, that she felt more calm, and going up to the coffin, opened the packet. She had hardly seen that a hammer and three long nails were its contents when suddenly

Woislaw's voice rang through the church, and broke the stillness of the aisles. Franziska started, but recognized the appointed prayer. She seized one of the nails, and with one stroke of the hammer drove it at least an inch into the cover. All was still; nothing was heard but the echo of the stroke. Taking heart, the maiden grasped the hammer with both hands, and struck the nail twice with all her might, right up to the head into the wood. At this moment commenced a rustling noise; it seemed as though something in the interior began to move and to struggle. Franziska drew back in alarm. She was already on the point of throwing away the hammer and flying up the steps, when Woislaw raised his voice so powerfully, and so entreatingly, that in a sort of excitement, such as would induce one to rush into a lion's den, she returned to the coffin, determined to bring things to a conclusion. Hardly knowing what she did, she placed a second nail in the centre of the lid, and after some strokes this was likewise buried to its head. The struggle now increased fearfully, as if some living creature were striving to burst the coffin. This was so shaken by it, that it cracked and split on all sides. Half distracted, Franziska seized the third nail; she thought no more of her ailments, she only knew herself to be in terrible danger, of what kind she could not guess: in an agony that threatened to rob her of her senses and in the midst of the turning and cracking of the coffin, in which low groans were now heard, she struck the third nail in equally tight. At this moment, she began to lose consciousness. She wished to hasten away, but staggered; and mechanically grasping at something to save herself by, she seized the corner of the coffin, and sank fainting beside it on the ground.

A quarter of an hour might have elapsed when she again opened her eyes. She looked around her. Above was the starry sky, and the moon, which shed her cold light on the ruins and on the tops of the old oak-trees. Franziska was lying outside the church walls, Woislaw on his knees beside her, holding her hand in his.

"Heaven be praised that you live!" he cried, with a sigh of relief.

. . . .

. . . On the following morning, Franziska rose earlier than she had done for a long time. She assured her friend it was the first time since her illness commenced that she had been really refreshed by her sleep, and, what was still more remarkable, she had not been troubled by her old terrible dream. Her improved looks were not only remarked by Bertha, but by Franz and the knight; and with Woislaw's permission, she related the adventures of the previous evening. No sooner had she concluded, than

Kipling's Vampire

Rudyard Kipling wrote this poem in 1897.

The Vampire

The verses—as suggested by the painting by Philip Burne-Jones, first exhibited at the new gallery in London in 1897.

A fool there was and he made his prayer
    (Even as you and I!)
To a rag and a bone and a hank of hair
(We called her the woman who did not care),
But the fool he called her his lady fair
    (Even as you and I!)

Oh the years we waste and the tears we waste
    And the work of our head and hand,
Belong to the woman who did not know
(And now we know that she never could know)
    And did not understand.

A fool there was and his goods he spent
    (Even as you and I!)
Honor and faith and a sure intent
(And it wasn't the least what the lady meant),
But a fool must follow his natural bent
    (Even as you and I!)

Oh the toil we lost and the spoil we lost
    And the excellent things we planned,
Belong to the woman who didn't know why
(And now we know she never knew why)
    And did not understand.

The fool was stripped to his foolish hide
    (Even as you and I!)
Which she might have seen when she threw him aside—
(But it isn't on record the lady tried)
So some of him lived but most of him died—
    (Even as you and I!)

Portrait of Rudyard Kipling by Philip Burne-Jones, 1899
(Harry Ricketts, Rudyard Kipling: A Life, *2000;*
Thomas Cooper Library, University
of South Carolina)

And it isn't the shame and it isn't the blame
    That stings like a white hot brand.
It's coming to know that she never knew why
(Seeing at last she could never know why)
    And never could understand.

—Kipling, *Poems and Ballads*
(New York & Boston: Caldwell,
1899), pp. 59–60

Woislaw was completely stormed with questions about such a strange occurrence.

"Have you," said the latter, turning towards his host, "ever heard of Vampires?"

"Often," replied he; "but I have never believed in them."

"Nor did I," said Woislaw; "but I have been assured of their existence by experience."

"Oh, tell us what occurred," cried Bertha eagerly, as a light seemed to dawn on her.

"It was during my first campaign in Hungary," began Woislaw, "when I was rendered helpless for some time by this sword-cut of a janizary across my face, and

another on my shoulder. I had been taken into the house of a respectable family in a small town. It consisted of the father and mother, and a daughter about twenty years of age. They obtained their living by selling the very good wine of the country, and the taproom was always full of visitors. Although the family were well to do in the world, there seemed to brood over them a continual melancholy, caused by the constant illness of the only daughter, a very pretty and excellent girl. She had always bloomed like a rose, but for some months she had been getting so thin and wasted, and that without any satisfactory reason: they tried every means to restore her, but in vain. As the army had encamped quite in the neighbourhood, of course a number of people of all countries assembled in the tavern. Amongst these there was one man who came every evening, when the moon shone, who struck everybody by the peculiarity of his manners and appearance; he looked dried up and deathlike, and hardly spoke at all; but what he did say was bitter and sarcastic. Most attention was excited towards him by the circumstance, that although he always ordered a cup of the best wine, and now and then raised it to his lips, the cup was always as full after his departure as at first."

"This all agrees wonderfully with the appearance of Azzo," said Bertha, deeply interested.

"The daughter of the house," continued Woislaw, "became daily worse, despite the aid not only of Christian doctors, but of many amongst the heathen prisoners, who were consulted in the hope that they might have some magical remedy to propose. It was singular that the girl always complained of a dream, in which the unknown guest worried and plagued her."

"Just the same as your dream, Franziska," cried Bertha.

"One evening," resumed Woislaw, "an old Sclavonian—who had made many voyages to Turkey and Greece, and had even seen the New World—and I were sitting over our wine, when the stranger entered, and sat down at the table. The bottle passed quickly between my friend and me, whilst we talked of all manner of things, of our adventures, and of passages in our lives, both horrible and amusing. We went on chatting thus for about an hour, and drank a tolerable quantity of wine. The unknown had remained perfectly silent the whole time, only smiling contemptuously every now and then. He now paid his money, and was going away. All this had quietly worried me—perhaps the wine had got a little into my head—so I said to the stranger: 'Hold, you stony stranger; you have hitherto done nothing but listen, and have not even emptied your cup. Now you shall take your turn in telling us something amusing, and if you do not drink up your wine, it shall produce a quarrel between us.' 'Yes,' said the Sclavonian, 'you must remain; you shall chat and drink, too'; and he grasped—for although no longer young, he was big and very strong—the stranger by the shoulder, to pull him down to his seat again: the latter, however, although as thin as a skeleton, with one movement of his hand flung the Sclavonian to the middle of the room, and half stunned him for a moment. I now approached to hold the stranger back. I caught him by the arm; and although the springs of my iron hand were less powerful than those I have at present, I must have gripped him rather hard in my anger, for after looking grimly at me for a moment, he bent towards me and whispered in my ear: 'Let me go: from the grip of your fist, I see you are my brother, therefore do not hinder me from seeking my bloody nourishment. I am hungry!' Surprised by such

words, I let him loose, and almost before I was aware of it, he had left the room. As soon as I had in some degree recovered from my astonishment, I told the Sclavonian what I had heard. He started, evidently alarmed. I asked him to tell me the cause of his fears, and pressed him for an explanation of those extraordinary words. On our way to his lodging, he complied with my request. 'The stranger,' said he, 'is a Vampire!'"

"How?" cried the knight, Franziska, and Bertha simultaneously, in a voice of horror. "So this Azzo was——"

"Nothing less. He also was a Vampire!" replied Woislaw. "But at all events *his* hellish thirst is quenched for ever; he will never return. But I have not finished. As in my country Vampires had never been heard of, I questioned the Sclavonian minutely. He said that in Hungary, Croatia, Dalmatia, and Bosnia, these hellish guests were not uncommon. They were deceased persons, who had either once served as nourishment to Vampires, or who had died in deadly sin, or under excommunication; and that whenever the moon shone, they rose from their graves, and sucked the blood of the living."

"Horrible!" cried Franziska. "If you had told me all this beforehand, I should never have accomplished the work."

"So I thought; and yet it must be executed by the sufferers themselves, while someone else performs the devotions," replied Woislaw. "The Sclavonian," he continued after a short pause, "added many other facts with regard to these unearthly visitants. He said that whilst their victim wasted, they themselves improved in appearance, and that a Vampire possessed enormous strength——"

"Now I can understand the change your false hand produced on Azzo," interrupted Franz.

"Yes, that was it," replied Woislaw. "Azzo, as well as the other Vampire, mistook its great power for that of a natural one, and concluded I was one of his own species. You may now imagine, dear lady," he continued, turning to Franziska, "how alarmed I was at your appearance when I arrived: all you and Bertha told me increased my anxiety; and when I saw Azzo, I could doubt no longer that he was a Vampire. As I learned from your account that a grave with the name Ezzelin von Klatka lay in the neighbourhood, I had no doubt that you might be saved if I could only induce you to assist me. It did not appear to me advisable to impart the whole facts of the case, for your bodily powers were so impaired, that an idea of the horrors before you might have quite unfitted you for the exertion; for this reason, I arranged everything in the manner in which it has taken place."

"You did wisely," replied Franziska shuddering. "I can never be grateful enough to you. Had I known

Letter from Philip Burne-Jones to Stoker, who had sent the painter a copy of Dracula
(Brotherton Collection, Leeds University Library)

what was required of me, I never could have undertaken the deed."

"That was what I feared," said Woislaw; "but fortune has favoured us all through."

"And what became of the unfortunate girl in Hungary?" inquired Bertha.

"I know not," replied Woislaw. "That very evening there was an alarm of Turks, and we were ordered off. I never heard anything more of her."

The conversation upon these strange occurrences continued for some time longer. The knight determined to have the vault at Klatka walled up for ever. This took place on the following day; the knight alleging as a reason that he did not wish the dead to be disturbed by irreverent hands.

Franziska recovered gradually. Her health had been so severely shaken, that it was long ere her strength was so much restored as to allow of her being considered out of danger. The young lady's character underwent a great change in the interval. Its former strength was, perhaps, in some degree diminished, but in place of that, she had acquired a benevolent softness, which brought out all her best qualities. Franz continued his attentions to his cousin; but, perhaps owing to a hint from Bertha, he was less

assiduous in his exhibition of them. His inclinations did not lead him to the battle, the camp, or the attainment of honours; his great aim was to increase the good condition and happiness of his tenants, and to this he contributed the whole energy of his mind. Franziska could not withstand the unobtrusive signs of the young man's continued attachment; and it was not long ere the credit she was obliged to yield to his noble efforts for the welfare of his fellow-creatures, changed into a liking, which went on increasing, until at length it assumed the character of love. As Woislaw insisted on making Bertha his wife before he returned to Silesia, it was arranged that the marriage should take place at their present abode. How joyful was the surprise of the Knight of Fahnenberg, when his daughter and Franz likewise entreated his blessing, and expressed their desire of being united on the same day! That day soon came round, and it saw the bright looks of two happy couples.

– The Penguin Book of Vampire Stories,
edited by Alan Ryan (New York:
Penguin, 1987), pp. 36–70

The *Britannica*'s Vampire

Stoker may have relied on the entry on Vampire *in the ninth edition of* Encyclopædia Britannica *(1888). In this article it is falsely reported that the vampire bat stands "alone from all other mammals as being fitted only for a diet of blood, and capable of sustaining life upon that alone."*

Vampire

VAMPIRE, a term, apparently of Servian origin *(wampir),* originally applied in eastern Europe to blood-sucking ghosts, but in modern usage transferred to one or more species of blood-sucking bats inhabiting South America.

In the first-mentioned meaning a vampire is usually supposed to be the soul of a dead man which quits the buried body by night to suck the blood of living persons. Hence, when the vampire's grave is opened, his corpse is found to be fresh and rosy from the blood which he has thus absorbed. To put a stop to his ravages, a stake is driven through the corpse, or the head cut off, or the heart torn out and the body burned, or boiling water and vinegar are poured on the grave. The persons who turn vampires are generally wizards, witches, suicides and those who have come to a violent end or have been cursed by their parents or by the church. But any one may become a vampire if an animal (especially a cat) leaps over his corpse or a bird flies over it. Sometimes the vampire is thought to be the soul of a living man which leaves his body in sleep, to go in the form of a straw or fluff of down and suck the blood of other sleepers. The belief in vampires chiefly prevails in Slavonic lands, as in Russia (especially White Russia and the Ukraine), Poland and Servia, and among the Czechs of Bohemia and the other Slavonic races of Austria. It became especially prevalent in Hungary between the years 1730 and 1735, whence all Europe was filled with reports of the exploits of vampires. Several treatises were written on the subject, among which may be mentioned Ranft's *De masticatione mortuorum in tumulis* (1734) and Calmet's *Dissertation on the Vampires of Hungary,* translated into English in 1750. It is probable that this superstition gained much ground from the reports of those who had examined the bodies of persons buried alive though believed to be dead, and was based on the twisted position of the corpse, the marks of blood on the shroud and on the face and hands—results of the frenzied struggle in the coffin before life became extinct. The belief in vampirism has also taken root among the Albanians and modern Greeks, but here it may be due to Slavonic influence.

Two species of blood-sucking bats (the only species known)—*Desmodus rufus* and *Diphylla ecaudata*—representing two genera, inhabit the tropical and part of the subtropical regions of the New World, and are restricted to South and Central America. They appear to be confined chiefly to the forest-clad parts, and their attacks on men and other warm-blooded animals were noticed by some of the earliest writers. Thus Peter Martyr (Anghiera), who wrote soon after the conquest of South America, says that in the Isthmus of Darien there were bats which sucked the blood of men and cattle when asleep to such a degree as to even kill them. Condamine, a writer of the 18th century, remarks that at Borja (Ecuador) and in other places they had entirely destroyed the cattle introduced by the missionaries. Sir Robert Schomburgk relates that at Wicki, on the river Berbice, no fowls could be kept on account of the ravages of these creatures, which attacked their combs, causing them to appear white from loss of blood. The present writer, when in South and Central America, had many accounts given him as to the attacks of the vampires, and it was agreed upon by most of his informants that these bats when attacking horses showed a decided preference for those of a grey colour. It is interesting to speculate how far the vampire bats may have been instrumental—when they were, perhaps, more abundant—in causing the destruction of the horse, which had disappeared from America previous to the discovery of that continent.

Although these bats were known thus early to Europeans, the species to which they belonged were not determined for a long time, several of the large frugivorous species having been wrongly set down as blood-suckers, and named accordingly. Thus the name *Vampyrus* was suggested to Geoffroy and adopted by Spix, who also considered that the long-tongued bats of the group *Glossophaga* were addicted to blood, and accordingly described *Glossophaga soricina* as a very cruel blood-sucker *(sanguisuga crudelissima),* believing that the long brush-tipped tongue was used to increase the flow of blood. *Vampyrus spectrum,* a large bat inhabiting Brazil, of sufficiently forbidding aspect, which was long considered by naturalists to be thoroughly sanguivorous in its habits, and named accordingly by Geoffroy, has been shown by the observations of travellers to be mainly frugivorous, and is considered by the inhabitants of the countries in which it is found to be perfectly harmless. Charles Waterton believed *Artibeus planirostris,* a common bat in British Guiana, usually found in the roofs of houses, and now known to be frugivorous, to be the veritable vampire; but neither he nor any of the naturalists that preceded him had succeeded in detecting any bat in the act of drawing blood. It fell to the lot of Charles Darwin to determine one of the blood-sucking species at least, and the following is his account of the circumstances under which the discovery of the sanguivorous habits of *Desmodus rufus* was made: "The vampire bat is often the cause of much trouble by biting the horses on their withers. The injury is generally not so much owing to the loss of blood as to the inflammation which the pressure of the saddle afterwards produces. The whole circumstance has lately been doubted in England; I was therefore fortunate in being present when one was actually caught

The vampire bat, native only to Central and South America, lives exclusively on blood. It was given its popular name by Spanish explorers who associated the bat's feeding habit with the vampires of European folklore.

on a horse's back. We were bivouacking late one evening near Coquimbo, in Chile, when my servant, noticing that one of the horses was very restive, went to see what was the matter, and, fancying he could detect something, suddenly put his hand on the beast's withers, and secured the vampire" (*Naturalist's Voyage Round the World*, p. 22).

Desmodus rufus, the common blood-sucking bat, is widely spread over the tropical and subtropical parts of Central and South America from Oaxaca to southern Brazil and Chile. It is a comparatively small bat, a little larger than the noctule, the head and body about 3 in. in length, the forearm 2½, with a remarkably long and strong thumb; it is destitute of a tail, and has a very peculiar physiognomy. The body is covered with rather short fur of a reddish-brown colour but varying in shade, the extremities of the hairs sometimes ashy. The teeth are peculiar and characteristic, admirably adapted for the purposes for which they are employed. The upper front teeth (incisors), of which there are only two, are enormously enlarged, and in shape obliquely triangular like small guillotines. The canines, though smaller than the incisors, are large and sharp; but the cheek-teeth, so well developed in other bats, are very small and reduced in number to two above and three below, on each side, with laterally compressed crowns rising but slightly above the level of the gum, their longitudinally disposed cutting edges (in the upper jaw) being continuous with the base of the canine and with each other. The lower front teeth (incisors) are small, bifid, in pairs, and separated from the canines, with a space in front. The lower cheek-teeth are narrow, like those in the upper jaw, but the anterior tooth is slightly larger than the others, and separated by a small space from the canines.

Behind the lower incisors the jaw is deeply hollowed out to receive the extremities of the larger upper incisors.

With this peculiar dentition there is associated as remarkable a departure from the general type in the form of the digestive apparatus. The exceedingly narrow oesophagus opens at right angles into a narrow, intestine-like stomach, which almost immediately terminates on the right, without a distinct pylorus, in the duodenum, but on the left forms a greatly elongated caecum, bent and folded upon itself, which appears at first sight like a part of the intestines. This, the cardiac extremity of the stomach is, for a short distance to the left of the entrance of the oesophagus, still very narrow, but soon increases in size, till near its termination it attains a diameter quite three times that of the short pyloric portion. The length of this cardiac diverticulum of the stomach appears to vary from 2 to 6 in., the size in each specimen probably depending on the amount of food obtained by the animal before it was captured.

The only other known species of blood-sucking bat, *Diphylla ecaudata,* inhabits Brazil, and appears to be much less abundant than *Desmodus rufus,* from which it is distinguished by its slightly smaller size, by the absence of a groove in the front of the lower lip, the non-development of the interfemoral membrane in the centre, and the presence of a short calcaneum (absent in *D. rufus*), but more particularly by the presence of an additional rudimentary cheek-tooth (?molar) above and below, and the peculiar form of the lower incisors, which are much expanded in the direction of the jaws and pectinated, forming a semi-circular row touching each other, the outer incisors being wider than the inner ones, with six notches, the thinner incisors with three each.

Thus constituted, these bats present, in this extraordinary differentiation of the manducatory and digestive apparatus, a departure from the type of other species of the family *(Phyllostomidae)* to which they belong unparalleled in any of the other orders of *Mammalia,* standing apart from all other mammals as being fitted only for a diet of blood, and capable of sustaining life upon that alone. Travellers describe the wounds inflicted by the large sharp-edged incisors as being similar to those caused by a razor when shaving: a portion of the skin is shaved off and, a large number of severed capillary vessels being thus exposed, a constant flow of blood is maintained. From this source the blood is drawn through the exceedingly narrow gullet—too narrow for anything solid to pass—into the intestine-like stomach, whence it is, probably, gradually drawn off during the slow process of digestion, while the animal, sated with food, is hanging in a state of torpidity from the roof of its cave or from the inner sides of a hollow tree.

—*Encyclopædia Britannica*, ninth edition, volume 24 (Edinburgh: Black, 1888), pp. 52–53

III. Contexts for *Dracula*

An appreciation of Dracula *is enriched through an awareness of its literary, social, and cultural contexts. The novel reveals the fears as well as the fascinations of late-Victorian England.*

Gothic and Irish Influences

British scholar Victor Sage places Dracula *in the context of the Gothic literary tradition.*

The Gothic Novel
Victor Sage

The Gothic Novel begins with the anonymous publication of collector, antiquarian, dilettante Horace Walpole's novel *The Castle of Otranto* (1764), subtitled "A Gothick Story." Walpole, who was also an MP, concealed himself behind layers of personae, teasingly framing the story as a fifteenth-century manuscript by one "Onuphrio Muralto," translated by "William Marshall, Gent." The critics were hostile, sensing a fake, but not quite sure. The public, however, was enthusiastic; the first edition sold out in a matter of months and Walpole was prevailed upon to reveal himself as the author.

The story of *The Castle of Otranto* reveals many of the preoccupations of the later Gothic Novel. It looks back to a feudal world, in this case, medieval Italy, in which the Lord of the Manor, Manfred, the first of a long line of Gothic villain/heroes, exercises seigneurial rights over the minds and bodies of his subjects. His

Illustration from the 1791 edition of Horace Walpole's The Castle of Otranto. *The supernatural power of the past to affect the present, here shown in the figure of an old man descending on the young from his portrait, is a central theme of the Gothic tradition and Bram Stoker's* Dracula *(drawing by John Masey Wright; Judith Wilt,* Ghosts of the Gothic, *1980; Thomas Cooper Library, University of South Carolina).*

castle, however, as part of an ancient prophecy, appears to be haunted by a gigantic suit of armour. His obsession with primogeniture, and the inability of his wife Hippolita to provide him with an heir, lead him, on the news of the death of his sickly son, Conrad, to offer himself in a peremptory, and vaguely incestuous, fashion to his quondam prospective daughter-in-law, Isabella. Isabella, the first of a line of intrepid Gothic heroines, refuses him indignantly and flees through the subterranean vaults of the castle, taking refuge in the local monastery church. In the end, Manfred is revealed as the son of a usurper of the line of Otranto, which is represented by a young peasant of noble bearing, Theodore, who defies him and with whom Isabella has in the meantime fallen in love.

This plot encodes various obsessions of the later Gothic: the "authenticating" pretence that the author is merely the editor of a found manuscript; the setting in medieval and "superstitious" Southern Catholic Europe; the expectation of the supernatural; the conflation of hero and villain; the decay of primogeniture and of feudal and aristocratic rights in general, and the rise of an ambitious bourgeoisie eager to exercise individual freedom in marriage and inheritance; the focus on the victimised, but often defiant, position of women; the use of confined spaces—castles, dungeons, monasteries and prisons, to symbolise extreme emotional states by labyrinthine incarceration—all these characteristic modalities spring into being, more or less fully formed, in Walpole's tale.

But Walpole's story exhibits a contradiction between subject matter and language which is uncharacteristic of the tradition it founded. Stylistically, it is dry, witty, terse, and suffused with the rational virtues of eighteenth-century prose—it has no Romantic expansiveness, and though it foregrounds extreme emotions, especially in the case of Manfred, its characters, generally speaking, are puppets without psychological depth and its action is screwed to a high pitch of melodrama. Walpole was personally close to the Enlightenment in France, and yet his antiquarianism and his dilettantism, beneath a humorous façade, revealed a more serious interest in neglected areas of historical scholarship and a willingness to speculate about alternative modes of awareness. In a famous account of the genesis of the tale, which proved interesting to André Breton and the French Surrealists in the 1930s, Walpole shows that he was indeed allowing his unconscious to dominate the writing process.

Mid-eighteenth-century aesthetics are built on Horace—polished, witty, decorous, and above all conscious, writing which is built on an aesthetics of product. But the Longinian aesthetics of the Sublime, revived also in the mid-century by Burke in his *A Philo-* *sophical Inquiry into the Origin of our Ideas of the Sublime and the Beautiful* (1757), are founded on an aesthetics of process, foregrounding the affective relationship between reader and text. Burke's treatise is a blueprint for an aesthetics of terror and horror, laying down a set of conditions for the excitement of the reader's passions. The artist's task was to evoke fear, grandeur and awe in the soul of the reader.

Walpole also invented other characteristics of the genre that were to endure: his "Gothic story" was ostensibly set back in the remote past in an age of "superstition" when emotions were freer and manners more direct and barbarous than in eighteenth-century polite society. But as with many later Gothic novels this "historical" content is relatively superficial, intentionally so, because the novel is essentially addressing changes of taste in its eighteenth-century audience. The expanded and expanding reading public (in large part female), despite the neo-classical strictures of the eighteenth-century establishment, craved popular entertainment, and Walpole, not without humour, was the first to provide it. The early Gothic novels are eighteenth-century costume-dramas that play with history.

After an apparent lull of almost two decades (during which time the magazines were highly active, as Mayo has shown), the Minerva Press, backed by the new circulating libraries, began to pour out Gothic three-deckers to a formula that derived in part from Walpole, but these writers' novels lacked his comic astringency of tone. Set in the medieval past, such novels were thought of at the time as subversive or childish "romances," according to one's point of view, and they inserted themselves, at the extreme end, into the critical debate between Novel and Romance which ran from the mid eighteenth-century to well on in the nineteenth century. By the end of the 1790s, the demand for such books had grown into an addiction, as Jane Austen's famous and brilliant Gothic parody both of this female readership, and of male attempts to control it, in *Northanger Abbey* (1818), proves.

The leading Gothic novelist of the eighteenth century, far surpassing her forerunners Sophia Lee and Clara Reeve in popularity and known as "the great enchantress," was Ann Radcliffe (her style and method of the "explained supernatural" also spoofed expertly by Austen), who kept a generation on edge with *The Mysteries of Udolpho* (1794). Two years later, Matthew Lewis, another Whig MP, published *The Monk,* whose camp sexuality and Faustian metaphysics proved a *succès de scandale* and had to be withdrawn under threat of blasphemy after a review by Coleridge. Ann Radcliffe replied to Lewis with *The Italian* (1797), half of which is set in the dungeons of the Roman Inquisition, and the Gothic genre was fully established, recognised in partic-

THE

MYSTERIES OF UDOLPHO,

A

ROMANCE;

INTERSPERSED WITH SOME PIECES OF POETRY.

BY

ANN RADCLIFFE,

AUTHOR OF THE ROMANCE OF THE FOREST, ETC.

IN FOUR VOLUMES.

Fate sits on these dark battlements, and frowns,
And, as the portals open to receive me,
Her voice, in sullen echoes through the courts,
Tells of a nameless deed.

VOL. I.

LONDON:
PRINTED FOR G. G. AND J. ROBINSON,
PATERNOSTER-ROW.
1794.

THE MONK:

A

ROMANCE.

Somnia, terrores magicos, miracula, sagas,
Nocturnos lemures, portentaque.
                              HORAT.

Dreams, magic terrors, spells of mighty power,
Witches, and ghosts who rove at midnight hour.

IN THREE VOLUMES.
VOL. I.

LONDON:
PRINTED FOR J. BELL, OXFORD-STREET.
M.DCC.XCVI.

THE

ITALIAN,

OR THE

CONFESSIONAL of the BLACK PENITENTS.

A ROMANCE.

BY

ANN RADCLIFFE,

AUTHOR OF THE MYSTERIES OF UDOLPHO, &c. &c.

He, wrapt in clouds of mystery and silence,
Broods o'er his passions, bodies them in deeds,
And sends them forth on wings of Fate to others:
Like the invisible Will, that guides us,
Unheard, unknown, unsearchable!

IN THREE VOLUMES.
VOL. I.

LONDON:
Printed for T. CADELL Jun. and W. DAVIES
(Successors to Mr. CADELL) in the STRAND.

1797.

*Title pages from three eighteenth-century novels that established many of the conventions of the Gothic
tradition (top, Library of Congress; bottom, right and left, Thomas Cooper Library,
University of South Carolina)*

ular by the Marquis de Sade, whose judgement in 1800 that these novels were "the necessary fruits of the revolutionary tremors felt by the whole of Europe" has proved highly influential in later critical debate, marking a tradition of linking the Gothic Novel with the French Revolution.

The 1790s were a turbulent decade and the Gothic novel was a focus for various cross-currents: English antiquarianism; Whig dilettantism; German influences from the sturm und drang; Jacobinism; occultism and radical Secret Societies; French Revolutionary propaganda; conservative English nationalism; anti-Catholicism; feudal nostalgia; Romantic diabolism; Godwinianism.

By 1820, thanks to the publication of parodies like Austen's *Northanger Abbey* and Peacock's *Nightmare Abbey* (1818), the influence of the Enlightenment relativism of Sir Walter Scott, and the rise of his "historical romance," the earlier novels had begun to seem somewhat *grand guignol*. In 1818, Mary Shelley, following in the footsteps of both her father, William Godwin (who produced two novels in the Gothic mode, *Caleb Williams,* 1794, and *St Leon,* 1799), and her mother, Mary Wollstonecraft (who also published novels influenced by the genre), brought forth what she later half-jestingly referred to as her "hideous progeny"—one of the most famous of all the Gothic novels, *Frankenstein.*

The plot of this novel, the story of a scientist who, having exultantly discovered the secret of artificial reproduction from corpses, creates a being and then, revolted by its apparent monstrosity, morally and physically abandons it, has become nothing less than a modern myth in the post-war period. Given the discovery and the use of the atom bomb, the subsequent Cold War and arms race, the developments in genetics and computers and the ethical issues raised by all these matters, this complex and ambiguously horrifying story prophetically codifies in miniature many of our contemporary concerns.

The publication of the Dublin writer Charles Maturin's extraordinary Faustian novel *Melmoth the Wanderer* (1820), which failed at the box office but was a great success in France, conventionally marks the end of the first phase of the tradition.

After 1820, the radicalism (as Maggie Kilgour has recently argued, Godwin is as much a model for the Gothic Novel as Burke), the confusion, and the anarchy of the "old Gothick" gives way to the new conservative "historical romance" of the Waverley era (roughly 1820–1837). The Minerva Press gives up the Gothic and turns to children's books. The Gothic Novel breaks up and becomes a more scattered but now permanent and widely influential

aspect of literary sensibility rather than a concerted genre or movement as such: a polarisation occurs between popular forms—the "Penny Dreadfuls" of Reynolds and of writers like Ainsworth and the popular melodrama, on the one hand; and, on the other, the literary tradition dominated by Scott.

Mrs Radcliffe survived into the Victorian period as a writer's writer, or a clumsy forerunner of Romanticism; but *Blackwood's Magazine* (1818–1880) and Henry Colburn's *New Monthly Magazine* (1814–1884) had kept alive the Gothic flame, and by the 1840s both Dickens and the Brontës were showing unmistakable signs of the influence of the Gothic. In America, Poe, following on from Radcliffe and Charles Brockden Brown, began to produce his tales. In Scotland, defiant of the Enlightenment rationalism of Scott, Hogg used the Gothic convention of the *doppelgänger*—probably derived from Hoffmann—to satirise the growth of evangelical Calvinism in his *The Private Memoirs and Confessions of a Justified Sinner,* and produced a truly schizophrenic text. Eventually Dickens planned a similar "confessional" structure for his last novel *The Mystery of Edwin Drood* (1870).

By the mid-century, the Gothic Novel as a genre was apparently extinct, and the term "Gothic," if used at all, was predominantly an architectural term. But paradoxically this diversified and underground role guaranteed its survival in the literary field. The cultural conditions in which it had first appeared—the unease about enlightenment modes of thought, about empirical science, and epistemological certainty inherited from the eighteenth-century, and the official, daylight definitions of national, and rational, Protestant culture, the criteria for "superstition"—all these elements of late eighteenth century cultural formation had survived, and indeed intensified in the nineteenth century. The Gothic mode had become decentred, a register available for writers of many different kinds, but its influence on Victorian writing was taken for granted, thanks to the currency of the magazines and the early immense popularity of Scott's Border Ballads.

Victorian culture, bolstered by recycled memories of Romantic poetry, became obsessed with the escapism and utopian romance of medieval pre-industrial society, which had a symbiotic and compensatory relationship to its own growing industrialisation and urbanisation. The traditional historical themes of the Gothic, mingled with the Arthurian "matter of Britain" and the Gothic revival in architecture, with its Catholic and anti-Catholic tensions and its claims to be a national style, reinforced the literary tradition. Many of these features are clearly evident in Bram Stoker's books at the end of the Victorian period.

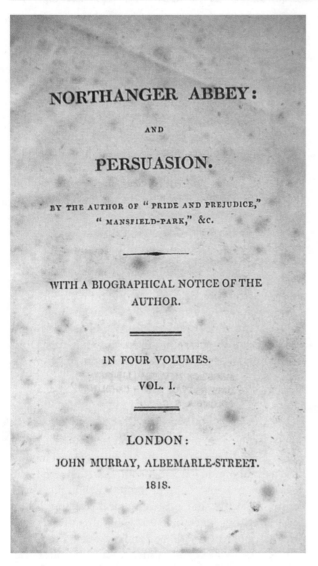

Title page for Jane Austen's fifth book, published the year after her death. In Northanger Abbey, *Austen parodies Gothic novels such as Ann Radcliffe's* Mysteries of Udolpho *as being too removed from normal reality (Thomas Cooper Library, University of South Carolina).*

Part of this currency of the mode is attributable to the Victorian pleasure in horror and darkness, and there is also a growing interest during the Victorian period in sexuality, sexual taboo and sex-roles.

The Shakespeare revival was also fully under way in the earlier eighteen hundreds and the heroic style of early Victorian acting added to the sense of a relation between theatre and the character in the novel. Dickens, in particular, employed a theatrical and melodramatic style, full of darkness, violence, and sudden horrors. Even his early comic work like *The Pickwick Papers* (1836–1837), as Jackson and others have argued, owes a good deal to Gothic prece-

dent—and later, after 1850, Dickens's London becomes a sublimely dark, disease-ridden labyrinth of courts and alleys flanking a Thames polluted and full of floating corpses. Dickens also experimented with Gothic characterisation—the symbolically "flat" rendition of aspects of a person—in his studies of repression and criminal mentalities, frequently employing in his later work (Arthur Clenham in *Little Dorrit,* 1855–1857, Jaggers and Wemmick in *Great Expectations,* 1860–1861 and Bradley Headstone in *Our Mutual Friend,* 1864–1865) subdued versions of the *doppelgänger* motif which Poe and Hogg had also developed.

Meanwhile, as Heilman first demonstrated, the Brontës internalised and psychologised the old Gothic, producing wild and dark accounts of the perversity of human passion, carrying on the Gothic tradition of the Satanic and Byronic Villain/Hero in the figures of Rochester and Heathcliff, set in a bleak Northern landscape of remote houses. Poe, in his magazine tales, in an intensely Schopenhauerian manner, also used the Gothic vocabulary of excess to explore an intense and suffocating inner world of psychological isolation and perversity, catalepsy and necrophilia, while at the same time using the tradition for philosophical purposes to satirise Cartesianism and parody the German Idealism which held for him such a fascination.

Precisely because it was not a concerted tradition, but a highly flexible register which could be employed as a shorthand in characterisation, setting, and narrative mode, a register which often hid itself in the respectable documentation of "historical romance," the Gothic became a frequent sub-code in the Victorian novel. It became important for a writer to try something in this darker, affective mode, even if only a tale, only an exercise—expectations of horror, fear, anxiety and *diablerie* were strong in the audience and the mode became part of the writerly range in the nineteenth century. This period sees also the rise of new popular genres like detective and science fiction which overlap with the Gothic.

Literary history used to crystallize the later Gothic under the heading of the Victorian "sensation school"—which included J. Sheridan Le Fanu, Wilkie Collins, and Charles Reade. The term "sensation" is a reference to the physiological effect that the reading of such authors is supposed to have had on the audience, which links it directly back to the tradition of the Sublime. The first two of these writers have undergone a revival of interest in the last ten years and now most of their works are currently available in paperback reprints. In particular, Le Fanu is seen as a major transmitter of the Gothic to later nineteenth-century writers like Bram Stoker and Ambrose

Bierce. His collection *In a Glass Darkly* (1872) contains the *doppelgänger* vampire story "Carmilla," which has always been a favourite of anthologists. In 1932 this story—as with several of the Gothic fictions of Poe—was made into a German expressionist film, *Vampyr*. Recent interest in lesbianism, vampirism, and perverse sexuality has revived the story, and given it currency again as a modern classic. Le Fanu's horror masterpiece, *Uncle Silas* (1864), has also been revived on stage and screen on several occasions from the 1920s onwards, while his particularly horrid chapter in *The House by the Churchyard* (1861–1863), "Narrative of a Hand," was transformed into another anthology classic, "The Beast with Five Fingers" by W. F. Harvey. Le Fanu is prized particularly by later horror writers like M. R. James, who edited him and on whose *Ghost Stories of an Antiquary* (1904), a leading representative of the genre in the Edwardian period, he had a great deal of influence.

Collins's *The Woman in White* (1860) owes also something to the Gothic tradition—in particular its sublime and dramatic opening scene in which a woman dressed in white is encountered wandering in a North London suburb near Hampstead Heath, having escaped incarceration. Both these writers carry on an important rhetorical tradition begun by Ann Radcliffe and developed into a sophisticated and "modern" art by Poe with their use of the "explained supernatural"—that of the deliberately excessive, and sometimes ironical, foregrounding of "explanation" as a mode of their documentary façade.

The later nineteenth century sees the steady production of minor classics in the horror tradition: Henry James's "The Jolly Corner" and *The Turn of the Screw* (1898), M. R. James's collections (1904, 1911, 1919), Bram Stoker's early stories and tales, Hawthorne's *The Scarlet Letter* (1850), Collins's *The Woman in White* and Dickens's *The Mystery of Edwin Drood* (1870). But the dominant piece of Gothic writing of this period is undoubtedly, Stevenson's novella *The Strange Case of Dr Jekyll and Mr Hyde* (1886). This narrative, which, following some of the

Illustration from the 1930 Bodley Head edition of Robert Louis Stevenson's The Strange Case of Dr. Jekyll and Mr. Hyde, *a work that, like* Dracula, *has been read as a metaphor for Victorian sexual repression (drawing by S. G. Hulme Beaman; Judith Wilt,* Ghosts of the Gothic, *1980; Thomas Cooper Library, University of South Carolina)*

earlier experiments of Poe and Le Fanu, presents itself rhetorically in the Gothic magazine mode as a "Strange Case," is often viewed by post-war writers on the Gothic Novel as a rich and penetrating analysis of Victorian repression, which anticipates Freud's work on the Ego and the Id. The story of the respectable, well-intentioned Doctor and his dwarfish, murderous "other half" has passed into popular mythology as a way of describing split personality, and contributes to the literature on the divided self in the modern period. This story too has been the subject of extensive visual representation.

The great coup of the nineteenth-century Gothic novel, however, comes at its end, with *Dracula* (1897) by Bram Stoker. This novel, together with Radcliffe's novels, Shelley's *Frankenstein,* Poe's tale "The Fall of the House of Usher," and Stevenson's *The Strange Case of Dr Jekyll and Mr Hyde,* represents the canon of the post-Second-World-War rehabilitation of the Gothic Novel. Stoker's novel creates single-handedly the literary myth of "Transylvania," the kingdom of vampires, portrayed as a vortex-like region of central Europe in which the Turks were originally repelled by the Magyars. Stoker's novel sites itself along the inflammatory metaphorical axis of invasion—geographical and bodily. The novel is a *farrago* of late Victorian beliefs; it is obsessed with the nature of the unconscious; the breaking of certain sexual taboos; the loss of Empire; the degeneration of the stock (i.e. the "blood") of Western Europe; the onset of the New Woman; the decadent reliance on Empirical Science at the expense of traditional religion.

The figure of the evil Count Dracula, the leader of the Undead, was largely ignored at the time of publication, but since the Second World War has become one of the most charismatic and visually reproduced characters in the popular tradition of the Gothic Novel, rivalling Mary Shelley's Victor Frankenstein and his Monster. Other texts from this period have been rehabilitated in the postwar period: Charlotte Perkins Gilman's *The Yellow Wallpaper* (1892), for example, a novella with Gothic overtones, has become a classic of the feminist modern tradition, reissued in paperback. In France, Gaston Leroux produced *The Phantom of the Opera* (1911), whose monstrous version of the Beauty and the Beast fairy-tale, recast as a post-Imperial historical romance, has also gained great currency in the post-war period, being turned into a world-touring popular musical.

With the exception of the Gothic strain in the shorter narratives of Kipling, Conrad, and Wells, the Edwardian period and the 1920s and 1930s see the Gothic retreat again into the magazines and anthologies, tapping an unease about Empire which Dickens had already shown himself aware of in his last novel, *The Mystery of Edwin Drood* (1870). The Gothic Novel appeared to decline, under threat from Modernism and the general reaction against Victorianism which took place after the First World War.

During this period, it is left to the cinema, and in particular the directors of the German expressionist cinema, to explore new forms of re-presentation, often using the settings, motifs and plots of the Gothic novels as a framework, and thus drawing a whole generation of readers back to the novels. This German movement also provided the studio training ground for Alfred Hitchcock, whose contribution to the tradition after the war is outstanding.

This period also saw the emergence of the first of a series of unifying, explanatory critical frameworks, which seem to fit the extreme case of the Gothic Novel, in the essay of Freud on "The Uncanny" (1919). This vastly influential piece of writing, which, using Hoffmann's eighteenth-century Gothic novels and stories as examples, seeks to explain the phenomena of readerly and writerly uncertainty by the unconscious projection of repressed fantasy on the part of both, brought commentary on the Gothic Novel onto a new level, a discursive field which has become part of the metalanguage of the postwar Gothic itself. Following Freud, the Surrealists also recognised the eighteenth-century English Gothic Novels as important forerunners of their own experiments with the unconscious, linking their comments to those of the Marquis de Sade already quoted.

American popular culture, which had thoroughly domesticated Freudian analysis by the end of the Second World War, found a new home for the Gothic Novel, which was marginalised during the postwar recovery period of the 1940s and 1950s in Britain. Important exceptions to this are the works of David Lyndsay, and two English Gothic Novels, between the late 1940s and 1960, the *Gormenghast Trilogy* (1946, 1950, 1959) of Mervyn Peake, and the pre-Wolfenden *doppelgänger* novel, *Radcliffe* (1963), by David Storey, a unique blend of naturalistic surface and Gothic motifs. The American interest in science and technology and the drive to demonise Eastern Europe during the Cold War period gave a new currency and availability to the shapes of Gothic fantasy, in conjunction with science fiction and detective fiction. The horror film was re-born, often deriving from magazine stories or novels of a Gothic type (like *Psycho* for example) or serving as remakes of the Gothic fictions themselves (such as the famous *Invasion of the Body Snatchers,* 1956, which makes allusion to a forgotten story by R. L. Stevenson). This change, supported by the popularity of the Hammer Films in Britain, in its turn encouraged some limited underground paperback re-publication of the Gothic Novels.

After the 1960s, both genre and commentary have, in a sense, expanded in symbiosis. Or at least, they have both increased exponentially. From the late 1960s on, we have seen the growth of new markets and new readers, which parallel, but far surpass, the market expansion of the original

Gothic Novels. Now, every book stall and airport bookstore has a pulp fiction section called "horror." The horror writer Stephen King was for a long time the world's best-selling author, and recently Anne Rice, another American author, has begun to rival him with the immense popularity of her *Interview with the Vampire* (1976), which forms the beginning of a series. There are many other strands of the postwar Gothic Novel, which has evolved its own complex map.

The critical interpretation of the Gothic Novel is also evolving. The earlier dominance of psychoanalytic explanation from the 1930s to the 1950s gave way to more historical, linguistic and socio-cultural approaches. From the 1960s onwards, the growth of interest in popular culture and the rise of feminism have changed and immensely broadened the literary and critical possibilities for the Gothic. Lively international and interdisciplinary debate as to the nature of the "subversiveness" of the Gothic Novel from the eighteenth century to the contemporary period is now under way, a debate which feeds round in a loop into the highly self-conscious fictional practice of such influential contemporary exponents as Angela Carter, whose sophisticated collection of stories *The Bloody Chamber* (1979), a blend of fairytale and traditional sadistic Gothic, itself fully aware of the theoretical and fictional possibilities of these overlapping traditions, teases mercilessly the expectations of its would-be commentators and devotee-readers alike.

—The Handbook to Gothic Literature, edited by Marie Mulvey-Roberts (New York: New York University Press, 1998), pp. 81–89

* * *

Bram Stoker and the Tradition of Irish Supernatural Fiction
Albert Power

Bram Stoker's *Dracula* is the most famous Irish supernatural horror novel. It represents the high point in a tradition of ghostly fiction in Ireland which owes its origin to the English Gothic novel of the second half of the eighteenth century. Beginning with Horace Walpole's *The Castle of Otranto* (1764), these novels featured vigorous villains, helpless heroines of surpassing beauty and unsullied virtue, and dashing heroes of limp imagination and questionable intelligence. Monastic corruption provided a plausible pillar for many of the plots. The most powerful of these novels are still read avidly, notably Ann Radcliffe's *The Mysteries of Udolpho* (1764) and *The Italian* (1797), Matthew Gregory Lewis's *The Monk* (1795), and, most famous of all, Mary Shelley's evocative *Frankenstein* (1818).

Ireland's prime contribution came on the ebb tide of this great wave of the Gothic. Charles Robert Maturin (1780–1824) was a graduate of Trinity College Dublin and became a Church of Ireland clergyman,

Charles Robert Maturin, the first Irish author to make a significant contribution to the tradition of the Gothic novel (frontispiece, Maturin, Melmoth the Wanderer *[London: Richard Bentley, 1892]; Thomas Cooper Library, University of South Carolina)*

holding the curacy of St. Peter's in Dublin for many years up to his death. Maturin achieved little immediate or lasting success with his first Gothic novel *The Family of Montorio; or, The Fatal Revenge* (1807). However, with his fifth novel, *Melmoth the Wanderer* (1820), Maturin produced a masterpiece. This lengthy book, penned in a series of interlocking sub-narratives, describes the endless wanderings of a Faust-like villain, an Irishman named John Melmoth, who buys a hundred and fifty years of extra life from the devil, and spends most of that time trying to barter it. Curiously, the author's main interest seemed to be in the histories of Melmoth's victims, rather than in the fate of the Wanderer himself. Working into the small hours, urged by indigence and inspired by brandy, Maturin produced effusive prose often attaining to a frenzied intensity.

Melmoth's own story, set in Ireland, forms the outer framework of the novel. The sub-narratives are many and widely scattered in terms of setting. Of these, the most effective is a lengthy segment called "The Spaniard's Narrative." This describes the ingenious attempts made by young Alonzo de Monçada, the eldest though illegitimate son of a distinguished Spanish family, to extricate himself from a Spanish monastery to which his parents have consigned him in an effort to hide his birth. Set in eighteenth century Madrid, it is a protracted story of deception and cruelty rich in vivid scenes of horror. Yet one is driven to wonder whether Maturin's inspiration may not have stemmed from closer to home. Support for this view is lent by Maturin's frequent bolstering of his lurid vignettes by footnoted allusions to similar scenes in Ireland, which either he himself had witnessed or else had had recounted to him. One such footnote relates the revolting butchery with pikes of Lord Arthur Kilwarden, Lord Chief Justice of Ireland, during Robert Emmet's abortive insurrection of 1803, a sight so shocking that it permanently blasted the mind of a neighboring artisan, who, unhappily, chanced to look out of his window at just the wrong moment.

The death scene of a descendant of Melmoth, in a dirty hovel on the coast of County Wicklow, features a

MELMOTH

THE

WANDERER:

A

TALE.

BY THE AUTHOR OF " BERTRAM," &c.

IN FOUR VOLUMES.

VOL. I.

EDINBURGH:
PRINTED FOR ARCHIBALD CONSTABLE AND COMPANY.
AND HURST, ROBINSON, AND CO. CHEAPSIDE,
LONDON.

1820.

Title page for Maturin's most acclaimed Gothic novel, in which the title character sells his soul to the devil for a longer life (Thomas Cooper Library, University of South Carolina)

grim parody of a certain Irish type—the Gombeen Man, also to be a leading character in Bram Stoker's earliest novel *The Snake's Pass* (1891).

Charles Robert Maturin died in 1824, having enjoyed little celebrity during his lifetime. The poet, James Clarence Mangan (1803–1848), who had known him, wrote:—

> He—in his own dark way—understood many people; but nobody understood him in any way. And therefore it was that he, this man of the highest genius, Charles Robert Maturin, lived unappreciated—and died unsympathised with, uncared for, uninquired after—and not only forgotten because he had never been thought about.[1]

Neither should we forget James Clarence Mangan himself, blood brother to the doom-depressed progenitors of the Irish ghost story. Best known now, if at all, for his poems, particularly "Dark Rosaleen," Mangan lived a dark, tormented life, a victim of alcohol, opium, and frustrated love. His several strange tales and exotic poems attest to an inner fire which drove and at last consumed him. In his later years, prematurely aged, he could be seen stalking around Trinity College Dublin, with his thin gaunt face, his wild grey hair thrown back, clad in a long white single-seam garment like a winding sheet.

Maturin's *Melmoth the Wanderer* represents the last great blossoming of the Gothic novel. Throughout the 1830s and 1840s the miniaturized horror tapestries of Edgar Allan Poe (1809–1849) were pointing in a new direction. Though preserving the dark embroideries of Gothic horror, Poe introduced a new personalized intensity and gave voice to his grim imaginings through the vehicle of the short story. It was through the short story also that the most famous Irish writer of ghostly fiction vented in literature his nightmare genius. This was Joseph Sheridan Le Fanu (1814–1873), a barrister turned journalist, like Maturin a Dublin-man and a graduate of Trinity College.

Le Fanu was born in Dublin, spent his youth in County Limerick, then returned to Dublin where he lived as a virtual recluse in Merrion Square, after the premature death of his young wife in 1858. His twin areas of specialty were the mystery novel, in which form he rivaled Wilkie Collins, and the supernatural short story where he is unparalleled. In his earlier years Le Fanu sought to specialize in the romantic historical novel, transferring to his own country the already proven techniques of Sir Walter Scott: hence his first two novels, *The Cock and Anchor* (1845), set in early eighteenth century Dublin, and *The Fortunes of Colonel Torlough O'Brien* (1847), a tale about the Jacobite Wars. His early short stories were first published in the Dublin University Magazine, then posthumously in book form as *The Purcell Papers* (1880). Through Fr. Francis Purcell, the character who links the various narratives, Le Fanu tackles, in allegorical fashion, the theme of the demise of the Great House and of the old Irish Catholic aristocracy. Though the writing style in these early tales lacks the terseness and refinement of his later work, the supernatural element in such stories as "The Drunkard's Dream" and "Schalken the Painter" is particularly chilling.

Le Fanu drew extensively on his childhood experience in County Limerick for some of his later folklore-based ghost stories. Tales such as "The White Cat of Drumgunniol," "The Child that Went with the Fairies," "Sir Dominic's Bargain," "Ultor de Lacey" and "Stories of Lough Guir" cleverly rework the legends and superstitions of the mid-West. However, his best writings are unrelated to the folk tradition. Unlike Poe, he avoids the usual trappings and style of the Gothic, and so, in large degree, his stories outlive the era in which they were written. Like Mangan's, Le Fanu's most memorable outpourings are tormented: his conscience-spawned spectres show us for the first time the ghost of the *mind,* which is yet, disquietingly, sometimes seen by others too, so that at the end we know not for certain whether the tormenting spirit comes from within or without.

In 1872, the year before his death, Le Fanu brought out a collection of short stories called *In A Glass Darkly.* These included "The Familiar," "Mr. Justice Harbottle," and "Green Tea" (ghost stories); "The Room in the Dragon Volant" (a long murder-mystery story); and "Carmilla" (a vampire tale). These stories are among Le Fanu's greatest, and indeed, rank, by any reckoning, among the foremost in the ghost story genre. "Carmilla" is of special significance as being the first treatment of the vampire legend by an Irish writer, and, arguably, was a crucial influence on Bram Stoker's *Dracula.*

Bram Stoker (1847–1912) embodies what might be termed the third generation in the tradition of Irish supernatural fiction. His background, middle-class Protestant, and graduate of Trinity College Dublin, closely resembles those of Maturin and Le Fanu. In 1879, after a lightning romance and hurried marriage to Florence Balcombe, formerly courted by Oscar Wilde, Stoker threw over his humdrum job as a civil servant in Dublin Castle to take on the strenuous role of manager of actor Henry Irving's Lyceum Theatre Company in London. It was a demanding job which involved long hours and often little

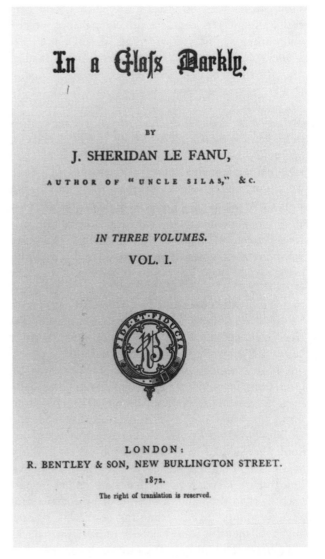

In a Glaſs Darkly.

BY

J. SHERIDAN LE FANU,

AUTHOR OF "UNCLE SILAS," &c.

IN THREE VOLUMES.

VOL. I.

LONDON:

R. BENTLEY & SON, NEW BURLINGTON STREET.

1872.

The right of translation is reserved.

Title page for a story collection that includes "Carmilla," the first vampire tale by an Irish author (from In A Glass Darkly *[New York: Arno, 1977]; Thomas Cooper Library, University of South Carolina)*

thanks, leaving Stoker with scant time to pursue his writing. Indeed, it was not until Irving's death in 1905 that Stoker became a full-time writer when the demise of the Lyceum Theatre Company left him with no other means of subsistence. Stoker himself died in 1912, so he had very little real opportunity to develop his skills as a writer. Consequently, one often finds an unevenness in Stoker's work. At times it is taut and vivid, at others tedious and turgid. Given the constraints under which Stoker labored for most of his life, it is little short of a marvel that he found time to write anything at all!

Stoker's writings can be divided, broadly, into three categories: romance novels, horror novels and short stories with supernatural elements, and general writings. His romance novels are ably written with strong sentimentalized plots. They include *The Watter's Mou'* (1894), *The Shoulder of Shasta* (1895), *Miss Betty* (1898), *The Man* (1905) and *Lady Athlyne* (1908). In part a romance novel, in part adventure story, and in part a disguised autobiography, is *The Mystery of the Sea* (1902), a lengthy novel set against the backdrop of Cruden Bay on the east coast of Scotland which Stoker had first discovered in 1890 and thereafter visited often, alternatively as a holiday resort and a scenic workshop. Here in Cruden Bay, he wrote much of what would become *Dracula*.

His general works include a two-volume *Personal Reminiscences of Sir Henry Irving* (1906), a lecture pamphlet *A Glimpse of America* (1885) and a collation of renowned historical frauds called *Famous Imposters* (1910). Unique among his general writings is his first published book, and one which best expresses his Irish roots, for it is, in fact, a reference book for Irish civil servants and law clerks: *The Duties of Clerks of Petty Sessions in Ireland* (1879). With its generous festooning of dull details, amply supported by quotations from statute and regulations, about dog licences, cattle trespasses, summonses and stamp duties, it could not be further removed from the Gothic world of *Dracula*. Stoker began writing this book after he had been appointed Inspector of Petty Sessions in 1876, essentially to ease the load of the unfortunate clerks who at that time had no reference works other than a mound of precedents and ancient statutes. By the time the book was eventually published by John Falconer of 53 Upper Sackville Street, Dublin, in 1879, Stoker was miles away in a new life with Irving at the Lyceum Theatre in London. In later years he was to look on this fledgling book as "dry as dust," and came to disregard it as a legitimate work altogether. Seemingly, though, the clerks of petty sessions found it helpful, and there is some evidence that when the British administration moved out of Dublin Castle, and left Ireland in 1922, copies of this seminal text found their way over to the Four Courts, where at least a few of them survived the bombing of the Civil War.

Though he had already published at least four short stories in his twenties, "The Crystal Cup" (1872), "The Primrose Path," "Buried Treasure" and "The Chain of Destiny" (all in 1875), Stoker's first book collection was a set of macabre supernatural fairy tales, *Under the Sunset* (1882). These tales, anticipating in darker hue the type of fables for which Oscar Wilde was later to become celebrated, are set in a remote never-never world called "The Land Under the Sunset." There is a lyrical, poetic touch to these stories, far removed from Stoker's heavily textured style in *Dracula* and the other horror novels. In essence, they are moral fables, probably intended for children, but rather grimmer than would appeal to the tastes of any normal child. For example, "The Castle of the King" tells of a grief-tormented poet who journeys through the Valley of the Shadow of Death to try and retrieve his deceased loved one, only to be stricken down himself; and "The Invisible Giant" deals with a deadly plague in the form of a sightless, unseen giant which overwhelms an entire city for its wickedness.

It has been suggested that in writing this collection, and in particular "The Invisible Giant," Stoker was influenced by an account earlier written by his mother, Charlotte Stoker, of a cholera epidemic in Sligo in 1832, which she had herself lived through as a child. Mrs. Stoker's report of how the cholera devastated half the town, and, especially, of the growing inhumanity in privation of former neighbors to each other, makes harrowing reading. Such descriptions as the following would not be amiss from the pen of Maturin:

> One action I vividly remember. A poor traveller was taken ill on the roadside some miles from the town, and how did those samaritans tend him? They dug a pit and with long poles pushed him living into it, and covered him up quick, alive. Severely, like Sodom, did our city pay for such crimes?

Stoker's next foray into the macabre came in 1891 with *The Snake's Pass,* a novel set in the West of Ireland. This combines a routine love interest with the sinister legend of the King of Snakes and a treasure lost by the French army in 1798. The Snake's Pass, called the Shleenanaher—a literal translation of the Irish *slí na n'athar*—is part of a mountain said to be the scene of a confrontation between St. Patrick and the King of the Snakes. The mountain is called Knockcalltecrore, an anglicization of the Irish words *cnoc na caillte coróin óir,* which mean, literally, "the hill of the lost crown of gold." The principal geological feature of this mountain is a treacherous shifting bog, which Stoker implies is the latter-day form assumed by the still active King of the Snakes. In his depiction of Black Murtagh, ("the Gombeen Man"), a greedy and unscrupulous moneylender, Stoker writes with particular vividness and intensity. In a sense, Black Murtagh is the archetype of evil and so prefigures, in character if not in power, the awesome Count Dracula himself.

An illustration personifying the plague for Stoker's "The Invisible Giant," in his first story collection, Under the Sunset
(drawing by Reverend William Fitzgerald; Barbara Belford, Bram Stoker: A Biography of the Author of
Dracula, 1996; Elizabeth Miller Collection)

Dracula was completed in 1897, though we now know this most famous of Stoker's novels took several years to research and write. Then came *The Jewel of Seven Stars* (1903), a novel with a theme of reincarnation: the wicked Queen Tera's complex plans for a second coming wreak havoc on the lives of the explorers who discover her hidden tomb in Egypt's Valley of the Sorcerer and take her mummified body back to London. *Snowbound,* a collection of short stories from a fictitious theatrical company, followed in 1908, and *The Lady of the Shroud* in 1909. This novel has a theme and setting not unlike *Dracula*. A beautiful young princess in the make-believe

Balkan kingdom of the Land of the Blue Mountains assumes the role of a she-vampire for political reasons. A young Scot, who inherits a castle there, falls in love with her and helps to deliver her people from the marauding Turks. This novel is distinguished by some highly improbable melodrama. An example is a frantic scene in which a character called the Gospodar jumps from a cliff, breaking his fall by clutching the branches of trees growing straight out from the cliff face, and lands safely on the ground after severing a Turkish invader's head with his scimitar while in mid-flight. Another scene, lending a quaintly (for the time) contemporary touch, involves a daring rescue operation by aeroplane, in which the aircraft contrives to land very adroitly on top of a prison wall!

Last came *The Lair of the White Worm* (1911), an extraordinary story about a huge white worm which has survived for thousands of years in a labyrinth of caverns in the south of England and transforms itself into a beautiful young woman, Lady Arabella March, who sports slinky white dresses and has an abiding dread of mongooses—the bane of snakes. This novel was written in a jerky, irregular style, likely indicative of the fact that Stoker was terminally ill at the time of its composition. It contains a wide gamut of highly unusual characters, including Oolanga, a baleful Negro, and Edgar Caswell, a local madman who owns a castle and flies a huge kite from its battlements—to scare away the birds.

At the time of his death, in April 1912, Stoker (according to his widow, Florence) had been planning the publication of three volumes of short stories that had appeared earlier piecemeal in various periodicals and magazines. One volume was published posthumously, with an introduction by Florence Stoker, under the title *Dracula's Guest and Other Weird Stories.* The opening story, "Dracula's Guest," may have originally been intended as an introductory sequence for the novel *Dracula,* excised at the behest of the publisher due to the novel's already considerable length. It is difficult to guess what might have formed the contents of Stoker's other two anthologies, since Stoker's writings in shorter form were multifarious and published in numerous different periodicals.

Likewise difficult to assess is the exact significance of his being Irish on Bram Stoker's writings. One can see it clearly enough in *Under the Sunset* and *The Snake's Pass,* but otherwise specifically Irish incursions are not easy to discern. True, there are Gaelic characterizations in *The Mystery of the Sea* and *The Watter's Mou',* and a large element of stage Irishness in *The Man from Shorrox's,* a semi-whimsical, semigrisly short story published in 1894. The charge of stage Irishness or blarney can be levelled at certain of Stoker's writings. Unlike Maturin and Le Fanu, Stoker spent most of his life in England, mingling in society circles, and so was out of touch with direct inspiration from his native country.

At one time it was fashionable to conjecture that during Le Fanu's later years and while Stoker was a young man living in Dublin the two must have met. Attractive though this speculation is, there seems to be no evidence to support it. That Le Fanu's writings may have influenced Stoker's is far more likely. Certainly, there is a close resemblance between Le Fanu's short story "An Account of Some Strange Disturbances in Aungier Street" (1853) and Stoker's "The Judge's House" (1891). Both concern the supernatural prowlings of a wicked "hanging judge"; in each case the house possesses a lurid portrait of the judge which exerts a disturbing influence on the house's occupants; and in each case also the judge becomes embodied in the form of a grotesque and menacing rat. Also, Le Fanu's "Carmilla" (1872), detailing the wiles of a female vampire, stirs parallel echoes in parts of "Dracula's Guest," and was demonstrably an inspiration for the novel *Dracula* itself.

But more compellingly than any of these literary comparisons, Bram Stoker's Irishness manifested in his staunch and generous personality which spilled over into his characterizations in fiction. Stoker was an archetype of uprightness, steadfastness and decency. He was ever a man of honor, a loyal friend, a tireless worker and unflagging supporter of those whose causes he espoused. Stories abound of his heroism and selflessness: how, for example, in 1882, he dived into the Thames from a steamer to try and save a man from drowning, but failed in the attempt; of his kindly advices to actresses Genevieve Ward and Ellen Terry when time could ill be spared for the giving of advice; of his tireless labors as Theatre Manager for actor Henry Irving, a man difficult to work for by all accounts, whom he served unstintingly for twenty-seven years.

Despite the erotic attributions of vampire blood-guzzling, which Stoker does not strive to conceal, the man himself was very much a moralist, a supporter of censorship, and a devoted idealizer of women—though the then conventional image of woman as a domestic, supportive entity to be protected would have appealed to his sense of the proper. In his obituary notice in *The Times* it was justly said of Stoker that "Few men have played the part of Fidus Achates to a great personality with more gusto." Nor was it without reason that Walt Whitman, the American poet whose works Stoker had so stoutly championed in his student days, referred to him as "a broth of a boy."

These personality traits inevitably seep into his writing. The romance novels drip with them. And even in the horror novels we invariably find a select group of staunch, high-principled men limbering themselves up to take on such diverse embodiments of evil as Black Murtagh, Dracula, and the White

Worm. In his choice of plot, Stoker is more akin to the Gothic writers than to Le Fanu. Unlike Le Fanu, he does not engulf us in half-hidden questions of metaphysics, nor trouble us with the torments of a supernaturally pestered conscience. The conflicts of which he treats are primal—good against evil, right against wrong. But for all that, he wrenches the reader into the thick of the struggle, forcing a keen emotional involvement with the outcome of the fray.

—revised by the author from *Dracula: Celebrating 100 Years,* edited by Leslie Shepard and Albert Power (Dublin: Mentor Press, 1997), pp. 58–67

1. Qtd. in Robert E. Loughy, *Charles Robert Maturin* (Lewisburg: Bucknell University Press, 1975), p. 87.
2. Qtd. in Harry Ludlam, *A Biography of Bram Stoker, Creator of Dracula* (London: New English Library, 1977), pp. 28–29.

* * *

British scholar Clive Leatherdale, the author of Dracula: The Novel & the Legend *(2001), has published several of Stoker's works through his publishing company, Desert Island Books.*

Dracula and Ireland
Clive Leatherdale

Stoker had the entire Gaelic tradition of folklore to call upon, for Ireland is among the most superstition-ridden lands of Europe. Its geographical position on the western extremity of the Continent has given it a unique heritage. Because Ireland escaped conquest by the Romans, the classical imprint so evident in the mythology found elsewhere in Europe is absent; yet, like the ripple effect on a pond, those continental myths that did filter through continued to circulate long after their disappearance from their points of origin. These European influences merged with the indigenous Irish folk tradition, and the consequent richness and diversity of Gaelic superstition has inspired many Irish authors.

St. Martin cutting his cloak in half for a beggar. In Ireland there is a folk belief that a blood sacrifice between Halloween and St. Martin's Day, 11 November, assures good luck for the year. Dracula's destruction on 6 November is thus in keeping with this tradition (David Self, The Loyola Treasury of Saints, *2003; Richland County Public Library).*

In Stoker's case, he had availed himself of the fund of folk tales collected by Sir William and Lady Wilde, both of whom published anthologies on Irish folklore.[1] His mother also provided an early stimulus for Stoker's fiction, and her graphic account of the 1832 Sligo cholera epidemic[2] (instancing premature burial and the deadly suspicion of strangers) had directly inspired one of his fairy tales. "The Invisible Giant," from *Under the Sunset,* told of a young girl who sees in the sky beyond the city "a vast shadowy Form, with its arms raised. It was shrouded in a great misty robe that covered it, fading away into the air so that she could only see the face and grim, spectral hands . . . the face was as that of a strong man, pitiless, yet without malice; and . . . the eyes were blind." A second tale from the collection can likewise be seen to anticipate *Dracula.* "The Castle of the King" relates a young poet's quest to find his beloved, who has apparently died in a strange castle. This quest is obstructed by various horrors, until the hero finally arrives at the castle—huge, dead, and shrouded in mist.

Although from a Protestant family, Stoker's homeland was, and is, overwhelmingly Catholic. It is a feature of Catholic lands across Europe that they are receptive to belief in vampires. The vampire is almost as entrenched in the folklore of Ireland as on the Continent, though divested of most of its usual macabre manifestations. The "deargdue" (the red bloodsucker) of ancient Ireland was reputed to use her beauty to tempt passing men and then suck their blood. Similarly, the "leanhaun shee" (the fairy mistress) was an eye-catching fairy whose charms were irresistible to men. Energy would be drawn from the ensnared male until he eventually wasted away, or else procured a substitute victim to take his place.[3] Irish fairies were presumed to be bloodless, and their abduction of humans intended to remedy that deficiency.[4]

It is possible to discern in *Dracula* other, non-vampire, elements from Irish folk superstition. The devil, for instance, is in Irish lore traditionally depicted in human guise—as opposed to the grotesque animalistic representations of Europe, or the spirit form familiar to the East. The Irish devil is also able to adopt feminine form and assume the role of temptress, but despite his powers he can nevertheless be outwitted.[5]

Children would often be abducted by the Irish spirit world, with "changelings" (deformed or senile fairies) left disguised in their place. As with vampires, changelings are said to be vulnerable to fire or water. Any children unbaptised ran an increased risk of abduction by the spirit world.

Some Irish fairies are gregarious. Others are solitary beings, for instance the "leprechaun" and the "cluricane"—the latter feared for its cunning and reputed ability to escape capture by becoming invisible. The "dullahan" is variously conceived as a headless ghost at the reins of a death coach which appears at midnight, or a black coach drawn by headless horses. Whichever guise it takes, the "dullahan" portends death.[6]

The bitter-sweet, tingling music of seduction with which Stoker arms his vampire ladies might have been suggested by the "banshee," the indecipherable female wailing which signals an impending death. Stoker's vampires are capable of transformation into phosphorescent specks, like those other Irish omens of death, the "water sheeries"—the souls of those refused permission to enter either heaven or hell. They frequent churchyards, can appear as dancing flames, and can be repelled with a crucifix.[7] Evil spirits may pass through narrow interstices, and certain plants or herbs—notably the rowan (mountain ash)—protect the bearer against the fairy world.

One clear instance of Irish lore discernible in *Dracula* concerns the climax of the novel. The Count is destroyed on 6 November. In Ireland, the feast of St Martin is celebrated on the 11th of that month, and it is the custom for blood to be shed during the interval following Halloween. If St Martin fails to receive his blood sacrifice, the neglectful family can expect ill luck in the year ahead.[8] Dracula's demise, occurring when it does, thereby fulfills the hunters' obligation to St Martin.

—*Dracula: The Novel & The Legend*
(Westcliff-on-Sea, U.K.: Desert Island
Books, 2001), pp. 80–82

1. See, for example. Sir William Wilde, *Irish Popular Superstition* (1853) and Lady Wilde, *Ancient Legends of Ireland* (1888).
2. Reproduced in Harry Ludlam, *A Biography of Bram Stoker, Creator of Dracula* (London: New English Library, 1977), pp. 27–34.
3. Peter Haining, *The Leprechaun's Kingdom* (London: Souvenir Press, 1979), pp. 91, 99.
4. Sean O'Sullivan, *The Folklore of Ireland* (London: Batsford, 1974), p. 72.
5. O'Sullivan, *Folklore,* pp. 21, 23.
6. Haining, *Kingdom,* pp. 21, 25, 39. Consider Harker's experience with Dracula's coach in Chapter 1 of *Dracula.*
7. *Haining, Kingdom,* p. 107.
8. O'Sullivan, *Folklore,* pp. 114–115.

An Early Gothic Story

Several stories in Stoker's first collection, Under the Sunset *(1881), had Gothic themes, as well as do other tales written in the early 1890s while he was working on* Dracula, *including "The Burial of the Rats," "The Squaw," and "The Judge's House."*

The following story was first published in the 5 December 1891 issue of Illustrated Sporting and Dramatic News.

The Judge's House
Bram Stoker

When the time for his examination drew near Malcolm Malcolmson made up his mind to go somewhere to read by himself. He feared the attractions of the seaside, and also he feared completely rural isolation, for of old he knew its charms, and so he determined to find some unpretentious little town where there would be nothing to distract him. He refrained from asking suggestions from any of his friends, for he argued that each would recommend some place of which he had knowledge, and where he had already acquaintances. As Malcolmson wished to avoid friends he had no wish to encumber himself with the attention of friends' friends, and so he determined to look out for a place for himself. He packed a portmanteau with some clothes and all the books he required, and then took ticket for the first name on the local time-table which he did not know.

When at the end of three hours' journey he alighted at Benchurch, he felt satisfied that he had so far obliterated his tracks as to be sure of having a peaceful opportunity of pursuing his studies. He went straight to the one inn which the sleepy little place contained, and put up for the night. Benchurch was a market town, and once in three weeks was crowded to excess, but for the remainder of the twenty-one days it was as attractive as a desert. Malcolmson looked around the day after his arrival to try to find quarters more isolated than even so quiet an inn as "The Good Traveller" afforded. There was only one place which took his fancy, and it certainly satisfied his wildest ideas regarding quiet; in fact, quiet was not the proper word to apply to it–desolation was the only term conveying any suitable idea of its isolation. It was an old rambling, heavy-built house of the Jacobean style, with heavy gables and windows, unusually small, and set higher than was customary in such houses, and was surrounded with a high brick wall massively built. Indeed, on examination, it looked more like a fortified house than an ordinary dwelling. But all these things pleased Malcolmson. "Here," he thought, "is the very spot I have been looking for, and if I can only get opportunity of using it I shall be happy." His joy was increased when he realised beyond doubt that it was not at present inhabited.

From the post-office he got the name of the agent, who was rarely surprised at the application to rent a part of the old house. Mr. Carnford, the local lawyer and agent, was a genial old gentleman, and frankly confessed his delight at anyone being willing to live in the house.

"To tell you the truth," said he, "I should be only too happy, on behalf of the owners, to let anyone have the house rent free for a term of years if only to accustom the people here to see it inhabited. It has been so long empty that some kind of absurd prejudice has grown up about it, and this can be best put down by its occupation–if only," he added with a sly glance at Malcolmson, "by a scholar like yourself, who wants its quiet for a time."

Malcolmson thought it needless to ask the agent about the "absurd prejudice"; he knew he would get more information, if he should require it, on that subject from other quarters. He paid his three months' rent, got a receipt, and the name of an old woman who would probably undertake to "do" for him, and came away with the keys in his pocket. He then went to the landlady of the inn, who was a cheerful and most kindly person, and asked her advice as to such stores and provisions as he would be likely to require. She threw up her hands in amazement when he told her where he was going to settle himself.

"Not in the Judge's House!" she said, and grew pale as she spoke. He explained the locality of the house, saying that he did not know its name. When he had finished she answered:

"Aye, sure enough–sure enough the very place! It is the Judge's House sure enough." He asked her to tell him about the place, why so called, and what there was against it. She told him that it was so called locally because it had been many years before–how long she could not say, as she was herself from another part of the country, but she thought it must have been a hundred years or more–the abode of a judge who was held in great terror on account of his harsh sentences and his hostility to prisoners at Assizes. As to what there was against the house itself she could not tell. She had often asked, but no one could inform her; but there was a general feeling that there was *something,* and for her own part she would not take all the money in Drinkwater's Bank and stay in the house an hour by herself. Then she apologised to Malcolmson for her disturbing talk.

"It is too bad of me, sir, and you–and a young gentleman, too–if you will pardon me saying it, going to live there all alone. If you were my boy–and you'll excuse me for saying it–you wouldn't sleep there a night, not if I had to go there myself and pull the big alarm bell that's on the roof!" The good creature was so manifestly in earnest, and was so kindly in her intentions, that Malcolmson, although amused, was touched. He told her kindly how much he appreciated her interest in him, and added:

"But, my dear Mrs. Witham, indeed you need not be concerned about me! A man who is reading for the Mathematical Tripos has too much to think of to be disturbed by any of these mysterious 'somethings,' and his work is of too exact and prosaic a kind to allow of his having any corner in his mind for mysteries of any kind. Harmonical Progression, Permutations and Combinations, and Elliptic Functions have sufficient mysteries for me!" Mrs. Witham kindly undertook to see after his commissions, and he went himself to look for the old woman who had been recommended to him. When he returned to the Judge's House with her, after an interval of a couple of hours, he found Mrs. Witham herself waiting with several men and boys carrying parcels, and an upholsterer's man with a bed in a cart, for she said, though tables and chairs might be all very well, a bed that hadn't been aired for mayhap fifty years was not proper for young bones to lie on. She was evidently curious to see the inside of the house; and though manifestly so afraid of the "somethings" that at the slightest sound she clutched on to Malcolmson, whom she never left for a moment, went over the whole place.

After his examination of the house, Malcolmson decided to take up his abode in the great dining-room, which was big enough to serve for all his requirements; and Mrs. Witham, with the aid of the charwoman, Mrs. Dempster, proceeded to arrange matters. When the hampers were brought in and unpacked, Malcolmson saw that with much kind forethought she had sent from her own kitchen sufficient provisions to last for a few days. Before going she expressed all sorts of kind wishes; and at the door turned and said:

"And perhaps, sir, as the room is big and draughty it might be well to have one of those big screens put round your bed at night—though, truth to tell, I would die myself if I were to be so shut in with all kinds of—of 'things,' that put their heads round the sides, or over the top, and look on me!" The image which she had called up was too much for her nerves, and she fled incontinently.

Mrs. Dempster sniffed in a superior manner as the landlady disappeared, and remarked that for her own part she wasn't afraid of all the bogies in the kingdom.

"I'll tell you what it is, sir," she said; "bogies is all kinds and sorts of things—except bogies! Rats and mice, and beetles; and creaky doors, and loose slates, and broken panes, and stiff drawer handles, that stay out when you pull them and then fall down in the middle of the night. Look at the wainscot of the room! It is old—hundreds of years old! Do you think there's no rats and beetles there! And do you imagine, sir, that you wont see none of them? Rats is bogies, I tell you, and bogies is rats; and don't you get to think anything else!"

"Mrs. Dempster," said Malcolmson gravely, making her a polite bow, "you know more than a Senior Wrangler! And let me say, that, as a mark of esteem for your indubitable soundness of head and heart, I shall, when I go, give you possession of this house, and let you stay here by yourself for the last two months of my tenancy, for four weeks will serve my purpose."

"Thank you kindly, sir!" she answered, "but I couldn't sleep away from home a night. I am in Greenhow's Charity, and if I slept a night away from my rooms I should lose all I have got to live on. The rules is very strict; and there's too many watching for a vacancy for me to run any risks in the matter. Only for that, sir, I'd gladly come here and attend on you altogether during your stay."

"My good woman," said Malcolmson hastily, "I have come here on purpose to obtain solitude; and believe me that I am grateful to the late Greenhow for having so organised his admirable charity—whatever it is—that I am perforce denied the opportunity of suffering from such a form of temptation! Saint Anthony himself could not be more rigid on the point!"

The old woman laughed harshly. "Ah, you young gentlemen," she said, "you don't fear for naught; and belike you'll get all the solitude you want here." She set to work with her cleaning; and by nightfall, when Malcolmson returned from his walk—he always had one of his books to study as he walked—he found the room swept and tidied, a fire burning in the old hearth, the lamp lit, and the table spread for supper with Mrs. Witham's excellent fare. "This is comfort, indeed," he said, as he rubbed his hands.

When he had finished his supper, and lifted the tray to the other end of the great oak dining-table, he got out his books again, put fresh wood on the fire, trimmed his lamp, and set himself down to a spell of real hard work. He went on without pause till about eleven o'clock, when he knocked off for a bit to fix his fire and lamp, and to make himself a cup of tea. He had always been a tea-drinker, and during his college life had sat late at work and had taken tea late. The rest was a great luxury to him, and he enjoyed it with a sense of delicious, voluptuous ease. The renewed fire leaped and sparkled, and threw quaint shadows through the great old room; and as he sipped his hot tea he revelled in the sense of isolation from his kind. Then it was that he began to notice for the first time what a noise the rats were making.

"Surely," he thought, "they cannot have been at it all the time I was reading. Had they been, I must have noticed it!" Presently, when the noise increased, he satisfied himself that it was really new. It was evident that at first the rats had been frightened at the presence of a stranger, and the light of fire and lamp; but that as the time went on they had grown bolder and were now disporting themselves as was their wont.

How busy they were! and hark to the strange noises! Up and down behind the old wainscot, over the ceiling and under the floor they raced, and gnawed, and scratched! Malcolmson smiled to himself as he recalled to mind the saying of Mrs. Dempster, "Bogies is rats, and rats is bogies!" The tea began to have its effect of intellectual and nervous stimulus, he saw with joy another long spell of work to be done before the night was past, and in the sense of security which it gave him, he allowed himself the luxury of a good look round the room. He took his lamp in one hand, and went all around, wondering that so quaint and beautiful an old house had been so long neglected. The carving of the oak on the panels of the wainscot was fine, and on and round the doors and windows it was beautiful and of rare merit. There were some old pictures on the walls, but they were coated so thick with dust and dirt that he could not distinguish any detail of them, though he held his lamp as high as he could over his head. Here and there as he went round he saw some crack or hole blocked for a moment by the face of a rat with its bright eyes glittering in the light, but in an instant it was gone, and a squeak and a scamper followed. The thing that most struck him, however, was the rope of the great alarm bell on the roof, which hung down in a corner of the room on the right-hand side of the fireplace. He pulled up close to the hearth a great high-backed carved oak chair, and sat down to his last cup of tea. When this was done he made up the fire, and went back to his work, sitting at the corner of the table, having the fire to his left. For a little while the rats disturbed him somewhat with their perpetual scampering, but he got accustomed to the noise as one does to the ticking of a clock or to the roar of moving water; and he became so immersed in his work that everything in the world, except the problem which he was trying to solve, passed away from him.

He suddenly looked up, his problem was still unsolved, and there was in the air that sense of the hour before the dawn, which is so dread to doubtful life. The noise of the rats had ceased. Indeed it seemed to him that it must have ceased but lately and that it was the sudden cessation which had disturbed him. The fire had fallen low, but still it threw out a deep red glow. As he looked he started in spite of his *sang froid*.

There on the great high-backed carved oak chair by the right side of the fire-place sat an enormous rat, steadily glaring at him with baleful eyes. He made a motion to it as though to hunt it away, but it did not stir. Then he made the motion of throwing something. Still it did not stir, but showed its great white teeth angrily, and its cruel eyes shone in the lamplight with an added vindictiveness.

Malcolmson felt amazed, and seizing the poker from the hearth ran at it to kill it. Before, however, he could strike it, the rat, with a squeak that sounded like the concentration of hate, jumped upon the floor, and, running up

the rope of the alarm bell, disappeared in the darkness beyond the range of the green-shaded lamp. Instantly, strange to say, the noisy scampering of the rats in the wainscot began again.

By this time Malcolmson's mind was quite off the problem; and as a shrill cock-crow outside told him of the approach of morning, he went to bed and to sleep.

He slept so sound that he was not even waked by Mrs. Dempster coming in to make up his room. It was only when she had tidied up the place and got his breakfast ready and tapped on the screen which closed in his bed that he woke. He was a little tired still after his night's hard work, but a strong cup of tea soon freshened him up and, taking his book, he went out for his morning walk, bringing with him a few sandwiches lest he should not care to return till dinner time. He found a quiet walk between high elms some way outside the town, and here he spent the greater part of the day studying his Laplace. On his return he looked in to see Mrs. Witham and to thank her for her kindness. When she saw him coming through the diamond-paned bay window of her sanctum she came out to meet him and asked him in. She looked at him searchingly and shook her head as she said:

"You must not overdo it, sir. You are paler this morning than you should be. Too late hours and too hard work on the brain isn't good for any man! But tell me, sir, how did you pass the night? Well, I hope? But, my heart! sir, I was glad when Mrs. Dempster told me this morning that you were all right and sleeping sound when she went in."

"Oh, I was all right," he answered smiling, "the 'somethings' didn't worry me, as yet. Only the rats; and they had a circus, I tell you, all over the place. There was one wicked looking old devil that sat up on my own chair by the fire, and wouldn't go till I took the poker to him, and then he ran up the rope of the alarm bell and got to somewhere up the wall or the ceiling—I couldn't see where, it was so dark."

"Mercy on us," said Mrs. Witham, "an old devil, and sitting on a chair by the fireside! Take care, sir! take care! There's many a true word spoken in jest."

"How do you mean? 'Pon my word I don't understand."

"An old devil! The old devil, perhaps. There! sir, you needn't laugh," for Malcolmson had broken into a hearty peal. "You young folks thinks it easy to laugh at things that makes older ones shudder. Never mind, sir! never mind! Please God, you'll laugh all the time. It's what I wish you myself!" and the good lady beamed all over in sympathy with his enjoyment, her fears gone for a moment.

"Oh, forgive me!" said Malcolmson presently. "Don't think me rude; but the idea was too much for me—that the old devil himself was on the chair last night!" And at the thought he laughed again. Then he went home to dinner.

This evening the scampering of the rats began earlier; indeed it had been going on before his arrival, and only ceased whilst his presence by its freshness disturbed them. After dinner he sat by the fire for a while and had a smoke; and then, having cleared his table, began to work as before. To-night the rats disturbed him more than they had done on the previous night. How they scampered up and down and under and over! How they squeaked, and scratched, and gnawed! How they, getting bolder by degrees, came to the mouths of their holes and to the chinks and cracks and crannies in the wainscoting till their eyes shone like tiny lamps as the firelight rose and fell. But to him, now doubtless accustomed to them, their eyes were not wicked; only their playfulness touched him. Sometimes the boldest of them made sallies out on the floor or along the mouldings of the wainscot. Now and again as they disturbed him Malcolmson made a sound to frighten them, smiting the table with his hand or giving a fierce "Hsh, hsh," so that they fled straightway to their holes.

And so the early part of the night wore on; and despite the noise Malcolmson got more and more immersed in his work.

All at once he stopped, as on the previous night, being overcome by a sudden sense of silence. There was not the faintest sound of gnaw, or scratch, or squeak. The silence was as of the grave. He remembered the odd occurrence of the previous night, and instinctively he looked at the chair standing close by the fireside. And then a very odd sensation thrilled through him.

There, on the great old high-backed carved oak chair beside the fireplace sat the same enormous rat, steadily glaring at him with baleful eyes.

Instinctively he took the nearest thing to his hand, a book of logarithms, and flung it at it. The book was badly aimed and the rat did not stir, so again the poker performance of the previous night was repeated; and again the rat, being closely pursued, fled up the rope of the alarm bell. Strangely too, the departure of this rat was instantly followed by the renewal of the noise made by the general rat community. On this occasion, as on the previous one, Malcolmson could not see at what part of the room the rat disappeared, for the green shade of his lamp left the upper part of the room in darkness, and the fire had burned low.

On looking at his watch he found it was close on midnight; and, not sorry for the *divertissement,* he made up his fire and made himself his nightly pot of tea. He had got through a good spell of work, and thought himself entitled to a cigarette; and so he sat on the great carved oak chair before the fire and enjoyed it. Whilst smoking he began to think that he would like to know where the rat disappeared to, for he had certain ideas for the morrow not entirely disconnected with a rat-trap. Accordingly he lit

Travelman Short Stories

Bram Stoker

The Judge's House

Suspense

Cover for a 1998 edition published for commuters (illustration by Ian McNee; Bruccoli Clark Layman Archives)

another lamp and placed it so that it would shine well into the right-hand corner of the wall by the fireplace. Then he got all the books he had with him, and placed them handy to throw at the vermin. Finally he lifted the rope of the alarm bell and placed the end of it on the table, fixing the extreme end under the lamp. As he handled it he could not help noticing how pliable it was, especially for so strong a rope, and one not in use. "You could hang a man with it," he thought to himself. When his preparations were made he looked around, and said complacently:

"There now, my friend, I think we shall learn something of you this time!" He began his work again, and though as before somewhat disturbed at first by the noise of the rats, soon lost himself in his propositions and problems.

Again he was called to his immediate surroundings suddenly. This time it might not have been the sudden silence only which took his attention; there was a slight movement of the rope, and the lamp moved. Without stirring, he looked to see if his pile of books was within range, and then cast his eye along the rope. As he looked he saw the great rat drop from the rope on the oak armchair and sit there glaring at him. He raised a book in his right hand, and taking careful aim, flung it at the rat. The latter, with a quick movement, sprang aside and dodged the missile. He then took another book, and a third, and flung them one after another at the rat, but each time unsuccessfully. At last, as he stood with a book poised in his hand to throw, the rat squeaked and seemed afraid. This made Malcolmson more than ever eager to strike, and the book flew and struck the rat a resounding blow. It gave a terrified squeak, and turning on his pursuer a look of terrible malevolence, ran up the chair-back and made a great jump to the rope of the alarm bell and ran up it like lightning. The lamp rocked under the sudden strain, but it was a heavy one and did not topple over. Malcolmson kept his eyes on the rat, and saw it by the light of the second lamp leap to a moulding of the wainscot and disappear through a hole in one of the great pictures which hung on the wall, obscured and invisible through its coating of dirt and dust.

"I shall look up my friend's habitation in the morning," said the student, as he went over to collect his books. "The third picture from the fireplace; I shall not forget." He picked up the books one by one, commenting on them as he lifted them. "*Conic Sections* he does not mind, nor *Cycloidal Oscillations,* nor the *Principia,* nor *Quaternions,* nor *Thermodynamics.* Now for the book that fetched him!" Malcolmson took it up and looked at it. As he did so he started, and a sudden pallor overspread his face. He looked round uneasily and shivered slightly, as he murmured to himself:

"The Bible my mother gave me! What an odd coincidence." He sat down to work again, and the rats in the wainscot renewed their gambols. They did not disturb him, however; somehow their presence gave him a sense of companionship. But he could not attend to his work, and after striving to master the subject on which he was engaged gave it up in despair, and went to bed as the first streak of dawn stole in through the eastern window.

He slept heavily but uneasily, and dreamed much; and when Mrs. Dempster woke him late in the morning he seemed ill at ease, and for a few minutes did not seem to realise exactly where he was. His first request rather surprised the servant.

"Mrs. Dempster, when I am out to-day I wish you would get the steps and dust or wash those pictures—specially that one the third from the fireplace—I want to see what they are."

Late in the afternoon Malcolmson worked at his books in the shaded walk, and the cheerfulness of the previous day came back to him as the day wore on, and he found that his reading was progressing well. He had worked out to a satisfactory conclusion all the problems which had as yet baffled him, and it was in a state of jubilation that he paid a visit to Mrs. Witham at "The Good Traveller." He found a stranger in the cosy sitting-room with the landlady, who was introduced to him as Dr. Thornhill. She was not quite at ease, and this, combined with the doctor's plunging at once into a series of questions, made Malcolmson come to the conclusion that his presence was not an accident, so without preliminary he said:

"Dr. Thornhill, I shall with pleasure answer you any question you may choose to ask me if you will answer me one question first."

The doctor seemed surprised, but he smiled and answered at once, "Done! What is it?"

"Did Mrs. Witham ask you to come here and see me and advise me?"

Dr. Thornhill for a moment was taken aback, and Mrs. Witham got fiery red and turned away; but the doctor was a frank and ready man, and he answered at once and openly:

"She did: but she didn't intend you to know it. I suppose it was my clumsy haste that made you suspect. She told me that she did not like the idea of your being in that house all by yourself, and that she thought you took too much strong tea. In fact, she wants me to advise you if possible to give up the tea and the very late hours. I was a keen student in my time, so I suppose I may take the liberty of a college man, and without offense, advise you not quite as a stranger."

Malcolmson with a bright smile held out his hand. "Shake! as they say in America," he said. "I must thank you for your kindness and Mrs. Witham too, and your kindness deserves a return on my part. I promise to take no more strong tea—no tea at all till you let me—and I shall go to bed to-night at one o'clock at latest. Will that do?"

"Capital," said the doctor. "Now tell us all that you noticed in the old house," and so Malcolmson then and there told in minute detail all that had happened in the last two nights. He was interrupted every now and then by some exclamation from Mrs. Witham, till finally when he told of the episode of the Bible the landlady's pent-up emotions found vent in a shriek; and it was not till a stiff glass of brandy and water had been administered that she grew composed again. Dr. Thornhill listened with a face of growing gravity, and when the narrative was complete and Mrs. Witham had been restored he asked:

"The rat always went up the rope of the alarm bell?"

"Always."

"I suppose you know," said the Doctor after a pause, "what the rope is?"

"No!"

"It is," said the Doctor slowly, "the very rope which the hangman used for all the victims of the Judge's judicial rancour!" Here he was interrupted by another scream from Mrs. Witham, and steps had to be taken for her recovery. Malcolmson having looked at his watch, and found that it was close to his dinner hour, had gone home before her complete recovery.

When Mrs. Witham was herself again she almost assailed the Doctor with angry questions as to what he meant by putting such horrible ideas into the poor young man's mind. "He has quite enough there already to upset him," she added. Dr. Thornhill replied:

"My dear madam, I had a distinct purpose in it! I wanted to draw his attention to the bell rope, and to fix it there. It may be that he is in a highly overwrought state, and has been studying too much, although I am bound to say that he seems as sound and healthy a young man, mentally and bodily, as ever I saw—but then the rats—and that suggestion of the devil." The doctor shook his head and went on. "I would have offered to go and stay the first night with him but that I felt sure it would have been a cause of offence. He may get in the night some strange fright or hallucination; and if he does I want him to pull that rope. All alone as he is it will give us warning, and we may reach him in time to be of service. I shall be sitting up pretty late to-night and shall keep my ears open. Do not be alarmed if Benchurch gets a surprise before morning."

"Oh, Doctor, what do you mean? What do you mean?"

"I mean this; that possibly—nay, more probably—we shall hear the great alarm bell from the Judge's House to-night," and the Doctor made about as effective an exit as could be thought of.

When Malcolmson arrived home he found that it was a little after his usual time, and Mrs. Dempster had gone away—the rules of Greenhow's Charity were not to be neglected. He was glad to see that the place was bright and tidy with a cheerful fire and a well-trimmed lamp. The evening was colder than might have been expected in April, and a heavy wind was blowing with such rapidly-increasing strength that there was every promise of a storm during the night. For a few minutes after his entrance the noise of the rats ceased; but so soon as they became accustomed to his presence they began again. He was glad to hear them, for he felt once more the feeling of companionship in their noise, and his mind ran back to

the strange fact that they only ceased to manifest themselves when that other—the great rat with the baleful eyes—came upon the scene. The reading-lamp only was lit and its green shade kept the ceiling and the upper part of the room in darkness, so that the cheerful light from the hearth spreading over the floor and shining on the white cloth laid over the end of the table was warm and cheery. Malcolmson sat down to his dinner with a good appetite and a buoyant spirit. After his dinner and a cigarette he sat steadily down to work, determined not to let anything disturb him, for he remembered his promise to the doctor, and made up his mind to make the best of the time at his disposal.

For an hour or so he worked all right, and then his thoughts began to wander from his books. The actual circumstances around him, the calls on his physical attention, and his nervous susceptibility were not to be denied. By this time the wind had become a gale, and the gale a storm. The old house, solid though it was, seemed to shake to its foundations, and the storm roared and raged through its many chimneys and its queer old gables, producing strange, unearthly sounds in the empty rooms and corridors. Even the great alarm bell on the roof must have felt the force of the wind, for the rope rose and fell slightly, as though the bell were moved a little from time to time, and the limber rope fell on the oak floor with a hard and hollow sound.

As Malcolmson listened to it he bethought himself of the doctor's words, "It is the rope which the hangman used for the victims of the Judge's judicial rancour," and he went over to the corner of the fireplace and took it in his hand to look at it. There seemed a sort of deadly interest in it, and as he stood there he lost himself for a moment in speculation as to who these victims were, and the grim wish of the Judge to have such a ghastly relic ever under his eyes. As he stood there the swaying of the bell on the roof still lifted the rope now and again; but presently there came a new sensation—a sort of tremor in the rope, as though something was moving along it.

Looking up instinctively Malcolmson saw the great rat coming slowly down towards him, glaring at him steadily. He dropped the rope and started back with a muttered curse, and the rat turning ran up the rope again and disappeared, and at the same instant Malcolmson became conscious that the noise of the rats, which had ceased for a while, began again.

All this set him thinking, and it occurred to him that he had not investigated the lair of the rat or looked at the pictures, as he had intended. He lit the other lamp without the shade, and, holding it up, went and stood opposite the third picture from the fireplace on the right-hand side where he had seen the rat disappear on the previous night.

At the first glance he started back so suddenly that he almost dropped the lamp, and a deadly pallor overspread his face. His knees shook, and heavy drops of sweat came on his forehead, and he trembled like an aspen. But he was young and plucky, and pulled himself together, and after the pause of a few seconds stepped forward again, raised the lamp, and examined the picture which had been dusted and washed, and now stood out clearly.

It was of a judge dressed in his robes of scarlet and ermine. His face was strong and merciless, evil, crafty, and vindictive, with a sensual mouth, hooked nose of ruddy colour, and shaped like the beak of a bird of prey. The rest of the face was of a cadaverous colour. The eyes were of peculiar brilliance and with a terribly malignant expression. As he looked at them, Malcolmson grew cold, for he saw there the very counterpart of the eyes of the great rat. The lamp almost fell from his hand, he saw the rat with its baleful eyes peering out through the hole in the corner of the picture, and noted the sudden cessation of the noise of the other rats. However, he pulled himself together, and went on with his examination of the picture.

The Judge was seated in a great high-backed carved oak chair, on the right-hand side of a great stone fireplace where, in the corner, a rope hung down from the ceiling, its end lying coiled on the floor. With a feeling of something like horror, Malcolmson recognized the scene of the room as it stood, and gazed around him in an awestruck manner as though he expected to find some strange presence behind him. Then he looked over to the corner of the fireplace—and with a loud cry he let the lamp fall from his hand.

There, in the judge's arm-chair, with the rope hanging behind, sat the rat with the Judge's baleful eyes, now intensified and with a fiendish leer. Save for the howling of the storm without there was silence.

The fallen lamp recalled Malcolmson to himself. Fortunately it was of metal, and so the oil was not spilt. However, the practical need of attending to it settled at once his nervous apprehensions. When he had turned it out, he wiped his brow and thought for a moment.

"This will not do," he said to himself. "If I go on like this I shall become a crazy fool. This must stop! I promised the doctor I would not take tea. Faith, he was pretty right! My nerves must have been getting into a queer state. Funny I did not notice it. I never felt better in my life. However, it is all right now, and I shall not be such a fool again."

Then he mixed himself a good stiff glass of brandy and water and resolutely sat down to his work.

It was nearly an hour when he looked up from his book, disturbed by the sudden stillness. Without, the wind howled and roared louder than ever, and the rain drove in sheets against the windows, beating like hail on the glass; but within there was no sound whatever save the echo of the wind as it roared in the great chimney, and now and then a hiss as a few raindrops found their way down the chimney in a lull of the storm. The fire had fallen low and had ceased to flame, though it threw out a red glow. Malcolmson listened attentively, and presently heard a thin, squeaking noise, very faint. It came from the corner of the room where the rope hung down, and he thought it was the creaking of the rope on the floor as the swaying of the bell raised and lowered it. Looking up, however, he saw in the dim light the great rat clinging to the rope and gnawing it. The rope was already nearly gnawed through—he could see the lighter colour where the strands were laid bare. As he looked the job was completed, and the severed end of the rope fell clattering on the oaken floor, whilst for an instant the great rat remained like a knob or tassel at the end of the rope, which now began to sway to and fro. Malcolmson felt for a moment another pang of terror as he thought that now the possibility of calling the outer world to his assistance was cut off, but an intense anger took its place, and seizing the book he was reading he hurled it at the rat. The blow was well aimed, but before the missile could reach him the rat dropped off and struck the floor with a soft thud. Malcolmson instantly rushed over towards him, but it darted away and disappeared in the darkness of the shadows of the room. Malcolmson felt that his work was over for the night, and determined then and there to vary the monotony of the proceedings by a hunt for the rat, and took off the green shade of the lamp so as to insure a wider spreading light. As he did so the gloom of the upper part of the room was relieved, and in the new flood of light, great by comparison with the previous darkness, the pictures on the wall stood out boldly. From where he stood, Malcolmsom saw right opposite to him the third picture on the wall from the right of the fireplace. He rubbed his eyes in surprise, and then a great fear began to come upon him.

In the centre of the picture was a great irregular patch of brown canvas, as fresh as when it was stretched on the frame. The background was as before, with chair and chimney-corner and rope, but the figure of the Judge had disappeared.

Malcolmson, almost in a chill of horror, turned slowly round, and then he began to shake and tremble like a man in a palsy. His strength seemed to have left him, and he was incapable of action or movement, hardly even of thought. He could only see and hear.

There, on the great high-backed carved oak chair sat the judge in his robes of scarlet and ermine, with his baleful eyes glaring vindictively, and a smile of triumph on the resolute, cruel mouth, as he lifted with his hands a *black cap*. Malcolmson felt as if the blood was running from his heart, as one does in moments of prolonged suspense. There was a singing in his ears. Without, he could hear the roar and howl of the tempest, and through it, swept on the storm, came the striking of midnight by the great chimes in the market place. He stood for a space of time

---

Alive with Rats

A few minutes later I saw Morris step suddenly back from a corner, which he was examining. We all followed his movements with our eyes, for undoubtedly some nervousness was growing on us, and we saw a whole mass of phosphorescence, which twinkled like stars. We all instinctively drew back. The whole place was becoming alive with rats.

—Dracula, chapter XIX,
Jonathan Harker's Journal,
1 October, 5 A.M.

Then he [Renfield] began to whisper: 'Rats, rats, rats! Hundreds, thousands, millions of them, and every one a life . . . ' He beckoned me to the window. I got up and looked out, and He raised his hands, and seemed to call out without using any words. A dark mass spread over the grass, coming on like the shape of a flame of fire; and then He moved the mist to the right and left, and I could see that there were thousands of rats with their eyes blazing red.

—Dracula, chapter XXI,
Dr. Seward's Diary,
3 October

---

that seemed to him endless still as a statue, and with wide-open, horror-struck eyes, breathless. As the clock struck, so the smile of triumph on the Judge's face intensified, and at the last stroke of midnight he placed the black cap on his head.

Slowly and deliberately the Judge rose from his chair and picked up the piece of the rope of the alarm bell which lay on the floor, drew it through his hands as if he enjoyed its touch, and then deliberately began to knot one end of it, fashioning it into a noose. This he tightened and tested with his foot, pulling hard at it till he was satisfied and then making a running noose of it, which he held in his hand. Then he began to move along the table on the opposite side to Malcolmson keeping his eyes on him until he had passed him, when with a quick movement he stood in front of the door. Malcolmson then began to feel that he was trapped, and tried to think of what he should do. There was some fascination in the Judge's eyes, which he never took off him, and he had, perforce, to look. He saw the Judge approach—still keeping between him and the door—and raise the noose and throw it towards him as if to entangle him. With a great effort he made a quick movement to one side, and saw the rope fall beside him, and heard it strike the oaken floor. Again the Judge raised the noose and tried to ensnare him, ever keeping his baleful eyes fixed on him, and each time by a mighty effort the student just managed to evade it. So this went on for many times, the Judge seeming never discouraged nor discomposed at failure, but playing as a cat does with a mouse. At last in despair, which had reached its climax, Malcolmson cast a quick glance round him. The lamp seemed to have blazed up, and there was a fairly good light in the room. At the many rat-holes and in the chinks and crannies of the wainscot he saw the rats' eyes; and this aspect, that was purely physical, gave him a gleam of comfort. He looked around and saw that the rope of the great alarm bell was laden with rats. Every inch of it was covered with them, and more and more were pouring through the small circular hole in the ceiling whence it emerged, so that with their weight the bell was beginning to sway.

Hark! It had swayed till the clapper had touched the bell. The sound was but a tiny one, but the bell was only beginning to sway, and it would increase.

At the sound the Judge, who had been keeping his eyes fixed on Malcolmson, looked up, and a scowl of diabolical anger overspread his face. His eyes fairly glowed like hot coals, and he stamped his foot with a sound that seemed to make the house shake. A dreadful peal of thunder broke overhead as he raised the rope again, whilst the rats kept running up and down the rope as though working against time. This time, instead of throwing it, he drew close to his victim, and held open the noose as he approached. As he came closer there seemed something paralysing in his very presence, and Malcolmson stood rigid as a corpse. He felt the Judge's icy fingers touch his throat as he adjusted the rope. The noose tightened—tightened. Then the Judge, taking the rigid form of the student in his arms, carried him over and placed him standing in the oak chair, and stepping up beside him, put his hand up and caught the end of the swaying rope of the alarm bell. As he raised his hand the rats fled squeaking, and disappeared through the hole in the ceiling. Taking the end of the noose which was round Malcolmson's neck he tied it to the hanging-bell rope, and then descending pulled away the chair.

When the alarm bell of the Judge's House began to sound a crowd soon assembled. Lights and torches of various kinds appeared, and soon a silent crowd was hurrying to the spot. They knocked loudly at the door, but there was no reply. Then they burst in the door, and poured into the great dining-room, the doctor at the head.

There at the end of the rope of the great alarm bell hung the body of the student, and on the face of the Judge in the picture was a malignant smile.

—Dracula's Guest, and Other Weird Stories
(London: Routledge, 1914), pp. 19–44

Stoker's Nonfiction

Stoker's body of work includes nonfiction pieces that have peripheral significance for the study of Dracula. *As a result of his American tours with the Lyceum between 1883 and 1885, he published* A Glimpse of America *(1885), and during his sojourn in America in 1887, Stoker several times delivered a lecture on Abraham Lincoln. Stoker's admiration for the United States is shown in* Dracula *through the inclusion of the young Texan adventurer, Quincey P. Morris. Among the most interesting nonfiction pieces Stoker wrote after the publication of* Dracula *are "The Censorship of Fiction," with its warnings about the dangers of portraying "sex impulses," and a section of* Famous Imposters *(1910) dealing with mesmerism, as hypnosis is an important motif in the novel.*

The following is the conclusion of Stoker's Lincoln lecture, inspired in part by Stoker's friendship with Walt Whitman. The manuscript of the lecture is located in the Special Collections of the University of Notre Dame Libraries.

Abraham Lincoln
Bram Stoker

Not long before his death, Walt Whitman said to me:

"No man knows—no one in the future can ever know Abraham Lincoln. He was much greater—so much vaster even than his surroundings.—What is not known of him is so much more than what is, that the true man can never be known on earth."

This we do know, that from the cradle to the grave, from that frontier cabin amid the wilderness where he first saw light, on to his throne in the hearts of a mighty Nation, and still to the victories of a hero and the death of a martyr, in the darkest hour of personal sorrow and National disaster, in the bold assertion of his Country's right to a high place amongst the Nations of the World, even in the wildest flush of victory when bell and bugle and cannon filled the air with clang and trill and roll of triumph from Eastern to Western sea, *no* voice was ever raised against the purity of his purpose, against his integrity, his honour or his truth.

If ever a man of the sons of men walked straight on his path in honourable, laborious worthy course, that man was Abraham Lincoln.

We look now from historic distance and can see with impartial eyes that every step which he ever took was consistent with every other which he had taken on his destined course. There was a distinct guiding purpose in his life from which his every action sprang. Every height which he won, every power which he achieved, every honour accorded to him was in distinct logical and dramatic sequence with his own efforts to a noble end.

It would be vain to try to tell of the grief of the Nation at his death. In his life he had taught nearly every lesson which it is given man to teach, of patience, of work, of purpose, of boldness, of courage, of honesty, of faith, of pity, of love; and his death was a worthy crown.

"Dulce est patria Mori," says the old Roman. After years of agony of anxiety to rest in such an honoured grave was sweet.

There was one lesson left to teach; but the cup of his glory was full and such was not for him, to go from his high place as the chief of a Nation back to his old simple life again, and, so, to teach to the ages the mighty lesson that in true democracy "the readiness is all."

Perhaps it was that his death had another lesson still and a sterner one, that he who would lift, howsoever worthily, the sceptre of Man's dominion over Man should know the many cares and perils of its sway, as it is wise in the economy of things that childhood should, now and again, stand face to face with the Mystery of the Open Grave.

–Robert J. Havlik, "Bram Stoker's
Lecture on Abraham Lincoln,"
Irish Studies Review,
10, no. 1 (2002): 27

* * *

America's Men

Dr. Seward praises Quincey Morris for his stoic acceptance of Lucy Westenra's passing.

. . . he bore himself through it like a moral Viking. If America can go on breeding men like that, she will be a power in the world indeed.

–*Dracula,* chapter XIII, Dr. Seward's Diary,
22 September

Abraham Lincoln

~~Ladies & Gentlemen~~

Since the American Civil War the condition of things, and still more of ideas, is so changed that it is hard to believe that within the recollection of us Slavery was not only an existing American institution, but that it aimed at a progressive power which, if carried into existence, would have changed the purposes and destinies of nations. With the experience of Lustres of freedom throughout the civilized world, we may well find it hard to realize that in our own time — amongst a people holding the same views which we hold in religion, in science, in literature, in art, in manners and morals — men and women, literally in millions were held in a state of bondage Comparing with which the isle of the prison and the strictest were worthiness. In these days the facts of Slavery were shameful enough — its own and its ends were dangerous in theory and in practice but its claims to indefinite extension were brought into such misery and danger to civilization that it is

Page from Stoker's lecture on Abraham Lincoln, which he delivered both in Great Britain and the United States (University of Notre Dame Libraries)

This essay was first published in the September 1908 issue of Nineteenth Century and After, *a London periodical.*

The Censorship of Fiction
Bram Stoker

There is perhaps no branch of work amongst the arts so free at the present time as that of the writing of fiction. There are no official prohibitions, no embarrassing or hampering limitations, no oppressive restraints. Subject and method of treatment are both free. A writer is under no special obligation, no preliminary guarantee; he may choose his own subject and treat it in his own way. In fact, his duty to the public—to the State—appears to be *nil*. What one might call the cosmic police do not trouble him at all. Under these conditions, hitherto possible by the self-respect of authors, a branch of the art of authorship has arisen and gone on perfecting itself in mechanical excellence, until it has become an important factor of the life of the nation. To-day if the supply of fiction were to be suddenly withdrawn the effect would be felt almost as much as the failure of the supply of breadstuffs. Happily fiction is not dependent on the existence of peace, or the flourishing of trade, or indeed on any form of national well-being. War and business worries—distress in any form—are clamorous in their own ways for intellectual antidotes; so that though the nature of the output may be of every varying kind, the supply is undiminished. Herein it is that the wide scope of the art of fiction proves its excellence; as no subject and no form of treatment is barred it follows that changing needs may find settlement in suitable opposites. And so imaginative work becomes recognised in the higher statecraft as a useful product.

But in the real world all things are finally relative. There is in reality, whose existence and progress must be based on cosmic laws, no such thing as absolute freedom. The needs and necessarily recognised rights of individuals and groups must at times become so conflicting that some sort of give-and-take rules or laws are necessary to the general good. Indeed we might put it in general form that freedom contains in its very structure the germs of restraint. The measure and method of that restraint have to be ascertained by experience, and in some measure by experiment, for if we wait till experience, following a simple course of *laissez faire,* has learned the worst that can happen, at least a part of the protective force of common sense is thrown away.

This is a philosophy too simple to be put in books, and has its existence in the brain of every sane individual. Let us apply it to the subject in question—the union or at least the recognition of two values, the excellences of imagination and of restraint. Restraint may be one of two kinds—either that which is compelled by external forces, or that which comes from within. In art the latter in its usual phase is known as "reticence." This is the highest quality of art; that which can be and is its chief and crowning glory. It is an attribute practically undefinable. Its conditions are so varying and so multitudinous, its degrees so finely graded, its workings so mysterious, its end so elusive, that it is not possible to explain it adequately by words which are themselves defective and yet of ever-varying meaning. Suffice it that it is recognisable, and recognised, by all true artists. In it consists largely, if not wholly, the ethics of art; and on it, or in it, depends that quality of art which brings it within the classification of "high" art. The measure of the ethics of the artist is expressed in the reticence shown in his work; and where such self-restraint exists there is no need for external compelling force. In fact, self-restraint is the bulwark of freedom, inasmuch as it makes other forms of restraint unnecessary. Some power must somewhere in the advance of things recognise the imperfection of humanity. When the integer of that great body recognises that imperfection and the evils consequent upon it, those evils are at their least.

This is especially so where imagination is concerned, for the bounds of such being vague, the restraint from within need only be applied to the hither or known edge of the area of demarcation; whereas if laws of restraint have to be made at all they must, in order to be of efficacy, be applicable to the whole area. This proposition may seem at first glance to be in some way a paradox; that as the object of the external power is to prevent a thing of possible good from straying into the region of evil, the mandate should be to prevent excursion beyond the outmost point of good. But it is no paradox at all. The object is not merely to prevent the straying from the region of good but to do so with the least measure of effort and at the smallest cost of friction. Whatever law, then, can be made or whatever application of force used to effect this—whether such law or force originate from within or from without—should in the first be as little drastic as possible and in the other as gentle as may prevail. Indeed, the difference between the internal and external forces thus applied is something like the difference between ethical and criminal laws. In the great world of fact, if ethical law be not observed the criminal law must come into operation, so that the balance of individual right be maintained and cosmic law vindicated.

Poster for the third of Jean Rollin's sex vampire movies (1970), one of many works that have exploited the vampire mythology widely publicized through Stoker's Dracula. *Stoker warned against drama that caters to "base appetites," in particular the harm "arising from sex impulses" (Barrie Pattison,* The Seal of Dracula *[London: Lorrimer, 1975]; Bruccoli Clark Layman Archives).*

I think this may be proved by the history of two great branches of fiction—the novel and the drama. By drama we must take drama when acted. Unacted drama is but the novel in another literary form. The novel we must accept in its old meaning as a story, quite irrespective of length or divisions. In the case of drama the necessity for an external controlling force has been illustrated throughout some three centuries, and by its history we may by a parity of reasoning gain some light upon the dangers of the other form of literary effort. Of course, primarily the controlling force comes into operation because the possibilities of trouble are multiplied by the fact that its mechanism of exploiting thoughts is by means of the human body; and inasmuch as poor humanity is likely to err in many ways, possibilities of error in this respect are superadded to the inherent possibilities of purely literary form. This is also another aspect of this control which must be mentioned before being set aside, lest it confuse issues in the case of the novel. This latter is the State aspect of censorship. It must be borne in mind that this is a State and not a political aspect. It came into existence and remains entirely for the protection of the King. The official who has to deal with the question is a State and not a political official, and has his bounds of jurisdiction regarding drama fixed *ipso facto* by the residence of the King. But in the matter of the general welfare of the public the censorship of the drama is based on the necessity of perpetually combating human weakness. This weakness is of two kinds—or rather in two forms: the weakness of the great mass of people who form audiences, and of those who are content to do base things in the way of catering for these base appetites. In fact, the quarrel rages round the standard of the higher law, made for the elevation as against the degradation of humanity; another instance of the war between God and devil. The vice of the many of the audience in this case is in the yielding to the pleasant sins or weaknesses of the flesh as against the restraining laws made for the protection of higher effort. The vice of the few who cater is avarice pure and simple. For gain of some form they are willing to break laws—call them conventions if you will, but they are none the less laws. The process of this mutual ill-doing is not usually violent. It creeps in by degrees, each one who takes a part in it going a step beyond his fellows, as though the violation of law had become an established right by its exercise. This goes on till a comparison between what was and what is shows to any eye, even an unskilled one, a startling fact of decadence. Then, as is too often observable in public matters, official guardianship of ethical values wakes up and

acts—when it is too late for any practical effect. To prevent this, censorship must be continuous and rigid. There must be no beginnings of evil, no flaws in the mason work of the dam. The force of evil, anti-ethical evil, is the more dangerous as it is a natural force. It is as natural for man to sin as to live and to take a part in the necessary strife of living. But if progress be a good and is to be aimed at in the organisation of national forces, the powers of evil, natural as well as arbitrary, must be combated all along the line. It is not sufficient to make a stand, however great, here and there; the whole frontier must be protected.

> For while the tired waves, vainly breaking,
>   Seem here no painful inch to gain,
> Far back, through creeks and inlets making,
>   Comes silent, flooding in, the main.

What use is it, then, in the great scheme of national life, to guard against evil in one form whilst in another form it is free to act? In all things of which suggestion is a part there is a possible element of evil. Even in imagination, of whose products the best known and most potent is perhaps fiction, there is a danger of corruption. For imagination is not limited to materials of a special kind; there is no assorted and approved stock of raw material for its use. The whole worlds of fact and fancy are open to it. This is its strength, and those who have imagination and believe in its power as a working factor in education—and so making for good—may well be jealous of its privileges, not the least amongst which is its freedom. Its weakness on its assailable side is that it is absolutely and entirely personal. To what Walt Whitman calls the '*en masse*' imagination does apply, does not appeal. If the '*en masse*' feels its effects it does so not as a unit but as a congeries of individuals; a wave there may be, but it is a wave of integers dominated by a common thought or purpose. This being so, the strongest controlling force of imagination is in the individual with whom it originates. No one has power to stop the workings of imagination, not even the individual whose sensoria afford its source. But the individual producer or recorder can control his own utterances; he may have to feel, but he need not of necessity speak or write. And so individual discretion is the first line of defence against such evils as may come from imagination—itself pure, a process of thought, working unintentionally with impure or dangerous material. To the drama as written this argument applies; to the play as acted it does not. The dramatist like any other person of imagination can control his output in the first instance. And like any other writer he has been, up to the present, free to print his work; his publishing it being simply subject to ordinary police control. It is on the stage and acting side that the censorship as existing comes in. Of course it must be borne in mind that if the evil is traceable to thoughts as set forth in words, the words must then come into the purview and under the knife of the censor. But up to the point of stage use the dramatist has the same freedom as any other writer of fiction.

Now as to the possible evils of imagination. Wherein or of what kinds are or may such be? We shall, I think, on considering the matter, find that they are entirely limited to evil effects produced on the senses. Here I speak only on the ethical side; there may be evils of revolt against political or social laws, but in such case the work of imagination, novel or drama, must be taken as an educational machine or medium only. Imagination does not appeal to a nation except through its units, and so must be taken as dealing with individuals only, though its effects may ultimately become of general, if not of universal import. As example, in a base play given in a crowded theatre, though many may be gratified and so debased by the exposition of lewd suggestion—either verbal or of movement or appearance—there are others who will be disgusted. It is through the corruption of individuals that the harm is done. A close analysis will show that the only emotions which in the long run harm are those arising from sex impulses, and when we have realised this we have put a finger on the actual point of danger. Practically in this country the danger from unacted plays has not up to the present existed. English people do not as a rule read plays; they prefer to see them acted. This is no doubt largely due to the fact that for a couple of centuries the plays that have been published, having already for stage purposes passed the censor, have had any passages considered objectionable or suggestive of evil deleted. As a practical matter they are as a rule but dull reading to those who look for salacious matter. Truly even the plays of the Restoration period and after, when Congreve, Wycherley, Farquhar and Mrs. Aphra Behn flourished, were written to suit a debased public taste; even these are but tame affairs compared with some of the work of our novelists. But if the growing custom continues of publishing as literary works stage plays forbidden for that purpose by the censor, the public may—will—end by reading them in the hope of finding offensive matter. They will bring to the study for evil motives an ardour denied for purposes of good.

I may perhaps here explain that I speak of "the censor" for purposes of clearness and brevity. We have a certain censorship over plays, but there is no such official as "the censor." By the Theatres Act the work of supervision of the stage is entrusted to the Lord Chamberlain, and it is a part of the duty of that functionary to issue the licence decreed by the Act as a necessary preliminary to the production of the play in a licensed theatre. For convenience—since he naturally cannot do such a mass of work himself—the Lord Chamberlain deputes a well-qualified gentleman to make the necessary examination of the plays submitted for licence. It is this gentleman to whom is applied the term "censor" by the writers of letters to newspapers and of articles in magazines who clamour against "oppression" and call aloud for absolute freedom of subject and treatment of stage productions.

Here we come to a point at which for our present purpose we may speak of "fiction" as containing both the forms of imaginative fiction, the novel and the drama. If we take it as "published" fiction we can exclude all considerations of the drama, as the word fiction will include all sorts of literary effort as applied to imaginative work, of which the drama is but an accepted form. Henceforth in this article we must take fiction to mean published fiction, irrespective of form or size. By this means the matter narrows itself down to its simplest form, and we find ourselves face to face with the question: Are we or are we not ultimately to allow fiction to be put forth without any form of restraint whatever? The question is not merely a civic or national one. It is racial, all-embracing, human. Fiction is perhaps the most powerful form of teaching available. It can be most potent for good; and if we are to allow it to work for evil we shall surely have to pay in time for the consequent evil effects. Let not anyone with a non-understanding or misapplied moral sense say or believe that fiction, being essentially based on something that is not true, should be excluded altogether from the field of morals. The highest of all teachers and moralists, Christ Himself, did not disdain it as a method or opportunity of carrying great truth. But He seemed to hold it as His chosen means of seeking to instil truth. What is a parable but a novel in little? A parable may be true in historical fact—its ethical truth may be complete, but if so the truth is accidental and not essential. When those who listened to the Master were told that "a sower went forth to sow," or that "a certain man planted a vineyard, and set an hedge about it," or "a certain man made a great supper, and bade many," or "two men went up into the Temple to pray," did they believe, or were they intended to believe, that they were being treated to a scrap of veracious history? No. The purpose of the Teacher was to win their hearts through the force of imagination. If there be any doubt about this, read the parable of Dives and Lazarus. Here the Master, who knew the workings of heart and brain, did not hesitate to give even presumably fictitious details which might enhance the force and conviction of His story—just as a novelist of to-day does. He followed the two men into the divisions of the "under world," and even heightened the scenic effect by the suggestion of a great gulf between the two. When Christ taught in such a way, are we to reprobate the method or even to forego it? Should we not rather encourage and protect so potent a form of teaching, and guard it against evil use?

The first question then is as to restraint or no restraint. That restraint in some form is necessary is shown by the history of the last few years with regard to works of fiction. The self-restraint and reticence which many writers have through centuries exercised in behalf of an art which they loved and honoured has not of late been exercised by the few who seek to make money and achieve notoriety through base means. There is no denying the fact nor the cause; both are only too painfully apparent. Within a couple of years past quite a number of novels have been published in England that would be a disgrace in any country even less civilised than our own. The class of works to which I allude are meant by both authors and publishers to bring to the winning of commercial success the forces of inherent evil in man. The word man here stands for woman as well as man; indeed, women are the worst offenders in this form of breach of moral law. As to the alleged men who follow this loathsome calling, what term of opprobrium is sufficient, what punishment could be too great? This judgment of work which claims to be artistic may seem harsh, and punishment may seem vindictive; the writer has no wish to be either harsh or vindictive—except in so far as all just judgment may seem harsh and all punishment vindictive. For look what those people have done. They found an art wholesome, they made it morbid; they found it pure, they left it sullied. Up to this time it was free—the freest thing in the land; they so treated it, they so abused the powers allowed them and their own opportunities, that continued freedom becomes dangerous, even impossible. They in their selfish greed tried to deprave where others had striven to elevate. In the language of the pulpit, they have "crucified Christ afresh." The merest glance at some of their work will justify any harshness of judgment; the roughest synopsis will horrify. It is not well to name either these books or their authors, for such would but make known what is better suppressed, and give the writers the advertisement which they crave. It may be taken that such works as are here spoken of deal not merely with natural misdoing based on human weakness, frailty, or passions of the senses, but with vices so flagitious, so opposed to even the decencies of nature in its crudest and lowest forms, that the poignancy of moral disgust is lost in horror. This article is no mere protest against academic faults or breaches of good taste. It is a deliberate indictment of a class of literature so vile that it is actually corrupting the nation.

. . . .

The sad part of the whole thing is the wantonness of it. Coarseness there has always been of some measure. Smollett, for instance, was undeniably and wantonly coarse; even Fielding's beautiful work was dyed with the colour of an age of luxury and unscrupulousness. But certain of the writers of our time claim absolute freedom of both subject and method of treatment, in order that they may deal what they call "problems." Now there is no problem which may arise to any human being in the long course between the cradle and the grave which need be forbidden to public consideration, and which may not be wholesomely dealt with. There is not a household which may not have its painful experiences of some of them, and they are solved to *some* end with boldness and decorum. But it may be feared that writers who deal with lewd subjects generally use the word "problem" either as a shelter for themselves or as a blind for some intention more base than mere honest investigation. The problem they have in reality set themselves is to find an easy and prosperous way to their desires without suffering from public ignomy, police interference, or the reproaches of conscience; with the inevitable result that they rightly incur the penalties distributable by all three. It is the same old problem which has tortured fallible humanity from the beginning, or, at any rate, since desire of many things found itself face to face with inadequate powers and insufficient opportunities for attainment.

Truth can always investigate in worthy fashion. Otherwise medicine and surgery would be obnoxious trades, and law and the administration of religion dangerous callings. As it is, those who prostitute their talents—and amongst them the fairest, imagination—must expect the treatment accorded to the class which they have deliberately joined. The rewards of such—personal luxury and perhaps a measure of wealth—may be theirs, but they must not expect the pleasures or profits of the just—love and honour, troops of friends, and the esteem of good men.

—*Nineteenth Century and After,* 47
(September 1908):
479–487

* * *

Stoker's last work of nonfiction, Famous Imposters, *was published in 1910. Stoker's interest in hypnotism is evident in* Dracula, *especially in the Count's mesmeric influence over Lucy and Van Helsing's induction of hypnotic trances in Mina.*

Mesmer
Bram Stoker

Although Frederic-Antoine Mesmer made an astonishing discovery which, having been tested and employed in therapeutics for a century, is accepted as a contribution to science, he is included in the list of impostors because, however sound his theory was, he used it in the manner or surrounded with the atmosphere of imposture. Indeed the implement which he used in his practice, and which made him famous in fashionable and idle society, was set forth as having magic properties.

. . . .

. . . He settled in the Hotel Bouret near the Place Vendôme and so in the heart of Paris; and at once undertook the treatment of patients hitherto deemed incurable. Fashion took up the new medical "craze" or "sensation," and he at once became the vogue. It was at this time of his life that Mesmer came to the parting of the ways between earnest science and charlatanism. So far as we know he still remained earnest in his scientific belief—as indeed he was till the end of his days. Inasmuch as fashion requires some concrete expression of its fancies, Mesmer soon used the picturesque side of his brain for the service of fashionable success. So he invented an appliance which soon became the talk of the town. This was the famous *baquet magique* or magic tub, a sort of covered bath, round which his patients were arranged in tiers. To the bath were attached a number of tubes, each of which was held by a patient, who could touch with the end of it any part of his or her body at will. After a

Mesmer treating a patient, with the apparatus Stoker describes as a "magic tub" in the foreground (Vincent Buranelli, The Wizard from Vienna *[New York: Coward, McCann & Geoghegan, 1975]; Richland County Public Library)*

while the patients began to get excited, and many of them went into convulsions. Amongst them walked Mesmer, clad in an imposing dress suggestive of mystery and carrying a long wand of alleged magic power; often calming those who had already reached the stage of being actually convulsed. His usual method of producing something of the same effect at private séances, was by holding the hand of the patient, touching the forehead and making "passes" with the open hand with fingers spread out, and by crossing and uncrossing his arms with great rapidity.

A well-attended séance must have been a curious and not altogether pleasant experience even to a wholesome spectator in full possession of his natural faculties. The whole surroundings of the place together with the previously cultured belief; the dusk and mystery; the "mysterious sympathy of numbers"–as Dean Farrar called it; the spasmodic snapping of the cords of tensity which took away all traces of reserve or reticence from the men and women present; the vague terror of the unknown, that mysterious apprehension which is so potent with the nerves of weak or imaginative people; and, it may be, the slipping of the dogs of conscience–all these combined to wreck the moral and mental stability of those present, most of whom it must be remembered were actually ill, or imagined themselves to be so, which came practically to the same thing. The psychical emotion was all very well in the world of pleasure; but these creatures became physically sick through nervous strain. As described by the historian, they expectorated freely a viscous fluid, and their sickness passed into convulsions more or less violent; the women naturally succumbing more readily and more quickly than the men. This absolute collapse–half epileptic, half hysterical–lasted varying periods according to the influence exercised by the presence of the calm, self-reliant operator. We of a later age, when electric force has been satisfactorily harnessed and when magnetism as a separate power is better understood, may find it hard to understand that the most advanced and daring scientists of the time–to whom Frederic-Antoine Mesmer was at least allied–were satisfied that magnetism and electricity were variants of the same mysterious force or power. It was on this theory that he seems to have worked his main idea to practical effect. The base of his system was animal magnetism, which could be superinduced or aided by mechanical appliances. . . . So far as we can gather his intentions from his acts, the main object in his scientific work was to simplify the processes of turning emotion into effect. Magnetism had already been largely studied, and means were being constantly sought for increasing its efficacy. . . . So far as we can follow after the lapse of time, Mesmer was consistent in his theories and their application. He held that the principle was one of planetary influence on the nervous system, and its manifestation was by a process of alternate intension and remission. It is possible that Mesmer–who held that the heavenly bodies floated in a limitless magnetic fluid and that he could make all substances, even such things as bread or dogs magnetic–had in his mind the wisdom of following the same theory in matters of lesser significance, though of more individual import, than those of astronomy and its correlated sciences. If so he was wise in his generation, for later electricians have found that the system of alternating currents especially at high tension, is of vast practical importance. . . .

It was distinctly to his disadvantage that Mesmer always kept at a distance the whole corps of savants such as the Faculty of Medicine and the Academy of Sciences–for they would no doubt have accepted his views, visionary though they were, if he could have shown any scientific base for them. True medical science has always been suspicious of, and cautious regarding, empiricism.

–*Famous Imposters* (New York:
Sturgis & Walton,
1910), pp. 95–100

Henry Irving and the Lyceum Theatre

In his own day, Bram Stoker was far better known as the manager of Henry Irving's Lyceum Theatre than as an author. The true nature of his relationship with Irving is debated by scholars, and it has even been suggested that Stoker's sublimated hostility toward Irving may have led him in some respects to model Dracula on the actor. The key source for examining the relationship between the two men is Stoker's Personal Reminiscences of Henry Irving *(1906). The accounts of Lyceum productions, Irving as actor, North American tours, and vignettes of contemporary celebrities during the last two decades of the nineteenth century also make this book an invaluable social history. It has been combed for possible resonances in* Dracula.

The following section includes extracts from Stoker's two-volume work, Personal Reminiscences of Henry Irving *(1906); Stoker describes an early encounter with Irving in 1876.*

A Wonderful Recitation

Thus it was that on this particular night my host's heart was from the beginning something toward me, as mine had been toward him. He had learned that I could appreciate high effort; and with the instinct of his craft liked, I suppose, to prove himself again to his new, sympathetic and understanding friend. And so after dinner he said he would like to recite for me Thomas Hood's poem *The Dream of Eugene Aram.*

A Brief Biography of Henry Irving

The Irving Society was established in 1996 to promote the understanding and appreciation of the theater in the age of the actor-manager Sir Henry Irving (1838–1905), and of his cultural and artistic contribution to the Victorian era.

Born in Somerset in 1838, the year of Victoria's Coronation, Irving's rise to prominence as an actor-manager was a slow and torturous one. Against his Methodist mother's wishes he chose a profession still much tarnished with the stigma of rogues and vagabonds. He began his acting career in 1856, appearing with various provincial Stock companies, playing during the following ten years over 600 parts. By 1866 he was established in London but it was to be another five years before he found over-night fame in *The Bells*.

For the next thirty years he was to be at the centre of Victorian Society. In 1895 he became the first actor to be knighted for his achievements, setting a standard of social respectability and professional integrity. Sadly his mother did not live to witness any of his success. Irving was also a man of letters with honorary doctorates from Cambridge, Dublin and Glasgow Universities. He became a Mason and was a close associate of leading politicians and the monarchy.

As a master of mise-en-scène he was at the forefront in the development of gaslight for his spectacular productions of Shakespearean and Romantic Melodrama at the Royal Lyceum Theatre, London, between 1871 and 1902 and was sole manager of that theatre from 1878 to 1899. During this period and until 1902 Ellen Terry was his leading lady. In 1904 the interior of Irving's theatre had to be demolished because it did not comply with new safety regulations. The new auditorium was designed by Bertie Crewe. In 1996 Apollo Leisure Group refurbished and re-opened Crewe's Lyceum.

Irving invited leading figures of the cultural world to contribute to his productions. These included the artists Telbin, Tadema and Burne-Jones, composers Mackenzie, Sullivan and Stanford, and authors Pinero, Tennyson, Albery, Sardou and Conan Doyle. He made eight major tours across North America between 1883 and 1904, setting new standards in visual presentations and ensemble playing. He regularly took his productions to the major cities in the U.K. In 1904 Irving started on a series of Farewell Tours with plans to retire in 1906, after celebrating fifty years on the stage. His sudden death on 13 October 1905 shocked and saddened the nation.

His was the age of Victorian values, which saw the exaltation of wealth in a new industrial society. It was an age that threw up a new middle class thirsting for knowledge and cultural experience. On these premises was founded a growing demand for theatre. The quality of Irving's performances and his stage management skills helped to feed and promote these attitudes. Irving became financially successful, socially popular and internationally famous. It was the essayist and critic Sir Max Beerbohm that dubbed him *The Knight from Nowhere*–the title of a little book of Pre-Raphaelite poems, a title he thought appropriate for an only son of a travelling salesman called Brodribb, who as Henry Irving had a personality that outshone his acting but never his 'Art.'

–courtesy of The Irving Society, London

That experience I shall never–can never–forget. The recitation was different, both in kind and degree, from anything I had ever heard; and in those days there were some noble experiences of moving speech.

. . . .

But such was Irving's commanding force, so great was the magnetism of his genius, so profound was the sense of his dominance that I sat spellbound. Outwardly I was as of stone; nought quick in me but receptivity and imagination. That I knew the story and was even familiar with its unalterable words was nothing. The whole thing was new, re-created by a force of passion which was like a new power. Across the footlights amid picturesque scenery and suitable dress, with one's fellows beside and all around one, though the effect of passion can convince and sway it cannot move one personally beyond a certain point. But here was incarnate power, incarnate passion, so close to one that one could meet it eye to eye, within touch of one's outstretched hand. The surroundings became non-existent; the dress ceased to be noticeable; recurring thoughts of self-existence were not at all. Here was indeed Eugene Aram as he was face to face with his Lord; his very soul aflame in the light of his abiding horror. Looking back now I can realise the perfection of art with which the mind was led and swept and swayed, hither and thither as the actor wished. How a change of tone or time denoted the personality of the "Blood-avenging Sprite"– and how the nervous, eloquent hands slowly moving, outspread fanlike, round the fixed face–set as doom, with eyes as inflexible as Fate–emphasised it till one instinctively quivered with pity. Then the awful horror on the murderer's face as the ghost in his brain seemed to take external shape before his eyes, and enforced on him that from his sin there was no refuge. After the climax of horror the Actor was able by art and habit to control himself to the narrative mood whilst he spoke the few concluding lines of the poem.

Henry Irving onstage (courtesy of Jeanne Youngson)

Let me say, not in my own vindication, but to bring new tribute to Irving's splendid power, that I was no hysterical subject. I was no green youth; no weak individual, yielding to a superior emotional force. I was as men go a strong man, strong in many ways.

. . . .

. . . he went into his room and after a couple of minutes brought me out his photograph with an inscription on it, the ink still wet:

"My dear friend Stoker. God bless you! God bless you!! Henry Irving. Dublin, December 3, 1876."

In those moments of our mutual emotion he too had found a friend and knew it. Soul had looked into soul! From that hour began a friendship as profound, as close, as lasting as can be between two men.

He has gone his road. Now he lies amongst the great dead; his battle won; the desire of his heart for the advancement of his chosen and beloved art accomplished; his ambition satisfied; his fame part of the history and the glory of the nation.

And the sight of his picture before me, with those loving words, the record of a time of deep emotion and full understanding of us both, each for the other, unmans me once again as I write.

———

I have ventured to write fully, if not diffusely, about not only my first meeting with Irving but about matters which preceded it and in some measure lead to an understanding of its results.

When a man with his full share of ambition is willing to yield it up to work with a friend whom he loves and honours, it is perhaps as well that in due season he may set out his reasons for so doing. Such is but just; and I now place it on record for the sake of Irving as well as of myself, and for the friends of us both.

For twenty-seven years I worked with Henry Irving, helping him in all honest ways in which one man may aid another—and there were no ways with Irving other than honourable.

Looking back I cannot honestly find any moment in my life when I failed him, or when I put myself forward in any way when the most scrupulous good taste could have enjoined or even suggested a larger measure of reticence.

—*Personal Reminiscences of Henry Irving,* 2 volumes
(New York: Macmillan, 1906),
volume 1, pp. 28–34

Then he collapsed half fainting.

———

There are great moments even to the great. That night Irving was inspired. Many times since then I saw and heard him—for such an effort eyes as well as ears are required—recite that poem and hold audiences, big or little, spellbound till the moment came for the thunderous outlet of their pent-up feelings; but that particular vein I never met again. Art can do much; but in all things even in art there is a summit somewhere. That night for a brief time in which the rest of the world seemed to sit still, Irving's genius floated in blazing triumph above the summit of art. There is something in the soul which lifts it above all that has its base in material things. If once only in a lifetime the soul of a man can take wings and sweep for an instant into mortal gaze, then that "once" for Irving was on that, to me, ever memorable night.

As to its effect I had no adequate words. I can only say that after a few seconds of stony silence following his collapse I burst into something like hysterics.

* * *

131

The Lyceum Productions

During Henry Irving's personal management of the Lyceum he produced over forty plays, of which eleven were Shakespeare's; *Hamlet, The Merchant of Venice, Othello, Romeo and Juliet, Much Ado About Nothing, Twelfth Night, Macbeth, Henry VIII., King Lear, Cymbeline,* and *Richard III. Coriolanus* was produced during his agreement with the Lyceum Company. He also reproduced six plays which he had before presented during his engagement by and partnership with the Batemans: *Eugene Aram, Richelieu, Louis XI., The Lyons Mail, Charles I., The Bells.* He also produced the following old plays, in most of which he had already appeared at some time: *The Lady of Lyons, The Iron Chest, The Corsican Brothers, The Belle's Stratagem, Two Roses, Olivia, The Dead Heart, Robert Macaire,* and a good many "curtain-raisers" whose excellences were old and tried.

The new plays were in some instances old stories told afresh, and in the remainder historic subjects treated in a new way or else quite new themes or translations. In the first category were *Faust, Werner, Ravenswood, Iolanthe* (one act). In the second were: *The Cup, The Amber Heart, Beckett, King Arthur, Madame Sans-Gêne, Peter the Great, The Medicine Man, Robespierre* and the following one-act plays: *Waterloo, Nance Oldfield,* and *Don Quixote. Dante* was produced after the Lyceum Company had been unable to carry out their contract with him.

This gives an average of two plays, "by and large" as the sailors say, for each year from 1878 to 1898, after which time he sold his rights to the Lyceum Theatre Company, Limited.

—*Personal Reminiscences,* volume 1, pp. 70–71

* * *

*The Lyceum Theatre on opening night (*The Graphic, *21 May 1881; Barbara Belford,* Bram Stoker: A Biography of the Author of *Dracula, 1996; Collection of Elizabeth Miller)*

Faust *was first produced by Irving in London in Decem-*
ber 1885. Stoker writes that it was performed eighty-seven times
in America.

Faust in America

When we played *Faust* in America, it was curious to note the different reception accorded to it
undoubtedly arising from traditional belief.

In Boston, where the old puritanical belief of a
real devil still holds, we took in one evening four
thousand five hundred and eighty-two dollars–
$4582–the largest dramatic house up to then known
in America. Strangely the night was that of Irving's
fiftieth birthday. For the rest the lowest receipts out
of thirteen performances was two thousand and ten
dollars. Seven were over three thousand, and three
over four thousand.

In Philadelphia, where are the descendants of
the pious Quakers who followed Penn into the wilderness, the average receipts were even greater.
Indeed at the *matinée* on Saturday, the crowd was so
vast that the doors were carried by storm. All the
seats had been sold, but in America it was usual to
sell admissions to stand at one dollar each. The
crowd of "standees," almost entirely women, began
to assemble whilst the treasurer, who in an American theatre sells the tickets, was at his dinner. His
assistant, being without definite instructions, went
on selling till the whole seven hundred left with him
were exhausted. It was vain to try to stem the rush
of these enthusiastic ladies. They carried the outer
door and the checktaker with it; and broke down by
sheer weight of numbers the great inner doors of
heavy mahogany and glass standing some eight feet
high. It was impossible for the seat-holders to get in
till a whole posse of police appeared on the scene
and cleared them all out, only re-admitting them
when the seats had been filled.

But in Chicago, which as a city neither fears
the devil nor troubles its head about him or all his
works, the receipts were not much more than half
the other places. Not so good as for the other plays
of the *répertoire* presented.

In New York the business with the play was
steady and enormous. New York was founded by
the Bible-loving righteous-living Dutch.

—Personal Reminiscences, volume 1, pp. 183–184

* * *

Mephistopheles, Faust, and Dracula

In this excerpt from her article "'For the Dead Travel Fast':
Dracula in Anglo-German Context," Diane Milburn finds par-
allels between Stoker's novel and Goethe's play.

. . . Stoker drew deeply on the themes of Goethe's
play. Both the Mephistopheles/Dracula and the
Faust/Dracula parallels need further investigation.
The vampire, like Mephistopheles, is unable to enter
a building unless invited to do so, and, like Goethe's
devil, has a certain affinity with animals: Mephistopheles transforms himself into a black poodle,
Dracula turns himself into "an immense dog" at
Whitby, for example. At the same time, there are
links with Faust himself: Faust was dissatisfied with
the limitations of conventional knowledge as he
knew it. We are told that Dracula in life was, like
Faust, an "alchemist": this was a branch of learning
which, as Van Helsing observes, "was the highest
development of the science-knowledge of his time.
He had a mighty brain, a learning beyond compare,
and a heart that knew no fear and no remorse. He
dared even to attend the Scholomance, and there
was no branch of knowledge of his time that he did
not essay" [chapter XXIII, Dr. Seward's Diary, 3
October]. Like Faust he sold his soul to the Devil, in
Dracula's case at the Scholomance above Lake Hermannstadt (now Sibiu),* where every tenth scholar
was retained by the Devil in return for the learning
he received there. The king of vampires thus was a
product of a Faustian pact.

—Dracula: The Shade and the Shadow,
edited by Elizabeth Miller
(Westcliff-on-Sea, U.K.:
Desert Island Books,
1998), pp. 43–44

---

*The Scholomance was not itself a German supersti-
tion, but was lifted by Stoker from Emily Gerard's
"Transylvanian Superstitions" (1885).

Bram Stoker, drawn by Alfred Bryan in 1885
(Shakespeare Centre Library,
Stratford-upon-Avon)

An American Reporter on Stoker

In "the twenty years covered by our tours of America" and "many hundreds" of interviews, Stoker writes that no reporter ever betrayed an off-the-record comment. His relations with reporters, however, were not without humor or mishap.

. . . more than twenty years ago we made a night journey from Chicago to Detroit. When we boarded our special train I found one strange young man with a gripsack who said he was coming with us. To this I demurred, telling him that we never took any stranger with us and explaining that, as all our company was divided into little family groups, they would not feel so comfortable with a stranger as when, as usual, they were among friends and comrades only. He said he was a reporter, and that he was going to write a story about the incidents of the night. I did not know what kind of incidents he expected! However, I was firm and would not let him come.

When we arrived in Detroit in the morning a messenger came on board with a large letter directed to me. It contained a copy of a local paper in which was marked an article on how the Irving company travelled—a long article of over a column. It described various matters, and even made mention of the appearance *en déshabille* of some members of the company. At the end was appended a note in small type to say that the paper could not vouch for the accuracy of the report as their representative had not been allowed to travel on the train. I give the whole matter from memory; but the way in which the writer dealt with myself was most amusing. It took up, perhaps, the first quarter of the article. It spoke of "an individual who *called himself* Bram Stoker." He was thus described:

" . . . who seems to occupy some anomalous position between secretary and valet. Whose manifest duties are to see that there is mustard in the sandwiches and to take the dogs out for a run; and who unites in his own person every vulgarity of the English-speaking race."

I forgave him on the spot for the whole thing on account of the last sub-sentence.

—*Personal Reminiscences,* volume 1, pp. 301–302

The Beefsteak Room, located behind a backstage stairway in the Lyceum Theatre, was the site of many dinner parties given by Irving with Stoker's assistance. Oak-paneled with a beamed ceiling, the room had walls adorned with Irving's favorite theatrical portraits.

The Beefsteak Room

The history of the Lyceum Theatre was for a quarter of a century a part of the social history of London. A mere list of Irving's hospitalities would be instructive. The range of his guests was impossible to any but an artist. As he never forgot or neglected his old friends there were generally at his table some present who represented the common-place or the unsuccessful as well as the famous or the successful sides of life. The old days and the new came together cheerily under the influence of the host's winning personality, which no amount of success had been able to spoil.

Sometimes the Beefsteak Room, which could only seat at most thirty-six people, was too small; and at such times we migrated to the stage. These occasions were interesting, sometimes even in detail. On the hundredth night of *The Merchant of Venice*, February 14, 1880, there was a supper for three hundred and fifty guests. On March 25, 1882, ninety-two guests sat down to dinner to celebrate the hundredth night of *Romeo and Juliet*.

The Prince of Wales dined there in a party of fifty on May 7, 1883. The table was a round one, and in the centre was a glorious mass of yellow flowers with sufficient green leaves to add to its beauty. This bouquet was thirty feet across, and was in the centre only nine inches in height, so that it allowed an uninterrupted view all round the table. I remember the Prince saying that he had never seen a more lovely table. On this as on other occasions there was overhead a great tent-roof covering the entire stage. Through this hung chandeliers. On three sides were great curtains of crimson plush and painted satin ordinarily used for tableaux curtains; and on the proscenium side a forest of high palms and flowers, behind which a fine quartette band played soft music.

The Beefsteak Room at the Lyceum Theatre, site of gatherings and dinner parties (English Illustrated Magazine, *September 1890; Barbara Belford,* Bram Stoker: A Biography of the Author of *Dracula, 1996; Elizabeth Miller Collection)*

Lyceum Guests

In Personal Reminiscences of Henry Irving, *Stoker provides a list of Lyceum guests that runs to more than one thousand names:* "There are but few to whom they all could be known; but many of them are known either in London or locally. Occasionally, when opportunity permitted and memory served, I jotted down—often on my copy of the* menu*—the names of some of my fellow guests; and as I usually kept these interesting souvenirs, I am able to give a somewhat suggestive list. It is, of course, only partial—incomplete; by comparison meagre; representative rather than comprehensive." *A few of these names are listed below.*

Rt. Hon. A.J. Balfour	Charles Dickens (the younger)
Ethel Barrymore	Edward Dowden
David Belasco	Sir Arthur and Lady Conan Doyle
Sarah Bernhardt	Right Hon. W.E. and Mrs. Gladstone
J.D. Beveridge	President W.R. Harper, Chicago University
W.A. Burdett-Coutts	Thomas Hardy
Sir Edward Burne-Jones	Julian Hawthorne
Sir Richard and Lady Burton	William Heinemann
Lord and Lady A. Campbell	Abbe Liszt
Dr. Charcot	James Whitcomb Riley
Lord and Lady Randolph Churchill	Sir Henry M. and Lady Stanley
S.L. Clemens ("Mark Twain")	Lord Strathcona
Rev. Henry Ward and Mrs. Beecher	Sir Arthur Sullivan
Alfred de Rothschild	Lord and Lady Tennyson

One charming night I remember in the Beefsteak Room when the Duke of Teck and Princess Mary and their three sons and Princess May Victoria, whose birthday it was, came to supper. In honour of the occasion the whole decorations of room and table were of pink and white May, with the birthday cake to suit. Before the Princess was an exquisite little set of *Shakespeare* specially bound in white vellum by Zaehnsdorf, with markers of blush-rose silk.

The ordinary hospitalities of the Beefsteak Room were simply endless. A list of the names of those who have supped with Irving there would alone fill chapters of this book. They were of all kinds and degrees. The whole social scale has been represented from the Prince to the humblest of commoners. Statesmen, travellers, explorers, ambassadors, foreign princes and potentates, poets, novelists, historians—writers of every style, shade and quality. Representatives of all the learned professions; of all the official worlds; of all the great industries. Sportsmen, landlords, agriculturists. Men and women of leisure and fashion. Scientists, thinkers, inventors, philanthropists, divines. Egotists, ranging from harmless esteemers of their own worthiness to the very ranks of Nihilism. Philosophers. Artists of all kinds. In very truth the list was endless and kaleidoscopic.

—*Personal Reminiscences,* volume 1, pp. 310–312

* * *

Stoker recalls the journalist and explorer Sir Henry Morton Stanley (1841–1904) after he had written How I Found Livingstone *(1872) and* Through the Dark Continent *(1878).*

Sir Henry Morton Stanley

Stoker first describes Stanley at a long dinner party in October 1882 at "the small private dining-room of the Garrick Club."

. . . It may of course have been that the dark face and the still eyes and that irregular white of the hair which speaks of premature stress on vitality conveyed by inference their own lesson; but most assuredly Henry Stanley had a look of the forest gloom as marked as Dante's contemporaries described of him: that of one who had traversed Heaven and Hell.

After a long time we broke up the set formation of the dinner table, and one by one in informal turn we each had a chat with the great explorer. He told us that he wanted some strong, brave, young men to go with him to Africa, and offered to accept any one whom I could recommend.

. . . .

Henry Morton Stanley in 1874 (Frank McLynn, Stanley:
The Making of an African Explorer *[Chelsea,
Mich.: Scarborough House, 1990]; Richland
County Public Library)*

*The entry on Arminius Vambery is of special interest, as
Stoker used the name "Arminius" in* Dracula *for the friend of
Abraham Van Helsing who was the source of information about
Count Dracula's background. The reference has led many scholars to
assume that Vambery was a vital source of information for Stoker as
he wrote the novel. No evidence supports this speculation, however.*

Arminius Vambery

Amongst the interesting visitors to the Lyceum and
the Beefsteak Room was Arminius Vambery, Professor at
the University of Buda-Pesth. On April 30, 1890, he came
to see the play, *The Dead Heart,* and remained to supper.
He was most interesting and Irving was delighted with
him. He had been to Central Asia, following after centuries the track of Marco Polo and was full of experiences
fascinating to hear. I asked him if when in Thibet he never
felt any fear. He answered:

"Fear of death—no; but I am afraid of torture. I protected myself against that, however!"

"However did you manage that?"

"I had always a poison pill fastened here, where the
lappet of my coat now is. This I could always reach with
my mouth in case my hands were tied. I knew they could
not torture me, and then I did not care!"

He is a wonderful linguist, writes twelve languages,
speaks freely sixteen, and knows over twenty. He told us
once that when the Empress Eugenie remarked to him
that it was odd that he who was lame should have walked
so much, he replied:

"Ah, Madam, in Central Asia we travel not on the
feet but on the tongue."

We saw him again two years later, when he was
being given a Degree at the Tercentenary of Dublin University. On the day on which the delegates from the various Universities of the world spoke, he shone out as a star.
He soared above all the speakers, making one of the finest
speeches I have ever heard. Be sure that he spoke loudly
against Russian aggression—a subject to which he had
largely devoted himself.

—*Personal Reminiscences,* volume 1, pp. 371–372

* * *

*This next observation of Stanley was drawn from a June
1890 dinner given in his honor by the publisher Edward Mas-
ton.*

. . . Stanley looked dreadfully worn, and much
older than when I had seen him last. The six years had
more than their tally of wear for him, and had multiplied themselves. He was darker of skin than ever; and
this was emphasised by the whitening of his hair. He
was then under fifty years of age, but he looked nearer
to eighty than fifty. His face had become more set and
drawn—had more of that look of slight distortion which
comes with suffering and over-long anxiety.

There were times when he looked more like a
dead man than a living one. Truly the wilderness had
revenged upon him the exposal of its mysteries.

—*Personal Reminiscences,* volume 1, pp. 367, 370

* * *

My Friend Arminius

*Professor Van Helsing refers to a man named Arminius in
telling his friends "something of the kind of enemy with which we
have to deal."*

". . . I have asked my friend Arminius, of Buda-
Pesth University, to make his record; and, from all the
means that are, he tell me of what he has been."

—*Dracula,* chapter XVIII, Mina Harker's
Journal, 30 September

---

431 Stevens st
    cor West.

Camden,
U. S. America. N. Jersey.
March 6 /76

'Bram Stoker,'
My dear 'young man,'

Your letters have been most welcome to me — welcome to me as Person, & then as Author — I don't know which most, — You did well to write to me so unconventionally, so fresh, so manly, & so affectionate too. I too hope, (though it is not Probable) that we shall one day personally meet each other. Meantime I send you my friendship & thanks.

Edward Dowden's letter containing among others your subscription for a copy of my new edition, has just been rec'd. I shall send the books very soon by express in a package to his address. I have just written to E. D.

My physique is entirely shatter'd — doubtless permanently — from paralysis & other ailments. But I am up & dress'd, & get out every day a little — live here quite lonesome, but hearty, & good spirits.

write to me again.
Walt Whitman

FACSIMILE LETTER FROM WALT WHITMAN

Letter from Walt Whitman to Stoker, long a defender of Whitman's poetry. The two men met on at least two occasions during the Lyceum's American tours (Stoker, Personal Reminiscences of Henry Irving, *1906; Thomas Cooper Library, University of South Carolina).*

Walt Whitman

In the early afternoon of Thursday, 20th March 1884, I drove with Irving to the house of Thomas Donaldson, 326 North 40th Street, Philadelphia. We went by appointment. Thomas Donaldson it was who had, at the dinner given to Irving by the Clover Club on December 6, 1883, presented him with Edwin Forrest's watch.

When we arrived Donaldson met us in the hall. Irving went into the "parlour"; Hatton, who was with us, and I talked for a minute or so with our host. When we went in Irving was looking at a fine picture by Moran of the Great Valley of the Yellowstone which hung over the fireplace. On the opposite side of the room sat an old man of leonine appearance. He was burly, with a large head and high forehead slightly bald. Great shaggy masses of grey-white hair fell over his collar. His moustache was large and thick and fell over his mouth so as to mingle with the top of the mass of the bushy flowing beard. I knew at once who it was, but just as I looked Donaldson, who had hurried on in front, said:

"Mr. Irving, I want you to know Mr. Walt Whitman." His anxiety beforehand and his jubilation in making the introduction satisfied me that the occasion of Irving's coming had been made one for the meeting with the Poet.

When he heard the name Irving strode quickly across the room with outstretched hand. "I am delighted to meet you!" he said, and the two shook hands warmly. When my turn came and Donaldson said "Bram Stoker," Walt Whitman leaned forward suddenly, and held out his hand eagerly as he said:

"Bram Stoker—Abraham Stoker is it?" I acquiesced and we shook hands as old friends—as indeed we were. "Thereby hangs a tale."

—

In 1868 when William Michael Rossetti brought out his Selected Poems of Walt Whitman it raised a regular storm in British literary circles. The bitter-minded critics of the time absolutely flew at the Poet and his work as watch-dogs do at a ragged beggar. Unfortunately there were passages in the *Leaves of Grass* which allowed of attacks, and those who did not or could not understand the broad spirit of the group of poems took samples of detail which were at least deterrent. Doubtless they thought that it was a case for ferocious attack; as from these excerpts it would seem that the book was as offensive to morals as to taste. They did not scruple to give the *ipsissima verba* of the most repugnant passages.

In my own University the book was received with homeric laughter, and more than a few of the students sent over to Trübner's for copies of the complete *Leaves of Grass*—that being the only place where they could then be had. Needless to say that amongst young men the objectionable passages were searched for and more noxious ones expected. For days we all talked of Walt Whitman and the new poetry with scorn—especially those of us who had not seen the book. One day I met a man in the Quad who had a copy, and I asked him to let me look at it. He acquiesced readily:

"Take the damned thing," he said; "I've had enough of it!"

I took the book with me into the Park and in the shade of an elm tree began to read it. Very shortly my own opinion began to form; it was diametrically opposed to that which I had been hearing. From that hour I became a lover of Walt Whitman.

—*Personal Reminiscences,* volume 2, pp. 92–94

* * *

Stephanie Moss, a specialist in Renaissance theater, is a co-editor of Disease, Diagnosis and Cure on the Early Modern Stage *(2004).*

Bram Stoker, Henry Irving and the Late-Victorian Theatre
Stephanie Moss

> We must not, however, forget that, according to some, the performance of the actor is hardly to be dignified by the name of an art, or, if it is, it is an art so paltry and unintellectual as wholly unworthy to be ranked with its sisters. The actor is usually subjected to destructive criticism in his dual capacity of artist and man. As an artist he is said to be the exponent of a form of mimicry little raised above that practised by the ape . . . as a man, he is said to be so corrupted by the inherent immorality of his calling and the vanity fostered in him by excessive adulation that he is unfitted to hold social intercourse with respectable or intellectual people.[1]

Henry Irving's disquiet about the social and artistic perception of the actor in late Victorian England was the result of his humble birth status and subsequent lifelong struggle for acceptance, a struggle in which Bram Stoker participated for almost half his life as Irving's business manager.[2] When Stoker died in 1912, he had spent twenty-seven of his sixty-four years with Irving, the actor-manager of the Lyceum Theatre who strove throughout his life to absolve actors of their tarnished image, by and large an unmediated vision that stretched back to Elizabethan vagrancy laws that punished actors unaffiliated with patronage as beggars. During his lifetime, Irving succeeded in raising the theatrical arts to a new cultural level, becoming in 1895 the first actor to be knighted and thereby at last shifting assumptions about the "strolling player" from vagabond to respected member of the British empire.

Stoker was Irving's partner in this task, not only handling the business end of the Lyceum but also working in concert with Irving to redefine the actor, the play, and the theatrical experience. As part of his contribution to this venture, Stoker published several articles about the social utility of theatre and its value as an intellectual and aesthetic exemplum. In an article about Ellen Terry, he wrote: "In art the truth is all in all," an artist seeks out truth with "intention, self-guidance, and restraint."[3] The concerted efforts on the part of the two men to rescue acting from its unsavory historical regard resulted in stunning theatre, and the Lyceum that Irving managed artistically and Stoker financially became one of the most important and well-respected social and artistic hubs in late Victorian England. As the Lyceum attracted more prominent audiences, both Stoker and Irving found themselves mingling with the upper classes, giving speeches at universities, the Royal Society, and various public openings, a fact that led Irving to comment in *Fortnightly Review* on a more democratic England:

> Those who have lent themselves to the promotion of the actor from the outskirts of social respectability, and have admitted him into the gilded saloons of the aristocracy in which he is, by some people, supposed to uneasily disport himself, have acted in obedience to the levelling spirit of an age that has broken down barriers which class distinctions or religious prejudice had set up . . . our social leaders are not likely to at present revoke the privilege accorded to him, at the bidding of those who represent him as a standing menace to a well-conducted household.[4]

The theatrical life Irving and Stoker shared manifests itself in Stoker's writing polysemously, ranging from transparent theatrical quotations of Lyceum productions to more subtle influences that inflect the subtext of *Dracula*. This article will sketch some of the obvious links between Irving, Stoker and their mutual profession along with those more shrouded and complex. I will first address the emerging trend in critical discussions of Stoker and the theatre to transform Irving's influence on Stoker into the author's pathological need to exact psychological revenge on Irving by creating Dracula in the actor's image.

When *Dracula* entered the academic canon in the 1970s, critics focused primarily on the Victorian sociosexual subtext of the novel, interpreting the vampires as an expression of the author's quintessentially Victorian sexual anxiety, an anxiety they believed seeped uncon-

sciously into the vampiric context of the novel. Virtually all of the early criticism on *Dracula* ignores Stoker's career and the impact of theatre on his oeuvre perhaps because there was little perception of the extent to which he immersed himself in that career. Theatre was (and continues to be) an all-consuming profession, demanding full-time devotion in order to create, rehearse, and perform the numerous productions that kept a repertory theatre such as Irving's Lyceum financially alive. Stoker attended six evening performances and additional matinees each week during the forty to fifty weeks per year that comprised the Lyceum season, taking care of financial operations, scheduling, and publicity. He juggled the two million pounds in ticket sales that accrued during the course of Irving's career,[5] many times ending his workday with after-hours chats with Irving that often went until dawn in the Beefsteak Room.

Although the influence of theatre on *Dracula* and Stoker's other novels and stories is ineluctable, it went unexplored until recently. Within approximately the last ten years both literary critics and biographers have discovered Stoker as a man of the theatre, exploring the nexus of performance, Shakespeare, melodrama, and acting that collected in his mind and impressed itself on his writing. In addition, Stoker's letters have become valuable to theatre historians. Russell Jackson's article in *Nineteenth Century Theatre Research* on the correspondence of G. E. Terry (Ellen Terry's brother) with Stoker during one of Irving's American tours searches Terry's letters for the minutia of quotidian theatrical life at the Lyceum. While etching Terry's dissatisfaction with the actress who occupied the Lyceum in Irving's absence, the letters also give "a recognizable picture of the frustrations of daily business in the theatre—the lavatories need repair, the taxes are due, a royal visitor arrives unannounced, a simple transaction becomes complicated. Meanwhile performances are being given and plans are being made."[6] Dealing with these every day frustrations was Stoker's job, and this included not only the menial chores mentioned above but also more laborious tasks such as counting the house each performance to make sure that the number of heads in the audience matched ticket receipts.[7]

Although recent criticism has finally acknowledged the influence of theatre and Irving on Stoker's writing, the initial impulse has been to profile the author as enthralled to the actor, a misunderstanding of Stoker's position in the Lyceum that also occurred at least once during his lifetime and that Stoker himself humorously noted. A reporter covering Irving during one of his eight American tours approached Stoker in Chicago, attempting to gain open access to Irving and the other actors in the troupe. When Stoker denied this

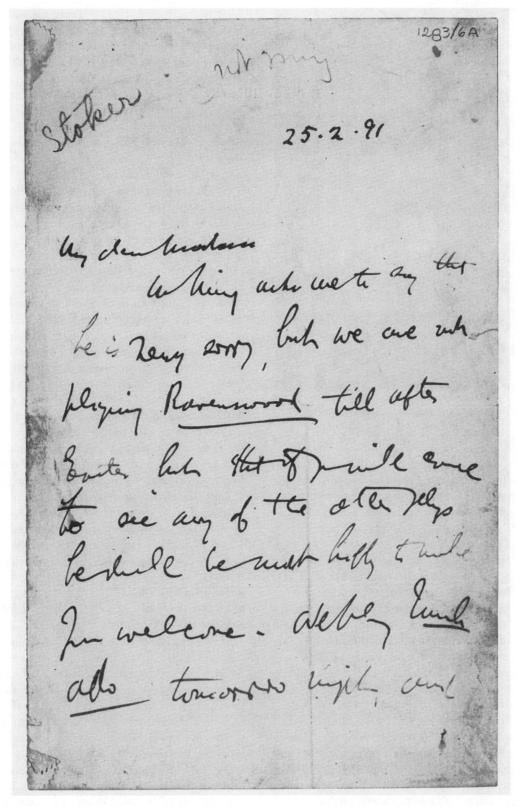

Page from a letter in which Stoker writes in his capacity as acting manager of the Lyceum Theater. His correspondent is
*unknown (*Bram Stoker's *Dracula:* A Centennial Exhibition at the Rosenbach Museum*
& Library, 1997; Elizabeth Miller Collection).

Ellen Terry, the Lyceum's leading lady, with Irving's dogs (Barbara Belford, Bram Stoker: A Biography of the Author of *Dracula, 1996; Richland County Public Library)*

request, the reporter wrote: "[Stoker] seems to occupy some anomalous position between secretary and valet, whose manifest duties are to see that there is mustard in the sandwiches and to take the dogs out for a run."[8] Condiments on sandwiches and dog exercise were part of Stoker's responsibilities, and his attention to these petty details, he knew, left the creative space of the actors undisturbed and therefore free for their craft.

The pressures of mounting productions given inadequate time, the physical demands of long days and nights of both acting and technical rehearsals, and the myriad stresses common to repertory performance at times made Irving "difficult," a term Stoker never would have used but that recurs in various ways in scholarly assessments of Irving as tyrannical actor-manager. Stoker's autobiographical paean to Irving, *Personal Reminiscences of Henry Irving,* however, clearly articulates his understanding of the actor and the temperament that often comes with the territory: "The artistic temperament is sensitive—almost super-sensitive; and the requirements of its work necessitate the form of quietude which comes from self-oblivion. . . . When in addition he has the cares of worries and responsibilities and labours and distractions of management to encounter daily and hourly, it is vitally necessary that he has

trustworthy and, to him, sufficing assistance."[9] Irving was a meticulous artist and his popularity rested not only on his innovative readings of such Shakespearean warhorses as *Macbeth, Hamlet,* and Shylock but also on his painstaking attention to production values that came to be one of his trademarks. Stoker's recognition that artists must be free to focus their energy on the act of creating impelled his loving attention to the smallest details of theatrical life as well as the devoted attention he lavished on Irving and Terry. This was his contribution to the creation of great art.

Dracula scholars, like the American reporter Stoker references in *Reminiscences,* have often misinterpreted these menial tasks and Stoker's seeming obsequiousness as evidence of Stoker's psychological enslavement to Irving. Biographer Barbara Belford, for example, over-reads Irving into *Dracula,* viewing Stoker as a kind of Renfield to Irving's Dracula; Irving "drained Stoker intellectually and emotionally" and "[a]ny understanding of Bram Stoker's life and the reason he wrote *Dracula* begins with [his] first meeting" with Irving. She continues: "Even more prophetic than the camaraderie forged that wet and chilly December evening was something Stoker would never admit: on that night he met Count Dracula. Irving as Dracula would grow into the evil paternal role, the most felicitous ever written for him."[10] This misapprehension of the personal and professional rapport between the two men results in a unilateral reading that slants Belford's biography, creating Irving as the wellspring for Stoker's vampire. Belford, however, is not alone in this misperception. Other critics make similar assumptions. In their Preface to the Norton edition of *Dracula,* editors David J. Skal and Nina Auerbach (two influential critics to whom *Dracula* scholars are greatly indebted for their research on the historical and gender contexts of the novel) conclude that "Irving was Stoker's indelible inspiration, not only for his vampire, but for the noble England Dracula threatened."[11]

It would be difficult to refute the influence Irving had on Stoker, but to demonize the relationship between the two men in light of *Dracula* creates the illusion that Stoker was somehow captive to Irving as Jonathan and Renfield are physically and psychically captive to the vampire. The understanding that Irving was a tyrant in fact disregards Stoker's own words on the subject, which portray Irving as a most generous and gifted artist who did not suffer fools easily but handled his position as actor-manager in a business-like way. As Stoker notes, "When any man was sincere with Irving, he too was always both sincere and sympathetic, even to an opposing view to his own."[12]

The tie between Irving, Stoker, the theatre, and *Dracula* therefore does not rest on the perception of

Dracula as an unconscious personal artifact of the life-long relationship between the two men. There is relevant evidence of theatre in *Dracula* that does not require a psychoanalytical lens to make visible. Alongside her overly reductive reading of the Stoker-Irving relationship, Belford correctly pinpoints many resonant images and theatricalized situations that are indeed overtly present in *Dracula,* shaping its narrative structure, dialogue, and language: "Shakespearean images motivate *Dracula's* epic action. Stoker's chapter outlines read like a theatre program."[13] She also notes Lucy's identification with Desdemona who writes the following to Mina about Quincey's proposal: "I sympathize with poor Desdemona when she had such a dangerous stream poured in her ear."[14] Other critics have noted the direct quotes (or misquotes) of Shakespeare's words such as Jonathan Harker's "'My tablets! quick, my tablets!/'Tis meet I that I put it down,' etc." (p. 41), and Seward's description of Van Helsing as a man with "an iron nerve, a temper of ice-brook, an indomitable resolution, self-command and toleration" (p. 106), a misquote this time of Othello's "I have another weapon in this chamber,/It is a sword of Spain, the ice-brook's temper."

Auerbach and Skal's annotated notes to *Dracula* point out many such references: for example, Jonathan's diary entry after a nightlong conversation with the vampire again refers to *Hamlet* (as well as to the recently translated *Arabian Nights*). Their conversation "seems horribly like the beginning of the 'Arabian Nights,' for everything has to break off at cock-crow—or like the ghost of Hamlet's father" (p. 35). Lucy Westenra's transformation to a vampire leaves Lady Macbeth-like traces, as Auerbach and Skal annotate: "Irving had staged a controversial *Macbeth* at the Lyceum in 1888. Stoker was haunted by Ellen Terry's unorthodox Lady Macbeth, as fragile, neurotic, and dreamily feminine a bloody creature as the stricken Lucy Westenra" (p. 38, n8). Auerbach and Skal also suggest that the pre-vampiric Lucy resembles the actual person of the actress who, like Lucy, "was a giggly, irresistible rose with an underlying wildness her male governors never subdued" (p. 160, n8). Many critics have mentioned the similarity between Lady Macbeth's steely resolve to pluck her nipple from the boneless gums of an imagined infant and then dash its brains out and the vampirized Lucy's treatment of a young child whom she has just clutched to her breast and then callously and demonically flung to the ground (p. 188). Stoker's reference to the three vampire brides as "weird sisters" (p. 51), well recognized by critics, once again embeds *Macbeth* in the text of *Dracula*.

Indeed, Auerbach and Skal's meticulous detailing of the theatrical references in the novel is comprehensive, and many of their annotations shift from noting direct [mis]quotations to references to more wide-ranging theatrical influences; for example, when Dracula drives the coach in the opening chapter, he repulses the encircling wolves by "sweeping his long arms," a theatrical gesture much like Irving's in his heroic roles (p. 20, n3). They also find residues of *Hamlet* (first staged at the Lyceum in 1874 and subsequently revived at the opening of the Lyceum in 1878) in Dracula's "dark clothes, his obsessive memories, and his rage against human gratification" (p. 31, n7). Theatre in fact penetrates Stoker's writing pluralistically, and the dynamic and specular relationship between performance and *Dracula* is not limited to specific quotations or theatrical gestures and costumes.

Both Irving and Stoker were enamored of technology, and if *Dracula* is a microcosm of nineteenth-century technology, Irving's Lyceum's was a microcosm of "the history of modern stage lighting." Irving's extensive use of lighting to create special effects, although already used sporadically in other theatres, encouraged managers to use lighting innovatively and thereby caused an "industry [to spring] into existence."[15] Irving was the first to darken the auditorium, eliminating the need for drop curtains to hide onstage scenery changes. Most famously, as Stoker notes, Irving's *Faust* in 1885 used electricity as a stage effect for the first time in theatre history:

> The fight between Faust and Valentine—with Mephistopheles in his supposed invisible quality interfering—was the first time when electric flashes were used in a play. This effect was arranged by Colonel Gouraud, Edison's partner, who kindly interested himself in this matter. . . . Two iron plates were screwed upon the stage at a given distance so that at the time of the fighting each of the swordsmen would have his right boot on one of the plates, which represented an end of the interrupted current. A wire was passed up the clothing of each from the shoe to the outside of the indiarubber glove, in the palm of which was a piece of steel. Thus when each held his sword a flash came whenever the swords crossed.[16]

Some of the most memorable scenes in Irving's effect-filled *Faust* have been translated almost in their entirety into descriptive passages in *Dracula*. In the opening moments of *Faust,* the stage went black except for the fireplace, and as the fire gradually died to embers, steam poured out of the grate. One theatregoer describes how the grate emitted "clouds of steam in the midst of which we bec[a]me aware of a grey mask, pale and sinister, a malevolent rictus, embodying the whole spirit of evil. Such was Irving's first appearance and from that moment he held us in his grip."[17] Like Mephistopheles emerging from the hearth, Dracula transforms into mist that grows "thicker and thicker." As he approaches Mina, the evanescent vapor first becomes a whirling "cloudy column," and then, with "the white energy of boiling water, [comes] pouring in, not through the window, but through the joinings of the door." Finally, Mina sees the red fire of vampire eyes in the fog. Like Mephistopheles emerging from the fire and steam of the fireplace, the "whirling mist in the moonlight" becomes Dracula (p. 227).

The spectacular centrepiece of Irving's *Faust* was the celebration of Walpurgis Night in scene four of the Lyceum production:

> The scene opens with Mephistopheles and Faust appearing in dim twilight over the top of a rocky peak. . . . What Stoker saw on opening night was a lurid vermilion Mephistopheles emerging from a cleft in the rocks, Faust clinging to him in fear. Lightning flashed, thunder rolled, and the air filled with inhuman sounds. A flight of witches on broomsticks crossed a yellow moon; owls flew into the stormy night. At the height of the frenzy 250 warlocks, demons, imps, and goblins pranced about and danced.[18]

Van Helsing's description of the environs of Dracula's castle creates a similar scene of spectral malevolence, reverberating with Irving's staged misty satanic ritual: "Do you know what the place is? Have you seen that awful den of hellish infamy–with the very moonlight alive with grisly shapes, and every speck of dust that whirls in the wind a devouring monster in embryo?" (p. 307).

Other instances of stage effects in Stoker's best known novel include aspects of Irving's production of *The Corsican Brothers* where the stage was blanketed by snow that was, as Stoker describes it:

> . . . all white and glistening in the winter sunrise. Snow that lay so thick that when the duelists, stripped and armed, stood face to face, they each secured a firmer foothold by kicking it away. Of many wonderful effects this snow was perhaps the strongest and most impressive of reality. The public could never imagine how it was done. It was *salt,* common coarse salt which was white in the appointed light and glistened like real snow.[19]

Like everyday mist and steam, snow in *Dracula* is vampiric. Engraved with a Holy circle drawn by Van Helsing, snow transforms into "the wheeling figures" that provide a "shadowy glimpse" of the three vampire brides. The "snow-flurries and the wreaths of mist t[ake] shape as of women with trailing garments." Snow also brings with it a silence, a "stilled air" that acts as a sounding board for preternatural aural phenomena. Mina's "long, low wail," like the howling of wolves,

seems unnaturally loud in the silence, and it wakes Van Helsing "like the sound of a clarion" (pp. 317, 316, 319). Indeed, the Transylvanian chapters of *Dracula,* like the stage in Irving's *Corsican Brothers,* are blanketed with snow. Stoker describes it sweeping in, glistening with "a light of some kind, as there ever is over snow" (p. 316). This description uses language similar to that which Stoker would later use in *Reminiscences* to describe the stage snow as "white in the appointed light and glisten[ing] like real snow." By the end of *Dracula,* snow is an elemental force, replacing the castle as a background for Gothic horror and indicating the mental traces of Lyceum productions lingering in Stoker's mind. Relocated to the setting of his vampire novel, the glinting whiteness of the *Corsican Brothers'* snow transforms purity into death and the virginal robes of the snow blanketed ground into a shroud.

Stoker deftly reconfigures into *Dracula* other aspects of theatre unconnected to Irving's Lyceum but relevant to his experiences in London's theatre district. Theatrical displays of magic had been present on the Victorian stage since the middle of the century. In 1864, the Davenport Brothers became the first successful stage mediums, and, sailing from America to England in 1865, they convinced audiences of their supernatural powers.[20] In a moment of what has been termed extreme stupidity, their agent offered one hundred pounds to any person who could duplicate their feats; it is at this point that Irving became involved in the incident. According to biographer, Austin Brereton, "This tempting bait appealed very strongly to a certain needy actor called Henry Irving" and on the afternoon of 25 February 1865, Irving appeared in the Library Hall of the Manchester Athenaeum performing a display of "preternatural philosophy" before 500 invited guests.[21] Before he produced a faithful impersonation of the Brothers' act, Irving addressed the audience:

> In introducing to your notice the remarkable phenomena which have attended the gentlemen who are not brothers–who are about to appear before you, I do not deem it necessary to offer any observations upon the extraordinary manifestations. I shall therefore at once commence a long rigmarole–for the purpose of distracting your attention, and filling your intelligent heads with perplexity. I need not tell this enlightened audience of the gigantic discoveries that have been made and are being made in the unfathomable abyss of science. . . . I need not tell this enlightened audience that the manifestations they are about to witness are produced by an occult power (the meaning of which I don't clearly understand).[22]

Although Stoker had not yet moved to London at the time of Irving's address at the Manchester Athenaeum, the actor's lampoon of the Davenports, had it not been so facetious, might have provided a model for Jonathan and Seward's incredulous response to supernatural phenomena. Irving and Stoker, however, differed in their attitudes toward the occult. Stoker was fascinated; Irving was unconvinced but pragmatically attuned to its theatrical possibilities. Stoker recorded in *Reminiscences* one late night conversation in 1891 in the Beefsteak Room:

> [T]he conversation turned towards weird subjects. [Hall] Caine told of seeing in a mirror a reflection not his own. Irving followed by telling us of his noticing an accidental effect in a mirror, which he afterwards used in the *Macbeth* ghost. . . . The evening was altogether a fascinating one; it was four o'clock when we broke up.[23]

This discussion between Stoker, Irving, and Hall Caine (the "hommy beg" to whom *Dracula* is dedicated) provides rare details about one of the customary post-performance discussions. The uncanny nature of mirrors is one of the most innovative metaphors in *Dracula*, and reflects not only this particular Beefsteak Room conversation but also some of the popular stage demonstrations of magic that were offered as entertainment in London.

An illusion called "Pepper's ghost," created by blackening the house, produced the impression that an object was present which was not. There were variant methods for fabricating this mirage. One such trick seated an audience member at an onstage table in a supposed cabaret. In the darkened theatre a spirit appeared as did a bottle and glass on the table. When the volunteer was asked to help himself to the liquid, the "performing spectator's idle gestures show[ed] that he certainly d[id] not see the glass, through which his hand passe[d] unobstructed."[24] Stoker embeds in *Dracula,* not the theatrical use of mirrors, but rather their uncanny and mythological nature, inscribing this ordinary stage illusion to create Jonathan's first encounter with the supernatural:

> Once there appeared a strange optical effect: when he [Dracula] stood between me and the flame he did not obstruct it, for I could see its ghostly figure all the same. This startled me, but as the effect was only momentary, I took it that my eyes deceived me straining through the darkness. (p. 19)

The science behind Jonathan's illusion is described by Albert A. Hopkins: a mirror is placed behind a transparent piece of glass. In between the two are shutters that can be opened and closed. An image is placed between the glass and the mirror and, when the

Irving as Mephistopheles in the Lyceum production (drawing by Sir Bernard Partridge; Victoria and Albert Museum, London)

shutter is opened and light placed on the mirror, the audience sees the interposed image. When the shutters are closed, the image vanishes. In this manner anything can be made to appear or disappear before the audience.[25] In *Dracula,* Jonathan hangs his shaving glass by the window, feels a hand on his shoulder and hears the Count's voice. However, he sees nothing reflected in the glass. In a reversal of the stage effect, Jonathan is startled, not because he sees something where there should be nothing but because he sees nothing where there should be something. Doubting the veracity of the mirror's non-reflection, Jonathan double checks, looking in the glass to see how he could be mistaken. "This time there could be no error, for the man was close to me, and I could see him over my shoulder. But there was no reflection of him in the mirror! The whole room behind me was displayed; but there was no sign of a man in it, except myself" (pp. 30–31).

Another instance of Stoker's absorption of stage performances in the theatre district occurs when he incorporates the Indian fakir as one of Van Helsing's examples of unexplainable phenomena:

> Can you tell me how the Indian fakir can make himself to die and have been buried, and his grave sealed and corn sowed on it, and the corn reaped and be cut and sown and reaped and cut again, and then the men come and take away the unbroken seal, and that there lie the Indian fakir, not dead, but that rise up and walk amongst them as before? (p. 172)

Indian fakirs had amazed London audiences since 1830, when the magician, Sheshal, demonstrated levitation by rising cross-legged into the air. In 1873, the "Fakir of Oolu" drew capacity crowds with his demonstration at the Egyptian Hall in London. Wearing a jeweled turban and a "shimmering" Indian robe, the magician verified the wonders of human magnetism by hypnotizing an assistant and suspending her horizontally in the air.[26] Indeed, the "wonder workers" of India were the originators of many stage illusions, and the magicians and illusionists of Europe and America were indebted to the Yogi and Mahatmas of India for many of their best tricks. The "Black Art," an act made famous by nineteenth century magicians Harry Keller and Alexander Hermann (who bore a remarkable resemblance to "His Satanic Majesty"), was filled with objects that materialized and faded away.[27] The impact of theatre on Stoker's psyche therefore extended beyond Irving's sway to the wider environs of Stoker's workday world. In an age captivated by spiritualism, theosophy, and the impact of Darwin on Christian theology, it is hardly surprising that theatre appropriated the performative elements of this fad and that both the philosophical and theatrical expression of theosophical phenomena found their way into Stoker's novel.

Perhaps one of the most interesting and least discussed particulars of Stoker's relationship with Irving, however, involves their conversations about the art of acting, particularly as acting connects to emerging notions of the mind articulated by the young Freud and by Jean-Martin Charcot, whom Stoker references in *Dracula* (p. 171). In some sense, the perception of the actor as a low-born "aper" rather than artist was abetted by a debate concerning the expression of passion in public that stretched back to Ancient Greek rhetoric and Plato's belief that artists should be banished from his ideal *Republic*. In juxtaposition to this perception of the expression of passion as social menace, a belief embraced by Puritans who succeeded in closing the theatres during the Commonwealth and whose voices were still strong in Stoker's time, Irving and Stoker expounded on acting as "scientific" art. Irving's theories focused inward on an analysis of the actor's mental mechanisms, which he later dubbed "dual conscious-

ness." The articulation of Irving's theories was impelled by a public discussion between the actor and rival French actor Constant Coquelin that addressed the exact nature of an actor's interiority while performing.

The foundation of the discussion lay in a psychological theory of acting initiated in the eighteenth century by Denis Diderot's *Le Paradoxe sur le comédien*. Diderot (1713–1784) who at first questioned the Cartesian duality of mind and body, posing the important question: "If the actor's mind and body constitute a single entity, then how can his mind coldly direct his body through sequences of passion without mentally experiencing the same emotions?" Diderot's answer to his own question strategically edged away from the mind-body monism posited in *Le Paradoxe*, and instead concluded the opposite: a great actor had a "freakish capacity to detach himself from his bodily machine, to divide himself into two personalities in performance, and so to direct the outward motions of his passions by an inward mental force, itself unmoved, undistorted by the physiological effect it oversees."[28] Diderot condemned the actor who experienced emotions while acting: "Extreme sensibility makes middling actors; middling sensibility makes the ruck of bad actors; in complete absence of sensibility is the possibility of a sublime actor."[29]

In 1887, the following defense of Diderot's *Paradoxe* appeared in *Harper's Magazine*:

> [I]n the actor the first self should be the master of the second; that the part of us which *sees* should rule as absolutely as possible the part of us which *executes* . . . [The actor] should be able to *see* what he is doing, to judge of his effects, and to control himself—in short, he should never feel the shadow of the sentiments to which he is giving expression at the very instant that he is representing them with the utmost power and truth.[30]

In other words, when acting a role, the soul of the actor must oversee the body, keeping the emotions in check. Irving's methodology was quite different, as Stoker cites in *Reminiscences*: "*If you cannot pass a character through your own mind it can never be sincere.*" Irving elaborates:

> Has not the actor who can . . . make his Feelings a part of his art an advantage over the actor who never feels, but makes his observations solely from the feelings of others? *It is necessary to this art that the mind should have, as it were, a double consciousness in which all the emotions proper to the occasion may have full swing, while the actor is all the time on the alert for every detail of his method.*[31]

Stoker was caught by the phrase "double consciousness" and its "endless possibilities" remained in his mind and are expressed in *Dracula*, particularly in his portrayal of Lucy as both a virgin and a whore.

Knowing, however, that Irving would have deprecated the psychological implications of his own theory, Stoker refrained from asking him to expound on it: "Men untrained to Mental Science and unfamiliar with its terminology are apt to place too much importance on abstract wide-embracing terms, and to find the natural flow of their true thought interrupted by disconcerting fears."[32] Unlike Irving, Stoker was not insecure in the dense intellectual realm of the subconscious and Charcot's neurological work, as stated earlier, is embedded in Van Helsing's defense of unexplained phenomena.[33]

Charcot's work was built on the work of Anton Mesmer and his immediate follower Armand Marie Jaques de Chastenet, Marquis de Puységur, who exposed the existence of a submerged and mysterious stratum within the mind. In 1784 during a session of "magnetic sleep," or hypnosis, Puységur discovered the subterranean layers of a patient's hidden neurosis. When the patient awoke, Puységur realized that what he had learned had occurred "without [the patient] having the slightest memory that he had given me this knowledge."[34] Puységur believed that he had discovered a sleep/waking consciousness that only emerged during somnambulism and only when an empathetic rapport between the doctor and patient had been established. Hypnosis, somnambulism, and dual consciousness centrally inform the narrative of *Dracula*. Lucy, like her father before her, had been a sleepwalker since childhood. Her somnambulism, reawakened by Dracula, marks the most recent research into the phenomena of the subconscious and her Lady Macbeth-like transformation indicates Stoker's awareness of a submerged stratum within her mind that Seward intuits in his diagnosis of her illness:

> [A]s there must be a cause somewhere, I have come to the conclusion that it must be something mental. She complains of difficulty in breathing satisfactorily at times, and of heavy lethargic sleep, with dreams that frighten her, but regarding which she can remember nothing. (p. 105)

In *The Bells,* first produced by Irving in November of 1871, Irving demonstrated the stratified mind, and the character of Mathias was a harbinger of what Irving would later dub double-consciousness. The role of Mathias established Irving's reputation as an actor, and while his rival Coquelin played the role as a criminal, Irving portrayed him as a man haunted by a guilty conscience. As Irving's contemporary and biographer, Austin Brereton, describes Mathias, the character lives "in two worlds, between which there [was] no link—an outer world which [was] ever smiling, an inner world which [was] purgatory."[35] Gordon Craig, Ellen Terry's

son (who would become one of the best-known stage designers of the twentieth century), describes one moment in *The Bells* that echoes Charcot's conversion reaction—the transformation of mental conflicts into muscular paralysis, distinguished by the assumption of a fixed posture due to contractions of the muscle, wide staring eyes, and the retention of whatever attitude may be given to the arms or legs:[36]

> It was . . . mesmeric in the highest degree . . . at the pace of the slowest and most terrified snail, the two hands still motionless and dead, were seen coming up the side of the leg . . . the whole torso of the man, also seemingly frozen, was gradually, and by an almost imperceptible movement, seen to be drawing up and back.[37]

The Bells was often revived and its expression of human interiority is not unlike the discourse that articulates the two Lucy Westenras. As Dracula approaches the shores of England, Lucy exhibits disassociative personality traits that Irving made visible in Mathias: "[T]here is an odd concentration about her which I do not understand; even in her sleep she seems to be watching me. She tries the door, and finding it locked, goes about the room searching for the key" (p. 73).

In addition to Stoker's exposure to this discourse through reading, acting theory, and *The Bells,* the theatre district in London was rife with hypnotic demonstrations as entertainment. These took place in auditoria such as London's St. James Hall and the Royal Aquarium where local actors were recruited and trained for the demonstration.[38] Medical researcher and reporter for *The Nineteenth Century* Ernest Hart describes one such performance where the hypnotized subject takes on bestial characteristics:

> She scratched, she mewed to perfection, she washed imaginary whiskers, she spat, she licked her hands, she lapped milk from a saucer; and when you "pressed the button" at her back she sat up rigid as on hind quarters and caressed her face with her paws with a truly feline grace.[39]

The behavior of this hypnotized subject, recorded in *The Nineteenth Century,* a periodical Stoker read regularly and often wrote for, suggests the animalistic behavior of the vampirized Lucy who "drew back with an angry snarl, such as a cat gives when taken unawares" (p. 188).

Many of the most striking aspects of *Dracula,* therefore, rest on topoi and metaphors inherent in Stoker's daily theatrical experience—the novel's expression of emerging psychoanalysis, for example, especially etched in the character of Lucy, or Van

Lyceum financial statement for Faust, *signed by Stoker as acting manager (Leslie Shepard Collection)*

Helsing's focus on hypnosis in his interrogation of consensual "reality," the demonic as another form of the everyday as in Dracula's ability to appear as mist or steam, and Transylvania as a metaphysical winter. The rich and abundant reconfigurations of Lyceum productions and events in and around the theatre district thus permeate Stoker's literary work. In this brief overview, I have suggested the intertextual nature of Stoker's career and his writing and the ubiquity of both the obvious and subtle influences of theatre in *Dracula*. This blend of theatre history and biographical data, at the moment, remains largely unharvested by scholars despite the importance of the information to Stoker's texts. To date, little has been published but that which delimits the influence of theatre and Irving to reading *Dracula* as a personal revenge novel or as a record of bits and pieces of Shakespearean dialogue that owe their origin to Irving's productions. A panoply of literary representational strategies (some of them discussed in brief by Belford, Auerbach and Skal but unmentioned here) are left to future excavation. The circularity of emphases, structures, causes, and effects thus make Stoker's lifelong career with Irving ripe for further, more complex investigation.

1. H.B. Irving, "The Art and Status of the Actor," in *Occasional Papers: Dramatic and Historical* (London: Bickers and Son, 1906), p. 72.

2. From 1878 to 1898, Irving headed the Lyceum as actor-manager, but in 1898 Irving sold his interest in the theatre to a syndicated company. The Lyceum began to lose money while the syndicate profited. Finally the new owners chose to convert the Lyceum into a music hall, and Irving became an actor without a theatre. Stoker and Irving remained friends, but Stoker saw less of Irving during the last seven years of the actor's life, which ended in 1905.

3. Bram Stoker, "The Art of Ellen Terry," *Cosmopolitan*, 31 (1901): 241, 242.

4. H.B. Irving, "Art," pp. 68–69. For a complete list of Stoker's theatre journalism and interviews, see William Hughes, *Bram Stoker: A Bibliography,* Victorian Fiction Guide 25 (1997).

5. Bram Stoker, "Dead-Heads," *Fortnightly Review*, 86 (1909): 649, 651.

6. Russell Jackson, "The Lyceum in Irving's Absence: G.E. Terry's Letters to Bram Stoker," *Nineteenth Century Theatre Research*, 6 (1978): 32.

7. Stoker, "Dead-Heads," p. 648.

8. Bram Stoker, *Personal Reminiscences of Henry Irving,* 2 vols. (London: Heinemann, 1906), vol. 1, p. 302.

9. Stoker, *Reminiscences*, vol. 1, pp. 148, 149.

10. Barbara Belford, *Bram Stoker: A Biography of the Author of Dracula* (New York: Knopf, 1996), pp. 99, 4, 5.

11. Nina Auerbach and David J. Skal, Preface to *Dracula* by Bram Stoker (New York: Norton, 1997), p. x. In *Ellen Terry, Player in her Time* (New York: Norton, 1987), Auerbach explores the relationship between Irving and Terry, correctly extending Irving's control over the Lyceum to control over Terry. Irving often marginalized the actress in her acting roles, ensuring that his onstage presence would overshadow hers. I'm not sure, however, that the nature of male-female relationships in the Victorian era that reinforced Irving's control over his leading lady can be applied to Stoker and Irving's business and personal relationship.

12. Stoker, *Reminiscences,* vol. 1, p. 146.

13. Belford, *Stoker,* p. 258.

14. Bram Stoker, *Dracula* (1897), eds. Nina Auerbach and David J. Skal (New York: Norton, 1997), p. 59. Cited hereafter in the text in parentheses.

15. Bram Stoker, "Irving and Stage Lighting," *Nineteenth Century,* 69 (1911): 903, 906.

16. Stoker, *Reminiscences,* vol. 1, p. 178.

17. H.A. Saintsbury and Cecil Palmer, eds., *We Saw Him Act: A Symposium on the Art of Sir Henry Irving* (New York: Benjamin Blom, 1939), p. 260. Stoker notes that *Faust* used "[s]team and mist" as "elements of the weird and supernatural effects of an eerie play" (*Reminiscences,* vol. 1, p. 177).

18. Belford, *Stoker,* p. 180.

19. Stoker, *Reminiscences,* vol. 1, pp. 160–161.

20. Milbourne and Maurine Christopher, *Illustrated History of Magic* (1973; Portsmouth: Heinemann, 1996), pp. 202–203.

21. Austin Brereton, *The Life of Henry Irving,* 2 vols. (London: Longmans, 1908), vol. 1, pp. 63–64.

22. Brereton, *Irving,* vol. 1, p. 65.

23. Stoker, *Reminiscences,* vol. 2, p. 122.

24. Albert A. Hopkins, ed., *Magic: Stage Illusions and Scientific Diversions, Including Trick Photography* (New York: Munn, 1898), p. 57.

25. Hopkins, *Magic,* p. 86.

26. Christopher, *History of Magic,* pp. 143, 159.

27. Hopkins, *Magic,* pp. 64, 22; Christopher, *History of Magic,* p. 217.

28. Joseph R. Roach, *The Player's Passions: Studies in the Science of Acting* (1985; Ann Arbor: University of Michigan Press, 1993), pp. 147, 148.

29. Qtd. in Stoker, *Reminiscences,* vol. 2, p. 18.

30. C[onstant] Coquelin, "Actors and Acting," *Harper's Magazine,* 74 (1886–1887): 903–904; emphasis his.

31. Stoker, *Reminiscences,* vol. 2, pp. 1, 20 (emphasis Stoker's).

32. Stoker, *Reminiscences,* vol. 2, p. 2.

33. Van Helsing asks Seward if he believes in hypnotism: "Yes," [Seward] said. "Charcot has proved that pretty well" (*Dracula,* p. 171).

34. Armand Marie Jacques de Chastenet, Marquis de Puységur, *Mémoires pour servir à l'histoire et l'établissement du magnétisme animal* (Paris: Denur, 1784), p. 36.

35. Brereton, *Irving,* vol. 1, p. 117.

36. Jean-Martin Charcot, "Magnetism and Hypnotism," *Forum,* 8 (1890): 572–573.

37. Qtd. in George Taylor, *Players and Performances in the Victorian Theatre* (Manchester: Manchester University Press, 1989), p. 155.

38. See Ernest Hart, "The Eternal Gullible," *Century Illustrated Month Magazine,* 48 (1894): 834, and Walter E. Houghton, *Wellesley Index to Victorian Periodicals: 1824–1900,* 5 vols. (Toronto: University of Toronto Press, 1966–1989), vol. 2, p. 941.

39. Ernest Hart, "The Revival of Witchcraft," *Nineteenth Century,* 33 (1883): 361.

* * *

Dracula and Shakespeare: The Count Meets the Bard
Elizabeth Miller

'Tis now the very witching time of night,
When churchyards yawn and hell itself breathes out
Contagion to the world. Now could I drink hot blood
And do such bitter business as the day
Would quake to look on. (*Hamlet,* III, ii)

It is hardly surprising that the text of *Dracula* reverberates with Shakespeare's influence. Bram Stoker's life-long association with the Bard can be traced to his days at Trinity College, where the renowned Shakespearean scholar, Edward Dowden, was one of his teachers. For many years, Stoker was involved with the production of Shakespeare's plays at the Lyceum Theatre; his intimate knowledge of Shakespeare's works may be credited to his association with Henry Irving, one of the most famous Shakespearean actors of the late nineteenth century. In *Personal Reminiscences of Henry Irving* Stoker records that forty plays were produced during Irving's management of the Lyceum. Eleven of them were by Shakespeare: *Hamlet, Macbeth, Othello, The Merchant of Venice, Romeo and Juliet, Much Ado about Nothing, Twelfth Night, King Lear, Henry VIII, Richard III,* and *Cymbeline.* With the exception of a brief allusion to *Julius Caesar,* all the references to Shakespeare in *Dracula* come from these plays.

Before examining specific Shakespearean resonances, note the cyclical tragic patterns in *Dracula* which are familiar to students of Shakespearean tragedy: the admission of villainy into a briefly glimpsed prelapsarian world, the tragic consequences of evil, and its eventual expulsion with the restoration of order. This pattern informs the tripartite structure of *Dracula,* which "first invites or admits a monster, then entertains or is entertained by monstrosity until in its closing pages it expels or repudiates the monster."[1] Like a Shakespearean tragedy, *Dracula* evokes a cathartic experience of suffering and an acute awareness of evil, but provides a sense of closure that restores our faith in the dignity of the human being and the power of civilization over bestiality.

The play most frequently cited in *Dracula* is *Hamlet.* Several days after their first meeting, Irving was honored at a "University Night" which included his appearance as the Prince of Denmark:

> In the philosophic passage "To be or not to be," and the advice to the players, there was a quiet, self-possessed dignity of thought. In the scene with Ophelia he acted as though inspired and in the play scene he stirred the house to such a state of feeling that there was a roar of applause.[2]

During Stoker's first year at the Lyceum Theatre, *Hamlet* was performed at least ninety-eight times. The play must have impressed him for he made numerous references to it in *Reminiscences*. Writing of an occasion in February 1887 when Irving performed a one-man version of *Hamlet*, he noted that "I have never had so illuminative an experience of the play. It was never to be forgotten."[3] In 1890 Irving addressed the Literary and Scientific Institute at Wolverhampton about *Hamlet*, just a month before Stoker scribbled his first notes on *Dracula*.

There are two direct references to *Hamlet* early in the novel, both focusing on the uncertain nature of reality and the act of writing itself. The first occurs after Harker has spent a long night with Dracula discussing Transylvanian history and the Count's ancestry. Although Harker is not yet aware that Dracula is a vampire, he has realized that he is a prisoner in the Castle. As morning approaches, Dracula ends his memoirs and Harker breaks off his diary "like the ghost of Hamlet's father."[4] This allusion to the supernatural helps set up the central tension of the novel: the tenuous boundaries between the rational world of science and the intuitive realm of the supernatural. Harker is not cut from the same intellectual cloth as Hamlet, but he faces the same task: the necessity of accepting the validity of the supernatural as a prerequisite for dealing with it. Following his escape and his return to England, Harker questions the reality of his experiences in Transylvania. Just as Hamlet accepted the appearance of his father's ghost, Harker gradually accepts that Dracula is a supernatural being. Of course, this can be extended to include readers of *Dracula*, who must be willing to accept the "reality" of Stoker's tale. The author reinforces this point in his preface to the Icelandic edition of the novel (1901) where he evokes Hamlet's oft-quoted statement to Horatio that: "there are more things in heaven and earth /than are dreamt of in your philosophy."[5]

The text of *Dracula* connects with that of *Hamlet* in a significant way as Harker quotes directly from *Hamlet*. Harker has undergone an unsettling experience: "But my very feelings changed to repulsion and terror when I saw the whole man [Dracula] slowly emerge from the window and begin to crawl down the castle wall over that dreadful abyss, face down, with his cloak spreading out around him like great wings" (p. 39). This is followed by an encounter with the three vampire women in Dracula's castle. Recalling the event, Harker questions his sanity and exclaims: "Up to now I never quite knew what Shakespeare meant when he made Hamlet say: 'My tablets! quick, my tablets! / 'Tis meet that I put it down'" (p. 41). Any student of Shakespeare will spot the mis-quotation. What Hamlet actually says is "My tables—meet it is I set it down / That one may smile, and smile, and be a villain" (I, v, 108–109). Whether this error is due to Stoker's carelessness, for there are a few careless errors in the text, or whether it was intended as an indication of Harker's agitated state of mind, is a matter of conjecture. It is quite likely that Stoker was merely reproducing what he had heard many times at the theatre, the "mangled Lyceum version" of Shakespeare's text that George Bernard Shaw deemed 'Bardicide'.[6] Like Hamlet, Harker turns to his journal for comfort and security, using the act of writing as a means of coping with the encroaching insanity of the world around him.

Hamlet's exclamation "'Tis meet that I put it down" expresses the sentiments of many of the narrators of *Dracula*, who record their thoughts, feelings and actions in order to deal with anxiety. After his harrowing experiences at Castle Dracula, Harker suffers what Sister Agatha calls "brain fever" and halts his journal entries. After reading them later, when Jonathan is safely back in England, Mina expresses doubt about their validity. But she finds a way to deal with her doubts: "I shall get my typewriter this very hour and begin transcribing" (p. 161). It is significant that Harker's journal survives the madness of Castle Dracula, to resurface in the rational environs of England as an important weapon in the fight against the Count. After Jonathan becomes convinced of the reality of his experiences and regains his composure, he returns to the act of writing. Thus, when Dracula's attack on Mina drives him to the brink of madness he exclaims, "As I must do something or go mad, I write this diary" (p. 252).

Other narrators also draw attention to the narrative processes. Mina, anxiously awaiting word from Jonathan, states that "it soothes me to express myself here; it is like whispering to one's self and listening at the same time" (p. 72). Dr. John Seward, who keeps his records on phonograph, uses writing for therapeutic as well as professional purposes. After Lucy rejects his offer of marriage, he records, "Cannot eat, cannot rest, so diary instead" (p. 61). Later, he discovers that his diary can do what drugs cannot. The Captain of the *Demeter* begins his Log because "things so strange [are] happening, that I shall keep accurate note henceforth till we land" (p. 81). And, near the end of the novel when Mina has come under Dracula's spell to such an extent that she cannot function as a recorder of events, Van Helsing urgently takes up the challenge "so each day of us may not go unrecorded" (p. 314). The writing and compiling of manuscripts becomes the means of self-preservation, as the collective effort of narration makes the defeat of Dracula possible.

Mina's scar is another resonance of *Hamlet*. It not only designates her as the monster's victim, but can be seen in the tradition of the mark of Cain. Her reference to it as a "mark of shame" on her "polluted flesh" (*Dracula*, p. 259) has the connotation of sexual defilement. This links it to Hamlet's declaration about Gertrude's pollution at the hands of the monstrous Claudius: "Such an act/takes off the rose/From the fair forehead of an innocent love,/And sets a blister there, makes marriage vows/As false as dicers' oaths" (III, iv, 40–45).

Madness is an important motif in both *Hamlet* and *Dracula*. The most obvious representation is found in the character of Renfield. Referring to his lunatic patient, Seward quotes Polonius as he says, "There is a method in his madness" (p. 69); and in a second allusion to *Hamlet* which resembles a comment Hamlet makes to his distracted mother, he claims that his treatment of Renfield forces him to be "cruel only to be kind" (p. 237). Renfield also illustrates how blurred the distinction between madness and sanity can be. The paradox of this "sane man fighting for his soul" is recognized by both Seward and Van Helsing. Seward's comment about "How well the man reasoned" (p. 71) expresses his ambivalence about Renfield's condition, also exemplified by the doctor's statements that "Renfield had become, to all intents, as sane as he ever was" (p. 169) and has "an unusual understanding of himself" (p. 215). Van Helsing is also impressed by this "lunatic who talk philosophy, and who reason so sound," and is forced to concede that "Perhaps I may gain more knowledge out of the folly of this madman than I shall from the teaching of the most wise" (p. 225).

According to Barbara Belford, Ellen Terry, who played the role of Ophelia, visited an asylum in order to observe a young mad woman.[7] An Ophelia-like character in *Dracula* exists in the person of Lucy Westenra who, in a letter to Mina, expresses concern about her fear of sleep with its unknown horrors: "Well, here I am to-night, hoping for sleep, and lying like Ophelia in the play, with 'virgin crants and maiden strewments'" (p. 122). Just as Ophelia was driven to madness over Hamlet's rejection of her love, Lucy is infected by the madness of Dracula's world. Thus, we have Lucy, lying in her bed decked with garlic and uncertain of her

survival through the night comparing herself ironically to the tragic Ophelia. The difference is that Lucy is still alive (at least for a while) while Ophelia at this point was being prepared for burial. Yet Lucy, like Ophelia, is powerless to prevent the tragedy that befalls her, as she slides inexorably towards death.

The concept of madness is also reinforced through references to *King Lear,* which ran for seventy-six nights during the season of 1892–1893 while Stoker was writing *Dracula*. The most significant is by Jonathan Harker who, fearing for his sanity as he confronts the horrors of Castle Dracula, steels himself by writing "out of that way lies madness indeed" (p. 41). This is a resonance of Lear's exclamation on the heath "O, that way madness lies; let me shun that!" (III, iv, 21). Harker's experience with the three vampire women led him to question whether he "be not mad already" (p. 41). Renfield's reference to "Rats and mice and such small deer" is taken almost verbatim from *King Lear,* where Edgar, disguised as the mad "poor Tom," strives to reaffirm a world of sanity. Van Helsing's declaration that "All men are mad in some way or the other" (p. 111) questions the distinction between madness and sanity, the thematic core of both *Hamlet* and *King Lear.*

The novel abounds in madness. Not only does one of the narrators operate a lunatic asylum, but much of the action of the novel occurs in or around this institution (including Dracula's attacks on Mina, while the "sane" men are off hunting or even sleeping). Almost every participant in the action questions his own as well as that of others. The Captain of the *Demeter* declares his mate "stark, raving mad" and "a raging madman, with his eyes rolling" (p. 83) and believes that he caused the deaths of other crew members. John Seward, pondering Van Helsing's theory that Lucy is the victim of a vampire, wonders "if his [Van Helsing's] mind can have become in any way unhinged" (p. 181). At one point Seward questions his own sanity, wondering whether his "long habit of life amongst the insane is beginning to tell upon my own brain" (p. 124). And we must not forget that Van Helsing's wife is deranged, "alive by Church's law, though no wits" (p. 158).

"Of all the plays of which Irving talked to me," wrote Stoker in *Reminiscences,* "I think *Macbeth* interested me most. . . . Its diction is so lordly, so poetical, so searching in its introspective power that it lifts the mind to an altitude which requires and expects some corresponding elevation of the senses."[8] It appears that Stoker and Irving spent considerable time discussing nuances of the play before its first production at the Lyceum in 1888, two years before Stoker began working on *Dracula*. Clive Leatherdale has noted several similarities between the two works,[9] including the presence of supernatural evil and the factor of human complicity.

Another noticeable parallel is the appearance of a trio of evil women who seduce a central male figure. The three witches of *Macbeth* are reincarnated as the three vampire women at Dracula's castle. Jonathan Harker's allusion to them as "those weird sisters" echoes several similar references in Shakespeare's play.

Two other points are worth noting. In *Ellen Terry: Player in her Time* (1987), Nina Auerbach sees Lucy as the sweet, almost likeable Lady Macbeth portrayed by Terry: "Lucy, a sleepwalker like Lady Macbeth might be Bram Stoker's tribute to his adored Ellen Terry's most audacious performance."[10] A resonance from *Macbeth* can be detected when Dracula himself, commenting on the passing of time, laments like the Scottish king, "The warlike days are over [it is] as a tale that is told" (p. 35).

A brief allusion to *Othello* occurs in one of Lucy's letters to Mina where she comments about one of her suitors, Quincey Morris, an adventurous American from Texas: "I sympathize with poor Desdemona when she had such a dangerous stream poured in her ear, even by a black man" (p. 59). While the allusion draws a parallel between Morris's and Othello's tales of adventure (which won Desdemona's heart but not Lucy's), it can be seen as an image of tainted blood. Othello was accused of using sorcery to win Desdemona's heart—foreshadowing Dracula's "poisonous" bites of sleeping victims (which, incidentally, echo Claudius's poisoning of the sleeping King Hamlet). And Lucy, like Desdemona, must be destroyed "lest she betray more men," for as the "bloofer lady" she abandons the female virtues of sexual passivity and nurturing motherhood.

In *Othello* racist and xenophobic remarks are part of the evil spread by the villainous Iago, but the perpetrators of similar comments in *Dracula* are intended as its heroes. Count Dracula has many attributes that are assigned to undesirable stereotypes: a foreign accent, an irresistible sexual potency and a foul smell. The fear of Dracula is in part "the embodiment of all the social forces that lurked just beyond the frontiers of Victorian middle class consciousness."[11] The fear that Dracula might create more like himself resembles fears encoded in *The Tempest,* with the possibility of an isle full of Calibans.

In *Dracula,* as in *Othello* and *The Tempest,* the landscape is symbolic of the contrast between the civilized and the primitive, the rational and the irrational, the ordered and the chaotic. Dracula is an outsider, a metaphoric "Turk" who threatens to invade civilized England (Venice). Transylvania serves a function similar to that of Cyprus in the symbolic geography of *Othello,* for it represents the barbaric, the primitive, the bestial. Dracula's plan to leave Transylvania and to travel to England invokes the fear of foreigners in the face of late-Victorian anxieties about imperialism and

---

Dracula and *Macbeth*

A casual glance shows the resemblance between *Dracula* and *Macbeth*. Both are centred around a lonely, desolate castle, to which an unsuspecting stranger is lured, then "visited" in his sleep. Both works have as their focus the personification of evil—not earthly, but supernatural evil. Macbeth and Dracula each receive a kind of immortality as a result of their pacts with supernatural forces. This evil is portrayed as more fascinating and more potent that the powers of good arrayed against it, for Macbeth's ultimate downfall, like Dracula's, cannot totally be accounted for by the ingenuity of his enemies. In both cases, their own schemes sow the seeds of their destruction. The contest between good and evil is shown to be unequal. The representatives of good lack mutual trust, undermining their strength. Furthermore, the evil which both works distil is dependent on complicity—the victim must willingly accept the touch of evil/vampirism.

Like Macbeth, Dracula was once a fearless warrior, grown to manhood through the spilled blood of his enemy's armies; a heroic figure for whom the fall from power to perpetrator of evil is a mystery. Both are, as it were, the first victims of the disease which spreads before them, until they are driven remorselessly back to the castle whence they came to have their throats slashed. The "contagion" in both works is combated by a team of adversaries skilled in medical science. Similarly, what motivates both principal characters is not a thirst for blood (either literally or metaphorically) but power and ambition. Nonetheless, the two works display blood as a central motif, and introduce three weird and evil women in symbolic form. The three witches that open *Macbeth* are reincarnated as vampires near the beginning of *Dracula*.

Two other comparisons deserve mention: first, the respective conclusions. With the death of Macbeth the cry is "The time is free." Following Dracula's demise the response is "The curse has passed away." Second, the historical elements of both are abstract rather than factual. The Scotland of *Macbeth* exists in the mind rather than as any geographical entity. The same could be said of Stoker's Transylvania.

—Clive Leatherdale, *Dracula: The Novel & the Legend,* pp. 86–87

British hegemony. By the end of the novel, the forces of Victorian England prevail. The threat of "reverse colonization"[12] is turned back as Dracula is chased back to Transylvania (where he belongs) and destroyed.

Another source of influence is *The Merchant of Venice,* a play Stoker must have known intimately, for Irving played the role of Shylock in an unbroken run of 250 nights. Over the twenty-six years that it remained in his repertoire, he played Shylock a thousand times. Stoker responded with the predictable stereotype in his comment about Irving's preparations for the role of Shylock:

> It has often amazed me to see the physiognomy of Shylock gradually emerge from the actor's own generous countenance. Though I have seen it done a hundred times I could never really understand how the lips thickened, with the red of the lower lip curling out and over after the manner of the typical Hebraic countenance; how the bridge of the nose rose into the Jewish aquiline; and how the eyes became veiled and glassy with introspection–eyes which at times could and did flash lurid fire.[13]

These images may have been in Stoker's mind when he wrote parts of *Dracula* that have been cited as antisemitic: Dracula's aquiline features and lurid red eyes; the zoo-keeper's comment about the Count's "'ook nose and pointed beard"; references to a Hebrew with "a nose like a sheep" and the smell of "ole Jerusalem" (pp. 126, 302, 201). Judith Halberstam makes a strong case for a deliberate connection between the presentation of Dracula with his "sexual and economic parasitism, and degeneracy" and the characterization of Shylock in Shakespeare's text and on the stage. In fact, she argues that Stoker's Dracula is a parodic inversion of Shylock's famous "I am a Jew" defense:

> Stoker epitomizes the differences between Dracula and his persecutors in the very terms that Shylock claims as common ground. Dracula's eyes and hands, his senses and passions are patently alien; he does not eat the same food, he is not hurt by the same weapons or infected by the same diseases, and when he is wounded he does not bleed.[14]

One could add that, whereas Shylock sought after Christian flesh, Dracula seeks Christian blood.

Dracula is clearly a novel written by a man who not only knew his theatre intimately, but was familiar with the work of its most famous son.

–revised by the author from *Reflections on Dracula*
(White Rock, B.C.: Transylvania Press,
1997), pp. 157–170

Henry Irving as Shylock in The Merchant of Venice
(*Laurence Irving,* Henry Irving: The Actor and
His World, *[London: Faber & Faber, 1951];
Library of Congress*)

1.　Christopher Craft, "'Kiss Me With Those Red Lips': Gender and Inversion in Bram Stoker's *Dracula*," in *Dracula: The Vampire and the Critics*, ed. Margaret L. Carter (Ann Arbor: UMI, 1988), p. 167.

2.　Bram Stoker, *Personal Reminiscences of Henry Irving* (1906; London: William Heinemann, 1907), p. 24.

3.　Stoker, *Reminiscences,* pp. 200–201.

4.　Bram Stoker, *Dracula* (1897), eds. Nina Auerbach and David J. Skal (New York: Norton, 1997), p. 35. Cited hereafter in the text in parentheses.

5.　Stoker misquotes Shakespeare here. Hamlet actually says, "There are more things in heaven and earth, Horatio,/ Than are dreamt of in your philosophy" (I,v,166–167).

6.　Qtd. in Bram Stoker, *Dracula,* ed. Maurice Hindle (London: Penguin, 1993), p. 511, n36.

7.　Barbara Belford, *Bram Stoker: A Biography of the Author of Dracula* (New York: Knopf, 1996), p. 110.

8.　Stoker, *Reminiscences,* pp. 68, 70.

9.　See Clive Leatherdale, *Dracula: The Novel & the Legend* (1985; rev. Westcliff-on-Sea, U.K.: Desert Island Books, 2001), pp. 86–87.

10.　Qtd. in Leonard Wolf, ed., *The Essential Dracula* (New York: Penguin, 1993), p. 221, n32.

11.　Burton Hatlen, "The Return of the Repressed/ Oppressed in Bram Stoker's *Dracula*," in *Vampire and Critics,* ed. Carter, p. 120.

12.　The phrase was coined by Stephen T. Arata in "The Occidental Tourist: *Dracula* and the Anxiety of Reverse Colonization," *Victorian Studies,* 33 (1990): 621–645.

13.　Stoker, *Reminiscences,* pp. 89–90.

14.　Judith Halberstam, "Technologies of Monstrosity: Bram Stoker's *Dracula*," *Victorian Studies,* 36 (Spring 1993): 348.

*Irving and Stoker leaving the Lyceum (*The Tatler, *9 October 1901; Barbara Belford,* Bram Stoker: A Biography of the Author of Dracula, *1996; Elizabeth Miller Collection)*

Social and Cultural Contexts

A close examination of Dracula *yields insights into a wide range of contemporary interests and concerns, including evolutionary theory, concepts of atavism and criminality, anxieties about the blurring of gender boundaries, and emerging scientific and technological advances.*

In her introduction to Dracula, *editor Glennis Byron suggests that the fields of science and technology may prove to be "the most fruitful of the new areas for further investigation" of the novel. In the following excerpt she cites Rosemary Jann's article "Saved by Science? The Mixed Messages of Stoker's* Dracula," *which was published in* Texas Studies in Literature and Language *(volume 31, 1989).*

Dracula, Science and Technology
Glennis Byron

. . . The technological advances of the time are clearly crucial to the defeat of the count. Without the telegraph, the typewriter, the phonograph, the railway, the newspapers, the necessary information could never have been collected, collated, transmitted. But as well as drawing on all the most recent technological advances, Stoker also engages with many of the most recent scientific debates. With his references to Jean-Martin Charcot, who had used hypnotism in his therapy at the Salpêtrière in the 1870s, to John Burdon Sanderson and David Ferrier, scientists involved in vivisection, with his use of the term "unconscious cerebration," his appropriation of telepathy, a term coined in 1882 by F.W.M. Myers, Stoker draws upon some of the most recent theories and developments in science. He participates in the contemporary debate between the empiricists and materialists and those who were reluctant to surrender belief in the spiritual or supernatural, who began to explore such new fields as spiritualism, theosophy, and, most importantly, mental physiology, the study of the workings of the mind, who attempted, in Rosemary Jann's words, to "expand the boundaries of the real beyond the merely physical" (274). Stoker's narrative, which juxtaposes Winchesters and crosses, telegraphs and telepathy, rail travel and somnambulism, seems to swing between the two sides of the debate. On the one hand, the text suggests it is "their very reliance on scientific rationality that makes the English so vulnerable to Dracula's threat" (Jann 274). As Van Helsing, "one of the most advanced scientists of his day," observes, "in this enlightened age, when men believe not even what they see, the doubting of wise men would be [Dracula's] greatest strength." On the other hand, the vampire hunters' use of technology, their superior deductive powers, their power over data, all these things are crucial to their eventual victory over the count.

—Dracula, edited by Glennis Byron
(Peterborough: Broadview, 1998),
pp. 22–23

* * *

Among the most striking episodes in Stoker's novel are the scenes in which Van Helsing administers blood transfusions to the dying Lucy Westenra. Given that three of Stoker's brothers were medical doctors, one would expect that the author of Dracula *had access to the most current medical practices. Apparently, however, he describes a procedure that was already falling into disuse. Stoker wrote his novel before the discovery of the existence of blood types.*

Blood Transfusion in the Nineteenth Century
Goldie Morgentaler

During the nineteenth century human-to-human blood transfusions were added to the physicians' arsenal of possible cures for disease. Beginning

Jonathan Harker's description of Dracula in Pitman shorthand, a system of shorthand in wide use in the United Kingdom in the late nineteenth century. Harker uses shorthand in part to keep his thoughts private from Count Dracula (transcription by Marion Gregory).

The Typewriter

Dr. Seward quotes Mina Harker.

" . . . See, I have tried to be useful. I have copied out the words on my typewriter."

> —*Dracula,* chapter XVII,
> Dr. Seward's Diary,
> 29 September

. . . I feel so grateful to the man who invented the 'Traveller's' typewriter, and to Mr. Morris for getting this one for me.

> —*Dracula,* chapter XXVI,
> Mina Harker's Journal,
> 30 October, evening

Poster by Lucien Faure, 1897 (Victoria and Albert Museum)

in 1818 and continuing with greater frequency in the second part of the nineteenth century, blood transfusions became a relatively common if uncertain way of saving lives. Nevertheless, it is one of the ironies of literary (and medical) history that by the time Bram Stoker published *Dracula* in 1897, British medicine had moved so far away from using blood for transfusions that the practice had come to be regarded as a holdover from medicine's dark ages.[1] What follows here is a history of how blood, the most symbolically weighted of bodily fluids—"the human being's finest juice" as a fifteenth-century Dutch physician called it—was demoted during the course of the nineteenth century from a substance promising revitalization in the early decades of the century to a second-rate bodily fluid, inferior even to salt water, in the century's last decade. That history is in turn related to the much longer history of how blood has been understood, and misunderstood, from ancient times.

The biblical Hebrews equated blood with life itself and considered it sacred. The Hebrew Bible mentions blood more than four hundred times. "The life of the flesh is in the blood," says Leviticus. Because of this, Jewish dietary law forbids the consumption of blood. It has been one of the sad ironies of Jewish history that the very people who have been banned by their religion from ingesting blood should have been the primary victims of blood libel, of the accusation that they spilled the blood of Christian children to make matzos.

Both the religious taboo against ingesting blood and the false accusation of blood libel illustrate the mystical power ascribed to blood from earliest times. The ancient Egyptians would bathe in blood as a restorative and in Roman times, gladiators drank the blood of their fallen opponents, because they believed that blood conveyed strength.[2] In order to preserve her youth, the sixteenth-century Hungarian countess Elisabeth Bathory took to bathing in the blood of virginal servant girls—several hundred of them, whom she murdered for the purpose—thus making literal the term "blood-bath."[3] Catholics drink transubstantiated wine—Christ's blood—as a way of attaining eternal life, and the practice follows logically from what was once the widespread belief that the characteristics of an individual were carried in his or her blood and could be passed on through drinking or transfusing that blood.

According to the ancient Greeks, good health depended on maintaining a balance of the humours. There were thought to be four of these humours or liquids that coursed through the body: blood, phlegm, choler (yellow bile) and melancholy (black

HMV Gramophone, 1896. In the novel, Dr. Seward keeps his diary "in phonograph." Mina Harker's transcription of his diary into typewritten notes enables the vampire hunters to learn more of Count Dracula's plans (Science Museum/Science and Society Picture Gallery, London).

bile). As Douglas Starr describes it, "blood, as the Paramount Humour, was considered the bearer of life, carrying its vital spirit through the body, ebbing and flowing through arteries and veins and sloshing through imagined pores in the heart."[4] Fevers and other bodily ailments were thought to result from too much blood flowing through the body. The fact that the body occasionally sheds blood naturally, during menstruation, for instance, or during a nosebleed, suggested that the cure for disease might be to drain off excess blood through bleeding the patient.

The theory of bodily humours as an explanation for disease proved to be remarkably long-lasting, despite the fact that it was given a check around the time of the Renaissance, when the Church relaxed its taboos against dissecting the human body. It was dissection that led William Harvey to conclude in 1628 that the heart functioned like a pump. Harvey's discovery that the blood circulates and that it does so in one direction only, and does not slosh back and forth through pores between arteries and veins, as was previously thought, redefined the metaphorical understanding of the most symbolically weighty organ of the body–the heart. Harvey's discovery suggested that the heart was not the seat of the soul, the source of all life, but simply a mechanical instrument. Har-

vey's discovery also suggested that the human body was transfusible and that blood might convey what was injected into it in much the same way as river currents can be used to transport matter from one point to another.

Harvey's contemporaries did indeed begin to inject various substances into the bodies of animals and experimented with blood transfusions from animals to human beings, although Harvey himself saw no future for transfusion. Harvey's colleagues in Oxford's Experimental Philosophy Club, Christopher Wren, later famous as the architect of St. Paul's Cathedral in London, and Robert Boyle, the founder of modern chemistry, conducted an experiment in which they used a hollow quill and bladder to inject opium and antimony into dogs. Since opium causes sleep and antimony induces vomiting, Wren and Boyle were able to show by the reactions of the dogs that the injected substances had had an effect. As Douglas Starr suggests, "that simple experiment yielded two striking results: the invention of the first intravenous syringe, and proof that the circulatory system, previously inviolate, could now be made open to interference from outside."[5]

Another early experimenter was a French doctor named Jean-Baptiste Denis who transfused the blood of a calf into a violent patient to make him

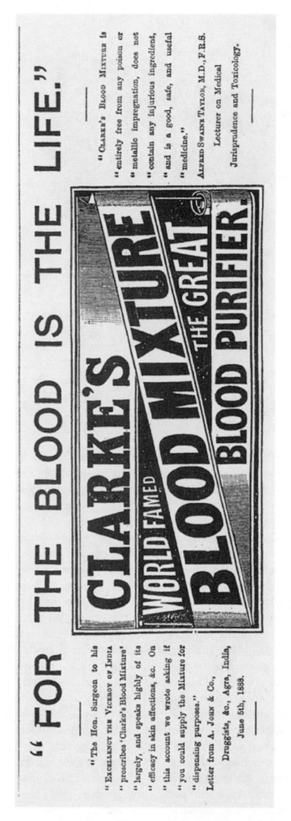

An advertisement from the 8 November 1890 issue of
Illustrated Sporting and Dramatic News. *The
slogan "For the Blood is the Life" was popularized
by Stoker's novel (British Library).*

docile, since it was believed that blood drawn from a creature of mild temperament could confer mildness and docility on the recipient. The first time Denis tried the experiment, it was a success and the patient did grow calmer, but the second time, the patient died. Denis was charged with manslaughter and brought to trial. He was acquitted, but the case resulted in a ban on transfusions throughout France, a ban that was soon extended to the rest of Europe, and remained in effect for 150 years.

During that century and a half, blood transfusion remained a subject of purely theoretical speculation. Although Erasmus Darwin suggested in 1794 that blood transfusions might alleviate fevers and malnutrition, the ban on transfusions was not broken until 1818. That year saw the first transfusion of human-to-human blood, and the beginning of the modern era in the history of blood transfusion. The transfuser was James Blundell, a Scottish doctor who worked as what was then called a man-midwife, or accoucheur. Blundell was a contemporary of Mary Shelley, whose *Frankenstein* was published in the same year as Blundell's first transfusion. The first piece of vampire fiction in English, John Polidori's "The Vampyre," appeared in print only a year later, in 1819.[6]

Blundell had been distressed at the high incidence of death from hemorrhaging in women who had just given birth. He cast about for a way to replace the blood that had been lost. After experimenting with animals, he decided that only human blood should be employed and that blood transfusions should not be used to cure madness or change characteristics, but only to replace lost blood.[7] Blundell first tried transfusion on a man with an ulcer, but this patient died. Blundell then became convinced that the procedure should be limited to women on the verge of death from uterine hemorrhage. In such cases, he believed, transfusion held great therapeutic promise. His experiments with blood transfusion made him realize that the procedure would not work to recover the dead. But he could save some of the dying, although his success rate by today's standards appears somewhat dubious—of the ten patients he transfused in eleven years, five died. Nothing daunted, Blundell wrote up his experiments in *The Lancet,* and this in turn led to a revival of interest in blood transfusion among other obstetricians.

Following Blundell's lead, a small group of these British obstetricians carried out transfusions on women who were hemorrhaging after childbirth. They published accounts of their efforts—many of them apparently successful—in medical journals like

We Began the Operation

As he spoke, he was dipping into his bag and producing the instruments for transfusion; I had taken off my coat and rolled up my shirt-sleeve. There was no possibility of an opiate just at present, and no need of one; and so, without a moment's delay, we began the operation.

                                                        —*Dracula,* chapter X,
                                                        Dr. Seward's Diary,
                                                        10 September

The Lancet. Successful case histories often told of how such women were veritably re-animated by the blood transfused into their veins. By 1825, transfusion's potential as an effective replacement for blood lost after childbirth had become the subject of intense debate in British medical circles.

In 1858, a group of obstetricians formed themselves into The Obstetrical Society of London, with the result that many of the chief advocates of blood transfusion came together in this one institutional body.[8] Thus it was that the history of blood transfusion began to march in tandem with the history of obstetrics. This in turn contributed to the gendering of the procedure throughout the early part of the century, when men were considered to be more acceptable donors because of the presumed "strength" of their blood, while women were viewed as passive recipients. This gendering of the act of blood transfusion becomes an important element in literary depictions of the procedure such as in George Eliot's "The Lifted Veil" and Bram Stoker's *Dracula.*

Harvey's discovery of the circulation of the blood had not put an end to the belief in the humours as the cause of disease, and bloodletting continued as the favorite cure for a wide variety of

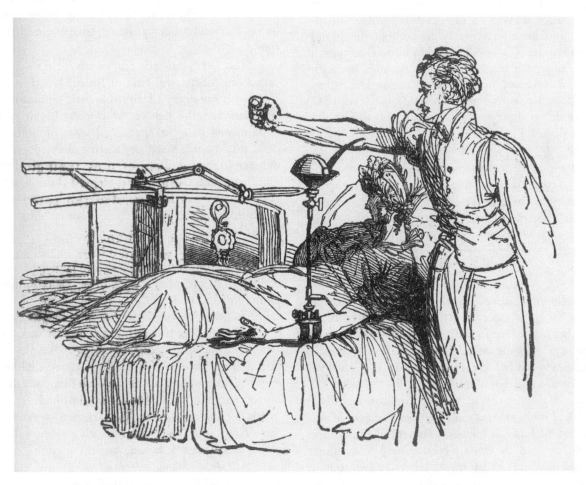

Blundell's Gravitator, an apparatus used for blood transfusion in the nineteenth century (Science Museum/ Science and Society Picture Library, London)

ailments throughout the nineteenth century. In fact, Mrs. Beeton's 1859 *Book of Household Management,* which became the bible of the Victorian housewife, contains instructions on the proper way to bleed the sick. (Always standing up or in a sitting position: Mrs. Beeton counsels against bleeding someone who is lying down, because there is then no way to revive the patient by placing him or her in a reclining position.) Thus the growing nineteenth-century interest in blood transfusion took place against a backdrop of medical practice that defined bloodletting as an all-purpose cure for whatever ailed. Bleeding was such a mainstay of medical care that it was even used to treat uterine hemorrhage. The persistence and tenacity of this practice may be seen in the fact that until the 1920s, country doctors in the United States would seasonally "breathe a vein" to keep patients in good health.[9]

As for blood transfusion, it remained a risky and uncertain procedure throughout the nineteenth century. There was as yet no knowledge of blood types, no consensus on the need to sterilize instruments and no effective way to prevent the blood from clotting. The result was that human-to-human transfusions remained a very questionable proposition. For instance, the Liverpool surgeon Dr. Alfred Higginson transfused seven patients between 1847 and 1856. Of these seven, five died. A study by the Polish doctor F. Gesellius conducted in 1873 found that 56 percent of all transfusions ended in death.

Despite the low success rate, physicians continued to resort to blood transfusions with increasing frequency as the century progressed. By the second half of the nineteenth century, transfusion had become quite common, with hundreds being reported throughout Europe. American doctors recorded two transfusions during the Civil War, both for leg amputations; one of the patients survived. During Canada's great cholera epidemics of the 1830s some doctors gave milk transfusions in the belief according to their reports that the "white corpuscles of milk were capable of being transformed into red blood corpuscles."[10] In fact, cholera proved a very tempting disease for transfusers, because its symptom of sudden copious vomiting mimicked hemorrhage, and, like hemorrhage, it too depleted the body of fluids. Treatment of cholera by transfusion led to experiments in which a saline solution augmented by alcohol was added to the blood. This new substance seemed to be just as effective as blood in reviving patients, although, again, success rates were low. All six of the cholera patients treated with saline solution by Dr. William

John Little during an epidemic in London in 1848 died. But others using this method were marginally more successful in saving lives, because the salino-alcoholic solutions worked to replace lost fluids.

In fact the persistent problem with clotting had caused blood to fall into disfavor among physicians. There were two proposed solutions: One was defibrination, which was an attempt to rid the blood of the fibrin that collected to form clots. Defibrination entailed whipping blood with a fork, stick or rod, so that the fibrin stuck to the whipping device and the blood remained fluid a little longer. The second approach to the problem was to construct a device that would permit the blood to pass as directly as possible from donor to recipient, so that it would avoid contact with the air. The primary proponent of this method was James Hobson Aveling, who invented an apparatus consisting of two silver tubes attached to a length of rubber tubing with a squeeze bulb in the middle that he carried around in his pocket for weight, years before using it successfully on a woman suffering from postpartum hemorrhage.[11]

The 1880s saw the end of what Kim Pelis has called the "obstetrical era" in British blood transfusion, with the entry of physiologists, biologists and surgeons into the debate.[12] Surgeons began to use transfusions to treat anemic patients of both genders. But the increased popularity of the procedure did not decrease its risks, many of which were ascribed to the persistent problem of clotting, which gummed up instruments and which could cause death through the introduction of an embolism into the patient's vein.

Because of the risks involved in using whole blood, doctors began to experiment with other kinds of infusions, including the salino-alcoholic infusion pioneered by Dr. Little. It was found that adding a saline solution to blood increased its quantity and made it easier to transfuse. A series of influential articles in the *British Medical Journal* by the physiologist William Hunter in the 1890s argued that blood was valuable only as a circulating fluid that transported nutrition around the body but had no value in itself. This being the case, Hunter argued, the same effect could be achieved with a saline solution alone, which, unlike blood, would not clot.

Hunter's articles were so persuasive that by 1900 the use of blood for transfusion had fallen into complete disfavor among British physicians, with the procedure routinely dismissed as a dangerous practice from medicine's ignorant past. As Kim Pelis has pointed out, Bram Stoker's *Dracula* appearing in 1897 was published just as medical belief in blood transfusion was at its lowest. Pelis suggests that Stoker's novel contrasted the "good and evil movement of blood in terms that would have been more familiar to Blundell than to Hunter."[13] Pelis further makes the point that Stoker's portrayal of blood transfusion, while out of character with contemporary medical practice, nevertheless "resonated with popular ideas about blood," specifically with the notion that blood had the power to reanimate.

The disuse of blood transfusion in Britain was so general by the early twentieth century, that even Karl Landsteiner's 1900 discovery of human blood types had no impact, because blood transfusion itself was no longer generally practiced. It was not until the American surgeon George Washington Crile's experiments with blood pressure in 1906 that it was discovered that blood and salt solutions were not equal in terms of the body's needs and uses. The centre of research into transfusion moved to the United States and the reanimating qualities of "the body's finest juice" remained unexploited in Britain until the First World War.

1. Kim Pelis, "Blood Clots: The Nineteenth-Century Debate over the Substance and Means of Transfusion in Britain," *Annals of Science,* 54 (1997): 357, n149. I wish to acknowledge my debt to Kim Pelis's two fine essays on nineteenth-century blood transfusion: "Blood Clots" and "Transfusion, with teeth," in *Manifesting Medicine: Bodies and Machines,* ed. R. Bud, B. Finn, and H. Troschler (Amsterdam: Harwood Academic Publishers, 1999). I am also indebted to Douglas Starr's *Blood: An Epic History of Medicine and Commerce* (New York: HarperCollins, 1998).
2. Starr, *Blood,* p. xiv.
3. For secondary sources on Bathory, see Pelis, "Clots," p. 332, n1.
4. Starr, *Blood,* p. 7.
5. Starr, *Blood,* p. 8.
6. For more on the link between galvanism and blood transfusion as represented in *Frankenstein* and "The Vampyre," see Pelis, "Transfusion."
7. Starr, *Blood,* pp. 36–37.
8. Pelis, "Clots," p. 341.
9. Starr, *Blood,* p. 17.
10. Starr, *Blood,* p. 38.
11. Starr, *Blood,* p. 37.
12. Pelis, "Clots," p. 350.
13. Pelis, "Clots," p. 359.

* * *

In this excerpt from Sesame and Lilies: Two Lectures Delivered at Manchester in 1864 *(1865), of which some forty-four thousand copies were sold by 1900, critic John Ruskin (1819–1900) discusses the place of women in Victorian society.* Dracula *scholars debate the extent to which Stoker accepted the traditional roles of men and women.*

From *Sesame and Lilies*

John Ruskin

Now their separate characters are briefly these. The man's power is active, progressive, defensive. He is eminently the doer, the creator, the discoverer, the defender. His intellect is for speculation and invention; his energy for adventure, for war, and for conquest, wherever war is just, wherever conquest necessary. But the woman's power is for rule, not for battle,—and her intellect is not for invention or creation, but for sweet ordering, arrangement, and decision. She sees the qualities of things, their claims, and their places. Her great function is Praise; she enters into no contest, but infallibly adjudges the crown of contest. By her office, and place, she is protected from all danger and temptation. The man, in his rough work in open world, must encounter all peril and trial;—to him, therefore, must be the failure, the offence, the inevitable error: often he must be wounded, or subdued; often misled; and *always* hardened. But he guards the woman from all this; within his house, as ruled by her, unless she herself has sought it, need enter no danger, no temptation, no cause of error or offence. This is the true nature of home—it is the place of Peace; the shelter, not only from all injury, but from all terror, doubt, and division. In so far as it is not this, it is not home; so far as the anxieties of the outer life penetrate into it, and the inconsistently-minded, unknown, unloved, or hostile society of the outer world is allowed by either husband or wife to cross the threshold, it ceases to be home; it is then only a part of that outer world which you have roofed over, and lighted fire in. But so far as it is a sacred place, a vestal temple, a temple of the hearth watched over by Household Gods, before whose faces none may come but those whom they can receive with love,—so far as it is this, and roof and fire are types only of a nobler shade and light,—shade as of the rock in a weary land, and light as of the Pharos in the stormy sea;—so far it vindicates the name, and fulfils the praise, of Home.

And wherever a true wife comes, this home is always round her. The stars only may be over her head; the glowworm in the night-cold grass may be the only fire at her foot; but home is yet wherever she is;

and for a noble woman it stretches far round her, better than ceiled with cedar, or painted with vermilion, shedding its quiet light far, for those who else were homeless.

This, then, I believe to be,–will you not admit it to be?–the woman's true place and power. But do not you see that, to fulfil this, she must–as far as one can use such terms of a human creature–be incapable of error? So far as she rules, all must be right, or nothing is. She must be enduringly, incorruptibly good; instinctively, infallibly wise–wise, not for self-development, but for self-renunciation: wise, not that she may set herself above her husband, but that she may never fail from his side: wise, not with the narrowness of insolent and loveless pride, but with the passionate gentleness of an infinitely variable, because infinitely applicable, modesty of service–the true changefulness of woman.

–Ruskin, "Of Queens' Gardens," in
The Works of John Ruskin, volume 18
(London: George Allen / New York:
Longmans, Green, 1905),
pp. 121–123

* * *

Mina on the New Woman

The movement for women's rights, both lauded and derided with the phrase "New Woman," was gaining momentum in the late nineteenth century. Mina makes light of the notion of women aspiring to the place of men.

. . . We had a lovely walk. Lucy, after a while, was in gay spirits. . . . We had a capital "severe tea" at Robin Hood's Bay in a sweet little old-fashioned inn, with a bow-window right over the seaweed-covered rocks of the strand. I believe we should have shocked the "New Woman" with our appetites. Men are more tolerant, bless them!

. . . .

She has more colour in her cheeks than usual, and looks, oh, so sweet. If Mr. Holmwood fell in love with her seeing her only in the drawing-room, I wonder what he would say if he saw her now. Some of the "New Women" writers will some day start an idea that men and women should be allowed to see each other asleep before proposing or accepting. But I suppose the New Woman won't condescend in future to accept; she will do the proposing herself. And a nice job she will make of it, too!

–*Dracula,* Chapter VIII, Mina Murray's
Journal, 10 August

"*Donna Quixote,*" *from* Punch *(28 April 1894), one of many satirical sketches aimed at the "New Woman," a term coined in 1893 and used by Stoker in his novel*
(Victoria and Albert Museum)

The Degeneration of Society
Glennis Byron

The advancements of Western civilization were not always viewed optimistically by all, and for many, the breakdown of traditional gender roles, the confusion of the masculine and feminine, was only one indication of cultural decay, of a more widespread "degeneration" of society. Evolutionary theories had dissolved the firm boundaries between human and animal, leading to the inevitable conclusion that if something–individual or nation–could evolve, it could also devolve or degenerate. The discourse of degeneration spanned many fields, including economics, psychiatry, statistics, eugenics, and criminal anthropology, and the source of the threat of degeneration accordingly varied. For some, such as the psychiatrist Henry Maudsley and the zoologist E. Ray Lankester, the threat came from the lower classes, from the growing number of the poverty-stricken individuals reduced to crime by social conditions; for others the threat was the decadence of the aristocracy. For such social commentators as the Earl of Dunraven, feeding the common fears of what was different and not understood, it was "The Invasion of Destitute Aliens." As Stephen Arata demonstrates, "*Dracula* enacts the period's most important and pervasive narrative of decline, a narrative of reverse colonization,"* a fantasy drawn upon by such late-Victorian popular writers as Rider Haggard, Rudyard Kipling, and H.G. Wells. One result of the expansion of empire was the subsequent entry into England of a whole range of peoples from different cultures, prompting a fear of racial degeneration, of the contamination of "Englishness."

. . . .

The discourse of degeneration clearly influenced Stoker in many ways. Indeed, he even makes direct reference to two of the key figures in the debate: the criminologist Cesare Lombroso, who used phrenology to demonstrate his theory that habitual criminals were throwbacks to primitive races, and the doctor and journalist Max Nordau, who extended Lombroso's arguments in his sensational *Degeneration* (1895) to suggest racial and artistic decline and attack many contemporary writers, such as Wilde, Ibsen, and Tolstoy, as having degenerated through excessive emotionality. Mina draws upon these two writers in her attempt to understand Dracula: responding to Van Helsing's prompting she identifies Dracula as

> a criminal and of criminal type. Nordau and Lombroso would so classify him, and *quâ* criminal he is of imperfectly formed mind. Thus, in a difficulty he has to seek resource in habit. . . . So he came to London to invade a new land. He was beaten, and when all hope of success was lost, and his existence in danger, he fled back over the sea to his home.

Drawing upon this particular discourse of degeneration, Dracula is read as an atavistic being and descriptions of such features as his "aquiline nose," "massive eyebrows," "pointed ears," and sharp white teeth can be seen to echo accounts of Nordau's degenerate or Lombroso's "born criminal." Dracula embodies more than just the primitive in this reading, however; he embodies the possibility of degeneration, the reversion to the primitive, in the other characters: Renfield . . . is derived from Lombroso's epileptic-criminal type; the vamped Lucy can equally be slotted into position, with her striking links to Lombroso and Ferrero's lunatic female offender.

–*Dracula* by Bram Stoker,
edited by Glennis Byron,
pp. 20, 21–22

———

*Stephen D. Arata, "The Occidental Tourist: Dracula and the Anxiety of Reverse Colonization," *Victorian Studies,* 33 (1990): 623.

* * *

The Italian criminologist Cesare Lombroso (1835–1909) established an international reputation through his studies of the relationship between mental and physical characteristics, including L'Uomo Delinquente *(The Criminal Man, 1876) and* Le Crime, Causes et Remèdies *(Crime, Its Causes and Remedies, 1899). In this excerpt from his introduction to his daughter's summarization of his ideas, published the year following his death, Lombroso explains the origin of his theory about criminality.*

A Theory of Criminality
Cesare Lombroso

I, therefore, began to study criminals in the Italian prisons, and, amongst others, I made the acquaintance of the famous brigand Vilella. This man possessed such extraordinary agility, that he had been known to scale steep mountain heights bearing a sheep on his shoulders. His cynical effrontery was such that he openly boasted of his crimes. On his death one cold grey November morning, I was deputed to make the "post-mortem," and on laying open the skull I found on the occipital part, exactly on the spot where a spine is found in the normal skull, a distinct depression which I named "median occipital fossa," because of its situation precisely in the middle of the occiput as in inferior animals, especially rodents. This depression, as in the case of animals, was correlated with the hypertrophy of the "vermis," know in birds as the middle cerebellum.

This was not merely an idea, but a revelation. At the sight of that skull, I seemed to see all of a sudden, lighted up as a vast plain under a flaming sky, the problem of the nature of the criminal—an atavistic being who reproduces in his person the ferocious instincts of primitive humanity and the inferior animals. Thus were explained anatomically the enormous jaws, high cheek-bones, prominent superciliary arches, solitary lines in the palms, extreme size of the orbits, handle-shaped or sessile ears found in criminals, savages, and apes, insensibility to pain, extremely acute sight, tattooing, excessive idleness, love of orgies, and the irresistible craving for evil for its own sake, the desire not only to extinguish life in the victim, but to mutilate the corpse, tear its flesh, and drink its blood.

–Cesare Lombroso, Introduction,
*Criminal Man, According to the
Classification of Cesare Lombroso,*
pp. xxiv–xxv

. . . .

The criminal is an atavistic being, a relic of a vanished race. This is by no means an uncommon occurrence in nature. Atavism, the reversion to a former state, is the first feeble indication of the reaction opposed by nature to the perturbing causes which seek to alter her delicate mechanism. Under certain unfavourable conditions, cold or poor soil, the common oak will develop characteristics of the oak of the Quaternary period. The dog left to run wild in the forest will in a few generations revert to the type of his original wolf-like progenitor, and the cultivated garden roses when neglected show a tendency to reassume the form of the original dog-rose. Under special conditions produced by alcohol, chloroform, heat, or injuries, ants, dogs, and pigeons become irritable and savage like their wild ancestors.

This tendency to alter under special conditions is common to human beings, in whom hunger, syphilis, trauma, and, still more frequently, morbid conditions inherited from insane, criminal, or diseased progenitors, or the abuse of nerve poisons, such as alcohol, tobacco, or morphine, cause various alterations, of which criminality—that is, a return to the characteristics peculiar to primitive savages—is in reality the least serious, because it represents a less advanced stage than other forms of cerebral alteration.

The aetiology of crime, therefore, mingles with that of all kinds of degeneration: rickets, deafness, monstrosity, hairiness, and cretinism, of which crime is only a variation. It has, however, always been regarded as a thing apart, owing to a general instinctive repugnance to admit that a phenomenon, whose extrinsications are so extensive and penetrate every fibre of social life, derives, in fact, from the same causes as socially insignificant forms like rickets, sterility, etc. But this repugnance is really only a sensory illusion, like many others of widely diverse nature.

–Gina Lombroso-Ferrero, *Criminal Man,*
According to the Classification of
Cesare Lombroso (New York &
London: Putnam, 1911),
pp. 135–136

* * *

This excerpt is from a translation of La donna delinquente *(1895), a work that Lombroso wrote with his son-in-law.*

From *The Female Offender*
Cesare Lombroso and William Ferrero

We see, then, that another characteristic of the female lunatic, and consequently of the criminal lunatic, is an exaggeration of the sexual instincts. These which in male lunatics are almost always in abeyance, lead in women, even in very old women as in quite young girls, to the most disgusting and unnatural excesses.

. . . .

Nymphomania transforms the most timid girl into a shameless bacchante. She tries to attract every man she sees, displaying sometimes violence, and sometimes the most refined coquetry. She often suffers from intense thirst, a dry mouth, a fetid breath, and a tendency to bite everybody she meets.

. . . .

Female lunatics in general surpass their male prototypes in all sexual aberrations and tendencies, and, after long years of observation, I am disposed to agree with Hergt, who affirmed that two-thirds of female lunatics suffer from maladies of the reproductive organs, which, by increasing reflex action and impairing psychical activity, bring on convulsions and produce abnormal sensations, which are transformed into illusions, hallucinations, delirium, or obscene impulses.

–*The Female Offender* (New York:
D. Appleton, 1898),
pp. 295–297

* * *

In Psychopathia Sexualis, *which was originally published in 1886, the German psychologist Richard von Krafft-Ebing compiles some 247 case studies, one of which involves vampirism.*

From *Psychopathia Sexualis*
Richard von Krafft-Ebing

Sadism in Woman.–That sadism–a perversion, as we have seen, frequent in men–is much less frequent in women, is easily explained. In the first place, sadism, in which the need of subjugation of the opposite sex forms a constituent element, in accordance with its nature, represents a pathological intensification of the masculine sexual character; in the second place, the obstacles which oppose the expression of this monstrous impulse are, of course, much greater for a woman than for a man. Yet sadism occurs in women; and it can only be explained by the primary constituent element,–the general hyper-excitation of the motor sphere.

Krafft-Ebing then cites the first of the two cases that he says "have thus far been scientifically studied."

Case 42. A married man presented himself with numerous scars of cuts on his arms. He told their origin as follows: When he wished to approach his wife, who was young and somewhat "nervous," he first had to make a cut in his arm. Then she would suck the wound, and during the act become violently excited sexually.

This case recalls the wide-spread legend of the vampires, the origin of which may perhaps be referred to such sadistic facts.

He then adds a footnote:

The legend is especially spread throughout the Balkan peninsula. Among the Greeks it has its origin in the myth of the *lamia* and *marmolykes,*—blood-sucking women. Goethe made use of this in his "Bride of Corinth." The verses referring to vampirism, "suck thy heart's blood," etc., can be thoroughly understood only when compared with their ancient sources.

—Krafft-Ebing, *Psychopathia sexualis,* authorized translation of the seventh enlarged and revised German edition by Charles G. Chaddock (Philadelphia & London: F. A. Davis, 1892), p. 87

* * *

The Paris-based journalist, writer, and physician Max Nordau popularized notions of racial and genetic decline in his book Die Entartung *(1893), which was translated as* Degeneration *in 1895.*

From *Degeneration*
Max Nordau

One epoch of history is unmistakably in its decline, and another is announcing its approach. There is a sound of rending in every tradition, and it is as though the morrow would not link itself with to-day. Things as they are totter and plunge, and they are suffered to reel and fall, because man is weary, and there is no faith that it is worth an effort to uphold them.

—pp. 5–6

. . . .

When under any kind of noxious influences an organism becomes debilitated, its successors will not resemble the healthy, normal type of the species, with capacities for development, but will form a new subspecies, which, like all others, possesses the capacity of transmitting to its offspring, in a continuously increasing degree, its peculiarities, these being morbid deviations from the normal form—gaps in development, malformations and infirmities. That which distinguishes degeneracy from the formation of new species (phylogeny) is, that the morbid variation does not continuously subsist and propagate itself, like one that is healthy, but, fortunately, is soon rendered sterile, and after a few generations often dies out before it reaches the lowest grade of organic degradation.

Degeneracy betrays itself among men in certain physical characteristics, which are denominated "stig-

mata," or brandmarks—an unfortunate term derived from a false idea, as if degeneracy were necessarily the consequence of a fault, and the indication of it a punishment. Such stigmata consist of deformities, multiple and stunted growths in the first line of asymmetry, the unequal development of the two halves of the face and cranium; then imperfection in the development of the external ear, which is conspicuous for its enormous size, or protrudes from the head, like a handle, and the lobe of which is either lacking or adhering to the head, and the helix of which is not involuted; further, squint-eyes, harelips, irregularities in the form and position of the teeth; pointed or flat palates, webbed or supernumerary fingers (syn- and poly-dactylia), etc.

—pp. 16–17

. . . .

In the mental development of degenerates, we meet with the same irregularity that we have observed in their physical growth. The asymmetry of face and

---

Lucy as a Vampire

"Arthur! Oh, my love, I am glad you have come! Kiss me!" Arthur bent eagerly over to kiss her; but at that instant Van Helsing, who, like me, had been startled by her voice, swooped upon him, and catching him by the neck with both hands, dragged him back with a fury of strength which I never thought he could have possessed, and actually hurled him almost across the room.

"Not for your life!" he said; "not for your living soul and hers!"

—*Dracula,* chapter XII,
Dr. Seward's Diary,
20 September

She [Lucy] still advanced, however, and with a languorous, voluptuous grace, said:—
"Come to me, Arthur. Leave these others and come to me. My arms are hungry for you. Come, and we can rest together. Come, my husband, come!"

—*Dracula,* chapter XVI,
Dr. Seward's Diary
(continued)

She seemed like a nightmare of Lucy as she lay there; the pointed teeth, the bloodstained, voluptuous mouth—which it made one shudder to see—the whole carnal and unspiritual appearance, seeming like a devilish mockery of Lucy's sweet purity.

—*Dracula,* chapter XVI,
Dr. Seward's Diary
(continued)

"good" and "evil," virtue and vice, are arbitrary distinctions; goes into raptures over evildoers and their deeds; professes to discover beauties in the lowest and most repulsive things; and tries to awaken interest in, and so-called "comprehension" of, every bestiality. The two psychological roots of moral insanity, in all its degrees of development, are, firstly, unbounded egoism, and, secondly, impulsiveness—i.e., inability to resist a sudden impulse to any deed; and these characteristics also constitute the chief intellectual stigmata of degenerates.

—Max Nordau, *Degeneration*
(New York: Appleton, 1895),
pp. 18–19

Max Nordau (David J. Skal, Vampires: Encounters with the Undead, *2001; Elizabeth Miller Collection)*

Cover for a 1907 German novel in which the vampire resembles Oscar Wilde (David J. Skal, V is for Vampire, *1996; Elizabeth Miller Collection)*

cranium finds, as it were, its counterpart in their mental faculties. Some of the latter are completely stunted, others morbidly exaggerated. That which nearly all degenerates lack is the sense of morality and of right and wrong. For them there exists no law, no decency, no modesty. In order to satisfy any momentary impulse, or inclination, or caprice, they commit crimes and trespasses with the greatest calmness and self-complacency, and do not comprehend that other persons take offence thereat. When this phenomenon is present in a high degree, we speak of "moral insanity" with Maudsley; there are, nevertheless, lower stages in which the degenerate does not, perhaps, himself commit any act which will bring him into conflict with the criminal code, but at least asserts the theoretical legitimacy of crime; seeks, with philosophically sounding fustian, to prove that

IV. The Writing of *Dracula*

The most important collection of primary documents concerning the composition of Dracula is "Bram Stoker's Original Foundation Notes & Data for His Dracula" (referred to henceforth as "Notes"). These unpublished Notes, comprising more than eighty handwritten and typed pages, are held at the Rosenbach Museum & Library in Philadelphia.

The provenance of Stoker's Notes has large gaps. The first and only time the Notes appeared in the auction record was when they were sold through Sotheby, Wilkinson & Hodge on 7 July 1913 to New York bookseller James F. Drake for £2, 2s. Nothing is known of the history of the Notes during the next twenty-five years, when they reappeared in the possession of Charles Scribner's Sons. The Notes are listed in four Scribner catalogues between 1938 and 1946, but the Scribner Archive provides no more information about the Notes or their purchaser. Again, nothing is known about the whereabouts of the Notes from 1946 until 1970, when the Rosenbach acquired them through the Philadelphia firm of Charles Sessler for an undisclosed price.

Much of the current misinformation about Dracula arises from critics and scholars who have indulged in speculation about Stoker and his sources without consulting the Notes. These papers offer insights into the early stages of the planning of the novel and

Stoker at work (Billy Rose Theatre Collection, New York Public Library for the Performing Arts, Astor, Lenox and Tilden Foundations)

include direct evidence about his key sources. Beyond the Notes, little is known about Stoker's work on the novel. All of his comments about Dracula *are comprised in one interview, one preface, and in passing remarks. A typescript of the novel, presumed to be the final copy from which the text was printed, is in the hands of a private collector and not currently accessible to researchers.*

Stoker's Notes for *Dracula*

The Notes: An Overview
Elizabeth Miller

Stoker's Notes comprise the most significant material for anyone interested in reconstructing the composition of *Dracula*. Located at the Rosenbach Museum & Library in Philadelphia, they were acquired from a local bookseller, Charles Sessler, in 1970. According to the Rosenbach, the provenance is hazy:

> Shortly after Stoker's death, his wife, Florence, sold them at a Sotheby's auction held in London on July 7, 1913. The notes were purchased by a Mr. Drake for slightly more than two pounds. Eventually, the Scribner's Company gained possession of the notes and offered them for sale at least twice, in 1938 and 1946. The asking price was a mere $500. Some years later, probably in 1969, the notes ended up in Philadelphia and were acquired by Sessler.[1]

The Notes remained in relative obscurity until they were fortuitously discovered in the mid-1970s by Raymond McNally and Radu Florescu, who had visited the Rosenbach to examine an original German woodcut of Vlad the Impaler:

> Then, like a bolt from the blue, the archivist asked us a startling question: might we also be interested in seeing the original notes that Stoker made while creating the novel Dracula?. . .
>
> At first we could not believe our ears. No scholar had ever found Stoker's notes. In fact no one knew where they were.[2]

Since then, the Notes have been the focus of intense scholarly debate, the subject of a number of publications, and the centrepiece of several popular exhibitions. They are now available for any researcher interested enough to go to Philadelphia to see them.

The Notes, composed between 1890 and 1896, provide an invaluable source of information about Stoker's earliest conception of his novel, as well as changes that he made in its structure, setting, plot, and characters. The following summary provided by the Rosenbach indicates the scope of these papers:

Manuscript and typescript notes, photographs, and a newspaper clipping, comprising both background research and an outline for the book. The first section consists of 49 leaves of manuscript: a list of characters, notes on vampires, outlines for the whole book and for most chapters (all 7 chapters for each of books 1–3 and ch. 26–27), chronologies, and miscellaneous notes on characters and events. The second section consists of 30 manuscript leaves tipped onto 10 sheets, 2 photographs, and a clipping: reading notes on vampires and werewolves; and shipwrecks, weather, geography, and language in the area of Whitby, North Yorkshire, where part of the story takes place. The last section consists of 37 leaves of typescript notes with manuscript corrections, being reading notes on various works about the history and geography of the Carpathians, dream theory, and tombstones at Whitby.[3]

As useful as they are, the Notes, however, pose distinct limitations:

1. Most of the sheets are undated, making it extremely difficult to establish a clear-cut sequence in the planning stages of the novel. Only the following sheets are dated: 8 March 1890 (early outline for Part 1); 14 March 1890 (early chapter outline); 30 July, 11 August, 13 August, 18 August, 21 August (sundry notes at Whitby in 1890); 15 October 1890 (short outline for Whitby ship coming ashore); 29 February 1892 (27-chapter outline); 2 February 1896 (dated clipping from *New York World*). In addition, there are several undated sheets of notes obviously taken at Whitby (notes from headstones, items from Coastguard, glossary, etc). A rough outline for Chapters 26 and 27, though undated, was written on stationery from the Stratford Hotel, Philadelphia. Stoker was with Irving in that city from 23 December 1895 to 4 January 1896; it is possible, though improbable, that he wrote this during an earlier visit in the winter of 1893.

2. Many sheets show no indication as to where they were written.

3. It is impossible to determine when he read the individual source-texts that he lists. As all of them were published prior to 1890, it is possible that he read some or all of them before he started working on the novel.

4. Several sheets contain revisions that were apparently added later. This can confuse researchers, especially as we find revisions of unknown date on a couple of the dated pages.

5. The handwriting is often illegible. As Stoker himself once observed, "I seldom wrote, in working times, less than fifty letters a day. Fortunately–for both myself and the readers, for I write an extremely bad hand–the bulk of them were short."[4] While perseverance and patience will render most of the handwritten Notes readable, there are a few phrases that will remain a challenge.

6. The Notes may be incomplete. Given Stoker's habit of jotting his notes on sundry scraps of paper, additional pages may have been lost.

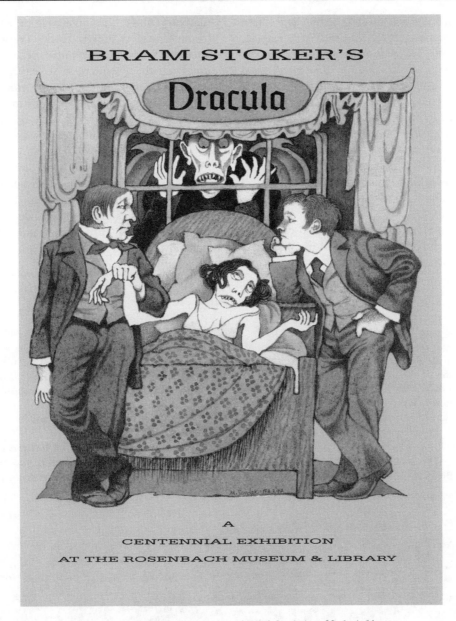

Cover for the catalogue that provides a detailed description of Stoker's Notes,
designed by Maurice Sendak (Elizabeth Miller Collection)

Another point of caution. While the Notes ought to be required reading for any *Dracula* scholar, they are not the "be-all-and-end-all" of the background for the novel. It would be foolhardy to claim that Stoker's sources are limited to what he mentions in his papers. But it is just as absurd to claim that he "must have" read this or that, when there is no supporting evidence. Serious investigators have a responsibility to separate the provable from the hypothetical.

      —revised by the author from *Dracula: Sense & Nonsense* (Westcliff-on-Sea, U.K.: Desert Island Books, 2000), pp. 17–21

1. Wendy Van Wyck Good, "*Dracula* Collections at the Rosenbach Museum & Library, Philadelphia, Pennsylvania," in *Bram Stoker's Dracula: Sucking Through the Century, 1897–1997,* ed. Carol M. Davison (Toronto: Dundurn, 1997), p. 406.
2. Raymond McNally and Radu Florescu, *The Essential Dracula* (New York: Mayflower, 1979), p. 17.
3. Rosenbach Museum & Library, "Catalogue Description of Bram Stoker's Notes for *Dracula,*" in *Bram Stoker's Dracula,* ed. Davison, p. 417.
4. Bram Stoker, *Personal Reminiscences of Henry Irving,* 2 vols. (London: Macmillan, 1906), vol. 1, p. 42.

***

Raymond McNally made a passing reference to the Notes in A Clutch of Vampires *(1975). Two years later, Joseph S. Bierman published the first article that examined the Notes in some detail. This essay was followed by Clive Leatherdale's book* The Origins of Dracula *(1987), which included for the first time a complete list of Stoker's sources as well as lengthy excerpts from several of them. By far the most comprehensive examination of the Notes is that undertaken by Christopher Frayling in* Vampyres: Lord Byron to Count Dracula *(1991).*

Bram Stoker's Working Papers for *Dracula*
Christopher Frayling

The first notes are dated "8/3/90" and consist of a brief outline of the opening section of the novel. At that early stage, the novel was to begin with a letter from "Count Wampyr" to the President of the Law Society, followed by much legal correspondence involving the President, a solicitor named Abraham Aaronson, and another letter from the Count, in Styria, asking Aaronson to come in person or send a trustworthy agent who, he stipulates, is not able to speak the German language.

[Abraham Aaronson was to become Peter Hawkins, solicitor of Exeter, and the published novel dealt with the Count's business transaction—the purchase of the estate at Purfleet—in flashback, during Chapter II of Harker's journal (entries for 5 and 7 May). The only legal document to survive the transition from notes to

---

The First Dated Note

The earliest date on any manuscript is 8 March 1890. This date is on a manuscript in Stoker's distinctive and almost illegible handwriting that is an outline for a first section of the novel which differs from the final version in only a few details. It is an outline for a novel in epistolary form like *Dracula,* and consists mainly of one line summaries of letters describing the action. Some of the letters are from an as-yet-unnamed Count to his Solicitor. The location of the Count's Castle is shown as Styria. The word "vampire" is not mentioned, but there are phrases, such as "describe old dead man made alive . . . waxen color." Although Jonathan Harker is not yet called by name, he is without doubt the male character in a sketch of the scene in the novel with the vampiresses in the Castle: "Young man goes out sees girls one tries to kiss him not on lips but throat Old Count interferes—Rage and fury diabolical—This man belongs to me—I want him—a prisoner for a time. . . ."

–Joseph S. Bierman, "The Genesis and Dating of
Dracula from Bram Stoker's Working Notes,"
Notes and Queries, 24 (1977): 39–41

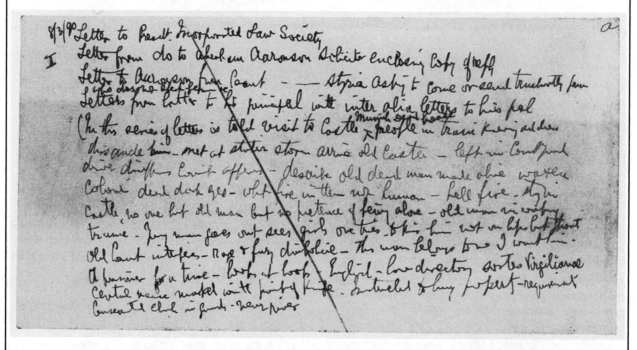

The earliest dated working document for Dracula *(Bram Stoker's* Dracula: A Centennial Exhibition
at the Rosenbach Museum & Library, 1997; Elizabeth Miller Collection)

finished text was a nine-line extract from Peter Hawkins's sealed letter, which the Count hands to Harker. Otherwise, the details all emerge from two conversations between Dracula and his guest. In these notes of March 1890, the Count evidently lives in Styria (where Le Fanu's *Carmilla* was set). Since Styria was largely German-speaking, the stipulation that the agent does not speak German was presumably to protect the Count from gossiping peasants. As historian Clive Leatherdale has pointed out, in Stoker's short story *Dracula's Guest* Jonathan Harker cannot speak German—"it was difficult to argue with a man," writes Harker, "when I did not know his language"—whereas in the final version of *Dracula* we are told on the first page that he has a "smattering of German . . . indeed, I don't know how I should be able to get on without it."]

Then there were to be letters from the trustworthy agent to his Principal, and to his girlfriend, describing the journey to the castle in Styria, including a visit to the Munich Dead House, followed by a train journey to Styria, where he is met by a coachman (who is really the Count) at the station.

[This Munich incident is developed by Stoker in subsequent notes. It involves Harker catching his first glimpse of the Count near a mortuary; only when Harker is safely back in England, and the Count has come to look exactly as he did in Munich, does the young solicitor realize the connection. The incident survived the change of locale from Styria to Transylvania.]

The letters would then describe the arrival at an ancient castle, the first appearance of the Count (as himself), with his devil-dark eyes, and the atmosphere in the castle where the old Count *seems* alone but clearly is not. There followed the incident with the girls who try to kiss him not on the lips but on the throat, culminating in the Count saying, "This man belongs to me I want him." After that, the young lawyer describes becoming a prisoner in the castle and, to pass the time, consulting his law directory for the Sortes Virgilianae: he has been instructed to buy a large property for the Count, with a consecrated church in the grounds, situated near a river.

[This is the earliest example of Bram Stoker extending the "rules" of the vampire genre: the Count, it seems, has to rest in consecrated earth. There will be many more such extensions.]

The next notes are, in effect, an early cast list for the novel. The cast (in spring 1890) includes Abraham Aaronson; the lawyer's clerk who goes to Styria; a mad doctor; a mad patient who has "a theory of perpetual life"; a "Philosophic Historian"; a German professor of history; a detective inspector; an undertaker; a girl who dies; another girl who is the young lawyer's bright and sceptical sister; and the Count's two servants in London (a silent man and a dumb woman), who are said to be controlled by the evil powers of the Count.

[In this cast list the character who was to become the Dutch Professor Abraham Van Helsing was no less than *three* separate characters: historian, German professor of history and detective inspector. In the event, Van Helsing was to become historian, philosopher, priest, detective and scientist. The detective-story element of the story was evidently to be stronger during the early stages: there are references in subsequent notes to "tracing the criminal" and to the conundrum caused to the Count's trackers because they are "in want of a clue to whereabouts." Also in this list the Count has two strange servants in London, whereas in *Dracula* one of Stoker's more atmospheric touches was to have the Count a shabby genteel aristocrat, without servants—he does all the domestic chores himself. Although the Count apologizes to Harker, "My people are not available," the young solicitor realizes that the Count has no "people" in his employ when he discovers his host making the bed and laying the dinner table. The Mina Harker character was at this stage to be the young lawyer's "shrewd, sceptical sister."]

Then comes a full chapter outline, written on Lyceum Theatre notepaper and dated "14/3/90." The outline consists of four "Books," headed *Styria to London*, *Tragedy*, *Discovery* and *Punishment*, each broken up into seven chapters. It reads like the synopsis page of a theatre programme.

Book I begins with the lawyer's correspondence, and the clerk's visit to Styria, via Munich (where he encounters "wolves" and "blue flame and c"). After arriving at the castle, he experiences "Loneliness, the Kiss 'this man belongs to me'." Then Dr Seward's diary takes over, with details of the old chapel and the Sortes Virgilianae ("notes in letter"), and of someone called the fly patient who, the notes add, is in love with death.

[The name "Styria" was written first by Stoker and then, at a later date, deleted to make way for "Transylvania." The names Seward, Lucy, Mina and

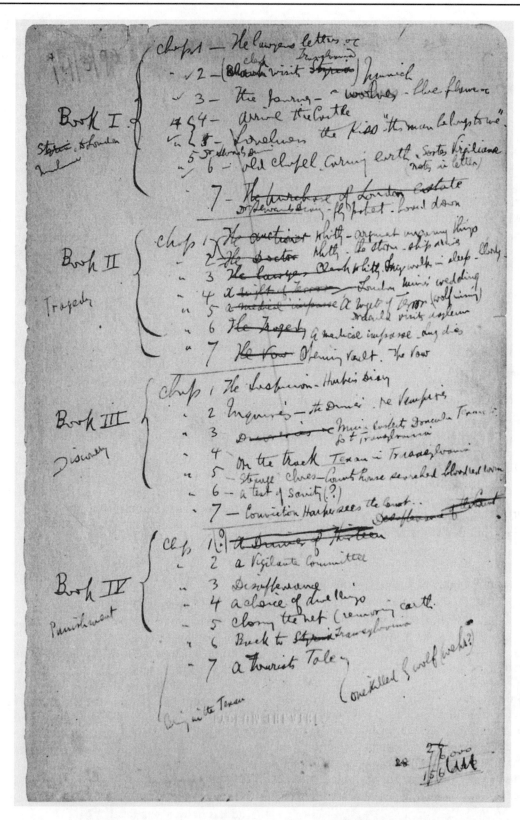

An early chapter outline for Dracula *(Bram Stoker's* Dracula: A Centennial Exhibition at the Rosenbach Museum & Library, *1997; Elizabeth Miller Collection)*

Harker were all written first time round. This may mean that between 8 March and 14 March 1890 Bram Stoker settled on these proper names. The Van Helsing character (or characters) does not appear at all in this outline.]

Book II begins at Whitby, Yorkshire, with arguments concerning uncanny happenings, a storm, the arrival of a ship and Lucy walking in her sleep. Then Mina's wedding takes place in London, followed by a night of terror ("wolf missing") and Count Dracula's visit to the lunatic asylum. It ends with the death of Lucy (the "tragedy" of the Book's title), the opening of the vault and a vow.

[The phrase "Count Dracula" was evidently added later, between Chapters 5 and 6 of Book II, as must have been another reference to "Dracula" in Book III, Chapter 3. In March 1890, he was still "Count Wampyr."]

Book III opens with Harker's diary, various suspicions and inquiries, and "The Dinner." Mina begins to suspect the Count, and the Texan goes on a visit to Transylvania, where he finds himself "on the track." The Count's house is searched for clues, and a "blood-red room" is discovered. The Count disappears, but at the end of the Book he is sighted by Harker.

[Bram Stoker originally had the idea of including a dinner-party scene (at Dr Seward's), in Book III, where each of the thirteen diners would be given a number and would be asked to tell something strange, the "order of numbers" making the story complete. The punch-line would be that the Count would enter the room. This strange variation on Lord Byron's "we will each write a ghost story" (at the end of which, in a sense, *The Vampyre* walked in) also, perhaps, relates to one of Stoker's odder performances, which was serialized on 30 January 1892 in the *Gentlewoman* magazine. It was Chapter 10 of *The Fate of Fenella,* the other nine chapters being written by "well-known writer(s) of Fiction, without consulting his or her collaborateurs, the result being a . . . literary curiosity"; they included Arthur Conan Doyle and F. Anstey. *The Fate of Fenella* was published, complete, later in the year. Stoker eventually junked the idea of the "dinner of thirteen." Later in Book III, the (as yet unnamed) Texan was to visit Transylvania on his own, and possibly be killed by a were-wolf. In the final version of *Dracula,* Quincey P. Morris falls victim to the "knives of the gypsies," but he has such a tangential relationship to the rest of the plot that

some commentators have even suggested he is secretly in league with the Count himself (in a kind of American-Transylvanian unholy alliance). Morris (at first named "Brutus") was also originally, to have been "an . . . inventor from Texas," a "Tourist" and a walking example of Yankee know-how who arms himself with the latest Maxim Gun for the final assault on the Castle. Stoker's reference to "a vigilante committee" and "a necktie party" suggest that the novel had more Western connections in the author's mind at one stage, in common with his novel *The Shoulder of Shasta,* published in October 1895.]

Book IV opens on another dinner party and a vigilante committee. The net closes on the Count ("remaining earth") and the scene shifts back to Styria. The last chapter, entitled "A Tourist's Tale," includes "one killed by a wolf (wehr?)," and finishes on the *aide-mémoire* "Bring in the Texan."

There follows another cast list, this time headed *Historiae Personae,* which includes some characters who were to appear in the finished novel: Dr Seward, the "Girl engaged to him," Lucy Westenra, the lawyer Peter Hawkins from Exeter, his clerk Jonathan Harker, Harker's fiancée, the pupil teacher Wilhelmina Murray, known as Mina, and a Texan named "Brutus Morris." It includes even more characters who were *not* to survive the drafting process: two lawyers called William Abbott and A. M. Young, a friend and schoolfellow of Mina called Kate Reed, the Count's two English servants, a detective named Cotford, a psychical research agent named Alfred Singleton, an American inventor from Texas (unnamed), a German professor named Max Windshoeffel and a painter named Francis Aytown. At this early stage, the Count was still to be called "Count Wampyr."

[In this cast list the Van Helsing character was still to be divided into three—only this time it was a detective, a psychical research agent and a German professor, and each of these characters had been given a name: Cotford, Alfred Singleton and Max Windshoeffel. Perhaps Professor Windshoeffel was based upon the other German professor called Max in Bram Stoker's life at the time—Professor Max Muller of Oxford. The appearance of the fine artist "Francis Aytown" may relate to the next two documents. Wilhelmina gets her full name for the first time, as does Lucy, and Mina's friend and confidante Kate Reed (later to be jettisoned) makes her first appearance. The phrase "Count Wampyr" was changed by Stoker to "Count Dracula" at a later date.]

An early list of characters for the novel. The list includes characters who were later dropped from Dracula *and shows
"Count Wampyr," changed to "Count Dracula" (*Bram Stoker's *Dracula:* A Centennial Exhibition
at the Rosenbach Museum & Library, *1997; Elizabeth Miller Collection).*

The next document, again written on Lyceum Theatre notepaper, consists of three short checklists of the "characteristics of Count Wampyr." According to Stoker's notes, the Count:

goes through life entirely by instinct;

must cross running water at the exact flood or slack of the tide;

has an influence over rats, and over the animals in the zoological gardens ("rage of lion, eagle and c . . . wolves, hyenas cowed");

absolutely despises death and the dead;

loves creating evil thoughts in others, and banishing good ones–thus destroying their will;

can see in the dark, and can even get through the thickest of London fogs by instinct;

is insensible to the beauties of music;

has "white teeth and c," and the magic power of making himself large or small;

must be carried, led, helped, or in some way welcomed over the threshold;

is enormously strong, even though he never–apparently–eats or drinks;

has an ambivalent attitude towards the icons of religion: he can be moved only by relics older than his own *real* date or century (that is, when he actually lived)–more recent relics leave him unmoved;

always uses for money his stores of old gold, which are eventually "traced to Salzburg banking house";

"Immortality–Gladstone" . . .

Where the Count's image is concerned:

painters can't make a likeness of him–however hard the artist tries, the subject always ends up looking like someone else;

equally, it is impossible to photograph (or "Codak") him–the resulting print always makes him appear "black or like skeleton corpse";

and there are no looking glasses in the Count's house–because he has no reflection and casts no shadow; the lights in his house must therefore be specially arranged "to give no shadow."

As to the Count's folkloric background:

a long branch of a wild rose must be placed in his coffin, to prevent him leaving it;

a swallow–or "galinele lui Dieu"–is considered lucky, as the fowl of the Lord;

so is a crow, notably when it flies over a person's head; St. George's Day is on 24 April ("our May 6th"), and the night before is, by tradition, a Witches' Sabbat.

[These three check-lists of Count Wampyr's "characteristics" (rather than those of vampires in general) include some predictable entries as well as some surprises. In addition to the "characteristics" of the folkloric vampire, they incorporate some plot elements (the Count at London zoo; the influence over rats and "lower" life forms; the London fog; the Count's favoured currency of old gold) which relate only to the story of *Dracula*. Other "characteristics," which Stoker did not in the end use, seem to belong to the world of *The Yellow Book* and have more to do with Oscar Wilde than folklore: the *fin-de-siècle* vampire is insensible to the beauties of music, he *loves* to create evil thoughts and "painters cannot paint him–their likenesses [are] always like someone else." This latter "characteristic" suggests a close family resemblance to Wilde's *The Picture of Dorian Gray* (which, in 1891, had just been published) and may also connect with the character "A Painter–Francis Aytown" in the previous cast list. Stoker was, of course, an acquaintance of Wilde, and a close friend of his neighbour in Cheyne Walk, Chelsea, James McNeill Whistler. Wilde's play *Salomé* was written in Paris in 1891. He decided to cast Sarah Bernhardt in the title role during a party at Henry Irving's (with Stoker probably present), and when *Salomé*, was published in February 1893, Wilde immediately sent a signed copy of it to Florence Stoker (this Salomé, especially in Beardsley's famous illustration, is a seductive little vampire, part-vampire and part vamp). The idea that vampires could be moved only by relics older than their own *real* date sounds ancient and folkloric, but appears to have been invented by Stoker. The more up-to-date idea that you cannot photograph (or "Codak") a vampire because he will come out looking like a corpse is logical–if that is the correct word in the circumstances–but also new. In *Dracula* Harker does use his "Kodak" to photograph the house at Purfleet (or rather "views of it from various points") but sadly, he never tries this relatively new process out on the Count himself. The references to the swallow as the fowl of the Lord, the crow as unlucky and the dates of St. George's Day are all taken verbatim from Gerard's *Transylvanian Superstitions*. The "Salzburg banking house" reference would suggest that these lists date from the time when the book was still to be set in Austrian Styria–that is, before February 1892; in the finished text Dracula's bankers are Herren Klopstock and Billreuth of Buda-Pesth. The bizarre line, "Immortality–Gladstone," unless it refers to the bag of that name, remains a puzzle, whatever the date. There is no mention of the fact that vampires are nocturnal creatures. That may be because Stoker chose to ignore this particular "rule"; Dracula can function in the daytime, although he is not at his best. When Stoker notes that the Count never eats or drinks, he must presumably be referring to solid food and vintage wine; in the novel itself, the Count does have a preferred beverage, but it has to be served at body temperature. After noting that he has never *seen*

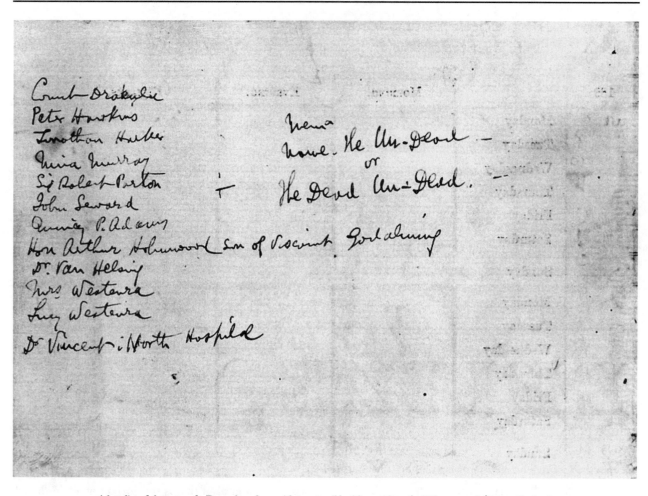

A late list of characters for Dracula, *along with two possible titles, neither of which was used (Bram Stoker's*
Dracula: A Centennial Exhibition at the Rosenbach Museum & Library, *1997;*
Elizabeth Miller Collection)

the Count eat or drink, Harker sensibly observes, "He must be a very peculiar man."]

Also appended to the document is a series of short notes concerning the visit of the lawyer's clerk to Munich, en route for the Castle. As he is walking past the Dead House in Munich, the young man is to see a waxen face among the funeral flowers. At first he thinks it is a corpse, but it turn out to be the face of a living man. Long afterwards, when the Count is in London–and when his "white moustache" has grown–Harker will recognize the Count's face as the one he saw among the flowers in Munich. Evidently, the face presented by the Count when he is in his castle is appreciably different–perhaps younger.

[In the published novel the Count has a "great white moustache," or a "heavy moustache"–as befits a retired military commander–when Harker first meets him at the Castle. There is the suggestion that

Dracula gets *younger* (rather than more ancient) as the story progresses.]

There follows a brief memo, dated "29/2/92," outlining the structure of the beginning of the novel. Harker's diary, with its Munich interlude, still forms Chapter 2. Chapter 1 consists of correspondence about "Purchase of Estate." Chapter 3 continues the Munich story (so it remains an extensive section of the narrative) and Chapter 4 takes us to "Bistritz–Borgo Pass–Castle." What happens there, as Stoker cryptically adds, is "Sortes Virgil. Belongs to Me."

[This revised structure is particularly significant for its references to "Bistritz–Borgo Pass." By the end of February 1892 Stoker had evidently decided to shift the location from Styria to Bistrita in Transylvania. Since his knowledge of the Borgo Pass (and of how to spell Romanian place-names) came from Charles Boner's *Transylvania,* and of local folklore from Gerard, it appears that he had read these two books by this date. He may also have known about the name "Dracula" as early as Summer 1890. So by 1892 all the key pieces of the jigsaw were already in place—*five years* before publication.]

Another memo represents a slight refinement of the outline structure of February 1892. It still opens on lawyers' letters about "Purchase of Estate" but is more explicit about "Harker's diary—Munich—Wolf" and "Harker's diary—Munich—death House," and cross-cuts between Harker's journey from "Bistritz to Castle Dracula" and Dr Seward's diary entries concerning the "Fly man," so that the "Fly man" (who was later to become Renfield) heralds Harker's arrival at the Castle rather than, as in the published version, the Count's arrival at his English residence. Also, the "Belongs to Me" incident appears to be cross-cut with events in Whitby. The most significant aspect of this memo is that it explicitly mentions "Castle Dracula" for the very first time.

The next document is a fully worked-out structure, letter by letter, of Book I. It begins with a letter from Sir Robert Parton, President of the Law Society, to Peter Hawkins of Cathedral Place, Exeter, stating that he has been contacted by one "Count Wampyr." Peter Hawkins, we learn from another letter, has gout and decides to let Harker handle the conveyancing of an estate to the Count (which he finds at Purfleet). Letter 6 is from Kate Reed to Lucy Westenra, telling Lucy about Harker's visit to a school to see pupil-teacher Mina Murray; there is a postscript in which Kate tells of "how she thought after waiting it would be well to ask Mina's permission before telling her story." Letter 7 continues this theme: "she knows it's all dead long ago, and that she goes to stay with her" on her summer holidays at Whitby. Letter 8 is a telegram from "Dracula to Hawkins," asking that Harker set out for Munich.

[Strangely, although the name "Count Wampyr" appears in Letters 1–5, later crossed out by Bram Stoker and superseded by the new name "Count Dracula," from Letter 8 onwards the name "Dracula" was written first time round—and continues that way throughout Stoker's summary. Perhaps the early chapters were being copied from a previous (but post-"Abraham Aaronson") version. Peter Hawkins's attack of gout, mentioned here for the first time, is still there in the finished novel. "An attack of gout," he writes in Chapter II, "from which malady I am a constant sufferer, forbids absolutely any travelling on my part."

The two letters from confidante Kate Reed seem to imply, first, that she has some "story" which is of interest to Mina and, second, that it is "all dead long ago," so they can remain friends. Could it possibly have been a romance with Jonathan? In the published version, he is *very* correct on such matters.]

The structure then changes from the letter form to "journal in shorthand of Jonathan Harker on his first journey abroad." Since this journal is being written especially to show Mina on Harker's return, all business matters have been deliberately omitted. Chapter 2 begins with the directions which have been sent by the Count, to go by the direct service to Munich and then to "stop at (Hotel Marienbad) Quatre Saisons and await instructions." On his first day, Harker visits the Pinakothek Museum "and c," and also the Dead House. There he catches sight of "old man on bier"—among some flowers—who seems at first to be a corpse but in fact isn't. He goes back to the Quatre Saisons hotel. The following morning he receives a wire from "Transylvania. Bistritz," giving him details of the next leg of his journey. Chapter 3 (still in journal form) describes the journey to Bistritz, where Harker checks into his hotel. The Count's name is well known there, for it was the hoteliers who sent on the telegram; but when they hear of the young man's destination, they become "all very sad and mysterious." There are some strange gifts for him ("see xix century"). [These 'gifts' are an explicit reference to Gerard's article in the *Nineteenth Century* magazine.] Harker is deposited at the Borgo Pass by the Diligence, where he is met by a "driver man muffled" on a carriage. The journey from the Borgo Pass to the Castle is eventful: some wolves surround the carriage, some blue flames are sighted, until, amid the howlings of wolves and dogs, thunder and other "weird sounds"—they eventually arrive at the castle at midnight. At this juncture, "enter Count-supper-to bed-describe room, etc." [Stoker's shorthand "enter Count" reads like a stage direction for Henry Irving!]

Chapter 4 continues Harker's account in his journal of his stay in the Castle. Although Harker is left all alone in the daytime, he feels he is a prisoner: "the books—Sortes Virgilianae—and the visitors—is it a dream—women stoop to kiss him. terror of death. Suddenly Count turns her away—'this man belongs to me'." [Later in this structure, at Book III, Chapter 7, Jonathan Harker "sees the Count—met him going into the Munich Death-House": clearly, for some reason, by then the Count's appearance has become the same as in Book I, Chapter 2. The "dinner of revenge" is also still there.]

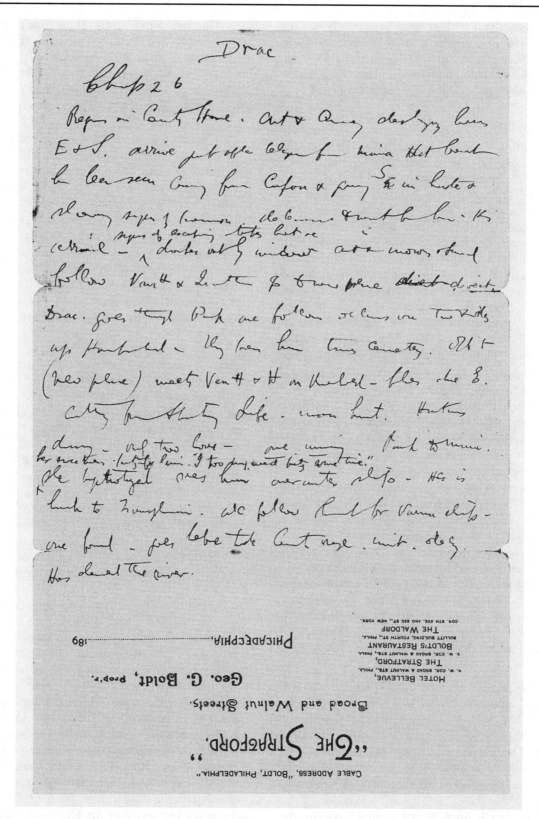

Stoker's outline for chapter 26 of the novel, evidently made when he was in the United States (Bram Stoker's Dracula: A Centennial Exhibition at the Rosenbach Museum & Library, 1997; Elizabeth Miller Collection)

Bram Stoker's final outline of the early part of the novel–the next document–is evidently an attempt to sort out the timescale of his story. It is written on a printed, all-purpose diary with no dates on it–just the headings *189–Mon–Sat, Morn Eve* and *Remarks*.

The outline begins on 16 March with Count Dracula's letter to Peter Hawkins (dated, Stoker adds, 4 March old style), then continues on 21 March with Sir Robert Parton's letter to Hawkins– the President of the Law Society to a senior solicitor. Hawkins's letter to the Count is written on Thursday, 23 March and the reply a week later (18 March old style). Jonathan Harker visits Purfleet on 12 April and starts his house-deeds search on Thursday, 13 April–the same day as Count Dracula writes to the *maître d'hôtel* of the Quatre Saisons in Munich. Two days later, Harker writes to Hawkins, and on Sunday, 16 April, he visits Mina at the school where she teaches.

[Either Stoker wasn't concentrating, or Mina taught at a boarding-school. Otherwise, why should she be visited at school on a Sunday?]

The following day, Katie writes to Lucy, and on Wednesday, 19 April, Hawkins writes to Dracula.

Following a telegram from Dracula dispatched on Monday, 24 April, Harker leaves London on the night of the 25th, arrives in Paris early the following morning, leaves Paris at 8.25 a.m. and arrives in Munich at 8.35 p.m. Having checked into the Quatre Saisons late on Wednesday, 26 April, Harker has his adventure with "snowstorm and wolf" on the following day, gets back to the Hotel early on the morning of the 28th and spends all 29 April recovering. On the evening of Sunday, 30 April, he goes to the opera to see Wagner's *Flying Dutchman*. Monday, 1 May, is the day of the Dead House incident, and is also the day after Walpurgis Night. Harker leaves Munich by train at 8.35 that evening. His destination is Vienna, via Salzburg.

[This Wagnerian curtain-raiser to the events in Transylvania provides a nice link with the world of Henry Irving (who performed W. G. Wills's version of the legend of the Flying Dutchman, *Vanderdecken,* from June 1878 onwards) and with Bram Stoker's personal interests. *Vanderdecken* was reviewed by Stoker: "the chief actor is not quick but dead . . . and in the last act . . . answers the question 'where are we?': 'Between the living and the dead'." After the opening night, Stoker helped Irving to "cut and alter the play," and in 1891–2 was involved in discussions

with Irving and Hall Caine about a new version of the story–which were to come to nothing. He was a great fan of Wagner's operatic music, and especially of Hans Richter's interpretations. In the 1890s, according to the *Personal Reminiscences,* "with my wife I attended the Wagner Cycle at Bayreuth . . . and heard Wagner's *Meistersinger* in all its magnificent perfection." Stoker was also to discuss the lighting effects in *The Flying Dutchman,* with Richter, over lunch on 24 October 1900. The events in Munich, according to this late timescale by Stoker, occur in an unexpected order. First, the adventure of the "snowstorm and wolf," then the visit to the opera, then Walpurgis Nacht, then the Dead House incident. On the first line of *Dracula* as published, all of this is reduced to "Left Munich at 8.35 p.m."; only the time of departure survives from the drafting stage.]

Tuesday, 2 May, is spent travelling: a change of trains at Vienna in the morning (arrive 6.45 a.m., depart 8.25 a.m.), another at Buda-Pesth over lunchtime (arrive 1.30 p.m., depart 2.00 p.m.), followed by arrival at Klausenburg at 10.34 p.m. After an overnight stay at Klausenburg (2–3 May), Harker leaves by the 8 a.m. train and arrives in Bistritz twelve hours later. After another overnight stay, he leaves Bistritz at 2 p.m.–by coach–and reaches the Borgo Pass seven hours later at 9.00 p.m. (or one hour earlier than the scheduled eight hours). Harker finally reaches the Castle, driven by the muffled and disguised coachman, in the early hours of Friday, 5 May. It takes him two days to realize that the Castle is in fact a prison, and on Tuesday, 9 May, he tries to write home about his experiences so far. On the Wednesday, he sees the Count crawling out of his window and down the wall of the Castle, and on Thursday, 11 May, he sees "the women kissing." Friday is spent in bed, writing letters. To judge by the crossings-out, Bram Stoker then changed his mind about the dating of the incidents in the Castle. He substituted the night of Saturday, 13 May, for the window incident, and Monday, 15 May, for "women kissing."

[On the manuscript of this timescale, Stoker wrote–just before the entry for Thursday, 11 May– "Jonathan Diary" as a heading. This would suggest that all the previous incidents were to be communicated in the form of a collection of documents: the legal letters, Katie's letter, Dracula's telegram, then letters home from the Castle. Stoker also wrote "Seward's Diary" against the dates Wednesday, 3 May, and Saturday, 6 May, so at one stage the account of the journey from Vienna to Transylvania

A calendar of events in the novel, set in the year 1893 (Bram Stoker's Dracula: A Centennial Exhibition at the Rosenbach Museum & Library, 1997; Elizabeth Miller Collection)

Works Consulted

Stoker referred to many sources in order to provide background for his story. Here follows an alphabetical list of the source texts identified in the Notes, a list first published by Clive Leatherdale in The Origins of Dracula *(1987). Asterisks have been added to indicate those from which it is known that Stoker took notes:*

Sabine Baring-Gould, *The Book of Were-Wolves: Being an Account of a Terrible Superstition* (1865)*

Sabine Baring-Gould, *Curious Myths of the Middle Ages* (1867)

Sabine Baring-Gould, *Germany, Past and Present* (1879)

Fletcher S Bassett, *Legends and Superstitions of the Sea and of Sailors – In All Lands and at All Times* (1879)

Isabella L Bird, *The Golden Chersonese* (1883)*

Charles Boner, *Transylvania: Its Products and its People* (1865)*

Sir Thomas Browne, *Religio Medici* (1643)*

Andrew F Crosse, *Round About the Carpathians* (1878)*

Rushton M Dorman, *The Origin of Primitive Superstitions: And Their Development into the Worship of Spirits and the Doctrine of Spiritual Agency among the Aborigines of America* (1881)

A Fellow of the Carpathian Society, *Magyarland: Being the Narrative of our Travels through the Highlands and Lowlands of Hungary* (1881)*

Emily Gerard, "Transylvanian Superstitions" (1885)*

Major E C Johnson, *On the Track of the Crescent: Erratic Notes from the Piraeus to Pesth* (1885)*

John Jones, *The Natural and the Supernatural: Or, Man – Physical, Apparitional and Spiritual* (1861)

William Jones, *Credulities Past and Present* (1880)

William Jones, *History and Mystery of Precious Stones* (1880)

Rev W Henry Jones and Lewis L Kropf, *The Folk-Tales of the Magyars* (1889)

Henry Charles Lea, *Superstition and Force – Essays on The Wager of Law, The Wager of Battle, The Ordeal and Torture* (1878)

Rev Frederick George Lee, *The Other World: Or, Glimpses of the Supernatural – Being Facts, Records and Traditions* (1875)

Henry Lee, *Sea Fables Explained* (1883)

Henry Lee, *Sea Monsters Unmasked* (1883)

Sarah Lee, *Anecdotes of Habits and Instincts of Birds, Reptiles and Fishes* (1853)

L F Alfred Maury (no titles given)

Herbert Mayo, *On the Truths Contained in Popular Superstitions – with an Account of Mesmerism* (1851)

Thomas Joseph Pettigrew, *On Superstitions connected with the History and Practice of Medicine and Surgery* (1844)

Rev Albert Reville, *The Devil: His Origin, Greatness and Decadence* (1871)

F C and J Rivington, *The Theory of Dreams* (1808)*

F K Robinson, *A Whitby Glossary* (1876)*

Robert H. Scott, *Fishery Barometer Manual* (1887)*

William Wilkinson, *An Account of the Principalities of Wallachia and Moldavia: with various Political Observations Relating to Them* (1820)*

–Elizabeth Miller, Dracula: Sense & Nonsense, *pp. 21–22*

may have been compiled from Harker's reminiscences to Dr Seward; or he may still have intended to cross-cut between the journey and Seward's simultaneous experiences. If "Jonathan Diary" *was* to begin on Thursday, 11 May, then its first page would have described "the women kissing" incident, which would, of course, have given it even more prominence in the story. The date he finally settled on for this incident, Monday, 15 May, was the same as in the published novel.

The whole of this detailed breakdown of the story outline into dates and times was evidently written *after* Stoker had made up his mind about the details of the story itself. It suggests that the initial legal correspondence was present until the final stages of drafting the novel, as was Katie Reed's correspondence with Lucy. Also Jonathan Harker's five-day stopover in Munich (why five days?) survived until a very late stage. As McNally and Florescu have pointed out, these dates and days correspond with the year 1893. It is quite possible that Stoker was already sorting out the timescale of *Dracula* in that same year, for we know that he wanted the events to seem "exactly contemporary."]

Appended to the timescale was a detailed timetable of train arrivals and departures from London to Paris, Paris to Munich, Munich to Vienna via Salzburg, Vienna to Budapest, Budapest to Klausenburg, Klausenburg to Bistritz and of the coach journey from Bistritz to the Borgo Pass. Stoker simply transposed this timetable (from Baedeker's) into his own order of events.

[He was evidently keen to establish an aura of "authenticity" around his story, by getting all the dates and timetables right, so that, as he put it in his opening words to *Dracula,* his history "may stand forth as simple fact." It was a passion shared by Count Dracula himself, who owns "such books of reference as the London Directory, the 'Red' and 'Blue' books, Whitaker's Almanack, the Army and Navy Lists, and . . . the Law List." Later, Jonathan Harker discovers the Count "lying on the sofa, reading, of all things in the world, an English Bradshaw's Guide." As Henry Irving's manager, Stoker would have had to look after the complex logistics of his national and international tours, involving constant reference to Bradshaw's and, for overseas, Baedeker's guides.]

–Vampyres: Lord Byron to Count Dracula (London: Faber & Faber, 1991), pp. 303–316

Vampire Lore

Stoker obtained his knowledge of vampire lore from many places. One of the source texts on his list—Herbert Mayo's On the Truths Contained in Popular Superstitions—*included a chapter on the vampire sightings of the early eighteenth century, including the Arnold Paul case. Stoker was familiar with at least some of the vampire fiction and poetry published earlier in his own century. His Notes allow for the identification of several specific sources that directly influenced the writing of* Dracula.

One of the most important of Stoker's sources is Emily Gerard's "Transylvanian Superstitions," an article published in the July 1885 issue of The Nineteenth Century, *which might well have convinced the author of* Dracula *to change the locale of his vampire's homeland from Styria to Transylvania. Stoker gleaned other bits and pieces of vampire lore from a variety of publications, including a New York newspaper he read while on one of the Lyceum's American tours.*

From "Transylvanian Superstitions"
Emily Gerard

Transylvania might well be termed the land of superstition, for nowhere else does this curious crooked plant of delusion flourish as persistently and in such bewildering variety. It would almost seem as though the whole species of demons, pixies, witches, and hobgoblins, driven from the rest of Europe by the wand of science, had taken refuge within this mountain rampart, well aware that here they would find secure lurking-places, whence they might defy their persecutors yet awhile.

There are many reasons why these fabulous beings should retain an abnormally firm hold on the soil of these parts; and looking at the matter closely we find here no less than three separate sources of superstition.

First, there is what may be called the indigenous superstition of the country, the scenery of which is peculiarly adapted to serve as background to all sorts of supernatural beings and monsters. There are innumerable caverns, whose mysterious depths seem made to harbour whole legions of evil spirits: forest glades fit only for fairy folk on moonlight nights, solitary lakes which instinctively call up visions of water sprites; golden treasures lying hidden in mountain chasms, all of which have gradually insinuated themselves into the minds of the oldest inhabitants, the Roumenians, and influenced their way of thinking, so that these people, by nature imaginative and poetically inclined, have built up for themselves out of the surrounding materials a whole code of fanciful superstition, to which they adhere as closely as to their religion itself.

–p. 130

. . . .

The spirit of evil (or, not to put too fine a point upon it, the devil) plays a conspicuous part in the Roumenian code of superstition, and such designations as the Gregynia Drakuluj (devil's garden), the Gania Drakuluj (devil's mountain), Yadu Drakuluj (devil's hell or abyss), &c. &c., which we frequently find attached to rocks, caverns, or heights, attest the fact that these people believe themselves to be surrounded on all sides by a whole legion of evil spirits.

The devils are furthermore assisted by witches and dragons, and to all of these dangerous beings are ascribed peculiar powers on particular days and at certain places.

–p. 131

. . . .

To different hours of the day are likewise ascribed different influences, favourable or the reverse. Thus it is always considered unlucky to look at oneself in the glass after sunset; also it is not wise to sweep the dust over the threshold in the evening, or to give back a sieve or a whip which has been borrowed of a neighbour.

The exact hour of noon is precarious on account of the evil spirit *Pripolniza,* and so is midnight because of the *miase nópte* (night spirit), and it is safer to remain within doors at these hours. If, however, some misguided peasant does happen to leave his home at midnight, and espies (as very likely he may) a flaming dragon in the sky, he need not necessarily give himself up as lost, for if he have the presence of mind to stick a fork into the ground alongside of him, the fiery monster will thereby be prevented from carrying him off.

–p. 132

. . . .

The Greek Church, to which the Roumenians exclusively belong, has an abnormal number of feast-days, to almost each of which peculiar customs and superstitions are attached. I will here only attempt to mention a few of the principal ones.

–pp. 132–133

. . . .

In the night preceding Easter Sunday witches and demons are abroad, and hidden treasures are said to betray their site by a glowing flame. No God-fearing peasant will, however, allow himself to be tempted by the hopes of such riches, which he cannot on that day appropriate without sin. On no account should he presume to absent himself from the midnight church service, and his devotion will be rewarded by the mystic qualities attached to the wax candle he has carried in

Emily Gerard and Transylvanian Superstitions

Emily Gerard, whose article "Transylvanian Superstitions" was a significant source for much of the folklore in Dracula. *She also wrote* The Land Beyond the Forest *(1888), a book Stoker may have read (courtesy of Lokke Heiss).*

"No one ever comes to Transylvania in cold blood . . ."

–Emily Gerard,
The Land Beyond the Forest

Emily Gerard was right. In her day, no one ever traveled to remote and distant Transylvania without a compelling reason. Her motives were many: she was a dutiful wife, a writer, and an amateur anthropologist who must have sensed that a trip to Transylvania was an opportunity for the adventure of a lifetime.

Born in Scotland near Airdrie (just east of Glasgow), Emily at the age of fourteen was sent to Switzerland to attend finishing school. While in Venice she met an Austrian cavalry officer, Miecislaus Laszowski, whom she married in 1869. While raising a family in Austria, she began a career as a writer, producing novels, essays and book reviews for British magazines and newspapers.

In 1885, Emily's husband was assigned for a two-year tour of duty in Transylvania. With their two children, Emily followed her husband from post to post, eventually publishing a book about her experiences, *Transylvania, The Land Beyond the Forest* (1888), a meticulous recording of local ethnic customs. A chapter from this book had been published separately as "Transylvanian Superstitions" in *The Nineteenth Century Magazine* in 1885. This article, with its elements about vampire lore (including the "nosferatu") was found by Bram Stoker during the course of his research for what would become *Dracula*.

Returning to Vienna, Emily became close friends with Samuel Clemens (Mark Twain) who was in Austria at the time. Spurred by this friendship, she returned to writing, producing novels and short stories about the "fin de siècle" world of the Habsburg Empire. Her husband died, after a long illness, in 1904. Only four weeks later, Emily succumbed to a fever at the age of 56.

Though her writings about Transylvania represent a small fraction of her total work, Emily Gerard will be best remembered as the woman who helped inspire Bram Stoker to establish Transylvania as the homeland of his vampire Count, and who gave the world the word "nosferatu."

–Lokke Heiss

his hand, and which when lighted hereafter during a thunderstorm will infallibly keep the lightning from striking his house.

The greatest luck which can befall a mortal is to be born on Easter Sunday while the bells are ringing, but it is not lucky to die on that day. The spoon with which the Easter eggs have been removed from the boiling pot is carefully treasured up, and worn in the belt by the shepherd; it gives him the power to distinguish the witches who seek to molest his flock.

Perhaps the most important day in the year is St. George's, the 23rd of April (corresponds to our 5th of May), the eve of which is still frequently kept by occult meetings taking place at night in lonely caverns or within ruined walls, and where all the ceremonies usual to the celebration of a witches' Sabbath are put into practice.

The feast itself is the great day to beware of witches, to counteract whose influence square-cut blocks of green turf are placed in front of each door and window. This is supposed effectually to bar their entrance to the house or stables, but for still greater safety it is usual here for the peasants to keep watch all night by the sleeping cattle.

This same night is the best for finding treasures, and many people spend it in wandering about the hills trying to probe the earth for the gold it contains. Vain and futile as such researches usually are, yet they have in this country a somewhat greater semblance of reason than in most other parts, for perhaps nowhere else have so many successive nations been forced to secrete their riches in flying from an enemy, to say nothing of the numerous veins of undiscovered gold and silver which must be seaming the country in all directions. Not a year passes without bringing to light some earthern jar containing old Dacian coins, or golden ornaments of Roman origin, and all such discoveries serve to feed and keep up the national superstition.

In the night of St. George's Day (so say the legends) all these treasures begin to burn, or, to speak in mystic language, to 'bloom' in the bosom of the earth, and the light they give forth, described as a bluish flame resembling the colour of lighted spirits of wine, serves to guide favoured mortals to their place of concealment. The conditions to the successful raising of such a treasure are manifold, and difficult of accomplishment. In the first place, it is by no means easy for a common mortal who has not been born on a Sunday nor at midday when the bells are ringing, to hit upon a treasure at all. If he does, however, catch sight of a flame such as I have described, he must quickly stick a knife through the swaddling rags of his right foot, and then throw the knife in the direction of the flame he has seen. If two people are together during this discovery they must not on any account break

silence till the treasure is removed, neither is it allowed to fill up the hole from which anything has been taken, for that would induce a speedy death. Another important feature to be noted is that the lights seen before midnight on St. George's Day, denote treasures kept by benevolent spirits, while those which appear at a later hour are unquestionably of a pernicious nature.

–pp. 133–135

....

The feast of St. Elias, the 20th of the July (August 1), is a very unlucky day, on which the lightning may be expected to strike.

If a house struck by lightning begins to burn, it is not allowed to put out the flames, because God has lit the fire and it would be presumption if man were to dare to meddle. In some places it is believed that a fire lit by lightning can only be put out with milk.

An approved method for averting the danger of the dwelling being struck by lightning is to form a top by sticking a knife through a piece of bread, and spin it on the floor of the loft during the whole time the storm lasts. The ringing of bells is likewise very efficacious, provided, however, that the bell in question has been cast under a perfectly cloudless sky.

As I am on the subject of thunderstorms, I may as well here mention the *Scholomance,* or school supposed to exist somewhere in the heart of the mountains, and where all the secrets of nature, the language of animals, and all imaginable magic spells and charms are taught by the devil in person. Only ten scholars are admitted at a time, and when the course of learning has expired and nine of them are released to return to their homes, the tenth scholar is detained by the devil as payment, and mounted upon an *Ismeju* (dragon) he becomes henceforward the devil's aide-de-camp, and assists him in "making the weather," that is to say, preparing the thunderbolts.

A small lake, immeasurably deep, lying high up among the mountains to the south of Hermanstadt, is supposed to be the cauldron where is brewed the thunder, and in fair weather the dragon sleeps beneath the waters. Roumenian peasants anxiously warn the traveller to beware of throwing a stone into this lake lest it should wake the dragon and provoke a thunderstorm. It is, however, no mere superstition that in summer there occur almost daily thunderstorms at this spot, about the hour of midday, and numerous cairns of stones round the shores attest the fact that many people have here found their death by lightning. On this account the place is shunned, and no Roumenians will venture to rest here at the hour of noon.

–pp. 135–136

....

The *Pomana,* or funeral feast, is invariably held after the funeral, for much of the peace of the defunct depends upon the strictest observance of this ceremony. At this banquet all the favourite dishes of the dead man are served, and each guest receives a cake (*colac*) and a jug (*ulcior*), also a wax candle, in his memory. Similar *Pomanas* are repeated after a fortnight, six weeks, and on each anniversary for the next seven years; also, whenever the defunct has appeared in dream to any member of the family, this likewise calls for another *Pomana;* and when these conditions are not exactly complied with, the soul thus neglected is apt to wander complaining about the earth, and cannot find rest. These restless spirits, called *Strigoi,* are not malicious, but their appearance bodes no good, and may be regarded as omens of sickness or misfortune.

More decidedly evil, however, is the vampire, or *nosferatu,* in whom every Roumenian peasant believes as firmly as he does in heaven or hell. There are two sorts of vampires—living and dead. The living vampire is in general the illegitimate offspring of two illegitimate persons, but even a flawless pedigree will not ensure anyone against the intrusion of a vampire into his family vault, since every person killed by a *nosferatu* becomes likewise a vampire after death, and will continue to suck the blood of other innocent people till the spirit has been exorcised, either by opening the grave of the person suspected and driving a stake

---

A Whirlpool of Superstition

Stoker's use of Gerard's "Transylvania Superstitions" is evident in his novel.

. . . I read that every known superstition in the world is gathered into the horseshoe of the Carpathians, as if it were the centre of some sort of imaginative whirlpool.
　　—*Dracula,* Chapter I, Jonathan Harker's
　　　　　　　　　　　　　　　Journal, 3 May

"Do you know what day it is?" I answered that it was the fourth of May. She shook her head as she said again:
"Oh, yes! I know that, I know that! but do you know what day it is?" On my saying that I did not understand, she went on:
"It is the eve of St. George's Day. Do you not know that to-night, when the clock strikes midnight, all the evil things in the world will have full sway? Do you know where you are going, and what you are going to?" She was in such evident distress that I tried to comfort her, but without effect. Finally, she went down on her knees and implored me not to go; at least to wait a day or two before starting.
　　—*Dracula,* Chapter I, Jonathan Harker's
　　　　　　　　　　　　　　　Journal, 4 May

. . . I asked him [Dracula] of some of the strange things of the preceding night, as, for instance, why the coachman went to the places where we had seen the blue flames. Was it indeed true that they showed where gold was hidden? He then explained to me that it was commonly believed that on a certain night of the year—last night, in fact, when all evil spirits are supposed to have unchecked sway—a blue flame is seen over any place where treasure has been concealed.
　　—*Dracula,* Chapter II, Jonathan Harker's
　　　　　　　　　　　　　　　Journal, 7 May

Van Helsing explains "the lore and experience of the ancients" to the vampire hunters as they close in on Lucy.

. . . for all that die from the preying of the Un-Dead become themselves Un-Dead, and prey on their kind. And so the circle goes on ever widening, like as the ripples from a stone thrown in the water. Friend Arthur, if you had met that kiss which you know of before poor Lucy die; or again, last night when you open your arms to her, you would in time, when you had died, have become *nosferatu,* as they call it in Eastern Europe.
　　—*Dracula,* Chapter XVI, Dr. Seward's
　　　　　　　　　　　　　　Diary—29 September

Arthur bent and kissed her, and then we sent him and Quincey out of the tomb; the Professor and I sawed the top off the stake, leaving the point of it in the body. Then we cut off the head and filled the mouth with garlic.
　　—*Dracula,* Chapter XVI, Dr. Seward's
　　　　　　　　　　　　　　Diary—29 September

. . . The Draculas were . . . a great and noble race, though now and again were scions who were held by their coevals to have had dealings with the Evil One. They learned his secrets in the Scholomance, amongst the mountains over Lake Hermanstadt, where the devil claims the tenth scholar as his due.
　　—*Dracula,* Chapter XVIII, Mina Harker's
　　　　　　　　　　　　　　　Journal, 30 September

through the corpse, or firing a pistol shot into the coffin. In very obstinate cases it is further recommended to cut off the head and replace it in the coffin with the mouth filled with garlic, or to extract the heart and burn it, strewing the ashes over the grave.

That such remedies are often resorted to, even in our enlightened days, is a well-attested fact, and there are probably few Roumenian villages where such has not taken place within the memory of the inhabitants.

First cousin to the vampire, the long exploded were-wolf of the Germans is here to be found, lingering yet under the name of the *Prikolitsch*. Sometimes it is a dog instead of a wolf, whose form a man has taken either voluntarily or as penance for his sins. In one of the villages a story is still told (and believed) of such a man, who driving home from church on Sunday with his wife, suddenly felt that the time for his transformation had come. He therefore gave over the reins to her, and stepped aside into the bushes, where, murmuring the mystic formula, he turned three somersaults over a ditch. Soon after this the woman, waiting in vain for her husband, was attacked by a furious dog, which rushed, barking, out of the bushes and succeeded in biting her severely, as well as tearing her dress. When, an hour later, this woman reached home alone she was met by her husband, who advanced smiling to meet her, but between his teeth she caught sight of the shreds of her dress which had been bitten out by the dog, and the horror of the discovery caused her to faint away.

–pp. 142–143

. . . .

We do not require to go far for the explanation of the extraordinary tenacity of life of the were-wolf legend in a country like Transylvania, where real wolves still abound. Every winter here brings fresh proof of the boldness and cunning of these terrible animals, whose attacks on flocks and farms are often conducted with a skill which would do honour to a human intellect. Sometimes a whole village is kept in trepidation for weeks together by some particularly audacious leader of a flock of wolves, to whom the peasants not unnaturally attribute a more than animal nature, and one may safely prophesy that so long as the real wolf continues to haunt the Transylvanian forests, so long will his spectre brother survive in the minds of the inhabitants.

Many ancient Roumenian legends tell us that every new church or otherwise important building became a human grave, as it was thought indispensable to its stability to wall in a living man or woman, whose spirit henceforward haunts the place. In later times people having become less cruel, or more probably,

because murder is now attended with greater inconvenience to the actors, this custom underwent some modifications, and it became usual in place of a living man to wall in his shadow instead. This is done by measuring the shadow of a person with a long piece of cord, or a ribbon made of strips of reed, and interring this measure instead of the person himself, who, unconscious victim of the spell thrown upon him, will pine away and die within forty days. It is an indispensable condition to the success of this proceeding that the chosen victim be ignorant of the part he is playing, therefore careless passers-by near a building place may often hear the warning cry "Beware, lest they take thy shadow!" So deeply engrained is this superstition that not long ago there were still professional shadow-traders, who made it their business to provide architects with the necessary victims for securing their walls. "Of course the man whose shadow is thus interred must die," argues the Roumenian, "but as he is unaware of his doom he does not feel any pain or anxiety, so it is less cruel than walling in a living man."

–pp. 143–144

. . . .

Rubbing the body with garlic is a preservative against witchcraft and the pest.

–p. 145

. . . .

The gipsies, one of whose principal trades is the burning of bricks and tiles, are often accused of occasioning lengthy droughts to suit their own purposes. When this has occurred, and the necessary rains have not been produced by soundly beating the guilty Tziganes, the Roumenians sometimes resort to the *Papaluga,* or Rain-maiden. This is done by stripping a young gipsy girl quite naked, and dressing her up with wreaths of flowers and leaves which entirely cover her up, leaving only the head visible. Thus adorned, the Papaluga is conducted round the villages in procession, to the sound of music and singing, and everyone hastens to water her copiously.

If also the Papaluga fails to bring the desired rain, then the evil must evidently be of a deeper and more serious nature, and is to be attributed to a vampire, who must be sought out and destroyed in the manner described above.

–p. 150

–Emily Gerard, "Transylvanian Superstitions," *The Nineteenth Century,* 18 (July 1885): 130–150

* * *

Isabella L. Bird (1831–1904), the best known of the Victorian "lady travelers," made a five-week tour of Malaysia in 1878–1879. Like her other popular travel books, The Golden Chersonese and the Way Thither (1883) *was made up of revised letters originally sent to her sister, Hennie, who remained in England.*

From *The Golden Chersonese and the Way Thither*
Isabella Bird

The following excerpt from Letter XXII was copied verbatim by Stoker into his Notes.

I never heard of any country of such universal belief in devils, familiars, omens, ghosts, sorceries, and witchcrafts. The Malays have many queer notions about tigers, and usually only speak of them in whispers, because they think that certain souls of human beings who have departed this life have taken up their abode in these beasts, and in some places, for this reason, they will not kill a tiger unless he commits some specially bad aggression. They also believe that some men are tigers by night and men by day!

The *pelīsit,* the bad spirit which rode on the tail of Mr. Maxwell's horse, is supposed to be the ghost of a woman who has died in childbirth. In the form of a large bird uttering a harsh cry, it is believed to haunt forests and burial-grounds and to afflict children. The Malays have a bottle-imp, the *polong,* which will take no other sustenance than the blood of its owner, but it rewards him by aiding him in carrying out revengeful purposes. The harmless owl has strange superstitions attaching to it, and is called the "specter bird"; you may remember that the fear of encountering it was one of the reasons why the Permatang Pasir men would not go with us through the jungle to Rassa.

A vile fiend called the *penangalan* takes possession of the forms of women, turns them into witches,

Frontispiece for Isabella Bird's The Golden Chersonese and the Way Thither, *one of several travel books that Stoker relied on in writing* Dracula *(Thomas Cooper Library, University of South Carolina)*

and compels them to quit the greater part of their bodies, and fly away by night to gratify a vampire craving for human blood. This is very like one of the ghoul stories in the *Arabian Nights Entertainments.* Then they have a specter huntsman with demon dogs who roams the forests, and a storm fiend who rides the whirlwind, and spirits borrowed from Persia and Arabia. It almost seems as if the severe monotheism to which they have been converted compels them to create a gigantic demonology.

–pp. 451–452

Bird's account includes the following description of the vampire bat. Whether Stoker read it is not known, though like Bird, he exaggerates the size of this particular species of bat.

The bat family is not numerous. The vampire flies high, in great flocks, and is very destructive to fruit. This frugiverous bat, known popularly as the "flying fox," is a very interesting-looking animal,

and is actually eaten by the people of Ternate. At the height of the fruit season, thousands of these creatures cross from Sumatra to the mainland, a distance never less than forty miles. Their strength of wing is enormous. I saw one captured in the steamer *Nevada,* forty-five miles from the Navigators, with wings measuring, when extended, nearly five feet across. These are formed of a jet black membrane, and have a highly polished claw at the extremity of each. The feet consist of five polished black claws, with which the bat hangs on, head downward, to the forest trees. His body is about twice the size of that of a very large rat, black and furry underneath, and with red foxy fur on the head and neck. He has a pointed face, a very black nose, and prominent black eyes, with a remorseless expression in them.

–Bird, *The Golden Chersonese and the Way Thither* (New York: Putnam, 1883), p. 11

* * *

While on tour in the United States in the winter of 1895–1896, Stoker came across this article in the New York World *(2 February 1896), which he clipped and pasted into his Notes. The description here of the small bat caught "in the act of sucking blood from the flank" of a horse is at odds with Quincey Morris's memory in the novel of one of "those big bats that they call vampires" that he blames for draining his mare of blood.*

Vampires in New England

Dead Bodies Dug Up and Their Hearts Burned
to Prevent Disease.

——

Strange Superstition of Long Ago.

——

The Old Belief Was that Ghostly Monsters Sucked the
Blood of Their Living Relatives.

——

Recent ethnological research has disclosed something very extraordinary in Rhode Island. It appears that the ancient vampire superstition still survives in that State, and within the last few years many people have been digging up the dead bodies of relatives for the purpose of burning their hearts.

Near Newport scores of such exhumations have been made, the purpose being to prevent the dead from preying upon the living. The belief entertained is that a person who has died of consumption is likely to rise from the grave at night and suck the

---

Stoker's Vampire Bat

The true vampire bat is quite small, only about three inches in length. The quantity of blood such a bat ingests is insufficient to harm a large animal. Stoker's bat is far more bloodthirsty.

Quincey Morris, when he is trying to understand Lucy Westenra's recurring need for blood transfusions, is the first to mention a vampire bat in Dracula.

. . . I have not seen anything pulled down so quick since I was on the Pampas and had a mare that I was fond of go to grass all in a night. One of those big bats that they call vampires had got at her in the night, and, what with his gorge and the vein left open, there wasn't enough blood in her to let her stand up.

–Chapter XII, Dr. Seward's Diary, 18 September

The following passage is from the scene in which Van Helsing is preparing Dr. Seward to accept the reality of vampires.

. . . Can you tell me why in the Pampas, ay and elsewhere, there are bats that come at night and open the veins of cattle and horses and suck dry their veins; how in some islands of the Western seas there are bats which hang on the trees all day, that those who have seen describe as like giant nuts or pods, and that when the sailors sleep on the deck, because that it is hot, flit down on them and then–and then in the morning are found dead men, white as even Miss Lucy was?

–*Dracula,* Chapter XIV, Dr. Seward's Diary, 26 September

blood of surviving members of his or her family, thus dooming them to a similar fate.

The discovery of the survival in highly educated New England of a superstition dating back to the days of Sardanapalus and Nebuchadnezzar has been made by George R. Stotson, an ethnologist of repute. He has found it rampant in a district which includes the towns of Exeter, Foster, Kingstown, East Greenwich and many scattered hamlets. This region, where abandoned farms are numerous, is the tramping-ground of the book agent, the chromo peddler and the patent medicine man. The social isolation is as complete as it was two centuries ago.

Here Cotton Mather and the host of medical, clerical and lay believers in the uncanny ideas of bygone centuries could still hold high carnival. Not merely the out-of-the-way agricultural folk, but the more intelligent people of the urban communities are strong in their belief in vampirism. One case noted was that of an intelligent and well-to-do head of a family who some years ago lost several of his children by consumption. After they were buried he dug them up and burned them in order to save the lives of their surviving brothers and sisters.

Two Typical Cases.

There is one small village distant fifteen miles from Newport, where within the last few years there have been at least half a dozen resurrections on this account. The most recent was made two years ago in a family where the mother and four children had already succumbed to consumption. The last of these children was exhumed and the heart was burned.

Another instance was noted in a seashore town, not far from Newport, possessing a summer hotel and a few cottages of hot-weather residents. An intelligent man, by trade a mason, informed Mr. Stotson that he had lost two brothers by consumption. On the death of the second brother, his father was advised to take up the body and burn the heart. He refused to do so, and consequently he was attacked by the disease. Finally he died of it. His heart was burned, and in this way the rest of the family escaped.

This frightful superstition is said to prevail in all of the isolated districts of Southern Rhode Island, and it survives to some extent in the large centres of population. Sometimes the body is burned, not merely the heart, and the ashes are scattered.

In some parts of Europe the belief still has a hold on the popular mind. On the Continent from 1727 to 1735 there prevailed an epidemic of vampires. Thousands of people died, as was supposed, from having their blood sucked by creatures that came to their bedsides at night with goggling eyes and lips eager for the life fluid of the victim. In Servia it was understood that the demon might be destroyed by digging up the body and piercing it through with a sharp instrument, after which it was decapitated and burned. Relief was found in eating the earth of the vampire's grave. In the Levant the corpse was cut to pieces and boiled in wine.

Vampirism a Plague.

There was no hope for a person once chosen as a prey by a vampire. Slowly but surely he or she was destined to fade and sicken, receiving meanwhile nightly visits from the monster. Even death was no relief, for—and here was the most horrible part of the superstition—the victim, once dead and laid in the grave, was compelled to become a vampire and in his turn to take up the business of preying on the living. Thus vampirism was indefinitely propagated.

Realize, if you please, that at that period, when science was hardly born and no knowledge had been spread among the people to fight off superstition, belief in the reality of this fearful thing was absolute. Its existence was officially recognized, and military commissions were appointed for the purpose of opening the graves of suspected vampires and taking such measures as were necessary for destroying the latter.

Vampirism became a plague, more dreaded than any form of disease. Everywhere people were dying from the attacks of the blood-sucking monsters, each victim becoming in turn a night-prowler in pursuit of human prey. Terror of the mysterious and unearthly peril filled all hearts.

Evidence enough as to the prevalence of the mischief was afforded by the condition of many of the bodies that were dug up by the commissions appointed for the purpose. In many instances corpses which had been buried for weeks and even months were found fresh and lifelike. Sometimes fresh blood was actually discovered on their lips. What proof could be more convincing, inasmuch, as was well known, the buried body of a vampire is preserved and nourished by its nightly repasts? The blood on the lips, of course, was that of the victim of the night before.

The faith in vampirism entertained by the public at large was as complete as that which is felt in a discovery of modern science. It was an actual

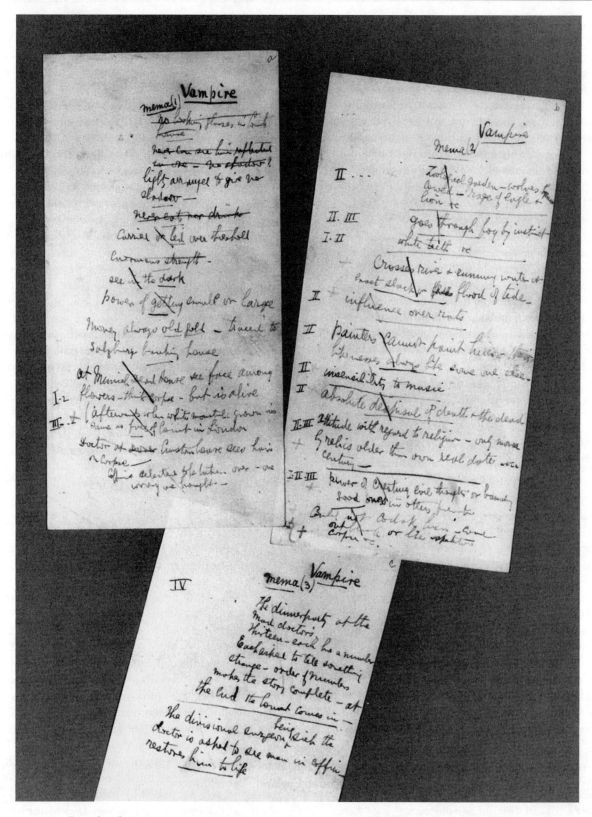

*Pages from Stoker's notes, listing vampire characteristics and describing a storytelling scene at a dinner party that does not appear in the novel (*Bram Stoker's *Dracula:* A Centennial Exhibition at the Rosenbach Museum & Library, *1997; Elizabeth Miller Collection)*

epidemic that threatened the people, spreading rapidly and only to be checked by the adoption of most drastic measures.

The contents of every suspected grave were investigated, and many corpses found in such a condition as that described were promptly subjected to "treatment." This meant that a stake was driven through the chest, and the heart, being taken out, was either burned or chopped into small pieces. For in this way only could a vampire be deprived of power to do mischief. In one case a man who was unburied sat up in his coffin, with fresh blood on his lips. The official in charge of the ceremonies held a crucifix before his face and saying, "Do you recognize your Saviour?" chopped the unfortunate's head off. This person presumably had been buried alive in a cataleptic trance.

Were They Buried Alive?

How is the phenomenon to be accounted for? Nobody can say with certainty, but it may be that the fright into which people were thrown by the epidemic had the effect of predisposing nervous persons to catalepsy. In a word, people were buried alive in a condition where, the vital functions being suspended, they remained as it were dead for a while. It is a common thing for a cataleptic to bleed at the mouth just before returning to consciousness. According to the popular superstition, the vampire left his or her body in the grave while engaged in nocturnal prowls.

The epidemic prevailed all over south-eastern Europe, being at its worst in Hungary and Servia. It is supposed to have originated in Greece, where a belief was entertained to the effect that Latin Christians buried in that country could not decay in their graves, being under the ban of the Greek Church. The cheerful notion was that they got out of their graves at night and pursued the occupation of ghouls. The superstition as to ghouls is very ancient and undoubtedly of Oriental origin. Generally speaking, however, a ghoul is just the opposite of a vampire, being a living person who preys on dead bodies, while a vampire is a dead person that feeds on the blood of the living. If you had your choice, which would you rather be, a vampire or a ghoul?

One of the most familiar of the stories of the Arabian Nights tells of a woman who annoyed her husband very much by refusing food. Nothing more than a few grains of rice would she eat at meals. He discovered that she was in the habit of stealing away from his side in the night, and, following her on one such occasion, he found her engaged in digging up and devouring a corpse.

Among the numerous folk tales about vampires is one relating to a fiend named Dakanavar, who dwelt in a cave in Armenia. He would not permit anybody to penetrate into the mountains of Ulmish Altotem to count their valleys. Every one who attempted this had in the night the blood sucked by the monster from the soles of his feet until he died.

At last, however, he was outwitted by two cunning fellows. They began to count the valleys, and when night came they lay down to sleep, taking care to place themselves with the feet of each under the head of the other. In the night the monster came, felt as usual and found a head. Then he felt at the other end and found a head there also.

"Well!" cried he, "I have gone through all of the three hundred and sixty-six valleys of these mountains and have sucked the blood of people without end, but never yet did I find one with two heads and no feet!" So saying he ran away, and never more was seen in that country, but ever since people have known that the mountains have three hundred and sixty-six valleys.

Belief in the vampire bats is more modern. For a long time it was ridiculed by science as a delusion, but it has been proved to be founded correctly upon fact. It was the famous naturalist Darwin who settled this question. One night he was camping with a party near Coquimbo, in Chili, and it happened that a servant noticed the restlessness of one of the horses. The man went up to the horse and actually caught a bat in the act of sucking blood from the flank of the animal.

While many kinds of bats have been ignorantly accused of the blood-sucking habit, only one species is really a vampire. It constitutes a genus all by itself. Just as a man is the only species of the genus homo, so the vampire bat is the only species of the genus desmodus. Fortunately, it is not very large, having a spread of only two feet. This is not much for a bat. The so-called "flying foxes" of the old world, which go about in flocks and ravage orchards, are of much greater size, and there is a bat of Java, known as the "kalong," that has a spread of five feet from wing tip to wing tip. The body of the true vampire bat weighs only a few ounces.

–_New York World_ (2 February 1896)

* * *

Stoker's description of Count Dracula—canine teeth, pointed fingernails, hairy palms, and heavy eyebrows—owes much to the werewolf as presented in Sabine Baring-Gould's The Book of Were-Wolves *(1865), a source from which Stoker took several notes. Baring-Gould is best known as the composer of the hymn "Onward, Christian Soldiers."*

The Characteristics of a Were-Wolf
Reverend Sabine Baring-Gould

In chapter 7 a French boy of thirteen, Jean Grenier, who claimed to be a werewolf and to have attacked and eaten little girls, is described.

The appearance of the lad was peculiar. His hair was of a tawny red and thickly matted, falling over his shoulders and completely covering his narrow brow. His small pale-grey eyes twinkled with an expression of horrible ferocity and cunning, from deep sunken hollows. The complexion was of a dark olive colour; the teeth were strong and white, and the canine teeth protruded over the lower lip when the mouth was closed. The boy's hands were large and powerful, the nails black and pointed like bird's talons.

–p. 88

. . . .

Chapter 8, "Folk-Lore Relating to Were-Wolves," gathers information from various cultures. The following description is a French belief.

A were-wolf may easily be detected, even when devoid of his skin; for his hands are broad, and his fingers short, and there are always some hairs in the hollow of his hand.

–p. 108

. . . .

This description is from a section of stories from Denmark.

. . . By day the were-wolf has the human form, though he may be known by the meeting of his eyebrows above the nose. . . . It is only when another person tells him that he is a were-wolf, or reproaches him with being such, that a man can be freed from the ban.

–p. 111

. . . .

Among the Bulgarians and Sloyakians the were-wolf is called *vrkolak*, a name resembling that given it by the modern Greeks. . . . The Greek were-wolf is closely related to the vampire. The lycanthropist falls into a cataleptic trance, during which his soul leaves his body, enters that of a wolf and ravens for blood. On the return of the soul, the body is exhausted and aches as though it had been put through violent exercise. After death lycanthropists become vampires. They are believed to frequent battlefields in wolf or hyena shapes, and to suck the breath from dying soldiers, or to enter houses and steal the infants from their cradles.

. . . .

The Serbs connect the vampire and the were-wolf together, and call him by one name *vlkoslak*. These rage chiefly in the depths of winter: they hold their annual gatherings, and at them divest themselves of their wolf-skins, which they hang on the trees around them. If any one succeeds in obtaining the skin and burning it, the vlkoslak is thenceforth disenchanted.

–pp. 115–116
–Sabine Baring-Gould, *The Book of Were-Wolves*
(London: Smith, Elder, 1865)

"A Very Marked Physiognomy"

Jonathan Harker first describes his host after Dracula has seated him comfortably by the fire and given him a cigar.

. . . His eyebrows were very massive, almost meeting over the nose, and with bushy hair that seemed to curl in its own profusion. The mouth, so far as I could see it under the heavy moustache, was fixed and rather cruel-looking, with peculiarly sharp white teeth; these protruded over the lips, whose remarkable ruddiness showed astonishing vitality in a man of his years. For the rest, his ears were pale and at the tops extremely pointed; the chin was broad and strong, and the cheeks firm though thin. The general effect was one of extraordinary pallor.

Hitherto I had noticed the backs of his hands as they lay on his knees in the firelight, and they had seemed rather white and fine; but seeing them now close to me, I could not but notice that they were rather coarse—broad, with squat fingers. Strange to say, there were hairs in the centre of the palm. The nails were long and fine, and cut to a sharp point.

–*Dracula*, Chapter II, Jonathan Harker's
Journal, 5 May

Notes on Russian Schooners

The notes in the Rosenbach Collection disclose that during a Whitby holiday in August 1890 Stoker gathered a mine of information, almost all of which he was to use in *Dracula*. Descriptions from the notes appear nearly verbatim in Chapters 6 and 7. On 11 August he recounts a conversation with a coastguard, who told him " . . . of various wrecks. A Russian Schooner 120 tons from Black Sea ran in with all sail main stay foresail jib nearly full tide Put out two anchors in harbor I look and she slewed round-against-pier–Another ship got into harbour Never knew how all hands were below praying. . . . Above Russian vessel was light ballasted with silver sand." In another note he adds, "On 24 October 1885 the Russian schooner 'Dimetry' about 120 ton was sighted off Whitby about 2 p.m. Wind northeast Force 8 (fresh gale) strong sea on coast (cargo silver sand–from mouth of Danube) ran into harbour by pure chance avoiding rocks. The following is extract from Log Book of the Coast Guard Station." For his novel, Stoker changed the details of the tale somewhat, but Dracula enters Whitby harbour in a violent storm on the ship *Demeter*.

–Bierman, "The Genesis and Dating of *Dracula* from Bram Stoker's Working Notes," *Notes and Queries*, 24 (1977): 39–41

The Dmitry, *a Russian vessel that beached near Whitby in October 1885, was the inspiration for the* Demeter *in* Dracula. *The vampire escaped the wreck by transforming himself into "an immense dog" (Barbara Belford,* Bram Stoker: A Biography of the Author of *Dracula, 1996; Richland County Public Library).*

Detail of Wrecks at Whitby

24th Octr 1885

On Her Majesty's Service.

At 1.0 P.M observed vessel apparently in Distress & making for harbour called out L.S.A. Company wind N.E. Force 8 & Strong Sea on Coast followed the Vessel along coast where most likely to strand - the Life Boat at same time was launched but drove ashore & became of no further use The Vessel Stranded at about 2.0 pm Got communication with 1st Rocket & landed 4 of the Crew by whip & buoy fearing the masts would go whip snatch Block getting out of order Sent of Hawser & landed safe the remaining 2 of Crew being 6 all told. During this service observed a Russian Schooner making for harbour & likely to drive back of South Pier Called out S Pier L.S.A Company & both Companys watched her progress on each side of harbour the "Russian" got in but became a wreck during the night Crew landed safe by their own personses the 1st L.S.A Company were out 5 hours & the 2nd L.S.A Company 4 hours on these services 125 fms of Rocket Line & 9 fms of Hawser was Expended on the 1st Service having cut the hawser with hawser Cutter When the 2nd Vessel was observed in Distress

Names of Ships

Mary & Agnes British

Dmitry Russian

Page from Stoker's notes about shipwrecks near Whitby (Rosenbach Museum & Library, Philadelphia)

Transylvania

Never having visited Transylvania, and apparently eager to provide a realistic backdrop for his tale of the supernatural, Stoker relied primarily on popular travel literature for information about place-names, geography, and local customs.

In his preface to his work on Transylvania, Charles Boner writes, "Any traveller in Transylvania will discover the difficulty of obtaining correct information on particular questions, owing to the influence of nationality and of political feeling." Boner's book is political in some respects, but Stoker was interested only in his descriptions of the land and its people.

From *Transylvania: Its Products and Its People*
Charles Boner

And away we go,—I on my hay throne, and my little shaggy team springing along at a good gallop. For awhile we passed a whole population all streaming into town. There were troops of women and cart-loads of peasants and young girls in holiday attire, nearly all in snow-white shifts with broad stripes of embroidery, red or blue, over the shoulders and round the sleeves; and large silver medals hanging from their necks over their bosom. Some wore

Map of Transylvania in Charles Boner's Transylvania: Its Products and Its People. *This map was probably Stoker's source for the Borgo Pass, the location he selected for Dracula's castle (Elizabeth Miller Collection).*

around their head a large white kerchief, but so full and long that it fell over them like a veil and flowed low down behind. There is something very graceful and feminine in this spotless head-gear, with its many and waving folds. Others had brighter-hued kerchiefs, but purple seemed to be the favourite colour. Anon came a chattering company in brand-new jackets of sheepskin without sleeves, all embroidered with red and green and blue leather, and having a very holiday air. Then others with a sort of scarlet fez upon their heads; and some with a covering having two horn-like corners rising in front, reminding you of Aaron's budding ornament. Now a gipsy passed, dark as a Hindoo; and though most of the wayfarers were clean and in their Sunday clothes, there were some who, it was evident, had no thought of merry-making, and everything about their persons was blackened, coarse, and dirty. Pleasing and picturesque as the simple clothing of these women is when fresh and tidy, in the contrary state it has an air of perfectly savage life. The "obrescha," being then almost black with dirt, and torn and entangled, looks like horsehair hanging and flying about, and has a most strange, uncomely appearance.* Now in the distance a whole bevy of young girls come stepping on, with shifts and head-gear white as the daisies of the field; and as they breast the morning breeze, the bright red "obrescha" streaming and fluttering in the wind, might almost make you think a flock of flamingoes was moving over the plain. Most of them had distaffs stuck in their girdle, and one with arms distended was winding off red yarn; the sun, too, was shining, and lighted up the bright figures, which quite illumined the sober-coloured autumn landscape. It is astonishing how they can spin as they walk, for they advance at a brisk rate, and their feet and merry tongue keep pace with each other.

What busts you see here, where stays are unknown, and there is nothing to cramp the full development of the figure! The linen covering does not conceal the beautiful outline of the bosom, but rather serves to define it; marking now an oval bud and now a full-rounded form. And the drapery falls over this loveliest feminine feature in a sharp angular line, as though beneath were firmest marble; and marble it is, but glowing with passionate lifes.

On our road my driver pointed out to me a point in the mountains where one evening he had seen "a gold fire."—"And what is that?" I asked. "'Tis a light which hovers over the spot where gold is buried."—"Of course you went and took possession of it," I said, laughing. "Yes, but being so far I could not find the exact spot, and therefore got nothing."

Carpathian Roads

The aspect of the Carpathians is very different in winter: all the heights are covered with snow, and the narrow roads with mud and large stones, rolled in the midst of them by the torrents, so as to render them almost impassable; mostly situated on the brinks of dreadful precipices, at the bottom of which rivers or torrents have formed their passage, one false step of the passenger is immediate death.

The Hospodars purposely neglect to repair these roads; the fear of creating suspicions at the Porte that they wish to facilitate the passage of foreign troops into the principalities, induces them to abstain from an undertaking, which in other respects has become so imperiously necessary.

—William Wilkinson, *An Account of the Principalities of Wallachia and Moldavia* (London: Longman, Hurst, Rees, Orme & Brown, 1820), p. 166

. . . I was told that this road is in summer-time excellent, but that it had not yet been put in order after the winter snows. In this respect it is different from the general run of roads in the Carpathians, for it is an old tradition that they are not to be kept in too good order. Of old the Hospadars would not repair them, lest the Turk should think that they were preparing to bring in foreign troops, and so hasten the war which was always really at loading point.

—*Dracula*, Chapter I, Jonathan Harker's Journal, 5 May

His two horses, which still went along bravely, had, he told me, cost him forty florins. We met a peasant who had bought a cow and her calf and was now driving them home. For both he had paid only eight florins; such was the effect of the dearth and drought in Hungary.

The road was even all the way, with wooded hills at a little distance on either side. The villages were neatly built, the houses good and solid-looking, and, if I remember rightly, often standing separate. They stood in a row far back from the roadside, so that an immense breadth was thus given to the street. Owing to this mode of building, a village spread to a considerable length. The neatness and regularity all gave evidence of former military supervision, and the road, too, was broad and smooth as a billiard-table.

"You'll see the difference when we get to Transylvania," said my man to me; "directly we get there, all is bad,—roads, bridges, everything."

—pp. 40–42

*The "obrescha" is the girdle worn by the women over the shift, and consists of a broad band of plaited twine-like cord, from which, before and behind, hangs a fringe reaching nearly to the ankle. It is much the same thing as that which savage tribes wear as their sole covering. It is of a bright red, and contrasts greatly with the white linen beneath.

. . . .

Bistritz is prettily situated on the plain, just where a range of hills, covered with orchards and beech-groves, rise beside it. It has nothing of that medieval look which distinguishes Hermannstadt or Schässburg; the streets are straight and broad, and nearly every building is of modern date, the place having suffered repeatedly by fire. From 1836 to 1850, there were five conflagrations, by which three hundred and twenty-five houses were destroyed. But in former days Bistritz suffered other fearful calami-

---

The Dark Side of Twilight

It was on the dark side of twilight when we got to Bistritz, which is a very interesting old place. Being practically on the frontier—for the Borgo Pass leads from it into Bukovina—it has had a very stormy existence, and it certainly shows marks of it. Fifty years ago a series of great fires took place, which made terrible havoc on five separate occasions. At the very beginning of the seventeenth century it underwent a siege of three weeks and lost 13,000 people, the casualties of war proper being assisted by famine and disease.
—*Dracula*, Chapter I, Jonathan Harker's Journal, 3 May

. . . Before us lay a green sloping land full of forests and woods, with here and there steep hills, crowned with clumps of trees or with farmhouses, the blank gable end to the road. There was everywhere a bewildering mass of fruit blossom—apple, plum, pear, cherry; and as we drove by I could see the green grass under the trees spangled with the fallen petals. In and out amongst these green hills of what they call here the "Mittel Land" ran the road, losing itself as it swept round the grassy curve, or was shut out by the straggling ends of pine woods, which here and there ran down the hillsides like tongues of flame. The road was rugged, but still we seemed to fly over it with a feverish haste. I could not understand then what the haste meant, but the driver was evidently bent on losing no time in reaching Borgo Prund.
—*Dracula*, Chapter I, Jonathan Harker's Journal, 5 May

---

ties,—sieges, oppression, hunger, and pestilence. Its neighbourhood to the frontier exposed it to the devastations of the Mongols and Tartars: the foe before the walls, the famine and disease within, carried off, in 1602, in the twenty days' siege, 13,000 of the inhabitants.

—p. 377

. . . .

The weather was beautiful, and I hardly think a Canadian winter could be more bright. To the east of Bistritz lies Borgó Prund, and thither I drove to see and to purchase some of the manufactures of the Roumain women. The country hereabouts reminded me at once of the scenery in the Valley of the Inn. Here, too, is the so-called "Mittel Land," a ridge of low hills rising in the vale between the higher mountains. Even now their bold forms and gentle slopes were most attractive; and in summer, when the woods on the upland are in full leaf, and the pastures green and enlivened with flocks and herds, the scene must be most lovely.

—pp. 417–418

. . . .

Still further on, towards the pass into Moldavia, the scenery increases in picturesqueness, and nothing can be better than the road thither.

In the neighbourhood of Prund lies a territory, the possession of which has led to the most flagrant outrages. Commission after commission has been appointed to decide peremptorily on the line of demarcation, and although the existing documents and the boundary marks all prove where it is—indeed there was never any doubt about it—the Wallacks will not give way, but come on their neighbour's land, plough it for their own purposes, or destroy the harvests which the Saxons have raised.

—pp. 419–420
—Charles Boner, *Transylvania: Its Products and Its People* (London: Longmans, Green, Reader & Dyer, 1865)

* * *

From *Round About the Carpathians*
A. F. Crosse

. . . later on I became familiar enough with the carts of the country; they are long-bodied, rough constructions, wonderfully adapted to the uneven roads. In this case there were four horses abreast, which sounds imposing, as any four-in-hand must always do.

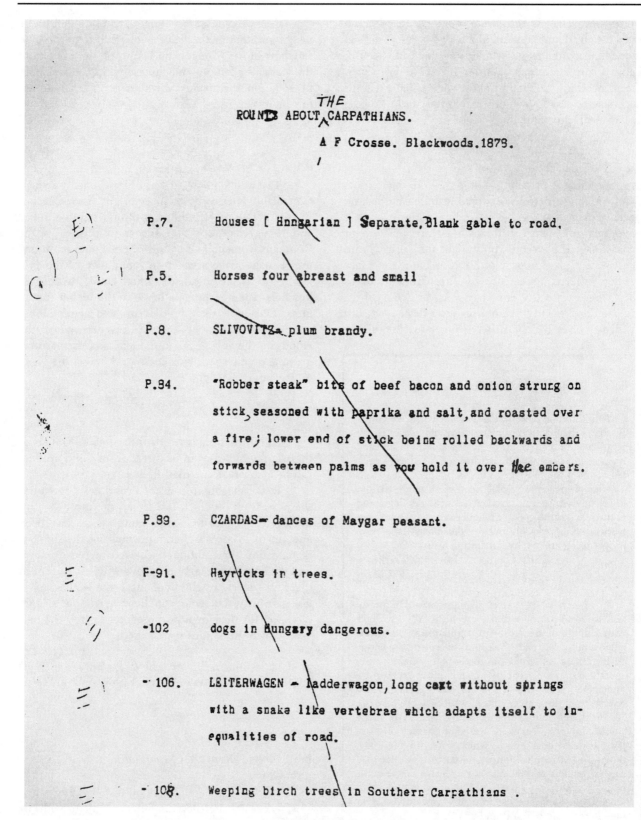

ROUND ABOUT THE CARPATHIANS.

A F Crosse. Blackwoods.1879.

P.7.   Houses [Hungarian] Separate,blank gable to road.

P.5.   Horses four abreast and small

P.8.   SLIVOVITZ plum brandy.

P.94.   "Robber steak" bits of beef bacon and onion strung on
        stick, seasoned with paprika and salt, and roasted over
        a fire; lower end of stick being rolled backwards and
        forwards between palms as you hold it over the embers.

P.99.   CZARDAS dances of Maygar peasant.

P-91.   Hayricks in trees.

-102   dogs in Hungary dangerous.

-106.   LEITERWAGEN - ladderwagon, long cart without springs
        with a snake like vertebrae which adapts itself to in-
        equalities of road.

-108.   Weeping birch trees in Southern Carpathians .

Page 54 of Stoker's notes, from A. F. Crosse's Round About the Carpathians
(Rosenbach Museum & Library, Philadelphia)

I now asked the Wallack in German if he could drive me to Oravicza, for I saw he had made up his mind to drive me somewhere. To my relief I found he could speak German, at all events a few words.

–p. 5

. . . .

Hungarian towns look like overgrown villages that have never made up their minds seriously to become towns. The houses are mostly of one story, standing each one alone, with the gable-end, blank and windowless, towards the road.

–p. 7

. . . .

The more civilization closes round one, the more enjoyable is an occasional "try back" into barbarism. This feeling made the mere fact of camping out seem delightful. Our first care was to select a suitable spot; we found a clearing that promised well, and here we made a halt. We deposited our *batterie de cuisine,* arranged our plaids, and then proceeded to make a fire with a great lot of dried sticks and logs of wood. The fire was soon crackling and blazing away in grand style, throwing out mighty tongues of flame, which lit up the dark recesses of the forest.

Now came the supper, which consisted of robber-steak and tea. I always stuck to my tea as the most refreshing beverage after a long walk or ride. I like coffee in the morning before starting–good coffee, mind; but in the evening there is nothing like tea. The robber-steak is capital, and deserves an "honourable mention" at least: it is composed of small bits of beef, bacon, and onion strung alternately on a piece of stick; it is seasoned with pinches of *paprika* and salt, and then roasted over the fire, the lower end of the stick being rolled backwards and forwards between your two palms as you hold it over the hot embers. It makes a delicious relish with a hunch of bread.

–pp. 84–85

. . . .

At length the whole party got off in sundry *leiterwagen,* a vehicle which has no counterpart in England, and the literal rendering of a ladder-waggon hardly conveys the proper notion of the thing itself. This long cart, it is needless to say, is without springs; but it has the faculty of accommodating itself to the inequalities of the road in a marvellous manner. It has, moreover, a snake-like vertebrae, and even twists itself when necessary.

–pp. 106–107

. . . .

. . . The pace was so slow that I confess it made me impatient, but our path through the forest was too narrow and too steep to do more than walk our horses in single file. The character of the vegetation visibly changed as we ascended. We left the oak and beech, and came upon a forest of pine-trees, and I thought of the lines–

> "This is the forest primeval. The murmuring pines and the hemlocks,
> Bearded with moss, and in garments green, indistinct in the twilight."

The grey moss which hangs in such abundant festoons from the fir-trees has a most singular effect, almost weird at times. These ancients of the forest, with their long grey beards and hoary tresses, look very solemn indeed in the gloaming.

What unheeded wealth in these majestic trees, which grow but to decay! Enormous trunks lay on every side: some had passed into the rottenness which gives new life; and here fungi of bright and varied hues, grey lichen, and green moss preserved together the contour of the gigantic stem, which, prostrate and decayed now, had once held its head high amongst the lordlings of the forest.

–pp. 110–111

. . . .

. . . The wines were excellent. We had golden Mediasch, one of the best wines grown in Transylvania, Roszamáber from Karlsburg and Bakatar. The peculiarity about the first-named wine is that it produces an agreeable pricking on the tongue, called in German *tschirpsen.*

–p. 120

. . . .

There are a great many "settled gipsies" in Transylvania. Of course they are legally free, but they attach themselves peculiarly to the Magyars, from a profound respect they have for everything that is aristocratic; and in Transylvania the name Magyar holds almost as a distinctive term for class as well as race. The gipsies do not assimilate with the thrifty Saxon, but prefer to be hangers-on at the castle of the Hungarian noble: they call themselves by his name, and profess to hold the same faith, be it Catholic or Protestant. Notwithstanding that, the gipsy has an incurable habit of pilfering here as elsewhere; yet they can be trusted as messengers and carriers–indeed I do not know what people would do without them, for they are as good as a general "parcels-delivery company" any day; and certainly

Traveling in Transylvania

Then our driver, whose wide linen drawers covered the whole front of the box-seat—"gotza" they call them—cracked his big whip over his four small horses, which ran abreast.

—*Dracula,* Chapter I, Jonathan Harker's Journal, 5 May

. . . I dined on what they called "robber steak"—bits of bacon, onion, and beef, seasoned with red pepper, and strung on sticks, and roasted over the fire, in the simple style of the London cat's-meat! The wine was Golden Mediasch, which produces a queer sting on the tongue, which is, however, not disagreeable.

—*Dracula,* Chapter I, Jonathan Harker's Journal, 4 May

. . . Now and again we passed a leiter-wagon—the ordinary peasant's cart, with its long, snake-like vertebra, calculated to suit the inequalities of the road. On this were sure to be seated quite a group of home-coming peasants, the Cszeks with their white, and the Slovaks with their coloured, sheepskins, the latter carrying lance-fashion their long staves, with axe at end.

—*Dracula,* Chapter I, Jonathan Harker's Journal, 5 May

. . . They [gypsies] are peculiar to this part of the world, though allied to the ordinary gipsies all the world over. There are thousands of them in Hungary and Transylvania, who are almost outside all law. They attach themselves as a rule to some great noble or *boyar,* and call themselves by his name.

—*Dracula,* Chapter I, Jonathan Harker's Journal—28 May

they are ubiquitous, for never is a door left unlocked but a gipsy will steal in, to your cost.

—pp. 146–147

. . . .

The market-day at Kronstadt is a most curious and interesting sight. The country-people come in, sitting in their long waggons, drawn by four horses abreast, they themselves dressed in cloaks of snow-white sheepskins, or richly-embroidered white leather coats lined with black fur.

—Andrew F. Crosse, *Round About the Carpathians* (London: Blackwood, 1878), p. 203

* * *

From *On the Track of the Crescent*
Major E. C. Johnson

The women wore a loose-sleeved white under-garment or chemisette, and over this a coloured apron called a Catrintsa, which descended both before and behind, and fitted so tightly as to show the figure. They also wore necklaces and large earrings, white cloths on the head which descended on the back of the neck, coloured stockings and ankle-boots. Some of the women wore that which I constantly saw afterwards in Transylvania—a broad belt or girdle, called an Obreska, tightly round the waist. It was handsomely embroidered in various colours, and had a thick fringe of black and red pendent from it to the bottom of the skirt, as if the other apron had been cut into strips; the wearers of this costume having coloured handkerchiefs instead of the white head-cloths. Among all the women, however, I saw nothing like a pretty face.

—pp. 118–119

. . . .

. . . We were now fairly in the country called by the Romans Transylvania, or "The land beyond the forests," and by the Hungarians Erdély, from "*erdö,* a forest," and by the Germans Siebenbürgen, or "Seven Fortresses." It is the most picturesque and romantic portion of Hungary.

This strange country, which was originally a part of Dacia, is inhabited by Magyars, Saxons, Wallachs, and Székelys. The Magyars inhabit the west, the Székelys the north and east, and the Saxons the south, with them the Wallachs—the descendants of the Dacians—being mixed in great numbers. The Székelys—who claim to be descended from Attila and the Huns—were found settled on the eastern frontier when the country was conquered by the Magyars, and the two races at once fraternised. . . . To replace the waste of inhabitants in the constant wars of which Transylvania was the theatre, colonists were brought from Germany, and these colonists were the ancestors of the present Saxons of that country.

—p. 205

. . . .

Immediately above us frowned an old tower, in which was a long slit rather than a window. This, the Baron informed me, had been the torture-chamber, whence the wretched prisoners, having been racked and otherwise tortured, were cast through a trap in the floor into a deep pit below, to writhe out the brief remnant of their existence. Openings of a similar kind in the other towers showed where the prisoners' dungeons had been, and even below the level of the moat human beings had passed weary years in damp and darkness, without a ray of light, or of hope. To complete the respectable antiquity of this tower, I need scarcely say that, of course, it is haunted. That monsters, capable of inflicting such fiendish cruelties on their fellow-men had lived, was already known to me, from having seen similar proofs in the castle of Nuremberg and elsewhere, and there is no doubt that in the Middle Ages such horrible practices were pretty general. This dismal thought, however, was dissipated by the reflection that they are no longer possible, and by the lovely scene before me. The bright, warm sunshine, the soft, well-kept lawn, the sweet-smelling flowers, the air teeming with every kind of insect life, from the brilliant and ubiquitous butterfly to the humming bee: all these rapidly asserted their power of charm, and I thoroughly enjoyed the scene.

Passing through the gardens, we now entered a wood, a path through which led to a shady nook which commanded a view of the whole valley. Here a convenient seat invited us to rest—an invitation which we accepted. The forest covered the side of the hill on which the castle was built, right down to the valley below, the white road here and there peeping through the trees as it gradually ascended. Along this road a herd of buffaloes was being driven in a cloud of dust. They looked like black-beetles, and their drivers mere specks. The hill on which the castle stood was so steep towards the Gallician frontier that it formed a very strong military position, which, if cleared for the use of modern artillery, would be impregnable by a *coup-de-main*. In front of us, as far as the eye could reach, was an interminable stretch of forest, right up to the base of the mountain range, brilliant in numberless shades of green, blue, and brown, and melting into a dusky purple as it became more stunted, and was lost in the haze surrounding the rocky crags. These towered range above range till they were crowned by the mighty "Isten-Szék" (God's Seat), the abode of eternal snow. This view reminded me strongly of my first sight of the Himalayan range from the Nepaulese frontier, and caused that awe-inspired feeling of the littleness of man, when face to face with the stupendous grandeur of nature, which I always experience when in the presence of mountains, and brought to my recollection Kant's grand idea, that the sublime effect of vast physical objects excites a consciousness of a moral power stronger than all nature, and I felt how right was this great analyser of psychological phenomena.

The Carpathians, towering aloft in their savage grandeur, are a spectacle not readily to be forgotten. They are almost inaccessible, and their steep and rocky sides are cut by numerous chasms, through which descend the waters which fertilise Transylvania. Immense mineral wealth is contained in these moun-

---

The People and the Carpathians

In the population of Transylvania there are four distinct nationalities: Saxons in the south, and mixed with them the Wallachs, who are the descendants of the Dacians; Magyars in the west, and Szekelys in the east and north. I am going among the latter, who claim to be descended from Attila and the Huns. This may be so, for when the Magyars conquered the country in the eleventh century they found the Huns settled in it.

—*Dracula,* Chapter I, Jonathan Harker's Journal, 3 May

. . . At every station there were groups of people, sometimes crowds, and in all sorts of attire. Some of them were just like the peasants at home or those I saw coming through France and Germany, with short jackets and round hats and home-made trousers; but others were very picturesque. The women looked pretty, except when you got near them, but they were very clumsy about the waist. They had all full white sleeves of some kind or other, and most of them had big belts with a lot of strips of something fluttering from them like the dresses in a ballet, but of course petticoats under them.

—*Dracula,* Chapter I, Jonathan Harker's Journal, 3 May

Beyond the green swelling hills of the Mittel Land rose mighty slopes of forest up to the lofty steeps of the Carpathians themselves. Right and left of us they towered, with the afternoon sun falling full upon them and bringing out all the glorious colours of this beautiful range, deep blue and purple in the shadows of the peaks, green and brown where grass and rock mingled, and an endless perspective of jagged rock and pointed crags, till these were themselves lost in the distance, where the snowy peaks rose grandly. Here and there seemed mighty rifts in the mountains, through which, as the sun began to sink, we saw now and again the white gleam of falling water. One of my companions touched my arm as we swept round the base of a hill and opened up the lofty, snow-covered peak of a mountain, which seemed, as we wound on our serpentine way, to be right before us:–

"Look! Isten szek!"–"God's seat!"–and he crossed himself reverently.

—*Dracula,* Chapter I, Jonathan Harker's Journal, 5 May

---

tains, but it has not, as yet, been developed as it might, and should, be.

—Major E. C. Johnson, *On the Track of the Crescent: Erratic Notes from the Pireus to Pest* (London: Hurst & Blackett, 1885), pp. 258–261

* * *

A leiter-wagon, described by Jonathan Harker in Dracula *as having a "long, snake-like vertebra, calculated to suit the inequalities of the road," a description Stoker found in A. F. Crosse's* Round About the Carpathians *(courtesy of Clive Leatherdale, Desert Island Books)*

These excerpts are from a book written by "A Fellow of the Carpathian Society."

From *Magyarland*

A road to the left leads us to a wild and beautiful gorge, which we gradually descend through stupendous pine forests; a swift mountain torrent, clear as crystal, which follows the roadway, accompanying the jingling of our horses' bells with a sweet and plaintive melody.

Here beauty and grandeur alternate in singular contrast. Now we see before us huge rock-fragments lying by our pathway which have been hurled from the heights above, and, anon frowning down upon us with forbidding aspect, are rugged peaks.

–p. 169

. . . .

According to the latest returns, there are 470,000 Rusniaks in the north-east portion of Hungary, and 2,000,000 Slovaks occupying the north-west; the former supposed to be the descendants of a band of Russians who "came in with Arpád."

During the two hours we spend here whilst our horses are being baited, we have ample opportunity of studying the exterior characteristics of both races. Their dress is almost identical, the only difference consisting in their head-gear. The Rusniaks, instead of the large "*sombreros*" which distinguish the Slovaks, wear ponderous caps made of black curly sheepskin, which from a distance look like the wearer's own hair combed erect, and give them a very wild and incongruous appearance.

Their garments consist of a loose jacket and large trousers, and are made of a coarse woollen material the colour of which is originally white, while their waists are encircled by enormous leather belts, more than half an inch thick and from twelve to sixteen broad, studded with brass-headed nails so arranged as to form a variety of patterns. In these belts they keep their knives, scissors, tobacco-pouch, a primitive arrangement for striking light and a number of other small useful articles.

–pp. 190–191

–Magyarland: Being the Narrative of our Travel through the Highlands and Lowlands of Hungary, 2 volumes (London: Sampson Low, Marston, Searle & Rivington, 1881)

* * *

The Slovaks

. . . The strangest figures we saw were the Slovaks, who are more barbarian than the rest, with their big cowboy hats, great baggy dirty-white trousers, white linen shirts, and enormous heavy leather belts, nearly a foot wide, all studded over with brass nails. They wore high boots, with their trousers tucked into them, and had long black hair and heavy black moustaches.

–*Dracula,* Chapter II, Jonathan Harker's Journal–3 May

As a consequence of Stoker's decision to have Transylvania as the homeland of Count Dracula, that region (now part of the modern state of Romania) has become fixed in the Western imagination as the land of vampires.

Typing Transylvania
Elizabeth Miller

And then away for home! away to the quickest and nearest train! away from this cursed spot, from this cursed land, where the devil and his children still walk with earthly feet!

–*Dracula,* Chapter IV, Jonathan Harker's Journal, 30 June

The "cursed land" of Jonathan Harker's journal is Transylvania, one of three former principalities (the others being Moldavia and Wallachia) which form the modern state of Romania. The name "Transylvania," from the Latin for "the land beyond the forest," was used in documents dating back to the ninth and tenth centuries to refer to the lands encompassed by the Eastern and Southern Carpathians and the Apuseni Mountains. Today, the term includes not only the original principality but the regions of Maramures, Crisana and the Banat—an area of some 39,000 square miles with a population of 7,000,000. This region, which ethnic Romanians consider the cradle of their modern nation, has had a turbulent history. Its inhabitants are a mix of ethnic groups: Saxons, Magyars, Szeklers and Romanians. In 1541 the Turks, having conquered central Hungary, established an autonomous Transylvanian state. It survived until the end of the seventeenth century when it was absorbed by the Habsburgs. By the time Bram Stoker wrote *Dracula* it had been annexed by Hungary. After the First World War Transylvania joined the united principalities of Moldavia and Wallachia to form the modern state of Romania.

Stoker's decision to select Transylvania as the homeland of his vampire Count was to have momentous consequences. Transylvania has been represented throughout twentieth century fiction and film as a mysterious and eerie realm, its geography reduced to dark forests, misty and remote valleys, and forbidding mountains. The inhabitants have fared no better: Transylvanians are still depicted as backward peasants who hold fast to their primitive and superstitious past, who still hang garlic on their windows to keep vampires away, and who would never venture out at night without crucifix in hand.

Contrary to popular assumption, this negative stereotyping did not begin with Stoker. The first reference to a Transylvanian in Western literature, in Shakespeare's *Pericles,* is none too flattering: "The poor Transylvanian is dead that lay with the little baggage" (IV, ii). But it was not until the nineteenth century and the rise of Gothic fiction that the region was selected as a suitable locale for supernatural creatures. A collection of tales by Alexandre Dumas (père), *Les Mille et un Fantomes* (1849), includes a story about a vampire who haunts the Carpathians; in "The Mysterious Stranger" (anonymous, 1860), a vampire Count terrorizes a family in this area. Best-known may be Jules Verne's romantic adventure, *The Castle of the Carpathians* (1892). Although the strange events in this novel admit to rational explanations, the narrator cites the prevalence of beliefs in a host of supernatural creatures, including vampires. But it was *Dracula* that firmly established Transylvania as a land of superstition and horror.

Dracula encodes in its representation of Transylvania the negative stereotypes that dominated much of nineteenth-century British travel literature, some of which Stoker consulted. Indicative of an increased interest in the remote parts of Europe, these accounts reveal and perpetuate an attitude that weaves its way insidiously through the pages of Stoker's novel, and from there into twentieth-century popular culture. Victorian travellers habitually presented their readers with invidious comparisons between Western progress, science and civilization and Eastern primitivism, superstition and barbarism. Transylvania is invariably described in terms of both remoteness and strangeness: a "hotch-potch of races," the "odd corner of Europe," which is "beyond the pale of Western civilization." Its geographical features inspire fear: the clouds are "grim" and "phantom-haunted," and there are "dreadful precipices."[1] The inhabitants and their way of life are continuously presented in condescending terms.

Singled out are the Wallachians (or Wallacks), most of whom were peasants and formed the majority of the population of nineteenth-century Transyl-

A twenty-first-century view of the Borgo Pass, bearing little resemblance to its description in the early pages of Dracula *as a wild, forbidding landscape (photograph by Elizabeth Miller)*

vania. John Paget, whose *Hungary and Transylvania* (1850) was for many years a staple text, maintains that the Wallachians in Transylvania "are generally considered treacherous, revengeful, and entirely deficient in gratitude" and that "the Wallack is idle and drunken it would be very difficult to deny."[2] Andrew Chalmers, while he praises the "beautiful country rich in all the blessings of soil, climate and scenery," criticizes its people with their "serf-like crouching aspect" and their "old women [who] closely resemble the typical witches in *Macbeth*." He states that "they have no drama and very little that deserves the name of art."[3] According to William Wilkinson, the Wallachians have "a dull and heavy disposition: with weak passions, no strength of mind, and betraying a natural aversion to a life of industry or of mental exertion." He also refers to the "absurdities of superstition" and how peasants "believe in all sorts of witchcraft, in apparitions of the dead, in ghosts."[4]

The "white man's burden" mentality is evident in much of the material. For example, Crosse comments that "If the Wallack could be raised out of the moral swamp of his present existence he might do something, but he must first feel the need of what civilisation has to offer him." He refers to the Wallachian villages as in "slatternly disorder" and notes that in one case a fire "licked the whole place clean—a condition not attainable by any other means." Their "wild, untamed . . . [horses] [are] hardly as wild as the Wallacks who led them, dressed in sheepskin, and followed each by his savage wolf-like dog."[5] To make matters worse, the Wallachian is "grossly superstitious" and "believes in ghosts, vampires and changelings, and spends much of his time in inventing charms against the machinations of the devil."[6] Johnson (whose work we know Stoker had read) comes up with this diatribe: "There are other and darker shades in the Wallach character, and in these, alas! he much resembles his Hibernian prototype. He is much given to treacherous revenge, and is capable of the most awful atrocities when aroused."[7]

Other ethnic groups are targeted as well. Crosse speaks of "other picturesque rascals, such as gipsies and Jews, and here and there a Turk, and, more ragged than all, a sprinkling of refugee Bulgarians."[8] Jews come in for their share of ethnic and racial slurs:

> There are no fewer than 190,000 Jews in this province alone, and one would suppose from the number that are met with everywhere that the whole neighbourhood must be given over into the hands of the Israelites. Standing about the principal street, or sitting in groups on the benches beneath the houses, where we turn we see these black-robed gentry: old Jews with snow-white ringlets; middle-aged Jews with iron-grey ringlets; boy Jews with black ringlets—the last, dressed like their elders in the long greasy toga, forming the most incongruous-looking objects in the universe.[9]

Or again,

> One thing which must strike every traveller in Hungary is the immense number of Jews, and no one who has been in the country can be still puzzled as to the whereabouts of the lost tribes; for at least one third of the Jews on the whole earth—some 3,000,000—are in Hungary and Poland. Who can mistake them? The oval face; the "parrotty" beak, out of all proportion to the other features; the stooping gait and long, flowing beard; the furtive glances from under the shaggy eyebrow, now cringing, now vindictive; the black skull-cap, from under which two oily "kiss-me-quick" curls protrude, brushed well forward over the ears on each side of the low, thoughtful brow; the protruding lower lip; the receding chin; the bony hands, accustomed to roll together, either in supplication, or satisfaction at having "done a Christian in the eye"; the tight-fitting cassock-like garment of seedy, shining cloth or threadbare silk, generally with tight sleeves, sometimes varied by a black or red sash round the waist, and always long skirts, lined with fur in winter reaching to the top of his high boots;—all these show unmistakably the Hungarian branch of that race "against whom is every man's hand," and who returns the compliment with compound interest.[10]

Little wonder that the author settled on Transylvania (a place he had never visited) and even less that some of the same attitudes permeate *Dracula*.

Stoker's original intention was to use Styria (in Austria) as Count Dracula's homeland, but as a result of his research, he made the change to Transylvania. One of his chief sources was "Transylvanian Superstitions" (1895) by Emily Gerard. "Nowhere else," Gerard writes, "does this crooked plant of delusion flourish as persistently and in such bewildering variety." Jonathan Harker notes, with a similar smugness, "I read that every known superstition in the world is gathered into the horseshoe of

the Carpathians, as if it were the centre of some sort of imaginative whirlpool." Similar sentiments can be found in Mina Harker's comment, when she travels to Transylvania to help hunt down Dracula: "the people . . . are *very, very* superstitious."[11] Gerard's article also provided Stoker with some of the folklore surrounding Dracula and his castle: St. George's Day, "the eve of which is still frequently kept by occult meetings taking place at night in lonely caverns or within ruined walls"; hidden treasures and "the light they give forth, described as a bluish flame"; and the wolf that "continues to haunt the Transylvanian forests."[12] And from Gerard came the term "nosferatu," which has become inexorably linked with the myth of Dracula.[13]

Dracula depicts Transylvania as a backward region inhabited by wild animals and superstitious peasants. What an appropriate residence for a monster who emerges from his lair to threaten Victorian England! The novel opens and closes in Transylvania. In spite of the fact that only Chapters 1–4 and part of Chapter 27 take place in Transylvania, it leaves an indelible impression on the reader.

---

1. See the following: A. F. Crosse, *Round About the Carpathians* (London: Blackwood, 1878), pp. 2, 19, 223; *Magyarland: Being the Narrative of our Travels through the Highlands and Lowlands of Hungary* (London: Sampson Low, 1881), vol. 2, p. 1; and William Wilkinson, *An Account of the Principalities of Wallachia and Moldavia* (1821; New York: Arno Press, 1971), p. 166. Stoker was familiar with all three sources.

2. John Paget, *Hungary and Transylvania*, 2 vols. (1850; New York: Arno Press, 1971), vol. 2, pp. 136, 138.

3. Andrew Chalmers, *Transylvanian Recollections: Sketches of Hungarian Travel and History* (London: Smart & Allen, 1880), pp. 2, 78.

4. Wilkinson, *Account*, pp. 128–129, 151, 156.

5. Crosse, *Carpathians*, pp. 141, 102.

6. Johnson, *Crescent*, p. 233; *Magyarland*, vol. 2, p. 129.

7. Johnson, *Crescent*, p. 251.

8. Crosse, *Carpathians*, p. 220.

9. *Magyarland*, vol. 1, p. 308.

10. Johnson, *Crescent*, pp. 200–201.

11. Emily Gerard, "Transylvanian Superstitions," *Nineteenth Century*, 18 (July 1885): 130; *Dracula*, pp. 10, 312.

12. Gerard, "Superstitions," pp. 134, 143.

13. Gerard, "Superstitions," p. 142. The word "nosferatu" does not exist in the Romanian language. Gerard apparently heard something else (possibly "nesuferit" or "nosophoros") which she transcribed as "nosferatu." For details, see Elizabeth Miller, *Dracula: Sense & Nonsense* (Westcliff-on-Sea, U.K.: Desert Island Books, 2000), pp. 48–49.

Creating Count Dracula

Many scholars and critics have sought to trace the influences that led Stoker to create Count Dracula. While such a search is often necessarily speculative, it is known where Stoker found the name "Dracula" and how he constructed a fictional "history" drawing upon several of the sources that are acknowledged in his Notes. As for a "model" for the Count, there is no clear indication that Stoker had any one person in mind.

Stoker probably encountered the name "Dracula" for the first time in William Wilkinson's book on Wallachia and Moldavia, which he found at the public library in Whitby in summer 1890. He included in his Notes not only the name of the library but also the call number of the book. He then decided to change the name for his vampire, discarding his previous choice, Count Wampyr. Wilkinson's book is the only known source of information that Stoker had about the historical Dracula, Vlad the Impaler, who is sometimes mistakenly cited as the inspiration for Count Dracula.

The Name "Dracula"
William Wilkinson

After being defeated in 1391 by the Turks under Sultan Bajazet, the military commander (voïvode) of the Wallachians was compelled to pay an annual tribute to his conquerors.

Wallachia continued to pay it until the year 1444; when Ladislas King of Hungary, preparing to make war against the Turks, engaged the Voïvode Dracula to form an alliance with him. The Hungarian troops marched through the principality and were joined by four thousand Wallachians under the command of Dracula's son.

The Hungarians being defeated at the celebrated battle of Varna, Hunniades their general, and regent of the kingdom during Ladislas's minority, returned in haste to make new preparations for carrying on the war. But the Voïvode, fearful of the Sultan's vengeance, arrested and kept him prisoner during a year, pretending thereby to show to the Turks that he treated him as an enemy. The moment Hunniades reached Hungary, he assembled an army and placed himself at the head of it, returned to Wallachia, attacked and defeated the Voïvode, and caused him to be beheaded in his presence; after which he raised to the Voïvodate one of the primates of the country, of the name of *Dan*.

The Wallachians under this Voïvode joined again the Hungarians in 1448, and made war on Turkey; but being totally defeated at the battle of Cossova, in Bulgaria, and finding it no longer possible to make any stand against the Turks, they submitted again to the annual tribute, which they paid until the year 1460, when the Sultan Mahomet II. being occupied in completing the conquest of the islands in the Archipelago, afforded them a new opportunity of shaking off the yoke. Their Voïvode, also

named Dracula*, did not remain satisfied with mere prudent measures of defence: with an army he crossed the Danube and attacked the few Turkish troops that were stationed in his neighbourhood; but this attempt, like those of his predecessors, was only attended with momentary success. Mahomet having turned his arms against him, drove him back to Wallachia, whither he pursued and defeated him. The Voïvode escaped into Hungary, and the Sultan caused his brother Bladus to be named in his place. He made a treaty with Bladus, by which he bound the Wallachians to perpetual tribute; and laid the foundations of that slavery, from which no efforts have yet had the power of extricating them with any lasting efficacy.

–Wilkinson, *An Account of the Principalities of Wallachia and Moldavia*, p. 17–19

---

* Dracula in the Wallachian language means Devil. The Wallachians were, at that time, as they are at present, used to give this as a surname to any person who rendered himself conspicuous either by courage, cruel actions, or cunning.

* * *

In Chapter II of the novel, Dracula gives Jonathan Harker an outline of his history. An examination of the Notes reveals where Stoker found his details.

Dracula's History

"We Szekelys have a right to be proud, for in our veins flows the blood of many brave races who fought as the lion fights, for lordship. Here, in the whirlpool of European races, the Ugric tribe bore down from Iceland the fighting spirit which Thor and Wodin gave them, which their Berserkers displayed to such fell intent on the seaboards of Europe, ay, and of Asia and Africa too, till the peoples thought that the were-wolves themselves had come. Here, too, when they came, they found the Huns, whose warlike fury had swept the earth like a living flame, till the dying peoples held that in their veins ran the blood of those old witches, who, expelled from Scythia had mated with the devils in the desert. Fools, fools! What devil or what witch was ever so great as Attila, whose blood is in these veins?" He held up his arms. "Is it a wonder that we were a conquering race; that we were proud; that when the Magyar, the Lombard, the Avar, the Bulgar, or the Turk poured his thousands on our frontiers, we drove them back? Is it strange that when Arpad and his legions swept through the Hungarian fatherland he found us here when he reached the frontier; that the Honfoglalas was completed there? And when the Hungarian flood

ACCOUNT OF THE PRINCIPALITIES OF WALLACHIA AND MOLDAVIA.ETC.

1820

Wm.Wilkinson late consul of Bukorest.Longmans.Whitby Library.O.1097.

1

P.19.   DRACULA in Wallachian language means DEVIL. Wallachians
        were accustomed to give it as a surname to any person
        who rendered himself conspicuous by courage,cruel actions
        or cunning.

P.18.19.The Wallachians joined Hungarians in 1448.and made war on
        Turkey,being defeated at battle of Cassova in Bulgaria
        and finding it impossible to make stand against the Turks
        submitted to annual tribute which they paid until 1460.when
        Sultan Mahomet II. being occupied in completing conquest
        of islands in Archipelogo gave opportunity of shaking off
        yoke. Their VOIVODE [DRACULA] crossed Danube and
        attacked Turkish troops Only momentarily success. Mahomet
        drove him back to Wallachia where pursued and defeated
        him. The VOIVODE escaped into Hungary.and the Sultan
        caused his brother ~~Bladus~~ *Bladus* *received* in his place. He
        made treaty with Bladus finding Wallachians to *perpetual*
        tribute and laid the foundations of that slavery not yet
        abolished.[1820]

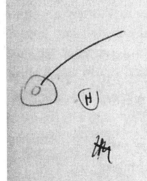

Page 71 from Stoker's notes, the only surviving document that shows the author's awareness of the historical Dracula
*(*Bram Stoker's *Dracula: A Centennial Exhibition at the Rosenbach Museum & Library,*
1997; Elizabeth Miller Collection)

swept eastward, the Szekelys were claimed as kindred by the victorious Magyars, and to us for centuries was trusted the guarding of the frontier of Turkey-land; ay, and more than that, endless duty of the frontier guard, for, as the Turks say, 'water sleeps, and enemy is sleepless.' Who more gladly than we throughout the Four Nations received the 'bloody sword,' or at its warlike call flocked quicker to the standard of the King? When was redeemed that great shame of my nation, the shame of Cassova, when the flags of the Wallach and the Magyar went down beneath the Crescent, who was it but one of my own race who as Voivode crossed the Danube and beat the Turk on his own ground? This was a Dracula indeed! Woe was it that his own unworthy brother, when he had fallen, sold his people to the Turk and brought the shame of slavery on them! Was it not this Dracula, indeed, who inspired that other of his race who in a later age again and again brought his forces over the great river into Turkey-land; who, when he was beaten back, came again, and again, and again. though he had to come alone from the bloody field where his troops were being slaughtered, since he knew that he alone could ultimately triumph? They said that he thought only of himself. Bah! what good are peasants without a leader? Where ends the war without a brain and heart to conduct it? Again, when, after the battle of Mohacs, we threw off the Hungarian yoke, we of the Dracula blood were amongst their leaders, for our spirit would not brook that we were not free. Ah, young sir, the Szekelys—and the Dracula as their heart's blood, their brains, and their swords—can boast a record that mushroom growths like the Hapsburgs and the Romanoffs can never reach. The warlike days are over. Blood is too precious a thing in these days of dishonourable peace; and the glories of the great races are as a tale that is told."

—*Dracula,* Chapter II, Jonathan Harker's Journal, Midnight

Sources for Dracula's History

We Szekelys . . .

. . . The Székelys—who claim to be descended from Attila and the Huns—were found settled on the eastern frontier when the country was conquered by the Magyars, and the two races at once fraternised. This was in the eleventh century, and from that time till 1526 the country was nominally a part of Hungary, being governed by an official who was appointed by the kings of Hungary.

—Johnson, *On the Track of the Crescent,* p. 205

the Ugric tribe

. . . Max Muller, by the unerring guide of language, has traced the original seat of this interesting people [Mag-

yars] to the Ural mountains which stretch upwards to the Arctic ocean; and pointing out the close affinity the Magyar tongue bears to the idiom of the Finnish race spoken east of the Volga, declares that the Magyars form the fourth branch of the Finnish stock, viz. the Ugric.

—*Magyarland,* volume 1, p. 45

their Berserkers

> *Baring-Gould discusses warriors dressed in wolf skins and the derivation of the term:*

. . . the word *berserkr,* used of a man possessed of superhuman powers, and subject to excesses of diabolical fury, was originally applied to one of those doughty champions who went about in bear-sarks.

—Sabine Baring-Gould, *The Book of Were-Wolves,* p. 36

they found the Huns

Geographically situated to be the "war ground" of Europe, these unfortunate Danubian provinces were open to inroads from all sides, and the barbarians made them happy hunting-grounds for human game. . . . In 376 A.D. the Huns paid Dacia a "morning call," and subdued it, driving out the Goths. These fierce Scythians are not flatteringly described by Gibbon, to whose delightful pages I must refer my readers for details of their personal appearance, & c.

—Johnson, *On the Track of the Crescent,* p. 106

Attila, whose blood is in these veins

They won, under their famous King Attila, a constant succession of victories against the Romans, till Attila's death in A.D. 543, and were then driven out of Dacia by the Gepidæ, a tribe of Goths. The country was afterwards successively held by the Lombards, Avars, and Bulgars.

—Johnson, *On the Track of the Crescent,* p. 106

Arpad and his legions

Hungary . . . has been peopled since the beginning of the Christian era, as we have already seen, by three distinct and separate colonies of barbarians, whose birthplace was in the regions of the frozen North. Here, led by Attila, the Huns established themselves between the third and fourth centuries, and hither a century or two later came the Avars, belonging to the same northern race. . . . Lastly . . . came the Magyars, the great conquering army with Arpád at its head, in whom the Ugro-Finnish type once more reappeared in all its pristine energy.

—*Magyarland,* volume 1, pp. 45–46

When the Magyars overran Pannonia in the tenth century, under the headship of the great Arpad, they appear to have found the Szeklers already in possession of part of the vast Carpathian horseshoe—that part known to us as the Transylvanian frontier of Moldavia. They claim to have come hither as early as the fourth century. It is known that an earlier wave of the Turanians had swept over Europe before the incoming of the Magyars, and the so-called Szeklers were probably a tribe or remnant of this invasion, the date of which, however, is wrapped in no little obscurity.

–A. F. Crosse, *Round About the Carpathians*, p. 205

the Honfoglalas

. . . the *honfoglalas,* as the conquest of the Hungarian fatherland by Arpád in the ninth century is called.

–*Magyarland*, p. 57

the Szekelys were claimed as kindred by the victorious Magyars

The Székelys have played a very important part in the history of Hungary and Transylvania. They were recognised as kindred by the Magyars on their first entering Hungary, and the two races have remained allies ever since. The Székelys also received certain privileges in return for their having guarded the frontier towards Moldavia and "Turkey-land." They became also the guardians of the national language, for they speak the purest Hungarian.

–Johnson, *On the Track of the Crescent*, p. 234

that great shame of my nation, the shame of Cassova

The Wallachians under this Voïvode joined again the Hungarians in 1448, and made war on Turkey; but being totally defeated at the battle of Cossova [Kosovo], in Bulgaria, and finding it no longer possible to make any stand against the Turks, they submitted again to the annual tribute.

–Wilkinson, *An Account of the Principalities of Wallachia and Moldavia*, p. 18

his own unworthy brother

The Voïvode [Dracula] escaped into Hungary, and the Sultan caused his brother Bladus to be named in his place. He made a treaty with Bladus, by which he bound the Wallachians to perpetual tribute.

–Wilkinson, *An Account of the Principalities of Wallachia and Moldavia*, p. 19

the battle of Mohacs

After the battle of Mohacs, which extinguished Hungarian independence, Transylvania fell into the hands of "the unspeakable," who made it an independent principality under the protection of the Porte; the country being governed by princes who were elected by the people, subject to the approval of the Sultan.

–Johnson, *On the Track of the Crescent*, pp. 205–206

* * *

Since the 1970s no issue has more interested scholars of Stoker's work than the nature of the relationship between the fictional Dracula and the historical Dracula, Vlad the Impaler. It has become commonplace to accept the hypothesis (first popularized in the 1970s) that Stoker was consciously suggesting a parallel between the sort of brutality the Romanian voïvode practiced and vampirism. Indeed, the belief that Stoker had intended this parallel increased respect for him as an artist and for his work.

The Historical Dracula: A Brief Biography
Elizabeth Miller

Vlad Tepes (the Impaler) was descended from Basarab the Great, a fourteenth-century prince who is credited with having founded the state of Wallachia, part of present-day Romania. The most famous of the early Basarabs was Vlad's grandfather, Mircea cel Batrin (Mircea the Old), who succeeded in consolidating an extensive Wallachian state which roughly comprises that part of present-day Romania between the southern range of the Carpathian Mountains and the Danube River. His entire reign was dominated by struggles against the Ottoman Empire and his attempts to exclude permanent Turkish settlement on Wallachian lands. There were no clear rules of succession in Wallachia. The council of "boyars" (nobility) had the power to select as voivode any son of a ruling prince. As a result, factional disputes were common, as branches of a family would fight for power. Mircea's death in 1418 led to one such struggle, especially between his illegitimate son Vlad and Dan, the son of one of Mircea's brothers.

In 1431, often cited as the year of Vlad the Impaler's birth, his father (also named Vlad) was stationed in Sighisoara as a military commander with responsibility for guarding the mountain passes from Transylvania into Wallachia from enemy incursion. That same year he was summoned to Nuremberg by Sigismund, the Holy Roman Emperor, to receive a signal honor. He was one of several princes and vassals initiated by the Emperor into the Order of the Dragon, an institution, similar to other chivalric orders of the time, modeled on the Order of St. George. Created in 1408 by Sigismund and his queen Barbara Cilli mainly for the purpose of gaining protection for the royal family, the Order of the Dragon also required its initiates to defend the Cross and to do battle against its enemies, principally the Turks. As an indication of his pride in the Order, Vlad took on the nickname "Dracul," a term derived from the Latin "draco" meaning "the dragon." The sobriquet later adopted by the younger Vlad ("Dracula" indicating "son of Dracul" or "son of the Dragon") also had a positive connotation.

In Romanian history, Vlad is usually referred to as Tepes (pronounced Tse-pesh), rather than Dracula. The name "Tepes," from the Turkish nickname "kaziklu bey" ("impaling prince"), was used by Ottoman chroniclers of the late fifteenth and early sixteenth centuries because of Vlad's fondness for impalement as a means of execution. The epithet, an indication of the fear that he instilled in his enemies, was embraced in his native country. No evidence exists to suggest that Vlad ever used it in reference to himself. By contrast, he did use the term "Dracula" (or linguistic variations thereof) in letters and documents that still survive in Romanian museums. Yet to this day, many Romanians are reluctant to refer to him as Dracula. Part of the reason is that this designation was widely used in the fifteenth- and sixteenth-century German manuscripts and printed texts that presented him in strongly negative terms. Furthermore, Bram Stoker's decision to appropriate the nickname for his vampire reinforced Romanian opposition.

Little is known about Vlad's early childhood in Sighisoara. His mother was apparently Cneajna, of a Moldavian princely family. He was the second of three sons; his brothers were Mircea and Radu. As his father was a strict governor who enforced the rules with brutality, it is likely that Vlad grew up accepting the necessity of brute force as a means of maintaining order and retaining power. The family remained in Sighisoara until 1436 when Vlad Dracul moved to Târgoviste to become voivode of Wallachia. After the move, young Vlad was educated at court, with training that was appropriate for knighthood. But his father's political actions were to have major consequences for him and his younger brother Radu. On the death of Sigismund, Vlad Dracul ranged from pro-Turkish policies to neutrality, depending on the stance he thought necessary to protect the interests of Wallachia. To ensure the reliability of Dracul's support, the Sultan required that two of his sons–Vlad and Radu–be held in Turkey as guarantees that their father would actively support Turkish interests. The two boys may have spent up to six years under this precarious arrangement. Young Vlad would have been about eleven years old at the time of the internment, while Radu would have been about seven.

It appears that the two boys were held for part of the time at the fortress of Egregoz, located in western Anatolia, and later moved to Sultan Murad's court at Adrianople. At times, the situation became quite tense. What effect this might have had on young Vlad and his concept of trust we cannot ascertain. Some historians claim that Vlad's later sadistic tendencies were due at least in part to these formative years spent in captivity. The younger brother Radu, a handsome lad who attracted the attention of the future sultan, fared better than Vlad, a factor that helps explain the bitter hatred

Vlad Tepes (circa 1431–1476), whose preferred name, "Dracula," Stoker used for his vampire (hand-colored fifteenth-century woodcut, Bamberg, 1491; Bram Stoker's Dracula: A Centennial Exhibition at the Rosenbach Museum & Library, *1997; Elizabeth Miller Collection)*

and rivalry that developed between the brothers later. After their subsequent release in 1448, Radu chose to remain in Turkey. But Vlad returned to Wallachia to find that his father had been assassinated and his older brother Mircea buried alive by the nobles of Târgoviste who had supported a rival claimant.

Vlad was voivode for three separate periods, totaling about seven years. Not too much is known of his first brief period of rule (in 1448). His reign was short-lived, and Vlad spent the next eight years plotting his return to power. Finally in 1456 he was successful and ruled for the next six years, the period about which most is known. After major battles against the Turks in 1462, he escaped across the mountains into Transylvania and was held as a prisoner by the Hungarian king Matthias Corvinus until the mid-1470s. He recovered the throne for a third time in 1476 but he was killed in battle during the subsequent winter.

Vlad's immediate priority when he regained his throne in 1456 was to consolidate his position in Wallachia. He was determined to break the political power of the boyars (nobles) who tended to support puppet (and often weak) leaders who would protect their interests. One of his earliest actions was taken against the nobles of Târgoviste whom he held responsible for the deaths of his father and brother. According to early Romanian chronicles, in the spring of 1457 Vlad invited the nobles and their families to an Easter feast. After his guests had finished their meal, Vlad's soldiers surrounded them: he impaled the old, while those who were young, together with their wives and children, all dressed up for Easter, he had taken to Poenari where they were forced to build a fortress.

A related internal problem that faced Vlad was the continuous threat from rival claimants to the throne, all of whom were descendants of Mircea cel Batrin. The solution was simple: to purge the existing boyar class of any potential opposition and to replace them with hand-picked men whose loyalty would be unflinching. Coupled with his determination to consolidate his own power was his extreme view of law and order. He did not hesitate to inflict the punishment of impalement on anyone who committed a crime, large or small. On the economic front, he was determined to break the hold that the Saxon merchants of southern Transylvania (especially Brasov) had on trade. Not only were these merchants ignoring his imposed customs duties, they were also supporting rival claimants to his throne.

It was inevitable that Vlad would finally have to confront the Turks, as Wallachia lay between Turkish-controlled Bulgaria and the rest of central and eastern Europe. The small principality of Wallachia had to stand against the might of Sultan Mehmed II, conqueror of Constantinople. Vlad precipitated the anger of the Sultan by refusing to honor an earlier arrangement to pay an annual tribute and to supply young Wallachian men for the Turkish army. After a period of raiding and pillaging along the Danube border, full-fledged war broke out during the winter of 1461–1462. Initially, Vlad met with remarkable success. His exploits drew the attention of several European rulers, including the Pope himself. The Turks launched a full counter-offensive. Badly outnumbered, Vlad employed every possible means to gain an advantage: drawing the enemy deep into his own territory through a strategic retreat, he burned villages and poisoned wells along the route; he employed guerilla tactics, using the local terrain to advantage; he may even have initiated a form of germ warfare, deliberately sending victims of infectious diseases into the Turkish camps.

On 17 June 1462, he led a raid known in Romanian history as the "Night Attack." But the Sultan's army continued onwards and reached the outskirts of Vlad's capital city, where Vlad used his most potent weapon–psychological warfare. The invaders were greeted with a gruesome sight: a forest of the impaled. The Sultan withdrew. But the war was not over. Mehmed threw his support behind Vlad's brother Radu, who with the support of defecting boyars and Turkish soldiers, pursued Vlad all the way to his mountain fortress at Poenari. According to oral legends that survive to this day in the village of Aref, near the fortress, Vlad was able to escape into Transylvania with the help of local villagers. But he was soon arrested by Matthias Corvinus, who had chosen to throw his support behind Radu, Vlad's successor.

Vlad did regain the throne briefly in 1476, but was killed in battle under circumstances that are unclear. A Russian source claims that he was mistaken by one of his own men for a Turk and consequently killed. More likely is that he was attacked by a rival claimant, Basarab Laiota (who succeeded him as voivode), and killed by a hired assassin. One story goes that he was beheaded, and his head was taken back to the Sultan in Constantinople and displayed as a trophy. Tradition has it that his body was taken by monks to the Snagov Monastery and buried there close to the altar, in recognition of the fact that he had supplied funds for the rebuilding of the monastery years earlier. However, excavations on the site during the early 1930s failed to uncover a burial site. Where are his remains? Some suggest that he was buried elsewhere on the monastery site where indeed remains were found. Others contend he is buried near the altar, but at a greater depth than was excavated. Yet others suggest he may have been interred in a different area altogether, such as Targsor or Cormana. To date, the mystery remains unsolved.

Vlad is best known today for the many atrocities that have been attributed to him by various sources. The material includes the following categories: German manuscript sources (including a narrative poem) from 1462–1463 while Vlad was still alive, along with a series of pamphlets printed between 1485 and 1500; Turkish chronicles detailing the military campaign of 1461–1462; Slavic manuscripts from the 1480s found in Russian archives; and a body of Romanian oral narratives collected and transcribed by chroniclers and folklorists. We find in these sources a variety of representations of Vlad, from a cruel, even psychopathic tyrant to a hero who put the needs of his country above all else. Consequently, it is virtually impossible to reconstruct his political and military activities with certainty.

***

Ruins of the palace at Târgoviste, where Vlad the Impaler ruled as voïvode of Wallachia (photograph by Elizabeth Miller)

The most widespread misconception about Stoker and the creation of Dracula is that Vlad the Impaler was the inspiration for Stoker's Count—that Stoker, familiar with accounts of Vlad's atrocities, found him a fitting model for his Dracula. The evidence, however, does not support such a claim.

Filing for Divorce:
Count Dracula vs Vlad the Impaler
Elizabeth Miller

In Chapter 18 of *Dracula,* Van Helsing says this of the Count: "He must, indeed, have been that Voivode Dracula who won his name against the Turk, over the great river on the very frontier of Turkey-land."[1] Very little attention was paid to the possible connection between the fictional Count and his historical namesake until 1972 when Radu Florescu and Raymond T. McNally's *In Search of Dracula* revealed to the world the story of the real Dracula—Vlad Tepes. This was closely followed by their fortuitous discovery that the Rosen-

bach Museum in Philadelphia had acquired Stoker's working papers for *Dracula,* which prove conclusively that he did know about the existence of a "Voivode Dracula." Dracula studies have not been the same since. Using the initial findings of Florescu and McNally (some of which the two historians have since revised), many enthusiasts have championed tenuous connections between Count Dracula and Vlad, to the point where it has become increasingly difficult to separate fact from hypothesis.

It has become commonplace to assume that Stoker was inspired by accounts of the Impaler's atrocities and deliberately modeled his Dracula on the life and character of Vlad. This has resulted in some fanciful and at times ludicrous statements: that "*Dracula* was the reshaping of four centuries of folk legends that had accreted around the historical Walachian warlord Prince Vlad Tepes"; that much of the story of Count Dracula "was drawn . . . from the ghastly doings of the Hungarian Prince Vlad who was a remote ancestor of Attila the Hun"; that the historical Dracula's abandonment of his Orthodox faith resulted in his becoming subject to punishment by Orthodox priests who "publicly laid the curse of vampirism" on him; and that the "first reported vampires were real historical figures . . . Elizabeth of Bathory and Vlad the Impaler."[2] Such claims are unfounded.

Investigations into possible connections between the Count and the Voivode began before the publication of *In Search of Dracula.* In 1958, Bacil Kirtley stated that "Unquestionably the historical past that Van Helsing assigns the fictional vampire Dracula is that of Vlad Tsepesh, Voivod of Wallachia."[3] In 1962, Stoker's first biographer, Harry Ludlam, asserted that Stoker had "discovered that the Voivode Drakula or Dracula . . . had earned for himself the title of 'the Impaler,' and that the story of his ferocity and hair-raising cruelty in defiance of the Turks was related at length in two fifteenth-century manuscripts, one of which spoke of him as 'wampyr'."[4] In 1966, Grigore Nandris connected the vampire Dracula with the historical figure, even claiming that available portraits of Vlad were "adapted by Bram Stoker to suit his literary purposes."[5] Building on these obscure references to a possible connection, Florescu and McNally embarked on a quest of their own, the results of which were published in *In Search of Dracula* (1972, revised 1994). While their historical research was thorough and well documented, the two authors speculated that the author of *Dracula* knew quite a bit about the historical figure, and that his sources included Arminius Vambéry (a Hungarian professor whom he met on at least two occasions) and various readings found at the British Museum. But is this the case? Exactly what *is* the connection between the Count and the Voivode? For the answer, we must go to two sources, the reliability of which cannot be questioned: Stoker's Notes at the Rosenbach Museum, and the novel itself.

We know from the Notes that by March 1890, Stoker had decided to write a vampire novel; in fact, he had already selected a name for his vampire–Count Wampyr. We are also certain that Stoker found the name "Dracula" (most likely for the first time) in a book by William Wilkinson that he borrowed from the Whitby Public Library in the summer of 1890. Stoker not only recorded the call number of the book but copied almost verbatim key passages.

The name "Dracula" appears just three times, two of which more accurately refer to Vlad's father (Vlad Dracul). What attracted Stoker was a footnote attached to the third occurrence: "Dracula in the Wallachian language means Devil. The Wallachians were, at that time, as they are at present, used to give this as a surname to any person who rendered himself conspicuous either by courage, cruel actions, or cunning." That Stoker considered this important is evident in that he copied into his own notes "DRACULA in Wallachian language means DEVIL" (emphasis his). The three references to "Dracula" in Wilkinson's text, along with the footnote, are the only occurrences of the name in all of the sources that we know that Stoker consulted.

Stoker's debt to Wilkinson is generally acknowledged, but a number of points are often overlooked: Wilkinson refers only to "Dracula" and "Voivode," never "Vlad," never "Vlad Tepes" or "the Impaler"; furthermore there are no specific references to his atrocities. It is no mere co-incidence that the same paucity of information applies to the text of *Dracula*. Yet the popular theory is that Stoker knew much more than what he read in Wilkinson–that his major sources were the Hungarian professor Arminius Vambéry, and readings in the British Museum.

In *Personal Reminiscences of Henry Irving,* Stoker gives a brief account of two meetings with Vambéry.[6] There is nothing to indicate that the topic of Dracula ever came up; Stoker does tell us, however, that Henry Irving was present at the first meeting, a meal that followed a performance of the play "The Dead Heart." Is it not more likely that the dinner conversation focused on the play, and (considering Irving's overpowering personality) on his performance? As the account of this dinner was written several years after the publication of *Dracula,* one would expect Stoker to have mentioned Vambéry's role (assuming he had one). Stoker notes that the Hungarian was "full of experiences [about a trip to Central Asia] fascinating to hear." Surely a discussion about the atrocities of Vlad the Impaler would have been as fascinating, had it occurred? Also signifi-

Vlad the Impaler (from Dracole Wayda, *1500; Radu Florescu and Raymond T. McNally,* Dracula: Prince of Many Faces, *1989; Elizabeth Miller Collection)*

cant is that this meeting took place in April 1890, *before* Stoker went to Whitby and read Wilkinson's book. As for the second encounter, Stoker provides even less information. "We saw him again two years later," records Stoker, "when he was being given a Degree at the Tercentenary of Dublin University. . . . He soared above all the speakers, making one of the finest speeches I have ever head [sic]." The only comment about the subject matter of the talk was that Vambéry "spoke loudly against Russian aggression." Nothing about Dracula.

The conviction that Stoker gleaned information from the Hungarian seems to be the residue of theories about Stoker's sources before the discovery of his Notes. As early as 1962, Ludlam was making the claim that "Bram sought the help of Arminius Vambéry in Budapest" and that "Vambéry was able to report that 'the Impaler' who had won this name for obvious reasons, was spoken of for centuries after as the cleverest and the most cunning, as well as the bravest of the sons of the 'land beyond the forest.'"[7] Florescu and McNally cemented the connection in 1972: "The two men [Stoker and Vambéry] dined together, and during the course of their conversation, Bram was impressed by the professor's stories about Dracula 'the impaler'. After Vambéry returned to Budapest, Bram wrote to him, requesting more details about the notorious 15th century prince and the land he lived in."[8] The only fact we have is that they dined together. Stoker makes no reference to Vambéry in his working papers. No documented evidence exists that Vambéry gave Stoker *any* information about Vlad, or for that matter, about vampires. Supporters of the Stoker-Vambéry link also go to the novel for textual evidence, claiming that what Vambéry told Stoker is revealed through what Arminius, Van Helsing's friend, tells Van Helsing. Van Helsing, the argument goes, is Stoker's alter-ego, and the insertion of Arminius is the author's tribute to Vambéry, or, as Florescu and McNally speculate, "Stoker's way of acknowledging his debt" and showing "what information and conclusions the professor had passed on to Stoker."[9] But the mere inclusion of the name proves no such thing. *Dracula* contains many names drawn from its author's friends and acquaintances: the name "Harker," for example, most likely came from one of the workers at the Lyceum, while "Swales" was taken from a tombstone that Stoker noted in Whitby.

But let us assume that what Arminius tells Van Helsing is an echo of what Vambéry told Stoker. What exactly does he say?

> I have asked my friend Arminius, of Buda-Pesth University, to make his record; and, from all the means that are, he tell me of what he has been. He must, indeed, have been that Voivode Dracula who won his name against the Turk, over the great river on the very frontier of Turkey-land. If it be so, then was he no common man; for in that time, and for centuries after, he was spoken of as the cleverest and the most cunning, as well as the bravest of the sons of the "land beyond the forest" . . . The Draculas were, says Arminius, a great and noble race, though now and again were scions who were held by their coevals to have had dealings with the Evil One. They learned his secrets in the Scholomance, amongst the mountains over Lake Hermanstadt, where the devil claims the tenth scholar as his due. In the records are such words as "stregoica"—witch, "ordog," and "pokol"—Satan and hell; and in one manuscript this very Dracula is spoken of as "wampyr," which we all understand too well. (p. 212)

All of the vital information in this passage can be traced to Stoker's own notes and sources: Wilkinson writes about Dracula and the Turks, as well as the Voivode's courage and cunning; "the land beyond the forest" was

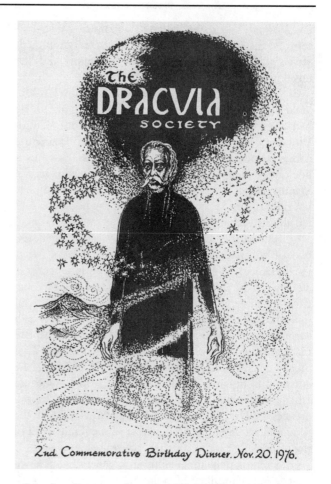

Cover for a dinner program, with a depiction of Dracula in which the artist has tried to render Stoker's Count accurately. The Dracula of the novel bears little physical resemblance to Vlad, Henry Irving, or to most of the Draculas of the movies (from a painting by Bruce Wightman; courtesy of The Dracula Society, London).

the heading of a chapter in Charles Boner's book on Transylvania (one of Stoker's known sources) as well as the title for a book by Emily Gerard, whose article "Transylvanian Superstitions" we know that Stoker read; the information about the Scholomance comes almost verbatim from Gerard's article; the terms "stregoica," "ordog," and "pokol" are listed in Stoker's notes as having come from *Magyarland* (1881); and "wampyr" was the name that Stoker originally intended to give his Count. Nothing remains to have come from Vambéry.

Arminius makes a second appearance in the text as Van Helsing reports on Dracula to the band of vampire hunters: "As I learned from the researches of my friend Arminius of Buda-Pesth, he was in life a most wonderful man" (p. 263). While he goes on to comment on his "mighty brain, a learning beyond compare, and a heart that knew no fear and no remorse," Arminius says nothing about his reputation as "the Impaler," certainly his most memorable characteristic. While the inclusion of the name of Arminius can be seen as Stoker's tribute to Vambéry, there is no evidence that the Hungarian provided Stoker with *any* information about Dracula.

But what about the "manuscript" in which "this very Dracula is spoken of as 'wampyr'"? Some have posited the theory that Stoker actually did see such a manuscript; or at the very least, during his research at the British Museum, "Stoker uncovered writings pertaining to Vlad the Impaler."[10] No doubt Stoker did do some research at the British Museum, but there is not a shred of evidence that he did any of it on the historical Dracula. Now, he *could* have. Christopher Frayling lists what would have been available at the time: included is one of the German printed pamphlets about Vlad published in Bamberg in 1491 with a woodcut. Could this be the mysterious document to which Arminius alludes? Frayling goes so far as to suggest that this is an "authentic model for Dracula" and that "Stoker must have seen the pamphlet or a reproduction of it."[11] This is, of course, speculation.

One result of all of this is that readers, accepting these hypotheses as fact, begin to look to the novel for corroborating evidence. First there is the assumption that Stoker drew his physical description of Count Dracula from either the woodcut portrait in the Bamberg pamphlet about Vlad or from a printed account of Vlad's physical appearance. It has been tempting, for example, to deduce that Stoker had access to the following description of Vlad, provided by a fifteenth-century papal legate who had met the voivode:

> He was not very tall, but very stocky and strong, with a cold and terrible appearance, a strong aquiline nose, swollen nostrils, a thin and reddish face in which the very long eyelashes framed large wide-open green eyes; the bushy black eyebrows made them appear threatening.[12]

That Stoker had access to this document is virtually impossible. Furthermore, the description offered in the novel differs significantly from the fifteenth-century account: Stoker describes Dracula as tall and thin rather than short and stocky; the Count's eyes are red, not green, and his complexion is pale. And as for Count Dracula's "eyebrows almost meeting over the nose," Stoker records in his notes that this came from Baring-Gould's *The Book of Were-Wolves*. In addition, anyone familiar with nineteenth-century Gothic literature knows that many of the features of Vlad described in the legate's account (such as the bushy eye-

brows and the aquiline nose) had become, by Stoker's time, common conventions in Gothic fiction.

Another popular piece of speculation began as early as 1956: that in creating the character Renfield, Stoker "seems to have adapted the legend" about Vlad's penchant for impaling mice while he was a prisoner in Hungary; Nandris connected the tradition about Vlad impaling birds saying it "is developed in Bram Stoker's *Dracula*."[13] This reappears several years later in Farson's biography of Stoker and is extended to Renfield:

> There is a story that he [Vlad] bribed his guards into bringing him small birds which he would mutilate and then impale on sticks in neat rows. If true, this was echoed by Stoker in his powerful characterisation of the lunatic Renfield, who caught flies to feed spiders to feed birds which he devoured himself.[14]

Equally far-fetched is the claim that Vlad's fondness for impaling his victims was Stoker's inspiration for his method of destroying the vampire—the use of the wooden stake.[15] This misleading connection overlooks three facts: that Bram Stoker had planned on writing a vampire novel before he ever came across the name of "Dracula"; that there is no definitive proof that Stoker knew anything about Vlad's fondness for impalement; and that the staking of vampires was a well-established motif both in folklore and in earlier Gothic fiction long before *Dracula*.

Another consequence of the insistence on connecting the two Draculas is the temptation to criticize Stoker for inaccurate "history." Why, some ask, did he make Dracula a Transylvanian Count rather than a Wallachian Voivode? Why was his castle situated in the Borgo Pass instead of at Poenari? Why is Count Dracula a "boyar," a member of the nobility which Vlad continuously struggled with? Why does Stoker make Dracula a "Szekely," descended from Attila the Hun, when the real Dracula was a Wallachian of the Basarab family? There is a very simple answer to these questions: Vlad Tepes is Vlad Tepes, while Count Dracula is Count Dracula. Considering the preposterous conclusions that the premises behind such questions have generated, a closer look seems warranted.

Although Stoker's knowledge of the historical Dracula was scanty, he did know that he was a voivode. His use of the title "count" was in keeping with the Gothic convention of drawing villains from the ranks of the aristocracy. A cursory glance shows a recurrence of villainous counts: Count Morano in *The Mysteries of Udolpho* (Radcliffe), Count de Bruno in *The Italian* (Radcliffe), Count Doni in *Ernestus Berchtold* (Polidori), Count Cenci in *The Cenci* (Shelley), Count Montonio in *The Fatal Response* (Maturin), Lord Byron's Count Manfred, and Wilkie Collins' Count Fosco.

The Gothic Villain

. . . His nose was aquiline, his eyes large, black and sparkling, and his dark brows almost joined together. . . . He bowed himself with humility to the audience. Still there was a certain severity in his look and manner that inspired universal awe, and few could sustain the glance of his eye, at once fiery and penetrating. Such was Ambrosio, abbot of the Capuchins, and surnamed "The Man of Holiness."
—Matthew Gregory Lewis, *The Monk: A Romance*, 3 volumes (London: Printed for J. Bell, 1796)

. . . His figure was striking, but not so from grace; it was tall, and, though extremely thin, his limbs were large and uncouth, and as he stalked along, wrapt in the black garments of his order, there was something terrible in its air; something almost super-human.
—Ann Radcliffe, *The Italian, or The Confessional of the Black Penitents* (London: Cadell & Davis, 1797)

Within, stood a tall old man, clean shaven save for a long white moustache, and clad in black from head to foot, without a single speck of colour about him anywhere.

. . . .

His face was a strong—a very strong—aquiline, with high bridge of the thin nose and peculiarly arched nostrils; with lofty domed forehead, and hair growing scantily round the temples, but profusely elsewhere. His eyebrows were very massive, almost meeting over the nose, and with bushy hair that seemed to curl in its own profusion.

—*Dracula,* Chapter II, Jonathan Harker's Journal, 5 May

Vampire counts in pre-Dracula fiction include Count Azzo von Klatka in "The Mysterious Stranger" and Countess Karnstein in Le Fanu's "Carmilla." The frequent occurrence of Counts in Gothic fiction links the temporal power of aristocrats, especially foreign aristocrats, with supernatural powers. As for references to the Borgo Pass, the "boyars" and the Szeklers, these are bits and pieces from sundry sources that Stoker mentions in his notes.

How much *did* Bram Stoker know about the historical Dracula? There is no doubt that some material was available. But how meticulous a researcher was Stoker? We know that he read and took notes from a number of books and articles (listed elsewhere in this volume) and that some of this material found its way into his novel almost verbatim. But his research seems to have been haphazard (though at times fortuitous) rather than scholarly. What he used, he used "as is," errors and confusions included. That his rendering of historical and geographical data is fragmented and at times erroneous can be explained by the fact that Stoker seemed content to combine bits and pieces of information from his sources without any concern for accuracy. After all, Stoker was writing a Gothic novel, not a historical treatise. And he was writing *Dracula* in his spare time, of which I doubt he had much. He may very well have found more material about the historical Dracula, had he had the time to look for it. But in the absence of any proof to the contrary, I am not convinced that he did. There is no conclusive evidence that he gleaned any information on Vlad from Vambéry, from material at the British Museum, or from anywhere else except that one book he found in Whitby—by William Wilkinson.

I have other reasons for taking this position. Let us assume for argument's sake that he *did* learn more from Vambéry, that he *did* conduct research on the historical Dracula beyond Wilkinson. Why, then, is Count Dracula in the novel never referred to as "Vlad" or "the Impaler"? Why are there no references to his atrocities, which would have been grist for the horror writer's mill? Why is Van Helsing reduced to stating that "He [Dracula] was in life a most wonderful man"? Why are there no references in Stoker's working notes to his having found any other material? And why, when queried about the historical basis of his novel, did Stoker not mention Vlad?[16] There are only two possible answers: either he knew more and chose not to use it, or else he used what he knew.

Was Stoker so sophisticated a novelist that he deliberately suppressed material for artistic purposes? One need only consider how greedily he gobbled up and reproduced a significant amount of rather trivial information. Are we to believe that he knew about Vlad's bloodthirsty activities but decided to discard such a history for his villainous Count in favor of the meager pickings gleaned from Wilkinson? One could argue that absence is as important as presence: that Stoker deliberately suppressed information in order to make his character more mysterious; or that Dracula's silence about his past is a consequence of the fact that the text denies him a narrative voice. Such interpretations are intriguing, but one must bear in mind that there is a difference between interpretation and fact.

As for the theories about the connections between the Count and the Voivode, they are (with the exception of the link to Wilkinson) based on circumstantial evidence, some of which is quite flimsy. I do not dispute that in using the name "Dracula" Stoker appropriated the sobriquet of the fifteenth-century Wallachian voivode. Nor do I deny that he added bits and pieces of obscure historical detail to flesh out a past for his vampire. But I do challenge the widespread view that Stoker was knowledgeable about the historical Dracula (beyond what he read in Wilkinson) and that he based his Count on the life and character of Vlad. While it is true that the resurgence of interest in *Dracula* since the early 1970s is due in no small measure to the theories about such connections, the theories themselves do not withstand the test of close scrutiny.

–revised by the author from *Dracula: The Shade and the Shadow,* edited by Elizabeth Miller (Westcliff-on-Sea, U.K.: Desert Island Books, 1998), pp. 165–179

1. Bram Stoker, *Dracula,* p. 212. All subsequent quotations are cited in parentheses.

2. See: Stefan Dziemianowicz, Introduction to *Weird Vampire Tales,* ed. Robert Weinberg, Stefan Dziemianowicz and Martin Greenberg (New York: Grammercy, 1992), p. 11; Manuela Dunn Mascetti, *Vampire: The Complete Guide to the World of the Undead* (New York: Viking, 1992), p. 274; Vincent Hillyer, *Vampires* (Los Banos: Loose Change, 1988), p. 17; and Victoria A. Brownworth and Judith M. Redding, Introduction to *Night Bites: Vampire Stories by Women,* ed. Victoria A. Brownworth (Seattle: Seal, 1996), p. ix.

3. Bacil Kirtley, "Dracula: The Monastic Chronicles and Slavic Folklore," in *Dracula: The Vampire and the Critics,* ed. Margaret L. Carter (Ann Arbor: UMI, 1988), p. 14.

4. Harry Ludlam, *A Biography of Bram Stoker, Creator of Dracula* (1962; London: New English Library, 1977), p. 113.

5. Grigore Nandris, "The Historical Dracula: The Theme of his Legend in the Western and Eastern Literatures in Europe," *Comparative Literature Studies,* 3 (1966): 375.

6. Bram Stoker, *Personal Reminiscences of Henry Irving* (1906; London: William Heinemann, 1907), p. 238.

7. Ludlam, *Biography,* p. 100.

8. Raymond McNally and Radu Florescu, *In Search of Dracula* (New York: Greenwich, 1972), p. 115.

9. McNally and Florescu, *Search,* p. 116.

10. Donald Glut, *The Dracula Book* (Metuchen, N.J.: Scarecrow, 1975), p. 55; see also Andrew Mackenzie, *Dracula Country* (London: Arthur Barker, 1977), p. 55.

11. Christopher Frayling, *Vampyres: Lord Byron to Count Dracula* (London: Faber & Faber, 1991), p. 421.

12. qtd. in Radu Florescu and Raymond McNally, *Dracula: Prince of Many Faces* (Boston: Little, Brown, 1989), p. 85.

13. Kirtley, "Dracula," p. 14; Nandris, "Historical Dracula," p. 391.

14. Daniel Farson, *The Man Who Wrote Dracula: A Biography of Bram Stoker* (New York: St. Martin's Press, 1975), p. 128.

15. See, for example, Glut, *Dracula Book,* p. 56.

16. See Jane Stoddard, "Mr. Bram Stoker: A Chat with the Author of *Dracula*," 1897, repr. in *Dracula,* ed. Glennis Byron (Peterborough: Broadview, 1998), pp. 484–488.

Possible Character Models

There has been a considerable preoccupation with finding models and/or inspirations for the fictional characters in Dracula *among Stoker's friends and acquaintances. Here are some of the more interesting candidates, with an indication of what evidence is–or is not–available to support the claims.*

A Dracula "Who's Who"
Elizabeth Miller

Count Dracula

Other than the common misconceptions about Vlad the Impaler, the most widespread assumption is that Stoker deliberately modeled Count Dracula on his employer, Sir Henry Irving. One frequently encounters the supposition that Stoker's hero-worship of Irving, as revealed in his *Personal Reminiscences of Henry Irving,* masks what Stoker was unable to admit to himself: that he resented the man under whose shadow he had labored for so long. Chief proponent of this view is Barbara Belford, whose biography of Stoker is built on the premise that "Dracula is all about Irving as the vampire," and that the novel was Stoker's "stunning but avenging tribute" to his employer.[1] Such claims are difficult to prove.

A much more likely possibility is that Irving's performances on stage helped Stoker's shaping of Dracula. One of the first to follow this path was Grigore Nandris, who drew attention to Stoker's comment about Irving's private recitation of "The Dream of Eugene Aram": "the awful horror on the murderer's face" and "the fixed face–set as doom, with eyes as inflexible as Fate."[2] Maurice Richardson adds that "Irving's saturnine appearance and the savage hiss . . . [may have] inspired the character of Dracula."[3] Irving's ability to capture the facial expressions of the great villains comes through on many occasions. Some of his most famous roles may have flashed across Stoker's mind as he was writing the novel: how as Shylock his eyes did "flash like lurid fire"; his features in *Don Quixote* "heightened by the resources of art to an exaggerated aquiline"; his exaggeration in speaking. But most significant may have been Irving's Mephistopheles in *Faust.* Considering that Irving played the role 792 times, Stoker must have had implanted in his mind images of Irving in the diabolical role.[4]

Abraham Van Helsing

Next to the Count, Van Helsing has been subjected to the most source-searching. First of all, the name. "Abraham" was, of course, the name of both Stoker ("Bram" was a shortened form) and his

Whitby, London and Environs

Though Transylvania is usually thought of as the setting of Dracula, *most of the story takes place in England, primarily London and environs but also the town of Whitby. Stoker spent the summer in Whitby in 1890, during which time he collected information that he incorporated into his novel, most notably coming across the name "Dracula." The novel is also replete with references to sites in and around the English capital, including the London Zoo, Piccadilly Circus, Hampstead Heath, and Purfleet. The use of landmarks familiar to contemporary readers lent the novel a verisimilitude that made its supernatural events more believable.*

At times Stoker, while not directly copying information, seems to adopt the tone of a traveler's handbook, as a comparison of the immediate following passages demonstrates.

Hampstead Heath (430 ft. above the sea-level) is one of the most open and picturesque spots in the immediate neighbourhood of London, and is a favourite and justly valued resort of holiday-makers and all who appreciate pure and invigorating air. The heath is about 240 acres in extent. Its wild and irregular beauty, and picturesque alternations of hill and hollow, make it a refreshing contrast to the trim elegance of the Parks. The heath was once a notorious haunt of highwaymen. In 1870 it was purchased by the Metropolitan Board of Works for the unrestricted use of the public. *Parliament Hill* (265 acres), to the S.E. of the heath proper, has also been acquired for the public. A supposed tumulus, known as "Queen Boadicea's Grave," was investigated here in 1895 with disappointing results. Near the ponds at the S.E. corner of the heath the Fleet Brook takes its rise. The garden of the *Bull and Bush Inn,* on the N. margin of the heath, contains a holly planted by Hogarth, the painter; and *"Jack Straw's Castle,"* on the highest part of the heath, near the flag-staff, is another interesting old inn. . . . On public holidays Hampstead Heath is generally visited by 25–50,000 Londoners and presents a characteristic scene of popular enjoyment.

. . . .

We leave Hampstead Heath at the N. end, near "Jack Straw's Castle," and follow *Heath* or *Spaniards' Road,* leading to the N.E. to Highgate. We soon reach, on the left, the *"Spaniards' Inn,"* the gathering-point of the

"No Popery" rioters of 1780, and described by Dickens in "Barnaby Rudge." The stretch of road between "Jack Straw's Castle" and this point is perhaps the most open and elevated near London.

–Karl Baedeker, *London and Its Environs. Handbook for Travelers,* twelfth revised edition (Leipsig: Karl Baedeker, 1900), pp. 372–373

24 *July. Whitby.*–Lucy met me at the station, looking sweeter and lovelier than ever, and we drove up to the house at the Crescent in which they have rooms. This is a lovely place. The little river, the Esk, runs through a deep valley, which broadens out as it comes near the harbour. A great viaduct runs across, with high piers, through which the view seems somehow further away than it really is. The valley is beautifully green, and it is so steep that when you are on the high land on either side you look right across it, unless you are near enough to see down. The houses of the old town–the side away from us–are all red-roofed, and seem piled up one over the other anyhow, like the pictures we see of Nuremberg. Right over the town is the ruin of Whitby Abbey, which was sacked by the Danes, and which is the scene of part of "Marmion," where the girl was built up in the wall. It is a most noble ruin, of immense size, and full of beautiful and romantic bits; there is a legend that a white lady is seen in one of the windows. Between it and the town there is another church, the parish one, round which is a big graveyard, all full of tombstones. This is to my mind the nicest spot in Whitby, for it lies right over the town, and has a full view of the harbour and all up the bay to where the headland called Kettleness stretches out into the sea. It descends so steeply over the harbour that part of the bank has fallen away, and some of the graves have been destroyed. In one place part of the stonework of the graves stretches out over the sandy pathway far below. There are walks, with seats beside them, through the churchyard; and people go and sit there all day long looking at the beautiful view and enjoying the breeze.

–*Dracula,* Chapter VI, Mina Murray's Journal

father; it may also have been selected for its biblical resonance, as Van Helsing serves the function of patriarchal leader in the world of the vampire hunters. As for his surname, it may come from Dr. Hesselius, the fictional narrator of Sheridan Le Fanu's *In a Glass Darkly* or "from the Danish name for Hamlet's famed castle Elsinore–Helsingor."[5] The name also closely resembles "Van Helmont," an ancient alchemist mentioned in T.J. Pettigrew's *On Superstitions*

Connected with the History and Nature of Medicine and Surgery, a book included in Stoker's list of sources.

Shortly after the publication of the novel, Stoker suggested that the professor "is founded on a real character." He seems to confirm this with the tantalizing remark in his preface to the Icelandic edition of *Dracula* (1901) that "the highly respected scientist, who appears here under a pseudonym, will also be too famous all over the educated world for his real name . . . to be hid-

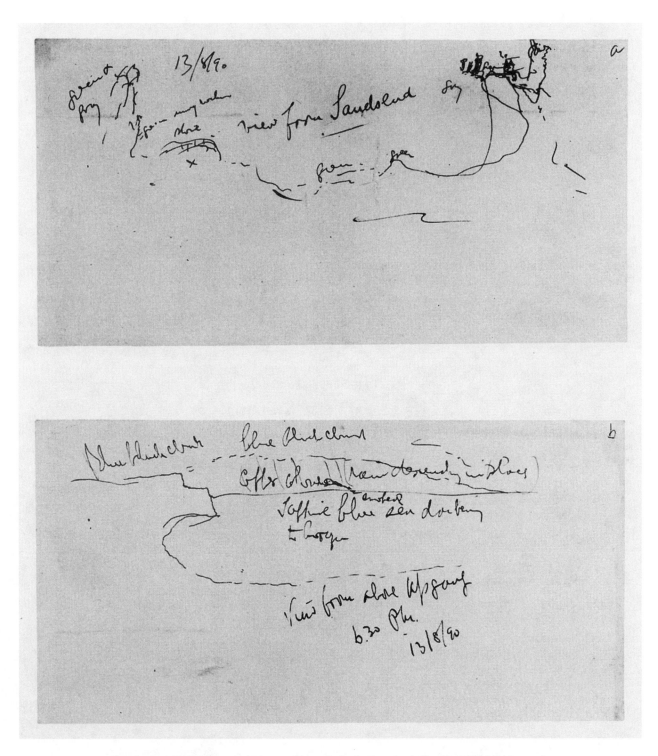

Two sketches of Whitby from Stoker's notes (Bram Stoker's Dracula: *A Centennial Exhibition at the Rosenbach Museum & Library, 1997; Elizabeth Miller Collection)*

(Whitby Tombstones)
10

SACRED

to the Memory of

THOMAS BAXTER

Who was killed on board of

H.M.S. SCOUT

by a shot from a Spanish Gunboat

Off Cape Trafalgar Novr.2nd 1807

ALSO

JOHN ROBINSON who

died Aug. 3rd 1827. aged 36 years

This Stone was erected out of

Affectionate remembrance by

Mary their surviving Widow.

ALSO

the above Mary their

Wife who died Oct.27. 1833.

Aged 36 years.

*One of several pages of notes that Stoker copied from Whitby tombstones. He used some of the names for minor characters
in his novel (Bram Stoker's* Dracula: *A Centennial Exhibition at the Rosenbach
Museum & Library, 1997; Elizabeth Miller Collection).*

The remnants of Whitby Abbey, described in Dracula *as "a most noble ruin, of immense size"*
(Elizabeth Miller Collection)

den from people."[6] We must keep in mind, however, that this is likely nothing more than the familiar pose of the Gothic novelist striving for credibility, especially considering another of Stoker's remarks (in the Icelandic preface) that "Jonathan Harker and his wife . . . are my friends and have been so for many years, . . . [and] I have never doubted that they were telling the truth."[7]

Some draw parallels between Van Helsing and Stoker. Not only do they share a common name, but most likely Dutch ancestry. Assuming Stoker had a model in mind for Van Helsing, a strong case can be made for a contemporary German professor at Oxford, Max Müller. Stoker's Notes show that the character of Van Helsing was originally conceived as three separate entities, one of whom was "a German professor of history"; elsewhere in the Notes this professor is given a name—Max Windshoeffel. The change from German to Dutchman was made later. One scholar adds that "the Oxford professor from Germany [Müller] was a specialist in religion and mythology."[8]

Jonathan Harker

The name "Harker" was most likely borrowed from Joseph Harker, a scenic designer at the Lyceum Theatre, who later wrote that "[Stoker] had appropriated my surname for one of his characters."[9] A second possibility is that the name came from Fanny Harker, Stoker's landlady in Whitby: a "Wm. Harker" is listed in Town and Parish records as a lodging house keeper at 7 Royal Crescent Avenue, where it is known that Stoker stayed while in Whitby. Like Van Helsing, Harker shares attributes of his literary creator: his Protestantism, his legal training, his research at the British Museum, his obsession with schedules, even his familiarity with lines from *Hamlet*.

Quincey P. Morris

In his earliest Notes, Stoker makes reference to "a Texan"; then he adds the name "Brutus Moris" [?] which is later changed to "Quincey P. Adams."[10] The most commonly held view is that Morris is Stoker's tribute to America. To some extent, he duplicates an earlier character in "The Squaw," a gun-toting American with "his quaint speech and his wonderful stock of adventures."[11] This short story, published in 1893, was written while Stoker was working on *Dracula*. Both Americans meet a tragic end, albeit in "The Squaw" it is more ignominious.

Lucy Westenra

Many suggestions have been put forth. Leatherdale proposes that the surname "possibly . . .

symbolizes the Light of the West," while Davies notes that Westenra is a family name from County Monaghan (137).[12] As for "Lucy," it is a common name, with the advantage of sounding like Lucifer.

Arthur Holmwood

The name "Arthur" might have recommended itself because of its chivalric connotations. As for "Holmwood," one plausible explanation: that Stoker had read an 1892 newspaper account of two men (a Mr. Holm and a Mr. Wood) who had broken into a vault and severed the head from a corpse.[13] Belford suggests that Godalming "is named after the town of Godalming, thirty-four miles southwest of London, among the first to use electricity for public lighting in 1881; in keeping with Stoker's love of double meanings, Lucy symbolizes light or Lucifer."

Mr. Swales

Apparently, Stoker plucked this name from a tombstone in Whitby. One of the entries in the "Whitby Tombstones" section of his Notes reads "Ann Swales. 6th Feb. 1795. aet 100."

Bersicker

This name given to the wolf at the zoo is obviously a dialectic corruption of "berserker," a term Stoker found in Baring-Gould's *The Book of Were-Wolves*: "used of a man possessed of superhuman powers, and subject to accesses [sic] of diabolical fury," an "object of aversion and terror to the peaceful inhabitants of the land," and "a species of diabolical possession."[14] That Baring-Gould was the source can be further substantiated by Van Helsing's reference to the "berserker Icelander" and the zoo-keeper's comment that the wolf "Bersicker" came from Norway.

From here, the pickings get slim. "My friend Arminius" was apparently a nod to Arminius Vambéry, whom Stoker met at the Lyceum; "Vanderpool" may have been borrowed from a Judge Vanderpoel, whose name appears on Stoker's list of Lyceum guests;[15] the term "bloofer lady" (the un-dead Lucy as described by the children she ensnares) seems to have come from Charles Dickens, who uses the almost identical term "boofer" twice in *Our Mutual Friend* as a childlike rendering of "beautiful lady."[16] Renfield is a bit of a mystery. Referred in the Notes only as "mad patient" or "the flyman," he must have, unlike the others, received his name very late in the composition process.

Maybe Stoker recalled "Rheinfeldt," the name of General Spielsdorf's niece in "Carmilla."

—revised by the author from *Dracula: Sense & Nonsense*, pp. 88–93

———

1. Barbara Belford, *Bram Stoker: A Biography of the Author of Dracula* (New York: Knopf, 1996), pp. 106, 270. A similar view is posited in: Nina Auerbach, *Ellen Terry: Player in Her Time* (New York: Norton, 1987), pp. 200–201; Peter Haining and Peter Tremayne, *The Un-Dead: The Legend of Bram Stoker and Dracula* (London: Constable, 1997), p. 173; and Roxanna Stuart, *Stage Blood: Vampires of the 19th Century Stage* (Bowling Green: Bowling Green State University Press, 1994), p. 190.

2. Bram Stoker, *Personal Reminiscences of Henry Irving*, 2 vols. (London: Macmillan, 1906), vol. 1, p. 30.

3. Maurice Richardson, "The Psychoanalysis of Count Dracula," in Christopher Frayling, *Vampyres: Lord Byron to Count Dracula* (London: Faber & Faber, 1991), p. 421.

4. Stoker, *Reminiscences*, vol. 1, pp. 140, 257, 175.

5. Robert Tracy, "Loving you all ways: Vamps, Vampires, Necrophiles and Necrofilles in Nineteenth-Century Fiction," in *Sex and Death in Victorian Literature*, ed. Regina Barreca (London: Macmillan, 1990), p. 40; Raymond McNally and Radu Florescu, *In Search of Dracula*, revised ed. (Boston: Houghton Mifflin, 1994), p. 147.

6. Jane Stoddard ("Lorna"), "Mr. Bram Stoker: A Chat with the Author of Dracula," 1897; repr. in *Dracula*, ed. Glennis Byron (Peterborough: Broadview, 1998), p. 487; Bram Stoker, "Author's Preface," *Makt Myrkranna*, 1901; repr. in *Bram Stoker Society Journal*, 5 (1993): 8.

7. Stoker, "Preface," p. 8.

8. Clemens Ruthner, "Bloodsuckers with Teutonic Tongues: The German-speaking World and the Origins of *Dracula*," in *Dracula: The Shade and the Shadow*, ed. Elizabeth Miller (Westcliff-on-Sea, U.K.: Desert Island Books, 1998), p. 61.

9. Joseph Harker, *Studio and Stage* (London: Nisbet, 1924), p. 135.

10. "Moris" is the common reading of this name in the Notes. However, Bernard Davies (in personal correspondence) makes a convincing argument that it reads "Marix."

11. Bram Stoker, "The Squaw," repr. in *Midnight Tales*, ed. Peter Haining (London: Peter Owen, 1990), p. 87.

12. Clive Leatherdale, *Dracula: The Novel & the Legend* (1985; rev. Westcliff-on-Sea, U.K.: Desert Island Books, 1993), p. 142; Bernard Davies, "Inspirations, Imitations and In-Jokes in Stoker's *Dracula*," in *Dracula: The Shade and the Shadow*, ed. Elizabeth Miller, p. 137.

13. Philip Temple, "The Origins of Dracula," *Times Literary Supplement*, 4 November 1983.

14. Sabine Baring-Gould, *The Book of Were-Wolves* (1865; New York: Causeway Books, 1973), pp. 36, 37, 39.

15. Stoker, *Reminiscences*, vol. 1, p. 316.

16. Charles Dickens, *Our Mutual Friend* (London: Chapman, Hall & Froude, 1870), pp. 384, 390.

* * *

The village of Whitby. The Abbey ruins can be seen atop the cliff, far right. In the novel Stoker writes, "Between it and the town there is another church, the parish one, round which is a big graveyard, all full of tombstones." It is in the graveyard that Dracula first attacks Lucy (Elizabeth Miller Collection).

Bernard Davies is the cofounder of the British Dracula Society.

Inspirations, Imitations and In-Jokes in Stoker's *Dracula*
Bernard Davies

There were many influences upon Bram Stoker during the years that he was thinking of writing his classic vampire novel, *Dracula*. Many of these were literary, such as the works of his fellow Irishman, Joseph Sheridan Le Fanu and the popular novelist, Wilkie Collins. But more obscure factors should also be considered, such as a number of people of Stoker's acquaintance whom he may well have had in mind as he penned certain passages in his book.

Certainly a major influence was Le Fanu. As an unpaid theatre critic, Stoker was working for Le Fanu during the last eighteen months of the latter's life, while he was part-owner of the Dublin *Evening Mail*. It is quite possible that they could have met. It is often incorrectly stated that Le Fanu became a total recluse after his wife's death. He certainly avoided socializing and he no longer entertained, but he still remained a busy working journalist and editor to the end. He preferred to

roam the print-rooms and taverns of Dublin after dark, and his habit of materializing suddenly out of the shadows and vanishing again earned him the nickname "The Invisible Prince." Stoker certainly revered Le Fanu and his works; yet, strangely enough, almost all the original inspirations for *Dracula* disappeared in subsequent revisions. Wise decisions actually, since in his early Working Notes they were rather obvious. Yet a few traces do remain.

The notion that vampires could function in daylight, though without special powers—correct in folklore—he took from "Carmilla"; in fact, in Le Fanu's story, some of the most erotic scenes take place in mid-afternoon. The detective duo, Professor Van Helsing and Dr. Seward, only developed once the professor had ceased to be a marginal commentator and Seward had been turned from hero-lover into a skeptical scientific side-kick. These roles clearly stemmed from Le Fanu's *In a Glass Darkly* (1872), especially from the tale "Green Tea." Van Helsing is a combination of Dr. Hesselius, a wandering psychiatrist, and his Dutch friend and correspondent, Professor Van Loo; Dr. Seward recalls Hesselius's amanuensis, who keeps notes and eventually publishes his cases. This young man, by the way, had his surgical career blighted by stabbing his hand with an infected dissecting knife, exactly the accident in which Seward saves Van Helsing's life by sucking poison from his wound. A further echo is surely that first glimpse we get of Count Dracula. Tall, pale-faced, dressed from head to foot totally in black, with nothing to relieve it except his flowing white hair, he is precisely Le Fanu's compelling hero, Uncle Silas, as young Maud Ruthyn first saw him.

Stoker was obviously influenced significantly by Wilkie Collins, especially by *The Woman in White*. Many of its motifs spill over into *Dracula:* Hampstead, asylums, the white apparition among the graves, and the similar pairs of heroines (Marion and Laura on the one hand, Mina and Lucy on the other). Stoker's novel may owe rather less to Collins's mystery novels. Although generally termed "epistolary" in style, these were not of the classic kind. Rather, the characters relate the part they played in the story as if giving a legal deposition before a notary, in the form of recollections made well after the events. The accounts often contradict each other or overlap, as contributors describe the same incidents from different viewpoints. Even Count Fosco gets his turn.

By contrast, Stoker's method is more original. He abandoned a series of letters planned as the opening for his novel and opted for revealing almost all of the story in the form of diary entries, written in shorthand at the end of the day or spoken directly into a phonograph. Thus the accounts are fresh, off-the-cuff, and often unguarded impressions made somewhat in haste. Each diarist covers only certain phases of the action. They do not overlap. Combined with a few letters and other items such as press clippings, they lend a vivid, slightly ragged immediacy to each narrative, in contrast to Collins's carefully crafted but more pedestrian style. Furthermore, Stoker's touches of realism are brilliant. For instance, when Harker insists on scribbling a quotation from memory, he invariably gets it slightly wrong, as people tend to. And after 30 September, the last day that Mina was allowed to transcribe and type them up, the narratives disintegrate slightly, with non-sequiturs and contradictions.

Stoker's Working Notes offer no clues as to literary influences. One obvious candidate is the German tale "The Mysterious Stranger" (1860); the resemblance between the lifestyles of Ezzelin von Klatka and Count Dracula (even down to their troops of wolves and the underground chapels) is quite pronounced. Another was Charles Collins's "The Compensation House" (1866): the narrator is interrupted while shaving on board a steam-ship by a fellow passenger who causes him to cut himself and then angrily seizes his shaving mirror and throws it out of the porthole. From

1892-1895, the popular *Strand Magazine* furnished subject matter and plot devices that could have been useful to Stoker. Mrs. L.T. Meade's monthly medical adventures included an episode in which catalepsy is suspected. In fact, the doctor announces that he is going to unscrew the girl's coffin in a bedroom piled high with white flowers. Another series, on Regent's Park Zoo, related a visit to the Wolf House, with sketches of its inmates and an interview with the original of Mr. Bilder.

The most important body of material of which all traces are entirely missing from Stoker's Working Notes is the sub-text which runs throughout *Dracula*, consisting of "in-jokes": references to events, places, people and institutions included solely for the benefit of certain relatives or friends. Many of these are obvious once one knows the background, while others still defy precise explanation. Such references would strike only the individual they were intended for, and were most likely inserted into the text fairly late in the writing process.

By far the most notable recipient of such honors was the philanthropist, Angela, Baroness Burdett-Coutts. She became the richest woman in England when still quite young, and was the friend of many of the famous men of her time: the Emperor Napoleon III, the Duke of Wellington, Charles Dickens, and Sir Henry Irving. But she seems to have found Bram Stoker, with his boyish sense of fun, more relaxing company than Irving (who had no sense of fun at all). Stoker inserted several little sallies into *Dracula* for her benefit. For example, he makes Van Helsing and Seward climb over the rear wall of the cemetery from the nursery-grounds next to her country residence, "Holly Lodge" at Highgate. He introduces the "white church," just behind Count Dracula's Piccadilly mansion; this was Christ Church, Down Street, which Angela largely paid for and where, in 1881, she had been married. Stoker also set many scenes in London's East End, where the Baroness had several favorite projects. One of the Count's hideaways was in a house in Chicksand Street, in Jack the Ripper territory, just off Brick Lane. Here Angela had established a Costermongers' Club, a social centre for the Cockney street-traders in fruit and vegetables. In fact, she even cajoled Henry Irving into giving recitals there.

After the shipwreck at Whitby, when Count Dracula leaps from the ship in the shape of a large dog and disappears in the lanes under the cliff, Stoker drags in the "Society for the Prevention of Cruelty to Animals," one of Angela's favorite causes (which her father had helped to found). Pleas to its members to help rescue the frightened German Shepherd were typical of Stoker's sense of comic irony: Dracula had already disemboweled one dog, and the picture of Whitby animal-lovers coaxing him out of hiding with tid-bits is frankly hilarious! Stoker also made play with the initials "A.B.C." by which the Baroness was known among her friends, by having Harker patronize the A.B.C. tea-rooms in Piccadilly, not far from her home. But his most outrageous leg-pull was to make her, as chief shareholder in Coutts and Company's Bank, Count Dracula's banker.

Other friends and colleagues were Stoker's targets as well. We know that he asked the Lyceum's chief scenic artist, Joseph Harker, if he might borrow his surname. But he also gave a presentation copy of _Dracula_ to Anthony Hope, author of _The Prisoner of Zenda;_ the copy was inscribed to "Anthony Hope Hawkins" (his real name), "Hawkins" being the name Stoker used for the old solicitor in his novel. Family members were not immune. Stoker chose for Count Dracula's town house the actual number 137 Piccadilly, only yards away from Hertford Street, Mayfair, where his younger brother, Dr. George Stoker, had his practice. Years before, George had been employed by Baroness Burdett-Coutts as chief of her medical mission attached to the Turkish Red Crescent during the Russo-Turkish War.

Stoker writes a scene in which Van Helsing and Seward visit a hospital in Hampstead, where the children bitten on the neck by the undead Lucy have been admitted, and speak with the doctor in charge. In the very year in which the events of the novel are set—1893—his cousin, Ernest Stoker, was appointed superintendent of a hospital in Hampstead. A few years later, Ernest became a partner in George Stoker's practice in Hertford Street, and when George retired to Ireland, he continued to run it with the telegraphic address "Stokeroid London." Two other cousins, William and James Stoker (both doctors), were working at the time within a few hundred yards of each other, in Walworth, South London. Not surprisingly, Walworth figures prominently as a setting in the latter half of _Dracula._

Such impish, cryptic sub-text, with its sly and private digs to his intimates may seem a trifle tiresome to today's reader. But Bram Stoker obviously enjoyed it; and more important, it serves a number of salutary purposes. First of all, it helps dispel any notion that Stoker wrote _Dracula_ as a man driven by the overwhelming impulse of his own, allegedly repressed sexuality. This is not to say that he did not betray certain predilections in his writing, but he was always in control. His grounding in Gothic literature and melodrama was so thorough that he could deploy all the conventional metaphor and symbolism with tongue firmly in cheek, knowing exactly what effect he wanted and how to obtain it.

Equally important is the further light that this throws on the controversy over whether the Hungarian orientalist, Arminius Vambéry, provided Stoker with material for his novel. In recent years there has been a marked reaction against the assumption that on 30 April 1890 (Walpurgis Night), over supper at the Lyceum, Stoker received from Vambéry the entire wisdom about Transylvania, its superstitions, vampires, and—most importantly—the notorious prince, Vlad the Impaler (Dracula). There is, of course, not a shred of evidence for this, nor has any correspondence between the two come to light. The consensus now is that Stoker did not need Vambéry to feed him such information. As for why he changed the opening setting, a close examination of Stoker's Notes shows that within eight weeks of that Lyceum supper, he severed the link with "Carmilla" and switched the opening from Styria to Transylvania, _before_ he even made the trip to Whitby where he discovered the name "Dracula."

Though the early claims about Vambéry's role were exaggerated, the fact that Van Helsing makes two references in the novel to "my friend Arminius" suggests that Stoker probably did feel some indebtedness to Vambéry, if only for pointing him in the right direction. A few moments of conversation about his proposed weird story partly set in Austria-Hungary must surely have engaged the interest of a citizen of that country. It need have drawn nothing more, except perhaps a well-meaning tip about the possibilities of those magical landscapes. "Take my advice, Mr. Stoker, and try Transylvania," is all Vambéry needed to have said. Nothing about vampires, and certainly nothing about Dracula. After a few weeks of research, Stoker started recasting his opening chapters. Maybe he felt that the Hungarian deserved a cheery acknowledgement or two.

Perhaps the most important effect of Stoker's interpolations is to explode the myth, first put forth by horror writer H.P. Lovecraft, that Stoker got into such a muddle writing _Dracula_ that he eventually found an American ghost-writer to finish it for him. Lovecraft, who spent his time ghosting other people's material, should have known better. An admirer of _Dracula,_ he unashamedly used its first four chapters for a whole section of his own book, _The Case of Charles Dexter Ward._ It is obvious that no British ghost-writer or editor, let alone an American, could have produced the text of _Dracula_ with all of its little nudges in the ribs. The only person who could have written it is Stoker himself.

The riddle that remains to be solved is what prompted Stoker to choose for one of his female characters, Lucy, the surname "Westenra." It is a name that has always defeated scriptwriters and directors who invariably change it to "Western" or "Weston." But it is a well known and respected Irish name, that of the present line of the barons Rossmore of County Monaghan. It derives from three Dutch brothers–Warner, Dirck, and Peter–who settled in Ireland in the 1660s. The line, distinguished by administrators, jurists, and soldiers, culminated in an irony that even Stoker could never have foreseen. In 1923, the London society wedding of the year was that of the heir to the Marquis of Cambridge (nephew of Queen Mary) and Dorothy, Isabella Westenra Hastings, grand-daughter of the 13th Earl of Huntingdon. The groom's father and Queen Mary were of the British-naturalized German house of Teck, descended from Alexander of Wurtemberg and his wife Claudine Rhédey, Countess Höhenstein of Kis-Rhédey in Transylvania. She was a direct descendant of Vlad Dracula's half-brother, Vlad the Monk. Did any of those who threw confetti realize that here was a Dracula groom and a Westenra bride? If Stoker had known, he would have been hysterical. But he had been dead for eleven years. However, I fancy that up at Golders Green Crematorium, his ashes did a little dance of glee!

　　　　　–*Dracula: The Shade and the Shadow*, pp. 131–137

The Mystery of "Dracula's Guest"

In 1914, two years after Bram Stoker's death, Florence Stoker published a collection of her husband's stories titled Dracula's Guest and Other Weird Tales. *Scholars and critics have questioned the contention that "Dracula's Guest" was actually, as Florence claims in her preface, the first chapter of* Dracula *excised at the request of the publisher.*

Dracula's Guest
Bram Stoker

When we started for our drive the sun was shining brightly on Munich, and the air was full of the joyousness of early summer. Just as we were about to depart, Herr Delbrück (the maître d'hôtel of the Quatre Saisons, where I was staying) came down, bareheaded, to the carriage and, after wishing me a pleasant drive, said to the coachman, still holding his hand on the handle of the carriage door:

"Remember you are back by nightfall. The sky looks bright but there is a shiver in the north wind that says there may be a sudden storm. But I am sure you will not be late." Here he smiled, and added, "for you know what night it is."

Johann answered with an emphatic, "Ja, mein Herr," and, touching his hat, drove off quickly. When

Preface to *Dracula's Guest and Other Weird Tales*

A few months before the lamented death of my husband–I might say even as the shadow of death was over him–he planned three series of short stories for publication, and the present volume is one of them. To his original list of stories in this book, I have added an hitherto unpublished episode from *Dracula*. It was originally excised owing to the length of the book, and may prove of interest to the many readers of what is considered my husband's most remarkable work. The other stories have already been published in English and American periodicals. Had my husband lived longer, he might have seen fit to revise this work, which is mainly from the earlier years of his strenuous life. But, as fate has entrusted to me the issuing of it, I consider it fitting and proper to let it go forth practically as it was left by him.

　　　　　　　　　　　–Florence A. L. Bram Stoker

we had cleared the town, I said, after signalling to him to stop:

"Tell me, Johann, what is to-night?"

He crossed himself, as he answered laconically: "Walpurgis nacht." Then he took out his watch, a great, old-fashioned German silver thing as big as a turnip, and looked at it, with his eyebrows gathered together and a little impatient shrug of his shoulders. I realized that this was his way of respectfully protesting against the unnecessary delay, and sank back in the carriage, merely motioning him to proceed. He started off rapidly, as if to make up for lost time. Every now and then the horses seemed to throw up their heads and sniffed the air suspiciously. On such occasions I often looked round in alarm. The road was pretty bleak, for we were traversing a sort of high, wind-swept plateau. As we drove, I saw a road that looked but little used, and which seemed to dip through a little, winding valley. It looked so inviting that, even at the risk of offending him, I called Johann to stop–and when he had pulled up, I told him I would like to drive down that road. He made all sorts of excuses, and frequently crossed himself as he spoke. This somewhat piqued my curiosity so I asked him various questions. He answered fencingly, and repeatedly looked at his watch in protest. Finally I said:

"Well, Johann, I want to go down this road. I shall not ask you to come unless you like; but tell me why you do not like to go, that is all I ask." For answer he seemed to throw himself off the box, so quickly did he reach the ground. Then he stretched out his hands appealingly to me, and implored me not to go. There was just enough of English mixed with the German for me to understand the drift of his talk. He seemed always just about to tell me something–the very idea of which evidently frightened him; but each time he pulled himself up, saying, as he crossed himself: "Walpurgis-Nacht!"

I tried to argue with him, but it was difficult to argue with a man when I did not know his language. The advantage certainly rested with him, for although he began to speak in English, of a very crude and broken kind, he always got excited and broke into his native tongue–and every time he did so, he looked at his watch. Then the horses became restless and sniffed the air. At this he grew very pale, and, looking around in a frightened way, he suddenly jumped forward, took them by the bridles and led them on some twenty feet. I followed, and asked why he had done this. For answer he crossed himself, pointed to the spot we had left and drew his carriage in the direction of the other road, indicating a cross, and said, first in German, then in English: "Buried him–him what killed themselves."

I remembered the old custom of burying suicides at cross-roads: "Ah! I see, a suicide. How interesting!" But for the life of me I could not make out why the horses were frightened.

Whilst we were talking, we heard a sort of sound between a yelp and a bark. It was far away; but the horses got very restless, and it took Johann all his time to quiet them. He was pale, and said: "It sounds like a wolf–but yet there are no wolves here now."

"No?" I said, questioning him; "isn't it long since the wolves were so near the city?"

"Long, long," he answered, "in the spring and summer; but with the snow the wolves have been here not so long."

Whilst he was petting the horses and trying to quiet them, dark clouds drifted rapidly across the sky. The sunshine passed away, and a breath of cold wind seemed to drift past us. It was only a breath, however, and more in the nature of a warning than a fact, for the sun came out brightly again. Johann looked under his lifted hand at the horizon and said:

"The storm of snow, he comes before long time." Then he looked at his watch again, and, straightway holding his reins firmly–for the horses were still pawing the ground restlessly and shaking their heads–he climbed to his box as though the time had come for proceeding on our journey.

I felt a little obstinate and did not at once get into the carriage.

"Tell me," I said, "about this place where the road leads," and I pointed down.

Again he crossed himself and mumbled a prayer, before he answered: "It is unholy."

Dust jacket for the collection published in 1914, two years after Stoker's death (courtesy of Jeanne Youngson)

"What is unholy?" I enquired.

"The village."

"Then there is a village?"

"No, no. No one lives there hundreds of years." My curiosity was piqued: "But you said there was a village."

"There was."

"Where is it now?"

Whereupon he burst out into a long story in German and English, so mixed up that I could not quite understand exactly what he said, but roughly I gathered that long ago, hundreds of years, men had died there and been buried in their graves; and sounds were heard under the clay, and when the graves were opened, men and women were found rosy with life, and their mouths red with blood. And so, in haste to save their lives (aye, and their souls!–and here he crossed himself) those who were left fled away to other places, where the living lived, and the dead were dead and not–not something. He was evidently afraid to

The Origins of "Dracula's Guest"

Stoker's Notes provide a few clues as to the origins of the narrative that was published in 1914 as "Dracula's Guest":

1. The chapter outline dated 14 March 1890 indicates Stoker's original intention to have "The lawyers' letters" as Chapter 1, followed by "clerk visits Styria" and "Munich" as Chapter 2.

2. Early outlines for Book 1, Chapters 1 and 2 (undated, but likely completed by 1892) include Harker about to "start for Munich" at the end of the first chapter. The second, set in Munich, includes Harker's arrival, his stay at the Quatre Saisons Hotel, and visits in the city to a museum and the "Dead House." There is nothing in this outline that resembles the episode related in "Dracula's Guest."

3. A full chapter-by-chapter outline dated 29 February 1892 reveals that by this time Stoker had fixed on two chapters (2 and 3) for the Munich events, preceded by an opening chapter dealing with the lawyers' letters.

4. Calendar of Events (undated, likely 1892–1893) notes several episodes to take place in Munich for the dates 27 April through May 1, one of which (for 27 April) is "adventure snowstorm and wolf" (the subject of "Dracula's Guest").

Two conclusions can be drawn from this information. First, that the incident that shapes the plot of "Dracula's Guest" was part of the original plan for the novel (though what form it took is another matter). Secondly, this incident was never intended as part of the first chapter.

–Elizabeth Miller

speak the last words. As he proceeded with his narration, he grew more and more excited. It seemed as if his imagination had got hold of him, and he ended in a perfect paroxysm of fear—white-faced, perspiring, trembling and looking round him, as if expecting that some dreadful presence would manifest itself there in the bright sunshine on the open plain. Finally, in an agony of desperation, he cried:

"Walpurgis nacht!" and pointed to the carriage for me to get in. All my English blood rose at this, and, standing back, I said:

"You are afraid, Johann—you are afraid. Go home; I shall return alone; the walk will do me good." The carriage door was open. I took from the seat my oak walking-stick—which I always carry on my holiday excursions—and closed the door, pointing back to Munich, and said, "Go home, Johann—Walpurgis-nacht doesn't concern Englishmen."

The horses were now more restive than ever, and Johann was trying to hold them in, while excitedly imploring me not to do anything so foolish. I pitied the poor fellow, he was so deeply in earnest; but all the same I could not help laughing. His English was quite gone now. In his anxiety he had forgotten that his only means of making me understand was to talk my language, so he jabbered away in his native German. It began to be a little tedious. After giving the direction, "Home!" I turned to go down the cross-road into the valley.

With a despairing gesture, Johann turned his horses towards Munich. I leaned on my stick and looked after him. He went slowly along the road for a while: then there came over the crest of the hill a man tall and thin. I could see so much in the distance. When he drew near the horses, they began to jump and kick about, then to scream with terror. Johann could not hold them in; they bolted down the road, running away madly. I watched them out of sight, then looked for the stranger, but I found that he, too, was gone.

With a light heart I turned down the side road through the deepening valley to which Johann had objected. There was not the slightest reason, that I could see, for his objection; and I daresay I tramped for a couple of hours without thinking of time or distance, and certainly without seeing a person or a house. So far as the place was concerned, it was desolation itself. But I did not notice this particularly till, on turning a bend in the road, I came upon a scattered fringe of wood; then I recognised that I had been impressed unconsciously by the desolation of the region through which I had passed.

I sat down to rest myself, and began to look around. It struck me that it was considerably colder than it had been at the commencement of my walk—a sort of sighing sound seemed to be around me, with, now and then, high overhead, a sort of muffled roar. Looking upwards I noticed that great thick clouds were drifting rapidly across the sky from North to South at a great height. There were signs of coming storm in some lofty stratum of the air. I was a little chilly, and, thinking that it was the sitting still after the exercise of walking, I resumed my journey.

The ground I passed over was now much more picturesque. There were no striking objects that the eye might single out; but in all there was a charm of beauty. I took little heed of time and it was only when the deepening twilight forced itself upon me that I began to think of how I should find my way home. The brightness of the day had gone. The air was cold, and the drifting of clouds high overhead was more marked. They were accompanied by a sort of far-away rushing sound, through which seemed to come at intervals that mysterious cry which the driver had said came from a wolf. For a while I hesitated. I had said I would see the deserted village, so on I went, and presently came on a wide stretch of open country, shut in by hills all around. Their sides were covered with trees which spread down to the plain, dotting, in clumps, the gentler slopes and hollows which showed here and there. I followed with my eye the winding of the road, and saw that it curved close to one of the densest of these clumps and was lost behind it.

As I looked there came a cold shiver in the air, and the snow began to fall. I thought of the miles and miles of bleak country I had passed, and then hurried on to seek the shelter of the wood in front. Darker and darker grew the sky, and faster and heavier fell the snow, till the earth before and around me was a glistening white carpet the further edge of which was lost in misty vagueness. The road was here but crude, and when on the level its boundaries were not so marked, as when it passed through the cuttings; and in a little while I found that I must have strayed from it, for I missed underfoot the hard surface, and my feet sank deeper in the grass and moss. Then the wind grew

stronger and blew with ever increasing force, till I was fain to run before it. The air became icy-cold, and in spite of my exercise I began to suffer. The snow was now falling so thickly and whirling around me in such rapid eddies that I could hardly keep my eyes open. Every now and then the heavens were torn asunder by vivid lightning, and in the flashes I could see ahead of me a great mass of trees, chiefly yew and cypress all heavily coated with snow.

I was soon amongst the shelter of the trees, and there, in comparative silence, I could hear the rush of the wind high overhead. Presently the blackness of the storm had become merged in the darkness of the night. By-and-by the storm seemed to be passing away: it now only came in fierce puffs or blasts. At such moments the weird sound of the wolf appeared to be echoed by many similar sounds around me.

Now and again, through the black mass of drifting cloud, came a straggling ray of moonlight, which lit up the expanse, and showed me that I was

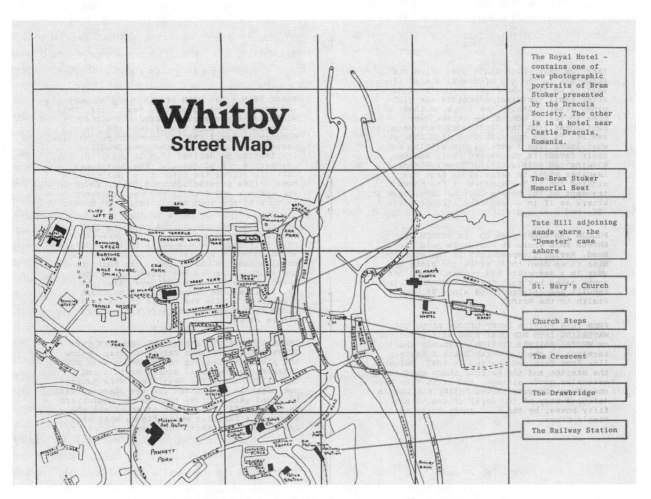

Map of Whitby, with the sites mentioned in Dracula *indicated (courtesy of Scarborough Borough Council; copyright Scarborough Borough Council)*

at the edge of a dense mass of cypress and yew trees. As the snow had ceased to fall, I walked out from the shelter and began to investigate more closely. It appeared to me that, amongst so many old foundations as I had passed, there might be still standing a house in which, though in ruins, I could find some sort of shelter for a while. As I skirted the edge of the copse, I found that a low wall encircled it, and following this I presently found an opening. Here the cypresses formed an alley leading up to a square mass of some kind of building. Just as I caught sight of this, however, the drifting clouds obscured the moon, and I passed up the path in darkness. The wind must have grown colder, for I felt myself shiver as I walked; but there was hope of shelter, and I groped my way blindly on.

I stopped, for there was a sudden stillness. The storm had passed; and, perhaps in sympathy with nature's silence, my heart seemed to cease to beat. But this was only momentarily; for suddenly the moonlight broke through the clouds, showing me that I was in a graveyard, and that the square object before me was a great massive tomb of marble, as white as the snow that lay on and all around it. With the moonlight there came a fierce sigh of the storm, which appeared to resume its course with a long, low howl, as of many dogs or wolves. I was awed and shocked, and felt the cold perceptibly grow upon me till it seemed to grip me by the heart. Then while the flood of moonlight still fell on the marble tomb, the storm gave further evidence of renewing, as though it was returning on its track. Impelled by some sort of fascination, I approached the sepulchre to see what it was, and why such a thing stood alone in such a place. I walked around it, and read, over the Doric door, in German—

COUNTESS DOLINGEN OF GRATZ
IN STYRIA
SOUGHT AND FOUND DEATH.
1801.

On the top of the tomb, seemingly driven through the solid marble—for the structure was composed of a few vast blocks of stone—was a great iron spike or stake. On going to the back I saw, graven in great Russian letters:

"The dead travel fast."

There was something so weird and uncanny about the whole thing that it gave me a turn and made me feel quite faint. I began to wish, for the first time, that I had taken Johann's advice. Here a thought struck me, which came under almost mysterious circum-stances and with a terrible shock. This was Walpurgis Night!

Walpurgis Night, when, according to the belief of millions of people, the devil was abroad—when the graves were opened and the dead came forth and walked. When all evil things of earth and air and water held revel. This very place the driver had specially shunned. This was the depopulated village of centuries ago. This was where the suicide lay; and this was the place where I was alone—unmanned, shivering with cold in a shroud of snow with a wild storm gathering again upon me! It took all my philosophy, all the religion I had been taught, all my courage, not to collapse in a paroxysm of fright.

And now a perfect tornado burst upon me. The ground shook as though thousands of horses thundered across it; and this time the storm bore on its icy wings, not snow, but great hailstones which drove with such violence that they might have come from the thongs of Balearic slingers—hailstones that beat down leaf and branch and made the shelter of the cypresses of no more avail than though their stems were standing-corn. At the first I had rushed to the nearest tree; but I was soon fain to leave it and seek the only spot that seemed to afford refuge, the deep Doric doorway of the marble tomb. There, crouching against the massive bronze-door, I gained a certain amount of protection from the beating of the hail-stones, for now they only drove against me as they ricochetted from the ground and the side of the marble.

As I leaned against the door, it moved slightly and opened inwards. The shelter of even a tomb was welcome in that pitiless tempest, and I was about to enter it when there came a flash of forked-lightning that lit up the whole expanse of the heavens. In the instant, as I am a living man, I saw, as my eyes were turned into the darkness of the tomb, a beautiful woman, with rounded cheeks and red lips, seemingly sleeping on a bier. As the thunder broke overhead, I was grasped as by the hand of a giant and hurled out into the storm. The whole thing was so sudden that, before I could realize the shock, moral as well as physical, I found the hailstones beating me down. At the same time I had a strange, dominating feeling that I was not alone. I looked towards the tomb. Just then there came another blinding flash, which seemed to strike the iron stake that surmounted the tomb and to pour through to the earth, blasting and crumbling the marble, as in a burst of flame. The dead woman rose for a moment of agony, while she was lapped in the flame, and her bitter scream of pain was drowned in the thundercrash. The last thing I heard was this mingling of dreadful sound, as again I was seized in the giant-grasp and dragged away, while the hailstones beat on me, and the air around seemed reverberant with the howling of wolves. The last sight that

I remembered was a vague, white, moving mass, as if all the graves around me had sent out the phantoms of their sheeted-dead, and that they were closing in on me through the white cloudiness of the driving hail.

Gradually there came a sort of vague beginning of consciousness; then a sense of weariness that was dreadful. For a time I remembered nothing; but slowly my senses returned. My feet seemed positively racked with pain, yet I could not move them. They seemed to be numbed. There was an icy feeling at the back of my neck and all down my spine, and my ears, like my feet, were dead, yet in torment; but there was in my breast a sense of warmth which was, by comparison, delicious. It was as a nightmare—a physical nightmare, if one may use such an expression; for some heavy weight on my chest made it difficult for me to breathe.

This period of semi-lethargy seemed to remain a long time, and as it faded away I must have slept or swooned. Then came a sort of loathing, like the first stage of sea-sickness, and a wild desire to be free from something—I knew not what. A vast stillness enveloped me, as though all the world were asleep or dead—only broken by the low panting as of some animal close to me. I felt a warm rasping at my throat, then came a consciousness of the awful truth, which chilled me to the heart and sent the blood surging up through my brain. Some great animal was lying on me and now licking my throat. I feared to stir, for some instinct of prudence bade me lie still; but the brute seemed to realize that there was now some change in me, for it raised its head. Through my eyelashes I saw above me the two great flaming eyes of a gigantic wolf. Its sharp white teeth gleamed in the gaping red mouth, and I could feel its hot breath fierce and acrid upon me.

For another spell of time I remembered no more. Then I became conscious of a low growl, followed by a yelp, renewed again and again. Then, seemingly very far away, I heard a "Holloa! holloa!" as of many voices calling in unison. Cautiously I raised my head and looked in the direction whence the sound came; but the cemetery blocked my view. The wolf still continued to yelp in a strange way, and a red glare began to move round the grove of cypresses, as though following the sound. As the voices drew closer, the wolf yelped faster and louder. I feared to make either sound or motion. Nearer came the red glow, over the white pall which stretched into the darkness around me. Then all at once from beyond the trees there came at a trot a troop of horsemen bearing torches. The wolf rose from my breast and made for the cemetery. I saw one of the horsemen (soldiers by their caps and their long military cloaks) raise his carbine and take aim. A companion knocked up his arm, and I heard the ball whizz over my

The steps from Whitby to the Abbey, described by Mina Harker as "endless" as she searches for Lucy (Barbara Belford, Bram Stoker: A Biography of the Author of *Dracula, 1996; Elizabeth Miller Collection)*

head. He had evidently taken my body for that of the wolf. Another sighted the animal as it slunk away, and a shot followed. Then, at a gallop, the troop rode forward—some towards me, others following the wolf as it disappeared amongst the snow-clad cypresses.

As they drew nearer I tried to move, but was powerless, although I could see and hear all that went on around me. Two or three of the soldiers jumped from their horses and knelt beside me. One of them raised my head, and placed his hand over my heart.

"Good news, comrades!" he cried. "His heart still beats!"

Then some brandy was poured down my throat; it put vigour into me, and I was able to open my eyes fully and look around. Lights and shadows were moving among the trees, and I heard men call to one another. They drew together, uttering frightened exclamations; and the lights flashed as the others came pouring out of the cemetery pell-mell, like men possessed.

Great Eastern Hotel in London, where Abraham Van Helsing
first stays when he is called in to aid Lucy Westenra
(photograph by Jeanne Youngson)

When the further ones came close to us, those who were around me asked them eagerly:

"Well, have you found him?"

The reply rang out hurriedly:

"No! no! Come away quick—quick! This is no place to stay, and on this of all nights!"

"What was it?" was the question, asked in all manner of keys. The answer came variously and all indefinitely as though the men were moved by some common impulse to speak, yet were restrained by some common fear from giving their thoughts.

"It—it—indeed!" gibbered one, whose wits had clearly given out for the moment.

"A wolf—and yet not a wolf!" another put in shudderingly.

"No use trying for him without the sacred bullet," a third remarked in a more ordinary manner.

"Serve us right for coming out on this night! Truly we have earned our thousand marks!" were the ejaculations of a fourth.

"There was blood on the broken marble," another said after a pause—"the lightning never brought that there. And for him—is he safe? Look at his throat!

See, comrades, the wolf has been lying on him and keeping his blood warm."

The officer looked at my throat and replied:

"He is all right; the skin is not pierced. What does it all mean? We should never have found him but for the yelping of the wolf."

"What became of it?" asked the man who was holding up my head, and who seemed the least panic-stricken of the party, for his hands were steady and without tremor. On his sleeve was the chevron of a petty officer.

"It went to its home," answered the man, whose long face was pallid, and who actually shook with terror as he glanced around him fearfully. "There are graves enough there in which it may lie. Come, comrades—come quickly! Let us leave this cursed spot."

The officer raised me to a sitting posture, as he uttered a word of command; then several men placed me upon a horse. He sprang to the saddle behind me, took me in his arms, gave the word to advance; and, turning our faces away from the cypresses, we rode away in swift, military order.

As yet my tongue refused its office, and I was perforce silent. I must have fallen asleep; for the next thing I remembered was finding myself standing up, supported by a soldier on each side of me. It was almost broad daylight, and to the north a red streak of sunlight was reflected, like a path of blood, over the waste of snow. The officer was telling the men to say nothing of what they had seen, except that they found an English stranger, guarded by a large dog.

"Dog! that was no dog," cut in the man who had exhibited such fear. "I think I know a wolf when I see one."

The young officer answered calmly: "I said a dog."

"Dog!" reiterated the other ironically. It was evident that his courage was rising with the sun; and, pointing to me, he said, "Look at his throat. Is that the work of a dog, master?"

Instinctively I raised my hand to my throat, and as I touched it I cried out in pain. The men crowded around to look, some stooping down from their saddles; and again there came the calm voice of the young officer:

"A dog, as I said. If aught else were said we should only be laughed at."

I was then mounted behind a trooper, and we rode on into the suburbs of Munich. Here we came across a stray carriage, into which I was lifted, and it was driven off to the Quatre Saisons—the young officer accompanying me, whilst a trooper followed with his horse, and the others rode off to their barracks.

When we arrived, Herr Delbrück rushed so quickly down the steps to meet me, that it was apparent

Piccadilly Circus in 1894. Jonathan Harker begins his search here for one of Dracula's London residences, which he discovers at No. 347 Piccadilly (Clare Haworth-Maden, Dracula: Everything You Always Wanted To Know about the Man, the Myth, and the Movies, *1992; Elizabeth Miller Collection).*

he had been watching within. Taking me by both hands he solicitously led me in. The officer saluted me and was turning to withdraw, when I recognized his purpose, and insisted that he should come to my rooms. Over a glass of wine I warmly thanked him and his brave comrades for saving me. He replied simply that he was more than glad, and that Herr Delbrück had at the first taken steps to make all the searching party pleased; at which ambiguous utterance the maître d'hotel smiled, while the officer pleaded duty and withdrew.

"But Herr Delbrück," I enquired, "how and why was it that the soldiers searched for me?"

He shrugged his shoulders, as if in depreciation of his own deed, as he replied:

"I was so fortunate as to obtain leave from the commander of the regiment in which I served, to ask for volunteers."

"But how did you know I was lost?" I asked.

"The driver came hither with the remains of his carriage, which had been upset when the horses ran away."

"But surely you would not send a search-party of soldiers merely on this account?"

"Oh, no!" he answered; "but even before the coachman arrived, I had this telegram from the Boyar whose guest you are," and he took from his pocket a telegram which he handed to me, and I read:

Bistritz.

"Be careful of my guest–his safety is most precious to me. Should aught happen to him, or if he be missed, spare nothing to find him and ensure his safety. He is English and therefore adventurous. There are often dangers from snow and wolves and night. Lose not a moment if you suspect harm to him. I answer your zeal with my fortune.–Dracula."

As I held the telegram in my hand, the room seemed to whirl around me; and, if the attentive maître d'hotel had not caught me, I think I should have fallen. There was something so strange in all this, something so weird and impossible to imagine, that there grew on me a sense of my being in some way the sport of opposite forces—the mere vague idea of which seemed in a way to paralyse me. I was certainly under some form of mysterious protection. From a distant country had come, in the very nick of time, a message that took me out of the danger of the snow-sleep and the jaws of the wolf.

　　　　　　　　—*Dracula's Guest and Other Weird Stories*
　　　　　　　　　(London: Routledge, 1914), pp. 1–18

* * *

"Dracula's Guest" and *Dracula*
Clive Leatherdale

In *Dracula: The Novel and the Legend* (1985) I put forward the case against the widely-held notion that "Dracula's Guest" was the excised first chapter of *Dracula*. Others have subsequently arrived at similar conclusions. This has not discouraged publishers, even prestigious ones, continuing as before, inserting "Dracula's Guest" with the rest of the novel, without explanation, let alone disclaimer.

The arguments against "Dracula's Guest" being the opening chapter of *Dracula* are part textual, part deduction from Stoker's working notes. First, the writer's styles in the two tales are quite distinct. *Dracula* is a series of diary entries, "Dracula's Guest" a straightforward first-person narrative. Second, the central motifs are contradictory. Wolves in *Dracula* are low-life creatures, servants of the Count. The wolf in "Dracula's Guest" is heroic, warming the body of the insensible guest to keep him alive.

Third, the narrator of "Dracula's Guest" is anonymous, and only identified as Jonathan Harker if one attaches a literary harness to join up the two stories. But this leads to a fourth problem. The narrator of "Dracula's Guest" is incompatible with the Jonathan Harker of *Dracula,* who is unworldly, introverted, accustomed to obey. The narrator of "Dracula's Guest" is brash, aggressive, shrugging off warnings that he stay indoors rather than venture off into the wild unknown. Jonathan Harker would never have been so foolhardy, and certainly not on Walpurgis Nacht.

Fifth, the crucial distinction between the two characters is that one speaks German while the other does not. The narrator in "Dracula's Guest" laments that his coach-driver "had forgotten that his only means of making me understand was to talk my language." English is his sole means of communication. But Stoker cannot allow such a shield for Jonathan Harker. It is vital that this naive solicitor, journeying from the safe insularity of England to open up Pandora's box, is denied the shield of linguistic igno-

rance. Harker cannot be simply an innocent messenger, but acts as an active agent in the spread of vampirism to England. In which case, Harker must be fully aware of what he is doing. He must face warnings and entreaties from the local inhabitants to return home, and he must reject them. Harker speaks German. Indeed, he says, "I don't know how I should be able to get on without it." Unlike Pontius Pilate, Jonathan Harker cannot wash his hands of the consequences of what he is destined to do.

The Siamese Twins linkage between "Dracula's Guest" and *Dracula* is dependent on chronology. The first words of the novel are "Left Munich at 8.35 p.m." As "Dracula's Guest" is set in Munich, it was considered natural that this was a prequel, and, as it does not appear in the published novel, that it was a deleted prequel. "Dracula's Guest" only came to light when published posthumously among other Stoker short stories in 1914.

With the discovery of Stoker's research notes, yet more evidence has come to light to separate these ill-fitting twins. Stoker's detailed calendar shows that various scenes from the planned beginning of the book were cut out. He intended the novel to begin on 16 March, not 3 May as in the published version. Seven weeks fell victim to the axe. The episode known as "Dracula's Guest"—or, as Stoker called it at the time, the adventure in a snow storm with a wolf—was one of three hair-raising escapades to befall the hapless solicitor en route to the Count. All three were to happen in Munich, the others being a visit to the opera to see a performance of *The Flying Dutchman,* and a spooky visit to a so-called Dead House. But even here the dates get chopped around, and with them the sequence of events. Originally, "Dracula's Guest" was scheduled to be the first of the three, to take place several days before Walpurgis Nacht. Irrespective of these changes, Stoker's notes reveal that whole swathes of the beginning of the novel, amounting perhaps to a hundred pages or more, fell under the author's or editor's axe. Of these, "Dracula's Guest" was just a part.

But if "Dracula's Guest" is not the original first chapter of *Dracula,* what is it? That is not so easy to answer. It is clear from the messy, typewritten manuscript of *Dracula* that surfaced in California in the 1980s that whole chunks of the early part of the novel were removed at a very late stage, after the manuscript had been submitted to the London publishers, Constable. One of those discarded chapters possibly did feature a version of the snow storm and the wolf. But in form and format it needed to be quite distinct from the tale that surfaced seventeen years later under the title "Dracula's Guest."

Two possibilities may be proposed here. The first is that "Dracula's Guest" properly belongs to the first draft of the novel, dating to between 1890 and 1892. An early note shows Dracula insisting that his English visitor be ignorant of German. At that stage in Stoker's planning the novel was to be sited in German-speaking Styria (part of modern Austria), the purpose of which was to prevent a German-speaking envoy being warned off his fool's errand. Once Stoker had shifted his location from Styria eastwards to Transylvania (which he did around 1892), he had less need to impose language restrictions on Harker. In Transylvania, Harker notes, the locals speak German "worse than my own." His fractured conversations in that language enable him to piece together elements of the dangers he is exposing himself to, but without comprehending the details. Stoker's literary style in "Dracula's Guest" also fits neatly into that exhibited in the early 1890s. That was a prolific period in his writing, producing what many critics contend are his finest short stories, including "The Squaw" and "The Judge's House."

A second possibility is that "Dracula's Guest" was not a first chapter of anything, but was a short story in its own right. It bears many hallmarks of a short story. Indeed, that was how it was first published and how it is mostly read. Although Stoker has no record of extending short stories into novels, this would fit the facts in this instance. "Dracula's Guest" was conceivably penned as a short story, but, rather than publish it as it stood, Stoker realized its potential and returned to construct a novel upon it.

What may be safely discounted is the assertion that in the final months of his life Stoker dug out the tale, reworked it as necessary, and cobbled together the story that surfaced after his death. "Dracula's Guest" is too good to allow such an explanation. Stoker's last years were marked by works such as *The Lair of the White Worm* (1911), which bears signs of an ailing mind, not to mention a laboured writing style at odds with the more youthful verve exhibited in "Dracula's Guest."

Of one thing we may be reasonably confident. "Dracula's Guest" dates not from Stoker's death-bed, nor even from the time of *Dracula* (1897). In whatever form, it belongs squarely with Stoker's output from the early 1890s.

—Dracula: The Shade and the Shadow, pp. 143–146

The Typescript

No manuscript for Dracula *has been found. There is, however, a typescript with holograph revisions, possibly the setting copy for the novel that Stoker delivered to his publisher, Constable. No galleys or page proofs have been found.*

Peter Haining and Peter Tremayne, two Dracula enthusiasts in Great Britain, investigated the matter of the typescript and published their findings in The Un-Dead *(1997). They note that the typescript for* Dracula, *which they here call the manuscript, was found "in an old trunk where it had been stored, forgotten" since the late nineteenth century. While respecting the privacy of the family who identified the typescript, Haining and Tremayne report the circumstances of the find, which took place in an old barn on a Pennsylvania homestead near Philadelphia, presumably in the early 1980s.*

The Discovery of the Typescript
Peter Haining and Peter Tremayne

. . . The barn had belonged to the same family since the end of the last [19th] century, and during much of this time was used purely for storage. In recent years, however, the building had fallen into a state of disrepair. When some members of the family were foraging around in the debris for anything that might be worth saving, they came across three old storage trunks, battered and grimy, which had clearly not been touched for years. The searchers decided to remove them for cleaning and perhaps using in the house.

The trunks were hauled into the daylight and prised open. In the first was an assortment of old clothes; in the second, some jumble and a large brown paper package. In the third, the searchers were horrified to find, were the corpses of several withered and dried-out dead rats! What these rodents were doing in the trunk and how they had got there was beyond anyone's immediate imagination and it was hastily shut. Not surprisingly, it was a little while before the unsettled group could bring themselves to go through the remaining two trunks.

They started by rummaging through the trunk containing the brown paper package.

Unwrapping the bundle revealed a bulky manuscript bearing the words 'THE UN-DEAD by Bram Stoker' with a list of the author's other titles and the words 'Copyright 1897'. When the new owners of one of the most fabulous manuscripts in literary history realised what they had found, the mystery of the dead rats took on an even more grisly fascination. But how they got into the trunk has defied all explanation, beyond the possibility that they might just have been nesting there when the trunk was last shut. Any direct connection with the manuscript about a vampire count seems unthinkable . . .

Cover for the catalogue showing the four black boxes that hold the 530-page
Dracula typescript (Elizabeth Miller Collection)

Title page for Stoker's final typescript for Dracula. *Stoker had not, even at this late stage, settled on the title of the novel (Christie's New York,* Bram Stoker's Dracula: The Original Typed Manuscript, *17 April 2002; Elizabeth Miller Collection).*

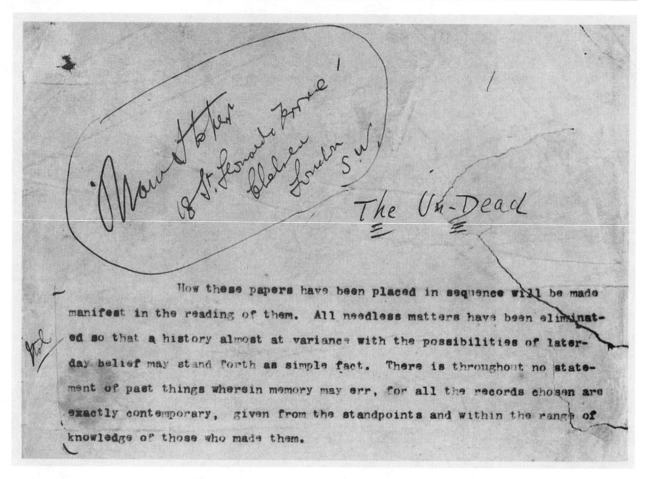

Preliminary note (Christie's New York, Bram Stoker's Dracula: The Original
Typed Manuscript, *17 April 2002; Elizabeth Miller Collection)*

That 'The Un-Dead' was, in fact, *Dracula* was confirmed for the family first by a local autograph dealer and then by another expert who compared the handwriting on the pages of the document with that on Bram Stoker's working papers which fortuitously happened to belong to the Rosenbach Foundation Library in nearby Philadelphia.
–Peter Haining and Peter Tremayne, *The Un-Dead: The Legend of Bram Stoker and Dracula* (London: Constable, 1997), pp. 22–23

* * *

As for how the typescript originally found its way from London to Pennsylvania, Haining and Tremayne suggest that Stoker gave it to Thomas Donaldson, a lawyer and collector who had first introduced him to the poet Walt Whitman in 1883. After Donaldson's death, it apparently went into the hands of relatives and somehow ended up in a trunk in a Pennsylvania barn. By 1984 the typescript had changed hands and was in the possession of John McLaughlin, a collector in California. In 2002

the typescript resurfaced and was auctioned at Christie's in New York. The purchaser—who paid $940,000 for the item—was unidentified, and whether scholars will ever get access to this valuable source of information about the making of Dracula *is uncertain. The following passages from the Christie's auction catalogue provide the most detailed description of the revised typescript available to date.*

Dracula: **The Original Typed Manuscript**
Chris Coover

STOKER, Abraham ("Bram") (1847–1912). Typescript of *The Un-Dead,* published as *Dracula* (London, 1897), with autograph additions, corrections and deletions in ink by the author, signed or initialed by Stoker in some 26 places, and with his name and address ("Bram Stoker, 17 St. Leonard's Terrace, Chelsea, London") on versos of some chapter endings, preceded by a hand-lettered title-page by Stoker (using the title *The Un-Dead*), dated 1897. Carbon and ribbon typescript (largely carbon, with some words, usually names of places or characters, typed

shadows as it flickered in the draught of the open door. The
old man with his right hand motioned me in with a courtly gesture, saying in excellent English, but with a strong intonation:

" Welcome to my house ! Enter freely and of your own
will." He made no motion of stepping to meet me, but stood
like a statue, as though his gesture of welcome had fixed him
into stone. The instant, however, that I had stepped over the
threshold, he moved impulsively forward, and holding out his
hand grasped mine with a strength which made me wince, an
effect which was not lessened by the fact that it seemed as
cold as ice - more like the hand of a dead man than a living one. Again he said:

" Welcome to my house. Come freely. Go safely and leave
something of the happiness you bring." The strength of the
handshake was so much akin to that which I had noticed in the
driver whose face I had not seen, that for a moment I doubted
if it were not the same person to whom I was speaking; so to
make sure, I said interrogatively:

" Count Dracula ?" He bowed in a courtly way as he replied:

" I am Dracula - and I bid you welcome, Mr Harker, to
my house. Come in, the night air is chill and you must need
to eat and rest." As he was speaking he put the lamp on a
bracket on the wall, and stepping out took my luggage and had
carried it in before I could forestall him. I protested, but

Page from chapter II (Christie's New York, Bram Stoker's Dracula: The Original Typed Manuscript,
17 April 2002; Elizabeth Miller Collection)

101

93

Besides it was all so confused, it seemed only a moment from his coming into the room till both his arms were round me and he was kissing me. I am very,very happy and I don't know what I have done to deserve it. I must only try in the future to show ~~that~~ that I am not ungrateful for all His Goodness to me in sending to me such a lover - such a husband - and such a friend.

                    Good bye.

                    Dr Seward's Diary
                    (Kept in phonograph)

25 April

Ebb tide in appetite today. Cannot eat, cannot rest — so diary instead. Since my rebuff of yesterday I have a sort of empty feeling; nothing in the world seems of sufficient importance to be worthy the doing . . . . As I knew that the only cure for this sort of thing was work, I went down amongst the patients. I picked out one who has afforded me a study of much interest. He is so quaint in his ideas and so unlike the normal lunatic, that I have determined to understand him as well as I can. Today I seemed to get nearer than ever before to the heart of his mystery.

I questioned ~~him~~ Renfield more fully than I had ever done with a view to making myself master of the facts of his hallucination. In my manner of doing it there was, I now see something of cruelty. I seemed to wish to keep him to the point of his madness - a thing which I avoid with the patients as I would the mouth of hell. Mem. under what circumstances would I not avoid the pit of hell. Omnia Romae venulia sunt. Hell has its prices. verb.sap. If there be anything behind this instinct it will be valuable to trace it afterwards accurately so I had better commence to do so, therefore,

R.M. Renfield aetat 59. Sanguine temperament - great physical strength - morbidly excitable - periods of gloom ending in some fixed idea which I cannot make out. I presume that the sanguine temperament itself and the disturbing influence ends in a mentally accomplished finish - a possibly dangerous man - probably dangerous if unselfish. In selfish men caution is as secure an armour for their foes as for themselves. What I think of on this point is, when self is the fixed point the

Page from chapter V, illustrating Stoker's cut-and-paste method (Christie's New York, Bram Stoker's Dracula: The Original Typed Manuscript, *17 April 2002; Elizabeth Miller Collection)*

which I shall show you later @ I felt the same vague terror which had

come to me before and the same sense of some presence. I turned to wake

Jonathan but found that he slept so soundly that it seemed as if he had

taken the sleeping _{potion} and not I. I tried but I could not wake him. This

caused me a great fear and I looked around terrified - and then indeed

my heart sank within me. - Beside the bed, as if he had stepped out of

the mist or rather as if the mist had turned into his figure for it had

entirely disappeared stood a tall, thin man all in black. I knew him

at once from the descriptions of the others. The waxen face, the high

aquiline nose on which the light fell in a thin white line, the parted

red lips with the sharp white teeth showing between and the red eyes that

I had seemed to see to see in the sunset on the windows of St.Mary's

I knew too the red scar on his forehead where Jonathan had struck him.

Church at Whitby. For an instant my heart stood still and I would have

---

Here he turned and spoke to us:

    "You think to baffle me,you - with your pale faces all in a row

there like sheep in a butcher's. You shall be sorry yet each one of you

- you think you have left me without a place to rest; but I have more.

My revenge has just begun! I spread it over centuries and time is on

my side. Your girls that you all love are mine already and through them

you and others shall yet be mine - my creatures to do my bidding and to

be my jackals when I want to feed - Bah !" and with a contemptuous sneer

he passed quickly through the door and we heard the rusty bolt creak as

he fastened it behind him and a door beyond open and shut. The first

of us to speak was the Professor as realizing the difficulty of follow-

ing him through the stable we moved towards the hall.

    "We have learnt something - much - notwithstanding his brave words

Passages from chapters XXI and XXII of the novel, typescript pages 422 and 429 (Christie's New York, Bram Stoker's
Dracula: The Original Typed Manuscript, 17 April 2002; Elizabeth Miller Collection)

directly into blank spaces), comprising Stoker's revised typescript used as the printer's setting copy, with the printer's occasional blue pencil markings. Probably typed by Stoker in London and perhaps in Cruden Bay, Scotland, 1890–97.

530 sheets (comprising unnumbered title and pp. 1–541, with irregularities), lacking 8 pp. (175, 233, 297, 521, 525, 532, 534, 537), pp. 177 and 295 skipped in pagination but text continuous. Typed on the rectos of sheets of wove paper of varying size (ranging from 8.5 to 14.5 inches in height). Stoker (like his contemporary, Arthur Conan Doyle) cut and reassembled some pages of his manuscript as part of the editorial process, often adding necessary connecting text in ink (see below under "Pagination"). Several marginal notes in the text are perhaps in the hand of William Thornley Stoker, the author's brother, some pencilled punctuation possibly added by an editor. A few marginal tears, not affecting text and without loss to paper, occasional minor soiling, otherwise in an excellent state of preservation throughout. Each leaf in protective mylar envelope, enclosed in four large half black morocco slipcases.

–p. 9

. . . .

Pagination

The existing pagination suggests much about Stoker's compositional method, providing concrete evidence of the complex rearrangements of text that the book underwent when Stoker, after seven years' work, prepared his finished typescript for the printer. Most of the typescript's pages bear at least three distinct sets of pagination: one typed and two in ink in Stoker's hand, which may suggest the existence of previous typescripts, or, at least, drastic rearrangement. The typed set of numerals and one of the handwritten sets are crossed out. The final numbered sequence commences with page 3 (preceded by Stoker's prefatory note and the first unnumbered page of text), and continues (with irregularities) to the last page (Stoker's "Note," an epilogue), which is numbered 541. Because of the cut-and-paste method Stoker used to assemble the manuscript, the numbering is irregular at times, and some pages in fact bear two consecutive numbers. The earlier numbering sequences strongly suggest that Stoker altered both the order of the chapters and the order of pages within chapters in the final stages of composition. Some chapters (19, 23–27) were originally separately numbered, the first page of each bearing the number 1. In keeping with contemporary typographical practice, the pages which begin Chapters (in Roman numerals) and sub-chapters (in Arabic numerals) are un-paginated by Stoker. The printer has numbered Chapters and sub-chapters in bold blue crayon; the same crayon has been used to mark the text at the end of each section. Stoker's

cut-and-paste manipulation of his typescript is evident in many places: some text pages consist of several strips pasted together, sometimes with additional handwritten connecting text added by Stoker to link them seamlessly. Further detailed analysis, it is likely, will permit at least a partial reconstruction of the pre-existing order of Stoker's text.

The Discarded Beginning

From the typescript and Stoker's preliminary notes it is apparent that Jonathan Harker's journey to Transylvania was not the novel's original beginning. Originally, Stoker's first chapter was to consist of the correspondence between Mr. Hawkins (Harker's employer) and Count Dracula concerning the purchase of residential property in London. In the second chapter, Harker was to have told of stopping in Munich to attend a performance of Richard Wagner's *The Flying Dutchman* (*Der Fliegende Hollander*), an appropriate choice, given its strong supernatural elements. In the present typescript, the chapter number of the first text page has been altered by Stoker from II to I. In addition, the first hand-numbered page bears the earlier typewritten number 103. It is clear that in the late stages of editing, Stoker deleted 102 pages of the earlier portion of the manuscript. The typescript and the published book now begin with Harker's diary entry dated May 3.

–p. 15

. . . .

The Typescript and Stoker's Emendations

. . . In preparing his novel for the printer, Stoker chose to use the newly invented manual typewriter. While the early typewriters were often cumbersome and difficult to maintain, the design was rapidly perfected and their use spread rapidly from 1880, as did the use of the carbon paper that made possible "manifold" or multiple carbon copies. Mina, in Chapter 14, expresses gratitude that she is able to use the "Traveller's typewriter," possibly a reference to the Columbia portable typewriter, weighing only six pounds, that came on the market in 1885. It is more than likely that Stoker himself typed the entire novel on such a machine. Alternatively, although there is no direct evidence to suggest it, he may possibly have employed one of the numerous typing agencies to transcribe a handwritten manuscript. (Oscar Wilde, Stoker's Dublin acquaintance and Trinity classmate, used the services of such agencies to prepare the sucessive typescripts of all of his successful plays at about the same date.) A careful study of the typescript, particularly in connection with Stoker's early notes, will certainly reveal a great deal about the genesis of the novel and Stoker's methods.

The Changed Ending

An interesting revelation provided by the typescript is that Stoker changed part of the ending. Originally, Dracula's castle was to be destroyed by natural forces. The published text reads: "The Castle of Dracula now stood out against the red sky, and every stone of its broken battlements was articulated against the light of the setting sun" (Chapter XXII, Mina Harker's Journal, 6 November). We may never know why this change was made, or even who made it—Stoker or his editor. Possibly Stoker had a sequel in mind, though given that he wrote no sequels to any of his other works (nor even reintroduces characters from one text to another), this seems unlikely.

—Elizabeth Miller

Page from the final chapter, showing the deletion of the passage describing the destruction of Castle Dracula (Christie's New York, Bram Stoker's Dracula: The Original Typed Manuscript, 17 April 2002; Elizabeth Miller Collection)

Cover for the catalogue in which the contracts for Dracula *were offered for sale as lot #100. The contracts, estimated to bring £30,000–50,000, went unsold (Sotheby's Literature, History & Illustrated Books, 10 July 2001; Thomas Cooper Library, University of South Carolina).*

Virtually every page of Stoker's typescript exhibits some revision by its author. In the case of pages that have been pasted together from fragments of other pages of typescript, Stoker has in some cases added a sentence or two in his small, spidery hand to link the previously unconnected narrative. The quotation from Burger's popular ballad, *Lenore,* "Denn die Todten reiten schnell" ("for the dead travel fast"), whispered by one of Harker's fellow coach passengers in Chapter 1, is here supplied in Stoker's hand.

In several places in the narrative where blood transfusions are administered to Lucy in hopes of saving her, Stoker's brother, the distinguished physician Sir William Thornley Stoker, has added a factual note in the margin, suggesting that Stoker showed the typescript to his brother, who resided in Dublin but frequently visited London, to be certain that his technical description of the unusual transfusion process was accurate. Interestingly, there are occasional typewritten emendations typed directly onto the pages of carbon typescript; these are readily distinguished by their darker appearance and appear to have been typed over

erasures or into blank places deliberately left in the typescript. The name of the zoophagous patient, Renfield, is left blank in some early appearances, in other places he is simply termed "Flyman," and his name is later filled in by hand, as are some place names and names of minor characters, such as Carfax (the abbey Dracula rents in England), Lord Godalming, Arthur Holmwood, Swales, and others, as well as the dates in the ship's log of the unfortunate *Demeter* (the vessel which brings the Count to Whitby). These blanks strongly suggest that Stoker remained undecided about the names of certain of the novel's minor characters and needed to fill these in at a relatively late stage.

Handwritten punctuation changes are quite frequent throughout the typescript; some are probably by Stoker, but many appear to be in a different, larger hand, perhaps that of an editor at the publishers, Archibald Constable & Co. From a close examination of several segments of Stoker's typescript and the published novel, it is apparent that a number of minor changes, including punctuation, paragraphing and occasional word substitutions were made subsequently to this typescript, probably at page proof or galley stage. No galleys or page proofs for the novel are extant, unfortunately.

–Christie's New York, *Bram Stoker's Dracula: The Original Typed Manuscript,* 17 April 2002, pp. 16–17

A Dramatic Reading of *Dracula*

On the morning of Tuesday, 18 May 1897, about a week before Dracula *was published, a script Stoker prepared from his novel was read at the Lyceum Theatre in London. Apparently held to protect the theatrical copyright of the work, the event attracted little attention. Sir Henry Irving's oft-quoted one-word review—"Dreadful!"—is likely apocryphal, for no reliable source has been found for the remark.*

In the following excerpts from her preface to Stoker's play, British theatre aficionado Sylvia Starshine discusses the manuscript and the circumstances surrounding the reading.

The Script and the Performance
Sylvia Starshine

The only copy of the manuscript in existence is that lodged in the Lord Chamberlain's Collection of Plays in the Department of Manuscripts at the British Library. The text itself is partly handwritten and partly pasted into place in sections cut from two proof copies stamped by Harris and Sons, Printers (a firm of bookbinders based in London). Wherever the typeset material did not fit, Stoker crossed out the offending words

The Original Publishing Contracts for "Dracula"

The "two contracts for the novel retained by the publisher, Archibald Constable & Co." are described and discussed in these passages from Sotheby's sale catalogue.

i) BRAM STOKER'S AUTOGRAPH MEMORANDUM OF AGREEMENT FOR "A WORK ENTITLED 'THE UN-DEAD'", written out entirely in his own hand, with corrections, initialled by him three times in the margin where changes have been made and signed by him in full as witness at the end, also witnessed by Charles E. Howson, Librarian (see below), 2 pages, folio, on paper watermarked "T H Saunders 1895," embossed "six pence" stamp in orange and white (dated 1–12–96) on first page, integral blank, numbered in red on the first page and on a label on the final verso "110," also docketed on the last verso "Bram Sto[ker] 'The Un-Dead' 1897," a space left in the contract for the day and month of the date, 1897

ii) TYPED MEMORANDUM OF AGREEMENT FOR "A WORK ENTITLED 'THE UN-DEAD'", with autograph alterations by Stoker, the changes initialled by him seven times in the margin, each page also initialled and dated by him (20–25/5/97) at the bottom, and signed in full by him at the end, also signed as witness by H. J. Loveday (see below), 3 pages, folio, watermarked "Waterlow & Sons / London," typed on rectos only, numbered in red on the first page and on a label on the last verso "113," also docketed on the final verso "Bram Stoker. May 21. 1897. Dracula," the date given in the text of the contract 20 May 1897

. . . .

The present surviving memoranda of agreement for the publishing of the novel show clearly that Stoker's contractual arrangements with Constable & Co. were technically completed at the last minute, since the typed version dated 25 May 1897 was finished only one day before the publication of *Dracula,* when the novel was actually distributed to booksellers. Presumably terms had already been agreed with Constable, who had published Stoker's two previous novels. . . . Yet even though these documents were simply a formality at the final stages of printing and binding, it is interesting to see how great a part the author himself played in their formulation, since he drafts out the first one in full himself, in his own somewhat hurried, ungainly script. It is, besides all else, a reminder that, as Irving's factotum at the Lyceum, Stoker, who became a qualified barrister in 1890, was accustomed to dealing in person with a variety of formal business matters, rather than delegating to secretaries. . . . It was evidently felt necessary to have a typed copy of Stoker's contract made as well (it was presumably the duly signed carbon-copy of this which the author himself retained for his own records). Both contracts were carefully and professionally scrutinised by Stoker and minor changes formally initialled in the margins.

Each of the contracts was formally witnessed by a second party, the two witnesses concerned both being members of the staff of the Lyceum Theatre and well known to Stoker. Charles Howson, who witnessed the manuscript contract, was (in Barbara Belford's words) "a near-destitute old actor forced to eke out a living by copying band parts at sixpence a time" who joined the Lyceum in 1878 as the theatre's accountant. . . . By 1897, as the present contract shows, Howson was calling himself a "Librarian," presumably a euphemism for "book-keeper." On the other hand, H. J. Loveday, who witnessed the final typed contract, was the Lyceum's well-known and well-respected stage manager, one who was totally devoted to Irving and had the actor's implicit trust and affection.

. . . .

The two present contracts have substantively identical texts and set out the relatively fair, though not inordinately generous, terms which a hitherto only modestly successful novelist in 1897, far from being a best-selling author, could reasonably have expected. The memoranda document an agreement between Archibald Constable & Co. and Bram Stoker, of 18 St. Leonard's Terrace, Chelsea, stipulating that the novel *The Un-Dead* will be printed in 1897 after the rights have been secured in the U.S.A.; that the first edition will have a print-run of at least 3,000 copies, published at the price of six shillings, and made available to the Book Trade at "Trade" terms; that after the first 1,000 copies sold the author will receive one shilling and sixpence per copy, and two shillings per copy after any possible run of 10,000 has been reached; that the publisher may, with the author's consent, publish "a Colonial edition (Canada being excepted)"; that unless terminated by mutual consent, this agreement will remain in force for ten years, with accounts settled every six months; that the agreement does not include Canada or any other country outside the United Kingdom and other British Dependencies; and that the copyright in the work belongs absolutely to Bram Stoker.

The contract also mentions that the novel should not be published "until the rights have been secured in the United States of America to the Author," but clearly this was not felt in practice to be an obstacle to immediate publication. Stoker had already secured the dramatic rights to the story by arranging for a pre-publication copyright reading of a dramatic version. . . . although he purchased the U.S. copyright of the novel, Stoker failed to comply with the technical requirement of registering two copies. Consequently Stoker received nothing from the first American printings in 1899, when the novel was serialised in several newspapers and then published separately by Doubleday & McClure. *Dracula* has, therefore, always remained in the public domain in the U.S.A.

—Peter Beal, item 100, Sotheby's catalogue,
10 July 2001

110

Memorandum of Agreement made this   Day of   one thousand eight hundred and ninety-seven between Archibald Constable and Company of 2 Whitehall Gardens Westminster hereinafter called the Publishers of the First part and Bram Stoker of 18 St Leonards Terrace Chelsea hereinafter called the Author of the Second Part **Whereby** *in consideration of the sums and conditions hereinafter mentioned it is agreed as follows*

1. *The Author having written a work entitled "The Un-Dead" and being prior to the signing of this Agreement possessed of all the rights therein agrees with the Publishers for its publication in the United Kingdom of Great Britain and Ireland and the British Dependencies (Canada being excepted) on the following terms*

2. *The Publishers shall print bind advertise and publish the work at their sole cost and shall publish it during the year 1897 but not until the rights have been secured in the United States of America to the Author. For the first edition of the said work the Publishers are to print at least three thousand copies. The sales are to be made to the Book trade at usual 'trade' and not 'net' terms.*

3. *The Publishers are not to pay the Author any royalty for the first one thousand copies sold but on each and every copy sold after the first one thousand they are to pay to the Author the sum of One shilling and Six pence sterling. The said work is to be published at the price of six shillings for each copy.*

4. *Should the sale of the said work reach Ten thousand copies the Publishers are to have the right to continue the publication paying to the Author a royalty of Two shillings sterling on each and every copy sold the other conditions of publishing remaining the same or they may bring this agreement to an end by a notice in writing leaving both parties to it free to act as they may decide*

5. *The Publishers may with the consent of the Author print and sell a Colonial edition (Canada being excepted from the operations of such*

Stoker's autograph contract for Dracula *under its original title, "The Un-Dead"*
(Sotheby's Literature, History & Illustrated Books, *10 July 2001;*
Thomas Cooper Library, University of South Carolina)

edition) at a price other than that already fixed but
such price and terms of royalty are to be subject to the
mutual consent expressed in writing of the parties to this
Agreement

6 This Agreement is to remain in force for Ten years unless earlier terminated
under clause four.

7 Accounts between the parties to this Agreement shall be taken and a
Settlement made half yearly being on the Thirtieth day of June and
the Thirty first day of December in each year and the party of the First
Part shall then pay to the party of the Second Part within thirty Days
any sums due to him as royalties on such account.

8 This Agreement does not include any place or country other than the
United Kingdom of Great Britain and Ireland and the British Dependencies
(Canada being excepted from such British Dependencies) and the said Author
shall be free to licence others than the said Publishers to publish the said
work in Canada and further this Agreement does not confer any
right on the Publishers other than the right to publish in the United Kingdom
of Great Britain and Ireland and the British Dependencies (Canada excepted)
as fixed in above clauses.

9 The Copyright and all other rights in the abovementioned work being
absolutely to the said Bram Stoker and if at any time after the publication
of the said work the party of the First Part shall become bankrupt or if their
business shall become merged in or incorporated with that of any
other firm or Company the licence hereby created and conferred
on the party of the First Part shall cease and determine and
all rights so created and conferred shall revert to the party
of the Second Part   In Witness

Bram Stoker

Witnessed by

Chas E Howson
    Librarian
53 Battersea Rise
    London S.W.

9.   The copyright and all other rights in the above
mentioned work belong absolutely to the said
BRAM STOKER and if at any time after the publication
of the said work the party of the First part shall
become Bankrupt or if their business shall become
merged in or incorporated with that of any other Firm
or Company the license hereby created and conferred
on the parts of the First part shall cease and
determine and all rights so created and conferred
shall revert to the party of the Second part.

Last page of the publishing agreement memo for Stoker's novel (Sotheby's Literature, History & Illustrated Books, 10 July 2001; Thomas Cooper Library, University of South Carolina)

and wrote in suitable amendments and bridging sections. That the effort was made in an almost indecent haste is evidenced by the fact that there are many traces of unblotted ink on the back of the single-sided pages.

Greater care does seem to have [been] taken when he began to write the Prologue, even if there is an overwhelming sense of the melodramatic. But Stoker was a busy man with a demanding job, and it soon becomes obvious that the initial creative intent to dramatise the novel properly soon gave way to the imperative of moving the plot along. There is also a favouring in the amount of stage time given to Van Helsing, suggesting that Stoker was rather preoccupied with the good doctor's ideas and thoughts.

As further evidence of haste, he omits naming some of the character parts and, in some scenes such as the encounter with the Un-Dead Lucy, large gaps

have been left in the text. Whether or not some of these gaps were aimed at avoiding the censor's wrath is unknown. But perhaps this is unlikely and we may speculate that the play probably passed through the censorship system on the understanding that it would only be read once and never be performed before a live audience.

–p. xii

. . . .

Bills announcing the play version of *Dracula: or The Un-Dead* were set out half an hour before the programme was due to start. It is usually assumed that seats were available at one guinea each–a fact borne out by Stoker's accounts which show a receipt of £2.2s. (two guineas, two tickets). Since this was the usual price for a private box, the natural surmise is that Stoker was not trying to encourage a full house, and we may assume that the audience mainly consisted of theatre staff and invited friends. The playbill, however, records the theatre's normal range of seat prices. If this performance had genuinely been presented for the paying public rather than as a legal device, we would have expected to see a more normal level of box office receipts. We must therefore conclude that only a token number of paying customers were required to satisfy the legal definition of public performance for copyright purposes.

–pp. xx–xxi

. . . .

Starshine notes that "Stoker chose his cast mainly from the younger supporting members of the Lyceum Company" (p. xxv).

With all of the talent, skills and services available to Stoker, there would be every reason to suppose that even the most hastily prepared script could have had a touch of that Lyceum magic. In addition to the cast, suitable music and scenery would have been available. Had it been properly written, the role of _Dracula_ would have offered Irving the chance to play a villain of epic proportions. But we must remember that Irving had already turned down an offer from Conan Doyle to play the part of Sherlock Holmes. He was in the final years of what had been a great career and he was content to continue in the roles which offered him the greatest security.

We are therefore left to conclude that this performance of _Dracula_ was nothing more than a straight reading. . . . it probably took place on the stage so that it could be classed as a performance for legal purposes with contemporary reports stating that it lasted for over four hours. Even if the text was cut, and there is no evidence for this, there would have been no time left for the niceties of scenery changes, costumes and music. Even an interval would have been unlikely.

One hundred years later, a second reading took place at the Spaniards Inn, Hampstead. Nine readers, including some professional actors, took on the task. They started with the best of intentions and tried to give some dramatic form to the reading. But it soon became apparent that if the reading was to be finished within a resonable time, it would have to be read at a breakneck speed, sharing the more difficult parts. Even so, it took six hours to read.

–pp. xxxiii–xxxiv
–_Dracula: or The Un-Dead: A Play in Prologue and Five Acts,_
edited by Sylvia Starshine (Nottingham:
Pumpkin, 1997)

* * *

Each of the following excerpts from the novel is followed by the corresponding section from the play.

The Novel and the Play

In the novel Dracula has warned Harker not to leave his rooms and fall "to sleep in any other part of the castle. It is old, and has many memories, and there are bad dreams for those who sleep unwisely."

Harker's Encounter with the Three Vampire Women

When I had written in my diary and had fortunately replaced the book and pen in my pocket I felt sleepy. The Count's warning came into my mind, but I took a pleasure in disobeying it. The sense of sleep was upon me, and with it the obstinacy which sleep brings as outrider. The soft moonlight soothed, and the wide expanse without gave a sense of freedom which refreshed me. I determined not to return to-night to the gloom-haunted rooms, but to sleep here, where of old ladies had sat and sung and lived sweet lives whilst their gentle breasts were sad for their menfolk away in the midst of remorseless wars. I drew a great couch out of its place near the corner, so that, as I lay, I could look at the lovely view to east and south, and unthinking of and uncaring for the dust, composed myself for sleep.

I suppose I must have fallen asleep; I hope so, but I fear, for all that followed was startlingly real–so real that now, sitting here in the broad, full sunlight of the morning, I cannot in the least believe that it was all sleep.

I was not alone. The room was the same, unchanged in any way since I came into it; I could see along the floor, in the brilliant moonlight, my own footsteps marked where I had disturbed the long accumulation of dust. In the moonlight opposite me were three young women, ladies by their dress and manner. I thought at the time that I must be dreaming when I saw them, for, though the moonlight was behind them, they threw no shadow on the floor. They came close to me and looked at me for some time, and then whispered together. Two were dark, and had high aquiline noses, like the Count, and great dark, piercing eyes, that seemed to be almost red when contrasted with the pale yellow moon. The other was fair, as fair as can be, with great, wavy masses of golden hair and eyes like pale sapphires. I seemed somehow to know her face, and to know it in connection with some dreamy fear, but I could not recollect at the moment how or where. All three had brilliant white teeth, that shone like pearls against the

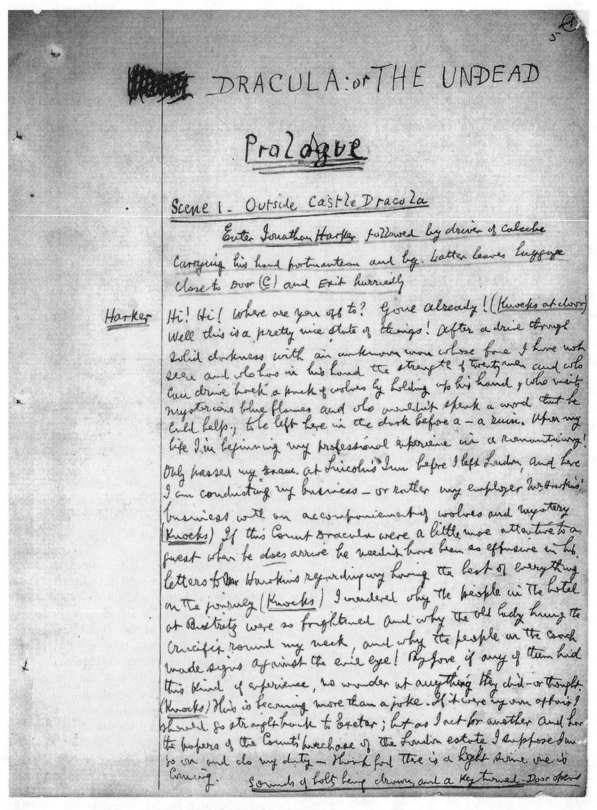

Opening page for the script of the dramatic reading of Dracula *in Stoker's hand (Additional Manuscript 53630,*
British Library Department of Manuscripts)

ruby of their voluptuous lips. There was something about them that made me uneasy, some longing and at the same time some deadly fear. I felt in my heart a wicked, burning desire that they would kiss me with those red lips. It is not good to note this down, lest some day it should meet Mina's eyes and cause her pain; but it is the truth. They whispered together, and then they all three laughed—such a silvery, musical laugh, but as hard as though the sound never could have come through the softness of human lips. It was like the intolerable, tingling sweetness of water-glasses when played on by a cunning hand. The fair girl shook her head coquettishly, and the other two urged her on. One said:—

"Go on! You are first, and we shall follow; yours is the right to begin." The other added:—

"He is young and strong; there are kisses for us all." I lay quiet, looking out under my eyelashes in an agony of delightful anticipation. The fair girl advanced and bent over me till I could feel the movement of her breath upon me. Sweet it was in one sense, honey-sweet, and sent the same tingling through the nerves as her voice, but with a bitter underlying the sweet, a bitter offensiveness, as one smells in blood.

I was afraid to raise my eyelids, but looked out and saw perfectly under the lashes. The girl went on her knees, and bent over me, fairly gloating. There was a deliberate voluptuousness which was both thrilling and repulsive, and as she arched her neck she actually licked her lips like an animal, till I could see in the moonlight the moisture shining on the scarlet lips and on the red tongue as it lapped the white sharp teeth. Lower and lower went her head as the lips went below the range of my mouth and chin and seemed about to fasten on my throat. Then she paused, and I could hear the churning sound of her tongue as it licked her teeth and lips, and could feel the hot breath on my neck. Then the skin of my throat began to tingle as one's flesh does when the hand that is to tickle it approaches nearer—nearer. I could feel the soft, shivering touch of the lips on the supersensitive skin of my throat, and the hard dents of two sharp teeth, just touching and pausing there. I closed my eyes in a languorous ecstasy and waited—waited with beating heart.

But at that instant another sensation swept through me as quick as lightning. I was conscious of the presence of the Count, and of his being as if lapped in a storm of fury. As my eyes opened involuntarily I saw his strong hand grasp the slender neck of the fair woman and with giant's power draw it back, the blue eyes transformed with fury, the white teeth champing with rage, and the fair cheeks blazing red with passion. But the Count! Never did I imagine such wrath and fury, even to the demons of the pit. His eyes were positively blazing. The red light in them was lurid, as if the flames of hell-fire blazed behind them. His face was deathly pale, and the lines of it were hard like drawn wires; the thick eyebrows that met over the nose now seemed like a heaving bar of white-hot metal. With a fierce sweep of his arm, he hurled the woman from him, and then motioned to the others, as though he were beating them back; it was the same imperious gesture that I had seen used to the wolves. In a voice which, though low and almost in a whisper, seemed to cut through the air and then ring round the room as he said:—

"How dare you touch him, any of you? How dare you cast eyes on him when I had forbidden it? Back, I tell you all! This man belongs to me! Beware how you meddle with him, or you'll have to deal with me." The fair girl, with a laugh of ribald coquetry, turned to answer him:—

"You yourself never loved; you never love!" On this the other women joined, and such a mirthless, hard, soulless laughter rang through the room that it almost made me faint to hear; it seemed like the pleasure of fiends. Then the Count turned, after looking at my face attentively, and said in a soft whisper:—

"Yes, I too can love; you yourselves can tell it from the past. Is it not so? Well, now I promise you that when I am done with him you shall kiss him at your will. Now go! go! I must awaken him, for there is work to be done."

"Are we to have nothing to-night?" said one of them, with a low laugh, as she pointed to the bag which he had thrown upon the floor, and which moved as though there were some living thing within it. For answer he nodded his head. One of the women jumped forward and opened it. If my ears did not deceive me there was a gasp and a low wail, as of a half-smothered child. The women closed round, whilst I was aghast with horror; but as I looked they disappeared, and with them the dreadful bag. There was no door near them, and they could not have passed me without my noticing. They simply seemed to fade into the rays of the moonlight and pass out through the window, for I could see outside the dim, shadowy forms for a moment before they entirely faded away.

Then the horror overcame me, and I sank down unconscious.

—Chapter III, Jonathan Harker's Journal,
16 May

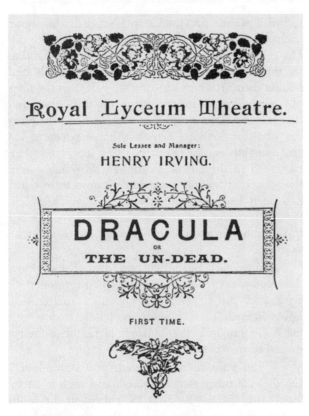

Program for the dramatic reading, apparently arranged to protect the theatrical copyright of the novel. There were no reviews of the production (courtesy of Jeanne Youngson).

For the corresponding scene in the play Stoker describes the setting: "A large room with big windows through which moonlight streams—splendid old furniture all in rags and covered with dust. Harker lies on sofa."

HARKER: Here I can rest. It was lucky that the door to this wing was not really locked but only appeared to be.

(Dozes.)

(Figures of three young women materialise from the moonlight and surround him.)

FIRST WOMAN: [*To blond*] Go on! You are first, and we shall follow; yours is the right to begin.

SECOND WOMAN: [*To blond*] He is young and strong; there are kisses for us all.

(Count suddenly appears beside them, and taking woman [blond] who is just fastening her lips on Harker's throat, by the neck hurls her away.)

DRAC: How dare you touch him, any of you? How dare you cast eyes on him when I had forbidden it? Back, I tell you all! This man belongs to me. Beware how you meddle with him, or you'll have to deal with me.

THIRD WOMAN [BLOND]: You yourself never loved; you never love!

DRAC: Yes, I too can love; you yourselves can tell it from the past. Is it not so? Well, now I promise you when I am done with him you shall kiss him at your will. Now go! go! I must awaken him, for there is work to be done.

FIRST WOMAN: Are we to have nothing to-night?

(Count points to bag which he has thrown on floor and which moves and a child's wail is heard. Women seize bag and disappear all at once. Count lifts up Harker who has fainted and carries him off. Darkness.)

—*Dracula: or The Un-Dead: A Play in Prologue and Five Acts,*
pp. 14–15

* * *

Comparing the following corresponding passages shows that much of the sexual innuendo of the novel has been expurgated in the play. Stoker, however, did not always revise in this fashion. For example, he left the equally suggestive bedroom scene in which Dracula and Mina exchange blood largely intact.

The Staking of Lucy

We all looked at Arthur. He saw, too, what we all did, the infinite kindness which suggested that his should be the hand which would restore Lucy to us as a holy, and not an unholy, memory; he stepped forward and said bravely, though his hand trembled, and his face was as pale as snow:—

"My true friend, from the bottom of my broken heart I thank you. Tell me what I am to do, and I shall not falter!" Van Helsing laid a hand on his shoulder, and said: –

"Brave lad! A moment's courage, and it is done. This stake must be driven through her. It will be a fearful ordeal—be not deceived in that—but it will be only a short time, and you will then rejoice more than your pain was great; from this grim tomb you will emerge as though you tread on air. But you must not falter when once you have begun. Only think that we, your true friends, are round you, and that we pray for you all the time."

"Go on," said Arthur hoarsely. "Tell me what I am to do."

"Take this stake in your left hand, ready to place the point over the heart, and the hammer in your right. Then when we begin our prayer for the dead–I shall read him, I have here the book, and the others shall follow–strike in God's name, that so all may be well with the dead that we love, and that the Un-Dead pass away."

Arthur took the stake and the hammer, and when once his mind was set on action his hands never trembled nor even quivered. Van Helsing opened his missal and began to read, and Quincey and I followed as well as we could. Arthur placed the point over the heart, and as I looked I could see its dint in the white flesh. Then he struck with all his might.

The Thing in the coffin writhed; and a hideous, blood-curdling screech came from the opened red lips. The body shook and quivered and twisted in wild contortions; the sharp white teeth champed together till the lips were cut, and the mouth was smeared with a crimson foam. But Arthur never faltered. He looked like a figure of Thor as his untrembling arm rose and fell, driving deeper and deeper the mercy-bearing stake, whilst the blood from the pierced heart welled and spurted up around it. His face was set, and high duty seemed to shine through it; the sight of it gave us courage, so that our voices seemed to ring through the little vault.

And then the writhing and quivering of the body became less, and the teeth ceased to champ, and the face to quiver. Finally it lay still. The terrible task was over.

The hammer fell from Arthur's hand. He reeled and would have fallen had we not caught him. The great drops of sweat sprang out on his forehead, and his breath came in broken gasps. It had indeed been an awful strain on him; and had he not been forced to his task by more than human considerations he could never have gone through with it. For a few minutes we were so taken up with him that we did not look towards the coffin. When we did, however, a murmur of startled surprise ran from one to the other of us. We gazed so eagerly that Arthur rose, for he had been seated on the ground, and came and looked too; and then a glad, strange light broke over his face and dispelled altogether the gloom of horror that lay upon it.

There, in the coffin lay no longer the foul Thing that we had so dreaded and grown to hate that the work of her destruction was yielded as a privilege to the one best entitled to it, but Lucy as we had seen her in life, with her face of unequalled sweetness and purity. True that there were there, as we had seen them in life, the traces of care and pain and waste; but these were all

dear to us, for they marked her truth to what we knew. One and all we felt that the holy calm that lay like sunshine over the wasted face and form was only an earthly token and symbol of the calm that was to reign for ever.

Van Helsing came and laid his hand on Arthur's shoulder, and said to him:–

"And now, Arthur, my friend, dear lad, am I not forgiven?"

The reaction of the terrible strain came as he took the old man's hand in his, and raising it to his lips, pressed it, and said:–

"Forgiven! God bless you that you have given my dear one her soul again, and me peace." He put his hands on the Professor's shoulder, and laying his head on his breast, cried for a while silently, whilst we stood unmoving. When he raised his head Van Helsing said to him:–

"And now, my child, you may kiss her. Kiss her dead lips if you will, as she would have you to, if for her to choose. For she is not a grinning devil now–not any more a foul Thing for all eternity. No longer she is the devil's Un-Dead. She is God's true dead, whose soul is with Him!"

Arthur bent and kissed her, and then we sent him and Quincey out of the tomb; the Professor and I sawed the top off the stake, leaving the point of it in the body. Then we cut off the head and filled the mouth with garlic. We soldered up the leaden coffin, screwed on the coffin-lid, and gathering up our belongings, came away.

–Chapter XVI, Dr. Seward's Diary,
29 September

The corresponding scene in the play.

[GODALMING:] My true friend, from the bottom of my broken heart I thank you. Tell me what I am to do, and I shall not falter.

[VAN HELSING:] Brave lad! A moment's courage, and it is done. This stake must be driven through her. It will be a fearful ordeal–be not deceived in that–but it will be only a short time, and you will then rejoice more than your pain was great, and from this grim tomb you will emerge as though you tread on air. But you must not falter when once you have begun. Only think that we, your true friends, are round you, and that we pray for you all the time.

ARTHUR: Go on. Tell me what I am to do.

[VAN HELSING:] Take this stake in your left hand, ready to place the point over the heart, and the hammer in your right. Then when we begin our prayer for the dead–I shall read him, I have here the book, and the others shall follow–strike in God's name, so that all may be well with the dead that we love, and that the Un-Dead pass away.

[Van Helsing begins to read. Godalming strikes with all his might. A hideous, blood-curdling screech comes from the open red lips– finally the body lies still and it is no longer a foul thing, but Lucy.]

[Van Helsing lays his hand on Godalming's shoulder.]

[VAN HELSING:] And now, Arthur, my friend, dear lad, am I not forgiven?

[GODALMING:] Forgiven! God bless you that you have given me peace, and my dear one her soul again.

[VAN HELSING:] And now, my child, you may kiss her. Kiss her dead lips if you will, as she would now have you to, if for her to choose. For she is not a grinning devil now, not a foul thing any more for all eternity. No longer she is the devil's Un-Dead. She is God's true dead, whose soul is with Him.

[Godalming bends and kisses her.]

–*Dracula: or The Un-Dead: A Play in Prologue and Five Acts,*
pp. 106–107

TUESDAY, MAY 18, 1897, AT A QUARTER-PAST TEN O'CLOCK A.M.,

WILL BE PRESENTED, FOR THE FIRST TIME,

DRACULA
OR
THE UN-DEAD
IN A PROLOGUE AND FIVE ACTS
BY
BRAM STOKER.

Count Dracula	....	Mr. JONES.
Jonathan Harker	....	Mr. PASSMORE.
John Seward, M.D. ...	....	Mr. RIVINGTON.
Professor Van Helsing	....	Mr. T. REYNOLDS.
Quincey P. Morris	....	Mr. WIDDICOMBE.
Hon. Arthur Holmwood (*afterwards Lord Godalming*)		Mr. INNES.
M. F. Renfield	....	Mr. HOWARD.
Captain Swales	....	Mr. GURNEY.
Coastguard	....	Mr. SIMPSON.
Attendant at Asylum	....	Mr. PORTER.
Mrs. Westenra	....	Miss GURNEY.
Lucy Westenra	....	Miss FOSTER.
Mina Murray (*afterwards Mrs. Harker*)	....	Miss CRAIG.
Servant	....	Miss CORNFORD.
Vampire Woman	....	Mrs. DALY.

Cast list for the first dramatic production of Dracula
(courtesy of Jeanne Youngson)

* * *

At the conclusion of the novel, Dracula's death takes away Mina Harker's curse.

The Final Scene

In the midst of this I could see that Jonathan on one side of the ring of men, and Quincey on the other, were forcing a way to the cart; it was evident that they were bent on finishing their task before the sun should set. Nothing seemed to stop or even to hinder them. Neither the levelled weapons or the flashing knives of the gypsies in front, or the howling of the wolves behind, appeared to even attract their attention. Jonathan's impetuosity, and the manifest singleness of his purpose, seemed to overawe those in front of him; instinctively they cowered aside and let him pass. In an instant he had jumped upon the cart, and, with a strength which seemed incredible, raised the great box, and flung it over the wheel to the ground. In the meantime, Mr. Morris had had to use force to pass through his side of the ring of Szgany. All the time I had been breathlessly watching Jonathan I had, with the tail of my eye, seen him pressing desperately forward, and had seen the knives of the gypsies flash as he won a way

through them, and they cut at him. He had parried with his great bowie knife, and at first I thought that he too had come through in safety; but as he sprang beside Jonathan, who had by now jumped from the cart, I could see that with his left hand he was clutching at his side, and that the blood was spurting through his fingers. He did not delay notwithstanding this, for as Jonathan, with desperate energy, attacked one end of the chest, attempting to prize off the lid with his great kukri knife, he attacked the other frantically with his bowie. Under the efforts of both men the lid began to yield; the nails drew with a quick screeching sound, and the top of the box was thrown back.

By this time the gypsies, seeing themselves covered by the Winchesters, and at the mercy of Lord Godalming and Dr. Seward, had given in and made no further resistance. The sun was almost down on the mountain tops, and the shadows of the whole group fell long upon the snow. I saw the Count lying within the box upon the earth, some of which the rude falling from the cart had scattered over him. He was deathly pale, just like a waxen image, and the red eyes glared with the horrible vindictive look which I knew too well.

As I looked, the eyes saw the sinking sun, and the look of hate in them turned to triumph.

Edith Craig, the first actress to play Mina Harker (photograph [1895] by Alfred Ellis; National Portrait Gallery, London)

But, on the instant, came the sweep and flash of Jonathan's great knife. I shrieked as I saw it shear through the throat; whilst at the same moment Mr. Morris's bowie knife plunged into the heart.

It was like a miracle; but before our very eyes, and almost in the drawing of a breath, the whole body crumbled into dust and passed from our sight.

I shall be glad as long as I live that even in that moment of final dissolution, there was in the face a look of peace, such as I never could have imagined might have rested there.

The Castle of Dracula now stood out against the red sky, and every stone of its broken battlements was articulated against the light of the setting sun.

The gypsies, taking us as in some way the cause of the extraordinary disappearance of the dead man, turned, without a word, and rode away as if for their lives. Those who were unmounted jumped upon the leiter-wagon and shouted to the horsemen not to desert them. The wolves,

which had withdrawn to a safe distance, followed in their wake, leaving us alone.

Mr. Morris, who had sunk to the ground, leaned on his elbow, holding his hand pressed to his side; the blood still gushed through his fingers. I flew to him, for the Holy circle did not now keep me back; so did the two doctors. Jonathan knelt behind him and the wounded man laid back his head on his shoulder. With a sigh he took, with a feeble effort, my hand in that of his own which was unstained. He must have seen the anguish of my heart in my face, for he smiled at me and said:—

"I am only too happy to have been of service! Oh, God!" he cried suddenly, struggling up to a sitting posture and pointing to me, "It was worth for this to die! Look! look!"

The sun was now right down upon the mountain top, and the red gleams fell upon my face, so that it was bathed in rosy light. With one impulse the men sank on their knees and a deep and earnest "Amen" broke from all as their eyes followed the pointing of his finger as the dying man spoke:—

"Now God be thanked that all has not been in vain! See! the snow is not more stainless than her forehead! The curse has passed away!"

And, to our bitter grief, with a smile and in silence, he died, a gallant gentleman.
–Chapter XXVII, Mina Harker's Journal, 6 November

[Gypsies and horsemen draw near.]

MORRIS: Halt!

[Horsemen fight with Gypsies and Morris and Harker throw box from cart and prise it open. Count seen. Fades away as knives cut off his head. Sunset falls on group. Morris is wounded and Harker holds up his head.]

MORRIS: I am only too happy to have been of any service! Oh, God! It was worth for this to die! Look! look!

[The sunset falls on Mina and they see her forehead stainless.]

[MORRIS]: Now God be thanked that all has not been in vain! See! the snow is not more stainless than her forehead! The curse has passed away.

CURTAIN
–*Dracula: or The Un-Dead: A Play in Prologue and Five Acts,*
pp. 192–193

V. Publication History of *Dracula*

The first reviews of Dracula *appeared in late May 1897. The steady, though not spectacular, sales of the novel led to new printings. Read as nothing more than a horror story, the novel received mixed reviews, ranging from high praise to condemnation. Yet, even the reviewers who found fault with the novel acknowledged its power. During Stoker's lifetime there were indications of enduring interest in the novel—it was published in America, brought out in an abridged edition in England, and translated into Icelandic and German—but the real popular appreciation and fascination with the work was not to begin to grow until well over a decade after Stoker's death.*

Reception in the U.K.

Mr. Bram Stoker's New Story
The Daily News (London), 27 May 1897

[PUBLISHED TO-DAY.]

What has become of the "general decay of faith" of which Parson Holmes reproachfully discoursed at Francis Allen's that night when the poet read aloud his fragment, "Morte d'Arthur," the noble precursor of "The Idylls of the King"? Have old beliefs really ceased to impress the imagination? It may be so; but our novelists are clearly experiencing a reawakened faith in the charm of the supernatural. Here, for the latest example, is Mr. Bram Stoker taking in hand the old-world legend of the Were-wolf or vampire, with all its weird and exciting associations of blood-sucking and human flesh devouring, and interweaving it with the threads of a long story with an earnestness, a directness, and a simple good faith which ought to go far to induce readers of fiction to surrender their imaginations into the novelist's hands. Of course the secret lies here. The story writer who would make others believe must himself believe, or learn at least to write as if he did. There must be no display of meaningless rhetoric, no selection of faded terrors out of the dusty scene-docks of the suburban theatres. The more strange the facts, the more businesslike should be the style and method of narration. Some there be who, in handling such themes, prefer to take shelter in a remote time; but the supernatural which cannot stand the present

day, and even the broad daylight of the world around us, stands a half confessed imposture. Mr. Stoker has not been unmindful of these canons of the art of the weird novel writer. His story is told in sections, in the form of letters or excerpts from diaries of the various personages, which is in itself a straightforward proceeding, investing the whole narrative with a documentary air. Ships' logs and medical practitioners' notebooks of cases also come in aid, with now and then a matter-of-fact extract from the columns of our contemporaries, "The Westminster" and "The Pall Mall Gazette," about mysterious crimes attributed to an unseen destroyer popularly known as "the Blooler [*sic*] Lady," the victims of whom are mostly little children whose throats are found marked with two little punctures, such as of old were believed to be made by the "Vampire Bat," who lives on human blood. These details are not the mere background of the story; for the mysteries of Lycanthropy, once devoutly believed in throughout Europe and the East, permeate the whole narrative and give their peculiar colouring to the web of romance with which they are associated. The author's artistic instincts have rightly suggested that the first step must be to attune the mind of the reader to the key of the story, for which purpose nothing could be more effective than the opening chapters, which are given up to the journal kept in shorthand by the hero, Jonathan Harker, the young solicitor who, leaving his fiancée, Mina Murray, behind in England, starts on a mission connected with the purchase of some estates and an ancient manor house in this country to the mysterious Count Dracula, a Transylvanian nobleman, who lives in a lonely castle in the Carpathians. The long drive from Buda-Pesth is graphically described, while a constantly-growing sense of some vague impending trouble is cleverly made to intensify the interest and curiosity of the reader. Sometimes it is the strange, anxious glances of innkeepers and attendants, who know that the traveller is on the way to sojourn at the Count's gloomy and almost inaccessible abode; at others it is a word let fall, which, though in the Servian or Slovak language, conveys to the mind of the traveller a

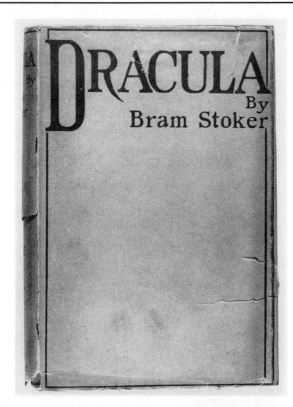
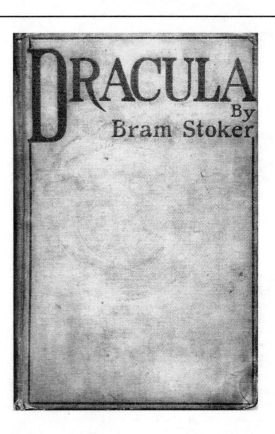
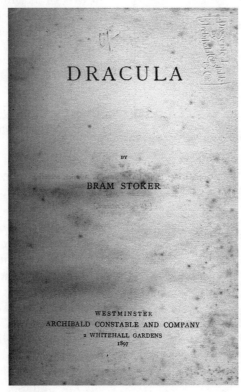

Dust jacket—acquired without a book (Bram Stoker's Dracula: *A Centennial Exhibition at the Rosenbach Museum & Library, 1997; Elizabeth Miller Collection); cover and title page (courtesy of Robert Eighteen-Bisang) for the first edition of Stoker's sixth novel*

The First *Dracula*

The first edition of Dracula *was published in a mustard-yellow cloth binding, with red lettering and red rules. The initial printing was 3,000 copies in May or June 1897; it was reprinted 1897, 1897, 1897, 1898, 1899, 1899, and 1904.*

Notes:

1. No one knows exactly when the first edition of *Dracula* was published. Possible dates range from late May to early June of 1897.

2. Unfortunately, Constable did not identify first editions or distinguish the reprintings of the editions in any systematic way. Early printings of *Dracula* bear the date "1897" on their title pages even when they are published in subsequent years.

3. Evidence from signed copies and presentation copies indicates that the first Constable edition does not have any advertising material after the text (p. 390).

4. A handful of first-edition copies carry the emboss-ment "Presented by Archibald Constable & Co." in the top right-hand corner of the title page.

5. Constable uses the word "edition" for what is actu-ally a reprinting. The so-designated "Fifth Edition" of "1898"–actually the fifth printing of the first edition–and all subsequent printings, state the edition and year of publication on the title page.

6. The "Eighth Edition" of 1904 was bound in a slightly smaller format (7 ¼" instead of 7½") and there are at least two variations with black cloth, red letter-ing, and red floral motifs, and one variation with red cloth, black lettering, and a black floral motif.

–Robert Eighteen-Bisang

sinister idea. One worthy old landlady at a post-house puts a rosary around her guest's neck, reminding him that it is the eve of St. George's Day, when at midnight all evil things have full sway, and after vainly imploring him to consider where he is going and what he is going to, places for protection a rosary round his neck. Even the crowd about the inn doors share in the worthy hostess's solicitude:

> When we started, the crowd round the inn door, which had by this time swelled to a considerable size, all made the sign of the Cross and pointed two fingers towards me. With some difficulty I got a fellow-passenger to tell me what they meant; he would not answer at first, but on learning that I was English he explained that it was a charm or guard against the evil eye. This was not very pleasant for me, just starting for an unknown place to meet an unknown man; but every one seemed so kind-hearted, and so sorrowful, and so sympathetic that I could not but be touched. I shall never forget the last glimpse which I had of the inn-yard and its crowd of picturesque figures, all crossing themselves, as they

stood round the wide archway, with its background of rich foliage of oleander and orange trees in green tubs clustered in the centre of the yard. Then our driver, whose wide linen drawers covered the whole front of the box-seat–"gotza," they call them–cracked his big whip over his four small horses, which ran abreast, and we set off on our journey. I soon lost sight and recollec-tion of ghostly fears in the beauty of the scene as we drove along, although had I known the language, or rather languages, which my fellow passengers were speaking, I might not have been able to throw them off so easily.

Strange, unearthly experiences indeed are in store for the young traveller in the chateau of the Count before this opening, which may be regarded as the prologue of the story, is concluded; but inter-est in a narrative whose effect depends so much on the feeling of curiosity must not be forestalled. For details, therefore, of how Jonathan Harker finally escaped from the castle and its terrible inmates to the shelter of a friendly convent in Buda-Pesth, where he is found by the faithful Mina suffering from brain fever; and also for the more marvellous incidents after their return to England, which form the chief substance of the narrative, we must send the reader to Mr. Bram Stoker's volume. Few stories recently published have been more rich in sensations or in the Websterian power of "moving a horror" by subtle suggestion.

* * *

Review of *Dracula*

The Daily Mail (London), 1 June 1897

It is said of Mrs. Radcliffe that when writing her now almost forgotten romances she shut herself up in absolute seclusion, and fed upon raw beef, in order to give her work the desired atmosphere of gloom, tragedy and terror. If one had no assurance to the contrary one might well suppose that a similar method and regimen had been adopted by Mr. Bram Stoker while writing his new novel "Dracula." In seeking for a parallel to this weird, powerful, and horrorful story our mind reverts to such tales as "The Mysteries of Udolpho," "Frankenstein," "Wuthering Heights," "The Fall of the House of Usher," and "Marjery of Quether." But "Dracula" is even more appalling in its gloomy fascination than any one of these.

We started reading it early in the evening, and followed Jonathan Harker on his mission to the Car-pathians with no definite conjecture as to what waited us in the castle of Dracula. When we came to the night journey over the mountain road and were chased by the wolves, which the driver, with apparently miraculous power, repelled by a mere gesture, we began to scent mystery, but were not perturbed. The first thrill of horrible sensation came with the discovery that the driver and the Count Dracula were one and the same person, that the count was the only human inhabitant of the castle, and that the rats, the bats, the ghosts, and the howling wolves were his familiars.

By ten o'clock the story had so fastened itself upon our attention that we could not pause even to light our pipe. At midnight the narrative had fairly got upon our nerves; a creepy terror had seized upon us, and when at length, in the early hours of the morning, we went upstairs to bed it was with the anticipation of nightmare. We listened anxiously for the sound of bats' wings against the window; we even felt at our throat in dread lest an actual vampire should have left there the two ghastly punctures which in Mr. Stoker's book attested to the hellish operations of Dracula.

The recollection of this weird and ghostly tale will doubtless haunt us for some time to come. It would be unfair to the author to divulge the plot. We therefore restrict ourselves to the statement that the eerie chapters are written and strung together with very considerable art and cunning, and also with unmistakable literary power. Tribute must also be paid to the rich imagination of which Mr. Bram Stoker here gives liberal evidence. Persons of small courage and weak nerves should confine their reading of these gruesome pages strictly to the hours between dawn and sunset.

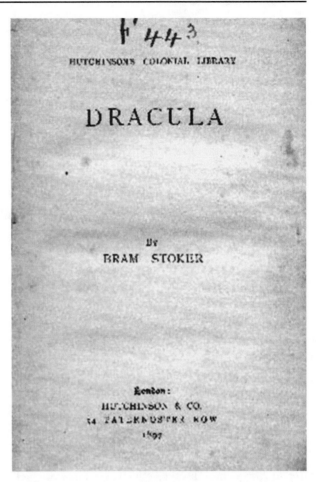

Title page for the only located copy of the colonial edition. The title page is a cancel (courtesy of Robert Eighteen-Bisang).

* * *

For Midnight Reading.
Pall Mall Gazette (London), 1 June 1897

Mr. Bram Stoker should have labelled his book "For Strong Men Only," or words to that effect. Left lying carelessly around, it might get into the hands of your maiden aunt who believes devoutly in the man under the bed, or of the new parlourmaid with unsuspected hysterical tendencies. "Dracula" to such would be manslaughter. It is for the man with a sound conscience and digestion, who can turn out the gas and go to bed without having to look over his shoulder more than half a dozen times as he goes upstairs, or more than mildly wishing that he had a crucifix and some garlic handy to keep the vampires from getting at him. That is to say, the story deals with the Vampire King, and it is horrid

---

The Colonial Edition

There are two known copies of Hutchinson's Colonial edition of Dracula, which was printed from the same plates as the Constable editions and has the same printer's colophon on page 390. The only observable differences are its binding, title page, and copyright page. The blood-red cover stipulates: "Hutchinson's Colonial Library"; the title page states: "Hutchinson & Co."; and the copyright page states: "This edition is issued for circulation in India and the British colonies only." Colonial editions provided an early source of profit for publishers and allowed the colonies, which did not have a large enough population to support their own publishing industries, a chance to enjoy the latest contemporary literature.

–Robert Eighteen-Bisang

and creepy to the last degree. It is also excellent, and one of the best things in the supernatural line that we have been lucky enough to hit upon. To expound the story in any detail would be grossly unfair to Mr. Bram Stoker, besides being utterly impossible, owing to the mass of corroborative detail and the tremendous complications, which, however, can be followed without a headache. It opens with the journey of a solicitor's clerk into the heart of the Carpathians, where the terror of the peasantry indicates that he is likely to meet with something uncommon. He does, and that something is—Dracula. Having once got through the first half-dozen pages, every one will finish the rest in as few sittings as possible, and, for reasons given above, we decline to tell what the rest is. It is enough to say that Mr. Bram Stoker has mastered the real secrets of a genuine "creep." A glance at your pipe-rack and evening paper will not save you, for Mr. Bram Stoker lays the main scenes of his tale in England and London, right up to date, with the type-writer, the phonograph, the *Pall Mall Gazette,* the Zoo, and all the latest improvements complete. That is the way to make a horror convincing. The mediæval is well enough in its way, but you don't care what sort of bogeys troubled your ancestors all that way back. And, again, Mr. Stoker understands how to sustain the interest. He gives you drops into the lifelike commonplace, which, nevertheless, tell upon the plot; and he sandwiches the various sides of his story in together at intervals of a few pages by means of an ingenious collection of diaries, newspaper extracts, &c., in chronological order. There are slight discrepancies, possibly, and the mechanism which helps the characters out is once or twice rather too obviously mechanism; but that is inevitable. And there is a creep in every dozen pages or so. For those who like that, this is a book to revel in. We did it ourselves, and are not ashamed to say so.

*　*　*

Books of the Day. Dracula.
W. L. Courtney
Daily Telegraph (London), 3 June 1897

　　Romance is dying—according to some littérateur, who seems to think that perennial forms of human thought are as transitory as fashion. Already the public is getting tired of romance, and is once more asking for the social problems and the deeper analysis into character which were temporarily obscured by the extravagances of the New Woman. It is odd that, under circumstances like these, one of

the most curious and striking of recent productions should be a revival of a mediæval superstition, the old legend of the "were-wolf," as illustrated and modernised by Mr. Bram Stoker, in the book which he entitles "Dracula." For there are two things which are remarkable in the novel—the first is the confident reliance on superstition as furnishing the groundwork of a modern story; and the second, more significant still, is the bold adaptation of the legend to such ordinary spheres of latter-day existence as the harbour of Whitby and Hampstead-heath. What is the good of telling us that romance is dead, or dying, when we see before our eyes its triumph and survival in ghost stories from the Highlands, and the scientific mysticism of the Psychical Society? How absurd to suppose that even the old gloomy and awe-inspiring melodrama of "The Castle of Otranto," has disappeared, when Mr. Bram Stoker invites us to sup on horrors, not only in the Carpathian Mountains but in the more cheerful and commonplace precincts of our metropolis! Superstition, whether we view it from the standpoint of folk-lore or in the shape in which it appealed to Dickens's fat boy, is apparently the deathless accompaniment of civilisation. It is not only the savage and the barbarian who likes to feel his flesh creep; it is the fashionable man or woman at the end of a century, who, sceptical of almost everything else, becomes anxious at the spilling of salt, and refuses to sit down at a table of thirteen.

　　"Dracula," at all events, is one of the most weird and spirit-quelling romances which have appeared for years. It begins in masterly fashion in the wilds of Transylvania, and introduces to us an ordinary solicitor's clerk, engaged on a mission to a Count who lives in its most remote fastnesses. How is it that in his progress to his destination the air seems to be full of omens? Why is it that the simple villagers at Bistritz press upon him branches of garlic and rosaries? Because it is the doom of Mr. Jonathan Harker, solicitor's clerk to Mr. Hawkins, to have to see a man-wolf, a Count Dracula, who from sunset to sunrise satisfies his thirst for human blood under appalling circumstances of secrecy and horror. Here is a commencement which lacks no element of the uncanny and the gruesome. We are at home in that precise corner of Europe which shelters the superstitions of the Middle Ages: we feel that anything can happen in the midst of the Carpathian Mountains, and Castle Dracula may be situated anywhere we please within the region which is the wildest and least known portion of the Continent. All the better if the narrator of the tale be nothing more or less than a solicitor's clerk. It is the juxtaposition of the

The Dedication

Dracula was dedicated "To My Dear Friend HOMMY-BEG," better known as Thomas Hall Caine, a prolific writer who, as this excerpt from Richard Dalby's profile indicates, in his time was far better known than Stoker. Stoker's dedication was in part reciprocal, for in 1893 Caine had dedicated a volume of three novellas to Stoker.

Thomas Hall Caine (1853–1931), born in Runcorn (Cheshire) and in later life the most famous inhabitant of the Isle of Man, was an incredible publishing phenomenon. He was undoubtedly the richest and most widely-read living novelist for thirty years in the late Victorian era up to the early 1920s. . . . he produced a series of graphic love stories of passion, seduction, divorce and illegitimacy, in both historical and near-contemporary settings. He was often controversial, especially when dealing with religious and political problems.

And yet now he is almost completely forgotten and all his novels are out-of-print, in spite of the timeless and often 'modern' themes of his novels, ranging from social injustice to racial conflict.

By a strange twist of fate, his major claim to fame today is as the dedicatee of *Dracula,* albeit under the disguised family nickname of "Hommy Beg"–Manx for "Little Tommy." It is a bizarre irony that Bram Stoker is now so much more famous internationally than Hall Caine–an unbelievable reversal of their roles one century ago.

Stoker devoted a complete chapter (LVII) to Hall Caine, a fervent admirer of Irving from 1874 onwards, in his *Personal Reminiscences of Henry Irving* (1906). According to Stoker, Irving "had a great opinion of Caine's imagination and always said that he would write a great work of weirdness some day. He knew already his ability and his fire and his zeal."

–Richard Dalby, "Hall Caine," *Bram Stoker Society Journal,* 11 (1999): 24–25

Thomas Hall Caine, the "Hommy Beg" of Stoker's dedication (Caine, Capt'n Davy's Honeymoon, *1893; Elizabeth Miller Collection)*

ordinary with the supernatural which gives the latter its significance. We accept the wildest adventures because the man who experienced them was only plain Mr. Jonathan Harker, engaged to Miss Mina Murray in England.

Were-wolf, Lycanthrope, Loup-garou–the name was familiar enough in Europe some centuries ago. The idea that a man can turn himself into a wolf begins early in recorded literature; we remember the story of Lycaon in Ovid's "Metamorphoses" and the noted wizard Mœris in Virgil's "Ecologues," who by the aid of Pontic poisons hid himself in the woods, and could bring the ghosts of dead men from their sepulchres. What has Mr. Bram Stoker been reading? Has he got hold of Richard Verstegan, who tells us in 1605 that it was a common thing in England for certain savage men to change at nighttime into wolves, and traverse the country seeking whom they could devour? Or is his authority Mr. Baring-Gould, who, in 1865, published "The Book of Were-wolves," together with every kind of rationalistic and perhaps not very convincing explanation that some specimens of the human race were born with a thirst for human blood? I seem also to remember that Mr. G. W. M. Reynolds, who posed as a Chartist some twenty or thirty years ago, and varied the task of founding *Reynolds's Newspaper* by addressing a crowd of homeless vagabonds on the iniquities of the income-tax, wrote a "London Journal" story on the were-wolf. At all events, history tells us that late in the sixteenth century a man called Gilles Garnier was arrested at Dôle, in France, on the charge of being a man-wolf, and that one of the means whereby human creatures could thus metamorphose themselves was a girdle of wolf-skin which they clasped round their loins. Naturally enough, however, the superstition was only prevalent so long as wolves themselves existed in the various countries. In England, for instance, James I. can tell us in his "Demonologie" that the old legend is an absurd one, while, as a matter of fact, it is not the wolf but the black cat, as a more familiar animal, which serves in our own country as the mystic instrument of witch-like juggleries. Not always is the wolf himself accepted in tradition as a destroying agency. It is true that in the shape of a grandmother he does his best to devour Little Red Ridinghood, but Rome owes it to a wolf that Romulus ever existed, and some forms of the story of Beauty and the Beast make the future husband of the beautiful heroine a wolf-like animal, susceptible of the fascination of flowers. Perhaps the were-wolf was in reality a metaphorical figure for the outlaw, the man who preferred a vendetta to all kinds of money composition for injuries, a man with a price set on his head as an enemy to society, whom at all hazards a developing civilisation had to destroy.

All this, doubtless, Mr. Bram Stoker is familiar with, but it leads to a point which concerns the mechanism of his tale. After Mr. Harker's episode in Transylvania and his escape from the castle of Count Dracula, the story changes to Whitby, and we discover a fresh arena for the maleficent energies of the were-wolf. The Count has purchased a little property in England, for no other reason than the desire to extend the range of his operations. Nor is his success less extraordinary than his nature. He infects with wolf-madness the body of Miss Lucy Westenra, engaged to Mr. Arthur Holmwood, and is the immediate cause of her melancholy demise. He makes a wolf desert the safe precincts of the Zoological Gardens and range at large for the express edification of the contemporary newspaper reporter. He fills the mad soul of a patient named Renfield with a lust for devouring flies and spiders, before aiming at higher game. Science is powerless before him. An Amsterdam specialist, Van Helsing, conspires with Dr. Seward to defeat his purposes, but these lights of modern knowledge have to fall back on the simpler remedies of garlic, crucifix, and consecrated wafer, and abjure the refinements of medical and pathological analysis. Poor Lucy Westenra, dead to human eyes, haunts the suburban heights of Hampstead and purloins the wandering children in the northern regions of the metropolis. Only when the wife of Jonathan Harker is herself tainted with the wolf poison can Van Helsing, Dr. Seward, Holmwood, and Quincey Morris succeed in tracking the monster to his lair. Count Dracula is killed at last before the sun reaches the horizon, and the world is once more at rest. Never was so mystical a tale told with such simple verisimilitude. We are not allowed to doubt the facts because the author speaks of them as mere matters of ascertained truth. Such is Mr. Stoker's dramatic skill, that the reader hurries on breathless from the first page to the last, afraid to miss a single word, lest the subtle and complicated chain of evidence should be broken; and though the plot involves enough and to spare of bloodshed, it never becomes revolting, because the spiritual mystery of evil continually surmounts the physical horror.

Nevertheless, there is no part of the book so good as the opening section. The reason is obvious. In telling a tale of romantic mystery the atmosphere, the mise-en-scène, the local colouring, are quite as important as the central incidents. When you are transported to an unknown region everything is possible. But the Château en Espagne—or, for the matter of that, the Castle in the Carpathian mountains—must not be transferred to the home of the railway and the phonograph. Besides, the legend of the were-wolf died in England when the wolf ceased to

---

A Reflection Not His Own

Hall Caine was good friends with Irving as well as with Stoker, who recalls an evening in 1891 when the conversation led to a anecdote that may have grown in Stoker's imagination.

. . . That night both Irving and Caine were in great form and the conversation was decidedly interesting. It began with a sort of discussion about Shakespeare as a dramatist—on the working side; his practical execution of his own imaginative intention. . . . Later on the conversation tended towards weird subjects. Caine told of seeing in a mirror a reflection not his own.

—Bram Stoker, *Personal Reminiscences of Henry Irving*, volume 2 (New York & London: Macmillan, 1906), p. 122

be a formidable enemy; it died, too, even in France after the end of the sixteenth century. There is yet another point which is a little confusing to the ordinary reader. The mechanism of thaumaturgy must always be rational, however ideal and supernatural may be the story. We resent the notion that a man or a woman can be turned into a wolf, unless he or she has shown wolf-like propensities. What had Lucy Westenra done that her pure soul should be contaminated? or Mina Harker, that she should be forced to drink Count Dracula's blood? Renfield we understand, because he was a madman; but if goodness can be turned into vice by a purely extraneous agency, the mystery of evil becomes too awful for us to contemplate. According to the older idea, this particular transformation was accomplished by Satanic agency, voluntarily submitted to because of an innate craving for human flesh. Macbeth could not have been tempted by the witches if he had not already conceived wicked schemes of ambition, nor could Faust have listened to the counsels of Mephistopheles if his own mind had not been infected with recrudescent passion. Such, at least, is our modern ethical principle, which we are loth to relinquish even in dealing with the sphere of transcendental mystery.

* * *

Review of *Dracula*

Glasgow Herald, 10 June 1897

It is an eerie and a gruesome tale which Mr Stoker tells, but it is much the best book he has written. The reader is held with a spell similar to that of Wilkie Collins's "Moonstone," and indeed in many ways the form of narrative by diaries and letters and extracts from newspapers neatly fitted into each other recalls Wilkie Collins's style. Mr Stoker's story begins in Transylvania, where a young English solicitor goes to take the instructions of Count Dracula as to an English estate which he has purchased. The solicitor's adventures in the remote castle at first are simply interesting; shortly they become horrible, for in the mysterious Dracula he finds one who is neither more nor less than a vampire, who dies daily and rises at night to gorge himself upon human bodies, who can creep up and down his outside walls like a lizard, and who has a hundred other fearful and blood-curdling peculiarities. When we have supped full of Transylvanian horrors, the author skilfully shifts the scene to England, where the appearance of Dracula, first in one locality and then in another, causes misery and terror to two or three households, which are exceedingly well imagined. Mr Stoker keeps his devilry well in hand, if such an expression is allowable; as strange event follows strange event, the narrative might in less skilful hands become intolerably improbable; but "Dracula" to the end seems only too reasonably and sanely possible. Henceforth we shall wreathe ourselves in garlic when opportunity offers, and firmly decline all invitations to visit out-of-the-way clients in castles in the South-East of Europe. "Dracula" is a first-rate book of adventure.

* * *

Review of *Dracula*

Manchester Guardian, 15 June 1897

A writer who attempts in the nineteenth century to rehabilitate the ancient legends of the were-wolf and the vampire has set himself a formidable task. Most of the delightful old superstitions of the past have an unhappy way of appearing limp and sickly in the glare of a later day, and in such a story as *Dracula,* by Bram Stoker (Archibald Constable and Co., 8vo, pp. 390, 6s.), the reader must reluctantly acknowledge that the region for horrors has shifted its ground. Man is no longer in dread of the monstrous and the unnatural, and although Mr. Stoker has tackled his gruesome subject with enthusiasm, the effect is more often grotesque than terrible. The Transylvanian site of Castle Dracula is skilfully chosen, and the picturesque region is well described. Count Dracula himself has been in his day a medieval noble, who, by reason of his "vampire" qualities, is unable to die properly, but from century to century resuscitates his life of the "Un-Dead," as the author terms it, by nightly draughts of blood from the throats of living victims, with the appalling consequence that those once so bitten must become vampires in their turn. The plot is too complicated for reproduction, but it says no little for the author's powers that in spite of its absurdities the reader can follow the story with interest to the end. It is, however, an artistic mistake to fill a whole volume with horrors. A touch of the mysterious, the terrible, or the supernatural is infinitely more effective and credible.

* * *

your book, meaning to cut it — & read after dinner — having some heavy revises to get through between 5.30 & 7 — I read & read till 7.15. Thank you greatly for the book, & its pretty inscription — We will talle of it more anon! when I have soberly read & meditated thereupon. I have done my humdrum little story of transfusion — in

June 23ᵈ 97

Dear Mr Stoker

You remember Sydney Smith's definition of a good novel! Well! I can honestly say that "Dracula" cut down my toilet-half-hour to a wish & a scramble of 15 minutes — I took up

First pages of Mary Elizabeth Braddon's letter to Bram Stoker thanking him for the gift of an inscribed copy of Dracula. *A popular practitioner of the novel of sensation, Braddon is chiefly remembered for* Lady Audley's Secret *(1862). At the bottom of the second page of the letter, Braddon refers to "my humdrum little story of transfusion"–a vampire tale, "Good Lady Ducayne," that she had published in 1896 (Brotherton Collection, Leeds University Library).*

In this negative assessment, the reviewer mistakenly labels the Dutchman Van Helsing as a German, an error made by more than one reviewer.

Review of *Dracula*
The Athenaeum, 26 June 1897

Stories and novels appear just now in plenty stamped with a more or less genuine air of belief in the visibility of supernatural agency. The strengthening of a bygone faith in the fantastic and magical view of things in lieu of the purely material is a feature of the hour, a reaction–artificial, perhaps, rather than natural–against late tendencies in thought. Mr. Stoker is the purveyor of so many strange wares that "Dracula" reads like a deter-mined effort to go, as it were, "one better" than others in the same field. How far the author is himself a believer in the phenomena described is not for the reviewer to say. He can but attempt to gauge how far the general faith in witches, warlocks, and vampires–supposing it to exist in any general and appreciable measure–is likely to be stimulated by this story. The vampire idea is very ancient indeed, and there are in nature, no doubt, mysterious powers to account for the vague belief in such beings. Mr. Stoker's way of presenting this matter, and still more the matter itself, are of too direct and uncompromising a kind. They lack the essential note of awful remoteness and at the same time subtle affinity that separates while it links our humanity with unknown beings and possibilities hovering on the confines of the known world. "Dracula" is highly sensational, but it is wanting in the constructive art as well as in the higher literary sense. It reads at times like a mere series of grotesquely incredible events; but there are better moments that show more power, though even these are never productive of the tremor such subjects evoke under the hand of a master. An immense amount of energy, a certain degree of imaginative faculty, and many ingenious and gruesome details are there. At times Mr. Stoker almost succeeds in creating the sense of possibility in impossibility; at others he merely commands an array of crude statements of incredible actions. The early part goes best, for it promises to unfold the roots of mystery and fear lying deep in human nature; but the want of skill and fancy grows more and more conspicuous. The people who band themselves together to run the vampire to earth have no real individuality or being. The German [_sic_] man of science is particularly poor, and indulges, like a German, in much weak sentiment. Still, Mr. Stoker has got together a number of "horrid details," and his object, assuming it to be ghastliness, is fairly well fulfilled. Isolated scenes and touches are probably quite uncanny enough to please those for whom they are designed.

* * *

This review was written under the Punch _pseudonym_ The Baron de Book-Worms.

Our Booking-Office

The Baron de B.-W.
Punch, 26 June 1897

"I wants to make your flesh creep," might Mr. BRAM STOKER well say as a preface to his latest book, named _Dracula,_ which he has given in charge of the CONSTABLES (& Co.) to publish. The story is told in diaries and journals, a rather tantalising and somewhat wearisome form of narration, whereof WILKIE COLLINS was a past-master. In almost all ghostly, as in most detective stories, one character must never be absent from the _dramatis personë_ and that is The Inquiring, Sceptical, Credulous Noodle. The Inquiring Noodle of Fiction must be what in comedy "CHARLES his friend" is to the principal comedian, "only more so," as representing the devoted, admiring slave of the philosophic astute hero, ever ready to question, ever ready to dispute, ever ready to make a mistake at the critical moment, or to go to sleep just when success depends on his remaining awake. "Friend JOHN" is Mr. BRAM STOKER's Noodle-in-Chief. There are also some secondary Noodles; Noodles of no importance. This weird tale is about Vampires, not a single, quiet, creeping Vampire, but a whole brood of them, governed by a Vampire Monarch, who is apparently a sort of first cousin to _Mephistopheles._

Rats, bats, wolves and vermin obey him, but his power, like that of a certain well-advertised soap, "which will _not_ wash clothes," has its limits; and so at last he is trapped, and this particular brood of vampires is destroyed as utterly as would be a hornets' nest when soused with hot pitch. It is a pity that Mr. BRAM STOKER was not content to employ such supernatural anti-vampire receipts as his wildest imagination might have invented without rashly venturing on a domain where angels fear to tread. But for this, the Baron could have unreservedly recommended so ingenious a romance to all who enjoy the very weirdest of weird tales.

* * *

The Trail of the Vampire

St. James' Gazette (London), 30 June 1897

There is no more fascinating theme for weird and mysterious fiction than that of the vampire or the were-wolf; and many admirable stories, among which the late Mr. Sheridan Le Fanu's "Carmilla" will always remain conspicuous, have been contrived about these mythical "creatures of the night." We doubt, however, whether any novelist has hitherto worked the mine so thoroughly as has Mr. Bram Stoker in this remarkable new story of his—"Dracula." Certainly we can recall no tale among those of recent date in which the possibilities of horror are more ingeniously drawn out. In the short story, of course, Mr. H. G. Wells can give Mr. Stoker points; but when we remember that "Dracula" fills some four hundred closely printed pages, through which horror follows horror with every wealth of accumulation, we have to confess that its author may fairly boast an achievement of a unique character. There are a hundred nightmares in "Dracula," and each is more uncanny than the last. Moreover, Mr. Stoker is fortunate in the skill with which he makes his imaginative impossibilities appear not only possible but convincing. In securing this end he has followed the method of Wilkie Collins, couching his tale in the form of diary and letter, and adding evidence to evidence with every circumstance of invoice, telegram, and legal document. The fact that this obliges him to represent his characters as writing their journals in the very moment of high emotional pressure may seem to the hypercritical to tax the reader's credulity too far; but, for ourselves, we are disposed to regard this little licence as abundantly justified by its results. Of the plot we have no intention of speaking in detail. Suffice it to say that a young lawyer's clerk is sent on a business errand to one Count Dracula in Transylvania, and that this Count is himself a prince among vampires. After experiencing the most hideous adventures, the young man escapes; but his tormentor follows him to England, tracks him out, and

---

Charlotte Stoker on *Dracula*

As Harry Ludlam notes in his biography of Stoker, the author's mother was enthusiastic and prophetic in her response to the novel.

'My dear,' she wrote from Ireland, 'it is splendid, a thousand miles beyond anything you have written before, and I feel certain will place you very high in the writers of the day—the story and style being deeply sensational, exciting and interesting.' And a few days later she added, 'I have seen a great review of "Dracula" in a London paper. They have not said one word too much of it. No book since Mrs Shelley's "Frankenstein" or indeed any other at all has come near yours in originality, or terror—Poe is nowhere. I have read much but I never met a book like it at all. In its terrible excitement it should make a widespread reputation and much money for you.'

—Harry Ludlam, *A Biography of Bram Stoker, Creator of Dracula* (London: New English Library, 1977), p. 122

---

works the death of an innocent and beautiful girl, whose spirit, by the law of the mystery, becomes a vampire in its turn, and is only laid by the intrepid courage of a very interesting German [*sic*] scientist. Gradually the circle of the vampire's influence is widened, and such homely spots as Whitby, Hampstead Heath, and Piccadilly become the scenes of midnight mysteries. Towards the close of the story, where the action quickens and strengthens in intensity, the narrative is remarkably exciting. Altogether "Dracula" is quite the best book Mr. Stoker has yet written, and does great credit alike to his imagination and to his descriptive power.

* * *

Review of *Dracula*
The Spectator, 31 July 1897

Mr. Bram Stoker gives us the impression—we may be doing him an injustice—of having deliberately laid himself out in *Dracula* to eclipse all previous efforts in the domain of the horrible,—to "go one better" than Wilkie Collins (whose method of narration he has closely followed), Sheridan Le Fanu, and all the other professors of the flesh-creeping school. Count Dracula, who gives his name to the book, is a Transylvanian noble who purchases an estate in England, and in connection with the transfer of the property Jonathan Harker, a young solicitor, visits him in his ancestral castle. Jonathan Harker has a terrible time of it, for the Count—who is a vampire of

immense age, cunning, and experience—keeps him as a prisoner for several weeks, and when the poor young man escapes from the gruesome charnel-house of his host, he nearly dies of brain-fever in a hospital at Buda-Pesth. The scene then shifts to England, where the Count arrives by sea in the shape of a dog-fiend, after destroying the entire crew, and resumes operations in various uncanny manifestations, selecting as his chief victim Miss Lucy Westenra, the fiancée of the Honourable Arthur Holmwood, heir-presumptive to Lord Godalming. The story then resolves itself into the history of the battle between Lucy's protectors, including two rejected suitors—an American and a "mad" doctor—and a wonderfully clever specialist from Amsterdam, against her unearthly persecutor. The clue is furnished by Jonathan Harker, whose betrothed, Mina Murray, is a bosom friend of Lucy's, and the fight is long and protracted. Lucy succumbs, and, worse still, is temporarily converted into a vampire. How she is released from this unpleasant position and restored to a peaceful post-mortem existence, how Mina is next assailed by the Count, how he is driven from England, and finally exterminated by the efforts of the league—for all these, and a great many more thrilling details, we must refer our readers to the pages of Mr. Stoker's clever but cadaverous romance. Its strength lies in the invention of incident, for the sentimental element is decidedly mawkish. Mr. Stoker has shown considerable ability in the use that he has made of all the available traditions of vampirology, but we think his story would have been all the more effective if he had chosen an earlier period. The up-to-dateness of the book—the phonograph diaries, typewriters, and so on—hardly fits in with the medieval methods which ultimately secure the victory for Count Dracula's foes.

* * *

Review of *Dracula*
The Observer (London), 1 August 1897

Those who are wishful for a veritable feast of horrors need seek no farther than the present work, for in it Mr. Stoker has been pleased to weave a romance of vampires and their habits. Not only is the subject gruesome, but the author's undoubted descriptive powers make the various ghastly experiences startlingly realistic, and engender a fascination which forces one to read on to the end. From start to finish the book, though long, is wildly exciting, and the account of the terrible midnight drive in the first chapter is one of a series of fierce struggles against the repulsive Count Dracula, which end only on the last page. The story is set forth in various diaries and letters, a style which is apt to prove somewhat confusing. It speaks well for the author's skill in this case that the plot is plainly traceable throughout. Notwithstanding the merits of the book, it is impossible to congratulate Mr. Stoker on his theme, which can but feel to be one quite unworthy of his literary capabilities.

* * *

Review of *Dracula*
Bookman, August 1897

Since Wilkie Collins left us we have had no tale of mystery so liberal in manner and so closely woven. But with the intricate plot, and the methods of the narrative, the resemblance to the stories of the author of "The Woman in White" ceases; for the audacity and horror of "Dracula" are Mr. Stoker's own. A summary of the book would shock and disgust; but we must own that, though here and there in the course of the tale we hurried over things with repulsion, we read nearly the whole thing with rapt attention. It is something of a triumph for the writer that neither the improbability, nor the unnecessary number of hideous incidents recounted of the man-vampire, are long foremost on the reader's mind, but that the interest of the danger, of the compli-

cations, of the pursuit of the villain, of human skill and courage pitted against inhuman wrong and superhuman strength, rises always to the top. Keep "Dracula" out of the way of nervous children, certainly; but a grown reader, unless he be of unserviceably delicate stuff, will both shudder and enjoy from p. 35 [39], when Harker sees the Count "emerge from the window and begin to crawl down the castle wall over that dreadful abyss, *face down,* with his cloak spreading out around him like great wings."

* * *

Dracula at the Beach

In "Chat About Books," the anonymously written column for the 6 August 1897 issue of Daily Mail, *the writer comments: "It is clear that holiday-makers prefer, on the whole, the merely entertaining novels rather than the didactic and the instructive." The reviewer then lists several books, including* Dracula, *by "authors at present most in vogue at the seaside" noting "a large demand."*

Sir Arthur Conan Doyle on *Dracula*

Stoker sent copies of his new novel to friends and acquaintances. This response by Sir Arthur Conan Doyle, dated 20 August 1897, is one of the few that have survived.

My dear Bram Stoker

I am sure that you will not think it an impertinence if I write to tell you how very much I have enjoyed reading *Dracula.* I think it is the very best story of diablerie which I have read for many years. It is really wonderful how with so much exciting interest over so long a book there is never an anticlimax. It holds you from the very start and grows more and more engrossing until it is quite painfully vivid. The old Professor is most excellent and so are the two girls. I congratulate you with all my heart for having written so fine a book.

With all kindest remembrances to Mrs Bram Stoker & yourself
    Yours very truly
    A Conan Doyle

  –Harry Ransom Humanities Research Center,
           University of Texas at Austin

Sir Arthur Conan Doyle, who became famous in the early 1890s for his Sherlock Holmes stories in The Strand *(David J. Skal,* Vampires: Encounters with the Undead, *2001; Elizabeth Miller Collection)*

Four Main Editions

As bibliographer Eighteen-Bisang explains, most subsequent editions of Stoker's novel are based on one of four editions: the 1897 Constable; the 1899 Doubleday, McClure; the abridged 1901 Constable; and the 1912 Rider.

Dracula is said to be the best-selling novel in the world. Bram Stoker's masterpiece has not been out of print since it was first published in 1897, and has been translated into dozens of languages. But *Dracula* is a bibliographer's nightmare. To begin with, there is an extensive pre-textual state that includes Bram Stoker's Notes and Papers, a copy of his manuscript, a play, and preliminary material that was excised before publication, some of which rose from the grave as "Dracula's Guest" (1914).

There are three important variations of the original text. The first American edition not only corrected some typographic errors, but included a phrase that does not appear in the original version. After Dracula thwarts the attack of his "Brides" on Jonathan Harker in Chapter Four, he warns them "To-night is mine. To-morrow night is yours!" This phrase, which appears on page 51 of the Doubleday and McClure text, was omitted from the first edition, which says: "To-morrow night, to-morrow night, is yours!" Possibly the suggestion of a homosexual relationship would have been excised by the original editor following the sensational trial of Oscar Wilde. William Rider and Son took over the British rights to Stoker's opus in 1911. Their edition, which made other editorial corrections, sold over a million copies by 1925. This version serves as the source for most British reprints. In 1901, Constable published an abridged, paperback version. Although this text was the basis for several translations of *Dracula*—such as early French and Italian editions—few copies have survived the ravages of time. In fact, most collectors were not aware of its existence until it was reprinted by Transylvania Press in 1994.

The source of most subsequent editions of *Dracula* can be determined by examining the first line of text:

Constable (1897): "3 *May. Bistritz.*–Left Munich at 8.35 p.m. on I[st] May . . . "

Doubleday (1899): "3 *May. Bistritz.*–Left Munich at 8:35 P.M., on I[st] May . . . "

Rider (1912): "3 *May. Bistritz.*–Left Munich at 8.35 P.M. on I[st] May . . . "

While basing their editions on one of these four major texts, editors of subsequent editions have sometimes corrected errors in spelling, grammar, and some of the erroneous dates that occur in letters and other communications in a catch-as-catch-can manner. After *Dracula* entered the public domain in 1962, editors have revised parts of the text that they deemed too violent or erotic. *Dracula* has also been entirely re-written for juvenile audiences. Stoker's creation has also inspired plays, movies, and comic books. What is more, the Count functions as the centrepiece of a diverse industry that revolves around myths about monsters that have returned from the grave. Almost everyone is familiar with the name "Dracula." Even children are aware that he is a "vampire" who is associated with "Transylvania." The extent to which the Count has captured our imaginations is reflected in the dust jackets and covers of more than five hundred editions.

–Robert Eighteen-Bisang

Recent Novels

The Times (London), 23 August 1897

Dracula cannot be described as a domestic novel, nor its annals as those of a quiet life. The circumstances described are from the first peculiar. A young solicitor sent for on business by a client in Transylvania goes through some unusual experiences. He finds himself shut up in a half ruined castle with a host who is only seen at night and three beautiful females who have the misfortune to be vampires. Their intentions, which can hardly be described as honourable, are to suck his blood, in order to sustain their own vitality. Count Dracula (the host) is also a vampire, but has grown tired of his compatriots, however young and beautiful, and has a great desire for what may literally be called fresh blood. He has therefore sent for the solicitor that through his means he may be introduced to London society. Without understanding the Count's views, Mr. Harker has good reason for having suspicions of his client. Wolves come at his command, and also fogs; he is also too clever by half at climbing.

Dracula in Translation

Dracula *has been translated into every major foreign language, including Chinese, Czech, Danish, Dutch, Estonian, Finnish, Flemish, French, Gaelic, German, Greek, Hebrew, Hungarian, Icelandic, Indonesian, Italian, Japanese, Korean, Lithuanian, Malaysian, Norwegian, Polish, Portuguese, Romanian, Russian, Spanish, Swedish, Ukrainian. For a detailed list of foreign editions, see J. Gordon Melton, "All Things Dracula," online at <www.cesnur.org/dracula_library.htm>.*

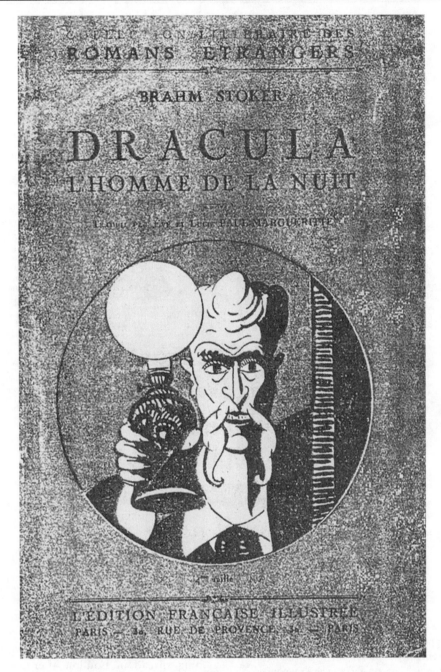

Front wrapper for the first French translation of Dracula. *Published in 1920, this edition was the first translation of the novel published after Stoker's death (courtesy of David J. Skal).*

There is a splendid prospect from the castle terrace, which Mr. Harker would have enjoyed but for his conviction that he would never leave the place alive:—

In the soft moonlight the distant hills became melted, and the shadows in the valleys and gorges of velvety blackness. The mere beauty seemed to cheer me; there was peace and comfort in every breath I drew. As I leaned from the window my eye was caught by something moving a storey below me, and somewhat to my left, where I imagined, from the lie of the rooms, that the windows of the Count's own room would look out. The window at which I stood was tall and deep, stone-mullioned, and, though weather-worn, was still complete, but it was evidently many a day since the casement had been there. I drew back behind the stonework and looked carefully out.

DRACULA

CAIBIDIL I

IRISLEABHAR SHEOIN ARCUR

(*Ón ngearrscríbhinn bhunaidh*)

3 *Beultaine, Bistritz.*—D'fhágas Munich ar 8.35 p.m. lá Beultaine, agus rángas Vienna i moiche maidne iarna bháireach ; ar 6.46 bhí an traen le bheith ann, acht bhí sí uair a chluig deidheanach. Cathair iongntach í Budapesth, a bhfaca ón dtraen di agus im scríb siubhail feadh na sráideanna. Níor mhuinghin liom dul ró fhada ón stáisiún, mar ná raibh an traen istigh in am agus go gcaithfeadh sí bogadh arís mar bhí beartuighthe dí. Ba mhalartú Iarthair ar Oirthear liom-sa é ; bhíomar imeasc iarsma smachta na dTurcach iar ndul dúinn thar an droichead is iartharaighe de dhroicheadaibh daingne na Donnabha, atá go leathan doimhin san áit sin.

Bhogamar in am is i dtráth, go rángamar Clausenburg le crónú na hoidhche. Chaitheas an oidhche ann ag an Hotel Royale. Leagadh romham chum dinnéir, nó suipéir ba chóra a rádh, sicín d'ullmhuigheadh ar chuma éigin le piobar dearg. Bhí sé go blasta bíodhgach bídheamhail acht bhí adhbhar íota go dóighte ann. (Caithfead fuirmle a fhulachta do sholáthar do Mhina). Chuireas a thuairisc ar an dáileamh agus dubhairt sé gur " paprika hendl " a thugtar air agus go mb'fhuiris dam a fhághail in aon áit i gcomhgar na gCarpátach, mar gur mhias náisiúnta é. Dá luighead den Ghearmáinis agam, bhaineas feidhm as san áit sin, agus is baoghal liom go mbeinn i bponc in a eughmais.

7

Dust jacket and first page of the Gaelic edition of the novel, published in 1933 (dust jacket courtesy of Ronald V. Borst/ Hollywood Movie Posters; text page courtesy of Robert Eighteen-Bisang)

What I saw was the Count's head coming out from the window. I did not see the face, but I knew the man by the neck and the movement of his back and arms. In any case, I could not mistake the hands, which I had had so many opportunities of studying. I was at first interested and somewhat amused, for it is wonderful how small a matter will interest and amuse a man when he is a prisoner. But my very feelings changed to repulsion and terror when I saw the whole man slowly emerge from the window and begin to crawl down the castle wall over that dreadful abyss, face down, with his cloak spreading out around him like great wings.

These scenes and situations, striking as they are, become commonplace compared with Count Dracula's goings on in London. As Falstaff was not only witty himself but the cause of wit in other people, so a vampire, it seems, compels those it has bitten (two little marks on the throat are its token, usually taken by the faculty for the scratches of a brooch) to become after death vampires also. Nothing can keep them away but garlic, which is, perhaps, why that comestible is so popular in certain countries. One may imagine, therefore, how the thing spread in London after the Count's arrival. The only chance of stopping it was to kill the Count before any of his victims died, and this was a difficult job, for, though several centuries old, he was very young and strong, and could become a dog or a bat at pleasure. However, it is undertaken by four resolute and highly-principled persons, and how it is managed forms the subject of the story, of which nobody can complain that it is deficient in dramatic situations. We would not, however, recommend it to nervous persons for evening reading.

Erstes Kapitel

Jonathan Harkers Tagebuch
(In Kurzschrift verfaßt)

3. Mai. Bistritz. Abfahrt von München am 1. Mai um 8.35 Uhr, Ankunft in Wien früh am nächsten Morgen; wir hätten um 6.46 Uhr eintreffen sollen, doch der Zug hatte eine Stunde Verspätung. Budapest ist anscheinend eine herrliche Stadt, nach dem flüchtigen Eindruck zu urteilen, den ich vom Zug aus und nach einem kurzen Gang durch die Straßen gewinnen konnte. Ich wagte nicht, mich allzuweit vom Bahnhof zu entfernen, da wir verspätet eingetroffen waren und so pünktlich wie möglich aufbrechen wollten. Ich hatte den Eindruck, den Westen zu verlassen und in den Osten zu kommen; die westlichste der prächtigen Brücken über die Donau, die hier von erhabener Breite und Tiefe ist, führte uns mitten in die Überlieferungen der türkischen Herrschaft.

Wir brachen recht pünktlich auf und trafen nach Einbruch der Dunkelheit in Klausenburg ein. Hier stieg ich für die Nacht im Hotel Royal ab. Zum Abendessen oder vielmehr zum Nachtessen gab es ein Hähnchen, das mit einer Art rotem Pfeffer zubereitet war; es war sehr gut, machte aber durstig. (*Nicht vergessen:* Mina Rezept mitbringen.) Ich fragte den Kellner, und er sagte mir, daß man es »Paprikahendl« nenne, und da es sich um ein Nationalgericht handele, könne ich es wohl überall in den Karpaten bekommen. Ich habe festgestellt, daß meine wenigen Brocken Deutsch mir hier sehr zustatten kommen; ich weiß wirklich nicht, wie ich ohne sie zurechtkommen sollte.

Da mir in London ein wenig Zeit geblieben war, hatte ich das Britische Museum besucht und Bücher und Landkarten der Bibliothek über Transsilvanien durchforstet; es war mir in den Sinn gekommen, daß gewisse Vorkenntnisse des Landes im Umgang mit einem ortsansässigen Adeligen mir durchaus von Nutzen sein könnten. Wie ich festgestellt habe, liegt der Distrikt, den er mir genannt hat, im äußersten Osten des Lan-

Opening page of the 1994 German edition of Dracula, *translated by Ulrike Bischoff. The novel was first translated into German in 1908, the second and last foreign edition of the work published during Stoker's lifetime (Elizabeth Miller Collection).*

Capitolul I

Jurnalul lui Jonathan Harker
(stenografiat)

3 mai. Bistriţa. Părăsit Münchenul la 8,35 seara, 1 mai. Sosit devreme la Viena, a doua zi dimineaţa. Ar fi trebuit să sosim la orele 6,46, dar trenul a avut o oră întîrziere. Budapesta pare un oraş minunat, după cîte mi-am putut arunca ochii din vagon şi după cele cîteva străzi pe care m-am plimbat, odată coborît din tren, însă mi-a fost teamă să mă depărtez prea mult de gară: în ciuda întîrzierii, trebuia să plecăm mai departe, după cum se prevăzuse. M-a încercat senzaţia că părăseam Occidentul spre a intra în Orient; Occidentul cel mai autentic, cu splendidele poduri peste Dunăre, care aici are cea mai nobilă lărgime şi adîncime, ne purta către tradiţiile dominaţiei turceşti.

Am părăsit Budapesta la timpul potrivit şi am ajuns la Klausenburg după căderea serii. M-am oprit aici ca să petrec noaptea la Hotel Royal. La masă, sau mai degrabă la cină, mi s-a servit pui fript cu boia-de ardei roşu, foarte bun, dar mi-a dat o sete! (*Mem.* Să cer reţeta pentru Mina!) L-am întrebat pe ospătar şi acesta mi-a spus că felul se numeşte „paprika hendl", şi că e o mîncare pe care am s-o găsesc pretutindeni de-a lungul Carpaţilor. De mare folos mi-a fost spoiala mea de germană; într-adevăr, nici nu ştiu cum m-aş fi descurcat fără ea.

La Londra, dispunînd de oarecare timp liber, vizitasem

First page of the 1993 Romanian edition of Dracula, *translated by Barbu Cioculescu and Ileana Verzea. Stoker's novel was banned in Romania during the Communist era (Elizabeth Miller Collection).*

American Reviews

Bram Stoker's Story
Detroit Free Press, 18 November 1899

It is almost inconceivable that Bram Stoker wrote "Dracula." Still, he must have done it. There is his name on the title page, and before the tale was bound up and offered us between covers it ran its length in various newspapers, and under the same name of authorship.

So there is no getting around it. Bram Stoker did write it.

Think of the story. It is a tale of ghouls, vampires and human imps all in direct communication with Satan. There are lunatics and idiots in it who feed flies to spiders, spiders to sparrows, and then, in lieu of a cat, devour the sparrows themselves. A weird count—the Dracula from whom the book is named—lies in a castle high among the Carpathians and weaves webs for ordinary folk—casts spells over pretty girls, and draws the strings tighter and tighter until they die—the girls, that is. An amazing man—Dracula. To achieve his fiendish ends he assumes many and divers forms. Now he is a spirit, visible but untangible, with two sharp front teeth and red eyes. Again, he is a dog, then a bat, in turn, a wolf at last. As a bat he goes about biting people in the neck. Of course they die. A Dutch specialist in physiological psychology sets out to solve the mystery of the strange deaths. In the end Dracula is worsted. His head is cut off and a stake is driven through his heart. There's an outline of the tale—such is what you may hope to find between the covers.

And it is a splendid story, too; done in a manner most convincing—by letters, diaries, and medical observations.

And Bram Stoker wrote it!

Think of him.

He—a great, shambling, good-natured, overgrown boy—although he is the business manager of Henry Irving and the Lyceum Theater—with a red beard, untrimmed, and a ruddy complexion, tempered somewhat by the wide-open, full blue eyes that gaze so frankly into yours! Why, it is hard enough to imagine Bram Stoker a business man, to say nothing of his possessing an imagination capable of projecting Dracula upon paper.

But he has done it. And he has done it well.

If you enjoy the weird, if you care for spinal titilations, "Dracula" is unstintingly recommended.

* * *

The following two reviews in San Francisco newspapers show the extreme responses Dracula engendered. Even the reviewer for The Wave, however, recognized the power of the novel to fascinate the reader.

The Insanity of the Horrible
The Wave, 9 December 1899

When an Englishman, or, for that matter, anyone of Anglo-Saxon blood, goes into degenerate literature of his own sort, he reveals a horrible kind of degeneracy. The works of the French degenerates possess a *verve,* a Gaelic attractiveness, indefinable but yet definite, the same subtle quality which, in another line, makes every Frenchwoman, young or old, attractive with a charm that pertains to the soul and not to the body or the mind. Now it goes without saying that the Anglo-Saxon has no such quality. When he becomes degenerate, it is degeneracy of a terrible sort—coarse, brutal, unlovely, its only attraction the fascination of

Cover for the first American edition, published in New York by Doubleday, McClure in 1899. A more attractive edition than that published by Constable, the American edition had fewer typographical errors. Forrest J. Ackerman owns a copy of this edition autographed by Bram Stoker, Bela Lugosi, and others (courtesy of Robert Eighteen-Bisang).

*Cover for the 1902 edition published in New York
by Doubleday, Page in a red binding
(courtesy of Robert Eighteen-Bisang)*

murder, one suicide, one lunatic with homicidal mania and a habit of eating flies, one somnambulist, one shipwreck, extent of fatalities not fully reported, one death by hysterical fright. Pleasant, isn't it? Well, these are only a sort of foretaste of incidents which I, being of a tender conscience, will forbear to harness on the imaginations of others.

There are two reasons of extended mention of this literary failure. The first is that the main cause of the failure shows so prominently as to furnish a beautiful object-lesson. This fault is the lack of artistic restraint. Stevenson, the century's greatest artist in fiction, happens to have used in two instances a theme like this one–in *Dr. Jekyll and Mr. Hyde*, and on the powerful short story *Oliala*. And anyone who wishes the lesson should put these two masterpieces, where the horror is suggested, hinted at, written around except for the one moment of the climax when it is brought home with an added force derived from the very fact that it has been hidden so long against this systematic piling-up of all the unwholesome and unpleasant things in the world. The other thing which makes the book worthy of notice is the fact that, in spite of it all, it holds to the end. It is true that the fascination is the same as that which would be possessed by a dissecting room, but it is there nevertheless.

If you have the bad taste, after this warning, to attempt the book, you will read on to the finish, as I did,– and go to bed, as I did, feeling furtively of your throat.

* * *

New Novels and Holiday Books
San Francisco Chronicle, 17 December 1899

One of the most powerful novels of the day and one set apart by its originality of plot and treatment is "Dracula," by Bram Stoker. The author is well known in the dramatic world for his long connection with Sir Henry Irving as manager. Several years ago he wrote a weird story of Irish life, but this is his first long romance. It is a somber study of a human vampire, the Count Dracula, who uses beautiful women as his agents and compasses the death of many innocent people. Theophile Gautier essayed the same subject, but his vampire, who was priest by day and ravening wolf by night, was not half so terrible as this malignant Count with the three beautiful female devils who do his bidding. Nothing in fiction is more powerful than the scene at the killing of the vampire in Lucy's tomb or that other fearful scene at the extinction of the malign power of the Count. The story is told in such a realistic way that one actually accepts its wildest flights of fancy as real facts. It is a superb tour de force which stamps itself on the memory.

horror. The difference is that between Whitechapel and the Moulin Rouge. I make no doubt that the existence of a Moulin Rouge in its midst is a greater menace to a people than the existence of a Whitechapel, but between the relative attractiveness of the two there is and can be no comparison at all. Swift and Hogarth are two very horrible examples of the Anglo-Saxon method of treating those things which our modern conventionalities decree shall be hidden.

Dracula, by an Englishman who calls himself "Bram Stoker," is an awful example. Here is a man who has taken the most horrible theme he could find in ancient or modern literature, the tradition regarding ghouls, or vampires, the beings, neither living nor dead, who creep in by night to suck the blood and damn the souls of their victims. He has then gone on to carry the thing out to all possible lengths. The plain horror were enough, perhaps, but the author goes farther, and adds insane asylums, dissecting rooms and unnatural appetites galore. No detail is too nauseating. In the first seventy pages, there are four cases of deaths caused by the preying of human vampires, one

Stoker on *Dracula*

Stoker's only substantial comments about Dracula *are found in his letter to former British prime minister William Gladstone, an interview with a local newspaper, and a preface to an Icelandic edition.*

The leader of the Liberal party, William Gladstone served as prime minister of Britain in 1868–1874, 1880–1886 and 1892–1894. He was a frequent guest of Irving's at the Beefsteak Room and liked to talk Irish politics with Stoker.

Bram Stoker to William Gladstone, 24 May 1897

My dear Gladstone,

May I do myself the pleasure of sending you a copy of my new novel *Dracula* which comes out on 26th. Perhaps at your leisure you may honour me by reading it. It is a story of a vampire—the old mediaeval vampire but recrudescent today. It has I think pretty well all the vampire legend as to limitations and these may in some way interest you who have made as bold a guess at "immortaliability". The book is necessarily full of horrors and terrors but I trust that these are calculated to "cleanse the mind by pity & terror." At any rate there is nothing base in the book and though superstition is brought in with the weapons of superstition I hope it is not irreverent. You will I know pardon my adding to the labour of your life by even the reading of one more letter. My regard for you and your work through all my thinking life has been such that I deem it a high privilege to be able to address you in the first person and to be able to put before you a book of my own, though it be only an atom in the intellectual kingdom where you have as long held sway.

Believe me

Your very sincere and respectful friend

Bram Stoker

—*Revue roumaine d'histoire*, 31 (1992): 175–178

* * *

William Gladstone, prime minister of Britain during the 1880s and 1890s. Stoker sent him a copy of Dracula *and a letter in which he claims the intent of the novel is to "cleanse the mind" (Barbara Belford,* Bram Stoker: A Biography of the Author of *Dracula, 1996; Elizabeth Miller Collection).*

First page of Bram Stoker's 24 May 1897 letter to William Gladstone (Manuscript 44525, 221-22, British Library)

The most extensive comments that Stoker made on Dracula *were recorded in a review and interview article that was published in* British Weekly *by "Lorna," the pseudonym for Jane Stoddard. Near the end of the article the interviewer asks Stoker about Queen Victoria's Diamond Jubilee, the celebration of the sixtieth anniversary of her accession to the throne.*

Mr. Bram Stoker. A Chat with the Author of *Dracula*
Jane Stoddard

One of the most interesting and exciting of recent novels is Mr. Bram Stoker's "Dracula." It deals with the ancient mediæval vampire legend, and in no English work of fiction has this legend been so brilliantly treated.

The scene is laid partly in Transylvania and partly in England. The first fifty-four pages, which give the Journal of Jonathan Harker after leaving Vienna until he makes up his mind to escape from Castle Dracula, are in their weird power altogether unrivalled in recent fiction. The only book which to my knowledge at all compares with them is "The Waters of Hercules," by E.D. Gerard, which also treats of a wild and little known portion of Eastern Europe. Without revealing the plot of the story, I may say that Jonathan Harker, whose diary first introduces the vampire Count, is a young solicitor sent by his employer to Castle Dracula to arrange for the purchase of a house and estate in England.

From the first day of his starting, signs and wonders follow him. At the "Golden Krone" at Bistritz the landlady warns him not to go to Castle Dracula, and, finding that his purpose is unalterable, places a rosary with a crucifix round his neck. For this gift he has good cause to be grateful afterwards. Harker's fellow-passengers on the stage-coach grow more and more alarmed about his safety as they come nearer to the dominions of the Count. Kindly gifts are pressed upon him: wild rose, garlic, and mountain ash. These are meant to be a protection against the evil eye. The author seems to know every corner of Transylvania and all its superstitions. Presently in the Borgo Pass a carriage with four horses drives up beside the coach. "The horses were driven by a tall man with a long brown beard, and a great black hat which seemed to hide his face from us. I could only see the gleam of a pair of very bright eyes, which seemed red in the lamplight as he turned to us. . . . As he spoke he smiled, and the lamplight fell on a hard-looking mouth, with very red lips and sharp-looking teeth as white as ivory. One of my companions whispered the line from Burger's 'Lenore': 'Denn die Todten reiten schnell' ('For the dead travel fast')."

This is the famous king vampire, Count Dracula, in ancient times a warlike Transylvanian noble. Jonathan Harker is conscious from the first that he is among ghostly and terrible surroundings. Even on the night journey to the Castle, wolves which have gathered round the carriage disappear when the terrible driver lifts his hand. On his arrival the guest is left waiting, and presently a tall old man, whom he suspects from the beginning to be none other than the driver himself, bids him welcome to his house. The Count never eats with his guest. During the day he is absent, but during the night he converses, the dawn breaking up the interview. There are no mirrors to be seen in any part of the ancient building, and the young solicitor's fears are confirmed by the fact that one morning, when the Count comes unexpectedly to his bedroom and stands looking over his shoulder, there is no reflection of him in the small shaving glass Harker has brought from London, and which covers the whole room behind. The adventures of Jonathan Harker will be read again and again; the most powerful part of the book after this is the description of the voyage of the *Demeter* from Varna to Whitby. A supernatural terror haunts the crew from the moment that they leave the Dardanelles, and as time goes on one man after another disappears. It is whispered that at night a man, tall, thin, and ghastly pale, is seen moving about the ship. The mate, a Roumanian, who probably knows the vampire legend, searches during the day in a number of old boxes, and in one he finds Count Dracula asleep. His own suicide and the death of the captain follow, and when the ship arrives at Whitby, the vampire escapes in the form of a huge dog. The strange thing is that,

although in some respects this is a gruesome book, it leaves on the mind an entirely wholesome impression. The events which happen are so far removed from ordinary experience that they do not haunt the imagination unpleasantly. It is certain that no other writer of our day could have produced so marvellous a book.

On Monday morning I had the pleasure of a short conversation with Mr. Bram Stoker, who, as most people know, is Sir Henry Irving's manager at the Lyceum Theatre. He told me, in reply to a question, that the plot of the story had been a long time in his mind, and that he spent about three years in writing it. He had always been interested in the vampire legend. "It is undoubtedly," he remarked, "a very fascinating theme, since it touches both on mystery and fact. In the Middle Ages the terror of the vampire depopulated whole villages."

"Is there any historical basis for the legend?"

"It rested, I imagine, on some such case as this. A person may have fallen into a death-like trance and been buried before the time. Afterwards the body may have been dug up and found alive, and from this a horror seized upon the people, and in their ignorance they imagined that a vampire was about. The more hysterical, through excess of fear, might themselves fall into trances in the same way; and so the story grew that one vampire might enslave many others and make them like himself. Even in the single villages it was believed that there might be many such creatures. When once the panic seized the population, their only thought was to escape."

"In what parts of Europe has this belief been most prevalent?"

"In certain parts of Styria it has survived longest and with most intensity, but the legend is common to many countries, to China, Iceland, Germany, Saxony, Turkey, the Chersonese, Russia, Poland, Italy, France, and England, besides all the Tartar communities."

"In order to understand the legend, I suppose it would be necessary to consult many authorities?"

Mr. Stoker told me that the knowledge of vampire superstitions shown in "Dracula" was gathered from a great deal of miscellaneous reading.

"No one book that I know of will give you all the facts. I learned a good deal from E. Gerard's 'Essays on Roumanian Superstitions,' [sic] which first appeared in the *Nineteenth Century,* and were afterwards published in a couple of volumes. I also learned something from Mr. Baring-Gould's 'Were-wolves.' Mr. Gould has promised a book on vampires, but I do not know whether he has made any progress with it."

Readers of "Dracula" will remember that the most famous character in it is Dr. van Helsing, the Dutch physician, who, by extraordinary skill, self-devotion, and

Cartoon of Stoker, wearing an "HMS Dracula" cap, with Pamela Colman Smith (far left), the artist, and Edith Craig,
the daughter of the Lyceum's leading lady, Ellen Terry, drawn on shipboard during the Lyceum's 1899 tour
(Ellen Terry Memorial Museum)

labour, finally outwits and destroys the vampire. Mr. Stoker told me that van Helsing is founded on a real character. In a recent leader on "Dracula," published in a provincial newspaper, it is suggested that high moral lessons might be gathered from the book. I asked Mr. Stoker whether he had written with a purpose, but on this point he would give no definite answer. "I suppose that every book of the kind must contain some lesson," he remarked; "but I prefer that readers should find it out for themselves."

In reply to further questions, Mr. Stoker said that he was born in Dublin, and that his work had lain for thirteen years in the Civil Service. He is an M.A. of Trinity College, Dublin. His brother-in-law is Mr. Frankfort Moore, one of the most popular young writers of the day. He began his literary work early. The first thing he published was a book on "The Duties of Clerks of Petty Sessions." Next came a series of chil-

dren's stories, "Under the Sunset," published by Sampson Low. Then followed the book by which he has hitherto been best known, "The Snake's Pass." Messrs. Constable have published in their "Acme" library a fascinating little volume called "The Watter's Mou," and this, with "The Shoulder of Shasta," completes Mr. Stoker's list of novels. He has been in London for some nineteen years, and believes that London is the best possible place for a literary man. "A writer will find a chance here if he is good for anything; and recognition is only a matter of time." Mr. Stoker speaks of the generosity shown by literary men to one another in a tone which shows that he, at least, is not disposed to quarrel with the critics.

Mr. Stoker does not find it necessary to publish through a literary agent. It always seems to him, he says, that an author with an ordinary business capacity can do better for himself than through any agent.

"Some men now-a-days are making ten thousand a year by their novels, and it seems hardly fair that they should pay ten or five per cent. of this great sum to a middleman. By a dozen letters or so in the course of the year they could settle all their literary business on their own account." Though Mr. Stoker did not say so, I am inclined to think that the literary agent is to him a nineteenth century vampire.

No interview during this week would be complete without a reference to the Jubilee, so I asked Mr. Stoker, as a Londoner of nearly twenty years' standing, what he thought of the celebrations. "Everyone," he said, "has been proud that the great day went off so successfully. We have had a magnificent survey of the Empire, and last week's procession brought home, as nothing else could have done, the sense of the immense variety of the Queen's dominions."

–*British Weekly,* 1 July 1897, p. 185

* * *

The first foreign-language edition of Dracula *was published in 1901 in Iceland as* Makt Myrkranna *(Powers of Darkness). An abridgment of the original novel, the volume includes the only preface that Stoker ever wrote for his novel. The English version of the preface was first published in* A Bram Stoker Omnibus *(1986).*

Author's Preface to the Icelandic Edition of *Dracula*

The reader of this story will very soon understand how the events outlined in these pages have been gradually drawn together to make a logical whole. Apart from excising minor details which I considered unnecessary, I have let the people involved relate their experiences in their own way; but, for obvious reasons, I have changed the names of the people and places concerned. In all other respects I leave the manuscript unaltered, in deference to the wishes of those who have considered it their duty to present it before the eyes of the public.

I am quite convinced that there is no doubt whatever that the events here described really took place, however unbelievable and incomprehensible they might appear at first sight. And I am further convinced that they must always remain to some extent incomprehensible, although continuing research in psychology and natural sciences may, in years to come, give logical explanations of such strange happenings which, at present, neither scientists nor the secret police can understand. I state again that this mysterious tragedy which is here described is completely true in all its external respects, though naturally I have reached a dif-

MAKT MYRKRANNA.

EFTIR

BRAM STOKER.

ÞÝTT HEFIR

VALDIMAR ÁSMUNDSSON.

ÚTGEFENDUR:

NOKKRIR PRENTARAR.

REYKJAVÍK.

PRENTUÐ Í FÉLAGSPRENTSMIÐJUNNI.

1901.

Title page for the abridged Icelandic edition of Dracula
(courtesy of Richard Dalby)

ferent conclusion on certain points than those involved in the story. But the events are incontrovertible, and so many people know of them that they cannot be denied. This series of crimes has not yet passed from the memory—a series of crimes which appear to have originated from the same source, and which at the time created as much repugnance in people everywhere as the notorious murders of Jack the Ripper, which came into the story a little later. Various people's minds will go back to the remarkable group of foreigners who for many seasons together played a dazzling part in the life of the aristocracy here in London; and some will remember that one of them disappeared suddenly without apparent reason, leaving no trace. All the people who have willingly–or unwillingly–played a part in this remarkable story are known generally and well respected. Both Jonathan Harker and his wife (who is a woman of character) and Dr. Seward are my friends and have been so for many years, and I have never doubted that they were telling the truth; and the highly respected scientist, who appears here under a pseudonym, will also be too famous all over the educated world for his real name, which I have not desired to specify, to be hidden from people–least of all those who have from experience learnt to value and respect his genius and accomplishments, though they adhere to his views on life no more than I. But in our times it ought to be clear to all serious-thinking men that

> "there are more things in heaven and earth
> than are dreamt of in your philosophy."

London, --- Street,
August 1898
B.S.

–*Bram Stoker Society Journal,* 5 (1993): 7–8

* * *

The Icelandic Edition of *Dracula*
Elizabeth Miller

The Icelandic text is divided into two parts of unequal length: Part I (pp. 5–167) corresponds to the first four chapters (Harker at Dracula's castle) in the British edition, and is fairly complete and intact. Part II (pp. 168–210) is a brief précis of the original chapters 5 to 27 (pp. 55–390 in the 1897 British edition).

What is significant about this book is that the publisher requested and included a special foreword from Stoker. This invaluable piece appears in no other edition, not even in Stoker's own abridgment of the novel that was published by Constable in 1901. That Stoker attached his name to this preface suggests that it was his intention to present a direct authorial statement.

He goes to great lengths to assure readers that "the events here described really took place," while at the same time he curiously distances himself as having "reached a different conclusion on certain points than those involved in the story." This approach, of course, is a common form of posturing for writers of supernatural fiction: the author both assists the reader in the willing suspension of disbelief and blurs the boundary between the worlds of fiction and reality.

Formáli höfundarins.

Lesarinn getur sjálfur séð, þegar hann les sögu þessa, hvernig þessum blöðum hefir verið raðað saman, svo að þau yrðu að einni heild. Eg hefi ekki þurft að gera annað en að draga úr þeim ýms óþörf smáatvik og láta svo söguafólkið sjálft skýra frá reynslu sinni i þeim sama einfalda búningi, sem blöðin upphaflega eru skrifuð i. Eg hefi, af augljósum ástæðum, breytt nöfnum manna og staða. En að öðru leyti skila eg handritinu óbreyttu, samkvæmt ósk þeirra, sem hafa álitið það stranga skyldu sína, að koma þvi fyrir almenningssjónir.

Eftir minni sannfæringu er það ekkert efamál, að þeir viðburðir, sem hér er lýst, hafi sannarlega átt sér stað, hversu ótrúlegir og óskiljanlegir sem þeir kunna að sýnast, skoðaðir eftir almennri reynslu. Og eg er sannfærður um, að þeir hljóta jafnan að verða að nokkru leyti óskiljanlegir, þó ekki sé óhugsandi, að áframhaldandi rannsóknir i sálfræðinni og náttúrufræðinni geti þegar minst varir skýrt bæði þessa og aðra leyndardóma, sem hvorki visindamenn né njósnarlögreglan hafa enn þá getað skilið. Eg tek það enn á ný fram, að þessi dularfulli sorgarleikur, sem hér er lýst, er fullkomlega sannur að þvi er alla ytri viðburði snertir, þó eg eðlilega hafi komist að annari niðurstöðu i ýmsum greinum en sögufólkið. En viðburðirnir eru ómótmælanlegir, og svo margir þekkja þá, að þeim verður ekki neitað. Þessi röð af glæpum er mönnum ekki úr minni liðin, röð af glæpum, sem virðast óskiljanlegir, en út leit fyrir að væru af sömu rót runnir, sem á sinum tima slógu jafnmiklum óhug á almenning som hin alræmdu morð Jakobs kviðristara, sem komu litlu seinna til sögunnar. Ýmsa mun reka minni til hinna merkilegu útlendinga, sem misserum saman tóku glæsilegan þátt i lifi tignarfólksins hér i Lundúnum, og menn muna eftir þvi, að annar þeirra að minsta kosti hvarf skyndilega og á óskiljanlegan hátt, án þess nokkur merki hans sæist framar.— Alt það fólk, sem sagt er að viljandi eða óviljandi hafi tekið þátt i þessari merkilegu sögu, er alþekt og vel metið. Bæði Tómas Harker og konan hans, sem er valkvendi, og dr. Seward eru vinir minir og hafa verið i mörg ár, og eg hefi aldrei efað, að þau segðu satt frá; og hinn mikilsmetni visindamaður, sem kemur hér fram með dularnafni, mun lika vera of frægur um allan hinn mentaða heim til þess að mönnum dyljist hið rétta nafn hans, sem eg hefi ekki viljað nefna, sizt þeim, sem af reynslu hafa lært að meta og virða snild hans og mannkosti, þótt þeir ekki fremur en eg fylgi lifsskoðunum hans. En á vorum dögum ætti það að vera ljóst öllum alvarlega hugsandi mönnum, að

„harðla margt er á himni og jörðu,
sem heimspekina dreymir ei um".

Lundúnum, —stræti, ágúst 1898.

B. S.

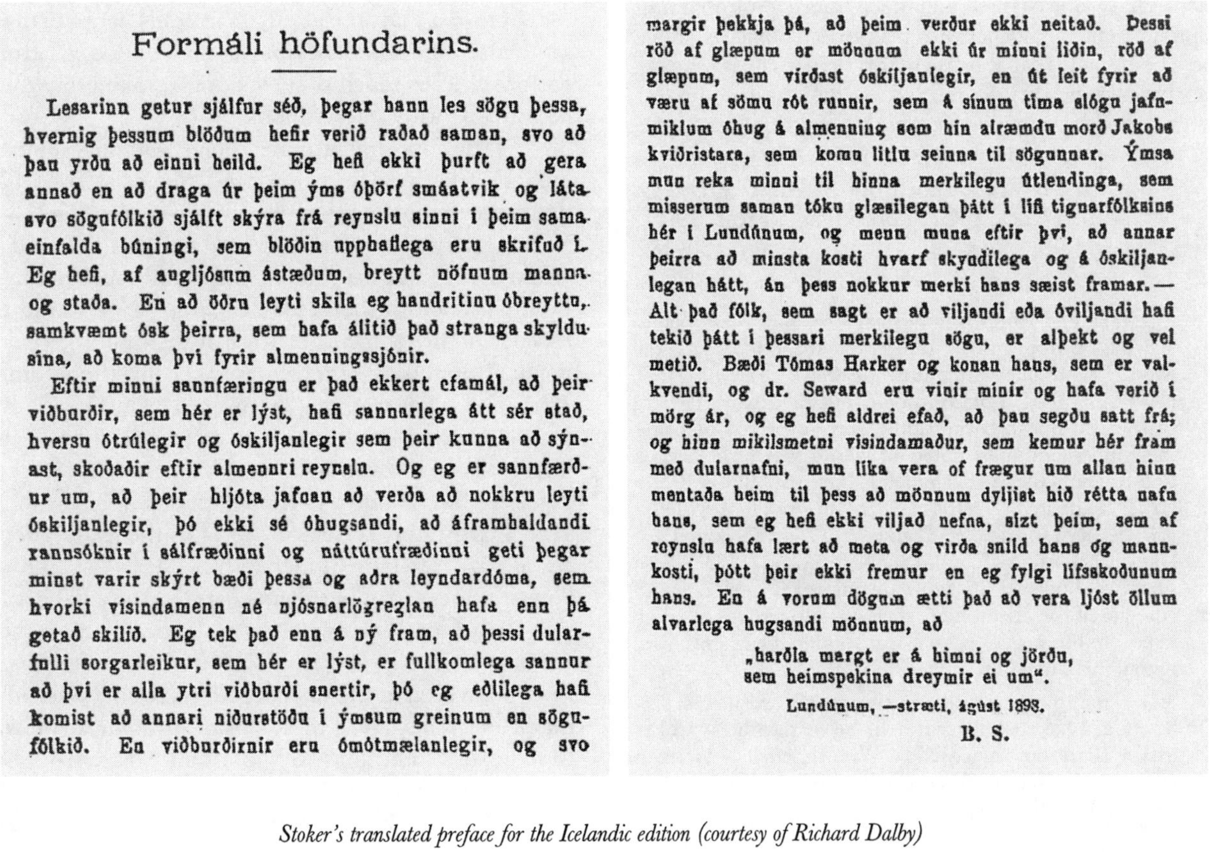

Stoker's translated preface for the Icelandic edition (courtesy of Richard Dalby)

More tantalizing is that Stoker provides clues as to the reality of both the crimes and the characters. What is one to make of these comments?

> This series of crimes has not yet passed from the memory–a series of crimes which appear to have originated from the same source, and which at the time created as much repugnance in people everywhere as the notorious murders of Jack the Ripper . . . Various people's minds will go back to the remarkable group of foreigners who for many seasons together played a dazzling part in the life of the aristocracy here in London; and some will remember that one of them disappeared suddenly without apparent reason, leaving no trace.

This is quite intriguing. Who are these foreigners? Are we to believe that one of them, a suspect in the "Ripper" murders, was yet another model for Count Dracula?[1] And what of the comment that "Jonathan Harker and his wife . . . and Dr. Seward are my friends and have been so for many years"? That "the highly respected scientist, who appears here under a pseudonym [Van Helsing], will also be too famous all over the educated world for his real name . . . to be hidden from people"?[2] While such leads may be worth pursuing (especially for anyone convinced that every character in *Dracula* has his/her counterpart in real life), they may very well be no more than the pose of a Gothic novelist intent on emphasizing that "the events are incontrovertible." Or if one wishes to take a more postmodernist approach, one might choose to believe that Stoker is stating these points in his capacity as author. Perhaps he is stepping into his own fictional world, forcing himself into the text (where all of the characters become his friends), thus operating on the same ontological level as the text itself.

–revised by the author from *Reflections on Dracula* (White Rock, B.C.: Transylvania Press, 1997), pp. 180–182

---

1.   McNally and Florescu note such a parallel, inasmuch as "an East European was among the suspected [Jack the Ripper] candidates at the time" (*Essential Dracula*, p. 156, n239). Carol M. Davison points out that many Jews of eastern European background were suspected of being the Ripper, the most noted of whom was Jack Pizer, a Polish Jew in the Whitechapel district; see "Blood Brothers: Dracula and Jack the Ripper," in *Bram Stoker's Dracula: Sucking Through the Century, 1897–1997,* edited by Davison (Toronto: Dundurn, 1997), pp. 147–172. These surmises, however, do not explain Stoker's reference to "the life of the aristocracy." Perhaps Stoker was alluding in part to the suspicions that surrounded the English aristocrat, the Duke of Clarence.

2.   Stoker may very well be referring to Max Müller, a professor at Oxford University. In his early notes, Stoker lists a character named Max Windshoeffel (a German professor) as one of three characters later combined to become Van Helsing.

Stoker's Abridgment

Shape-Shifting *Dracula:*
The Abridged Edition of 1901
Elizabeth Miller

The abridged edition of *Dracula,* published by Constable in 1901, has until recently gone virtually unnoticed.[1] Constable published it as a cheap "popular" book, aimed at less affluent, less sophisticated readers than those who bought regularly priced volumes. As was often the case with the books in Constable's sixpence series, *Dracula* was reduced in length both to keep down production costs and to make the text more accessible for the general reader. Whether the revisions were made by Stoker himself, by an editor, or by both is not certain. What we do know is that the original text was reduced by about 15 percent (approximately 25,000 words). Every chapter of the novel is affected: some undergo only minor alterations, while significant cuts are made in others. In his foreword to the 1994 reprint of the 1901 text, Robert Eighteen-Bisang notes that "most authorities agree that the revised edition of *Dracula* is more readable and, hence, more enjoyable than the common, well-known text." Raymond McNally concurs, commenting in his introduction to the same text that "the abridgment reads better than the original."[2] But such assessments may be too generous; the novel loses much of its texture, resulting in what I consider a vastly inferior book.[3]

True, we might have done without some of Stoker's lengthy descriptions and conversations which dominate the first edition. Few would mourn the loss of Van Helsing's detailed analysis of Dracula's "child-brain" and the "bloom and blood" account given by the captain of the *Czarina Catherine.*[4] Nor would the absence of the following concern anyone but the "trivial pursuit" enthusiast: the routes taken by the steamers *Emma* and *Scarborough* (p. 75), tea at Robin Hood's Bay (p. 86), lunch at Mulgrave Woods (p. 90), the fact that Van Helsing was staying at the Great Eastern Hotel (p. 106),[5] tidbits about Thomas Bilder and his wife (p. 125), Hardy's broken finger (p. 142), the list of attendees at Mr. Hawkins's funeral service (p. 154), and the illness of the Vice-Consul at Galatz (p. 301). Except for the purist for whom every scrap of text is sacred, these are dispensable.

I am certain the novel could have survived other minor deletions, albeit these do add in some small way to its texture: allusions to Spohr and MacKenzie, Disraeli, Ellen Terry, and Hans Andersen (pp. 90, 102, 160, 295); Van Helsing's references to Harker's "true grit" and Quincey's head "in plane with the horizon" (pp. 202, 257); "Count de Ville" (p. 239); the beautiful

Cover for the first paperback edition of the novel, published in 1901, by "Nathan." This abridgment cuts the text by about 15 percent and includes editorial alterations (courtesy of Robert Eighteen-Bisang).

girl in a big cart-wheel hat (p. 155). Much of the legal material in the text was eliminated: Dracula's questions about British solicitors and the disposition of property (p. 36), the ramifications of a ship's tiller being held by a dead hand (p. 79), the regulations of the Board of Trade (p. 80), and the disposition of Mrs. Westenra's estate (p. 151). While the removal of these passages has no effect on the plot, it lessens the richness of the text by eliminating details about contemporary Victorian England.

The scissors did yeoman work on the many literary allusions that dot the original, resulting in the loss of much of the novel's intertextuality. Significant among such deletions are the quotation from Bürger's poem "Lenore" (p. 17) and the line "As idle as a painted ship upon a painted ocean" from Coleridge's "The Rime of the Ancient Mariner" (p. 76). Into the discard

heap goes the majority of the Shakespearean intertext, including several references to *Hamlet, Macbeth, Othello, Romeo and Juliet,* and *King Lear.* Some of these I consider vital, such as Harker's misquotation of Hamlet–"My tablets! quick, my tablets! / 'Tis meet that I put it down" (p. 41)–while others (for example, the allusion to Malvolio on page 235) seem insignificant. Stoker (or his editor) did not seem to have drawn such distinctions. Other somewhat erudite allusions are also cut: a brief mention of *Arabian Nights* (p. 35), the Latin phrase from Tacitus (p. 275), the short reference to Archimedes (p. 296), as well as lines from Thomas Hood and Byron (pp. 147, 174).[6] Biblical allusions, on the other hand, fared better, with most of them remaining intact. Obviously, someone considered much of the intertext expendable for the projected readership.

We are considering much more than elimination of relatively insignificant details and esoteric allusions. While most of the memorable scenes in the novel are left intact in the 1901 abridgment (Jonathan's seduction by the three vampire women, the Count crawling head-first down the castle wall, the ship's Log, the blood transfusions, Lucy's appearances as the "bloofer lady" and her subsequent staking, Mina's "baptism of blood," the final chase), there are a few notable exceptions. The role of bats and rats is diminished. Gone is Quincey Morris's anecdote about the vampire bat on the Pampas (p. 138), as well as a scene at Carfax that presents one of the most horrifying images in the novel:

A few minutes later I saw Morris step suddenly back from a corner, which he was examining. We all followed his movements with our eyes, for undoubtedly some nervousness was growing on us, and we saw a whole mass of phosphorescence which twinkled like stars. We all instinctively drew back. The whole place was becoming alive with rats.

. . . In the minute that had elapsed the number of the rats had vastly increased. They seemed to swarm over the place all at once, till the lamplight, shining on their moving dark bodies and glittering, baleful eyes, made the place look like a bank of earth set with fireflies. . . . The rats were multiplying in thousands, and we moved out. (p. 222)

Significant deletions occur in the early part of the novel (Chapters 1–4), Jonathan Harker's journal of his sojourn in Transylvania. What may be seen as Stoker's over-reliance on his sources (he squeezes much detail into those four opening chapters) may well be their strength. Details about the history, geography and local customs not only give the text its richness but successfully ground it in the real world. Transylvania is both real and mysterious, setting up the central dichotomy of the novel. Much of this effect (though not all) is lost in

Winston Churchill, who cited his appreciation of Dracula *as one reason he acceded to Stoker's request for an interview in 1908 (Roy Jenkins,* Churchill: A Biography *[New York: Farrar, Straus & Giroux, 2001]; Thomas Cooper Library, University of South Carolina)*

Introduced by Dracula

At the beginning of his article "Mr. Winston Churchill talks of his Hopes, his Work, and his Ideals to Bram Stoker," Stoker explains how the interview was arranged.

When I wrote to Mr. Winston Churchill asking for an appointment to interview him he replied: "I would very much rather not; but if you wish it I cannot refuse you." When I met him in his library he explained more fully in words:

"I hate being interviewed, and I have refused altogether to allow it. But I have to break the rule for you, for you were a friend of my father." Then he added gracefully another reason, personal to myself: "And because you are the author of 'Dracula.'" This latter was a vampire novel I wrote some years ago, which had appealed to his young imagination.

—The Daily Chronicle, 15 January 1908, p. 38

---

the 1901 text, as a result of deletions. Most conspicuous is the disappearance of the following: the references to various local dishes (p. 9), some of the history of Bistritz (p. 11), the entire entry on the "robber steak"

(p. 13), the "Cszeks and Slovaks, all in picturesque attire" (p. 15), the leiter-wagon with its "long, snake-like vertebra calculated to suit the inequalities of the road" (p. 15), and the custom of the gypsies to "attach themselves . . . to some great noble or boyar" (p. 45). Gone also is the description of the Carpathians as "endless perspective of jagged rock and pointed crags . . . lost in the distance, where the snowy peaks rose grandly" (p. 15).

There are two significant deletions from the concluding chapter. The first occurs immediately after Van Helsing stakes the three female vampires: "For, friend John, hardly had my knife severed the head of each, before the whole body began to melt away and crumble into its native dust" (pp. 320–321). This result prepares readers for a similar occurrence in the case of Dracula, though one could argue that the text is improved by reserving the description of disintegration for the Count alone. Secondly—and this cut is certainly no improvement—a decision was made to delete the references to the "look of peace" on Dracula's face at the final moment and the last image of Castle Dracula:

I shall be glad as long as I live that even in that moment of final dissolution, there was in the face a look of peace, such as I never could have imagined might have rested there.
The Castle of Dracula now stood out against the red sky, and every stone of its broken battlements was articulated against the light of the setting sun. (p. 325)

While the removal of the first sentence may help to eliminate any possible ambiguity concerning the evil nature of the Count, the deletion of the second sentence is a major loss.

It has often been stated that the characters in *Dracula* (with the exception of the Count and possibly Mina and Renfield) are flat and uninteresting. If that is the case, then the 1901 text makes them even more so. Several nuances that introduce ambiguity into the characterization are missing. Jonathan Harker, for example, no longer makes the condescending comment about the peasant women, that they "looked pretty, except when you got near them" (p. 11). Nor, having admitted to a "wicked, burning desire" while being seduced by the three female vampires, does he think "It is not good to note this down; lest some day it should meet Mina's eyes and cause her pain" (p. 42). Arthur Holmwood loses his line "I would give the last drop of blood in my body for her" (p. 113) as well as his melodramatic outcry, "Oh, Jack! Jack! What shall I do! The whole of life seems gone from me at once, and there is nothing in the wide world for me to live for" (p. 152). Seward's momentary longing for the "modern Morpheus" (p. 97) is removed. Quincey Morris is made even more insignificant, with the removal of Seward's observation that he is a "moral Viking" and that "If America can go on breeding men like that, she will be a power in the world indeed" (p. 156). The complexity of Renfield is lessened with the exclusion of Van Helsing's astute observation that "Perhaps I may gain more knowledge out of the folly of this madman than I shall from the teaching of the most wise" (p. 225).

In fact, a somewhat different Van Helsing emerges. In the revised text he has lost much of his sense of humor (along with his entire "King Laugh" speech). On the other hand, the removal of the insensitive remark (made in Mina's presence) "Do you forget . . . that last night he banqueted heavily, and will sleep late?" (p. 258) takes some of the edge off his abrasiveness. We lose that tantalizing allusion to his wife, "dead to me, but alive by church's law, though no wits" (p. 158) as well as the indication that he has also lost a son.

Some of the deletions render the band of vampire hunters somewhat less reprehensible. Dr. Seward no longer offers to falsify Renfield's death certificate by claiming the cause of death a "misadventure in falling from bed" (p. 253). Nor does Quincey Morris offer the employee at Doolittle's Wharf "something from his pocket which crackle as he roll it up" (p. 275). And Jonathan does not make the comment in Varna that "this is the country where bribery can do anything. . . . Judge Moneybag will settle this case, I think!" (p. 290). On the other hand, some examples of questionable ethical behavior do remain. Although Lord Godalming retains his reservations about Jonathan's involvement in the break-and-entry scheme because of possible censure by the Incorporated Law Society, he is still not

Dust jacket for the 1916 printing of the edition originally published in London by Rider in 1912 (courtesy of Robert Eighteen-Bisang)

averse to using his title "to make it all right with the locksmith, and with any policeman that may come along" (p. 261).

Count Dracula, too, is affected. He loses the line "Come in; the night air is chill, and you must need to eat and rest" (p. 22), as well as the following eloquent passage with its Shakespearean resonance: "The warlike days are over. Blood is too precious a thing in these days of dishonourable peace; and the glories of the great races are as a tale that is told" (p. 35). He no longer gives his fascinating explanation of the "blue flame" (p. 27). Lost is his association with "the strangeness of the geologic and chemical world" (p. 278). We are given less information about his past with the removal of the following remarks by Van Helsing:

I have studied, over and over again since they came into my hands, all the papers relating to this monster; and the more I have studied, the greater seems the necessity to utterly stamp him out. All through there

---

Florence Stoker's Foreword to the 1926 Serialization

In 1926, Dracula *was serialized in* The Argosy: The World's Best Short Stories *(London), and Bram Stoker's widow wrote this note for the first installment.*

Of all the amazing tales that came from the pen of my late husband, "Dracula" has invariably been acknowledged as the most fascinating and enthralling. It is now being serialized for the first time, and even the early chapters are sufficient to justify the claim that the story has no equal in the realms of mystery and imagination.

It has been described as "the weirdest of weird tales," more powerful and more appalling than "Wuthering Heights," "Frankenstein," or "The Fall of the House of Usher," and I think that such judgments are not inadequate. My late husband used to read his stories over to me as they were written, and "Dracula" was by no means least among those which revealed to me the supernormal imagination of the author. Because this astonishing work will undoubtedly please and thrill a new generation of readers I have willingly given my permission to the Editor to republish it in serial form.

(Mrs.) F.A.L. Bram Stoker.

---

are signs of his advance; not only of his power, but of his knowledge of it. As I learned from the researches of my friend Arminius of Buda-Pesth, he was in life a most wonderful man. Soldier, statesman, and alchemist—which latter was the highest development of the science-knowledge of his time. He had a mighty brain, a learning beyond compare, and a heart that knew no fear and no remorse. He dared even to attend the Scholomance, and there was no branch of knowledge of his time that he did not essay. (p. 263)

More crucial is the effect this omission has on the reader's response to the Count, especially with the disappearance of Van Helsing's assessment that "He [Dracula] was in life a most wonderful man." When one couples this with the elimination of Mina's earlier comment "I suppose one ought to pity any thing so hunted as is the Count" (p. 202), much of the potential sympathy for Dracula is lost.

The character altered the most by the deletions is Mina. Much of the interpretation of her character rests on the occasional touches of ambivalence that the text supplies. For example, both of her references to the "New Woman" are removed (pp. 86–87), and along with them the enticing possibility that Mina

may have felt an affinity with the "New Woman." Neither does she retain her desire to "practice interviewing" (p. 163) or her interest in Seward's phonograph (p. 195). But some of the changes may be for the better. She no longer is concerned about being seen with bare feet (p. 89). She is spared the line, "I went to bed when the men had gone, simply because they had told me to" (p. 226), as well as her comment about "some of the taste of the original apple that remains still in our mouths" (p. 164) and her observation that "We women have something of the mother in us that makes us rise above smaller matters when the mother-spirit is invoked" (p. 203). The perceptive reader need no longer be doubtful about her declaration that "I felt a thrill of joy through me when I *knew* that no other woman was a cause of trouble" (p. 99). And, as noted above, her sympathy for Dracula also takes a direct hit.

Occasionally, a deletion actually improves the text. One example is the elimination of Van Helsing's use of "my child" in reference to Arthur, a wise decision considering the professor is about to ask Arthur if he can "cut off the head of dead Miss Lucy" (p. 184). But other changes are more puzzling. Why, for example, was Dracula's straw hat removed? The "hat of straw" which the Count is seen wearing as he hurries to make preparations on the *Czarina Catherine* (p. 276) becomes in the 1901 text merely "a hat"—a peculiar omission, as it renders the next phrase "which suit not him or the time" rather meaningless. Another minor inconsistency resulted from the decision to remove Van Helsing's statement to Arthur that "You shall kiss her once before it is done" (p. 114) but to leave in on the following page "You may take that one little kiss."

The preceding discussion has focused primarily on deletions. But in a few cases, there were changes and even additions. Most of these were occasioned by the need for new transitions to accommodate the removal of portions of text and do not merit any comment. However, that Stoker (or his editor) read at least parts of the text carefully for this abridgment is evident in the fact that some of the errors are corrected: "Hopwood" (p. 62) is corrected to "Holmwood," and "gloated" (p. 221) to "gorged." That Dracula no longer addresses his newly arrived guest as "Mr. Harker" (p. 22) may indicate a realization that at this stage the Count was still expecting Mr. Hawkins and not his employee. Somebody caught the inconsistency in the journal entries for 30 September: in the original text, Seward had stated that the Professor had called a meeting for "nine o'clock" while Mina had said "two hours after dinner, which had been at six o'clock" (p. 208); the first reference

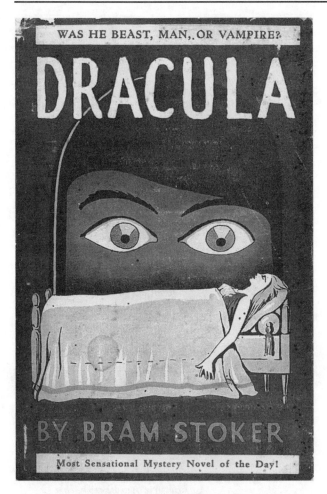

WAS HE BEAST, MAN, OR VAMPIRE?

DRACULA

BY BRAM STOKER

Most Sensational Mystery Novel of the Day!

Dust jacket for the 1928 reprint published in New York by Grosset & Dunlap. The back of the dust jacket reads: "A novel that has held two generations in fascination and terror. This is the book on which the play was based" (courtesy of Robert Eighteen-Bisang).

that the women were "clumsy about the waist" (p. 11), that the dinner at the Golden Krone in Bistritz was "in the simple style of the London cat's-meat" (p. 9), that the trains were late and the roads bad. Also removed was of one of the key lines of text, the oft-quoted "The impression I had was that we were leaving the West and entering the East" (p. 9). As great an impact would have been made on feminist readings. Not only were all references to the "New Woman" removed, but so was the familiar declaration made by Lucy: "Why can't they let a girl marry three men, or as many as want her, and save all this trouble?" (p. 60).

Is it possible that Stoker or his editor was aware of the subtexts in his novel and was deliberately eliminating some of them? This could explain the removal of a line such as "as it would have been to have stripped off her clothing in her sleep whilst living" (p. 176), and the omission of Van Helsing's reference to Lucy as a "polyandrist" (p. 158), a euphemism for "prostitute" in Stoker's time. Yet one of the most erotic sections of the novel, Jonathan's seduction by the three voluptuous females, is left in. An examination of the changes suggests that the decisions were somewhat arbitrary, with no clear rationale beyond cutting text that was (at least at that time) considered expendable.

—revised by the author from articles previously published in *Reflections on Dracula* (White Rock, B.C.: Transylvania Press, 1997), pp. 171–198; and *The Fantastic Vampire,* edited by James Craig Holte (Westport, Conn.: Greenwood Press, 2002), pp. 3–10

appears in 1901 but is changed to "eight."[7] Unfortunately, these errors remain in later editions, which followed the 1897 text or its other successors.

Had the 1901 text of *Dracula* been the one that went into hundreds of reprints, the whole course of *Dracula* scholarship might have been altered. New historicists would have a text without the two references to Charcot (p. 171). With the removal of the Hebrew with "a nose like a sheep" (p. 302), those who see the text as anti-Semitic would have a weaker case. Lucy's racist remark that she sympathizes with "poor Desdemona [in *Othello*] when she had such a dangerous stream poured in her ear, even by a black man" (p. 59) is no longer there. Post-colonialist criticism would be affected, with the elimination of some of the condescending remarks about Transylvania:

1. Martin Riccardo's bibliography, *Vampires Unearthed* (New York: Garland, 1983), lists it as just another reprint, while Richard Dalby in *Bram Stoker: A Bibliography of First Editions* (London: Dracula Press, 1983) calls it merely the "first paperback edition" (p. 27).

2. *Dracula: The Rare Text of 1901,* ed. Robert Eighteen-Bisang (White Rock, B.C.: Transylvania Press, 1994), n.p.

3. I would make one qualification: the superb cover illustration, which depicts Count Dracula crawling, batlike, down the castle wall.

4. *Dracula,* pp. 263–264, 275–276. All quotations from the novel, henceforth cited in the text, are from the Norton Critical Edition (1997).

5. Though in this instance, maybe someone had a flash of insight and noted the inconsistency (drawn to our attention by Leonard Wolf in *The Essential Dracula,* New York: Plume/Penguin, 1993, p. 49, n22) that later on, the professor is at the Berkeley.

6. One key Byronic reference remains: the phrase "decay's effacing fingers" (p. 207) is from *The Giaour,* the poem which contains Byron's famous "vampire curse."

7. However, the same "somebody" missed the dating error of Seward's diary entry of "25 April" (p. 80).

The 1901 Edition: Key Deletions

These passages were cut from the first edition of the novel for the 1901 abridgment.

Buda-Pesth seems a wonderful place, from the glimpse which I got of it from the train and the little I could walk through the streets. I feared to go very far from the station, as we arrived late and would start as near the correct time as possible. The impression I had was that we were leaving the West and entering the East; the most Western of splendid bridges over the Danube, which is here of noble width and depth, took us among the traditions of Turkish rule.

    –Chapter I, Jonathan Harker's Journal, 3 May

I had for dinner, or rather supper, a chicken done up some way with red pepper, which was very good but thirsty. (*Mem.*, get recipe for Mina.) I asked the waiter, and he said it was called "paprika hendl," and that, as it was a national dish, I should be able to get it anywhere along the Carpathians.

    –Chapter I, Jonathan Harker's Journal, 3 May

I had to hurry breakfast, for the train started a little before eight, or rather it ought to have done so, for after rushing to the station at 7.30 I had to sit in the carriage for more than an hour before we began to move. It seems to me that the further East you go the more unpunctual are the trains. What ought they to be in China?

    –Chapter I, Jonathan Harker's Journal, 3 May

Some of them were just like the peasants at home or those I saw coming through France and Germany, with short jackets and round hats and home-made trousers; but others were very picturesque. The women looked pretty, except when you got near them, but they were very clumsy about the waist.

    –Chapter I, Jonathan Harker's Journal, 3 May

There are many odd things to put down, and, lest who reads them may fancy that I dined too well before I left Bistritz, let me put down my dinner exactly. I dined on what they called "robber steak"–bits of bacon, onion, and beef, seasoned with red pepper, and strung on sticks and roasted over the fire, in the simple style of the London cat's-meat! The wine was Golden Mediasch, which produces a queer sting on the tongue, which is, however, not disagreeable. I had only a couple of glasses of this, and nothing else.

    –Chapter I, Jonathan Harker's Journal, 5 May

Dust jacket for an undated edition published by Doubleday, circa 1928 (courtesy of Ronald V. Borst/Hollywood Movie Posters)

One of my companions whispered to another the line from Burger's "Lenore:"–

"Denn die Todten reiten schnell"–
("For the dead travel fast.")

The strange driver evidently heard the words, for he looked up with a gleaming smile. The passenger turned his face away, at the same time putting out his two fingers and crossing himself.

    –Chapter I, Jonathan Harker's Journal, 5 May

Once there appeared a strange optical effect: when he stood between me and the flame he did not obstruct it, for I could see its ghostly flicker all the same. This startled me, but as the effect was only momentary, I took it that my eyes deceived me straining through the darkness. Then for a time there were no blue flames, and we sped onwards through the

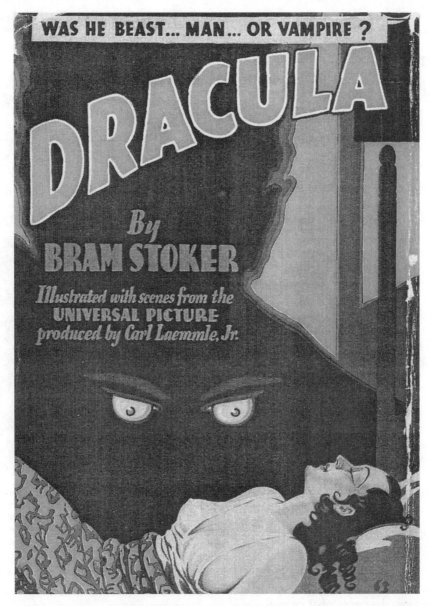

Dust jacket for the 1930 printing published in New York by Grosset & Dunlap. The back of the dust jacket features a photograph of Bela Lugosi. This edition also has a frontispiece and still photographs from the Universal picture produced by Carl Laemmle Jr. As the first "Bela Lugosi Edition" it is a highly sought-after collector's item (courtesy of Robert Eighteen-Bisang).

gloom, with the howling of the wolves around us, as though they were following in a moving circle.

    –Chapter I, Jonathan Harker's Journal, 5 May

  He then explained to me that it was commonly believed that on a certain night of the year–last night, in fact, when all evil spirits are supposed to have unchecked sway–a blue flame is seen over any place where treasure has been concealed. "That treasure has been hidden," he went on, "in the region through which you came last night, there can be but little doubt; for it was the ground fought over for centuries by the

Wallachian, the Saxon, and the Turk. Why, there is hardly a foot of soil in all this region that has not been enriched by the blood of men, patriots or invaders. In old days there were stirring times, when the Austrian and the Hungarian came up in hordes, and the patriots went out to meet them–men and women, the aged and the children too–and waited their coming on the rocks above the passes, that they might sweep destruction on them with their artificial avalanches. When the invader was triumphant he found but little, for whatever there was had been sheltered in the friendly soil."

    –Chapter II, Jonathan Harker's Journal, 7 May

"The warlike days are over. Blood is too precious a thing in these days of dishonourable peace; and the glories of the great races are as a tale that is told."
—Chapter III, Jonathan Harker's Journal, 8 May

It is not good to note this down, lest some day it should meet Mina's eyes and cause her pain; but it is the truth.
—Chapter III, Jonathan Harker's Journal, 16 May

These Szgany are gipsies; I have notes of them in my book. They are peculiar to this part of the world, though allied to the ordinary gipsies all the world over. There are thousands of them in Hungary and Transylvania, who are almost outside all law. They attach themselves as a rule to some great noble or _boyar,_ and call themselves by his name. They are fearless and without religion, save superstition, and they talk only their own varieties of the Romany tongue.
—Chapter IV, Jonathan Harker's Journal, 28 May

If it were not that I have made my diary a duty I should not open it to-night. We had a lovely walk. Lucy, after a while, was in gay spirits, owing, I think, to some dear cows who came nosing towards us in a field close to the lighthouse, and frightened the wits out of us. I believe we forgot everything, except, of course, personal fear, and it seemed to wipe the slate clean and give us a fresh start. We had a capital "severe tea" at Robin Hood's Bay in a sweet little old-fashioned inn, with a bow-window right over the seaweed-covered rocks of the strand. I believe we should have shocked the "New Woman" with our appetites. Men are more tolerant, bless them!
—Chapter VIII, Mina Murray's Journal, 10 August

If Mr. Holmwood fell in love with her seeing her only in the drawing-room, I wonder what he would say if he saw her now. Some of the "New Women" writers will some day start an idea that men and women should be allowed to see each other asleep before proposing or accepting. But I suppose the New Woman won't condescend in future to accept; she will do the proposing herself. And a nice job she will make of it, too!
—Chapter VIII, Mina Murray's Journal, 10 August

I am weary to-night and low in spirits. I cannot but think of Lucy, and how different things might have been. If I don't sleep at once, chloral, the modern Morpheus—$C_2HCl_3O \cdot H_2O$! I must be careful not to let it grow into a habit. No, I shall take none to-night! I have thought of Lucy, and I shall not dishonour her by mixing the two. If need be, to-night shall be sleepless.
—Chapter VIII, Dr. Seward's Diary, 19 August

Dust jacket created by the influential designer Edward McKnight Kauffer in 1940 (courtesy of Ronald V. Borst/Hollywood Movie Posters)

I do believe the dear soul thought I might be jealous lest my poor dear should have fallen in love with any other girl. The idea of _my_ being jealous about Jonathan! And yet, my dear, let me whisper, I felt a thrill of joy through me when I _knew_ that no other woman was a cause of trouble.
—Chapter IX, Letter, Mina Murray to Lucy Westenra, 24 August

"Tell me, and I shall do it. My life is hers, and I would give the last drop of blood in my body for her." The Professor has a strongly humorous side, and I could from old knowledge detect a trace of its origin in his answer:—
"My young sir, I do not ask so much as that—not the last!"
—Chapter X, Dr. Seward's Diary, 7 September

"I have not seen anything pulled down so quick since I was on the Pampas and had a mare that I was

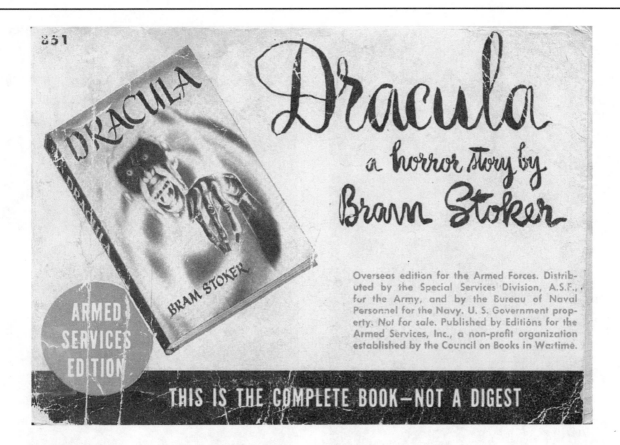

DRACULA by Bram Stoker

For sheer, stalking, horrendous terror there is no match for *Dracula* in the English language. It has made millions of hardened mystery-readers and avid movie fans squirm with dread. But few people seem to know anything about the author—"Oh yes, Stoker; wasn't he the guy who wrote *Dracula?*" So here is the best chance to tell you something about him.

Bram Stoker was born in Dublin nearly a hundred years ago. He was a sickly child and could not walk until he was seven. Instead he lay on his back and did a good deal of thinking. However, before he was twenty, he had staged a comeback, and was considered the athletic champion of Dublin University.

Ten dreary years as a civil servant were followed by experience as a journalist, a barrister, and as the manager of the famous actor, Henry Irving. With Irving, he toured America and wrote fifty letters a day. Subsequently, he was on the literary staff of the London *Telegraph.* Though he wrote other novels, *Dracula* is certainly his best-known.

This special edition of Dracula *by Bram Stoker has been made available to the Armed Forces of the United States through an arrangement with the original publisher, Doubleday, Doran and Co., Inc., New York.*

Editions for the Armed Services, Inc., a non-profit organization established by the Council on Books in Wartime

Front and back covers for the edition that was distributed free of charge to servicemen during World War II (Elizabeth Miller Collection)

Covers for English mass-market paperback publications in 1958 and 1962 (courtesy of Ronald V. Borst/Hollywood Movie Posters)

fond of go to grass all in a night. One of those big bats that they call vampires had got at her in the night, and, what with his gorge and the vein left open, there wasn't enough blood in her to let her stand up, and I had to put a bullet through her as she lay."
–Chapter XII, Dr. Seward's Diary, 18 September

What a fine fellow is Quincey! I believe in my heart of hearts that he suffered as much about Lucy's death as any of us; but he bore himself through it like a moral Viking. If America can go on breeding men like that, she will be a power in the world indeed.
–Chapter XIII, Dr. Seward's Diary, 22 September

I could not resist the temptation of mystifying him a bit–I suppose it is some of the taste of the original apple that remains still in our mouths–so I handed him the shorthand diary. He took it with a grateful bow, and said:–

"May I read it?"

"If you wish," I answered as demurely as I could. He opened it, and for an instant his face fell. Then he stood up and bowed.

"Oh, you so clever woman!" he said. "I long knew that Mr. Jonathan was a man of much thankfulness; but see, his wife have all the good things. And will you not so much honour me and so help me as to read it for me? Alas! I know not the shorthand." By this time my little joke was over, and I was almost ashamed; so I took the typewritten copy from my workbasket and handed it to him.
–Chapter XIV, Mina Murray's Journal, 25 September

"I suppose now you do not believe in corporeal transference. No? Nor in materialisation. No? Nor in astral bodies. No? Nor in the reading of thought. No? Nor in hypnotism–"

Other Noteworthy Editions

Some significant editions of the novel, in addition to those pictured elsewhere in this chapter, are listed below. For a more complete list of editions, see Richard Dalby and William Hughes, Bram Stoker: A Bibliography, *2004.*

Dracula. New York: Pocket Books, July 1947. Paperback. Cover: A caricature of Bela Lugosi hovers over a female in bed. This is the first mass-market edition.

Dracula. New York: Limited Editions Club, 1965. Hardback. Slipcase. Illustrated with wood engravings by Felix Hoffman (some color). "Introduction" by Anthony Boucher, p. v–[xi]. 1,500 numbered copies, signed by the illustrator. The first illustrated edition, it was reprinted in slightly smaller formats by both Heritage Press and Easton Press.

The Annotated Dracula. New York: Clarkson N. Potter, 1975. Hardback. Dust jacket. Edited, with an introduction, notes, a bibliography, and additional material by Leonard Wolf. Illustrated by Sätty. Reprinted 1976 as a trade paperback. The first annotated edition of *Dracula* offers a mixture of fact and speculation about the origin and meaning of Bram Stoker's creation. Revised and updated as *The Essential Dracula* in 1993.

The Essential Dracula: A Completely Illustrated and Annotated Edition of Bram Stoker's Classic Novel. New York: Mayflower, 1979. Hardback. Dust jacket. Frontis. Illustrated with photographs. Edited by Raymond McNally and Radu Florescu, with an introduction, bibliography, filmography, and additional material. Reprinted as a trade paperback, London: Penguin, 1993. This annotated edition by the authors of *In Search of Dracula* is the first edition to restore the missing chapter "Dracula's Guest."

Dracula. Parsippany, New Jersey: Unicorn, 1985. Black cloth binding with an inlay depicting Dracula and Lucy in Whitby. Edited by Jean L. Scrocco. Color Frontispiece and illustrated (some color) by Greg Hildebrandt. Introduction by Frank Langella.

Bram Stoker's Dracula Unearthed. Westcliff-On-Sea, U.K.: Desert Island Books, 1998. Hardback. Dust jacket. Edited, with an introduction, notes, and other material by Clive Leatherdale. This edition provides many insights into Victorian England and is part of the first annotated set of Bram Stoker's works. *The Jewel of Seven Stars, The Lady and the Shroud* and *The Lair of the White Worm* all have some connection with vampirism.

Dracula. Denver: Micawber, 2001. Hardback. Frontispiece & color illustrations by Griff Jones. "Afterword" by Robert L. Dean. Limited to 65 copies: 50 copies numbered 1–50 and 15 copies *hors commerce* with additional drawings and other material.

–Robert Eighteen-Bisang

"Yes," I said. "Charcot has proved that pretty well." He smiled as he went on: "Then you are satisfied as to it. Yes? And of course then you understand how it act, and can follow the mind of the great Charcot–alas that he is no more!–into the very soul of the patient that he influence. No? Then, friend John, am I to take it that you simply accept fact, and are satisfied to let from premise to conclusion be a blank? No? Then tell me–for I am student of the brain–how you accept the hypnotism and reject the thought-reading. Let me tell you, my friend, that there are things done to-day in electrical science which would have been deemed unholy by the very men who discovered electricity–who would themselves not so long before have been burned as wizards."

–Chapter XIV, Dr. Seward's Diary, 26 September

I am so glad that I hardly know how to contain myself. It is, I suppose, the reaction from the haunting fear which I have had: that this terrible affair and the reopening of his old wound might act detrimentally on Jonathan. I saw him leave for Whitby with as brave a face as I could, but I was sick with apprehension. The effort has, however, done him good. He was never so resolute, never so strong, never so full of volcanic energy, as at present. It is just as that dear, good Professor Van Helsing said: he is true grit, and he improves under strain that would kill a weaker nature. He came back full of life and hope and determination; we have got everything in order for to-night. I feel myself quite wild with excitement. I suppose one ought to pity any thing so hunted as is the Count. That is just it: this Thing is not human–not even beast. To read Dr. Seward's account of poor Lucy's death, and what followed, is enough to dry up the springs of pity in one's heart.

–Chapter XVII, Mina Murray's Journal, 30 September

He grew quite hysterical, and raising his open hands, beat his palms together in a perfect agony of grief. He stood up and then sat down again, and the tears rained down his cheeks. I felt an infinite pity for him, and opened my arms unthinkingly. With a sob he laid his head on my shoulder, and cried like a wearied child, whilst he shook with emotion.

We women have something of the mother in us that makes us rise above smaller matters when the mother-spirit is invoked; I felt this big sorrowing man's head resting on me, as though it were that of the baby that some day may lie on my bosom, and I stroked his hair as though he were my own child. I never thought at the time how strange it all was.
–Chapter XVII, Mina Murray's Journal, 30 September

Once I got a fright, for, seeing Lord Godalming suddenly turn and look out of the vaulted door into the dark passage beyond, I looked too, and for an instant my heart stood still. Somewhere, looking out from the shadow, I seemed to see the high lights of the Count's evil face, the ridge of the nose, the red eyes, the red lips, the awful pallor. It was only for a moment, for, as Lord Godalming said, "I thought I saw a face, but it was only the shadows," and resumed his inquiry, I turned my lamp in the direction, and stepped into the passage. There was no sign of any one; and as there were no corners, no doors, no aperture of any kind, but only the solid walls of the passage, there could be no hiding-place even for *him*. I took it that fear had helped imagination, and said nothing.

A few minutes later I saw Morris step suddenly back from a corner, which he was examining. We all followed his movements with our eyes, for undoubtedly some nervousness was growing on us, and we saw a whole mass of phosphorescence, which twinkled like stars. We all instinctively drew back. The whole place was becoming alive with rats.
–Chapter XIX, Jonathan Harker's Journal, 1 October

Unconsciously we had all moved towards the door, and as we moved I noticed that the dust had been much disturbed: the boxes which had been taken out had been brought this way. But even in the minute that had elapsed the number of the rats had vastly increased. They seemed to swarm over the place all at once, till the lamplight, shining on their moving dark bodies and glittering, baleful eyes, made the place look like a bank of earth set with fireflies. The dogs dashed on, but at the threshold suddenly stopped and snarled, and then, simultaneously lifting their noses, began to howl in most lugubrious fashion. The rats were multiplying in thousands, and we moved out.
–Chapter XIX, Jonathan Harker's Journal, 1 October

When Dr. Van Helsing and Dr. Seward had come back from seeing poor Renfield, we went gravely into what was to be done. First, Dr. Seward told us that when he and Dr. Van Helsing had gone down to the

Cover for a 1979 English edition (courtesy of Ronald V. Borst/ Hollywood Movie Posters)

room below they had found Renfield lying on the floor, all in a heap. His face was all bruised and crushed in, and the bones of the neck were broken.

Dr. Seward asked the attendant who was on duty in the passage if he had heard anything. He said that he had been sitting down–he confessed to half dozing–when he heard loud voices in the room, and then Renfield had called out loudly several times, "God! God! God!" After that there was a sound of falling, and when he entered the room he found him lying on the floor, face down, just as the doctors had seen him. Van Helsing asked if he had heard "voices" or "a voice," and he said he could not say; that at first it had seemed to him as if there were two, but as there was no one in the room it could have been only one. He could swear to it, if required, that the word "God" was spoken by the patient. Dr. Seward said to us, when we were alone, that he did not wish to go into the matter; the question

Illustrations by Greg Hildebrandt in the 1985 Unicorn edition of Dracula
(courtesy of Spiderwebart gallery <www.spiderwebart.com>)

of an inquest had to be considered, and it would never do to put forward the truth, as no one would believe it. As it was, he thought that on the attendant's evidence he could give a certificate of death by misadventure in falling from bed. In case the coroner should demand it, there would be a formal inquest, necessarily to the same result.

–Chapter XXII, Jonathan Harker's Journal, 3 October

"Not so!" said Van Helsing holding up his hand.
"But why?" I asked.
"Do you forget," he said, with actually a smile, "that last night he banqueted heavily, and will sleep late?"

Did I forget! Shall I ever–can I ever! Can any of us ever forget that terrible scene! Mina struggled hard to keep her brave countenance; but the pain overmastered her and she put her hands before her face, and shuddered whilst she moaned. Van Helsing had not intended to recall her frightful experience. He had simply lost sight of her and her part in the affair in his intellectual effort. When it struck him what he had said, he was horrified at his thoughtlessness and tried to comfort her. "Oh Madam Mina," he said, "dear, dear Madam Mina, alas! that I of all who so reverence you, should have said anything so forgetful. These stupid old lips of mine and this stupid old head do not deserve so; but you will forget it, will you not?" He bent low beside her as he spoke; she took his hand, and looking at him through her tears, said hoarsely:–

"No, I shall not forget, for it is well that I remember; and with it I have so much in memory of you that is sweet, that I take it all together. Now, you must all be going soon. Breakfast is ready, and we must all eat that we may be strong."

–Chapter XXII, Jonathan Harker's Journal, 3 October

"I have studied, over and over again since they came into my hands, all the papers relating to this monster; and the more I have studied, the greater seems the necessity to utterly stamp him out. All through there are signs of his advance; not only of his power, but of his knowledge of it. As I learned from the researches of my friend Arminius of Buda-Pesth, he was in life a most

Cover for the 1997 edition, in which the editors draw a clear parallel between Count Dracula and Henry Irving (Elizabeth Miller Collection)

wonderful man. Soldier, statesman, and alchemist—which latter was the highest development of the science-knowledge of his time. He had a mighty brain, a learning beyond compare, and a heart that knew no fear and no remorse. He dared even to attend the Scholomance, and there was no branch of knowledge of his time that he did not essay."

–Chapter XXIII, Dr. Seward's Diary, 3 October

"Were another of the Un-Dead, like him, to try to do what he has done, perhaps not all the centuries of the world that have been, or that will be, could aid him. With this one, all the forces of nature that are occult and deep and strong must have worked together in some wondrous way. The very place, where he have been alive, Un-Dead for all these centuries, is full of strangeness of the geologic and chemical world. There

are deep caverns and fissures that reach none know whither. There have been volcanoes, some of whose openings still send out waters of strange properties, and gases that kill or make to vivify. Doubtless, there is something magnetic or electric in some of these combinations of occult forces which work for physical life in strange way; and in himself were from the first some great qualities. In a hard and warlike time he was celebrate that he have more iron nerve, more subtle brain, more braver heart, than any man. In him some vital principle have in strange way found their utmost; and as his body keep strong and grow and thrive, so his brain grow too."

–Chapter XXIV, Mina Murray's Journal, 5 October

For, friend John, hardly had my knife severed the head of each, before the whole body began to

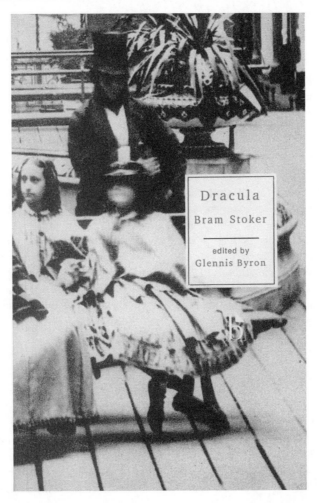

Cover for a 1998 Canadian edition published by Broadview Press (Elizabeth Miller Collection)

melt away and crumble into its native dust, as though the death that should have come centuries agone had at last assert itself and say at once and loud "I am here!"

 –Chapter XXVII, Dr. Van Helsing's Memorandum, 5 November

I shall be glad as long as I live that even in that moment of final dissolution, there was in the face a look of peace, such as I never could have imagined might have rested there.

The Castle of Dracula now stood out against the red sky, and every stone of its broken battlements was articulated against the light of the setting sun.

The gypsies, taking us as in some way the cause of the extraordinary disappearance of the dead man, turned, without a word, and rode away as if for their lives. Those who were unmounted jumped upon the leiter-wagon and shouted to the horsemen not to desert them. The wolves, which had withdrawn to a safe distance, followed in their wake, leaving us alone.

 –Chapter XXVII, Mina Murray's Journal, 6 November

VI. The Legacy of *Dracula*

Although Bram Stoker's Dracula *continued to be read in the early twentieth century, the catalysts for the apotheosis of Dracula as a popular culture icon were its stage and screen adaptations. In the 1920s* Dracula *inspired the celebrated German movie* Nosferatu *and was adapted for popular stage productions, first in Great Britain and then on Broadway. Since the first major Hollywood production based on the novel in 1931, Stoker's count has permeated every facet of Western culture, from comic books to ballet productions to breakfast cereals to children's shows. The importance of Stoker's* Dracula *as the basis for this phenomenon has led scholars and critics back to the text, and since the 1970s the novel has received serious attention.*

The First Movies

The first two movies Dracula *inspired were made in the early 1920s: the first was lost and the second barely survived the best efforts of Stoker's wife to destroy it.*

Discovery of a Hungarian *Drakula*
Lokke Heiss

What country gets credit for the first screen version of *Dracula*? Germany, with the release of *Nosferatu* in 1922 has long claimed this honor. However a filmbook has recently been found in the Budapest National Library that strongly suggests that the Hungarians got there first.

It has long been known that a Hungarian film titled *Drakula* was made in the early 1920s by a director named Károly Lajthay. But the film is long lost. Out of the hundreds of Hungarian films made between 1901 and 1930, less than thirty survive in complete form. With this bleak historical backdrop, the search for the film itself has long been considered hopeless.

Jenö Farkas, a Hungarian Dracula scholar, took a different approach. Instead of looking for the film itself, he looked for material generated by the film. While in the Hungarian National Library, he found a filmbook, published in 1924, titled *The Death of Drakula*. Filmbooks attempted to translate a film onto the printed page to give the story a different form of accessibility to the public. Since these adaptations were frequently fleshed-out versions of the film's script, the story-lines

in the books and films were usually similar if not identical. Filmbooks were then, and are now (in their modern incarnation as paperback novels), a popular way for those involved in the production of the film to make additional revenues. With this book, Farkas was able to reconstruct the probable plot of the original film. *The Death of Drakula* filmbook gives us a detailed narrative, which in part answers the question as to whether this film was or was not an adaptation of the Stoker novel.

The story begins as Mary Land, an innocent sixteen-year old orphaned seamstress, lives by herself in a small mountain village in Austria. She visits a mental hospital once a week to see her adopted father, who has had a nervous breakdown after the death of his wife. On Christmas Eve, Mary receives word that her father's health is failing. Her loyal boyfriend George, a local forest ranger, takes her to the hospital. Inside the hospital, Mary meets a once-famous composer who was once her music instructor. He has since gone mad and now claims to be the evil Drakula. (The spelling with a "k" was used perhaps to give the name a more local touch.) Mary tries to talk to her former teacher: "Try to remember, Mr. Professor . . . I was there, second row . . . you stroked my hair as a sign of approval."

"I am Drakula, the immortal one," the man responds. "I have been around a thousand years, and I shall live forever. . . . Immortality is mine. . . . Men can die, the world can be destroyed, but I live, I shall live forever!" Shaken by this encounter, Mary is seized and abducted by two patients who think they are doctors. They tie her up on a table with the intent of operating on her eyes. The plot is broken up by the staff of the hospital, and Mary is untied. She arrives at her father's side just in time for him to die in her arms.

Mary Land, spending the night at the asylum after these horrible events, has a terrible dream. Her music instructor, now calling himself Drakula, kidnaps her and takes her away to his castle. Twelve brides gather around her and escort her to a black magic marriage ceremony. Mary realizes that she going to be Drakula's new bride. At the last moment, Mary lifts up the crucifix she is carrying around her neck. "The cross! The cross!" Drakula yells, backing away. The rest of the evil spirits are repulsed. Mary runs out of the castle and into the woods.

Half-frozen, Mary is found by friendly villagers, and they call for a doctor. As Mary hovers near death, Drakula comes to her bedside and tries to hypnotize her. He approaches Mary with "a hellish face, blazing eyes, satanic features and hands ready to squeeze." The real doctor has been through a fiendish ride on a dark winding road to get to Mary. Now he arrives and with his help, Mary fights off Drakula's mesmerizing gaze. A lamp overturns, and the house catches on fire. Mary again runs out into the cold night, but now she wakes up to find herself back at the mental hospital. Was this all a dream? she ponders.

Meanwhile the insane inmates are playing games in the hospital garden. "Funnyman," a man wearing a pointed hat and thick glasses, has found a loaded gun. He aims it at Drakula, who seeing a chance to prove his immortality, urges him to pull the trigger. "When the shot finally rang out, it penetrated Drakula's heart and killed him instantly. His blood spilled out and left a bright red stain on the freshly fallen snow." Mary recovers, and as her fiancé George comes to pick her up from the hospital, they see Drakula's body being carried out on a stretcher. Papers fall out of the dead man's pocket titled "Diary of My Immortal Life and Adventures." Mary does not want to see the diary, and George throws the book away. Mary never tells George of her terrible ordeal. She thinks to herself: was it all a dream, or did it really happen?

An article about *The Death of Drakula* appeared in a Hungarian trade journal written in 1921. The journal includes two pictures from the film, one of Mary's abduction and the other of the wedding. The details seen in the photographs and in the text match the above storyline precisely. This evidence strongly supports that the book's narrative is similar to that of the film.

The larger issue remains: does this story contain the essence of Bram Stoker's novel? The answer depends on the issue of what constitutes a vampire. Vampires are quintessential seducers, and seductive men and women have been a staple of films from almost the beginning. With this very broad definition, you could find vampires lurking in many if not most films. In an attempt to be more selective, many vampirologists resort to more literal definitions to sort out the vampire from the vamp. Is he or she real or supernatural? For this film in particular, does Drakula have fangs, and does he suck blood?

On first consideration, the *Death of Drakula* fails this "bite 'em in the neck" litmus test. The film is not, in effect, a realization of the novel itself; it is more a commentary on the pervasive impact of Stoker's creation.

Cover for the filmbook for the lost Hungarian movie The Death of Drakula *(courtesy of Lokke Heiss and the Hungarian National Library)*

Lajthay evokes the image of Dracula as an evil character already familiar to the public. In only twenty-four years from the novel's publication, Dracula is already familiar enough for Lajthay to use as a symbol of evil repelled by a crucifix.

There is no evidence in the filmbook of any deliberate attempt to associate *Drakula* with the historical Dracula, Vlad the Impaler. Vlad was part of Romanian history and culture, not Hungarian, and Vlad's ties to Stoker's fictional character are tenuous at best. However, it is an open question as to if this connection was made by some of the audience familiar with the legends surrounding Vlad. Of note is that when the filmbook was published in 1925 it was published in Transylvania. Lajthay was also from Transylvania which until 1918 was still part of Hungary.

The narrative from *The Death of Drakula* models itself not from any historical event but from the fictional stories circulating in the early part of this century. Svengali-like stories of powerful dynamic men hypnotizing pure innocent girls were one of the staples of popular melodrama. Indeed, since Mary is kidnapped by her former music teacher, one could argue that the story is closer to Gaston Leroux's *Phantom of the Opera* than to anything Stoker visualized.

Still, there is the matter of the fangs. The front cover of the filmbook portrays a wonderful drawing of Drakula, displaying very sharp and deadly teeth. The image could be a display of wishful thinking by the artist. This would make the art-work part of a long tradition of posters and advertisements that promise more than is delivered. Or perhaps Drakula did have fangs, but only in the dream. If this is the case, the film itself begs the question of whether Drakula is real. This plot device is lifted directly from *The Cabinet of Dr. Caligari,* of which this film has more than a passing familiarity. Freud was one of Vienna's most famous citizens, and his influence can be felt throughout the story, chock-a-block full of symbols and neurotic dreams about substitute fathers.

According to records located by Farkas, the exterior locations of *The Death of Drakula* were shot near Vienna, and the interiors filmed in Corvin studios in Budapest. Paul Askonas was cast in the pivotal role as Drakula. Askonas was in many Austrian films in the twenties but as these films did not reach wide distribution outside of central Europe, his work is obscure. Those interested can look for his brief but menacing role as a butler in the 1924 German film *The Hands of Orlac.*

Newspaper accounts confirm that *The Death of Drakula* opened in Vienna in February 1921. *Nosferatu* premiered thirteen months later, in Berlin in March 1922. On these grounds alone, *The Death of Drakula* is clearly the first film adaptation relating to Stoker's novel. Perhaps the Austrians should get some of the bragging rights as to which country produced the first screen Dracula. The film is clearly an Austro-Hungarian collaboration, since the film was both partly shot and premiered in Vienna, and Paul Askonas (who played Drakula) is Austrian. This "Hungarian Drakula" certainly has more than a little Germanic blood.

A trade journal reporting on the 1921 opening in Vienna mentions that the lead female role was played by a Serbian actress named Lene Myl. The film next resurfaces in Budapest in 1923 with the lead actress named as Margit Lux. Although this might be simply the result of a marketing decision designed to highlight different actresses, the possibility exists that Lajthay recut or reshot the film to star Margit Lux, making the 1923 film an alternative version.

Károly Lajthay wrote and acted in more than twenty films and he directed at least twelve. All of his work from the silent era is lost. The Hungarian film industry in the 1920s was a victim of the bitter political landscape that existed in the country after the First World War. Internecine fighting and lack of money combined to cripple the chances for talented filmmakers

to make movies in their country. Many quit the business or became expatriates. Lajthay went back to his first training with the theatre and was away from film for almost twenty years. Lajthay returned to film-making briefly before he died in 1945. He was involved in the production of two sound films. The second, which he co-directed in 1943, was *Yellow Casino,* a comedy-suspense thriller in the Hitchcock tradition. A man has a jealous rage over a woman he loves, and finds himself in an insane asylum ("yellow room" is

Max Schreck as the vampire in Nosferatu *(1922), the first movie clearly based on Stoker's novel, considered a classic of German expressionism (courtesy of Ronald V. Borst/Hollywood Movie Posters)*

Florence Stoker and the Survival of *Nosferatu*

Bram Stoker's widow Florence sold Stoker's working notes for *Dracula* at auction in 1913 and received approximately two pounds, or about ten dollars, for them. The following year she published *Dracula's Guest and Other Weird Tales,* a collection of short pieces. Florence was, at this point, living in reduced circumstances. When Bram was in the employ of Henry Irving, the Stoker home on Cheyne Walk was elegantly furnished and their circle of friends was, to quote Miss Jean Brody, "la crème de la crème" of society. Now, on William Street in Knightsbridge, Florence had to depend on the small amounts that dribbled in from *Dracula* and on handouts from her son, Noel, who was working as an accountant. Since their relationship had always been rather strained, she did not expect, nor did she receive, much financial assistance from him.

Once during an interview, Vincent Price told about going to Florence Stoker's mews house for tea and recalled that her precious memorabilia included portraits by Rossetti, Burne-Jones, and her old flame, Oscar Wilde. She also had presentation copies of books by the greatest authors of the day, and, Price added with a sigh, she was still very beautiful. As it turned out, she was also a tiger when sinking her teeth into the problem which surfaced when she heard that a German film company had, without permission, used her husband's story in a movie entitled *Nosferatu*. In 1922 she joined the British Incorporated Society of Authors, presumably to recruit their support in what was to become a major and most unpleasant and tiresome conflict.

. . . .

Florence Stoker was relentless in pursuing her legal case. Members of the British Incorporated Society of Authors which she had joined correctly surmised that the only reason she had become a member was to enlist their support with the *Nosferatu* problem. G. Herbert Thring was the secretary of the society and, as such, had to take the brunt of Florence's incessant nagging. He and the society eventually put the matter into the hands of their German attorney, Dr. Wronker-Flatow, who lived and worked in Berlin. Florence Stoker was angry. Florence Stoker was persistent. Florence Stoker wanted justice. Above all, Florence Stoker wanted money.

In August of 1922, Thring contacted Florence and told her that the society was doing all it could but. . . ! Reading between the lines, Florence knew that the society really didn't care. Undaunted, she still had some irons in the fire, and immediately took advantage of certain influential friends who had ties within the society. On 22 August 1922, a Power of Attorney was sent to Dr. Wronker-Flatow in Berlin. At this point, Florence discovered that the movie was being shown in Budapest, which—if this were possible—further incensed her. She had been told that the film company had declared bankruptcy, and yet they were now collecting money from the movie, money that was rightfully hers. Was there no end to their insolence?

The situation dragged on and on. The society and poor G. Herbert became more and more exasperated. And still no conclusions were reached. Florence Stoker was trying to obliterate what was already being considered a classic movie and many people were involved. As we have already seen, Florence Stoker was a determined woman. And why not? By now the copyrighted *Dracula* was virtually her only means of support.

Eventually on 20 July 1925, word came from Berlin assuring the beleaguered society and a jubilant Florence Stoker that all prints and negatives of *Nosferatu* were to be destroyed. Florence breathed a sigh of relief, but—alas!—all too soon. Almost immediately, she heard that a British Film Society was being formed and one of the movies on its schedule was none other than *Dracula* by F. W. Murnau! Now, along with everything else, they were claiming authorship. The weary British Incorporated Society of Authors advised her to send a registered letter forbidding any showing of the film anywhere, anytime, any place, by anyone. More letters and phone calls followed, advising the film society that the movie was "stolen goods." And then, incredibly, there was more. The movie was being offered to theatres throughout England—and no one was able to locate those responsible for this development. Was reality imitating art? The cinematic vampire had flapped over country and channel and could obviously turn up whenever it wished. The vampire had achieved a life of its own and could move throughout the world at will.

—Jeanne Youngson, "Nosing Around *Nosferatu*," in
Dracula: Celebrating 100 Years, edited by
Leslie Shepard and Albert Power
(Dublin: Mentor, 1997),
pp. 120–125

Hungarian for mad-house). Artists frequently return to themes important to them, and this film, which happily survives, turns out to be a recasting of elements from *The Death of Drakula.* So although the original film is probably lost forever, Lajthay's vision lives on in a remake of sorts.

Those who insist that their Counts live in coffins and suck blood can rest assured that the German *Nosferatu* still qualifies as the first attempt to film Stoker's novel. The rest of us who like life with its complications and ambiguities can point instead to Hungary. It is only fitting that the country that was the birthplace of Bela Lugosi also gave us the first filmed Dracula.

Dracula on the Stage

Count Dracula became famous, not because of Nosferatu, *but as a result of two stage adaptations that ran in the United Kingdom and the United States during the mid- to late 1920s.*

'His Hour Upon the Stage':
Theatrical Adaptations of *Dracula*
David J. Skal

> Yet who would have thought the old man to have had so much blood in him?

> *—Macbeth* (V, i)

Although Dracula is best known to the public as a quintessential Hollywood icon and only secondarily as the fictional creation of Bram Stoker, our modern image of the king of vampires is largely a creation of the legitimate theatre. Stoker himself had a strong sense of the book's theatrical possibilities. By the time of its publication he had served as the acting manager of the Lyceum Theatre for seventeen years, the right-hand man and confidante of its impresario, the great Victorian actor Sir Henry Irving.

Stoker, born in Clontarf, Dublin, in 1847 and educated at Trinity College, had long been drawn to the exaggerated reality of the debating team and the theatre, and to literature and individuals who embodied dramatic, archetypal qualities. He positively idolized Walt Whitman, defending the poet at the height of the controversy over *Leaves of Grass,* writing the poet long, emotionally revealing letters.[1] Whitman responded, and the two eventually met.

But the most significant adoration of Stoker's life–indeed, most commentators agree that the relationship eclipsed even his marriage–was Henry Irving. In

Hamilton Deane, the British actor and producer who first successfully adapted Dracula *for the stage. He played Van Helsing in the first production, which was initially performed at the Grand Theatre, Derby, in August 1924 (courtesy of Jeanne Youngson).*

1876 Stoker was working as a civil servant in Dublin, but also contributing unpaid theatre reviews to the *Dublin Mail.* His glowing appraisals of Irving's Shakespearean performances attracted the attention of the thespian himself, who felt under-appreciated in Ireland and requested an introduction. After their second dinner together, Irving recited a grisly dramatic monologue, Thomas Hood's "The Dream of Eugene Aram," in which a murderer is overcome by guilt and the fear of God. Stoker himself was overcome by the force of Irving's acting, and "burst into something like hysterics."[2]

Irving was impressed ("Soul had looked into soul!" wrote Stoker. "From that hour began a friendship as profound, as close, as lasting as can be between two men."[3]) and a few seasons later claimed the young man as his own, at least professionally. Stoker became the acting manager of Irving's new venture, London's Lyceum Theatre, in December 1878. Irving was both commanding as a performer and demanding as an employer; Stoker's own language in describing their crucial encounter evokes a sense of the demonic, using phrases like "commanding force," "the magnetism of his genius," "so profound was the sense of his dominance that I set spellbound. . . ."[4] By the time Stoker began to work on the novel that would become *Dracula,* Irving had been playing the role of Mephistopheles in *Faust* for five years. Both Stoker and the public had become accustomed to Irving in the role of a showy devil, and, at some point during *Dracula*'s composition, Stoker decided his vampire might have the potential to be a signature Irving characterization.

According to veteran Chicago drama critic Frederick Donaghey who made the writer's acquaintance during one of the Lyceum's American tours around the turn of the century, "When the late Bram Stoker told me that he had put endless hours in trying to persuade Henry Irving to have a play made from *Dracula* and to act in it, he added that he had nothing in mind save the box office. 'If,' he explained, 'I am able to afford to have my name on the book, the Governor certainly can afford, with business bad, to have his name on the play. But he laughs at me whenever I talk about it; and then we have to go out and raise money to put on something in which the public has no interest.'"

Stoker went on to tell Donaghey his conception of Irving in the role of king vampire: "The Governor as Dracula would be the Governor in a composite of so many of the parts in which he has been liked—Matthias in 'The Bells,' Shylock, Mephistopheles, Peter the Great, the Bad Fellow in 'The Lyons Mail,' Louis XI, and ever so many others, including Iachimo in 'Cymbeline.' But he just laughs at me!" In Donaghey's recollection, Stoker's grandiose theatrical ambitions were countervailed by a literary humility. "He knew he had written, in 'Dracula,' a shilling shocker, however successful a one, and was frank about it," Donaghey wrote in 1929.[5]

Assuming that the Chicago critic is quoting Stoker accurately, it seems immediately apparent that issues of power, control, and Stoker's ambivalence about his own creative abilities are more important issues than box-office receipts. While there is no documentation that Stoker may have grown to resent Irving, many of Stoker's chroniclers find in *Dracula* an allegory of an unequal, draining relationship between the two

men; Stoker locked up in the Lyceum castle, as it were, serving a master's wishes while having his own attempts at written expression inhibited. Harker's letters are confiscated; Stoker's direct dramatic collaboration with Irving is never realized.

Dracula is filled with overreaching allusions to Shakespeare; in addition to the roles mentioned by Stoker in his conversation with Donaghey, there are ample references to *Macbeth* (Irving's favorite role): a cursed warrior-king in a desolate castle, three weird sisters, somnambulism, and blood imagery. The shipwreck in a storm and Dracula's ability to drive the elements seem dark reflections of *The Tempest;* Dracula's funereal Puritanism—his black clothing, his rejection of ordinary human pleasures like food, his inveighing against mirrors and human vanity—all darkly conjure the character of Hamlet, metamorphosed into a ghost like his father. There are passing quotations from and references to *King Lear, Twelfth Night,* and *The Merchant of Venice.* And Stoker's admission that he had Irving's Shylock in mind underscores the tacit anti-Semitism in Dracula's physical appearance, a Transylvanian variation on villainous literary Jews like Svengali and Fagin.

Stoker prepared a dramatic abridgement of his book entitled *Dracula: or The Un-Dead,* which was given a staged reading at the Lyceum on 18 May 1897. Ostensibly for purposes of protecting the novel's dramatic copyright, the marathon event may have also been something of an exercise in vanity—or simply a vain, last attempt to favorably impress Henry Irving. The Lyceum briefly became Stoker's macabre toy theatre, though brevity may have seemed an eternity; the reading was stupefyingly long—a prologue followed by five acts in forty-seven scenes, lasting over five hours. A formal program was printed, showing that the reading was elaborately cast with fifteen actors, drawn primarily from the second tier of Lyceum actors. Dracula was portrayed by a "Mr. Jones," Jonathan Harker by an actor named Herbert Passmore, and Van Helsing by Tom Reynolds, a popular character actor in Irving's employ. Edith Craig, the daughter of Ellen Terry, Irving's leading lady, took the role of Mina. The program credits the Lyceum's musical director, Meredith Ball, suggesting at least an overture or entr'acte accompaniment. The script indicates twenty separate scenes. The standing sets at the Lyceum the day of Stoker's reading were those of the comedy *Madame Sans-Gêne* by Victorien Sardou and Emile Moreau.

The "script" that Stoker later submitted to the Lord Chamberlain's Office on 31 May 1897 is a cut-and-paste of printer's proofs of the book, with numerous handwritten additions and emendations. Presumably, this is the only copy that ever existed,[6] and it is reasonable to assume that the actors read from it at a

II - 12

RENFIELD   The Fly - my dear sir - has one striking feature, its wings are typical of the aerial powers of the psychic faculties. The ancients did well - when they typified the soul as a butterfly !

SEWARD   Oh, it's a 'soul' you are after now - is it ?

RENFIELD   Oh no - oh no - I want no 'souls'. Life is all I want - and Blood is the life ! Life is a positive and perpetual entity, and by consuming a multitude of live things - no matter how low in the scale of creation, one may indefinitely prolong life - but I don't want any souls - indeed I don't - they would be no use to me - I couldn't eat them or - - -

SEWARD   But how are you to get the life, without getting the soul also ?

             RENFIELD looks puzzled.

A nice time you'll have some day when you are flying out there, with the souls of thousands of flies and spiders, and birds and cats, buzzing and twittering and miauing all round you. You've got their lives you know - and you must put up with their souls !

             RENFIELD puts his fingers in his ears, and shuts his eyes screwing them up tightly.

RENFIELD   To hell with you and your souls. Why do you plague me about souls ? Haven't I got enough to worry and distract me already without thinking of souls !

SEWARD   Renfield !

RENFIELD   Forgive me, Doctor, I forgot myself : I am so worried in my mind that I am apt to be irritable. If you only knew the problem I have to face - you would pity and pardon me. Please don't put me in a "strait-jacket", I want to think, and I can't think freely when my body is confined !

SEWARD   Well, come now - wouldn't you like some sugar to spread out for your flies ?

RENFIELD   Flies ! (A look of animation comes over his face - then passes) Oh flies are but poor things !

Page from Deane's script for Dracula *(courtesy of David J. Skal)*

lectern; it cannot be determined whether the stage directions were read aloud or indicated, but it can probably be safely assumed: certain scenes, such as Dracula's crawling down the wall of his castle, would make no sense unless the action was somehow described, if not actually staged.

Stoker's abridgement is only fitfully theatrical, and he seems to have been hampered by the same difficulties with which later adaptors would also wrestle. The book's vast geographical sweep and outdoor scenes, with breakneck carriage chases, shipwrecks, and gypsies on horseback, are obviously unsuited to the stage. Stoker is forced to provide Jonathan Harker with a breathless opening speech that is almost a parody of Victorian melodramatic exposition:

> Enter Jonathan Harker followed by driver of Calèche carrying his hand portmanteau and bag. Latter leaves luggage close to door (c) and Exit[s] hurriedly.

HARKER: Hi! Hi! Where are you off to! Gone already! (*knocks at door*) Well this is a pretty nice state of things! After a drive through solid darkness with an unknown man whose face I have not seen and who has in his hand the strength of twenty men and who can drive back a pack of wolves by holding up his hand; who visits mysterious blue flames and who wouldn't speak a word that he could help, to be left here in the dark before a—a ruin. Upon my life I'm beginning my professional experience in a romantic way! Only passed my exam at Lincoln's Inn before I left London, and here I am conducting my business—or rather my employer Mr. Hawkins's business with an accompaniment of wolves and mystery. (*knocks*) If this Count Dracula were a little more attentive to a guest when he *does* arrive he needn't have been so effusive in his letters to Mr. Hawkins regarding my having the best of everything on the journey. (*knocks*) I wondered why the people in the Hotel at Bistritz were so frightened and why the old lady hung the Crucifix round my neck and why the people on the coach made signs against the evil eye! By Jove, if any of them had this kind of experience, no wonder at anything they did—or thought. (*knocks*) This is becoming more than a joke. If it were my own affair I should go straight back to Exeter; but as I act for another and have the papers of the Count's purchase of [a] London estate I suppose I must go on and do my duty—thank God there is a light, someone is coming.[7]

Overall, Stoker's treatment of the scenes in Transylvania are the most successful from a dramatic standpoint, though most of the speeches are still far too long to be stageworthy. Nonetheless, some effects are striking; following Dracula's confrontation with the vampire women about to attack Harker, the Count picks up the fainted solicitor like another bride and carries him off into darkness (an action that underscores the homoerotic aspects of the novel that have recently been the

subject of several critical studies). One of Lucy's encounters with the vampire in the Whitby cemetery is indicated with remarkable theatrical economy and impact: *Enter Lucy sleepwalking in nightdress, and reclines on seat. Moonlight and shadow alternate. When a shadow moves Count Dracula is seen bending over her and with his face on her throat.* And when Mina interrupts his feast: *Shadow. Dracula raises his head, sees her, and sinks down through tombstone.*[8] Stoker was evidently quite familiar with "the vampire trap," a sprung opening in the stage so-named for its original use in James Robinson Planché's melodrama *The Vampire, or, The Bride of the Isles* (1820). The vampire trap effected dramatic entries and exits of supernatural characters and was first employed at the Lyceum (then the English Opera House) for Planché's thrilling play.

In the end, any hopes Stoker may have had about impressing Henry Irving with his dramaturgical skills came to naught in a possibly apocryphal scene recounted by Stoker's biographer and great-nephew Daniel Farson: "Legend has it that Sir Henry entered the theatre during the reading and listened for a few moments with a warning glint of amusement. 'What do you think of it?' someone asked him unwisely, as he left for his dressing room. *'Dreadful!'* came the devastating reply, projected with such resonance that it filled the theatre."[9]

Stoker, of course, was correct in his intuition that *Dracula* deserved a dramatic afterlife, though it would not come to pass in his own lifetime. He staged another "copyright reading" of his 1898 novel *Miss Betty,* once more using members of the Lyceum company. Following the death of Henry Irving in 1905 and his own recovery from a debilitating stroke, Stoker seems to have at least considered donning an Irving-like mantle in the American theatre. On 1 April 1906, a columnist for the *San Francisco Chronicle* revealed some of the details. Referring to an account published in a New York newspaper, the item noted that "Stoker, for many years, directed the business end of Irving's tours. There has never been word of Stoker's taking more than casual interest in the actual staging of plays, yet it is said, and apparently in good faith, that he has been invited to become the stage manager of one of the 'artistic' theatres which 'society,' in the whirligig of its jealousies, plans to build in this city." The unsigned piece went on, a bit cynically, concerning the current state of theatre in San Francisco, where Irving, and Stoker, had toured. "Before Stoker is pressed for a contract it might be profitable to come here and report on conditions as they exist. . . . But Mr. Stoker has a weakness for a joke that may lead him to accept the offer. This is as much to be desired as the other. In either pole his geniality would add to the diversion which the public already is

Raymond Huntley, who performed the role of Count Dracula more than two thousand times on the stage. In his early twenties, when he first played the part for Deane's struggling company, Huntley was required to provide his own costumes (courtesy of Jeanne Youngson).

finding in these proposed temples of high art."[10] A few weeks later the question was rendered moot as San Francisco was destroyed by one of the most theatrical natural disasters in history.

Whatever theatrical ambitions Stoker may have harbored went unrealized in his remaining years, which were difficult, physically and financially. Despite three decades of loyal service, Stoker was not included in Irving's will. In *Personal Reminiscences of Henry Irving,* published in two volumes in 1906, Stoker did manage to achieve a final "collaboration" with his dead employer, if only by superimposing his own biography over that of Irving, fusing their lives forever in print.

Stoker died on 20 April 1912. His widow was left with few tangible assets, save her husband's copyrights, and the only one that continued to generate income was *Dracula.* Forced into genteel poverty, she clung to the demon jealously. *Dracula* became Florence Stoker's guardian angel, of a kind, providing a steady if meager sustenance. She was determined to make money from stage and motion picture rights, but interlopers vexed her. A now-obscure 1920 film called *Drakula,* a Hungarian production filmed in Berlin by Károly Lajthay, apparently escaped her notice. But when *Dracula* was pirated by German filmmakers, the widow Stoker launched a protracted legal war against F. W. Murnau's now-classic *Nosferatu: Eine Symphonie des Grauens* (1922). With the aid of the British Society of Authors, she won a judgment from the German courts ordering the destruction of all copies. Fortunately, the film and its negative survived in scattered fragments; reconstituted, it was eventually recognized as a masterpiece of German expressionism.

Tired and infuriated by unauthorized encroachments, Florence Stoker granted the first license for a stage adaptation of *Dracula* to a touring actor-manager named Hamilton Deane, whose family had known Stoker's in Dublin. Deane had quite a following in the provinces, but almost no reputation in London; his barnstorming style was decidedly at odds with prevailing taste in the West End. Deane's *Dracula,* first produced in 1924, was conceived as a touring vehicle for less sophisticated regional audiences.

Stoker's novel, however theatrical its intentions, had built-in problems for would-be stage adaptors. For reasons of physical and economic practicality, the play needed to be reduced to the dimensions of a drawing-room mystery melodrama with minimal scenery and stage effects. (Deane originally included a Transylvanian prologue in which Dracula emerged from a castle window in half-human form, but never produced it because of cost.) Dracula himself presented difficulties: for most of the novel, Stoker's monster is an offstage presence who never interacts with the main characters in anything resembling a normal fashion. To work as a drawing-room mystery, Dracula would have to be reconfigured as the kind of character who might be reasonably invited into a drawing room to begin with. And thus began an essential dichotomy in the evolution of *Dracula,* which served practical, dramatic, and commercial considerations while working against Stoker's original vision.

Deane conceived the now-familiar appearance of Dracula as a kind of devilish vaudeville magician in evening dress and an opera cloak, who insinuates himself into the lives of the human characters by feigning neighborly interest in Mina's mysterious anemia. The associations with stage magic were especially appropriate given the variety-show effects Deane employed: flash boxes; demonstrations of hypnotism; and a trick coffin for Dracula's ultimate destruction, built along the lines of a standard conjurer's cabinet.

Deane originally wanted to play Dracula himself, but eventually realized that Van Helsing was the meatier role. An actor named Edmund Blake inaugurated the part and was succeeded by Raymond Huntley, who took the role to London's West End in 1927, where it was a surprise hit. As Deane feared, the critics did their best to drive a stake through *Dracula,* but audiences flocked to the Little Theatre, Adelphi, despite a decidedly second-class production. In 1989, not long before his death, Huntley told this writer that the production was so threadbare that he was required to provide his own evening clothes. When the production was forced to move to the larger Duke of York's, the London *Evening News* noticed, with some amazement, "while glittering productions costing thousands of pounds have wilted and died after a week or so in the West End, 'Dracula' has gone on drinking blood nightly."[11]

The flamboyant American publisher and producer Horace Liveright, ever on the prowl for properties with sensational possibilities, liked the premise of *Dracula* but disliked the stiff dialogue of Deane's original script. He enlisted the American journalist and dramatist John L. Balderston, who had recently scored a success as coauthor (with J. C. Squire) of the supernatural romance *Berkeley Square,* to rewrite the dialogue completely and improve the structure for Broadway.

Thereafter, and until World War II, *Dracula* was performed in two distinctly different versions, one for British audiences and one for Americans. (In strict point of fact there were three existing versions—Florence Stoker commissioned yet another adaptation from a playwright named Charles Morrell. This version she owned outright; she resented paying adaptor's royalties. But the Morrell play was static and talky, retaining long speeches taken verbatim from the novel as Stoker did in his 1897 dramatic abridgment, and was only performed briefly.) Hamilton Deane's version is notable for introducing most of the standard trappings we now associate with *Dracula:* the enveloping, crimson-lined cape; French doors; fog machines; secret panels; and, perhaps most memorably, easily hypnotized maids who can be relied upon to remove a range of annoyances ranging from crucifixes to garlic flowers to noxious necklaces of vampire-repelling wolfbane. One familiar costume detail, the exaggerated stand-up collar on Dracula's cape, had a particular stage function: to hide the back of the actor's head while he slipped through a trap door or panel, leaving the other company members holding the empty cloak. Though the collar had no function in motion pictures, where camera tricks replaced trap doors, it has nonetheless become a signature feature of vampire costuming in all media.

Liveright wanted the British actor Raymond Huntley to reprise his West End role on Broadway, but the actor refused the skimpy salary offered—$150 a week. Rebuffed, Liveright offered even less money to a

---

The London Premier

Hamilton Deane Adaptation of *Dracula*
Little Theatre, London, 14 February 1927

Cast of Characters

Dracula	Raymond Huntley
Van Helsing	Hamilton Deane
Seward	Stuart Lomath
Harker	Bernard Guest
Quincey Morris	Frieda Hearn
Lord Godalming	Peter Jackson
Renfield	Bernard Jukes
Mina	Dora Mary Patrick
The Maid	Betty Murgatroyd

—Leonard Wolf, *Dracula: The Connoisseur's Guide,*
p. 299

---

hungry expatriate actor from Lugos, Hungary, who was in no position to turn down work. And so Béla Ferenc Dezsö Blasko, known professionally as Bela Lugosi, became the strangest matinee idol the New York theatre had ever seen, and soon was one of the most instantly identifiable presences in theatrical history. Liveright understood the implied Freudian aspects of the story and their potential Jazz Age appeal; terms such as "libido" and "death wish" were bandied about routinely in smart Manhattan conversation, and Lugosi's weird characterization—patent-leather hair, patent-leather shoes, a continental accent, and bilious green makeup—was the perfect amalgam of Rudolph Valentino and the grave.

Dracula enjoyed a two-week tryout in New Haven, Hartford, and other nearby venues in late September 1927 before opening on Broadway on October 15. The sheer audacity of the production guaranteed a large box office. Here was a new kind of mystery play, which, contrary to prevailing stage conventions, did not attempt to "explain away" its terrors as the result of nefarious human agency. *Dracula,* the press release warned, "deals frankly with the supernatural." Liveright's theatrical manager Louis Cline, a wizard at publicity stunts, had a field day with outrageous and attention-getting promotions. As in London, lobby nurses and fainting patrons were both provided by the management—a conflict of interest, perhaps, but one which drew no serious complaint.

Dracula ran for thirty-three weeks in New York, followed by two simultaneous tours, one on the West Coast with Bela Lugosi, the other covering the rest of the country, with Raymond Huntley. The success of

Punch on Deane's *Dracula*

Deane feared the reaction of critics to his production when it premiered in London at the Little Theatre.

The late Mr. Bram Stoker's *Dracula,* which I understand has for many years been a cause of frequent nightmares in the unsophisticated, has been done into a play by Mr. Hamilton Deane, and I am bound to say that he has made a mirth-provoking affair of it—in parts. It is true this vampire business is not primarily designed for mirth, and no doubt the apparatus of suddenly-opened doors, clocks that tick eerily, howling lunatics who eat flies and white mice, pink-eyed bats (not induced by alcohol), magnesium flashes, swirling mists which don't smell at all like mists, pale-faced aristocratic aliens whose bodies are not reflected in plane mirrors and whose hair is twisted into devilish horns may very well be more seriously alarming between the pages of a book than they are in the three-dimensional medium of the stage. If this had all been played in a full-blooded transpontine manner, and if everything had not been said seven times, laughter would have been even more easy, though I admit there was something especially diverting in watching a company of grave conscientious actors in the West-End manner heroically pretending to take it all seriously.

Of course *Jonathan Harker* was asking for trouble when he shared a semi-detached house with *Doctor Seward,* who apparently kept or didn't keep his loosely-controlled lunatics in the other half of it. And it was tempting Providence to let the house on his other side to so obviously sinister a person as *Count Dracula,* with his mysterious packing-cases, his horned hair, red eyes and gaping fangs. But he couldn't be expected, I suppose, to realize that his sister-in-law would fade away to the grave, after I know not how many unavailing transfusions of blood, with those queer tiny wounds in her throat. And it was certainly rough luck that his own wife should apparently be going the same dreadful way. Not at all surprising that *Doctor Seward* (who looked and talked less like a medical man than seemed humanly possible) should be puzzled. Mere mumps would have puzzled him, I feel sure.

But help is at hand. *Professor Abraham van Helsing,* the Dutchman—psychologist, psycho-analyst, hypnotist and were-wolf specialist—arrives. His diagnosis is that a vampire is at work. Nonsense? Not at all. We scientific men know a good many queer things, let us tell you. He interviews the deplorable *Count,* having learnt about the packing-cases, which from his specialized knowledge he recognizes as the lairs or changing-places necessary to every self-respecting practising vampire; offers him garlic, a herb notoriously fatal to vampires (and other non-Fascists), and sees the violent convulsions into which it throws him; after which he brilliantly concludes that the red-eyed nobleman may have something to do with the sad business. "Of course I can't be sure, mind you, but ———"; the cautious scientific attitude in fact. This is, as you have guessed, a frightfully scientific play.

The heroine is visibly sinking. Shall we be in time to save her? The astute *Van Helsing,* having further cheered the patient and her friends by explaining what a perfectly terrible condition she is in and how lucky she is to have him there; having removed and sterilized (with garlic) all the *Count's* lairs but the one in the coach-house next-door; having explained to *Lord Godalming* that it is necessary that his late *fiancée, Lucy,* must have her tomb broken into and a stake driven into her heart in order to prevent her going about as a "beau'ful lady" (a were-wolf in fact), nibbling the throats of the Hampstead young—she is "undead" and must be made "true dead"; having carefully decorated poor *Mrs. Harker* with garlic and hung a cross about her neck, which the maid, hypnotized by *Dracula,* removes in a trance, thus leaving the vampire free for his hasty evening meal; having with his three friends surrounded the *Count* aforesaid and tried vainly to impress him with four fore-fingers dramatically levelled at him, he countering with a firework, under cover of which he makes his escape—it only remains for the four heroes to track the beast to his lair in the coach-house and at the precise hour of sunset to shine four green bulls'-eyes upon him and plunge a stake into his heart so that his tortured soul may leave his body with a fizz in a cloud of smoke.

For us it only remains to sidle quietly into the Adelphi, wondering sadly why this sort of thing should be supposed to be adequate entertainment for adults in this year of grace in one of the world's capital cities.

T.

—Punch, 23 February 1927

the stage play (which earned over $2 million in America alone) brought *Dracula* to the attention of Hollywood, which had shied away from the novel because its sensational horrors had always been considered unfilmable. But a film based on the much tamer thrills of the play would be another matter entirely. Following two years of tempestuous negotiations among Florence Stoker, Hamilton Deane, John L. Balderston, their agents, and the studios of Universal, Metro-Goldwyn-Mayer,

Columbia, and Fox Films, Universal purchased the film rights to the novel and all three stage versions for $40,000 in the summer of 1930. The studio planned a "super-production" starring the silent screen's "Man of a Thousand Faces," Lon Chaney, in one of his first talking roles. Chaney, however, was stricken with terminal cancer and Universal's plans went into a tailspin. The mounting economic realities of the deepening Depression forced the financially strapped

Cartoon from the 14 December 1927 issue of The Tatler *depicting replacement cast members Frederick Keen and Dora Jay*
(David J. Skal, Hollywood Gothic, *1990; Bruccoli Clark Layman Archives)*

studio to develop a script based almost exclusively on the stage play and to turn to Bela Lugosi for a part they originally intended for an established film star. Lugosi was paid a total of $3,500 for seven weeks of work on the film and never received additional payment related directly to Universal's 1931 film, despite his lifelong identification with the part.[12]

Dracula, directed by Tod Browning, was a major moneymaker for Universal and has been credited with rescuing the studio from the jaws of bankruptcy. The film's success sparked a renewed interest in the stage play; released to stock in 1930, Deane and Balderston's *Dracula* has been in almost continuous performance somewhere in the world ever since, a permanent fixture of the regional, college, and community theatre circuits.

To understand the popularity and persistence of *Dracula,* it is necessary to appreciate the novel's essential theatricality, beginning with its origins in Bram Stoker's problematic relationship with a major theatrical figure of the nineteenth century, and continuing with crucial twentieth-century embellishments, which first and foremost served the purposes of the theatre.

While popularizing *Dracula,* the theatre has also, ironically, created a powerful secondary set of images and expectations which have made a definitive dramatic adaptation on stage or screen virtually impossible from a commercial standpoint. Even the most careful dramatic reproduction of the book, the 1977 BBC television miniseries, refrained from depicting Dracula as the repulsive monster Stoker described, instead casting actor Louis Jourdan as an update on Bela Lugosi's ambiguously attractive aristocrat. Francis Ford Coppola's misleadingly titled film *Bram Stoker's Dracula* (1992) also refused to face the primal horror of Stoker's count in favor of a romantic/Byronic image of the vampire popularized in the early-nineteenth-century theatre, but unequivocally rejected by Stoker at the fin de siècle.

Dramatic Adaptations: A Checklist

The following list includes significant theatrical adaptations owing a true debt to Stoker, omitting casual spoofs, versions intended for amateurs, children's groups, and so on.

1897

Bram Stoker, *Dracula; or The Un-Dead*. Lyceum Theatre, London, 18 May 1897. A lengthy reading of Stoker's novel to secure theatrical copyright protection, this cumbersome manuscript (held by the Lord Chamberlain's Collection, British Library Department of Manuscripts) anticipates the difficulties later adaptors would encounter while attempting to translate the complex story to other media.

1924–1927

Hamilton Deane, *Dracula*. The first licensed adaptation of Stoker's novel toured the English provinces successfully for three years before opening in a slightly revised form at London's Little Theatre in February 1927.

Charles Morrell, *Dracula*. An alternate stage adaptation, commissioned by Stoker's widow, evidently to preserve "literary" qualities of her husband's book not included in Hamilton Deane's version. Produced briefly in September 1927, the script proved unstageworthy, but Universal Pictures purchased motion picture rights to this adaptation, as well as the Deane/Balderston play and novel itself; a few lines from Morrell were, in fact, used in the 1931 film, directed by Tod Browning.

Hamilton Deane and John L. Balderston, *Dracula* [*The Vampire Play*]. Plymouth Theatre, New York, October 1927. American journalist and playwright Balderston adapted Deane's British script for Broadway, retaining the dramatic structure but almost completely rewriting the dialogue. The 1977 Broadway stage revival starring Frank Langella added new lines for Dracula, including borrowings from the 1931 film version (for example, "I never drink . . . wine.")

1970

Leon Katz, *Dracula: Sabbat*. A ritualistic performance piece, attracting highly laudatory reviews from the national press during its run at the Judson Poet's Theatre in New York City.

1972

Ted Tiller, *Count Dracula*. Tiller's adaptation is similar in many respects to Deane and Balderston's, but includes considerably more comic relief and was quite successful on the regional and amateur theatre circuits in the 1970s. Arguably more influenced by the earlier play than by Stoker.

1977

Bob Hall and David Richmond, *The Passion of Dracula*. Commercially successful in New York and London, this

version retains the stagebound drawing-room conventions as established by Hamilton Deane.

1978

Douglas Johnson and John Aschenbrenner, *Dracula: A Musical Nightmare*. The best of many attempts at setting *Dracula* to music. A "concept" production combining the story of a third-rate English touring company and its production of *Dracula* with music-hall song-and-dance numbers. Johnson (book and lyrics) and Aschenbrenner (music) received excellent notices.

1983

Richard Sharp, *Dracula: The Story You Thought You Knew*. A critically acclaimed production, in repertory for two seasons at the Oregon Shakespeare Festival, Sharp's adaptation, which included elaborate stage effects, received additional praise when it was restaged as a commercial production in a San Francisco church in 1985.

1985

Liz Lochhead, *Dracula*. One of the most critically praised adaptations, written by a noted Scottish poet/playwright, largely jettisoning the traditional drawing-room settings for a more fluid and theatrically evocative physical production. To date, produced only in Scotland.

1994

Mac Wellman, *Mac Wellman's Dracula*. Produced by New York's SoHo Rep, a postmodernist interpretation of Stoker's novel.

1999

Richard Ouzounian, *Dracula: a Chamber Musical*. With book and lyrics by Richard Ouzounian and music by Marek Norman, this faithful adaptation of Stoker's novel played to full houses for six straight months at the Stratford Festival (Ontario, Canada) during their 1999 season.

2001

Des McAniff, *Dracula, the Musical*. Book and lyrics by Christopher Hampton and Don Black, music by Frank Wildhorn. Premiered at La Jolla Playhouse in California in October 2001. Opened in New York in the fall of 2002.

–Revised with the approval of the author from *Dracula*,
edited by Nina Auerbach and David J. Skal
(New York: Norton, 1997), pp. 371–381

---

1. Stoker's letters to Whitman are included in Horace Traubel, *With Walt Whitman in Camden*, vol. 4 (Philadel-

phia: University of Pennsylvania Press, 1953), pp. 181–185.

2. Bram Stoker, *Personal Reminiscences of Henry Irving,* 2 vols. (New York: Macmillan, 1906), vol. 1, p. 31.

3. Stoker, *Reminiscences,* vol. 1. p. 33.

4. Stoker, *Reminiscences,* vol. 1. pp. 29–30.

5. Frederick Donaghey, review of Deane and Balderston's *Dracula, Chicago Daily Tribune,* 3 April 1929, p. 37.

6. For the full text of this dramatization, see *Dracula: or The Un-Dead,* ed. Sylvia Starshine (Nottingham: Pumpkin, 1997). The original manuscript is in the British Museum.

7. Starshine, *Dracula,* p. 1.

8. Starshine, *Dracula,* pp. 37–38.

9. Daniel Farson, *The Man Who Wrote Dracula* (New York: St. Martin's Press, 1975), p. 164.

10. "Things Theatrical," *San Francisco Chronicle Sunday Supplement,* 1 April 1906, p. 9.

11. Harry Ludlam, *A Biography of Dracula: The Life Story of Bram Stoker* (London: Foulsham, 1962), p. 161.

12. Lugosi's identification with the Dracula persona was so complete that the role followed him even after death: he was buried in August 1956 in full vampire regalia.

* * *

As rewritten by John D. Balderston, the new Dracula *debuted in New York in 1927 and was an immediate hit. Its success led to a 1931 movie, also starring Bela Lugosi as the Count, that was largely based on the play. Because of the popularity of the play and the movie, Deane and Balderston's portrayal of the vampire as a predatory cape-wielding gentleman villain became the Dracula of American popular culture—not Stoker's original. The play has only two settings, Dr. Seward's parlor and Carfax Abbey, and Count Dracula at first is a welcome guest in the Seward home, where he comes offering aide to the doctor's daughter, Lucy.*

From *Dracula: The Vampire Play*

from Act 1

VAN HELSING: I'm not likely to laugh. . . .

[*Gently, without answering, he unwinds scarf from her throat. She puts hand up to stop him and cries, "No, no." A look at* HARKER *when her neck is bare. As* VAN HELSING *does so he starts, then quickly opens a small black bag on the table and returns with microscope; examines two small marks on throat.* LUCY *with eyes closed. Controlling himself with difficulty,* VAN HELSING *puts microscope back in bag, closes it, puts back chair by desk.*]

And how long have you had these little marks on your throat?

[SEWARD *and* HARKER *start violently and come to divan. They look at each other in horror.*]

LUCY: Since . . . that first morning.

Liveright's Production

Deane-Balderston Adaptation of *Dracula*
Fulton Theater, New York, 4 October 1927

Cast of Characters

Dracula	Bela Lugosi
The Maid	Nedda Harrigan
Harker	Terrence Neill
Seward	Herbert Bunston
Van Helsing	Edward Van Sloan
Renfield	Bernard Jukes
Lucy Seward	Dorothy Peterson

—Leonard Wolf, *Dracula: The Connoisseur's Guide,*
p. 300

HARKER: Lucy, why didn't you tell us?

SEWARD: Lucy, you've worn that scarf around your throat . . . to hide them!

[LUCY *makes convulsive clutch at throat.*]

VAN HELSING: Do not press her. Do not excite her. [*To* LUCY.] Well?

LUCY: [*Constrained; to* SEWARD *and* HARKER.] I was afraid they'd worry you, for I knew that . . . Mina had them.

VAN HELSING: [*With assumed cheerfulness.*] Quite right, Miss Lucy, quite right. They're nothing, and old Van Helsing will see that these . . . dreams trouble you no more.

MAID: [*Appears at door.*] Count Dracula.

[DRACULA *enters. He is a tall, mysterious man of about fifty. Polished and distinguished. Continental in appearance and manner.* LUCY *registers attraction to* DRACULA.]

SEWARD: Ah, good evening, Count.

DRACULA: Gentlemen [*He bows to men; then goes to the divan and bows in courtly fashion.*] Miss Seward, how are you? You are looking more yourself this evening.

[LUCY *registers thrill. Alternate moods of attraction and repulsion, unaccountable to herself, affect* LUCY *in* DRACULA's *presence. But this should be suggested subtly.*]

Horace Liveright, the publisher and Broadway producer who purchased the American rights to the Deane play and commissioned John L. Balderston to revise the script (frontispiece, Walker Gilmer, Horace Liveright: Publisher of the Twenties [New York: Lewis, 1970]; Thomas Cooper Library, University of South Carolina)

LUCY: [*Quite natural.*] I feel better already, Count, now that father's old friend has come to help me.

[DRACULA *turns to* VAN HELSING. LUCY *looks up at* DRACULA, *recoils, and turns to* HARKER.]

SEWARD: Count Dracula, Professor Van Helsing.

[*The two men bow.*]

DRACULA: A most distinguished scientist, whose name we know even in the wilds of Transylvania. [*To* SEWARD.] But I interrupt a consultation.

SEWARD: Not at all, Count, It's good of you to come, and we appreciate your motives.

HARKER: Doctor Seward has just told me of your offer, and I can't thank you enough.

DRACULA: It is nothing. I should be grateful to be permitted to help Miss Lucy in any way.

LUCY: But you do, Count. I look forward to your visits. They seem to make me better.

VAN HELSING: And so I arrive to find a rival in the field.

DRACULA: [*Crosses to* LUCY.] You encourage me, Miss Seward, to make them more frequent, as I should like to.

LUCY: [*Looking at him fixedly.*] I am always glad to see you.

DRACULA: Ah, but you have been lonely here. And my efforts to amuse you with our old tales will no longer have the same success, now that you have Professor Van Helsing with you, and especially now that Mr. Harker is to remain here.

HARKER: How did you know I was going to stay, Count?

DRACULA: [*Little start.*] Can the gallant lover ask such a question? I inferred it, my friend.

HARKER: You're right. Nothing is going to shift me now until Lucy's as fit as a fiddle again.

DRACULA: Nothing?

LUCY: Please come as before, Count, won't you?

[DRACULA *bows to her; kisses her hand.* VAN HELSING *meanwhile has been talking to* MAID.]

VAN HELSING: . . . you understand, you will not answer bells. She must not be alone for a single moment under any circumstances, you understand.

[*As* DRACULA *crosses to below desk,* LUCY *leans toward him, extends her hand, then recovers herself.* VAN HELSING *registers that he sees her look at* DRACULA.]

MAID: Yes, sir.

VAN HELSING: [*To* LUCY.] Good. Your maid will take you to your room. Try to rest for a little, while I talk to your father.

[MAID *comes to divan to get* LUCY. *Pause, as* LUCY *looks at* DRACULA.]

SEWARD: Wells, remember, don't leave her alone for a moment.

MAID: Oh, no, sir.

[LUCY *exchanges a long look with* DRACULA *as* MAID *takes her out.*]

DRACULA: Professor Van Helsing, so you have come from the land of the tulip, to cure the nervous prostration of this charming girl. I wish you all the success.

VAN HELSING: Thank you, Count.

DRACULA: Do I appear officious, Doctor Seward? I am a lonely man. You are my only neighbors when I am here at Carfax, and your trouble has touched me greatly.

SEWARD: Count, I am more grateful for your sympathy than I can say.

VAN HELSING: You, like myself, are a stranger in England, Count?

DRACULA: Yes, but I love England and the great London . . . so different from my own Transylvania, where there are so few people and so little opportunity.

VAN HELSING: Opportunity, Count?

DRACULA: For my investigations, Professor.

SEWARD: I hope you haven't regretted buying that old ruin across there?

DRACULA: Oh, Carfax is not a ruin. The dust was somewhat deep, but we are used to dust in Transylvania.

HARKER: You plan to remain in England, Count?

DRACULA: I think so, my friend. The walls of my castle are broken, and the shadows are many, and I am the last of my race.

HARKER: It's a lonely spot you've chosen . . . Carfax.

DRACULA: It is, and when I hear the dogs howling far and near I think myself back in my Castle Dracula with its broken battlements.

HARKER: Ah, the dogs howl there when there are wolves around, don't they?

DRACULA: They do, my friend. And they howl here as well, although there are no wolves. But you wish to consult the anxious father and the great specialist. . . . May I read a book in the study? I am so anxious to hear what the Professor says . . . and to learn if I can be of any help.

SEWARD: By all means, Count. [DRACULA *bows; exits.* SEWARD *watches him leave. Dogs howl offstage.*] Very kind of Dracula, with his damned untimely friendliness, but now what about my daughter?

HARKER: Yes, Professor, what do you think is the matter with Lucy?

VAN HELSING: [*Crosses to window, looks out. Long pause before he speaks.*] Your patient, that interesting Renfield, does not like the smell of wolfsbane.

SEWARD: Good Heavens. What has that got to do with Lucy?

VAN HELSING: Perhaps nothing.

HARKER: In God's name, Professor, is there anything unnatural or occult about this business?

SEWARD: Occult? Van Helsing! Oh . . .

VAN HELSING: Ah, Seward, let me remind you that the superstitions of today are the scientific facts of tomorrow. Science can now transmute the electron, the basis of all matter, into energy, and what is that but the dematerialization of matter? Yet dematerialization has been known and practiced in India for centuries. In Java I myself have seen things.

SEWARD: My dear old friend, you can't have filled up your fine old brain with Eastern moonshine.

VAN HELSING: Moonshine?

SEWARD: But anyway, come now, what about my daughter?

VAN HELSING: Ah! Seward, if you won't listen to what will be harder to believe than any Eastern moonshine, if you won't forget your textbooks . . . keep an open mind, then, Seward. Your daughter's life may pay for your pig-headedness.

HARKER: Go on, go on, Professor!

SEWARD: I am listening.

VAN HELSING: Then I must ask you to listen calmly to what I am going to say. Sit down. [VAN HELSING *crosses to window; closes curtains.* SEWARD *and* HARKER *exchange glances, then both look at* VAN HELSING *as they sit.*] You have both heard the legends of Central Europe, about the Werewolf, the Vampires?

SEWARD: You mean ghosts, who suck the blood of the living?

VAN HELSING: If you wish to call them ghosts. I call them the undead.

HARKER: [*Quickly.*] For God's sake, man, are you suggesting that Mina, and now Lucy . . .

SEWARD: [*Interrupting.*] Of course, I have read these horrible folk tales of the Middle Ages, Van Helsing, but I know you better than to suppose . . .

VAN HELSING: [*Interrupting.*] That I believe them? I *do* believe them.

SEWARD: [*Incredulously.*] You mean to tell us that vampires actually exist and . . . and that Mina and Lucy have been attacked by one?

VAN HELSING: Your English doctors would all laugh at such a theory. Your police, your public would laugh. [*Impressively.*] *The strength of the vampire is that people will not believe in him.*

SEWARD: [*Shaking head.*] Is this the help you bring us?

VAN HELSING: [*Much moved.*] Do not despise it.

HARKER: [*To* SEWARD.] Doctor, this case has stumped all your specialists. [*To* VAN HELSING.] Go on, Professor.

VAN HELSING: Vampires are rare. Nature abhors them, the forces of good combine to destroy them, but a few of these creatures have lived on for centuries.

HARKER: [*Excited.*] What *is* a vampire?

VAN HELSING: A vampire, my friend, is a man or woman who is dead and not yet dead. A thing that lives after its death by drinking the blood of the living. It must have blood or it dies. Its power lasts only from sunset to sunrise. During the hours of the day it must rest in the earth in which it was buried. But, during the night, it has the power to prey upon the living. [*Incredu-*

lous move from SEWARD.] My friend, you are thinking you will have to put me amongst your patients?

SEWARD: Van Helsing, I don't know what to think but I confess I simply can't follow you.

HARKER: What makes you think that Lucy has been attacked by such a creature?

VAN HELSING: [*From now on dominating them.*] Doctor Seward's written account of these ladies' symptoms at once aroused my suspicion. Anæmia? The blood of three men was forced into the veins of Miss Mina. Yet she died from loss of blood. Where did it go? Had your specialist any answer? The vampire attacks the throat. He leaves two little wounds, white with red centers. [HARKER *rises slowly.*] Seward, you wrote me of those two marks on Miss Mina's throat. An accident with a safety pin, you said. So I thought, I suspected, I did not know, but I came on the instant, and what do I find? These same wounds on Miss Lucy's throat. Another safety pin, Doctor Seward?

SEWARD: Do you mean to say that you've built up all this nightmare out of a safety pin? It's true I can't make out why she hid those marks from us.

VAN HELSING: I could tell you that.

SEWARD: [*Pause.*] What! I don't believe it. Of course Lucy's trouble can't be *that.*

HARKER: I do believe it. This theory accounts for all the facts that nobody has been able to explain. We'll take her away where this thing can't get at her.

VAN HELSING: She will not want to go.

SEWARD: What!

VAN HELSING: If you force her, the shock may be fatal.

HARKER: But why won't she go if we tell her that her life depends on it?

VAN HELSING: Because the victim of the vampire becomes his creature, linked to him in life and after death.

SEWARD: [*Incredulous, shocked; rises.*] Professor, this is too much!

HARKER: Lucy become an unclean thing, a demon?

VAN HELSING: Yes, Harker. *Now* will you help me?

HARKER: Yes, anything. Tell me what to do.

VAN HELSING: It is dangerous work. Our lives are at stake, but so is Miss Lucy's life, so is her soul. We must stamp out this monster.

HARKER: How can we stamp it out now?

VAN HELSING: This undead thing lies helpless by day in the earth or tomb in which it was buried.

SEWARD: A corpse, in a coffin?

VAN HELSING: A corpse, if you like, but a living corpse, sustained by the blood of the living. If we can find its earth home, a stake driven through the heart destroys the vampire. But this is our task. In such a case the police, all the powers of society, are as helpless as the doctors. What bars or chains can hold a creature who can turn into a wolf or bat?

HARKER: A wolf! Doctor Seward, those dogs howling! I told you they howl that way in Russia when wolves are about. And a bat . . . Renfield said there was a bat.

SEWARD: Well. What of it?

VAN HELSING: [*Reflectively.*] Your friend Renfield does not like the smell of wolfsbane.

SEWARD: But what in the world has your wolfsbane to do with all this?

VAN HELSING: A vampire cannot stand the smell of wolfsbane.

HARKER: You suspect that lunatic?

VAN HELSING: I suspect no one and everyone. . . . Tell me, who is this Count Dracula?

SEWARD: Dracula? We really know very little about him.

HARKER: When I was in Transylvania I heard of Castle Dracula. A famous Voivode Dracula who fought the Turks lived there centuries ago.

VAN HELSING: I will make inquiries by telegraph. No, but after all this Thing must be English. Or at least have died here. His lair must be near enough to this

Photo from the Liveright stage production of Dracula, *with Bela Lugosi and Dorothy Peterson (David J. Skal,* Hollywood Gothic, *1990; Bruccoli Clark Layman Archives)*

house for him to get back there before sunrise. [*To* SEWARD] Oh my friend, I have only the old beliefs with which to fight this monster that has the strength of twenty men, perhaps the accumulated wisdom and cunning of centuries.

HARKER: This all seems a nightmare. But I'm with you, Professor.

VAN HELSING: And you, Doctor Seward?

SEWARD: It all seems preposterous to me. But everyone else has failed. The case is in your hands at present.

VAN HELSING: [*Sternly.*] I need allies, not neutrals.

SEWARD: Very well, then, do what you will.

VAN HELSING: Good. Then bring your daughter here.

SEWARD: What are you going to do?

Poster by Vernon Short for the first Broadway production of
Dracula (*David J. Skal,* Hollywood Gothic, *1990;*
Bruccoli Clark Layman Archives)

VAN HELSING: To set a trap. Miss Lucy is the bait.

HARKER: My God, we can't let you do that!

VAN HELSING: There's no other way. I believe
this Thing knows that I plan to protect Miss Lucy.
This will put it on its guard and the first moment she
is alone it will no doubt try to get at her, for a vampire must have blood or its life in death ceases.

HARKER: No, I forbid this.

SEWARD: She's my daughter, and I consent. We'll
show the Professor he's mistaken.

. . . .

from Act 2

[VAN HELSING, *alone, registers as tired and exhausted,*
and walks slowly across the room, looking at his drawn face in
mirror. DRACULA, *with stealthy tread, in evening dress and*
cloak as before, enters from window and walks slowly to directly
behind VAN HELSING.]

VAN HELSING: [*Looking at himself, touching face, shakes*
head.] The devil.

DRACULA: Come. [VAN HELSING *turns suddenly to*
him and looks back into the mirror.] Not as bad as that.
[*Suave, cold, ironical.*]

VAN HELSING: [*Long look in mirror, then turns to*

DRACULA. *Controlling himself with difficulty.*] I did not
hear you, Count.

DRACULA: I am often told that I have a light footstep.

VAN HELSING: I was looking in the mirror. Its
reflection covers the whole room, but I cannot see . . .

[*Pause. He turns to mirror.* DRACULA, *face convulsed by*
fury, picks up a small vase with flowers from stand, smashes mir-
ror, pieces of mirror and vase tumbling to the floor. VAN
HELSING *steps back; looks at* DRACULA *with loathing*
and terror.]

DRACULA: [*Recovering composure.*] Forgive me, I dislike
mirrors. They are the playthings of man's vanity. . . .
And how's the fair patient?

VAN HELSING: [*Meaningly.*] The diagnosis presents
difficulties.

DRACULA: I feared it might, my friend.

VAN HELSING: Would you care to see what I have
prescribed for my patient?

DRACULA: Anything that you prescribe for Miss
Lucy has the greatest interest for me.

[VAN HELSING *crosses to table to get box.* DRACULA
crosses, meets VAN HELSING *coming back with box.* VAN
HELSING *deliberately turns away from him, goes to small*
table right of arch, turns front as he opens pocketknife and, in
cutting string of parcel, cuts his finger. He gives a slight exclama-
tion of pain; holds up finger covered with blood. DRACULA
starts for VAN HELSING *with right hand raised, then keep-*
ing control with difficulty, turns away so as not to see blood.
VAN HELSING *stares at him a moment, then walks up and*
sticks bleeding finger in front of him.]

VAN HELSING: The prescription is a most unusual one.

[*DRACULA, baring teeth, makes sudden snap at finger. VAN HELSING turns away quickly; ties handkerchief around it. DRACULA again regains poise with an effort.*]

DRACULA: The cut is not deep . . . I . . . looked.

VAN HELSING: [*Opening parcel.*] No, but it will serve. Here is my medicine for Miss Lucy. [*DRACULA comes up to VAN HELSING, who quickly holds handful of wolfsbane up to his face. DRACULA leaps back, face distorted with rage and distress, shielding himself with cloak. Putting wolfsbane back in box.*] You do not care for the smell?

DRACULA: You are a wise man, Professor . . . for one who has not lived even a single lifetime.

VAN HELSING: You flatter me, Count.

DRACULA: But not wise enough to return to Holland at once, now that you have learned what you have learned.

VAN HELSING: [*Shortly.*] I preferred to remain. [*Meaningly.*] Even though a certain lunatic here attempted to kill me.

DRACULA: [*Smiling.*] Lunatics are difficult. They do not do what they are told. They even try to betray their benefactors. But when servants fail to obey orders, the Master must carry them out for himself.

VAN HELSING: [*Grimly.*] I anticipated as much.

DRACULA: [*Gazing at him intently.*] In the past five hundred years, Professor, those who have crossed my path have all died, and some not pleasantly. [*Continues to gaze at VAN HELSING; lifts his arm slowly; says with terrible emphasis and force.*] Come . . . here. [*VAN HELSING pales, staggers, then slowly takes three steps toward DRACULA. Very slight pause as VAN HELSING attempts to regain control of himself, then takes another step toward DRACULA; pauses, places hand to brow, then completely regains control of himself and looks away.*] Ah, your will is strong. Then I must come to you. [*Advances to VAN HELSING, who takes out of breast pocket small velvet bag. DRACULA stops.*] More medicine, Professor?

VAN HELSING: More effective than wolfsbane, Count.

DRACULA: Indeed? [*Starts for VAN HELSING's throat. VAN HELSING holds bag out toward him. DRACULA's face becomes convulsed with terror and he retreats left before VAN HELSING, who follows him.*] Sacrilege.

VAN HELSING: [*Continuing to advance.*] I have a dispensation.

[*VAN HELSING has cut him off from the door and remorselessly presses him toward window. DRACULA, livid with rage and snarling, backs out of the window. As DRACULA is just outside the window he spreads his cape like a bat and gives a long satirical laugh as he makes exit. VAN HELSING almost collapses; puts bag back in pocket; crosses himself; mops perspiration from brow with handkerchief. A shot is heard. VAN HELSING leaps up; rushes to window. Bat circles almost into his face. He staggers back. SEWARD hurries in, carrying newspaper.*]

SEWARD: God, Van Helsing, what was that? [*Dropping newspaper on table.*]

VAN HELSING: A revolver shot. It came as a relief. That at least is something human.

SEWARD: Who broke the mirror?

VAN HELSING: I.

[*HARKER enters.*]

HARKER: Sorry if I startled you. I saw that infernal bat around this side of the house. I couldn't resist a shot.

SEWARD: Did you hit it?

HARKER: Why I . . .

VAN HELSING: The bullet was never made, my friend, that could harm *that* bat. *My* weapons are stronger.

. . . .

from Act 3

A vault.

Absolute darkness. Coffin right center and back of gauze drop. Flash of electric torch seen coming slowly downstairs center. Coffin contains body of DRACULA.

VAN HELSING'S VOICE: For God's sake, be careful, Seward.

SEWARD'S VOICE: These stairs go down forever.

How The New York Critics Regard
DRACULA
New York's Newest Shudder!!!

"NOTHING MORE BLITHELY BLOOD-CURDLING SINCE 'THE BAT.'" —*Percy Hammond, Herald-Tribune.*

"SEE IT AND CREEP"—*John Anderson, Post.*

"WAS ENJOYED TO THE HILT—AUDIENCE QUAKED DELIGHTEDLY AT THE FULTON." —*Alexander Woollcott, World.*

"Shivery as You Could Possibly Wish and Very Well Played." —*Burns Mantle, News.*

"AN EVENING RICH IN HORROR." —*Frank Vreeland, Telegram.*

"A Series of Spine-Creeping Thrills." —*Walter Winchell, Graphic.*

"Brought Chills to Many Distinguished First Nighters." —*Robert Coleman, Mirror.*

"SHOULD BE SEEN BY ALL WHO LOVE THEIR MARROWS JOLTED, THEIR HAIR RAISED AND THEIR SLUMBERS TRAMPLED." —*Gilbert Gabriel, Sun.*

"DRACULA IS THE UNUSUAL IN PLAYS" —*Arthur Pollock, Brooklyn Eagle.*

"IN A CLASS BY ITSELF! After Seeing About Every Thriller on Broadway in the Last 15 Years, This Is the First and Only One That Actually THRILLS for Three Acts." —*Wall Street Journal.*

Promotional handbill distributed by Horace Liveright Productions for the original Fulton Theatre run of the play in 1927, as well as for the touring engagements (courtesy of David J. Skal)

VAN HELSING'S VOICE: May God protect us.

SEWARD'S VOICE: Is Harker there?

VAN HELSING'S VOICE: He's gone for a lantern.

SEWARD'S VOICE: I've got to the bottom.

VAN HELSING'S VOICE: Be careful. I'm right behind you.

[*Torch flashes around vault and they walk about slowly.*]

SEWARD'S VOICE: What can this place be?

VAN HELSING'S VOICE: It seems an old vault. [*Stifled scream from* SEWARD. *Torch out. The torch is seen to jerk back.*] What is it? Oh, where are you, man?

SEWARD'S VOICE: Sorry. I'm all right. A big rat ran across my foot.

[*Light seen coming downstairs.* HARKER *appears carrying lighted lantern which reaches floor; partially illuminates bare vault. He has stake and hammer in left hand.*]

HARKER: Where are you? What is this place?

VAN HELSING: We can't see.

[HARKER *moves with lantern.*]

HARKER: The place smells horribly of bats.

VAN HELSING: It has an animal smell, like the lair of a wolf.

HARKER: That's what it is.

SEWARD: [*Still flashing torch about.*] There is absolutely nothing here.

HARKER: [*At extreme left with lantern.*] Here's another passage.

VAN HELSING: [*Moving left.*] I thought so. That must lead to Carfax. The sixth earth box is hidden somewhere here.

HARKER: And the monster is in it.

SEWARD: You can't be sure. [*As he speaks, light from his torch falls on* RENFIELD, *stretched on floor.* RENFIELD *screams as light falls on him; scurries off right into darkness.*] Renfield!

[HARKER *and* VAN HELSING *hurry across.*]

VAN HELSING: Where is he?

SEWARD: Over there somewhere. Even if Renfield knew about this place, that doesn't prove the vampire's here.

VAN HELSING: [*As* SEWARD *is speaking* VAN HELSING *moves right; seizes* RENFIELD.] It is the vampire's life or yours! [*Drags* RENFIELD *into light of lantern.*] Look at him, man, look at him. He knows.

RENFIELD: I know nothing. Let me go! Let me go, I say! [*Breaks away; goes right.*]

VAN HELSING: He was stretched out here, but he wouldn't let me drag him back. Ah! Here it is. Quick, that stake.

[HARKER *and* VAN HELSING, *with stake, pry up stone slab and open coffin. The three men gaze in horror and triumph at coffin.*]

SEWARD: What a horrible undead thing he is lying there!

HARKER: Let me drive it in deep!

A *Dracula* Revival

Deane-Balderston Adaptation of *Dracula*
Martin Beck Theater, New York, 15 October 1977

Cast of Characters

Dracula	Frank Langella
Lucy Seward	Ann Sachs
Harker	Alan Coates
Renfield	Richard Kavanaugh
Seward	Dillon Evans
Van Helsing	Jerome Dempsey
Wells (the Maid)	Gretchen Oehler

–Leonard Wolf, *Dracula: The Connoisseur's Guide,*
p. 300

[VAN HELSING *takes stake from* HARKER, *lowers it into the coffin.* RENFIELD *stands at right end of coffin.*]

VAN HELSING: [*Almost in a whisper.*] That's over the heart, Doctor?

SEWARD: [*Back of coffin.*] Yes. [VAN HELSING *hands hammer to* HARKER. HARKER *raises hammer high over head; pounds stake with full force. Low groan. Silence. Stake remains fixed in* DRACULA'*s body.*]

VAN HELSING: See his face now … the look of peace.

SEWARD: He is crumbling away.

RENFIELD: Thank God, we're free!

LUCY: [*Comes down stairway and halts at bottom.*] Father, Father, John!

HARKER: Lucy!

VAN HELSING: [*Takes handful of dust; scatters it over the body.*] Dust to dust … ashes to ashes…

CURTAIN

[*The curtain rises again and the entire cast comes downstage before a black drop for curtain speech.*]

VAN HELSING: [*To* AUDIENCE.] Just a moment, Ladies and Gentlemen! Just a word before you go. We hope the memories of Dracula and Renfield won't give you bad dreams, so just a word of reassurance. When you get home tonight and the lights have been turned

Ticket to the Broadway production of Dracula, *starring Frank Langella as the Count, that ran for 925 performances from October 1977 to January 1980 (courtesy of Jeanne Youngson)*

out and you are afraid to look behind the curtains and you dread to see a face appear at the window . . . why, just pull yourself together and remember that after all *there are such things.*

THE CURTAIN FALLS

—Dracula: The Ultimate, Illustrated Edition of the World-Famous Vampire Play, *edited by David J. Skal (New York: St. Martin's Press, 1993)*

Dracula as a Screen Star

The popularity of Dracula, *the 1931 movie starring Bela Lugosi, brought the Count to an even wider audience than the stage performances had reached. Moviemakers have since been inspired again and again by Stoker's creation, producing movies that are sometimes based, at least in part, on Stoker's novel and, more often, that only invoke the name "Dracula" in their titles. In* Hollywood Gothic: The Tangled Web of Dracula from Novel to Stage to Screen *(1990), David J. Skal notes that the character "has been depicted in film more times than almost any fictional being, with the single possible exception of Sherlock Holmes, and has now so pervaded the world of communications and advertising that it is no longer necessary to read the novel or see one of its film adaptations to be thoroughly acquainted with the Count and his exploits."*

Film Adaptations of *Dracula*
James Craig Holte

Dracula has always had success in the dark. In Bram Stoker's novel, the Count loses his supernatural powers in the daylight hours. One result is that the most dramatic scenes in *Dracula* occur in moon-washed mountains, storm-lashed seas, or candle-lit rooms, long after the sun has set. Little wonder then that the most powerful images of Count Dracula are those that have been projected into the darkened rooms of theatres. People throughout the twentieth century experienced the Count far more as a creature of the screen than of the page. Cinematic adaptations, rather than the novel, have shaped the Dracula of popular culture, from the silent film's haunting *Nosferatu* through the theatrical *Dracula* of Hollywood's golden age, the psychological *Draculas* of the 1950s and 1960s, the erotic and comedic *Draculas* of the 1970s to the romantic, revisionist and grand *Draculas* of the end of the century.[1]

Nosferatu, Eine Symphonie des Gauens
1922, Prana Films
Dir. F. W. Murnau

The earliest surviving film adaptation of Stoker's novel,[2] *Nosferatu* is considered by many critics and historians to be the most successful of all cinematic representations of *Dracula.* An outstanding example of post-war German expressionism, the film uses extreme non-realistic sets, lighting, and photography to create an atmosphere of horror. In order to transform Stoker's long epistolary novel into a coherent screenplay, as well as to give the film a more German flavor, director F. W. Murnau and screenwriter Henrik Galeen made major changes in characterization, setting, and plot. Count Dracula becomes Graf Orlok, Mina becomes Ellen, Harker becomes Hutter, Renfield becomes Knock, and Van Helsing becomes Bulwer; the other major characters are omitted. London is changed to Bremen, and the final dramatic return chase to Transylvania is cut. What remains, however, is the basic narrative thrust and thematic power of Stoker's novel.

Nosferatu succeeds because Murnau recognized that *Dracula* is ultimately a horror story, a fact that the film emphasizes. Murnau is especially effective in creating the mystery and unease of the vampire's castle in Transylvania, the horrors of the storm-tossed voyage to the West, and the mental disintegration of the vampire's victims. The most successful aspect of the film, however, is the character of the vampire himself, played as a personification of plague-like evil by Max Schreck. Unlike most later cinematic Draculas, Schreck portrayed the vampire as neither handsome nor seductive. Instead, his vampire is an ugly emaciated horror with a rat-like face that brings death and disease with him wherever he goes. In the final scene (a departure from Stoker's novel), Ellen offers herself as a sacrifice in order to kill the vampire, displaying heroism that is emphasized by the hideousness of the Count.

Although the movie was a commercial success in Germany and France upon its release, it received mixed reviews in the United States. Stoker's widow, upon discovering its existence, claimed copyright infringement and took legal action. In 1925, an order was issued that all copies of *Nosferatu* be destroyed. Fortunately they were not, and it has survived as a masterpiece of the silent cinema. In addition to a remake (1979), it inspired *Shadow of the Vampire* (2000), directed by E. Elias Merhige and starring John Malkovich and Willem Dafoe, which is built on the conceit that Max Schreck was actually a vampire playing an actor playing a vampire.

Dracula
1931, Universal
Dir. Tod Browning

Arguably the most influential of all cinematic versions of *Dracula,* this movie firmly implanted the image of Bela Lugosi as the quintessential Count. In the late 1920s Universal Studios Producer Carl Laemmle Jr. set out to film a series of horror films and selected *Dracula* as a major production to inaugurate the series. After lengthy negotiations, Universal purchased the rights to *Dracula* and the authorized Deane/Balderston stage version of the novel that had been a success in London, New York, and on tour in both the United States and Great Britain. Laemmle hired Tod Browning, who had a record of creating successful fantastic films at Metro-Goldwyn-Mayer, to direct the film. After an exhaustive and public search for the actor to play Count Dracula, the nod finally went to Hungarian actor Bela Lugosi, who had played the vampire in the Broadway production.

Relying on the Deane/Balderston script rather than on Stoker's novel, Browning's film is a much simplified rendering of the story. Although the opening scenes from the novel, Jonathan Harker's trip to Transylvania and the encounter with Count Dracula in his

A poster by Albin Grau for the 1922 movie directed by F. W. Murnau (courtesy of Ronald V. Borst/Hollywood Movie Posters)

castle, are included in the adaptation, most of the rest of the film follows the play fairly closely. Secondary characters are cut, settings changed to achieve dramatic unity and the final return to the Castle and the dramatic destruction of Dracula omitted. The result is an uneven production, but one that does manage to retain some of the power of the novel.

The movie is not without limitations. The first is that much is cut. Not only do Quincey Morris and Arthur Holmwood disappear, but Lucy's role, so central to the power of the original book, is eliminated. Seward is transformed from Lucy's young suitor to Mina's father, and Jonathan Harker is given nothing to do. Furthermore, the editing is at times inept: scenes are not fully developed; props are misplaced within scenes; and significant dramatic events, including the destruction of Dracula, take place off screen. Nevertheless, the film was popular with audiences, although not with critics, and it has influenced many of the later adaptations of Stoker's novel. Despite his failings, Browning did manage to capture two key elements of *Dracula,* atmosphere and character.

Browning's introduction of the vampire and his castle is a cinematic masterpiece. His vision of the vampire as an aging aristocrat in evening dress and cape inhabiting an empty, vermin-infested gothic castle has become the iconic representation of Dracula. Lugosi plays the Count as a rich, exotic, disreputable lover, a gothic seducer, and in doing so foregrounds the erotic elements of Stoker's creation, in contrast to the horrific elements emphasized in *Nosferatu*. Two other outstanding performances are given: Edward Van Sloan as Professor Van Helsing, an aging patriarch who must summon all his strength and wisdom to confront an alien evil provides an excellent balance to Lugosi's seductiveness; and Dwight Frye as the manic, eye-rolling Renfield, still the standard by which all other cinematic Renfields are measured.

Although the Universal *Dracula* is not a great production, it is, perhaps, the most influential adaptation of Stoker's novel. Wide distribution and re-releases in theatres and on television as well as endless product placements and marketing promotions have firmly placed the image of Bela Lugosi as Dracula in the popular imagination.

Dracula (Spanish-language version)
1931, Universal
Dir. George Mellford

Using the same sets (and filming at night), Universal produced a version of their *Dracula* in Spanish. Though based on the same script as the more famous Lugosi movie, this *Dracula* is quite different in how it utilizes the sets, its camera angles, and its more suggestive sexuality. Carlos Villarias played the Count, while other cast members included Lupita Tovar, Barry Norton and Eduardo Arozamena. Forgotten for decades until it resurfaced in the 1970s, this movie is fascinating to compare with the Browning version.

Drakula Istanbul'da[3]
1953, Turkey
Dir. Mehmet Muhtar

Thought for decades to be lost, this film resurfaced in the late 1990s on television in Turkey. The screen-play was from Riza Seyfi's novel *The Impaling Voivode,* which was itself a loose adaptation of Stoker's 1897 novel. The plot follows the general outline of the original *Dracula,* with a journey to Castle Dracula complete with all the trappings (though just one vampire bride). Then the action shifts as the vampire Count makes his way to contemporary Istanbul, and sets his sights on an exotic dancer (the "Mina" character). Dracula is played by Atif Kaptan, whose bald head is reminiscent of Max Schreck and who sports a fine set of fangs. Apparently, this was the first of the Dracula films to include the dramatic scene of the Count crawling down the castle wall. It is also the first movie to mention (in passing) the historical Dracula—Vlad the Impaler.

Dracula (Horror of Dracula)
1958, Hammer
Dir. Terence Fisher

The British company Hammer Films was well situated to provide viewers with popular, well-made genre films, appealing to a growing international youth market. Hammer had under contract a number of professional actors, writers, and technicians, access to the latest color and sound technology, and a willingness to adapt the successful gothic horror films made successful by American Universal Studios in the 1930s. The result was a number of popular movies, including a series of eight *Dracula* films. The best of these was the first, the 1958 *Dracula* (released in the U.S. as *Horror of Dracula*) starring Christopher Lee as the Count and Peter Cushing as Van Helsing. Like the Universal film, it is not faithful to Stoker's narrative, borrowing instead from the Deane/Balderston script. The film also drops several of Stoker's characters, including both Renfield and Seward, and moves the setting from London to a nameless town across a border from a mysterious castle.

Although the Hammer *Dracula* loses the rich texture of the London scenes and the uncanny horrors of Dr. Seward's Sanitarium, it successfully creates clearly defined characters, a lush, gothic setting, and a dramatic plot. In this adaptation the conflict between Dracula and society is again simplified. Jonathan Harker journeys to Dracula's castle to kill the vampire, but is instead turned into a vampire by the Count after destroying the bride of Dracula. Seeking revenge, Dracula hunts and kills Harker's love, Lucy, turning her into a vampire. Both Harker and Lucy are destroyed by Van Helsing, who then confronts Dracula to save the life and soul of Mina Holmwood. Van Helsing then chases Dracula to his castle where he dispatches the monster.

The Hammer *Dracula* is a better film than this plot summary would indicate. In the first place, Terence Fisher combines the sexuality, violence and horror that were essential parts of the novel. In addition, Christopher Lee and Peter Cushing play Dracula and Van Helsing with energy and enthusiasm. Cushing's Van Helsing is a modern, scientific vampire hunter, and Lee's Dracula is a strong, attractive menacing monster with none of the affected mannerisms of earlier Draculas. The confrontation between Van Helsing's controlled, authoritarian professional-

Bela Lugosi in the title role of Dracula and Helen Chandler as Mina Seward in the 1931 movie produced by Universal Pictures,
the first major Hollywood version of Stoker's novel (Cinema Bookshop, London)

ism and Dracula's violent sexual domination creates the dynamic conflict that made this film popular on both sides of the Atlantic.

El Conde Dracula (Count Dracula)
1970, Feniz/Korona
Dir. Jesus Franco

Christopher Lee returned to his role as Count Dracula in this film and Franco returned to the original novel for his inspiration. This time, Lee's appearance much more closely resembles the physical description of the Count given by Stoker. Not only is he initially an older man (who sports a mustache), but he gradually appears more youthful as he consumes the blood of his victims. In fact, the story-line of the film (at least for the first half) closely follows the original novel, and successfully captures the atmosphere of Harker's initial journey into Transylvania and his encounter with Dracula. But as the movie progresses, the departures from the text increase and the film degenerates into tedium.

Dracula
1973, Universal
Dir. Dan Curtis

Dan Curtis, who developed the popular gothic television series *Dark Shadows,* teamed up with novelist Richard Matheson, author of *I Am Legend,* for a made-for-television version of *Dracula* that used neither the Deane/Balderston script nor the Universal and Hammer adaptations. Curtis selected veteran actor Jack Palance to portray Dracula. The result was a film that was both faithful to Stoker's text and interesting in its own right. The film shows the influence of not only the novel but the work of Raymond McNally and Radu Florescu, whose *In Search of Dracula* (1972) had associated Stoker's vampire with the fifteenth-century Wallachian warlord, Vlad the Impaler.

Palance plays Dracula as a creature of power and menace who will destroy anyone who attempts to oppose him. Yet because of his long life and great suffering, he invites a degree of sympathy. The plot suggests that Mina is the reincarnation of Dracula's medieval love and that the vampire is motivated by desire as well as revenge. As a result, Dracula is a more complex character than he is in earlier film adaptations. Palance neither resorts to parody nor attempts humor in his creation of the Count; in this film Dracula is a monster, but he is a monster with a history. Unfortunately, because the film was produced for television rather than theatrical release, there was no budget to provide for appropriate special effects and sets. The result is a flat background for an interesting interpretation of the novel that has received little attention by film critics or students of Stoker.

Count Dracula
1978, BBC
Dir. Philip Saville

In 1978 the BBC produced a stylish adaptation of the novel starring Louis Jourdan, who redefined the character of the vampire count. Like the earlier Curtis adaptation, the BBC production was aimed at a television audience, but unlike the former, this production was well funded, attracted relatively large audiences, and received many favorable reviews. Jourdan, who had a long career of playing romantic leads, portrays Count Dracula as a long-suffering tragic romantic hero, emphasizing the pain and loneliness only hinted at in the novel, and downplaying the violence and the blood thirst. Jourdan's performance helped to establish the vampire as a romantic figure in twentieth-century film, and it paved the way for several of the successful adaptations that followed.

The film closely follows the plot of Stoker's novel, using all of the major characters, and even shooting the Whitby sequences on location. In fact, it is considered by most scholars to be the most faithful cinematic adaptation of Stoker's original novel yet produced.

Dracula
1979, Universal
Dir. John Badham

This film starred Frank Langella as the Count, with a supporting cast including Sir Laurence Olivier as Professor Van Helsing and Kate Nelligan as Lucy Seward. The script used a revised stage version of the Deane/Balderston play, but with a fundamental difference. The Count is sensual, seductive and bloodless. In his film Badham emphasizes the romantic aspects of *Dracula,* downplaying the horror and

Carlos Villarias in the 1931 Spanish-language version of Dracula *produced by Universal Pictures on the same sets as used in the Bela Lugosi version (courtesy of Ronald V. Borst/Hollywood Movie Posters)*

including elements of camp and humor. Because Badham's film is essentially a re-creation of a play rather than an adaptation of the novel, it cuts characters and scenes. Like the 1931 Universal adaptation, this film includes the dramatic scenes from Dracula's Castle in the first part of the narrative, but then moves to the intimacy of the character-driven drama provided by Balderston and Deane. Basing his screen performance on his stage performance, Langella consciously plays against the iconic vampire established by Lugosi.

In this adaptation, with sets by Edward Gorey, Frank Langella portrays Count Dracula as a vampire without fangs but with an awareness of his own semi-tragic situation. He can fall in love but never consummate that love and he will live long after his loves are dead. His character is that of a suffering, vulnerable vampire, who is all too aware of his own limitations (as well as his powers) and his alienation from the world around him. The film remains one of the more effective adaptations of *Dracula* available.

Nosferatu the Vampyre (Nosferatu: Phantom der Nacht)
1979, 20th Century-Fox
Dir. Werner Herzog

In 1979 Werner Herzog, a major European director who considered himself a successor of the German expressionist movement, produced and directed an acclaimed remake of Murnau's 1922 *Nosferatu,* casting Klaus Kinski as the vampire. The film captures much of the power of Murnau's original, notably the repulsive impact of Schreck's Count Orlock and the violent, horrific, and animalistic nature of the vampire. Herzog did, however, make two significant changes: he used color rather than black and white photography; and he changed the ending. Instead of the successful resolution of the sacrificial bride with the destruction of the vampire, Herzog has a more sinister ending as Jonathan, who has been bitten by the vampire, rides away to spread the infection.

Bram Stoker's Dracula
1992, Columbia
Dir. Francis Ford Coppola

By far the most ambitious film adaptation of *Dracula* is Francis Ford Coppola's lavish 1992 production, *Bram Stoker's Dracula.* Based on a screenplay by James V. Hart, the movie not only plays into the sympathetic vampire that characterizes several late-twentieth-century renderings, but incorporates more fully the historical Dracula. Though the connections between Stoker's Count and his historical namesake are tenuous at best, in this film the two become one and the same. Indeed, the motivation for the Count's vampirism is found in his human existence as Vlad, for the suicide of his wife and her subsequent damnation by the church send him to seek the powers of darkness.

Coppola, the acclaimed director of the *Godfather* series and *Apocalypse Now,* saw Dracula as a complex tragic hero who sacrifices himself and is ultimately saved by the power of love. With a star-studded cast (including Gary Oldman, Anthony Hopkins, Winona Ryder, Keanu Reeves and Tom Waits), extravagant sets, lavish costumes, and an exceptional soundtrack, the film won three Academy Awards. The attempt to create a film that captured the multiple points of view, shifting centres of consciousness, and the numerous themes of the novel, in addition to grafting on the historical Vlad Tepes narrative, was ambitious. Unfortunately, despite its positive features, Coppola's *Bram Stoker's Dracula* is

Atif Kaptan as Dracula in Drakula Istanbul'da, *a movie produced in Turkey in 1953 (courtesy of Ronald V. Borst/Hollywood Movie Posters)*

not Bram Stoker's *Dracula.* Stoker's novel is a complex work of horror that balances attraction and repulsion, but Coppola's film, with its emphasis on reincarnation and the redemptive power of love, is essentially a romance, a version of "Beauty and the Beast" in which love transforms a monster into a handsome prince.

Dracula has also been the subject of comic treatment. Two in particular draw quite substantially either from Stoker's novel or from earlier adaptations on stage and screen. *Love at First Bite,* directed by Stan Dragoti and starring George Hamilton as Dracula, was released in 1979. Hamilton, ironically best known for his tan, provides an energetic performance as a contemporary Dracula who moves to New York after being forced to leave his Transylvanian home by the communist government of Romania. *Dracula: Dead and Loving It,* directed by Mel Brooks and starring Leslie Nielsen as Dracula, was released in 1995. Brooks's enjoyable parody includes references to not only Stoker's novel but also several of the earlier film adaptations.

For over one hundred years Dracula has haunted the darkened rooms of theatres and homes,

Christopher Lee on Stoker's Dracula

As far as my character was concerned, there was some Stoker in the first one [*Horror of Dracula*], and not in the second [*Dracula: Prince of Darkness*], because I refused to speak the lines of the script . . . I kept on saying, well look, here's the book, look at these great lines, look at these great things. Can't we slip them in somewhere? No. They never agreed and that is why they became progressively less and less interesting and that is why I was determined to stop them.

–Christopher Lee, *Bram Stoker Society Journal*, 6 (1994): pp. 7–8

adapting to large screens and small ones, silent films, black-and- white movies, and wide-screen color spectaculars. Filmmakers have consistently gone to *Dracula* as a source for their narratives, continually reworking Stoker's vampire to reflect and represent the fears and desires of contemporary society. In part because of the power of Stoker's novel, Dracula never really dies but continues to survive on the screen, remaining ever popular, even to those who have never read the book. It is difficult, after all, to kill the undead.

1. For a more detailed analysis of the Dracula movies, see the following: James Craig Holte, *Dracula in the Dark: The Dracula Film Adaptations* (Westport, Conn.: Greenwood Press, 1997); Robert Marrero, *Vampire Movies: An Illustrated Guide to Seventy-Two Years of Vampire Movies* (Key West, Fla.: Fantasma, 1994); David J. Skal, *Hollywood Gothic: The Tangled Web of Dracula From Novel to Stage to Screen* (New York: Norton, 1990).
2. A lost Hungarian film, *Death of Drakula* (1921), was apparently the first film to have been inspired by Stoker's fictional character, though it was probably not an adaptation of the novel.
3. For a commentary on this obscure film, see Kaya Ozkaracalar, "*Drakula Istanbul'da*: Little Known Aspects of a Forgotten Movie," *The Borgo Post*, 3 (December 1997): 3.

* * *

Filming *Dracula*:
Vampires, Genre, and Cinematography
Jörg Waltje

On a Tuesday morning Katje discovered that Dr. Weyland was a vampire, *like the one in the movie she had seen last week*.[1]

Films that belong to the same genre are like the links of a chain, yet any generic type of film will also mark its difference from its predecessors. These films remain aware of their heritage and draw on earlier examples by modifying and reinterpreting certain aspects that are generically coded, with differing results. Accordingly, Ken Gelder points out:

Each new vampire film engages in a process of familiarisation and defamiliarisation, both interpellating viewers who already "know" about vampires from the movies (and elsewhere), and providing enough points of difference (in the narrative, in the "look" of the vampire, and so on) for newness to maintain itself.[2]

Films of a particular genre have the ability to do more than merely propagate received motifs and structures. They also comment on the art form of film itself, and how it has changed over a period of time. An analysis of stylistic and technical devices entails information not only about the progress of cinematography, but also about the self-awareness of film as a medium that makes use of a certain apparatus—an apparatus of which the audience is generally kept unaware in other filmic genres.[3] I will look closely at three vampire films, Friedrich Wilhelm Murnau's *Nosferatu* (1922), Tod Browning's *Dracula* (1931), and Francis Ford Coppola's *Bram Stoker's Dracula* (1992), and in an analysis of their filmic techniques work out how the two earlier films constituted what was then to become a genre, and how the structure of genre is closely related to the parameters of myth. My thesis can be summarized as follows: Stylistic/formal features that were developed in *Nosferatu* and *Dracula* with their combined influence molded the vampire films to come and found a preliminary culmination point in Coppola's treatment of the Dracula subject. I will focus on the depiction of the vampire through gestures and make-up, lighting and editing techniques as well as special effects and framing. Lastly, I will point out how vampire films and fictions, like myths, mirror the structure underlying our psychic apparatus. The fact that Dracula is a prototype of myth as well as an ideal representative of genre is responsible for our conscious and unconscious attraction to the figure of the vampire.

Especially in the overtly self-reflexive horror subgenre of the vampire film, the (postmodern) technique of including intertextual references into texts can only be savored by those familiar with earlier horror films, who in turn will enjoy watching early films because of their interrelation with the contemporary oeuvre. In the manner of a hermeneutic circle, each film bears the possibility of enriching the experience of the other, regardless of its ability to create suspense and terror. The epigraph introducing this article stems from Suzy Charnas's 1980 novel *The Vampire Tapestry,* and perfectly

Christopher Lee in Horror of Dracula, *1958, and* Count Dracula, *1970*
(courtesy of Ronald V. Borst/Hollywood Movie Posters)

Louis Jourdan played Dracula as a romantic hero in Count Dracula, *produced for BBC-TV in 1978 (courtesy of Ronald V. Borst/Hollywood Movie Posters)*

illustrates that modern people derive their knowledge about vampires from the cinema. A random person who grew up in the western hemisphere, when asked for the name of a vampire, would almost certainly respond with "Dracula," although not that many people might be aware of the fact that the name originated in a novel by the Anglo-Irish writer Bram Stoker. But where did the original audience for a film like *Nosferatu* get its information about vampires? Were those people who had not read Stoker's novel *tabulae rasae* when they entered the movie theatre? This is what often is assumed when we are thinking about the beginnings of a genre (any genre), disregarding the fact that a whole intertextual set of vampire depictions was already in existence all over Europe, for example through popular theatre plays and operas, the Grand Guignol, woodcuts and book illustrations. Nevertheless, it seems safe to say that after the appearance of the vampire on film, all subsequent depictions are more or less heavily influenced

by the earliest examples of cinematic adaptation of Stoker's master text. Since the beginnings of cinematography, literally hundreds of vampire films have been made, with no end in sight.[4] Murnau's *Nosferatu* is generally considered the first full-fledged cinematic treatment of the vampire, while more recent examples are Francis Ford Coppola's *Bram Stoker's Dracula* (1992), Neil Jordan's *Interview with the Vampire* (1994), Wes Craven's *Vampire in Brooklyn* (1995), Stephen Norrington's *Blade* (1998), and John Carpenter's *Vampires* (1998).

According to the credits in *Nosferatu*, the script by Henrik Galeen was "adapted from the novel by Bram Stoker," but Galeen and Murnau ignored the existing copyright. In turn, Stoker's widow procured a court injunction against this unauthorized version of *Dracula* and almost succeeded in having all copies of the film destroyed. Several copies were saved since they had already been exported abroad.[5] However, this German version bears only a nominal resemblance to its source. Murnau and Galeen had changed the original names and transferred the locale to Bremen. The tale has been stripped and simplified, and although the plot of *Nosferatu* like *Dracula* consists of three principal parts (namely: Jonathan's voyage to Transylvania, his and Dracula's race to Bremen, Dracula's influence and demise), the last part revised Stoker's fiction considerably. As Judith Mayne rightfully insists, it is not the case that literature provides an "unquestioned master code" that has to be translated into some cinematic equivalent. Every kind of *Verfilmung* creates a relationship between two texts, "a dynamic encounter rather than a static rendering of a story line from one medium to another."[6] Thus, this first film version of *Dracula* not merely deviates from the original, it appropriates the predecessor to the new medium.

The narrative structure in Stoker's work calls attention to itself; the book comes in the form of an epistolary novel which has no narration but rather presents letters and diary-entries from several people. The point-of-view is constantly changing, and Murnau transfers this pivotal feature by using point-of-view (POV) shots, subjective camera, and cross-cutting sequences to construct his narrative. The most impressive scene illustrating this technique occurs halfway through the film. When Jonathan hears a clock strike midnight, he gets agitated and runs to the door.[7] As he opens it a crack, we share his POV. In a long shot, Dracula is visible at the end of a long, dark corridor. A dissolve brings him closer, his shadow lurking behind him, and although we have seen his ghastly figure before, for the first time he wears no hat in this scene, and we perceive his bald head with pointed ears, while his long arms like claws stick threateningly out of his sleeves. He is the centre of this tableau, framed by light in a coffin shape and by the darkness that surrounds him—indeed, it almost seems to radiate from him. This framing motif recurs throughout the film in different variations, often as Gothic arches, creating a feeling of confinement and enclosure, which is emphasized by the conventional use of the iris and masked shots. Harker attempts to hide in his room, but the door flies open, and out of the darkness the vampire approaches, halts under the arched doorway and is framed by it. Through crosscutting, Murnau depicts simultaneous events in Bremen. Mina wakes up with fear in her eyes and walks to the balcony in a "somnambulistic dream" as an intertitle informs us. The sequence continues with crosscutting: Harker is hiding under his bedcovers, the shadow of the Count can be seen on the wall behind Harker, with hands held high and pointed ears. Mina screams, and as the shadow recedes, the camera cuts to the Count who turns his head around to look over his shoulder, as if he had heard the scream. The reaction shot is set up so slowly that it is almost suffocating, but this is the normal speed at which the Count moves, and when the camera cuts back to Mina, an eyeline match makes it appear as if she is looking straight at the vampire, who walks out of the room with the door closing itself behind him.

This is a sequence only a film can represent; although Stoker changes narrative perspective throughout the novel, he cannot depict two (or more) scenes going on simultaneously as Murnau does at times. There are other advantages film has over the written word. The immediacy of the medium enables effects that operate instantly on the beholder. What follows is the description Jonathan Harker gives of Count Dracula early in the novel:

His face was a strong—a very strong—aquiline, with high bridge of the thin nose and peculiarly arched nostrils; with lofty domed forehead, and hair growing scantily round the temples but profusely elsewhere. His eyebrows were very massive, almost meeting over the nose, and with bushy hair that seemed to curl in its own profusion. The mouth, so far as I could see it under the heavy moustache, was fixed and rather cruel looking, with peculiarly sharp white teeth; these protruded over the lips, whose remarkable ruddiness showed astonishing vitality in a man of his years. For the rest his ears were pale, and at the tops extremely pointed; the chin was broad and strong, and the cheeks firm though thin. The general effect was one of extraordinary pallor. . . . [The hands] were rather coarse—broad with squat fingers. Strange to say, there were hairs in the centre of the palm. The nails were long and fine, and cut to a sharp point.[8]

A purist might criticize the fact that Max Schreck's physique as Graf Orlok in *Nosferatu* has very little in common with Harker's depiction of Dracula. Yet, what counts is that Schreck's first appearance out of a dark tunnel underneath an archway sets up his persona instantaneously. One look is enough to create an aura of terror around him, an effect even the most imaginative reader will not derive from the passage quoted above and that only film can achieve. With literature, the text lies between the reader and the image; description can only unfold over time. Film, however, can work directly on the viewer, although for film theorists the medium can function as a filter in other respects.

Many of the scenes and effects Murnau created for *Nosferatu* went on to become tropes of the genre: the use of shadows as the harbingers of doom, shots and reverse shots from the perspective of the vampire approaching its victim and the victim shrinking from him, the extremely slow gait of the vampire, his threatening gestures with his right hand raised and his claw reaching out, the twitching and jerking portrayal of madness in Renfield, and the use of reaction shots to portray the effect of a statement or noise on the listeners (Dracula's name, the clock striking midnight, the herald's announcement, etc.). Murnau's repeated use of the relatively open form in which the action is not contained or completed within the frame also indicates the potential off-screen menaces.

As is fitting for a film that deals with the supernatural, *Nosferatu* repeatedly makes use of special effects: doors opening by themselves; superimpositions and dissolves of the vampire; his erect rising from his coffin; the under-cranked stop-motion technique that results in sped-up, jerky movements when Dracula's coach first approaches Harker, and later when the Count loads his coffins on a cart. Finally, the scene in the film which probably has received the most critical attention is an insertion of negative footage creating an effect of surrealistic distortion as the hearse-like carriage enters "the land of the phantoms," the latter perhaps an apt description of cinema itself.

While there are many scenes that could be singled out as precursors of the genre, there is another aspect in *Nosferatu* that is worth investigating more fully. Murnau's film is extremely self-conscious, and in numerous instances the spectator is made aware of the fact that s/he is watching a film. *Dracula* was published in 1897, and although the novel repeatedly refers to contemporary technologies like the typewriter and the phonograph, it ignores the fact that the cinema was emerging at the same time. Murnau, however, constantly alludes to film as an art form.

Nosferatu not only relates the story of vampiric contamination, but at the same time also comments on the medium of film itself. Dr. Van Helsing appears in an almost non-diegetic insert, his prominent role in the

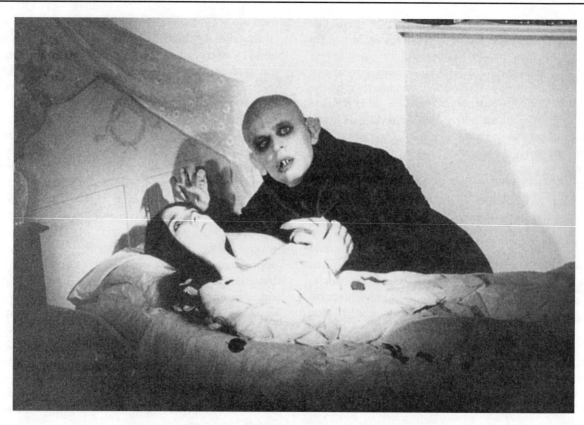

Klaus Kinski and Isabel Adjani in a scene from Nosferatu: Phantom der Nacht, *director Werner Herzog's 1979 remake of the 1922 classic (courtesy of Ronald V. Borst/Hollywood Movie Posters)*

novel having been reduced so much that he seems dispensable for the unfolding of the events. The short scene in which he is lecturing to a group of men about "natural" vampires is not important in furthering the plot, but rather contains a subtle comment on the medium. Metaphorically, the polyp under Van Helsing's microscope represents the vampire as we have seen him in superimpositions—"transparent and without substance" as the intertitle lets us know. But does this insert not stand as an allegory for the medium of film itself? The film strip is transparent: whatever is projected against the screen has no substance and represents merely a play of light and shadow, a *Lichtspiel,* as films were called in German at the time of the Weimar Republic when *Nosferatu* was released. The recurrent use of light falling in from a window alludes on the one hand to offscreen space as an outside world free from lurking evil, and on the other, to filmmaking itself. What else is film, if not light that falls through an opening and is captured on a piece of celluloid?

Tod Browning's *Dracula,* the first sound version of the vampire tale, was not directly derived from Stoker's novel, but based on an adaptation by Hamilton Deane and John Balderston. Their *Dracula: The Vampire Play* had stripped Stoker's novel to the core so that the central conflict could be portrayed on a stage almost in accordance with the Aristotelian notions of unity in the drama. *Dracula: The Vampire Play* was set in merely two locales, Dr. Seward's parlor and Carfax Abbey. Jonathan Harker's travel to Transylvania, the voyage on the *Demeter,* and the Crew of Light's pursuit of the Count to Transylvania had been eliminated. The play had enjoyed continuous success after its opening in New York in 1927 and prompted Universal to produce a film version. With Bela Lugosi as Count Dracula and Edward van Sloan as Dr. Van Helsing, Browning cast two actors who had already portrayed their characters on the stage. The whole film has a theatrical flair; entirely shot in the studio, many of the scenes seem staged and static, like tableaux captured by a camera. Yet, in some portions of the film the apparatus is put to work, especially in the portrayal of the vampire, which owes a lot to camera and lighting techniques but also to the theatrical artifice of the protagonist, Bela Lugosi. His portrayal of Dracula as a foreign predator in the guise of aristocratic sophistication became the role model for many vampires to come.

Early in the movie, in a sequence of high and low angle shots/reverse shots, the relation between Dracula and his victim Renfield is set up: vampire and prey, or master and servant as will become clear at a later point. In frames that contain both Dracula and another person, there is always an imaginary diagonal between the two heads. Even when Dracula is not standing a few steps up on a staircase, he is always taller; looking down on his counterpart he has an air of authority and danger. He is in control; when he leans forward, almost into the faces of the other characters, he appears ready to pounce on them. While the vampire in *Nosferatu* is mostly depicted by long and medium shots that kept him at a distance, Browning uses close-ups and low-angles to give Dracula a fearful appearance.[9] Low key and underlighting, as well as the recurring use of an eye-light, emphasize the hypnotic power of the vampire and often create a dramatic effect of horror by distorting Lugosi's facial features.

It is noticeably quiet through these scenes (the film has no score that supplies nondiegetic sound), but we must not forget that sound is available.[10] In contrast to *Nosferatu*, this vampire has a voice, and a striking one at that. Many of Lugosi's utterances have found their way into the successors of Browning's *Dracula*. Lugosi's low voice, his staccato rhythm, and the extreme slowness of his articulation have often been mimicked and parodied, yet these features form another thread running through the genre. "I am—Dracula," he introduces himself nonchalantly to a baffled Renfield; when offscreen howling is heard he comments "Listen to them, the children of the night—what music they make," and when he serves wine to his guest he explains "I never drink—wine." His pronunciation is guttural, rolling his R's he sounds as if a dangerous animal is hiding underneath the surface of the well-groomed aristocrat, and his Hungarian accent characterizes the Count as the dangerous, intrusive foreigner that he is coded as being.

Like Murnau's *Nosferatu,* Tod Browning's *Dracula* is aware of its construction as a film and covertly alerts the viewer to this fact. Framing and editing call attention to themselves and foreground the apparatus whenever we see a character walking from one frame into the next without a cut on movement. It is striking that Browning wholly abstains from the use of special effects. The pans and cuts that circumvent the vampire's transformation from a bat to human shape and his rising from the coffin make no effort to create an illusion of verisimilitude. Browning plays with the medium and with the spectator. Instead of using dissolves and superimpositions, he consciously calls attention to framing and editing. Scenes the spectator is most eager to perceive are always relegated off-screen, under-

mining the expectations of the audience and mocking them by compromising their visual pleasure.

The fact that this vampire, unlike the one in *Nosferatu,* has no mirror-image finally presents us with a paradox. When Van Helsing opens the cigarette box, a close-up of the mirror shows Mina but no image of Dracula. If the screen is considered a mirror, a representation of the vampire would be impossible, yet we can see him throughout the film. Indeed, we can only see him because of the screen: only film makes the vampire representable. In a way, film lends itself to be the medium of the vampire just as the figure of the vampire connotes the nature of film. An interplay of light and darkness—the *Lichtspiel*—defines the vampire as well as the audience. The vampire only comes out in the dark and spends the rest of the time in his coffin. The spectators voluntarily sit in a coffin (the darkened cinema), watching a screen on which not only light but also (within and between every frame) darkness is projected. Having turned themselves into vampires, they are waiting for the film-vampire to come out and join them. Furthermore, film has the same hypnotic power over its audience as Dracula in Browning's version has over his victims.

The notions of transformation and constancy, of novelty and recognition, not only define the vampire but also its medium, film. Browning takes up the conventions Murnau had brought to life in his treatment of *Nosferatu* and expands on them. A coded use of lighting, editing techniques like crosscutting, the gestures, poise, and gait of the vampire, his pallid make-up and mascara-eyes, these are only some of the features Browning adapted from his predecessor. The portrayal of the Count as an aristocrat, mobile framing, tracking and craning shots, and most importantly the use of sound, both on-screen and off-screen, add a new dimension to the awaking genre. Creaking doors, howling wolves, the vampire's metaphorical association with vermin and rodents, and the ominous utterances of Lugosi became stock features for vampire films to come.[11] Both *Nosferatu* and *Dracula* are more or less conscious of their construction and their cinematic apparatus, and make

Frank Langella played a romantic vampire in director John Badham's 1979 movie, Dracula. *He also played Dracula on Broadway (Cinema Bookshop, London).*

at least subtle efforts to communicate this self-reflexivity to the spectator.

A sense of film history reflected in intertextual references as well as the preoccupation with the cinematic apparatus became a token of the vampire genre and finds its climax in Francis Ford Coppola's *Bram Stoker's Dracula,* a film which not only covertly reflects on the medium, but rather makes film history and cinematic apparatus one of its central concerns. Seventy years after *Nosferatu,* Coppola's version of *Dracula* seemingly takes the audience back to the original concept. The film, which opened on Friday, 13 November 1992, on almost 2500 screens throughout the United States and Canada, provided Columbia Pictures with its largest release ever.[12] *Bram Stoker's Dracula* had the seventh best opening for any film in history, which goes to show that the interest in vampire fiction runs high, a fact that is further documented by the number of vampire films which have appeared in its wake. Silver and Ursini point out that this ultimate version of the Drac-

ula legend is "both the highest budgeted and largest grossing vampire film ever made."[13]

Bram Stoker's Dracula was greeted with sarcasm by many critics although it not only revitalized the genre, but in certain respects—by rediscovering and foregrounding the eminent traits of the genre—it also redefined some of the crumbling generic boundaries. For Stoker purists it quickly became a very controversial movie, since Coppola and his screen writer James V. Hart claim that they adhered as closely as possible to Bram Stoker's original, while only including changes they deemed necessary to improve on the original story's plausibility and cohesiveness.

Mainly, it was that no one had ever done the book. I'm amazed, watching all the other Dracula films, how much they held back from what was written or implied, how they played havoc with the characters and their relationship. . . . Aside from the one innovative take that comes from history—the love story between Mina and the Prince—we were scrupulously true to the book.[14]

Francis Ford Coppola on Reading *Dracula*

I had read the book when I was pretty young and loved it. Then as a teenager, I was the drama counselor at a camp in upstate New York, and had a bunk of eight- and nine-year-old boys. I would read aloud to them at night, and one summer we read *Dracula*. And when we got to that chilling moment—when Harker looks out the window and sees Dracula crawling across the face of the wall like a bug—even those little boys knew, this was going to be good!

–Francis Ford Coppola, *Bram Stoker's Dracula: The Film and the Legend* (New York: Newmarket Press, 1992), p. 2

There is certainly more than just one "innovative take" in this film's treatment of the original novel. Yet it is fairly obvious that Coppola and Hart felt compelled to draw on seventy years of vampiric cinematography. With a plethora of intertextual references, they are paying homage to their predecessors while trying to provide stimulating material to the devotees of the genre.

Ken Gelder's comment (noted above) is worth restating here: "Each new vampire film engages in a process of familiarisation and defamiliarisation, . . . providing enough points of difference . . . for newness to maintain itself." For David Glover the "protean durability of the un-dead" is exemplified in the vampire's ability to "reproduce itself in a seemingly endless series of copies, always resourcefully different from previous incarnations, frequently altering the rules of the genre in order to secure a new lease on life."[15] This oscillation between new and old motifs, and the allusion to familiar, yet sometimes unconscious features and sentiments, seems to be what we find at the core of any genre fiction. In the case of *Bram Stoker's Dracula* the technique of alluding to recurring staples of the genre, a trademark of any generic fiction, and the tendency for intertextual references has nevertheless met with on-going criticism ever since the production first opened.

Bram Stoker's Dracula emerges "like a music video directed by Dario Argento. It's post-modern allusionism, a welter of things to make reference to without any of them mattering much." It "revives the most tiresome of monster motivations . . . : the search for the reincarnation of the lost love," instead of providing new impulses to a faltering genre. Like other recent horror fictions, notes one critic, the film merely embodies "plagiarism and theft, dignified as 'post-modernist'."[16]

Such harsh criticism clearly disregards the importance of what has to be defined as the *sine qua non* of generic fiction: repetition and recognition of familiar elements. "[The] rediscovery of what is familiar, 'recognition,' is pleasurable," Freud points out, and pleasurable effects arise from "a repetition of what is similar, a rediscovery of what is familiar."[17] It is also worthwhile to recall Wellek and Warren's dictum that both "novelty and the sense of recognition" are responsible for our pleasure when consuming (literary) fictions.[18] In *Bram Stoker's Dracula* the pleasures of recognition indeed work on several levels: recognition of familiar elements of the *Dracula* story; recognition of the allusions to other treatments of the story (intertextual recognition); recognition of one's own entanglement in the narrative (the underlying, repetitive structure of the genre mirroring the structure of our unconscious). Thus, I would claim, one is doing the movie an injustice by dismissing it so peremptorily. Indeed, as a prototype of generic fiction, the film has many redeeming qualities, one of which is Coppola's uncanny ability to synthesize the materials of his predecessors.

Many characters and incidents from Bram Stoker's novel which have never before found their way onto the screen are included in Coppola's version, and the frequent exercise of mis- and re-naming the characters has been avoided. The narrative technique, at least in the first two thirds of the film, directly reflects Stoker's epistolary style. Multiple strands of narrative, told by the use of varying technologies (Jonathan's diary entries, Seward's phonograph records, Mina's typewritten accounts, letters, newspaper-clippings, etc.) are held together by voice-overs, captions, maps, visual and aural cues, and links.

The frequent, almost excessive, use of superimpositions and dissolves enables and enhances the depiction of multiple points of view and the unceasing flow of information, which the novel presents in a somewhat formal, almost pedantic manner. *Bram Stoker's Dracula* makes use of many of the formal elements we have determined as indispensable for the vampire genre in our earlier discussion of *Nosferatu* and *Dracula*. At the same time it incorporates the later Hammer Film tradition (1960s to 1970s) in its use of coded colors and visible blood, and feeds on film versions of *Dracula* and other vampires. Examples include the motif of Dracula's search for his lost love (used in Dan Curtis's 1974 *Dracula* with Jack Palance), and the cut to roast beef (from Tony Scott's 1983 *The Hunger*).

The prominent use of shadows anticipating or announcing the arrival of evil, fast crosscutting enabled by increased editing technology, the familiar gestures, poise, and gait of the vampire, the pseudo-Hungarian accent, the pointed fingernails (we are even treated to the hairy palms of Gary Oldman's Dracula), the frequent use of low angle, (medium) close-up shots for

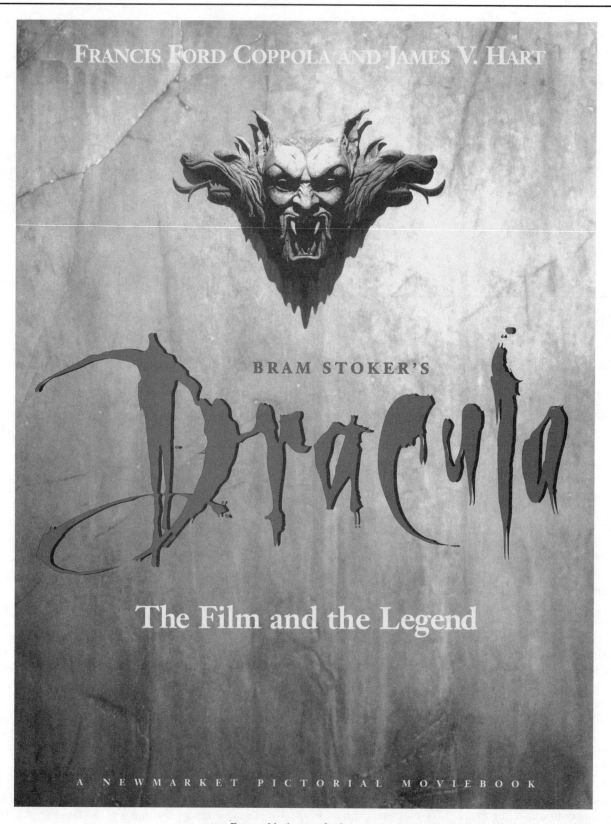

Front and back covers for the companion book to director Francis Ford Coppola's 1992 movie,
Bram Stoker's Dracula *(Bruccoli Clark Layman Archives)*

A Deathless Tale, Retold by a Master Filmmaker

*B*ram Stoker's Dracula is director Francis Ford Coppola's epic retelling of a story that has inspired many films—but never one so true to Stoker's 1897 novel and its historical background.

James V. Hart's screenplay opens in 1462, when the Roumanian prince Vlad Dracula (Gary Oldman) saves his country from the Turks but loses his great love, and swears an unholy oath to avenge her. Four centuries later, a young Englishman, Jonathan Harker (Keanu Reeves), visits the Transylvanian castle of an eccentric old count—and the classic tale unfolds. How Dracula terrorizes Harker and then takes ship for England, where he seduces Harker's fiancée Mina (Winona Ryder) and her best friend Lucy, and enslaves the madman Renfield (Tom Waits); and how he is finally vanquished by Dr. Van Helsing (Anthony Hopkins) and his fellow Vampire Killers. Unique to this *Dracula* is the love story between the vampire prince and Mina, the reincarnation of his lost princess.

This book contains the complete shooting script, excerpts from the original novel, and more than 160 photos, 100 in color, of the production, with its brilliant costumes and evocative sets. Sidebars explore behind-the-scenes details, the director's innovative methods, and the film's literary and historical links. With an introduction by Coppola, notes by screenwriter Hart, and an afterword by Dracula scholar Leonard Wolf, this is the only official companion book to this landmark film.

Newmarket Press
New York   **$14.95**

ISBN 1-55704-139-3

90000

9 781557 041395

Dracula, the claustrophobic framing of the vampiric world with the help of irises and arches, tracking and craning shots, the quasi-expressionist *chiaroscuro*-lighting, and many other allusions to its generic predecessors, combine and refine the now standardized elements of vampire cinema in the Coppola film.

While both *Nosferatu* and *Dracula* were already covertly conscious of their construction as film and communicated their self-awareness of being an art form to the spectator, *Bram Stoker's Dracula* makes film and the cinematic apparatus a central issue in its portrayal of Dracula's sojourn in London. An under-cranked, jerky scene filmed in faded colors with a Pathé camera gives an impression of documentary material, and at the same time addresses the dichotomies between the real and illusory, representation and recognition for which both the vampire and its medium stand. We are (once again) made aware of the fact that a vampire has no mirror image, since the film shows us the reflection of a newspaper in a window pane which seems to float through the air where Dracula should be. Yet after a cut, the screen reverts to a depiction of the vampire, for it is the screen alone which makes the vampire visible for us. The sequence leads up to Dracula's first encounter with Mina and their subsequent visit to the cinematograph. With its inserts and backdrops of film-within-film the sequence embodies another, and this time highly foregrounded, self-reflexive acknowledgment of the art form and its conventions.

The most striking reflection concerning the paradox of the vampire's non-representability, however, is an earlier segment in which Mina comes upon the rape of Lucy in the maze at Hillingham. The wolf-like creature into which Dracula has metamorphosed turns towards Mina and the spectators, who share her POV. For just a few frames (too fast to be *consciously* recognized) the "human" features of the vampire are superimposed on the wolf's face, and both Mina and the audience are ordered "Do not see me!" Only the screen can depict the vampire; although film is its medium, our recognition here is explicitly forbidden. Once again this scene reveals the paradox of the vampire's unrepresentability, at the same time that it addresses the hypnotic power both the vampire and film can have on the perceiver.[19]

Some of the outstanding novel elements contained in *Bram Stoker's Dracula* are the costume designs by Eiko Ishioko and the use of extra-diegetic sound to link scenes and characters. Both the costumes with their crests and insignia and the soundtrack by Wojciech Kilar add to the film as a *Gesamtkunstwerk,* a complete and integrated work of art in which all elements are directed toward the same end. With their recurrent themes and motifs and by means of intra-textuality, they reinforce the film's underlying repetitive structure. The combination of tactile, visual, and aural elements, as for example in Dracula's undulating blood-red cloak and Lucy's floating orange gown when she falls prey to the vampire in the garden during a thunderstorm, can be singled out here. The gentle musical cues of the love-theme, Dracula's and Mina's dance among a myriad of candles, and the thunderous, angry instrumentation of Lucy's final bloodletting crosscut with Mina's and Jonathan's wedding in the Romanian convent, which at the same time reverberates with subtle musical cues from the above-mentioned love-theme—all these elements combine to provide the spectator with heretofore unknown synaesthetic pleasure, appealing more to the body than to the mind. The story itself as vampiric fiction contains no surprises and adheres to Stoker, with the exception of Van Helsing's meta-narrative of Dracula's fight against the Turks and both the pseudo-historical and the contemporary love connection between Mina and her "Prince." The way in which it is filmed and edited, however, is imaginative, and, at times, even breathtaking.

In Coppola's film, not only the forces of good and evil but also centrifugal and centripetal forces are battling against each other. The figure of Dracula is the centre of the narrative, yet at the same time the film tries to break away from its centre in an attempt to include all possible features of the generic tradition. The abstract concept "Dracula" has taken on a life of its own and represents a certain master-narrative, despite—but also in addition to—the fact that it simultaneously functions as a reconfiguration of other mythological and artistic motifs.

Richard Dyer has alluded to the film's discreet references to Christian mythology. In Coppola's and Hart's treatment of what I shall loosely refer to as the Dracula myth, the figure of Dracula becomes an inversion of Christ. Deserted by God in his darkest hour, the defender of Christendom turns into a vampire, and thus becomes like Jesus, "a dead man who has eternal life."[20] The idea that for the vampire blood becomes the life reverberates with the Christian dogma of transubstantiation. "The vampire has baptized her with his own blood," Van Helsing remarks when Mina begins to turn. As in the Christian belief system, redemption through love appears possible in *Bram Stoker's Dracula*. In the final scenes (and even earlier on a portrait in Dracula's castle), the vampire's gory features metamorphose for fleeting moments into the bearded, long-haired figure which traditional Christian iconography depicts as the semblance of Christ.

Leslie Nielsen as the Count in Dracula: Dead and Loving It, *directed by Mel Brooks in 1996*
(courtesy of Ronald V. Borst/Hollywood Movie Posters)

"Love Never Dies" announces the original poster for the film's release, combining the public's interest in romantic stories, our preoccupation with the vampire, and our fascination with death, immortality, and reincarnation. The back cover of Coppola and Hart's *Dracula: The Film and the Legend,* a companion piece to the film which includes, among other things, stills and the original shooting script, defines its contents as "A Deathless Tale." Immortality here not only describes but inscribes the essential trait of the narrative, which strikes me as important insofar as the notion of immortality is closely related to the term "myth," a concept which Dracula has by now become.

"Mythic thought is especially concerned to deny and negate the effect of death and to affirm the unbroken unity of life," states David Bidney. For Marina Warner, myth's multiple functions consist of bringing binary oppositions into accord by "defining the forbidden and the alluring, the sacred and the profane, conjuring demons and heroes, saying who we are and what we want, telling a story which makes sense of things"[21] *Dracula* is indeed a prototype of myth as well as an ideal representative of genre. As vampire fiction the subject combines both the return of the repressed and the compulsion to

repeat; thus it mirrors the structure underlying the psychic apparatus which is responsible for our conscious and unconscious attraction to the genre.

The simultaneous presence of folktales, medical case-histories, socio-historical and psychological insights, and twentieth century obsessions make up what has become the myth of the vampire, reflecting universal and innate fears, desires, and the structure of our mind. This is why any comprehensive version of *Dracula* unavoidably becomes a "maelstrom of sensations," or "millenial rock'n'roll with all the stops out."[22] By now the vampire is a twentieth century myth, and its favored medium is film.

Yet, not only the preferred medium of the vampire has undergone some changes over the last century, the figure of the vampire itself has metamorphosed or been worked over again and again. In a fairly recent development, it has split into two halves, with its double leaving the realm of fiction. I am referring here to the figure of the serial killer, who embodies many of the traits of the vampire but presses closer to home and can be considered an updated and less "playful" version of one of our oldest obsessions. There has been a flood of commercially successful serial killer fictions in recent years, which in my view reflect and exploit many of the traits

---

Dracula Spinoffs

A partial list of movies having "Dracula" in their titles, but with little or no connection to Stoker's novel.

Dracula's Daughter (1936)
Son of Dracula (1943)
House of Dracula (1945)
Return of Dracula (1957)
Brides of Dracula (1960)
Dracula: Prince of Darkness (1964)
Billy the Kid vs Dracula (1966)
Batman Fights Dracula (1967)
Dracula Has Risen from the Grave (1968)
The Blood of Dracula's Castle (1969)
Dracula Sucks (1969)
Countess Dracula (1970)
The Scars of Dracula (1970)
Taste the Blood of Dracula (1970)
Dracula vs Frankenstein (1970)
Dracula AD 1972 (1972)
Blacula (1972)
The Satanic Rites of Dracula (1973)
Andy Warhol's Dracula (1973)
The Seven Brothers Meet Dracula (1974)
Old Dracula (1975)
Dracula, père et fils (1976)
Zoltan, Hound of Dracula [Dracula's Dog] (1977)
Dracula's Widow (1988)
Dracula Rising (1992)
Dracula 2000 (2000)

---

set up by the vampire cinema but cater even more directly to the underlying repetitive structure of our mind and our innate desires, anxieties, and fears. Over the last one hundred years, the image of the vampire has proven itself to be highly adaptable and it is far from being depleted. It will certainly be around for the next century, and as soon as the pendulum swings back from the blood-and-gore extremes, a definitive version of Bram Stoker's novel would be more than welcome by most fans of the genre.

– *Journal of Dracula Studies*, 2 (2000): 24–33

---

1. Suzie McKee Charnas, *The Vampire Tapestry* (New York: Tor, 1986), pp. 3-4; emphasis added.
2. Ken Gelder, *Reading the Vampire* (London: Routledge, 1994), p. 86.
3. "Apparatus" here is understood as the formal elements which make up a film and the effect their use might have on the audience. Varying use of lenses, light, camera angles, *mise en scène*, editing, sound, a particular film stock, etc. can be employed to evoke certain reactions/emotions in the audience, and a trained observer will be aware of that.
4. For the most comprehensive listings of vampire films, see Alain Silver and James Ursini, *The Vampire Film: From Nosferatu to Bram Stoker's Dracula* (New York: Limelight Editions, 1993); and J. Gordon Melton, *VideoHound's Vampires on Video* (Detroit: Visible Ink, 1997).
5. David J. Skal, *Hollywood Gothic* (New York: Norton, 1990) provides a detailed account of Florence Stoker's fights to block the Murnau film and later attempts to transfer *Dracula* from the written word to stage and screen.
6. Judith Mayne, "Dracula in the Twilight: Murnau's *Nosferatu* (1922)," in *German Film and Literature,* ed. Eric Rentschler (New York: Methuen, 1986), p. 25.
7. Depending on the print, the characters come with different names: Dracula/Graf Orlok, Mina/Ellen, Jonathan Harker/Thomas Hutter, Renfield/Knock, Van Helsing/Prof. Bulwer.
8. Bram Stoker, *Dracula,* pp. 23-24. All quotations are cited from the Norton Critical Edition, 1997.
9. A shift in film history becomes perceptible here, namely the move from more traditional and almost "primitive" film relying on a "proscenium arch" composition towards the establishment of close-ups and editing. For more information compare David Bordwell, Kristin Thompson, Janet Staiger, *The Classical Hollywood Cinema: Film Style and Mode of Production to 1960* (New York: Columbia University Press, 1985), pp. 194-213.
10. In 1999, sixty-eight years after its original release, Philip Glass composed a score for *Dracula*. Universal Home Videos now makes *Dracula* available with this soundtrack played by the Kronos Quartet as part of their "Classic Monster Collection."
11. The use of diegetic sound is, indeed, one of the most striking features of the horror film in general: in well-executed horror films the soundtrack is always part of the narrative (diegesis).
12. See J. Gordon Melton, *The Vampire Book: The Encyclopedia of the Undead* (Detroit: Visible Ink, 1994), p. 124.
13. Silver and Ursini, *The Vampire Film,* p. 155.
14. Francis Ford Coppola and James V. Hart, *Bram Stoker's Dracula: The Film and the Legend* (New York: Newmarket, 1992), p. 3.
15. David Glover, "Travels in Romania: Myths of Origin, Myths of Blood," *Discourse,* 16 (Fall 1993): 126-127.
16. See: Richard Dyer, "Dracula and Desire," *Sight and Sound,* (January 1993): 18; Kim Newman, "Bloodlines," *Sight and Sound,* (January 1993): 13; and Iain Sinclair, "Invasion of the Blood," *Sight and Sound,* (January 1993): 15.
17. Qtd. in David Bidney, "Myth, Symbolism, and Truth," in *Myth and Literature,* ed. John B. Vickery (Lincoln: University of Nebraska Press, 1996), p. 128.
18. Rene Wellek and Austin Warren, *Theory of Literature* (New York: Harcourt, Brace, 1956), p. 225.
19. "See me now!" Dracula orders Mina/the viewer a little later, and in the subsequent scene at the cinematograph Mina articulates our uncanny recognition of the vampire: "My God, who are you? I know you."
20. Dyer, "Dracula and Desire," p. 10.
21. Bidney, "Myth," p. 10; Marina Warner, *Six Myths of Our Time* (New York: Vintage, 1995), p. 87.
22. Dyer, "Dracula and Desire," p. 10; Sinclair, "Invasion," p. 15.

The Spreading Influence

Revampings of Dracula in Contemporary Fiction
Margaret L. Carter

Although Count Dracula is slain in the final pages of Bram Stoker's 1897 novel, throughout the subsequent century he has enjoyed innumerable resurrections in film and literature. Many of these incarnations might be unrecognizable to Stoker as the character he created. Fictional treatments of Dracula, especially those that have appeared within the past thirty years, reflect changes in attitudes toward vampires in general. In contrast to the characterization of vampires in Stoker's own fiction and that of his contemporaries, in recent decades various authors have rendered these "monsters" sympathetically.

Earlier nineteenth-century works do contain a few hints of sympathy for their vampire characters. They inspire sympathy or attraction, however, despite their inhuman nature rather than because of it. They still must be destroyed. The eponymous monster in *Varney the Vampyre* (1847) displays remorse for his bloodthirsty past and finally commits suicide by leaping into a volcano. Carmilla, in J. Sheridan Le Fanu's novella (1872), presents herself initially as victim rather than predator, and the narrator, Laura, finds her attractive, yet Carmilla's existence nevertheless ends in violent destruction. Nina Auerbach characterizes pre-Stoker vampires as "not demon lovers or snarling aliens . . . but singular friends" in a literary period when "it was a privilege to walk with a vampire." This "sinister, superior sharer" enjoys an "intimate intercourse with mortals," even though a "dangerously close" one.[1]

Auerbach views Stoker's novel as introducing a new quality of alienation into the portrayal of the undead; his vampires "blend with mortals only at intervals" and display a "soullessness" that "bars them from human space."[2] The text of *Dracula* strongly implies that the soulless, bloodsucking revenant is a different individual from the dead person who was put into the grave. Dr. Seward emphatically refuses to identify the night-prowling Lucy with the woman he loved. "Is this really Lucy's body," he asks, "or only a demon in her shape?" and he labels the revenant "the foul Thing which had taken Lucy's shape without her soul" (p. 190). Both Lucy and Dracula himself, after their destruction, take on a peaceful expression that seems to indicate the return of the "true" soul after the expulsion of an invading vampiric demon. Mina anticipates the "joy" Dracula will experience "when he, too, is destroyed in his worser part that his better part may have spiritual immortality" (p. 269).

Cover for Jon J. Muth's 1986 graphic novel based on Stoker's novel (courtesy of Anne Fraser)

Some of the very traits that made vampires monstrous to readers of the 1890s, oddly, account for their appeal to the mindset of the late twentieth century. Many critics have noted the revulsion with which Stoker's male characters regard the blatant sexuality of the vampirized Lucy. This "voluptuous" quality (to use one of Stoker's favorite words), shared by Dracula's brides, does not extend to the Count himself. Instead, he exemplifies blasphemous defiance of religion (having studied, according to Van Helsing, at the Scholomance, the Devil's school) and ruthless exercise of power. Carol Senf points out, in the vampire fiction of the post-1970 period, an "increasing emphasis on the positive aspects of the vampire's eroticism and on his or her right to rebel against the stultifying constraints of society."[3] Combined with the frequent appearance of literary vampires who "are less bloodthirsty than ordinary human beings," this stress on the "positive" dimension of traits considered negative by nineteenth-century authors and readers produces attractive, even admirable bloodsuckers. One of the earliest illustrations of this trend appeared in the television series *Dark Shadows*

(1966-71) with Barnabas Collins, who began life (or undeath) as a Gothic villain and grew into a popular and sympathetic character. Portrayal of Dracula as a character in popular fiction has shifted focus along with these changes in writers' and audiences' perception of vampirism.

Bloomian "misreadings" of Stoker's novel, of course, began in the 1920s with the stage play by Hamilton Deane and John L. Balderston, which transformed the Count into a romantic melodrama villain. As David J. Skal notes, this drama created an "image of the master vampire in evening dress and opera cloak . . . polite enough to be invited into a proper Knightsbridge living room" and "able to interact with the characters, rather than merely hang outside their bedroom windows."[4] Yet this Dracula, though more alluring than Stoker's, cannot be mistaken for anything but the villain, just as in the Bela Lugosi film (1931). True, Lugosi's Dracula quotes Swinburne's line about "worse things waiting for man than death," a remark one would not expect to hear from Stoker's Count. But despite this touch of pathos and the erotic overtones of the film, he remains unmistakably diabolical, as do vampires in general and Dracula in particular until the early 1970s. (I exclude humorous and parodic treatments, of course.)

Raymond Rudorff's *The Dracula Archives* (1971), for example, chronologically stands on the cusp dividing the traditional, diabolical undead from the "new" vampire, allowed to be morally neutral or even good. Dracula himself does not appear "onstage" until the very end of the novel. Rudorff's story, a prelude to Stoker's, unfolds a long, complex process of preparation for the advent of the vampire lord. Dracula returns to unnatural life by possessing the body of a young man whose mother had succumbed to a vampire embrace and been destroyed, like Lucy, by staking. Like Lucy, Adelaide in *The Dracula Archives* is framed as a victim whose true innocence is restored when her vampiric nature is exorcised by the stake. Rudorff's novel makes an interesting contrast with a much later prequel to *Dracula,* Jeanne Kalogridis' "Diaries of the Family Dracul" trilogy, beginning with *Covenant with the Vampire* (1994). Here Dracula himself, unmistakably evil, demands blood sacrifices from his subjects and relatives, yet individual vampires can choose to resist the descent into darkness inherent in the loss of their humanity. The vampire remains the person he or she was before transformation. In Rudorff's 1971 novel, as in Stoker, rebirth in vampire form simply obliterates the humanity of the transformed victim.

The year before Anne Rice brought the sympathetic vampire to the attention of readers outside the genre, another novel narrated a vampire's apologia on tape in his own words. The 1970s, according to Auerbach, constitute "a halcyon decade for vampires, one in which they not only flourished, but reinvented themselves."[5] Fred Saberhagen's *The Dracula Tape* (1975), one instance of such reinvention, portrays Count Dracula as a misunderstood nobleman persecuted by a gang of superstition-addled men under the direction of a bigoted, hardheaded Professor Van Helsing. This favorable treatment of Dracula recurs in several other works of fiction during the 1970s and 1980s, in accordance with that period's general tendency to characterize fictional monsters as simply different kinds of people. Echoes from the civil rights movement resonate in fantastic fiction, with vampires and other inhuman beings shown as another misjudged minority group. Saberhagen's book, which became the first in a still-continuing series, foreshadowed and helped to create this trend. The Count Dracula portrayed on screen by Frank Langella in 1979, for instance, resembles Saberhagen's hero more than he does the Bela Lugosi or Christopher Lee Dracula. Auerbach describes Langella's Dracula as "sad and wise and far-seeing, erotically easy in his animal self," clearly superior to the "scurrying little mortals" who harass him.[6]

The predominance of the sympathetic vampire, however, has been countered in recent years by a "backlash" toward viewing the vampire as evil monster, a trend Auerbach links to the emergence of AIDS (among other cultural phenomena), as illustrated by the dominance of the disease metaphor in many recent novels. Yet these works do not merely revert to the nineteenth-century view of the vampire as demonic and worthy only of destruction. Following upon decades of highly successful novels and stories foregrounding "good" vampires, these recent backlash works tend to take a more nuanced approach. An outstanding example is *Anno-Dracula* (1992), by Kim Newman.

The typical fictional vampire of the 1970s and beyond is humanized rather than demonic. The product of a secular world-view, he or she no longer necessarily constitutes a threat to the victim's immortal soul—and may even possess a soul him- or herself. Even if still conceived as a supernatural being returned from the dead, this kind of vampire has free will and may choose to behave ethically. Saberhagen's *The Dracula Tape* not only endows Dracula with free will but merges Stoker's character with the historical Vlad Tepes and recreates both in positive rather than negative terms. This Dracula is the hero of the tale instead of the villain, not only a nobleman but a gentleman, telling his side of the story in an urbane, sardonic tone. The first-person narrative incorporates all the "facts" established in Stoker's epistolary novel but reinterprets them from Dracula's point of view. His goal is not to

Stills from two movies based on Anne Rice's popular vampire chronicles: Tom Cruise in the 1994 movie Interview
with the Vampire *(© Duhamel Francois/Corbis Sygma) and Stuart Townsend and Aaliyah in
the 2002 movie* Queen of the Damned *(Getty Images)*

invade and conquer England but to be fully and unquestioningly accepted in the normal world as human. Lucy and Mina freely give him their blood in highly erotic encounters. He backs away from a brandished eucharistic wafer, not because he fears holy objects, but because he prefers not to desecrate them with his enemies' gore. Van Helsing, not the vampire, commits sacrilege by misusing sacred symbols. Lucy dies from transfusions of incompatible blood, not from Dracula's feeding, and he doses her with his transforming blood in an attempt to save her life. She preys upon children, Dracula theorizes, because her traumatic death has damaged her mind. The scar on Mina's forehead results from the hypnotic force of Van Helsing's personality acting upon her own guilt, not from God's curse. The staking of an undead revenant does not liberate a soul from Satan but constitutes simple murder. Vampirism, in short, becomes a morally neutral trans-

formation, leaving the subject's free will intact. Dracula maintains, "It is the *forcing* of death, or of a change in life, that's criminal, whether the force be applied by vampire fang, or wooden stake, or means more subtle used against a vulnerable mind or heart"[7]—an obvious allusion to human beings' frequently inhumane treatment of their fellow men and women. Since, like many recent literary vampires, Saberhagen's Vlad Dracula is less violent and cruel than his mortal adversaries, he has, as Joe Sanders puts it, "something to teach breathing humans about choosing honor and compassion as they live their uncertain lives in a chaotic world."[8]

The Dracula Tape anticipates not only Rice's subjective, internalized presentation of the vampire as protagonist but also the heroic, attractive Count Saint-Germain of Chelsea Quinn Yarbro. This character, who first appears in *Hotel Transylvania* (1978), may be described as a mirror image of Dracula. Saint-Germain, like Stoker's villain, is a Transylvanian Count who sleeps on his native earth, casts no reflection, and transforms his donors by sharing his own blood with them. But Yarbro's vampire, unlike Stoker's, is generous, self-sacrificing, and highly ethical. Religious symbols have no negative effect on him; in fact, a scene in *Hotel Transylvania,* in a deliberately ironic reversal of roles, shows him warding off a gang of Satanists with a holy object. Yarbro, by the way, has also created her own version of Dracula, in her recent trilogy dealing with the vampire's three "brides." Her Dracula, based directly on Stoker's, belongs to the more recent phase of fictional vampirism. Though ruthless and evil, he appears so from free choice rather than diabolical compulsion, and the women he transforms make their own ethical choices after initiation into the new existence of undeath.

In the 1990s readers have seen a reversion to the unequivocally "evil" vampire (though the more benign type has not, of course, vanished). This "backlash" predator, however, freely chooses to defy the laws of God and society rather than acting under compulsion from the indwelling of a diabolical force. *Dracula Unbound* (1991), by Brian Aldiss, most nearly approaches framing the vampire as inherently evil. Aldiss' monsters, reptilian parasites operating on instinct rather than intelligence, cannot make moral choices. They feed on human victims from the same innate drive that any other subhuman predator does. Dracula himself appears "horned and gigantic, more devil than man," but the "devilish" quality is metaphorical, not literal. Bram Stoker, as a character in this metafictional novel, scorning the suggestion that vampires might be "one more oppressed minority" (as many post-1970 works characterize them), classifies them as "simply . . . a bad lot–a disease, in short."[9] This book contains no "good" vampires. In keeping with the preoccupations of the late twentieth century, however, the "evil" of vampirism arises from biological rather than supernatural roots.

Another reinterpretation of vampirism as disease instead of demonic possession appears in Dan Simmons' *Children of the Night* (1992). Set partly in Romania after the fall of Communism, Simmons' novel propounds its theory of vampirism against the background of AIDS-infected children left to the overstressed mercy of the state. In this case, the genetic disorder that causes vampirism carries positive as well as negative qualities. If properly harnessed, this mutation has the potential to confer benefits on humanity, including a treatment for AIDS. The "vampire" most visible to the reader is not only innocent but helpless–a baby boy, seen through the viewpoint of his foster mother. As for Dracula, he works behind the scenes, a ruthless tyrant, killer, and capitalist, motivated not by the Devil but by pragmatic self-interest.

Kim Newman's alternate history, begun in *Anno Dracula,* depicts Europe and England in the late nineteenth century and the first half of the twentieth as dominated by vampires. Newman rewrites the conclusion of Stoker's narrative to reveal that Dracula survived his conflict with Van Helsing's band and married the widowed Queen Victoria. Now that Dracula (identified with Vlad Tepes) has become Prince Consort of Great Britain, the vampire minority holds sway over the "warm" majority. Ordinary human citizens retain their civil rights, but vampires have a near-monopoly on political power and social chic. As Elizabeth Hardaway notes, Stoker's Dracula, "a grotesquely romantic outsider," becomes in Newman's novel "a power-mad politician and despot who has made England safe for vampires."[10] Dracula himself, not seen in person until the end of the novel, is a loathsome monster, an undead bloodsucker of the most gruesome type, enthroned naked except for an "ermine-collared black velvet cloak, ragged at the edges" and "his body thickly coated with matted hair, blood clotting on his chest and limbs."[11] Sadistically cruel to Queen Victoria, whom he keeps chained at his side, he retains negative traits that originated in his human lifetime; "barely a generation away from his mountain bully-boy ancestors," he displays "the philistine avarice of a true barbarian."[12] Although supernatural as well as depraved, he is not, however, literally diabolical. Hardaway remarks upon Newman's "secularization of Dracula and, even more importantly, of vampires in general," observing that, "The Dracula that haunts *Anno Dracula* . . . is grotesque, violent, and corrupt, but ultimately secular," and that vampiric violence "differs only in degree, not kind, from the violence and cruelty found in the human heart."[13]

In Newman's fiction vampirism as such is not inherently evil. While some of the undead spring from "debased bloodlines," such as the "polluted" bloodline of Vlad Tepes, others escape this curse. One of the principal villains, Jack the Ripper, turns out to be the completely human Dr. John Seward, driven mad by the death of Lucy. And we find upright, ethical characters among the vampire population. Genevieve Dieudonne, for example, devotes her time to charitable works. She even aids a human secret agent, Charles Beauregard, in his attempt to assassinate the Prince Consort. Genevieve, as Auerbach puts it, "is a harmonizing alternative to Dracula's sick spawn."[14] Hardaway points out that the novel emphasizes the parallels between vampires and ordinary people more than their differences, conveying as its subtext "a philosophy that values 'humanity' (warm and undead alike) over such external constructs as government or other power-based entities."[15]

Fictional reinterpretations of Dracula as a character have thus evolved over the past century from Stoker's original characterization of the Count as satanic through various stages corresponding to the overall evolution of the literary vampire. When the typical vampire of the popular imagination became humanized in the 1970s, Fred Saberhagen created a Dracula who epitomized this trend and helped to catalyze its growth. Later, when the vampire as ruthless predator ascended to renewed popularity (though the sympathetic vampire has not, of course, vanished), Draculas of this type proliferated, as illustrated by the works of Jeanne Kalogridis, Dan Simmons, and Kim Newman. Since these novelists wrote after the significant shift in the fictional vampire from undead corpse animated by the Devil to a humanized being with free will and moral responsibility, however, they did not create vampires who were simply evil. In the fiction of these more recent writers, a more nuanced approach allows the possibility of "good" vampires, even though the archetypal vampire, Dracula, is depicted as evil.

– Journal of Dracula Studies, 3
(2001), pp. 15–19

1. Nina Auerbach, *Our Vampires, Ourselves* (Chicago: University of Chicago Press, 1995), p. 13.
2. Auerbach, p. 105.
3. Carol A. Senf, *The Vampire in Nineteenth-Century English Literature* (Bowling Green: Bowling Green University Popular Press, 1988), p. 163.
4. David J. Skal, *Hollywood Gothic* (New York: Norton, 1990), pp. 69–70.
5. Auerbach, p. 131.
6. Auerbach, p. 145.
7. Fred Saberhagen, *The Dracula Tape* (New York: Warner, 1975), p. 103.
8. Joe Sanders, "The Pretense that the World is Sane: Saberhagen's Dracula," in *The Blood is the Life: Vampires in Literature,* eds. Leonard Heldreth and Mary Pharr (Bowling Green: Bowling Green University Popular Press, 1999), p. 118.
9. Brian Aldiss, *Dracula Unbound* (New York: HarperCollins, 1991), pp. 159, 181.
10. Elizabeth Hardaway, "Ourselves Expanded: The Vampire's Evolution from Bram Stoker to Kim Newman," in *The Blood is the Life,* p. 179.
11. Kim Newman, *Anno-Dracula* (New York: Carroll & Graf, 1992), p. 342.
12. Newman, p. 346.
13. Hardaway, p. 185.
14. Auerbach, p. 178.
15. Hardaway, p. 181.

* * *

Dracula: The Ever Widening Circle
Elizabeth Miller

And so the circle goes on ever widening, like as the ripples from a stone thrown in the water."

–Van Helsing in *Dracula,* Chapter XVI,
Dr. Seward's Diary, 29 September

Today, Count Dracula is everywhere: Halloween masks, breakfast cereal, t-shirts, video games, posters, comic books, "Sesame Street," postage stamps, TV ads, musicals, ballets. The list goes on. The name "Dracula" has become synonymous with "vampire"; the characteristics and limitations of the vampire as presented by Stoker in his novel are known world-wide.

What follows is an across-the-spectrum overview of how Stoker's character has permeated just about every aspect of Western culture.

Box front for the breakfast cereal that debuted in 1971. Count Chocula was the first of a line of so-called Monster Cereals produced by General Mills (Elizabeth Miller Collection).

Sanitizing Dracula

The following is a partial list of vampire fiction for children and youth.

Molly Albright, *Meet Miss Dracula* (1988)
Victor Ambrus, *Count Dracula* (1991)
Ambrus, *Dracula* (1980)
Ambrus, *Dracula's Bedtime Story Book* (1981)
Ambrus, *Dracula's Late-Night TV Show* (1990)
Ambrus, *Read with Dracula* (1993)
Ambrus, *Son of Dracula* (1986)
Ambrus, *Spot Dracula* (1993)
Ambrus, *What's the Time Dracula?* (1991)
Pat Arthur, *Dracula's Castle* (1982)
Alan Benjamin, *Let's Count, Dracula* (1994)
Terence Blacker, *Ms Whiz Loves Dracula* (1992)
J. H. Brennan, *Dracula's Castle* (1986)
Vic Crume, *The Mystery in Dracula's Castle* (1973)
Keith Faulkner, *Dracula: A Spooky Lift-the-Flap Book* (1993)
John Goldthwaite, *Dracula Spectacula* (1975)
Gertrude Gruesome, *Drak's Slumber Party* (1995)
Jayne Harvey, *Great-Uncle Dracula* (1992)
Mary Hoffman, *Dracula's Daughter* (1988)
Mary Howath, *Could Dracula Live in Woodford?* (1983)
Ann Jungman, *Count Draco Down Under* (1996)
Jungman, *Vlad the Drac* (1982)
Jungman, *Vlad the Drac Down Under* (1989)
Jungman, *Vlad the Drac Goes Traveling* (1994)
Jungman, *Vlad the Drac Returns* (1984)
Jungman, *Vlad the Drac, Superstar* (1985)
Jungman, *Vlad the Drac Vampire* (1988)
Elizabeth Levy, *Dracula Is a Pain in the Neck* (1983)
Stella Maidment, *Little Dracula's Fantastic Fun Book* (1992)
David Orme, ed., *Dracula's Auntie Ruthless and Other Petrifying Poems* (1994)
Kin Platt, *Dracula Go Home!* (1979)
Chris Powling, *Dracula in Sunlight* (1992)
Jean Rudegeair, *Dracula's Castle* (1982)
Tom B. Stone, *Camp Dracula* (1995)
Robert Swindells, *Dracula's Castle* (1990)
Martin Waddell, *Little Dracula at the Seashore* (1987)
Waddell, *Little Dracula Goes to School* (1987)
Waddell, *Little Dracula's Christmas* (1986)
Waddell, *Little Dracula's Fiendishly Funny Joke Book* (1992)
Waddell, *Little Dracula's First Bite* (1986)

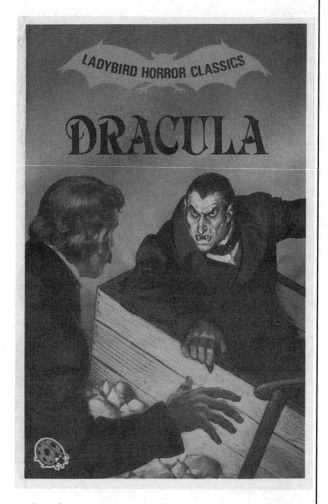

Cover for a 1984 adaptation of Dracula *for children, illustrated by Angus M. McBride (Elizabeth Miller Collection)*

Waddell and Joseph Wright, *Little Dracula's Monstrous Poster* (1992)
Jan Wahl, *Dracula's Cat* (1978)

–J. Gordon Melton and Robert Eighteen-Bisang, "Vampire Fiction for Children and Youth, 1960–Present," *Transylvanian Journal,* 2 (Spring/Summer 1996): 24–30

Vampires in fiction

Several of the hundreds of published novels and short stories dealing with vampires are directly linked to Stoker's novel. The best known is probably Fred Saberhagen's *The Dracula Tape* (1975), which is essentially a retelling of the original story from Count Dracula's point of view. Stoker's vagueness about Dracula's origins (especially how he became a vampire) and the perceived ambiguity of his ending have inspired other fiction writers to offer prequels and sequels. One of the best known among the former is the "Family Dracul" trilogy of Jeanne Kalogridis, in which the author connects the Count with Vlad the Impaler and creates a history for the intervening years for both Dracula and

Count von Count, *a character on* Sesame Street *who teaches children their numbers (© Sesame Workshop)*

Abraham Van Helsing. Peter Tremayne has created a pre-history for Stoker's Count in three novels beginning with *Dracula Unborn*. And Chelsea Quinn Yarbro has written a trilogy about the three female vampires in Dracula's Castle: who they were, how they ended up at the castle, and what happened to them before Jonathan Harker showed up. Sequels include Marie Kiraly's *Mina, Dracula the Undead* by Freda Warrington, *Blood to Blood* by Elaine Bergstrom, and *Quincey Morris, Vampire* by P. N. Elrod. Other authors have integrated the Count into alternative histories: best known is Kim Newman's *Anno Dracula* in which Dracula (in this case both Vlad and vampire) is the husband of Queen Victoria.

The phenomenal spread of *Dracula* is evident in a flood of vampire literature for children. This is not too surprising, for popular culture has appropriated the vampire as one of the icons of Halloween. In addition to adaptations of the original novel, Dracula shows his influence in dozens of children's books. Much of this fiction offers a greatly sanitized vampire, one that is almost unrecognizable to readers of Stoker. For example, in 1979 Deborah and James Howe introduced what is probably the most lovable vampire of all time, a vegetarian vampire rabbit named Bunnicula. In the 1980s, German author Angela Sommer-Bodenberg published a series of four books about a young vampire named Rudolph, his vampire sister, and a human friend. Such books continue to be popular to this day. J. Gordon Melton explains this phenomenon as follows:

> The success of the vampire in the last quarter of the twentieth century is due in large part to its development as both a positive creature and an anti-hero with great range and depth of character. The vampire no longer exists solely as an evil destructive force totally driven by the need for blood. It has continued to manifest an unexpected malleability with a seemingly infinite possibility for adaptation to different settings. As

Clubs, Organizations, and Awards

Transylvanian Society of Dracula

Formed in Romania in 1991, the Transylvanian Society of Dracula is a historical-cultural organization devoted to the serious study of Dracula, both the fictional and the historical. With chapters in several countries, the TSD organizes annual symposia/congresses as well as Dracula tours in Romania. The Canadian Chapter publishes the *Journal of Dracula Studies.*

The Dracula Society

Based in London, England, the Dracula Society has been in operation since 1973. They have organized several tours to Romania as well as other sites associated with Gothic literature, and they hold local meetings. Each year the society names the winners of its "Children of the Night" literary awards.

The Bram Stoker Society

Formed in 1980 in Dublin, this society strives to bring to Bram Stoker the recognition he deserves as a native son. The society issues regular newsletters as well as the *Bram Stoker Journal.* It works closely with the Bram Stoker Dracula Organization (Clontarf) and its annual Summer School.

The Vampire Empire

Formerly the Count Dracula Fan Club, this is the largest of the Dracula organizations. Based in New York, it offers numerous services to its members including regular newsletters and a variety of publications. It was founded in 1965 by Dr. Jeanne Youngson who still serves as its president.

Bram Stoker Heritage Centre

Opened in 2003, the centre is located near Stoker's birthplace in Clontarf (Dublin). It is a focal point for the study of Stoker and his works, especially *Dracula,* as well as Gothic literature in general. Its museum and library contain a vast collection of books, papers and memorabilia. "The Dracula Experience" enables visitors to enjoy some of the scenes from Stoker's most famous novel.

Bram Stoker Awards

Every year, the Horror Writers Association of America grants these awards in a number of categories. Among the winners have been Stephen King, Thomas Harris, Christopher Lee, Vincent Price, Peter Straub, Ray Bradbury, Robert Bloch, Richard Matheson, and Robert McCammon.

---

the vampire has been unique among monsters for its possession of rationality and feeling, and has shown itself possessed of an ambiguous and complicated personality fully capable of making moral decisions. They may assume a variety of sympathetic and even heroic roles. This malleability is very vividly portrayed in the books designed for young people.[1]

One could argue that all post-*Dracula* vampire fiction has been written in the shadow of Stoker's novel. But some works show the influence more pointedly than others. Stephen King, for example, has referred to *'Salem's Lot* as his own tribute to *Dracula:*

> When I conceived of the vampire novel which became *'Salem's Lot,* I decided I wanted to try to use the book partially as a form of literary homage. . . . So my novel bears an intentional similarity to Bram Stoker's *Dracula,* and after awhile it began to seem to me what I was doing was playing an interesting–to me, at least–game of literary racquet ball: *'Salem's Lot* itself was the ball and *Dracula* was the wall I kept hitting it against, watching to see how and where it would bounce, so I could hit it again. As a matter of fact, it took some pretty interesting bounces, and I ascribe this mostly to the fact that, while my ball existed in the twentieth century, my wall was very much a product of the nineteenth.[2]

Typical of tributes paid to the seminal influence of *Dracula* is this comment by Brian Aldiss, popular writer of science fiction, in his *Trillion Year Spree: The History of Science Fiction:* "*Dracula* is a remarkably good book of its sensational kind, carrying more conviction by far than any of Stoker's other rather feeble novels, and crammed with dramatically conceived terrors which are scarcely diminished by re-reading."[3]

On the other hand, much of the vampire fiction of the second half of the twentieth century delineates a conscious departure from Stoker. Beginning with authors such as Saberhagen, Anne Rice, Chelsea Quinn Yarbro and Suzy McKee Charnas, the vampire has taken on the mantle of a more ambivalent (even sympathetic) character, a reflection of the changing perception of an absolute "good versus evil" in our more secular world. In recent fiction, vampires come in many guises: no longer foreign aristocrats, they are college professors, police detectives, hospital workers, art dealers, rock musicians, nightclub dancers and even aliens from other planets.[4]

Not surprisingly, images from Stoker's novel have found their way into works of more mainstream literature. James Joyce's *Ulysses,* for example, contains a number of allusions to the vampire, including "He comes, pale vampire, through storm his eyes, his bat sails bloodying the sea, mouth to her mouth's kiss."[5] Also, T. S. Eliot, in *The Waste Land* (1921), incor-

---

frequently noted, the vampire is the horror creature that most closely resembles a normal human being, and thus is most capable, even as an evil entity, of living a somewhat normal existence in everyday human society. As developed through two centuries of literature,

Cover of a German model kit for Dracula (design by Peter Feierabend; courtesy of Anne Fraser)

porates the scene in Dracula where the Count climbs down the castle wall: "And bats with baby faces in the violet light / Whistled, and beat their wings / And crawled head downward down a blackened wall."

Vampires in the movies

In addition to films loosely based on Stoker's novel there are dozens of others that use "Dracula" in their titles. Some, such as the recent *Dracula 2000* (released in Europe as *Dracula 2001*), pick up on a few of the motifs of the original book, while others share nothing but the name of the Count. The list of the latter seems endless. Furthermore, there are about six hundred others that offer a variety of vampires.[6] Some of the best known of these include the following: *Near Dark, Fright Night, Dance of the Damned, The Hunger, The Vampire Lovers, The Lost Boys, Innocent Blood, Subspecies, From Dusk to Dawn, Blade, Interview with the Vampire* and *John Carpenter's Vampires.*

Vampires on TV

Vampires have also invaded the world of television. Some of the most successful early series were *Dark Shadows* (a Gothic soap opera featuring Jonathan Frid as Barnabas Collins) which ran for well over one thousand episodes, *The Munsters* (a comedy with its Dracula-like Grandpa), and *Count Duckula* (a children's cartoon featuring a vegetarian vampire). The 1990s saw two very popular series: *Forever Knight* which featured a vampire who was a police detective and who used his powers to help defeat criminals; and perhaps the most successful of all–*Buffy the Vampire Slayer* (which even ran an episode pitting Buffy against the Count himself). Television has also provided many documentaries on the whole Dracula phenomenon. Many of these, unfortunately, have the appearance of having been "slapped together" with sensationalism often taking priority over accuracy. Arguably the best from a literary standpoint is a documentary titled

---

Renfield's Syndrome

Psychologist Richard Noll, author of *Vampires, Were-wolves, and Demons,* says that the clinical cases of vampirism have things in common with fiction and folklore, and in fact these people go much further in terms of brutality than the vampire tales record. "Man's actual capacity for evil," he says in *Bizarre Diseases of the Mind,* "far outstrips any imaginary evils."

Noll is noted for his suggestion to rename clinical vampirism Renfield's syndrome. Contrary to some popular notions, Dracula's visit to England [in Stoker's novel] had nothing to do with Renfield's desire to drink blood. This lunatic was already a patient under Dr. Seward's care before Dracula arrived in that country. Seward had made many notes in his journal about Renfield's zoophagy, or desire to consume lives, starting with flies and working up to more complicated life-forms like cats.

Given his unstable frame of mind, Renfield becomes the person that Dracula exploits in order to gain entrée into the asylum. He gets Renfield to let him in and then commands him as a slave. Noll points out that this is consistent with a notion that the devil hones in on those suffering from delusions, as described in Johann Wier's *De Praestigiis Daemonum* from 1593. He believes that Stoker provided a human counterpart to the vampire, both of whom desire to absorb lives, and Noll names clinical vampirism after Renfield because clinical vampires are living humans.

To get right to it, people having the symptoms of this syndrome are primarily male, and they tend to endow blood with mystical qualities, as if it could somehow enhance their lives or empower them. Noll, a professor of clinical psychology, described the typical progression into this mental condition:

Renfield's syndrome is a psychiatric syndrome. . . . The first stage involves some event that happens before puberty where the child is excited in a sexual way by blood injury or the ingestion of blood. At puberty it becomes fused with sexual fantasies, and typically the person with Renfield's syndrome begins with autovampirism. That is, they begin to drink their own blood and then move on to other living creatures. That's the zoophagous element that Dr. Seward talks about in *Dracula.* The typical progression in many cases is ingesting blood from other people. That's what we know from the few cases we have on record. It has fetishistic and compulsive components to it and it's more than likely that if you used the *DSM-IV* for diagnosis, you would classify it as one of the paraphilias.

. . . .

In his book, Noll adds that blood will sometimes take on a mystical significance as a symbol of life and power. Ingesting it produces an experience of well-being. In short Renfield's syndrome is a sexual compulsion in which blood drinking is a necessary component.

While many professionals, Noll among them, believe that clinical vampirism is predominantly a male phenomenon, there have certainly been cases of women who developed an erotic attraction to blood. Often they didn't attack people, so they may not have come to the attention of doctors on psychiatric wards. Yet several women have talked freely to reporters about how they were treating a bruised knee or applying bandages to their own cuts when they grew excited over the act. After that, they sought out ways to lick a wound and imagined themselves partaking in a sacred ritual. The experience made them feel more alive.

–Katherine Ramsland, *The Science of Vampires*
(New York: Berkley, 2002),
pp. 116–119

Dracula, presented in the United States on The Learning Channel in 1999 as part of its "Great Books" series.

Centennial celebrations

The year 1997, which marked the centenary of the publication of the novel *Dracula,* saw numerous special events. First and foremost was "Dracula 97: A Centennial Celebration" sponsored by the Transylvanian Society of Dracula and the Count Dracula Fan Club. Held in Los Angeles, it drew hundreds of participants from all over the world. This unique event was actually a combination of scholarly conference and fan convention. It featured academic papers, guest writers and artists, films, role-playing games, a massive merchandise room, and even a masquerade ball.

Other events to mark the centenary included conferences in Boston and New York; special tours in Whitby, England and Transylvania, Romania; and the issuing of commemorative postage stamps in the United States, Canada, Britain and Ireland.

Dracula and the Arts

Dracula has appeared many times throughout the century in stage plays, beginning in the 1920s. But a more recent phenomenon is the Count's invasion into other forms of artistic expression. In 1999, a version of Stoker's *Dracula* as a chamber musical was presented at Canada's Stratford Festival. Directed by Richard Ouzounian with music by Marek Norman, it played to full and enthusiastic houses over a period of six months. In August 2004, *Dracula, the Musical* (Des McAniff and Frank Wildhorn) opened on Broadway.

Since 1997, at least three major productions of *Dracula* have been choreographed for professional bal-

Scene from The Munsters, *a 1960s television comedy with characters inspired in part by Stoker's* Dracula *and Mary Shelley's* Frankenstein. *Left to right, Al Lewis as Grandpa, Yvonne De Carlo as Lily, and Fred Gwynne as Herman Munster* (© *John Springer Collection/Corbis*).

let. America's Houston Ballet (choreography by Ben Stevenson to the music of Franz Liszt) and Britain's Northern Ballet (by Christopher Gable and Michael Pink, with original music by Philip Feeney) presented successful versions. But perhaps the most popular (with its eighty full-length performances to date) is the adaptation offered by Canada's Royal Winnipeg Ballet. Clearly inspired by Stoker's novel rather than movie versions of the story, this ballet was choreographed by Mark Godden to the music of Gustav Mahler, part of whose "Resurrection" Symphony (which premiered in 1895 while Stoker was writing *Dracula*) is used in the production. This ballet had a highly successful cross-Canada tour, and was also performed in several venues in the United States and throughout Asia. In 2002, a film adaptation, "Dracula: Pages from a Virgin's Diary," directed by Guy Maddin, was aired on CBC-TV in Canada, and won an International Emmy award for Arts Programming.

Clubs and Organizations

Several societies and fan clubs have sprung up around the world: the Transylvanian Society of Dracula (a cultural-historical society based in Romania with chapters in several countries); the Vampire Empire in the United States (formerly the Count Dracula Fan Club); the Lord Ruthven Assembly (a constituent part of the International Association for the Fantastic in the Arts); the Dracula Society (U.K.); the Bram Stoker Society (Dublin); and Stoker's Dracula Organization (Dublin).

Dracula Tourism

Places associated with Bram Stoker and his famous novel have become popular tourist destinations. In Dublin, one can visit the area where Stoker was born and spent his childhood, the university he attended, and the church in which he was married. London is the setting for most of the novel, as well as where Stoker lived and worked for most of his life.

The star of the television show Buffy the Vampire Slayer, *Sarah Michelle Gellar (1998; Getty Images)*

One of the most popular destinations is Whitby, which finds its way into the pages of the novel in most dramatic fashion. Visitors taking the "Dracula Trail" can sit on the Bram Stoker Memorial Seat and share the view of the town described in the early part of Chapter 6 of the novel. They can also climb the one hundred and ninety-nine steps to Eastcliff, view the ruins of Whitby Abbey, and walk through the graveyard immortalized by Stoker as the site of the Count's first attack on Lucy. And further north is the Scottish town of Cruden Bay where Stoker vacationed and may well have written parts of the novel.

Most famous of all Dracula sites is, of course, Transylvania, a region of Romania. Dracula tourism has been somewhat slow in developing, given the reluctance on the part of many Romanians to capitalize on an icon that is essentially not part of their culture.[7] Given that Stoker never visited Transylvania, it is not surprising that its most important site (for fans of the novel), the Borgo Pass, bears slight resemblance to the craggy, forbidding landscape that greets Jonathan

Harker. There is, of course, no Castle Dracula in the Borgo Pass; however, local entrepreneurs have constructed, for the benefit of tourists, a Castle Dracula Hotel, complete with vaults and a coffin. As for future plans, the Romanian Ministry of Tourism is promoting the building of Dracula Park, a vampire theme park that will most likely be constructed near the city of Bucharest.

Dracula in the Ivory Tower

Once ignored and even scorned as "inferior," *Dracula* is now included on the reading lists of many courses in Literature, Film Studies and Popular Culture throughout the Western world. The influence of Stoker's novel on mainstream literature is being recognized. Articles on vampire literature appear regularly in leading scholarly journals and periodicals, while papers on Stoker and *Dracula* (and on the vampire phenomenon in general) are common at academic conferences. In Romania, a World Dracula Congress is held at regular intervals, with smaller symposia scheduled for each of the intervening years. Stoker and his novel are well represented at university libraries by several highly regarded full-length studies.

A Dracula Miscellany

Dracula and vampire aficionados have been inundated with all kinds of merchandise and collectibles: Dracula jewelry, t-shirts, greeting cards, stuffed Draculas, vampire wine, even vampire teeth. Count Dracula and his kin make appearances in comic books, fan-zines, video and computer games, as well as in role-playing games such as the popular "Vampire: The Masquerade." The influence of vampires can be found in musical lyrics such as "Bela Lugosi's Dead" (Bauhaus), "Moon Over Bourbon Street" (Sting), "Bloodletting" (Concrete Blonde) and "Love Song for a Vampire" (Annie Lennox). For web surfers, a search for "Dracula" will bring up thousands of web sites and homepages.

Dracula shows up in the most unusual of places: a genus of orchids labeled "dracula"; an anticoagulant drug derived from the saliva of vampire bats patented as "draculin"; "vampire crime"; the "Dracula" helicopter; the "Dracula look" in fashion; and "Renfield's syndrome" (a psychiatric disorder characterized by a craving for blood).[8]

1. J. Gordon Melton, "The Vegetarian Vampire: On Introducing Dracula to Children," *Transylvanian Journal*, 2 (Spring/Summer 1996): 23.

2. Stephen King, *Danse Macabre* (New York: Berkley, 1983), p. 25.

3. Brian Aldiss, *Trillion Year Spree: The History of Science Fiction* (New York: Atheneum, 1986), p. 144.

4. In addition to those already noted above, here is a partial list of contemporary writers of vampire fiction: Nancy Baker, Poppy Z. Brite, Nancy Collins, Barbara Hambly, Laurell Hamilton, Tanya Huff, Nancy Kilpatrick, Tanith Lee, Brian Lumley, Robert McCammon, Christopher Moore, Yvonne Navarro, Michael Romkey, Dan Simmons, S. P. Somtow, and Lois Tilton.

5. James Joyce, *Ulysses* (New York: Random House, 1933), p. 48.

6. For a comprehensive list of vampire movies up to 1998, see J. Gordon Melton, *Vampires on Video* (Detroit: Visible Ink, 1997).

7. We must keep in mind that the Count Dracula of Stoker's novel is not Romanian. He is identified as "szekely," an ethic group related to the Magyars whose language was Hungarian. Transylvania, when Stoker wrote Dracula, was not part of Romania, but comprised part of the Austro-Hungarian Empire.

8. For details on "Renfield's syndrome" see Richard Noll, *Vampires, Werewolves and Demons: Twentieth Century Reports in the Psychiatric Literature* (New York: Brunner/Mazel, 1992), and Katherine Ramsland, *The Science of Vampires* (New York: Berkley, 2002).

* * *

The Search for Castle Dracula
Elizabeth Miller

In *Dracula,* Jonathan Harker declares that he was "not able to light on any map or work giving the exact locality of the Castle Dracula." Yet, the search for the "real thing" is ongoing. Several candidates have been put forth, with credentials from improbable to preposterous.

Bran Castle

Located near the city of Brasov in southern Transylvania, Bran Castle looks as if it could belong to Dracula. Photos of Bran Castle frequently appear with the caption "Castle Dracula." It is highly unlikely that Stoker knew of Bran Castle. To begin with, he never visited Transylvania. Nor did any of his known sources make reference to Bran. As for the historical Dracula, the links between this edifice and Vlad the Impaler are tenuous at best, limited to a possible overnight stay or two.

For years, Romanian authorities have deliberately promoted Bran as Dracula's Castle. The site has been visited by thousands of tourists who remain

Postcard of the Count Dracula Hotel, built in the Borgo Pass in Transylvania to cater to tourists
(Elizabeth Miller Collection)

blissfully unaware that they have been deceived. If one does not know the difference, it is easy to be misled. This thirteenth-century structure certainly is impressive, and it has all of the features tourists want to see in a medieval castle: battlements, towers, a Gothic chapel, a winding staircase and a secret underground passage. And of course, it happens to be located in Transylvania. Despite all of this (and an abundance of Dracula–both voivode and vampire–souvenirs at the stalls near the entrance), Bran Castle is *not* Castle Dracula.

The false representation apparently stems from the fact that when Western tourists began coming to Romania in search of Dracula, the Romanian tourist board took the opportunity to showcase some of its historic sites. Unlike Vlad's fortress at Poenari, Bran Castle is a magnificent edifice that is easily accessible from a major highway. At the World Dracula Congress in 1995 the curator of the Bran Castle Museum, Ioan Prahoveanu, pointed out that American tourists usually want to visit as many countries as possible in a short time and, with only two days in Romania, insist on seeing Dracula's Castle. "As Bran was the only Transylvanian castle included in this type of tour, they projected everything they knew about Transylvania and Dracula on [it]." Concomitantly, some guides began catering to this excitement and travel agencies were more than happy to promote it as "Castle Dracula." The present official position is to discourage the Dracula connection; yet it is still easy to find postcards and t-shirts of Bran that proudly proclaim it as "Dracula's Castle."

There are those who argue that Bran Castle is similar to the castle described in *Dracula,* that the analogies between Stoker's mythical Castle Dracula and the real Castle Bran are simply too close to be coincidental.[1] The resemblance, such as it is, is completely coincidental. In fact, a close comparison of the features of Bran with Stoker's description reveals more differences than similarities. Jonathan Harker describes his first view of Castle Dracula as "a vast ruined castle, from whose tall black windows came no ray of light, and whose broken battlements showed a jagged line across the moonlit sky." Bran is not a ruin, has windows that are more rectangular than tall, and shows not a sign of a broken battlement. While Bran, like Castle Dracula, is perched on a rock, it can hardly be said to be "on the very edge of a terrible precipice." True, Bran shares with Stoker's castle certain features–a courtyard, winding stairs and narrow passages. But then, so do most castles.

The Fortress at Poenari

This structure is a partially restored ruin situated on a crag some 1200 feet (a climb of about 1500 steps) above a gorge that runs from the Arges Valley through the mountains that separate Wallachia and Transylvania. (Actually, this "Castle Dracula" is in Wallachia, not Transylvania.) The fortress was rebuilt by Vlad the Impaler in the late 1450s and used as a mountain retreat during Turkish invasions. Virtually unknown until 1972 when its presence was brought to light by the two historians Florescu and McNally, it gained additional prominence during the 1970s when the Romanian government began to re-establish Vlad's reputation as one of the country's national heroes.

The gruesome story of the construction of this fortress is well documented. One Easter in the late 1450s, Vlad Dracula invited the boyars (nobles) whom he held responsible for the death of his elder brother, Mircea, to a feast in Târgoviste. After his guests finished their meal Vlad's soldiers surrounded them, rounded up the able-bodied and marched them fifty miles up the Arges River to Poenari, where they were forced to build his mountain fortress. His prisoners labored under very difficult conditions for many months. Those who survived the grueling ordeal were impaled. For Vlad, its inaccessibility served well as a refuge from encroaching enemies, while its strategic location afforded advance warning of attack. When the Turks attacked Poenari in 1462, Vlad fled to Transylvania where he was taken prisoner by the Hungarian king Matthias Corvinus.

This locale has nothing whatsoever to do with Stoker's *Dracula.* That Bram Stoker even knew of it is virtually impossible. It is referred to in Romania not as "Castle Dracula" but as "Cetatea [Fortress] Poenari." The label "Castle Dracula" was first assigned to it by Boston College historians Radu Florescu and Raymond McNally, in their best-selling book *In Search of Dracula.* Though they used it with reference to Vlad, the common assumption that Stoker based his Count on Vlad has led to the erroneous connections between this site and Stoker's novel.

Slains Castle

One prime candidate for the designation "Castle Dracula" is not in Romania at all, but on the northeast coast of Scotland. Slains castle, near Cruden Bay, is now being touted, especially by local tourism promoters, as the inspiration for Stoker's castle. There is no doubt that Stoker was intimately familiar with Cruden Bay. He first stayed at the village in August 1893,[2] and returned for a number of subsequent visits. We know that both *The Watter's Mou'* and *Crooken Sands* as well as "The Man from Shorrox'" were set there. It is also likely that he worked on portions of *Dracula* during these visits, though we have no way of knowing how much or which sections.

Illustration for Stoker's story "Castle of the King," which resembles the Castle Dracula described by Stoker in his novel
(drawing by Rev. William Fitzgerald; Stoker, Under the Sunset, *1881; Elizabeth Miller Collection)*

How similar is Slains to Stoker's castle? Clive Leatherdale reminds us Stoker paints Castle Dracula with considerable attention to detail:

> An architect could draw its likeness pretty accurately, with its courtyard, its ornate gates, the tower from which Dracula summons the wolves, its various wings linked by straight or winding staircases, the broken battlements, the decorous ladies' quarters at the rear, the ruined chapel open to the elements, the precipice that plunges into the void on the south side.[3]

A comparison between the two suggests very little resemblance. Stoker's Castle Dracula is more of a fortification, while Slains is akin to a palace:

> Photographic images of it in the 1890s present no Gothic ruin, rather the sumptuous home of the Earl of Erroll. The lawns are neat, the flower beds tidy, and nothing less vampirish could be imagined. Even the specifics are wrong. Slains has no courtyard, the layout is different, and all it has in common with Dracula's Castle are the vertiginous cliffs that plunge into the depths behind it.[4]

Cruden Bay, with its legends and its brooding landscapes, may well have played a role in the creation of *Dracula*. But the argument that Stoker deliberately modeled Castle Dracula on Slains is flimsy.

Was there, then, any specific source of inspiration for Castle Dracula? Stoker chose to locate it in the Borgo Pass, not because he knew the region but most likely because he came across the name on a map in Charles Boner's *Transylvania: Its Products and Its People*. (There is now a Hotel Castle Dracula in the Borgo Pass. Clearly named for Stoker's Count, it opened in the early 1980s to cater to Western tourists coming to the region with Stoker's novel in hand, looking for the castle.)

What is often overlooked is the fact that the description of Castle Dracula is similar to that of typical castles to be found throughout eighteenth- and nineteenth-century Gothic novels. The gloomy castle, with its broken battlements against a backdrop of rolling clouds, steep precipices and tumultuous streams, is part of the common stock of Gothic motifs that dominated the pages of late-eighteenth-century and nineteenth-century Gothic fiction. Jules Verne's *The Castle of the Carpathians* is another possibility. Or maybe Stoker had in mind an illustration of a castle used in one of his own earlier books, *Under the Sunset* (1882)–the gloomy castle of the King of Death, sketched by William Fitzgerald, which certainly bears some resem-

The Gothic Castle

. . . Mountains, whose shaggy steeps appeared to be inaccessible, almost surrounded it . . . the long perspective of retiring summits . . . the towers and battlements of a castle, that spread its extensive ramparts along the brow of a precipice above.

> –Ann Radcliffe, *The Mysteries of Udolpho*
> (London: Robinson, 1794)

. . . The road, therefore, was carried high among the cliffs, that impended over the river, and seemed as if suspended in air; while the gloom and vastness of the precipices, which towered above and sunk below it, together with the amazing force and uproar of the falling waters. . . .

> –Radcliffe, *The Italian, or The Confessional of the Black Penitents* (London: Cadell & Davies, 1797)

. . . jagged rock and pointed crags . . . mighty rifts in the mountains, through which . . . we saw now and again the white gleam of falling water. . . .

> –*Dracula,* Chapter I, Jonathan Harker's Journal, 5 May

. . . The castle is on the very edge of a terrible precipice. A stone falling from the window would fall a thousand feet without touching anything! As far as the eye can reach is a sea of green tree-tops, with occasionally a deep rift where there is a chasm.

> –*Dracula,* Chapter II, Jonathan Harker's Journal, 8 May

blance. And Barbara Belford reminds us that he would have seen plenty of castles, turrets and towers in his native Ireland.[5]

Or he could have made it up!

> –revised by the author from *Dracula: Sense & Nonsense* (Westcliff-on-Sea, U.K.: Desert Island Books, 2000), pp. 156–170

1. Raymond T. McNally and Radu Florescu, *In Search of Dracula* (Greenwich, Conn.: Graphic Society, 1972), p. 86.
2. Apparently, he first glimpsed Cruden Bay while visiting Scotland in 1888 with members of the Lyceum Theatre who were making preparations for *Macbeth*. See Barbara Belford, *Bram Stoker: A Biography of the Author of Dracula* (New York: Knopf, 1996), p. 204.
3. *Dracula Unearthed,* ed. Clive Leatherdale (Westcliff-on-Sea, U.K.: Desert Island Books, 1998), p. 12.
4. *Dracula Unearthed,* p. 13.
5. Belford, *Bram Stoker,* p. 234.

* * *

In 1995, the Transylvanian Society of Dracula, an historical-cultural organization in Romania, hosted the first World Dracula Congress. The conference attracted much attention from the media both within and outside of Romania. The varying responses illustrate the dilemma facing many Romanians whose homeland has become a prime attraction for fans of Stoker's novel.

Schizophrenic Dracula: Romania, the Media, and the World Dracula Congress
Elizabeth Miller

Bram Stoker's novel, though well known throughout most of the world, has until recently been practically unheard of in Romania. Today, more than ten years after the ban on the novel was finally lifted and the first Romanian edition was published, the book generates much controversy. Widespread resentment exists towards Stoker, who is accused of having stigmatized Romania as the "land of vampires" and, even worse, for having denigrated one of the country's leading historical figures (Vlad the Impaler) by using him as the foundation for his vampire. Most of the novel's critics fail to recognize two facts. First of all, Stoker did not set the novel in Romania at all. In 1897, Transylvania was not part of Romania (that did not occur until after the end of the First World War) but was a territory within the Austro-Hungarian empire. As to the second accusation, Stoker did little more than borrow the name "Dracula" from an obscure book, and certainly did not base the character on the historical figure.

The clash between the two Draculas first surfaced in Romania during the 1970s, a time when the current leader, Nicolae Ceausescu, was attempting to revive the reputation of Vlad the Impaler as a national hero. In addition to the raising of statues, the issuing of commemorative stamps, and restorative work on his ruined fortress at Poenari, monographs and articles extolling his heroic deeds were published. In 1978, Nicolae Stoicescu singled out the Stoker novel:

> Whoever knows something about Vlad Tepes may smile on reading such nonsense, but this nonsense ascribed to *Dracula* is highly popular and overshadows the true image of the Prince of Wallachia. . . . Those who would like to go on cultivating Dracula the vampire are free to do it without, however, forgetting that he has nothing in common with the Romanian history where the real Vlad Tepes whom we know by his deeds holds a place of honour.[1]

This collision came to a head on the occasion of the First World Dracula Congress which opened in

Bucharest on 24 May 1995. Organized by the Transylvanian Society of Dracula (a Romanian-based cultural-historical organization) with the co-operation of the Romanian ministries of Tourism and Culture, the Institute of Military History (Bucharest), and the Santa Barbara (California) Institute of Humanistic Studies, the Congress had as its primary purpose the exploration of the many aspects of the Dracula phenomenon in history, myth, and popular culture. Its chief feature was the presentation of about thirty papers by leading Dracula scholars from Canada, the United States, Great Britain, France, Italy, Sweden, and Romania. But the Congress was more than just another academic conference; it was clearly intended as a showpiece for Romanian tourism. At the opening ceremonies in Bucharest, Romanian Minister of Tourism, Dan Matei Agaton, expressed the hope that "the interest in the Congress . . . will have good results for the development of tourism." Indeed, the whole Congress was taken "on the road" with the presentation of papers accompanied by visits to sites associated with both Draculas, culminating in closing ceremonies at the Castle Dracula Hotel in the Borgo Pass. Included among the more than 200 people who made the trek through Dracula country were dozens of representatives of the media from around the world. It is hardly surprising that such an event attracted their attention. But what was fascinating were the focal points of the various media, as well as how Romanian coverage differed substantially from Western.

In many respects, coverage by the Western press was predictable, as reporters drew *ad nauseam* on the standard clichés and endless overworked puns to which those of us in the field have long since become accustomed. Consider, for example, the following headlines: "Cash-Thirsty Romania Taking Tourists for a Bite"; "World Dracula Congress: Batty Fans Up for the Count"; and "Sex, Blood and Death Hot Topics at Dracula Summit." While headlines are generally regarded as mechanisms for drawing the attention of readers, unfortunately much of the same tone is to be found in some of the articles themselves. A Reuters story carried in (among others) the *Chicago Tribune* (26 May) opened with "Fans of Dracula descended on Romania . . . to lay wreaths of garlic at his Transylvanian shrine," while the same feature referred to participants in the Congress as "a ghoulish gathering of horror aficionados" who had come to Romania to discuss "a subject closest to their hearts (and throats)." "Witchcraft cast a spell over Dracula fans of blood and horror in a weekend Transylvania pilgrimage," declared another Reuters contribution (Baltimore *Sun,* 29 May), continuing that during the "weird five days . . . [the participants] were treated to red meat dinners on

Logo for the conference sponsored by the Transylvanian Society of Dracula, Romania (Elizabeth Miller Collection)

spikes, blood-colored cocktails and other impaling themes."

Not surprisingly, most members of the media chose to ignore the centre-piece of the Congress—the scholarly papers. The result was a rather superficial representation of what the Congress was all about. As for television coverage, there was a tendency for the cameramen to seek out the bizarre: after all, a Beverly Hills vampire aficionado dressed in black garb makes a far more interesting subject than a scholar lecturing on "The Ambiguous Nature of Violence in *Dracula*." Even Jim Bitterman of ABC News (whose feature coverage was on the whole quite comprehensive) could not resist inventing a title for a paper—"Dracula's Sex Life"—that was not even on the program.

Not all of the Western media, however, trivialized the event. Perhaps the most comprehensive coverage of the Congress proceedings was provided by Tim Radford in his article "Pilgrimage to Castle Dracula" published in *The Guardian* (29 May 1995): the origins of the novel, the

Plaque on the Bram Stoker Memorial Seat, Whitby. Stoker knew the English settings he described, unlike the fantastic domain of the Count in Romania, which he almost wholly invented (photograph by David J. Skal).

explosion of the Dracula phenomenon in the 20th century, contemporary interpretations of Stoker's text, the confusion between the two Draculas, how Dracula is viewed in Romania, and the sensitive issue of using Dracula as a draw for Romanian tourism. But most perceptive was an article by John Marks in *U.S. News & World Report* (29 May 1995) who sounded a serious note of caution about promoting Dracula as a tourist attraction: "In exchange for exploiting the vampire myth . . . Romanians may be bartering away their history." The article quotes Romanian historian Stefan Andreescu who presumably refused an invitation to participate in the Congress on the grounds that "participants aren't coming to learn about the true history. They are coming here to confirm an image, to verify the idea of the vampire." The fear is that such tourist promotion would ultimately affect Romanians who would be led to accept "an imported and ridiculously distorted version of their national his-

tory." The same article also comments on the political implications of what it calls a troubling precedent: "In a country where ethnic tensions between Hungarians and Romanians simmer, where the natives grumble about their old enemies, the Turks, buying up businesses in Bucharest and where national myths have a way of becoming political reality, allowing vampires to eclipse the real Vlad Dracula is one step toward making history a means to an end."

While the Western media were focusing on Dracula's return to his homeland (with fans in tow), the Romanian press faced a more formidable task: coping with the invasion of a "native son" who was never theirs to begin with. This anomaly did not go unnoticed by Radford who astutely observed that "at last he [Count Dracula] has just colonised the only place that had never heard of him. He is back in Transylvania, introducing himself to his puzzled subjects." The bewilderment—even the resentment—of the association of the vampire Dracula with Romania in general and Transylvania in particular was an underlying theme in Romanian media coverage.

From the outset, Romanian reporters were skeptical about the Congress. Following a press conference held by the organizers in Bucharest in early March (more than two months before the actual event) many comments appeared in local newspapers. One article (in *Ziua*) anticipated the event by declaring that the participants will be "vampirologists," a blanket term that hardly covered adequately the occupations of the large majority of those who took part. But the skepticism which dominated these early reports was directed more specifically at the Minister of Tourism, Dan Matei Agaton. An item in *Azi* (10 March) reported that "the baron of Romanian tourism made his appearance, without fangs or cloak. The Minister took a seat at the head of the table with his eyes fixed hypnotically towards the future," a clear allusion to the Minister's assertion that the Congress would launch a major offensive on the part of Romanian tourism. The 10 March edition of *Ziua,* in an article with the subtitle "Romania will be haunted by . . . flocks of vampires," included this comment: "Five years after the death of the 'national vampire' Ceausescu, the Ministry of Tourism took the bull by the horns, after realizing that the only solution to attracting tourists to Romania is aggressive publicity." The story is accompanied by a photograph of the Minister with the caption "Dan Matei Agaton, ocrotitorul vampirilor (protector of vampires)" as well as a cartoon depicting two vampires at an open refrigerator filled with bottles, with one saying to the other "Ce zici de niste singe rece?" ("How about some cold blood?")

The most interesting of the pre-Congress coverage was that in *Romania Libera* on 21 March, a rather scathing commentary by Octavian Paler titled "Patriotic, nu?" written in fine satirical and rhetorical style. This essay addressed the crux of much of the subsequent criticism of the Congress:

> Whether we like it or not, we are the "country of Dracula." So, we will nurse our own dignity which is hurt by the ignorance and indifference of foreigners, by showing the world that at least in one domain we have no rivals! Nobody can compare with us in the "vampire field." What other country can organize spectacles with walking skeletons? What other minister of tourism (excluding ours, of course) can aspire to be the "knight of Count Dracula"? The ghosts of Scottish castles do not come close to what we can offer: cups of fresh blood.

Later in the article he states, "Dracula is not a Romanian myth. It is a myth that was imposed on us. But since the madness has become worldwide with fan clubs and universities that have departments of vampirology without knowing too well where Romania is, why should we not transform Dracula into an agent of tourism?" And one final passage: "I also doubt that the participants of the Congress will be willing to listen to serious historians and to assent that the legend of Dracula has paralyzed and falsified a historical reality. The vampirologists need vampires, not the truth." In spite of some rather sweeping generalizations resulting from a lack of knowledge of the purpose of the Congress, Octavian Paler does address a major concern: the fear that the Congress and tourist promotion in general will serve to exacerbate even further the general misconceptions that exist in the West both about Romania and vampires, about Vlad the Impaler and Count Dracula.

During the Congress itself, several pieces appeared in the local press. While some of the coverage tended to belittle the event (as was the case in the West), one Romanian newspaper (*Curierul National*) came up with an original headline: "Vampirologi din toata lumea, uniti-va!" ("Vampirologists of the world, unite!") Much of the satire in the Romanian press was once again aimed at the Minister of Tourism, who may very well have invited some of it as a result of his remark to one reporter that "If tourists want hands rising out of coffins, we'll give it to them" (*Baltimore Sun,* 29 May). *Evenimentul Zilei* (30 May) noted (with tongue firmly planted in cheek) that "At twelve o'clock on the last night of the Congress, Dan Matei was given the title of Knight of the Dracula Order. The ceremony was, contrary to expectations, not at all bloody. . . . The mantle of the Count—black, obviously—was placed on the minister's shoulders. . . ." In fact, Dan Matei was for the Romanian media the star of the show; consequently, most Romanian readers did get a distorted view of the Congress.

The second category of responses includes comments that supported the drive for tourism, though some of these did raise some basic questions about the country's preparedness for a major influx of tourists. *Capital* (1 June) conceded that though the Congress failed to "correct the balance between myth and historical truth," it did turn the eyes of the world to Romania. Now, this was obviously a major goal of the Congress, in the minds of some local entrepreneurs surpassing the more esoteric objective of the scholarly exchange of ideas. A couple of vital questions must be raised here. Does Romania want to build on the Dracula theme? The advantages are obvious: hundreds of thousands of tourists—yes, some of whom do not know (and maybe do not

A London tavern that is decorated inside in the style imagined to be that of Dracula's Dungeon. The toilets are behind a secret door in a false bookcase (photograph by Jeanne Youngson).

verted into a popular horror icon was in evidence in several articles. But what many of the reporters overlooked was that this issue *was* debated at the Congress. For example, military historian Mircea Dogaru, in his paper titled "The Psychological Component in Vlad Dracula's Warfare," stated quite clearly that the myth of Count Dracula the vampire "has nothing to do with the Romanian prince." But other views were also presented: Radu Florescu, co-author of *In Search of Dracula,* the book that first cemented the connection between the Count and the Voivode, stated categorically, "I exploited the vampire to promote Vlad"; expanding on this in an interview for a local newspaper he added "Through the vampirization of Vlad . . . we managed to bring our voivode to the attention of the entire world." Florescu's co-author, Raymond McNally, took an even more controversial stand (which brought no smiles to the faces of the military historians) as he asserted that "the glorification and idealization of past historical figures is a disease."

For many in the West (including hundreds of tourists who flock to Romania in search of their favorite movie monster), Vlad the Impaler and Count Dracula are one and the same. That such a confusion has permeated Western culture is widely evident: for example, the television documentary "Attila the Hun" (1994) presented by A&E as part of its *Biography* series makes a clear statement that Vlad the Impaler is "better known as Count Dracula"; and an entry in *Let's Go: The Budget Guide to Eastern Europe* (1995) records that the city of Bucharest was "first mentioned in a document dated 1459 and signed Vlad Tepes (*Count Dracula*)" (emphasis added).

The issue of a tourist initiative based on Dracula has resurfaced in recent times as a debate over the building of "Dracula Park." The arguments are the same. On the one hand, Romania is badly in need of the economic benefits that a flourishing tourist industry can bring; and certainly the country has much more to offer than Dracula. But not only is it competing against the major attractions of Western and central Europe; Romania has not fully recovered from the years of bad press that it received during the 1970s and 1980s. An aggressive drive for tourists using Dracula as a drawing card might turn the tide, but success will come only at a price, and maybe one that is more than the country is willing to pay.

As many tourists have been (and will continue to be) drawn to Romania because of the Dracula connection, there is the tendency on the part of the host country to cater to this, often at the expense of its own

want to know) the difference between the Count and the Voivode; money, business opportunities and all of the spinoffs associated with a tourist industry. If the answer is to be yes, then Romania has much to do to present itself as a viable tourist destination, especially with respect to its infrastructure. The only nightmares encountered by Congress participants in Romania were logistical, a feature not lost on some of the local reporters. *Adevarul* lauded Dan Matei's good intentions but noted that the Congress "excelled in confusion," due to what it called "Romanian timing" and "Romanian style."

But not all Romanians support a tourist initiative that centers on the Dracula theme. Much of the negative commentary in Congress coverage focused on what was expressed so succinctly in one headline: "Vlad Tepes a fost voievod si nu vampir!" ("Vlad the Impaler was a voivode and not a vampire!") Resentment about how the historical figure of Dracula has been appropriated by the West and con-

history and culture. Examples of the supremacy of crass commercialism over culture abound. A salesperson in the medieval square of Sighisoara was selling small portraits of Vlad with fangs and was quoted in a local paper as saying "I sell it only to foreigners—Romanians would be angry"; a copy of the item did make its way into at least two Romanian newspapers. The vendors' stalls near the entrance to Bran Castle are replete with souvenirs which deliberately perpetuate the confusion between the two Draculas: for example, a postcard of Bran labeled "Dracula's Castle" complete with a small icon of a Western-style vampire with widow's peak and black cape; and even worse, a t-shirt depicting Vlad with fangs extended, leaning over a bare-breasted and willing female victim. Such crass commercialism which flies in the face of both history and culture serves only to exacerbate the resentment that many Romanians already feel about Dracula-centred tourism.

How, then, can this paradox of Dracula be resolved? As far as tourism is concerned, all the history books in the world are not going to change the fact that for most Westerners (and thus most tourists) Dracula means Count Dracula, and Romania is the center of his world. Maybe what needs to be recognized is that Romania can use Dracula as a starting point from which to present to tourists its own history and culture. Those tourists who know (or want to know) that there is a difference will glean a greater understanding of the power of both history and myth; as for the others, at least they will leave their money behind. Some success has already been achieved, as current Dracula tours include visits to sites associated with both Draculas, along with some of Romania's other attractions (such as the world-famous Painted Monasteries and the Black Sea resorts). In addition, a small Dracula industry is developing which offers quality merchandise (local porcelain, crystal, leather goods, wine) as an alternative to some of the more questionable items on display at Bran and elsewhere. Finally, scholarly initiatives, such as the World Dracula congresses, need to be taken seriously and given widespread support. More constructive dialogue is needed between Western and Romanian historians, folklorists, and literary critics to achieve a common goal: to explore and to appreciate more fully the Dracula myth in all its manifestations.

1. Nicolae Stoicescu, *Vlad Tepes* (Bucharest: Editura Academiei Republicii Socialiste Romania, 1978), pp. 178–179.

Dracula Scholarship

Prior to the 1970s, academics paid little attention to Dracula, *a circumstance that changed dramatically in a few years, spurred in some measure by the publication of McNally and Florescu's* In Search of Dracula *(1972) and their association of Stoker's vampire with Vlad the Impaler. The general challenge to the exclusivity of the traditional literary canon combined with the popularity of psychoanalytic criticism also brought new attention to Stoker's novel.* Dracula *is now widely accepted as a significant novel. Indeed, its links with a wide range of academic disciplines, including anthropology, biology, history, law, literature, medicine, political science, psychology, religion, and sociology, have led to exciting scholarship and criticism.*

American scholar and editor J.P. Riquelme provides this overview of Dracula *criticism. All of the works cited in this article are included in the "Checklist for Reference and Further Reading" provided at the end of this volume.*

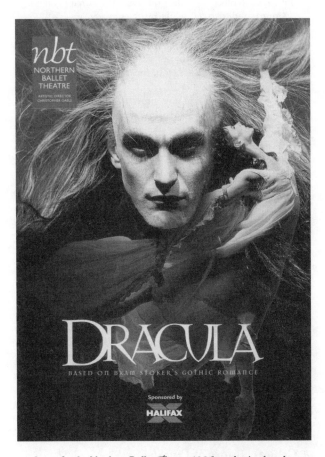

Cover for the Northern Ballet Theatre 1996 production based on Stoker's novel starring Denis Malinkine as Dracula and Shannon Lilly as Lucy (photograph by Anthony Crickmay; courtesy of NBT)

The Flaws of *Dracula*

Plagued by discrepancies in small matters such as the color of Lucy's hair—described initially as "sunny ripples" (Norton Critical Edition, p. 146) and later as "dark" (p. 187)—Dracula also has significant internal inconsistencies and gaps. Here are four examples to ponder.

1. Van Helsing, the resident vampire expert, assures the other hunters that Dracula sleeps in "his earth-home, his coffin-home, his hell-home, the place unhallowed" (p. 212). Yet, just a few moments later, the professor makes this comment: "For it is not the least of its terrors that this evil thing is rooted deep in all good; in soil barren of holy memories it cannot rest" (p. 213). So which is it—unhallowed or sacred?

2. Does everyone bitten by a vampire become a vampire? Van Helsing's declaration that "all that die from the preying of the Un-Dead become themselves Un-Dead" (p. 190) allows for the hope that the victim may be saved while he or she still lives. Presumably, if the vampire is destroyed while the victim yet lives, all will be well—which is the case with Mina, from whom the curse is lifted when Dracula is destroyed. This theory also seems to hold for the child on the Heath, who apparently escapes serious harm despite being attacked by Lucy as the "bloofer lady."

Professor Van Helsing, however, complicates the issue by stating that, had Arthur received Lucy's kiss, he "would in time . . . have become *nosferatu*" (p. 191)—although when he said this, Lucy was just about to be staked. To confuse matters even more, the circumstances surrounding the "turning" of the three vampires in the Castle are not explained; but one can assume from Dracula's comment to them,—"I too can love; you yourselves can tell it from the past" (p. 43)—that they were once the recipients of his bite. What other people has he fed on in the centuries since he graduated from the Scholomance? Did any or all become vampires after death? If not, why not? If so, where are they?

3. Van Helsing is unequivocal on two points: that a vampire must be invited in; and that it can enter a house at will after that first invitation: "He may not enter anywhere at the first, unless there be some one of the household who bid him to come; though afterwards he can come as he please" (p. 211). It appears that Lucy admitted Dracula into her abode in Whitby; whether or not the Count needed a new invitation for Hillingham, the London estate,

is unclear. As for access to Mina at Seward's asylum, that is provided by Renfield. But there is one puzzle here. Renfield asserts that Dracula has been urging him to "ask him to come in" (p. 244) even though the Count has already visited Mina's room.

4. Jonathan Harker is clear on what must be done to the Count to get rid of him forever: "Van Helsing and Seward will cut off his head at once and drive a stake through his heart" (p. 290). This method is consistent with what has been both preached and practised to this point in the text. The vampire hunters drive a wooden stake through Lucy's heart and decapitate her, and Van Helsing follows the same procedure in dispatching Dracula's three "brides." His lecture to the group in Chapter 18 reiterates the need for the staking and decapitation, and Mina recalls this procedure when she asks whether the same thing will be done to her if she becomes a vampire (p. 287). But, as many readers have observed, the method of Dracula's destruction is at variance with the prescription in the instance when the reader most expects the ritual to be applied. After a desperate chase, Count Dracula is attacked with two knives, a kukri and a bowie: "But on that instant came the sweep and flash of Jonathan's great knife. I shrieked as I saw it shear through the throat; whilst at the same moment Mr. Morris's bowie knife plunged into the heart. It was like a miracle; but before our very eyes, and almost in the drawing of a breath, the whole body crumbled into dust and passed from our sight" (p. 325).

The perceived weaknesses of Dracula *have been turned into strengths by ardent defenders of the novel. Internal inconsistencies have been represented as marks of originality with significant implications: that Lucy's hair becomes dark suggests her metamorphosis from a young innocent woman to a creature of darkness; that Dracula is dispatched not with a wooden stake, a remnant of East-European superstition, but with weapons that are emblematic of British imperialism is part of Stoker's intention.*

The simpler explanation, though, is that Stoker was at times a careless writer who could have benefited from an experienced copyeditor. He was an extremely busy man with a demanding job and did his fiction writing in his spare time. And in the case of Dracula, *he wrote the novel intermittently over a period of several years, which in itself would account for many of the errors, omissions, and discrepancies.*

—Elizabeth Miller

A Critical History of *Dracula*[1]
J. P. Riquelme

Dracula has spawned a rich progeny of speculative critical responses since its publication in 1897, so many and so various that a brief critical history can

provide only an outline with examples of the main types that have emerged. The fact that the book does not conform to the conventions of realism helps account for the variety and intensity of the interpretive speculations, which a less fantastic, less allegorical narrative would likely not generate. Following the ini-

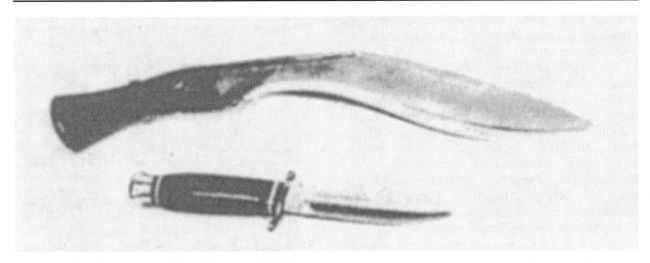

The knives that dispatch Count Dracula: a kukri (top) and a bowie (Leonard Wolf, The Annotated Dracula, *1975;*
Bruccoli Clark Layman Archives)

tial reviews, which were mixed in their judgments of the book's quality, *Dracula* attracted little attention from literary scholars and critics for much of the twentieth century. Beginning in the 1950s and increasingly since the 1970s, it has drawn responses from academic critics interested in a wide range of topics and perspectives, including historical and literary sources, narrative technique, psychoanalysis, gender roles, anthropology, Victorian culture, capitalism, the history of Gothic writing, poststructuralism, imperialism, postcolonialism, and Irish studies.[2] Broadly speaking, recent critics have responded to the book from two general orientations. Some have focused primarily on details that invite and support psychoanalytic readings, while others have staked out, explicitly or implicitly, a contrasting conceptual territory that emphasizes history or society rather than mind. Whether the specific approach gives precedence to issues of mind or issues of history, or tries to assign comparable weight to both, many critics read *Dracula* as either supporting values and tendencies of late-nineteenth-century British culture or reflecting on them with significant independence.

Initial Reactions and Developing Critical Acceptance

The psychological and social contours of critical writing about *Dracula* emerged only late in the twentieth century, after over half a century of dispute and, sometimes, disparagement concerning its literary quality. When *Dracula* appeared it was reviewed widely but with a mixed response in major British newspapers and periodicals, including the *Athenaeum,* the *Bookman,* the *Daily Mail,* the *Pall Mall Gazette, Punch,* and the *Spectator.* The reviewer in the *Bookman* (12 August

1897) compares the work to the popular tales of Wilkie Collins (1824–1889), a well-regarded writer of narratives involving mystery, crime, and suspense, but maintains that the audacity and horror of *Dracula* are distinctive. Like many later readers, the reviewer understands the narrative as a heroic, conservative tale "of human skill and courage pitted against inhuman wrong and superhuman strength." The review in the *Athenaeum* (26 June 1897) is less laudatory, claiming that Stoker's skill and imaginative conceptions are not sufficient to make his book high literature. From then until the 1950s critics treated *Dracula* as a minor but vivid and enduring piece of popular writing that had both contributed to and tapped a cultural fascination with the vampire. Dorothy Scarborough, herself a writer of fiction involving Gothic motifs, singles out *Dracula* as "the tensest, most dreadful modern story of vampirism,"[3] a book she warns against reading alone late at night. Montague Summers includes *Dracula* in *The Vampire: His Kith and Kin* (1928), but complains that Stoker's book is too long and prolix. For him, *Dracula*'s appeal arises from the vampire as subject, not Stoker's accomplishments as a writer. In *Supernatural Horror in Literature* (1939), H. P. Lovecraft, himself a well-published writer of strange tales, expresses a low opinion of Stoker's artistic achievement in many of his books, though he admits that *Dracula* is the best of them.

More extended and admiring treatments of *Dracula* began to appear when critics examined in detail the book's relation to folkloric and historical sources and its narrative techniques. Source studies and commentaries concerned with literary form provided a backdrop against which later critics could treat *Dracula* seriously from psychological and social perspectives. Significant source studies were first published in the 1950s. In one of the earliest of these, "*Dracula,* The Monastic Chronicles and Slavic Folklore" (1956), Bacil F. Kirtley identifies Vlad the Impaler, Prince of Wallachia, as an important model for Count Dracula and discusses both Vlad's life and Romanian vampire legends. He also identifies Arminius Vambéry, a famous Hungarian linguist and Orientalist scholar, whom Stoker met in London, as the model for Van Helsing's friend, Arminius. Kirtley's essay and the many later attempts to identify Stoker's sources and his transformations of them establish that the author of *Dracula* was a well-informed writer who had spent substantial time doing research for the book, which he wrote over a period of seven years, while also working as a theatre manager. Grigore Nandris's "The Historical Dracula: The Theme of His Legend in the Western and in the Eastern Literatures of Europe" (1966) contains a more extensive discussion of Vlad and vampire legends. Raymond McNally and Radu Florescu provide the most elaborate historical study of Vlad in relation to Count Dracula, *In Search of Dracula* (1972), speculating that the bloody career of Countess Elizabeth Bathory also provided Stoker with a model.[4] These explorations of sources and related studies published in the 1970s and 1980s reflect the growing scholarly interest in *Dracula* and make available relevant historical, folkloric, and literary information.

Critics writing about narrative technique in *Dracula* eventually challenged the negative literary judgments in the reviews and the early criticism, which suggested that the book was not, in fact, literature. They did so by arguing that what had appeared to some early readers as stylistic flaws were instead marks of originality with significant implications. These defenses of the artistic merit of *Dracula* regularly maintain that some of the narration's dissonant, inconsistent aspects encourage us to question the vampire hunters' views. Among the earliest influential commentaries of this kind is Carol Senf's "*Dracula:* The Unseen Face in the Mirror" (1979). Senf brings out the self-interested motives of Stoker's narrators and catalogues resemblances between the vampire and the vampire hunters to establish similarities between the forces of "good" and "evil." She argues that the vampire hunters turn away from recognizing that the vampire is the unacknowledged self. In "The Narrative Method of *Dracula*" (1985), David Seed draws on Stoker's notes to describe his careful shaping of the material formally.[5] Identifying elements of the book's pervasive doubling structure, Alan P. Johnson argues for the significant ordering of the narrative in "Bent

Commemorative postage stamp issued in the United States in 1997, the centennial year of Dracula *(Elizabeth Miller Collection)*

and Broken Necks: Signs of Design in Stoker's *Dracula*" (1987). Johnson focuses in particular on the doubling between male and female characters (Swales and Lucy; Renfield and Mina). He maintains as well that Dracula is the counterpart for the central female characters' unconscious rebellious desires and for the oppressive egotism of the male characters. Rebecca Pope describes *Dracula*'s narration as polyphonic, or multivocal, in "Writing and Biting in *Dracula*" (1990), a commentary that combines feminist and Marxist perspectives with reflections on narrative form. Relying on M. M. Bakhtin's ideas about the dialogical, open aspects of literature, she concentrates on Mina as the arranger of a text that refuses to conform to conventional social hierarchies of patriarchal power; instead, the book avoids the implications and illusions of a single continuous authorial voice. In this Bakhtinian reading, what some readers might regard as a flawed style becomes a virtue; because it is multiple and dialogical rather than singular and monological it can prevent narrative closure. Despite these and other defenses of the book's complex stylistic and conceptual achievements, some critics and editors still hesitate to acknowledge Stoker's artistic accomplishment.

The writings pertinent to *Dracula* by Devendra Varma during the 1970s and 1980s combine source studies with textual interpretation and, like the critical work concerned with narrative technique, argue for *Dracula*'s significance. He outlines briefly the book's sources in folklore, history, and Stoker's life in "The Genesis of *Dracula:* A Re-Visit" (1975). In his introduction to the reprinting (1970) of John Malcolm Rymer's Gothic serial, *Varney the Vampyre; or, The Feast of Blood* (1847), Varma places *Dracula* within the history of Oriental and European vampiric folklore and presents a more complicated, engaging evocation of the Count than do earlier critics. Varma celebrates Stoker's achievement in creating Dracula as an "essentially human" figure "not totally evil" in whom we recognize something that lives "within us all."[6] Varma's later essay "Dracula's Voyage: From Pontus to Hellespontus" (1986) interprets the Count's trip to England in relation to Coleridge's *The Rime of the Ancient Mariner*. Clive Leatherdale carries further Varma's work

toward establishing *Dracula* as a text that warrants scholarly attention. In the face of what he calls a lack of "serious critical study"[7] for most of the century, Leatherdale champions *Dracula*'s importance by providing a lengthy review of the book's sources, a detailed commentary on the major characters, and a series of chapters concerning the most revealing trends in the criticism. His book, *Dracula: The Novel & the Legend,* marks an important moment in the study of *Dracula* because of its attempt to span the range of critical responses, beginning with Montague Summers in the 1920s, from whom Leatherdale takes his epigraph for part one, through David Punter in the 1980s, from whose well-regarded history of Gothic literature, *The Literature of Terror* (discussed below), Leatherdale chooses a passage to bring his own commentary to conclusion. Leatherdale's list of articles and books pertinent to interpreting *Dracula* in his "Select Bibliography," which later critics build on, indicates that a significant critical response had already begun by the time of his own study, despite the comparative lack of attention to Stoker's writings. The catalogue of Stoker's sources, taken from his working notes for *Dracula,* in Leatherdale's bibliography confirms the range of Stoker's research and presents a reliable list of books that Stoker consulted.[8]

In *The Origins of Dracula* (1987), Leatherdale publishes relevant extracts from Stoker's sources, for which he provides informative headnotes. Christopher Frayling includes a briefer selection of source material in "The Genesis of Dracula," part of his work *Vampyres: Lord Byron to Count Dracula,* where he also presents the most detailed, cogent published account of the Rosenbach Museum's collection of Stoker's working papers. Like Leatherdale and Frayling, in *Dracula: Sense & Nonsense* (2000) Elizabeth Miller contributes to the reevaluation of Stoker's accomplishment by challenging a range of misunderstandings and misrepresentations, especially concerning Stoker's sources and his life. The appearance of Barbara Belford's biography, *Bram Stoker: A Biography of the Author of Dracula* (1996) also marks the greater acceptance of Stoker's accomplishments. Her account is by far the most thorough and carefully researched of the three biographies. Harry Ludlam's *A Biography of Dracula: The Life Story of Bram Stoker* (1962) draws on information provided by Stoker's son Noel, but it does not identify sources or substantiate many of its claims. Daniel Farson's *The Man Who Wrote Dracula: A Biography of Bram Stoker* (1975), written by Stoker's great-nephew, challenges some of the psychoanalytic speculations about Stoker based on his fiction, but he also makes speculative assertions without supporting them. Although Belford's biography is often more per-

A Vision of
Monstrous and Meaningless Happenings

Dracula, then, is a novel that lurches toward greatness, stumbling over perceived and unperceived mysteries: Christianity, insanity, identity, a spectrum of incest possibilities, marriage, homosexuality, immortality and death. All of them are bound together in the inclusive meanings of blood. If I claim greatness for this strange book, it is because, after nearly three generations, it continues to pulse with sometimes coherent, more often dismembered symbolic material of the sort that makes up what Jung has called "primordial experience which surpasses man's understanding, and to which he is therefore in danger of succumbing." Stoker's achievement is that he put all this *stuff* into his book with such skill that a headlong reader as well as one capable of worrying over the signs and portents is always in the grip of the narrative line. To put it another way, Stoker, organizing the tale of the vampire and his enemies, did not create impediments to our appreciation of "the disturbing vision of monstrous and meaningless happenings that in every way exceed the grasp of human feeling."

–Leonard Wolf, *A Dream of Dracula* (1972)

suasive and consistently better researched than its predecessors, Elizabeth Miller is right that "there is still much we do not know (and may never know) about his life."[9] Her point is confirmed by W. N. Osborough's "The Dublin Castle Career (1866–78) of Bram Stoker" (1999), in which he argues that existing records cast doubt on some of Stoker's representations about his education, representations that have been largely accepted as fact.

Psychoanalytic Readings

Psychoanalytic interpretations of *Dracula* begin in the 1950s with readings that understand the book's details as symptoms of the author's psychic tendencies. By the 1980s, however, psychoanalytic critics develop textual interpretations that are largely independent of claims about the author. Maurice Richardson's essay "The Psychoanalysis of Ghost Stories" (1959) contains the first of many critical readings of *Dracula* based on psychoanalytic concepts. Relying on strategies developed from Freud, Richardson maintains that details of the narrative arise from the author's repressed fantasies concerning perverse sexuality and incest. He turns in particular to Freud's notion that the history of the human species involves a primal horde struggling in an Oedipal way against the father who wants to keep all the women to himself.

Like many later critics, Richardson sees Dracula and Van Helsing as doubles, the bad father and the good one. In his reading, Van Helsing leads the younger men, as if they were the sons in Freud's psychoanalytic narrative, to defeat his evil antagonist and satisfy their sexual appetites in legitimate ways. In memorably extravagant statements that later critics cite or echo, Richardson says that Count Dracula proffers "a vast polymorph perverse bisexual oral-anal-genital sado-masochistic timeless orgy" and that the narrative is "a kind of incestuous necrophilous, oral-anal-sadistic all-in wrestling match" located in "a sort of homicidal lunatic's brothel in a crypt."[10] One measure of Stoker's achievement is the surprising recurrence in the critical response beginning with Richardson of language and claims that are, like *Dracula,* simultaneously excessive and revealing. Essays less rhetorically extravagant than Richardson's but presenting related readings appeared in the journal *American Imago* in the 1970s and 1980s. In "*Dracula:* Prolonged Childhood Illness and the Oral Triad" (1972), Joseph Bierman draws psychoanalytic conclusions about the author based on textual and biographical details. He reads the narrative as if it were a dream in which Stoker could fulfill his wish to undo a threat of loss by staging other men's loss of women. In "The Vampire Myth" (1980), James Twitchell follows Richardson by interpreting *Dracula* as an adolescent fantasy involving antagonism toward the possessive father.[11] While stressing the prevalence and significance of the vampire, Twitchell ascribes comparatively low artistic merit to *Dracula.*

The attractions and persistence of the psychoanalytic perspective for critics of *Dracula* are evident in several influential essays published in the journal *Literature and Psychology* during the 1970s and 1980s by Christopher Bentley, Thomas Byers, and Phyllis Roth. These commentators, however, rely on psychoanalytic concepts primarily to interpret the narrative rather than the author's psyche. In "The Monster in the Bedroom: Sexual Symbolism in Bram Stoker's *Dracula*" (1972), Bentley draws on the work of Freud and Ernest Jones as he catalogues at length what he considers the book's repressed displays of perverse sexuality, some of which tend, he suggests, toward the homoerotic. Incidental to the psychoanalytic interpretation, Bentley comments that the medicalizing of vampirism in Stoker's narrative is modern society's response to the threatening unknown by turning it into a disease amenable to treatment. In "Good Men and Monsters: The Defenses of *Dracula*" (1981), Byers argues that the Count and his relations with the vampire hunters represent a fear of male dependence and vulnerability that necessitates the destroying of the

...There lay the Count, but looking as if his youth had been half-renewed, for the white hair and moustache were changed to dark iron-grey; the cheeks were fuller, and the white skin seemed ruby-red underneath; the mouth was redder than ever, for on the lips were gouts of fresh blood...

Dracula
Bram Stoker

Clúdach Chéad Lae

Series of commemorative stamps issued in Ireland in 1997 (Elizabeth Miller Collection)

vampire in order to deny the dependence and protect the patriarchal hierarchy. He does so, however, without suggesting, as Bierman and others had earlier, that fears and wishes expressed in the narrative are symptoms of Stoker's psychic state.

Although psychoanalytic in its approach, Roth's influential "Suddenly Sexual Women in Bram Stoker's *Dracula*" (1977) considers the narrative's representations of gender roles in ways that make it also a feminist interpretation. Instead of describing the book as involving primarily an Oedipal struggle against the father to possess the mother, Roth argues for a pre-Oedipal ambivalent drama of desire for the mother and for her destruction. The narrative's central ambivalences are, in her view, pre-Oedipal in their "hostility toward the mother" and "toward female sexuality." She reads the parallel but contrasting stories of Lucy and Mina as two symbolic confrontations with the mother, in the first of which she is destroyed and in the second of which she is saved, as part of a structure that works through "the desire to destroy the threatening mother . . . who threatens by being desirable."[12] By means of her psychoanalytic method, Roth argues for antifeminist elements in *Dracula,* ones that invite the reader to accept the victimizing of women. In that regard, her essay complements a feminist reading published in the same year that bases its argument primarily on literary history rather than psychoanalytic concepts. Judith Weissman's "Women as Vampires: *Dracula* as a Victorian Novel" contrasts the largely comic portrayal of woman as sexually voracious in eighteenth-century fiction with the fearful presentation of women in *Dracula*. Stoker's narrative is, in

Sex without Mention

The myth is loaded with sexual excitement; yet there is no mention of sexuality. It is sex without genitalia, sex without confusion, sex without responsibility, sex without guilt, sex without love–better yet, sex without mention.

–James Twitchell, "The Vampire Myth" (1980)

Vampires in the Bedroom

. . . it must be assumed that he [Stoker] was largely unaware of the sexual content of his book. In common with almost all respectable Victorian novelists, Stoker avoids any overt treatment of the sexuality of his characters. The obscenity laws, the tyranny of the circulating libraries, and the force of public opinion were, throughout the greater part of the nineteenth century, powerful constraints on any author who wrote for the general public; but it is probably that for many writers, including Stoker himself, an even stronger reason for avoiding sexual matters was a personal reticence amounting to repression. Stoker's "living" characters (that is, those other than vampires) are, both the women and the men, models of chastity. One male-female relationship, that of Jonathan Harker and Mina Murray, is of primary importance to the story, and they marry at an early stage of the plot, but the sexual elements that presumably exist in their relationship are never revealed, much less discussed. However, what is rejected or repressed on a conscious level appears in a covert and perverted form through the novel, the apparatus of the vampire superstition, described in almost obsessional detail in *Dracula,* providing the means for a symbolic presentation of human sexual relationships.

–Christopher Bentley, "The Monster in the Bedroom: Sexual Symbolism in Bram Stoker's *Dracula*" (1972)

Weissman's view, ultimately about male control over women and their terrifying appetites in the nineteenth century.

Later critics have brought the work of Jacques Lacan, the French psychoanalyst and reinterpreter of Freud, to bear on *Dracula*. In "Dracula as Totemic Monster: Lacan, Freud, Oedipus and History" (1979), Richard Astle presents in a post-Freudian way the determining place of Oedipal psychic tendencies in nineteenth-century British culture by mapping relations among the characters in light of one of Lacan's structures, *schéma R*. By contrast, Elisabeth Bronfen's Lacanian reading in "Hysteric and Obsessional Discourse: Responding to Death in *Dracula*" (1992) emphasizes neither Oedipal relations nor a pre-Oedipal antagonism toward the mother. Instead, she invokes Lacan's contrast between "hysteric" discourse, associated with the feminine and the fluidity of the unconscious, and "obsessional" discourse, associated with the masculine and the clarity of logical thought. Bronfen argues that the vampire's bite induces hysteric thinking and behavior that obsessional tendencies have to eradicate because the hysteric represents the threat of death. Like Roth, she sees a reassertion of stability in the narrative but argues that it is undermined by the unstable character of the documents as they are arranged into the book's own fluid discourse. Bronfen's turn to instabilities of style and structure emerges from a poststructuralist engagement with psychoanalytic thinking about the book's details. In "'The little children can be bitten': A Hunger for Dracula" (2002), Dennis Foster draws on Lacan and Freud but ultimately takes his reading in a political direction. Foster brings out the competing values in *Dracula* and in our response through a reading that evokes divisions in the psyche, oral and anal stages, the death drive, and the sublimating of instincts, while suggesting that we are as likely as the characters in Stoker's narrative to fall under the sway of powerful and destructive leaders.

Among the many other psychoanalytic readings and the longer studies focusing on vampires, Laurence A. Rickels's *The Vampire Lectures* (1999) deserves special mention. This lengthy volume is comprised of twenty-six lectures from Rickels's course "Vampirism in German Literature and Beyond," which is also an introduction to psychoanalytic theory. Although Rickels is a scholar of German literature, he chooses not to present his views in a conventional academic form with a scholarly apparatus of detailed references and step-by-step argument. He proceeds instead by shifting, often rapidly, from text to text and from film to film, all relevant to *Dracula* through their influence on the text or their having been influenced by it, and from perspective to perspective within a wide range of psychoanalytic thought. The extravagant and frag-

Women and Vampires

[Stoker's] band of trusty men, loyal and chaste, are not simply trying to destroy Dracula, who has come to England to "create a new and ever-widening circle of semi-demons to batten on the helpless." Their fight to destroy Dracula and to restore Mina to her purity is really a fight for control over women. It is a fight to keep women from knowing what the men and women of the Middle Ages, the Renaissance, the seventeenth and eighteenth centuries knew, and what people of the nineteenth century must also have known, even if they did not want to–that women's sexual appetites are greater than men's.

–Judith Weissman, "Women and Vampires: *Dracula* as a Victorian Novel" (1977)

mented aspects of the writing in *The Vampire Lectures* are in the spirit of pop culture in various forms, in the spirit of Richardson's description of *Dracula,* and in the spirit of *Dracula* itself. The book's title has dual implications, suggesting both lectures *about* the vampire and lectures *by* him. The first seven lectures are most directly relevant to *Dracula* and to early film versions of it, especially F. W. Murnau's *Nosferatu* (1922). In lectures four through six, Rickels orients us to the Oedipal, heroic interpretation of the vampire hunters. He challenges and displaces that reading by offering various speculative, often revealing correlations between vampirism, media technology, and psychoanalysis with respect to representations of women and to psychoanalytic meditations on mourning. Rickels brings out the multiple associations of the vampire hunters with developments in media and technology (as does Jennifer Wicke without a psychoanalytic emphasis in "Vampiric Typewriting" [1992]). Based on those associations, he suggests that the vampire hunters constitute a "double of vampirism,"[13] pointing toward the future and implicating us. He moves beyond the Oedipal reading by suggesting the relevance of psychoanalytic writing about the uncanny and about melancholia for responses to *Dracula.*

Cultural, Historical, and Social Readings

Although some critical readings of *Dracula* that emphasize psychoanalytic concepts also engage historical and social issues, such as Roth's "Suddenly Sexual Women," more frequently psychoanalytic and social perspectives produce significantly different specific readings based on distinct general orientations. In "The Vampire in the Mirror: The Sexuality of *Dracula*" (1988), John Allen Stevenson attempts explicitly to develop an alternative to psychoanalytic interpretations of sexual conflict in the narrative by turning instead to anthropological concepts. By contrast with psychoanalytic descriptions of mind, anthropological descriptions of culture provide a conceptual vocabulary for understanding incest and miscegenation as a matter of racial differences, not just desire. In Stevenson's reading, *Dracula*'s threat projects an undermining of the cultural rules for exogamy and endogamy, which determine how far out from the tribe and how close to the tribe men and women can find appropriate sexual partners. The concern about exogamy, or marriage with foreigners, does not have an obvious psychoanalytic source, or not only such a source, since it arises from Victorian constructions of racial difference, which occur in the historical situation of a white, European imperial society in regular contact abroad and increasingly at home with people from other cultures.

Cover of program for the Royal Winnipeg Ballet production of Dracula *(1998), with dancers Tara Birtwhistle as Lucy and Zhang Wei-Qiang as Dracula (Royal Winnipeg Theatre)*

Although Stevenson relies in his essay on our taking historical contexts into account, he stops short of a historicist interpretation by claiming that the fears embodied in *Dracula* are more universal than they are historical. Generally speaking, historicist critics tend to avoid making universal claims, which they object to in psychoanalytic readings. The direction that Stevenson takes enables readings of the narrative that describe and interpret it not primarily with reference to incest, desire, and an intimate, forbidden family romance; for such a critic, the book reflects processes occurring on a large historical stage rather than in the theatre of the mind. Further, the narrative need not be read as narrowly reflecting those processes in a deterministic way; it can be a reflection *on* the processes as well. Like psychoanalytic critics, those working from other assumptions regularly face the question of the extent to which *Dracula* is conservative or liberatory in its tendencies. Many critics emphasizing social relations argue that the narrative largely supports already existing structures, which have determined its shape and its attitudes, while some suggest that it enables the imagining, by contrast with its own social context, of quite different relations that have yet to come fully into being.

Franco Moretti's influential Marxist commentary on *Dracula,* "Dialectic of Fear" (Italian 1978; English 1983), argues that the book is politically conservative. Orienting his reading on Marx's description of the capitalist as vampiric, sucking the life out of labor, Moretti identifies Dracula with monopoly capitalism. Count Dracula resembles the apparently long-buried money that Harker sees in the castle. The money that has come back from the grave is, according to Moretti, capital embarking "on the conquest of the world: . . . the story of Dracula the vampire." At the same time that he resembles money, however, Dracula takes an ancient form that threatens the vampire hunters, bourgeois defenders of a status quo bound up with capitalism. For Moretti the book is an allegory of monopoly capital, whose "ambition is to subjugate the last vestiges of the liberal era and destroy all forms of economic independence."[14] He claims that Dracula as a monopolist is both the distant past and the foreign future of late Victorian capitalist competition, something that appears to be feudal but that will produce new forms of monopoly to displace and overwhelm the economic forms of the present. Moretti argues, in effect, that Stoker's narrative affirms the bourgeois delusion, described by Marx, that the self-destructive consequences of capitalism can be avoided. The effect on the reader, in his view, is to identify with the vampire hunters and to be grateful that the dominance of the indefensible, self-serving system Dracula threatened is reasserted.

Other critics who attempt to situate Stoker's narrative in relation to nineteenth-century social institutions and intellectual developments have argued for his reliance on Victorian science and for his critical reflections on it. John L. Greenway brings out the deluded, ineffective character of Seward's science, which he sees as expressing "sentimental conventions" in ways that amount to ignorance of a structured kind.[15] Anne McWhir focuses more on the blurred structure of categories in the narrative than on specific debts to Victorian science in "Pollution and Redemption in *Dracula*" (1987). The constant breakdown of categories, such as science and myth, civilized and savage, she argues, reveals the primitive basis of modern scientific thinking. Despite the pervasive blurring of

Costume designs by Douglas Paraschuk for Dracula: A Chamber Musical, *staged at the Stratford Festival in Canada, 1999 (courtesy of Douglas Paraschuk and the Stratford Festival)*

boundaries in *Dracula,* she finds a reassertion of clear boundaries in the book's ending.

In her study of Victorian medical discourse and other Victorian representations of health and illness, Athena Vrettos interprets *Dracula* with reference to consumption, not as an economic matter but as a nutritional metaphor signifying imperial expansion. In comparison with Moretti, she reaches a mixed conclusion about the book's acceptance of a hierarchical status quo. Having established "correlations between racial fitness and imperial aggression" in Victorian thinking, Vrettos points out a displacement of the correlations in *Dracula* onto a foreign intruder who seems to be from a superior species. In her view, Stoker pushes Victorian links between diet and evolutionary stage to the absurd conclusion that cannibalism indicates the highest level of evolution, with the vampire as the "'master' carnivore." This development undermines the goal of evolutionary progress in a way that resembles the self-defeating contradiction that Marxists assert capitalism harbors. Vrettos also argues that *Dracula* reflects the contradictory connection between

The Worst Horror

Though it draws on ancient myths of femininity, Stoker's gothic is quintessentially Victorian: the worst horror it can imagine is not Dracula at all but the released, transforming sexuality of the Good Woman.

–Gail B. Griffin, "'Your Girls That You Love Are Mine': *Dracula* and the Victorian Male Sexual Imagination" (1980)

spiritualism and scientific inquiry, evident in Victorian theories of degeneration and criminal anthropology. Although Stoker's text makes the contradictions visible, it does so for her in a way that "legitimizes more than it attacks." Like his society, Stoker was, Vrettos concludes, "deeply divided about the politics of empire and the morality of science."[16] David Glover's commentary on Stoker's entire writing career, *Vampires, Mummies, and Liberals: Bram Stoker and the Politics of Popular Fiction* (1996), takes a similar stand. He explores the interplay of fantasy and realism in Stoker's writings as evidence that Stoker was responding to the decline of progressive politics and to the disputed character of science in late Victorian England.

Other divisions in Victorian society that critics find reflected in *Dracula* concern the roles of men and women. Readings that place primary emphasis on issues involving gender have, as we have seen, sometimes relied on psychoanalytic categories, but frequently they interpret the book largely in relation to categories and concepts involving society. In "*Dracula: Stoker's Response to the New Woman*" (1982), Carol A. Senf argues for the ambivalent character of Stoker's response to the New Woman novelists of the 1890s and to the political issues they raise concerning

Dracula and Jonathan Harker

. . . the novel's opening anxiety, its first articulation of the vampiric threat, derives from Dracula's hovering interest in Jonathan Harker; the sexual threat this novel first evokes, manipulates, sustains, but never finally represents is that Dracula will seduce, penetrate, drain another male. . . . Always postponed and never directly enacted, this desire finds evasive fulfillment in an important series of heterosexual displacements.

–Christopher Craft, "'Kiss Me with Those Red Lips': Gender and Inversion in Bram Stoker's *Dracula*" (1984)

women's rights. In her view, Lucy and Mina split the unattractive and attractive aspects of the New Woman, with Lucy embodying the unattractive aggression. As a woman who works and who thinks independently, Mina also represents the New Woman, though in a form that is comparatively conservative and unthreatening. In "Corruption of the Blood and Degeneration of the Race: *Dracula* and Policing the Borders of Gender" (2002), Sos Eltis considers Mina in relation to late-nineteenth-century fears about degeneration and gender identity. In her reading, Stoker presents through Mina not a reactionary response to the cultural panic of his time but an attractively modern merging of masculine and feminine elements. Many other suggestive feminist readings of *Dracula* have appeared that are not psychoanalytic in their orientation, including commentaries by Bram

Male Homosexuality in *Dracula*

. . . the fears and fantasies in which *Dracula* invites the reader to participate are exclusively male. Because the fundamental ambivalences motivating the novel revolve around an issue which few fin de siècle texts could discuss explicitly, male homosexuality, *Dracula* uses the feminine to displace and mediate the anxiety-causing elements of masculine character, representing the forbidden desires that men fear in themselves as monstrous femininity.

–Marjorie Howes, "The Mediation of the Feminine: Bisexuality, Homoerotic Desire, and Self-Expression in Bram Stoker's *Dracula*" (1988)

Dijkstra and Gail B. Griffin. Often feminist readings argue that, rather than staging antifeminist tendencies for us to recognize and judge, the book embodies misogynistic Victorian attitudes in ways that invite us to accept or even enjoy the victimizing of women.

Among the most suggestive of the socially oriented interpretations focusing on issues of male gender and the crossing of gender boundaries is Christopher Craft's "'Kiss Me With Those Red Lips': Gender and Inversion in Bram Stoker's *Dracula*" (1984). Craft builds on earlier psychoanalytic readings concerning the book's sexual implications by critics such as Roth and Bentley, but he focuses on the contrasts between cultural expectations concerning male and female behavior and the actions of Stoker's characters. Craft draws homoerotic implications from some of the book's prominent details. He argues that *Dracula* includes repeated instances of male homosex-

Failed Masculinity in *Dracula*

Dracula . . . is a text obsessed, as are its characters, with the definition of masculinity. . . . However, although these enthusiastic tributes do act to establish a definition of ideal manhood, it is a standard which the heroes often fail to achieve. *Dracula,* then, struggles as hard to define and control manhood as it does to restrict women to the masculinist roles of angel and demon, and with the same limited success.

–Katie Harse, "'Stalwart Manhood': Failed Masculinity in *Dracula*" (1998)

Illustration from the 2001 Micawber edition of Dracula *(drawing by Griff Jones; courtesy of Micawber Fine Editions)*

ual desire displaced onto a heterosexual structure because of the fear of homosexuality. In his view the female characters mediate forbidden relations between males. In this reading, the monstrous heterosexuality of Lucy, Mina, and the three female vampires implicitly represents a forbidden homoerotic desire as an inversion of conventional gender relations. The female vampires seem to represent female sexuality, but they actually threaten penetration of the male. According to Craft, forbidden desire lies just below the narrative's surface in the relations of the Count and Harker and among the male vampire hunters. Craft links the narrative strategy of displacement to the nineteenth-century discourse of inversion, with its reliance on heterosexual paradigms to gloss male desire. For him, *Dracula* participates in a Victorian horror of fluid gender roles. Although Craft recognizes the crossing of gender boundaries in the book, he reads the ending as a conventionally Gothic rejection of the monstrous and reassertion of generally accepted values. Later essayists, including Marjorie Howes in

Producing the Text of *Dracula*

What has been little remarked about the structure of *Dracula* is precisely how its narrative is ostensibly produced, its means of production. A narrative patchwork made up out of the combined journal entries, letters, professional records and newspaper clippings that the doughty band of vampire hunters had separately written or collected, it is then collated and typed by the industrious Mina. . . . All of these . . . emanate from radically dissimilar and even state-of-the-art media forms. *Dracula,* draped in all its feudalism and medieval gore, is textually completely au courant.

–Jennifer Wicke, "Vampiric Typewriting: *Dracula* and Its Media" (1992)

"The Mediation of the Feminine" (1988) and Talia Schaffer in "'A Wilde Desire Took Me': The Homoerotic History of *Dracula*" (1994), extend Craft's reading of the book as an instance of "queer Gothic." Schaffer shifts the focus from parallels in the intellectual discourse of the time to an actual historical situation. Instead of associating Count Dracula with Henry Irving, Stoker's employer (as critics who read *Dracula* from the perspective of Stoker's biography have often done), Schaffer links the Count to Oscar Wilde, Stoker's younger Irish contemporary, and sees the narrative as responding to the notorious trial and conviction of Wilde in the mid-1890s on charges of illegal homosexual behavior.

Nina Auerbach develops a critical position that challenges the socially and historically oriented commentaries described above. Her views are distinctly and provocatively at odds with many critics' characterizations of *Dracula.* She expressly opposes the historicist readings of Moretti and Craft (mentioned above) and those of Halberstam and Arata (mentioned below), which situate the book in relation to its historical context. Auerbach prefers instead to examine both material that antedates the book and later

---

Dracula's Border Crossings

Dracula's crossing of boundaries is relentless: returning from the past he tyrannises the present, uncannily straddling the borders between life and death and thereby undoing a fundamental human fact. In crossing the borders between East and West he undoes cultural distinctions between civilisation and barbarity, reason and irrationality, home and abroad. Dracula's threat is his polymorphousness, both literally, in the shapes he assumes, and symbolically in terms of the distinctions he upsets.

—Fred Botting, *Gothic* (1996)

---

developments, including films and our own contemporary situation. Her commentary still responds to social and historical issues, but they are not those that interest new historicist critics. Auerbach's interpretation of earlier literary representations of vampires enables her to argue that Count Dracula is not a transgressive figure. She defends her refusal to confine him to his own century with the claim that he is "a harbinger of a world to come, a world that is our own."[17] Although Auerbach reads *Dracula,* necessarily, in retrospect, she insists on doing so not by reconstructing the context of the past but by keeping in view the future frame of reference that the book helps create, a world that we inhabit.

Recent Developments: History of the Gothic, Postcolonial Perspectives, and Irish Studies

Dracula's standing in literary criticism has changed in part because the standing and the critical descriptions of Gothic literature have also changed. The history of Gothic narrative has received more serious consideration by literary critics in the past

---

Stoker on Seward

Dr. Seward is the only male pursuer of Dracula to have nuance to his character. . . . Collectively, the male stalwarts form an emblem of Victorian establishment: Seward, the scientist; Harker, the lawyer; Arthur, the aristocrat; and Quincey, the expendable American adventurer. As the scientist, however, Seward's failure to make inferences he should have made contributes to the growing power of Dracula, and implies an ironic attitude toward him on Stoker's part.

—John L. Greenway, "Seward's Folly: *Dracula* as a Critique of 'Normal Science'" (1986)

---

three decades than at any earlier period. In his synoptic study, *The Literature of Terror* (1980; revised, expanded edition 1996), by contrast with many earlier critics of *Dracula,* David Punter assesses Stoker's work in a highly positive way. He argues that the violating of "taboo" in *Dracula* involves boundary crossings that raise the question of what it means to be human. His argument is part of his general reinterpretation of the Gothic, which he claims to be not escapist literature but a response to anxieties that are simultaneously psychological and social. Although Punter shifts the critical focus away from the author's psyche and toward social matters in his study, he does so while retaining his commitment to psychoanalytic concepts, which regularly inform his readings. He says memorably that from a Freudian perspective, Dracula is the "passion which never dies, endless desire of the unconscious for gratification," but that, at the same time, from a Marxist perspective, he is the "final aris-

---

Stoker's Compelling Lapses

Stoker's lapses and inconsistencies are what make his writing so compelling, for they show his novels and stories to be the work of a transitional figure, an author nervously glancing back at the past as he strides out into the future. . . . there is always a strong reminder that the old Liberal certainties are failing, that something solid is slipping away.

—David Glover, *Vampires, Mummies, and Liberals* (1996)

---

tocrat," who threatens the late-nineteenth-century bourgeois family.[18]

Many essays and books that focus on either nineteenth- or twentieth-century Gothic narratives attend to the book's place in the history of Gothic writing. Kathleen Spencer reads *Dracula* as an important example of "urban gothic" in "Purity and Danger: *Dracula,* the Urban Gothic, and the Late Victorian Degeneracy Crisis" (1992). This kind of Gothic writing, which developed late in the nineteenth century, presents its strange events close to home and in the present. Spencer identifies Victorian concerns about degeneration in *Dracula,* as do Daniel Pick (1988) and Laura Croley (1995). Chris Baldick sets *Dracula* briefly but incisively in a line of nineteenth-century writing stretching from Mary Shelley's *Frankenstein* (1818; revised 1831) through Robert Louis Stevenson's *The Strange Case of Dr Jekyll and Mr Hyde* (1886) and Oscar Wilde's *The Picture of Dorian Gray* (1891). He sketches the connection to *Frankenstein,* a text he is unwilling to classify as Gothic, and also to Conan Doyle's presentation of the antagonism between Sherlock Holmes and Moriarty by describing Van Helsing and Dracula as doubles, "twin halves of a single, perversely sexualized Frankensteinian transgressor."[19] Baldick compares Van Helsing's violence to female bodies with Victor Frankenstein's destruction of the female monster he was creating. His comparison of *Dracula* to *Frankenstein,* a text that has achieved canonical status, indicates the increase in critical acceptance of *Dracula,* which began in the 1970s. Despite the evident irony in *Dracula,* which Baldick recognizes, that the chief vampire hunter is Count Dracula's double, he concludes that the book is conservative, since no perspective emerges to explicitly counter Van Helsing's militancy. He reads the ending as consonant with a Gothic tradition that antedates *Frankenstein,* in which the values of the bourgeoisie dominate.

In her essay "Technologies of Monstrosity" (1993) and her subsequent book *Skin Shows: Gothic Horror and the Technology of Monsters* (1995), Judith Halberstam puts *Dracula* at the center of her reconsidered history of the Gothic from *Frankenstein* to *The Silence of the Lambs.* Explicitly distancing herself from the frequent blind spot about society in psychoanalytic criticism, Halberstam challenges those who interpret *Dracula* as conservative and complicit. In a reading of *Dracula* that combines racial, sexual, and economic perspectives, she convincingly examines the relationship of Stoker's vampire to nineteenth-century anti-Semitic discourse. Halberstam defines the Gothic as a technology of monstrosity that creates the monstrous from fragments of class, race, and gender discourse not accepted by the dominant ideology, while

Cover for S. S. Prawer's scholarly study of Werner Herzog's 1979 movie (Bruccoli Clark Layman Archives)

simultaneously exposing the constructed character of what that dominant ideology labels the monstrous. The notion that the Gothic contains a critique of the culture it draws on for its elements, which it presents in exaggerated form, opens the possibility of interpreting *Dracula* as less determined by cultural expectations than many critics have allowed. In "Toward a History of Gothic and Modernism: Dark Modernity from Bram Stoker to Samuel Beckett" (2000), an essay influenced by poststructural and postcolonial writings, I draw conclusions that are at odds with conservative interpretations of the narrative, since I find in *Dracula* "a model, replicated in later works, for the emergence of hybridity as the character of the future and of modern experience."[20] By hybridity, I mean an in-between condition that tends to blur the clear distinctions between apparent opposites, distinctions on which hierarchies of value and power depend. I argue as well for the centrality of *Dracula* in the shift from Victorian to modernist writing.

In "Gothic Criticism" (2000), their metacritical commentary on critical writing about Gothic narra-

---

Transylvania and Ireland

Transylvania is at a minimum a metaphor for Ireland, as both Transylvania and Ireland are frontier territories on the fringes of the empire, fought over often by foreigners. The term "the land beyond the forest" has the meaning of the unknown "land beyond the clouds" where almost anything can happen. The common people are as superstitious and as "wild" as Irish peasants were thought to be. The dominant class to which Dracula belongs is alien to the common people. . . . Dracula resides in his decaying Big House with its battered battlements.

–Raymond T. McNally, "Bram Stoker and Irish Gothic" (2002)

Realigning Boundaries

The occult cannot be said therefore to be the only source of instability in the novel: the medical content enjoys a markedly similar function throughout. The rhetorical strategy of *Dracula* therefore is one of realignment, an assertion of coexistence rather than of an Absolute. Boundaries become blurred as the Christian and the scientific move to accommodate the occult, and as the demarcations between pathological conditions, pharmacopoeias and techniques break down.

–William Hughes, *Beyond Dracula: Bram Stoker's Fiction and Its Cultural Context* (2000)

tives, Chris Baldick and Robert Mighall, like Nina Auerbach, express their dissatisfaction with some prevalent strategies used by those who write about the Gothic. In particular, they object to a reductive tendency in historicist criticism of the Gothic to characterize British culture as anxiety-ridden and Stoker's narrative as subversive. Although they admit that David Punter's insights are often judicious, Baldick and Mighall cite his work on the Gothic as a prime example of the tendency to psychologize a historical situation without sufficient justification. Of special concern to them is the overuse of the word *subversive* in the service of political correctness, though they do not call it that. Focusing on responses to *Dracula*, they play on their category *Gothic criticism* by suggesting that the criticism has itself become *Gothic* since it projects a melodramatic conflict between the embattled outsider and social forces of repression. The strictures that Baldick and Mighall bring to bear are in many regards salutary, particularly as a warning to readers about some questionable tendencies in the response to *Drac-*

Dracula as Racial Threat

That Dracula is in some sense coded as racial threat is obvious: we may note his strong, if ambivalent, sexuality; his offensive odor; his corruption of the blood of his victims. But if this is true, what kind of racial threat does he suggest? Here it is necessary to remind ourselves that Dracula immigrates to England and becomes the invisible threat within. It is reasonable to associate him, therefore, with the most tangible alien immigrant threat of the time, the eastern European Jew.

–H. L. Malchow, *Gothic Image of Race in Nineteenth-Century Britain* (1996)

ula. They complain that frequently critics claim to rely on historical knowledge to reverse the heroic reading of *Dracula* as the story of good people conquering an evil monster but that the historical framework for reading the narrative as the liberated monster's battle against repressive foes needs substantiating. In their view, the reversal says more about the critics' political views than about the book's implications. Baldick and Mighall's complaints, however, are less convincing about critical arguments that find mixed evidence in the narrative for its relation to cultural concerns and expectations and about interpretations that argue for the resemblances between the monster and those who struggle against him.

Mighall attempts to provide an alternative to the tendencies he and Baldick criticize in "Sex, History and the Vampire" (1998) and in the longer chapter on

Dracula and Jack the Ripper

As the Jack the Ripper and *Dracula* narratives essentially played out a constellation of . . . fears ranging from syphilis to alien invasion, I take a certain poetic licence in describing these two predators as blood brothers. However, unlike the "blood brother" crusaders in Stoker's novel who oppose Dracula and seal a fraternal pact through a series of Christ-like blood transfusions intended to save Lucy Westenra's life, Jack the Ripper and Dracula are bloodthirsty siblings whose kinship is sealed with degenerate, anti-Christian, "black mass"-style acts involving sexual perversion, infection, and death.

–Carol M. Davison, "Blood Brothers: Dracula and Jack the Ripper" (1997)

Dracula and the postscript of his *A Geography of Victorian Gothic Fiction* (1999). Setting the vampire in the late Victorian discourse concerning pathological sexuality, Mighall argues that Van Helsing is a sexologist in reverse, imputing supernatural meanings to events that a Victorian sexologist would interpret differently. He argues for keeping the discourses of sexology and horror fiction separate, rather than blurring the boundaries between discourses as new historicists do, in order to exclude the sexual reading of vampirism and see the vampire as literally a monster rather than a figure for something else. William Hughes also explores the cultural discourses of Stoker's time in *Beyond Dracula: Bram Stoker's Fiction in Its Cultural Context* (2000), in which he adduces religious contexts, depictions of masculinity and femininity, and medical writings to explain how they influenced Stoker's thinking and also how their collisions in Stoker's texts produce new meanings. His study is noteworthy for its reading of Stoker's writings in new frames of reference. In particular, Hughes's account of *Dracula* deals not with blood considered medically and racially, a topic treated by earlier critics, but with the symptoms the vampire's victims exhibit in relation to medical works of the time and with vampirism in relation to abnormal medical conditions.

Largely lacking from critical responses to *Dracula* before 1990 is a recognition of the narrative's relation to the history of the British Empire, especially with respect to the Irish situation. In recent decades attitudes toward British and Irish writings from the

---

Evolution and the Fear of Degeneration

The cultural preoccupation around 1900 with the struggle of evolutionary progress against the forces of bestiality and degeneration was dramatized most coherently and consistently . . . in *Dracula*. In Stoker's novel, virtually all elements of the dream of future evolutionary possibility and all aspects of the period's suspicions about the degenerative tendencies in women have been brought together in such an effortless fashion that it is clear that for the author these were not so much a part of the symbolic structures of fantasy as the conditions of universal truth.

–Bram Dijkstra, *Idols of Perversity: Fantasies of Feminine Evil in Fin-de-Siècle Culture* (1987)

---

latter part of the nineteenth century, during the decline of the British Empire, have changed. Critics who use imperial and Irish contexts for interpreting literary texts now often invoke British views about nonwhite foreigners, the situation of the Irish under long-term British rule, and political issues involving empire. They tend to rely on the work of theorists such as Edward Said, Gayatri Spivak, and Homi Bhabha concerning colonialism's history and effects and concerning the character of postcolonialism. Patrick Brantlinger places *Dracula* in the context of the literature of empire when he identifies a strand of late-nineteenth-century Gothic narratives that he calls the "imperial Gothic" in an article of that title (1985) and in his later book, *The Rule of Darkness: British Literature and Imperialism, 1830–1914* (1988). He argues that British fears of atavism appear in adventure literature, including *Dracula,* as a Gothic dimension that includes occult elements. W. J. McCormack places *Dracula* in

---

Dracula and the Gothic Psyche

Like other Gothic novels such as *Frankenstein* and *The Strange Case of Dr. Jekyll and Mr. Hyde, Dracula* figures the ways the psyche fails to develop into integrity (what Jung calls the process of individuation) and instead risks the open mental boundaries and self-fragmentation of schizophrenia. Like Jung, Stoker shows the importance of recognizing and integrating the unknown inner selves of the psyche as revealed in dreams. Also, like Jung, Stoker dramatizes the psychological damage that results when the conscious personality denies either its shadow or its contrasexual aspects and thus produces a monstrous decentering of the Self.

–Matthew C. Brennan, *The Gothic Psyche: Disintegration and Growth in Nineteenth-Century English Literature* (1997)

---

the history of Irish writing that he calls the "Irish Gothic" in his essay introducing a section of the second volume of *The Field Day Anthology of Irish Writing* (1991). More recently, in "Bram Stoker and Irish Gothic" (2002), Raymond McNally has elaborated on McCormack's term, especially in relation to *Dracula*. Because of these and related critical developments, the previous lack of attention to imperial and Irish implications in the response to *Dracula* has begun to be filled.

A Reaffirmation of Christianity

It might seem superfluous to claim that *Dracula* is a Christian parody. Everything that Christ is meant to be Dracula either inverts or perverts. Christ is Good: Dracula is Evil–an agent of the devil. Christ was a humble carpenter: Dracula a vainglorious aristocrat. Christ offers light and hope, and was resurrected at dawn: Dracula rises at sunset and thrives in darkness. . . . Christ offered his own life so that others might live: Dracula takes the lives of many so that *he* might live. . . . The link between Christ and Dracula is made explicit through the Count's recoiling from crucifixes, holy wafer, and other symbols of Christianity.

A basic lesson of the novel was to reaffirm the existence of God in an age when the weakening hold of Christianity generated fresh debate about what lay beyond death.

–Clive Leatherdale, *Dracula: The Novel & the Legend* (1985)

Since *Dracula* stands at the intersection of literature with an imperial aspect, Gothic narratives, and Irish writing, the book's critics have begun linking in various ways concerns related to the decline of empire, motifs and structures characteristic of Gothic writing, aspects of the Irish situation, and Stoker's background as Anglo-Irish. Among the most influential readings of *Dracula* to take the history and literature of empire into consideration is Stephen Arata's "The Occidental Tourist: *Dracula* and the Anxiety of Reverse Colonization" (1990). For Arata, *Dracula* expresses the fear of reverse colonization, specifically the anxiety that the imperial homeland will be invaded by savage, foreign, colonized peoples. He draws on Said's writings about Orientalism to describe the Count's traveling west as a reversal of Harker's traveling east that, by mimicking the prejudicial Orientalist attitudes of the West toward the East, redirects them as Occidentalist attitudes held by someone from the East toward the West. In an explicit turn away from psychoanalytic interpretation, Arata focuses on the book's fusing of the travel narrative with the Gothic for their mutual transformation. He argues compellingly that the expectations of the imperial tourist are turned upside down when the travel narrative becomes Gothic and that the usual Gothic reassertion of stability is undermined at the end of *Dracula*. Because the traveler's expectations are never convincingly restored, Arata suggests, the closing invites us to reject Van Helsing's concluding statement as hollow. Arata's reading of the ending as the undoing of a conventional Gothic closing sets his interpretation in opposition to the assertions by Craft, Baldick, and others who claim that the ending restores stability in a conservative way.

A political cartoon titled "The Irish Vampire," by John Tenniel, in the 24 October 1885 issue of Punch. *It was viewed as an attack on the motivation of Charles Stewart Parnell, the most prominent advocate of Home Rule, and is a central image for scholars who argue for the importance of Stoker's Irish background in his work (Elizabeth Miller,* Dracula, *2000; Elizabeth Miller Collection).*

The Bourgeois View of Dracula

From the bourgeois point of view, Dracula is . . . a manic individualist; from his own point of view . . . he is the bearer of the promise of true union, union which transcends death. From the bourgeois point of view, Dracula stands for sexual perversion and sadism; but we also know that what his victims experience at the moment of consummation is joy, unhealthy perhaps but of a power unknown in conventional relationships. Dracula exists and exerts power through right immemorial; Van Helsing and his associates defeat him in the appropriate fashion, through hard work and diligent application, the weapons of a class which derives its existence from labour.

–David Punter, *The Literature of Terror* (1980)

Writing in the wake of Arata's ground-breaking essay, Cannon Schmitt identifies the fear of invasion more narrowly than does Arata as English anxiety about the Irish and about miscegenation. In "Mother Dracula: Orientalism, Degeneration, and Anglo-Irish National Subjectivity at the Fin de Siècle" (1994), a commentary that relies on the work of Edward Said, Schmitt argues that *Dracula*'s Orientalism, in its opposition of East to West, actually refers to another set of oppositions, Irish to English. Schmitt links the rise of the literary vampire with English imperial collapse, associating it with a fin de siècle discourse of degeneration and decline. For Schmitt, Stoker's text embodies an insistent rejection of racial impurity at a time when a civilization supposedly in decline needed rejuvenation from outside. In "Landlord and Soil: *Dracula*," attending to the concern with property in Gothic narratives and drawing on Terry Eagleton's characterization of Stoker's narrative, Seamus Deane identifies Count Dracula with an absentee Irish landlord "running out of soil."[21] He argues that *Dracula* presents in terms of

Modernization and the Law in *Dracula*

Of the host of folkloric and fictional vampires extant by the close of the nineteenth century, only Dracula survived the transition from the gothic to the (post) modern. Modernity is *Dracula's* strength. It represents more than new tools to fight old vampires or new strategies of a smart vampire needing *lebensraum*. It functions as a touchstone of change, a crystal reflecting and refracting images of science, morality and law in complex linked facets. The *fin-de-siecle* Darwinian pessimism played out in fears of alterity, moral degeneration and racial decay also underlay professional debates about the modernisation of the legal professions. These fears are embodied in Count Dracula.

–Anne McGillivray, "'He Would Have Made a Wonderful Solicitor': Law, Modernity and Professionalism in Bram Stoker's *Dracula*" (2003)

land, soil, and speech the overcoming of demons and deviations in a way that mystifies aspects of the Irish situation. Locating the book within "Gothic and Celtic twilights," he asserts its relation to the cultural nationalism of the 1890s and to "a whole series of Irish nineteenth-century novels."[22] In "Ambivalence and Ascendancy in Bram Stoker's *Dracula*" (2002), Gregory Castle attends to Stoker's in-between situation as an Anglo-Irish Protestant, that is, as Irish but not Catholic and Protestant but not English. He brings out in compelling detail ways in which prominent aspects of *Dracula*, such as Van Helsing's use of sacramental language and emblems, express contradictions in the compromised position of the Anglo-Irish.

In "The Irish Vampire: *Dracula,* Parnell, and the Troubled Dreams of Nationhood" (1997), Michael Valdez Moses elaborates at length the book's Irish connection. He argues for numerous echoes of late-nineteenth-century Irish history and culture in *Dracula,* in particular details from the life and political strategies of Charles Stuart Parnell (1846–1891), the Irish political leader who advocated Home Rule. Although his argument is more satisfying in general than in some of its specifics, Moses does present suggestively a mass of historical material that Stoker would have been aware of, material that might well have influenced the sometimes contradictory presentation of the Count, Van Helsing, and other major characters. One implication to be drawn from Moses's essay is indisputable: that part of the book's continuing fascination arises from its evocation of a conflicted political situation involving a clash of national identities, an evocation that resonates with a significant

aspect of our own time, the conflicted constructing of national identities in the postcolonial aftermath of the fall of empires.

Joseph Valente's *Dracula's Crypt: Bram Stoker, Irishness and the Question of Blood* (2001) provides the first sustained critical commentary informed by postcolonial and poststructural thinking that persuasively addresses the Irish aspects of *Dracula*. Like Auerbach, Baldick, and Mighall, Valente takes issue with readings of *Dracula* from a historicist perspective, in particular, deterministic interpretations that argue for a direct, causal relation between an Irish cultural situation that Stoker experienced and the details and implications of his narrative. Valente persuasively suggests that the Irish character of *Dracula* and its author are in need of more nuanced description than earlier critics have provided. Drawing on the work of the postcolonial theorist Homi Bhabha, Valente sketches the metrocolonial situation of Ireland at Stoker's time, marked by its proximity to the metropolitan center of the British Empire and by the racial identity its inhabitants shared with the British. Framing his reading of *Dracula* in the complex texture of Stoker's in-between status as Anglo-Irish but with a strong native Celtic dimension on his mother's side, Valente identifies various contradictions in the narrative. Those contradictions suggest that the Count frequently embodies antithetical perspectives while his antagonists are presented not as his opposites but as his doubles. By combining psychoanalytic and postcolonial insights, Valente is able to trace the contradictory implications of *Dracula* in ways that undermine readings of the book's Irish character that put Stoker on one side or the other of a two-way struggle for political control. Future critics will have to attend to Valente's rich formulations about the book's pervasive ambiguous doublings.

The recent developments in the response to *Dracula* carry forward the concerns of earlier interpreters with psychological and social issues, but they frame them in new ways within a reconsidered history and conception of Gothic writing and within the dynamics of imperialism and postcolonialism. In these new readings, we recognize *Dracula* as a book whose continuing relevance to our modernity we are just beginning to understand.

---

1. This essay is a revised, updated version of the essay of the same title that appears in *Dracula,* ed. John Paul Riquelme (Boston & New York: Bedford/St. Martin's, 2002), pp. 409–433, and is reprinted as changed with the permission of Bedford/St. Martin's. I wish to thank Theodora Goss for substantial assistance in the research for the original version of the essay and for her response to a late draft of that version. I am also grateful for helpful responses to drafts by Joseph Valente, Dennis Foster, and Gregory Castle. Timely

advice from Elizabeth Miller improved the coherence and accuracy of the new version.

2. Many of the most suggestive and persuasive readings of *Dracula* through the mid-1990s have been reprinted in critical collections focused on the book or on Stoker's writings in general. Twenty-five essays on *Dracula* published before 1990, including many of the most influential ones, are available in two collections, *Dracula: The Vampire and the Critics,* ed. Margaret L. Carter (Ann Arbor: UMI, 1988), and *The Critical Response to Bram Stoker,* ed. Carol A. Senf (Westport, Conn.: Greenwood, 1993). The latter volume also includes reviews of *Dracula* and essays and reviews about other works by Stoker. A more recent critical casebook, *Dracula: Bram Stoker,* ed. Glennis Byron (New York: St. Martin's, 1999), complements these earlier volumes, since the majority of the essays it reprints appeared originally in the 1990s. More recently, sixteen reviews and critical essays on *Dracula,* including several originally published after 2000, have been reprinted in volume 144 of *Twentieth-Century Literary Criticism* (2004), edited by Janet Witalec. Commentators on the criticism of *Dracula* have framed their descriptions using sets of categories that differ from mine. Carter, for example, divides the critical responses into the following emphases: "historical, political, psychosexual, metaphysical, or structural (i.e., focusing on narrative technique, not necessarily adhering to a 'structuralist' school of criticism)" (Carter, p. 2). Clive Leatherdale, in *Dracula: The Novel & the Legend* (1985; rev. Westcliff-on-Sea, U.K.: Desert Island Books, 2001) identifies five main emphases in the criticism: sexual repression, psychoanalysis, religious motifs, occult and mythic elements, and social and political tendencies. Byron's selected bibliography of the criticism is organized under the following headings: formalist, psychoanalytic, Marxist and historicist, and feminist and gender issues.

3. Dorothy Scarborough, *The Supernatural in Modern English Fiction* (New York: Putnam's, 1917), p. 163.

4. McNally and Florescu have together and separately published other volumes focusing on the history and legends that stand behind the figure of Dracula, including their *The Essential Dracula* (New York: Mayflower Books, 1979) and McNally's *Dracula Was a Woman* (London: Hale, 1984). I have not included these books in the review of criticism, since their subjects are more historical than literary. Some of their claims about the relation of Stoker's Count to historical figures, especially Vlad the Impaler and Elizabeth Bathory, have been challenged by Leatherdale, *Novel & Legend,* and Elizabeth Miller, *Dracula: Sense & Nonsense* (Westcliff-on-Sea, U.K.: Desert Island Books, 2000).

5. In their catalogue for an exhibition at the Rosenbach Museum & Library in Philadelphia celebrating the centenary of *Dracula*'s publication, Michael Barsanti and Wendy Good describe the pre-publication material that Seed works with in his essay. See also Christopher Frayling, *Vampyres: Lord Byron to Count Dracula* (London: Faber & Faber, 1991).

6. Devendra Varma, "The Vampire in Legend, Lore, and Literature," Introduction to *Varney the Vampyre; or, The Feast of Blood* by James Malcolm Rymer, 3 vols. (New York: Arno, 1970), p. xxviii.

7. Leatherdale, *Novel & Legend,* p. 9.

8. Alongside Leatherdale's work toward consolidating *Dracula*'s reputation have come various editions of the book with the elaborate annotations of a committed editor or with more succinct ones produced by established scholars of Victorian and modern literature. Leatherdale's own *Dracula Unearthed* (Westcliff-on-Sea, U.K.: Desert Island Books, 1998) is the most heavily annotated edition, with many references to Stoker's sources. Leonard Wolf's edition of the book, *The Essential Dracula* (New York: Plume, 1993), also provides extended glosses, and several editions by academic critics have appeared in the past decade. The increased availability of the book in reliable editions and the more frequent, more various scholarly writing about *Dracula* suggest that it has crossed into the canon of literature regularly taught and discussed in university classrooms, as Mary Shelley's *Frankenstein* did in the 1970s.

9. Miller, *Sense & Nonsense,* p. 57.

10. Maurice Richardson, "The Psychoanalysis of Ghost Stories," *The Twentieth Century,* 199 (1959): 427, 429.

11. The essay anticipates Twitchell's books *The Living Dead: A Study of the Vampire in Romantic Literature* (1981), a survey of vampirism as an element in nineteenth-century representations of art and the artist beginning with literary Romanticism, and *Dreadful Pleasures: An Anatomy of Modern Horror* (1985), which includes chapters not only about the vampire but about other monsters important in popular culture, including the Wolfman and Frankenstein.

12. Phyllis Roth, "Suddenly Sexual Women in Bram Stoker's *Dracula,*" *Literature and Psychology,* 27 (1977): 113, 120.

13. Laurence A. Rickels, *The Vampire Lectures* (Minneapolis: University of Minnesota Press, 1999), p. 51.

14. Franco Moretti, "Dialectic of Fear," in his *Signs Taken for Wonders: Essays in the Sociology of Literary Forms* (London: Verso, 1983), pp. 91, 92.

15. John L. Greenway, "Seward's Folly: *Dracula* as a Critique of 'Normal Science'," *Stanford Literature Review,* 3 (1986): 220, 230.

16. Athena Vrettos, "Physical Immunity and Racial Destiny," in his *Somatic Fictions: Imagining Illness in Victorian Culture* (Stanford: Stanford University Press, 1995), pp. 163, 166, 174.

17. Nina Auerbach, *Our Vampires, Ourselves* (Chicago: University of Chicago Press, 1995), p. 63.

18. David Punter, *The Literature of Terror: A History of Gothic Fictions from 1765 to the Present Day,* 2 vols. (1980; rev. London: Longman, 1996), vol. 2, pp. 19, 17.

19. Chris Baldick, "Dangerous Discoveries and Mad Scientists: Some Late-Victorian Horrors," in his *In Frankenstein's Shadow: Myth, Monstrosity, and Nineteenth-Century Writing* (Oxford: Clarendon, 1987), p. 147.

20. John Paul Riquelme, "Toward a History of Gothic and Modernism: Dark Modernity from Bram Stoker to Samuel Beckett," *Modern Fiction Studies,* 46 (Fall 2000): 591.

21. Deane cites Eagleton's *Heathcliff and the Great Hunger: Studies in Irish Culture* (pp. 215–216) as the source for his allegorizing of Count Dracula as an absentee landlord whose property is slipping away.

22. Seamus Deane, "Landlord and Soil: *Dracula,*" in his *Strange Country: Modernity and Nationhood in Irish Writing since 1790* (Oxford: Clarendon, 1997), pp. 90, 94, 91.

Checklist for Reference and Further Reading

Biographies

Belford, Barbara. *Bram Stoker: A Biography of the Author of* Dracula. New York: Knopf, 1996.

Farson, Daniel. *The Man who Wrote* Dracula: *A Biography of Bram Stoker*. New York: St. Martin's Press, 1975.

Ludlam, Harry. *A Biography of Dracula: The Life Story of Bram Stoker*. London: Foulsham, 1962. Republished as *A Biography of Bram Stoker, Creator of Dracula*. London: New English Library, 1977.

Murray, Paul. *From the Shadow of* Dracula: *A Life of Bram Stoker*. London: Jonathan Cape, 2004.

Whitelaw, Nancy. *Bram Stoker: Author of* Dracula. Greensboro, N.C.: Reynolds, 1998.

Bibliographies

Carter, Margaret L. *The Vampire in Literature: A Critical Bibliography*. Ann Arbor, Mich.: UMI, 1989.

Dalby, Richard. *Bram Stoker: A Bibliography of First Editions*. London: Dracula Press, 1983.

Dalby and William Hughes. *Bram Stoker: A Bibliography*. Westcliff-on-Sea, U.K.: Desert Island Books, 2004.

Eighteen-Bisang, Robert, and J. Gordon Melton. Dracula: *A Century of Editions, Adaptations and Translations*. Santa Barbara, Cal.: Transylvanian Society of Dracula, 1998.

Hughes. *Bram Stoker: A Bibliography,* Victorian Fiction Research Guide 25. Australia: University of Queensland, 1997.

Riccardo, Martin V. *Vampires Unearthed: The Complete Multi-Media Vampire and Dracula Bibliography*. New York: Garland, 1983.

Annotated Editions of *Dracula*

Auerbach, Nina, and David J. Skal, eds. *Dracula,* Norton Critical Edition. New York: Norton, 1997.

Byron, Glennis, ed. *Dracula*. Peterborough, U.K.: Broadview, 1998.

Leatherdale, Clive, ed. *Bram Stoker's* Dracula *Unearthed*. Westcliff-on-Sea, U.K.: Desert Island Books, 1998.

McNally, Raymond T., and Radu Florescu. *The Essential* Dracula: *A Completely Illustrated and Annotated Edition of Bram Stoker's Classic Novel*. New York: Mayflower, 1979.

Riquelme, J. P., ed. *Dracula: Complete, Authoritative Text with Biographical, Historical, and Cultural Contexts, Critical History, and Essays from Contemporary Critical Perspectives,* Case Studies in Contemporary Criticism. Boston: Bedford/St. Martin's Press, 2002.

Wolf, Leonard, ed. *The Annotated* Dracula. New York: Potter, 1975. Revised as *The Essential* Dracula: *The Definitive Annotated Edition of Bram Stoker's Classic Novel*. New York: Penguin, 1993.

Backgrounds and Context for *Dracula*

Allen, Vivien. *Hall Caine: Portrait of a Victorian Romancer*. Sheffield, U.K.: Sheffield Academic Press, 1997.

Auerbach, Nina. *Ellen Terry: Player in Her Time*. New York: Norton, 1987.

Baedeker, Karl. *London and Its Environs*. London: Dulau, 1898.

Barber, Paul. *Vampires, Burial, and Death*. New Haven: Yale University Press, 1988.

Baring-Gould, Sabine. *The Book of Were-Wolves,* 1865. Republished, New York: Causeway, 1973.

Beckson, Karl. *London in the 1890s: A Cultural History*. London: Norton, 1992.

Bell, Michael. *Food for the Dead: On the Trail of New England's Vampires*. New York: Carroll & Graf, 2001.

Bird, Isabella L. *The Golden Chersonese*. London: Murray, 1883.

Boner, Charles. *Transylvania: Its Products and Its People*. London: Longmans, Green, Reader & Dyer, 1865.

Brereton, Austin. *The Life of Henry Irving,* 2 volumes. London: Longmans, Green, 1908.

Bunson, Matthew. *The Vampire Encyclopedia*. New York: Crown, 1993.

Burton, Isabel. Preface. *Vikram and the Vampire,* edited by Richard Burton. London: Tylston & Edwards, 1893. Republished, New York: Dover, 1969.

Caine, Hall. "Bram Stoker: The Story of a Great Friendship," *Daily Telegraph,* 24 April 1912, p. 16.

Calmet, Dom Augustin. *Dissertation on those Persons who Return to Earth Bodily, the Excommunicated, the Oupires or Vampires, Vroucolacas, Etc,* 1850. Republished as *Treatise on Vampires & Revenants, the Phantom World*. Westcliff-on-Sea, U.K.: Desert Island Books, 1993.

Carter, Margaret L. *Shadow of a Shade: A Survey of Vampirism in Literature*. New York: Gordon, 1975.

Chitimia, Silvia. "Les traces de l'occulte dans le folklore roumain," in *Le Défi Magique,* volume 2. N.p.: Presses Universitaries de Lyon, n.d., pp. 135–148.

Clery, E. J., and Robert Miles, eds. *Gothic Documents: A Sourcebook, 1700–1820*. Manchester, U.K.: Manchester University Press, 2000.

Copper, Basil. *The Vampire in Legend and Fact,* 1973. Republished, Secaucus, N.J.: Citadel, 1974.

Crosse, A. F. *Round About the Carpathians*. London: Blackwood, 1878.

Cunningham, Gail. *The New Woman and the Victorian Novel*. New York: Barnes & Noble, 1978.

Daly, Teri. "The Medieval Vampire," *Tournaments Illuminated,* 20 (Autumn 1996): 20–23.

Day, William Patrick. *In the Circles of Fear and Desire: A Study of Gothic Fantasy*. Chicago: University of Chicago Press, 1985.

Dresser, Norine. *American Vampires: Fans, Victims and Practitioners*. New York: Vintage, 1990.

Dundes, Alan, ed. *The Vampire: A Casebook*. Madison: University of Wisconsin Press, 1998.

Eagleton, Terry. *Heathcliff and the Great Hunger: Studies in Irish Culture.* London & New York: Verso, 1995.

Ellman, Richard. *Oscar Wilde.* New York: Knopf, 1988.

Faivre, Tony. *Les Vampires: Essai historique, critique et littéraire.* Paris, 1962.

Fellow of the Carpathian Society. *Magyarland: Being the Narrative of our Travels Through the Highlands and Lowlands of Hungary,* 2 volumes. London: Sampson Low, Marston, Searle & Rivington, 1881.

Frost, Brian. *The Monster with a Thousand Faces: Guises of the Vampire in Myth and Literature.* Bowling Green, Ohio: Bowling Green State University Popular Press, 1989.

Gerard, Emily. "Transylvanian Superstitions," *Nineteenth Century,* 18 (July 1885): 130–150.

Girouard, M. *The Return to Camelot: Chivalry and the English Gentleman.* London: Yale University Press, 1981.

Glut, Donald F. *True Vampires of History.* New York: HC Publishers, 1971.

Gordon, Joan, and Veronica Hollinger, eds. *Blood Read: The Vampire Metaphor in Contemporary Culture.* Philadelphia: University of Pennsylvania Press, 1997.

Guiley, Rosemary. *The Encyclopedia of Vampires, Werewolves and Other Monsters.* New York: Checkmark Books/Facts on File, 2004.

Guiley. *Vampires Among Us.* New York: Pocket Books, 1991.

Guiley and J. B. Macabre. *The Complete Vampire Companion.* New York: Macmillan, 1994.

Harker, Joseph. *Studio and Stage.* London: Nisbet, 1924.

Hart-Davies, Rupert, ed. *The Letters of Oscar Wilde.* New York: Harcourt, Brace & World, 1962.

Hatlen, Burton. "The Return of the Repressed/Oppressed in Bram Stoker's *Dracula,*" *Minnesota Review,* 15 (1980): 80–97.

Haworth-Maden, Clare. *Dracula: Everything You Always Wanted to Know about the Man, the Myth, and the Movies.* New York: Crescent, 1992.

Heiss, Lokke. "Madame Dracula: The Life of Emily Gerard," *Journal of the Fantastic in the Arts,* 10 (1999): 174–186.

Hurwood, Bernhardt J. *Vampires.* New York: Quick Fox, 1981.

Introvigne, Massimo. "Antoine Faivre: Father of Contemporary Vampire Studies," in *Ésotérisme, Gnoses & Imaginaire Symbolique: Mélanges offerts à Antoine Faivre,* edited by Richard Caron, Joscelyn Godwin, Wouter J. Hanegraaff, and Jean-Louis Vieillard-Baron. Leuven [Louvain], Belgium: Peeters, 2001, pp. 595–610.

Introvigne. "Satanism Scares and Vampirism," *Transylvanian Journal,* 2 (Spring/Summer 1996): 31–45.

Irving, Laurence. *Henry Irving, the Actor and His World.* London: Faber & Faber, 1951.

Johnson, Major E. C. *On the Track of the Crescent: Erratic Notes from Pireus to Pesth.* London: Hurst & Blackett, 1885.

Jones, Ernest. *On the Nightmare,* 1931. Republished, New York: Liveright, 1971.

Kilgour, Maggie. *The Rise of the Gothic Novel*. New York: Routledge, 1995.

Kilgour. "Vampiric Arts: Bram Stoker's Defence of Poetry," in *Bram Stoker: History, Psychoanalysis and the Gothic,* edited by William Hughes and Andrew Smith. London: Macmillan, 1998, pp. 47–61.

King, Stephen. *Danse Macabre*. New York: Berkley, 1983.

Krafft-Ebing, Richard von. *Psychopathia Sexualis: A Medico-Forensic Study,* translated by F. S. Klaf. New York: Bell, 1965.

Lombroso, Cesare, and William Ferraro. *The Female Offender*. London: Fisher Unwin, 1895.

Lombroso-Ferrero, Gina. *Criminal Man According to the Classification of Cesare Lombroso*. London: Putnam, 1922.

Lovecraft, H. P. *Supernatural Horror in Literature,* 1939. Republished, New York: Dover, 1973.

Lyon, David T. "The Symbolic Significance of Blood in the Old Testament," *Fort Hayes Studies,* 5 (1985): 51–54.

MacAndrew, Elizabeth. *The Gothic Tradition in Fiction*. New York: Columbia University Press, 1979.

Malchow, H. L. *Gothic Images of Race in Nineteenth-Century Britain*. Stanford, Cal.: Stanford University Press, 1996.

Marigny, Jean. *Le Vampire dans la Littérature Anglo-Saxonne*. Paris: Atelier National de Reproduction des Theses, 1985.

Masters, Anthony. *The Natural History of the Vampire*. New York: Putnam, 1972.

Mayo, Herbert. *On the Truths Contained in Popular Superstitions with an Account of Mesmerism,* 1851. Republished, Westcliff-on-Sea, U.K.: Desert Island Books, 2003.

McCormack, W. J. *Sheridan Le Fanu and Victorian Ireland*. Dublin: Lilliput, 1991.

McNally. *A Clutch of Vampires*. New York: Warner Paperback Library, 1975.

Melton, J. Gordon. *The Vampire Book: The Encyclopedia of the Undead,* 1994. Revised edition, Detroit: Visible Ink Press, 1999.

Mulvey-Roberts, Marie, ed. *The Handbook to Gothic Literature*. New York: New York University Press, 1998.

Murgoci, Agnes. "The Vampire in Roumania," *Folklore,* 37 (1926): 320–349.

Noll, Richard. *Bizarre Diseases of the Mind*. New York: Berkley, 1990.

Noll. *Vampires, Werewolves, and Demons: Twentieth Century Reports in the Psychiatric Literature*. New York: Brunner/Mazel, 1992.

Nordau, Max. *Degeneration*. London: Heinemann, 1896.

Paget, John. *Hungary and Transylvania,* 2 volumes, 1850. Republished, New York: Arno, 1971.

Pascu, Stefan. *A History of Transylvania,* translated by D. Robert Ladd. New York: Dorset Press, 1982.

Perkowski, Jan L. *The Darkling: A Treatise on Slavic Vampirism*. Columbus, Ohio: Slavica, 1989.

Pick, Daniel. *Faces of Degeneration: A European Disorder, 1848–1918*. Cambridge: Cambridge University Press, 1989.

Pirie, David. *The Vampire Cinema*. London: Hamlyn, 1977.

Power, Albert. "Bram Stoker and the Tradition of Irish Supernatural Literature," *Bram Stoker Society Journal,* 3 (1991): 3–21.

Punter, David. *The Literature of Terror: A History of Gothic Fictions from 1765 to the Present Day. Volume I: The Gothic Tradition; Volume II: The Modern Gothic,* 1980. Revised edition, London & New York: Longman, 1996.

Ramsland, Katherine. *Piercing the Darkness: Undercover with Vampires in America Today.* New York: HarperPrism, 1998.

Ramsland. *The Science of Vampires.* New York: Berkley, 2002.

Richardson, Maurice. "The Psychoanalysis of Ghost Stories," *Twentieth Century,* 166 (1959): 419–431.

Rondina, Christopher. *Vampire Legends of Rhode Island.* North Attleborough, Mass.: Covered Bridge, 1997.

Ruskin, John. *Sesame and Lilies.* London: Dent, 1907.

Sage, Victor. "Gothic Novel," in *The Handbook to Gothic Literature,* edited by Marie Mulvey-Roberts. New York: New York University Press, 1998, pp. 81–89.

Senn, Harry A. *Were-Wolf and Vampire in Romania.* New York: Columbia University Press, 1982.

Shepard, Leslie. "The Library of Bram Stoker," in *Bram Stoker's Dracula: Sucking through the Century, 1897–1997,* edited by Carol M. Davison. Toronto: Dundurn, 1997, pp. 411–414.

Shepard. "A Note on the Death Certificate of Bram Stoker," in *Bram Stoker's Dracula: Sucking Through the Century, 1897–1997,* edited by Davison. Toronto: Dundurn, 1997, pp. 414–415.

Showalter, Elaine. *Sexual Anarchy: Gender and Culture at the Fin de Siècle.* London: Viking, 1990.

Silver, Alain, and James Ursini. *The Vampire Film: From* Nosferatu *to* Bram Stoker's Dracula. New York: Limelight Editions, 1993.

Skal, David J. *V Is for Vampire: An A to Z Guide to Everything Undead.* New York: Plume, 1996.

Stoddard, Jane (Lorna). "Mr Bram Stoker: A Chat with the Author of *Dracula,*" 1897. Republished in *Dracula* by Stoker, edited by Glennis Byron. Peterborough, U.K.: Broadview, 1998, pp. 484–488.

Stuart, Roxana. *Stage Blood: Vampires of the 19th-Century Stage.* Bowling Green, Ohio: Bowling Green State University Press, 1994.

Summers, Montague. *The Vampire: His Kith and Kin.* London: Routledge, 1928.

Summers. *The Vampire in Europe,* 1929. Republished, New Hyde Park, N.Y.: University Books, [1961].

Symons, John Addington, and Havelock Ellis. *Sexual Inversion.* London: Wilson & Macmillan, 1897.

Twitchell, James. *Dreadful Pleasures: An Anatomy of Modern Horror.* New York: Oxford University Press, 1985.

Twitchell. *The Living Dead: A Study of the Vampire in Romantic Literature.* Durham, N.C.: Duke University Press, 1981.

Twitchell. "The Vampire Myth," *American Imago,* 37 (1980): 83–92.

Whitehead, Gwendolyn. "The Vampire in Nineteenth-Century Literature," *University of Mississippi Studies in English,* 8 (1990): 243–248.

Wilkinson, William. *An Account of the Principalities of Wallachia and Moldavia,* 1820. Republished, New York: Arno, 1971.

Wilson, Katharina. "The History of the Word 'Vampire,'" *Journal of the History of Ideas,* 45 (1985): 577–583.

Wright, Dudley. *Vampires and Vampirism.* London: William Rider & Son, 1914.

Dracula Criticism

Alexander, Brian. "*Dracula* and the Gothic Imagination of War," *Journal of Dracula Studies,* 2 (2000): 15–23.

Andriano, Joseph. "The Unholy Circle: A Jungian Reading of *Dracula,*" in *The Dark Fantastic,* edited by C. W. Sullivan III. Westport, Conn.: Greenwood Press, 1997, pp. 49–55.

Appleby, Robin S. "Dracula and Dora: The Diagnosis and Treatment of Alternative Narratives," *Literature and Psychology,* 39 (1993): 16–37.

Arata, Stephen D. "The Occidental Tourist: *Dracula* and the Anxiety of Reverse Colonization," *Victorian Studies,* 33 (1990): 621–645.

Aristodemou, Maria. "Casting Light on *Dracula:* Studies in Law and Culture," *Modern Law Review,* 56 (1993): 760–765.

Astle, Richard. "Dracula as Totemic Monster: Lacan, Freud, Oedipus and History," *Sub-Stance,* 8 (1979): 98–105.

Auerbach, Nina. *Our Vampires, Ourselves.* Chicago: University of Chicago Press, 1995.

Baldick, Chris. "Dangerous Discoveries and Mad Scientists: Some Late-Victorian Horrors," in his *Frankenstein's Shadow: Myth, Monstrosity, and Nineteenth-Century Writing.* Oxford: Clarendon Press, 1987, pp. 141–162.

Baldick and Robert Mighall. "Gothic Criticism," in *A Companion to the Gothic,* edited by David Punter. Oxford: Blackwell, 2000, pp. 209–228.

Barclay, Glen St. John. "Sex and Horror: Bram Stoker," in *Anatomy of Horror: The Masters of Occult Fiction.* London: Weidenfeld & Nicolson, 1978, pp. 39–57.

Barsanti, Michael J., and Wendy Van Wyck Good. *Bram Stoker's* Dracula: *A Centennial Exhibition.* Philadelphia: Rosenbach Museum & Library, 1997.

Bentley, Christopher F. "The Monster in the Bedroom: Sexual Symbolism in Bram Stoker's *Dracula,*" *Literature and Psychology,* 22 (1972): 27–34.

Bhalla, Alok. *Politics of Atrocity and Lust: The Vampire Tale as a Nightmare History of England in the Nineteenth Century.* New Delhi: Sterling, 1990.

Bierman, Joseph S. "A Crucial Stage in the Writing of *Dracula,*" in *Bram Stoker: History, Psychoanalysis and the Gothic,* edited by William Hughes and Andrew Smith. London: Macmillan, 1998, pp. 151–172.

Bierman. "*Dracula:* Prolonged Childhood Illness, and the Oral Triad," *American Imago,* 29 (1972): 186–198.

Bierman. "The Genesis and Dating of *Dracula* from Bram Stoker's Working Notes," in *Dracula: The Vampire and the Critics,* edited by Margaret L. Carter. Ann Arbor, Mich.: UMI, 1988, pp. 51–55.

Blinderman, Charles S. "Vampurella: Darwin and Count Dracula," *Massachussetts Review,* 21 (1980): 411, 428.

Boone, Troy. "'He is English and therefore adventurous': Politics, Decadence and *Dracula,*" *Studies in the Novel,* 25 (1993): 76–91.

Botting, Fred. *Gothic.* London: Routledge, 1996.

Boucher, Anthony. Introduction to *Dracula* by Stoker. New York: Limited Editions Club, 1965.

Brantlinger, Patrick. "Imperial Gothic: Atavism and the Occult in the British Adventure Novel, 1880–1914," *ELT,* 28 (1985): 243–252.

Brennan, Matthew C. *The Gothic Psyche: Disintegration and Growth in Nineteenth-Century English Literature.* Columbia, S.C.: Camden House, 1997.

Brennan. "Repression, Knowledge and Saving Souls: The Role of the 'New Woman' in Stoker's *Dracula* and Murnau's *Nosferatu,*" *Studies in the Humanities,* 19 (1992): 1–10.

Bronfen, Elisabeth. "Hysteric and Obsessional Discourse: Responding to Death in *Dracula,*" in her *Over Her Dead Body: Death, Femininity and the Aesthetic.* New York: Routledge, 1992, pp. 313–322.

Byers, Thomas B. "Good Men and Monsters: The Defenses of *Dracula,*" *Literature and Psychology,* 31 (1981): 24–31.

Cain, Jimmie E. "'With the Unspeakables': *Dracula* and Russophobia—Tourism, Racism and Imperialism," in *Dracula: The Shade and the Shadow,* edited by Elizabeth Miller. Westcliff-on-Sea, U.K.: Desert Island Books, 1998, pp. 104–115.

Carlson, M. "What Stoker Saw: An Introduction to the History of the Literary Vampire," *Folklore Forum,* 10 (1977): 26–32.

Carter, Margaret L. "Share Alike: *Dracula* and the Sympathetic Vampire in Mid-Twentieth-Century Pulp Fiction," in *Bram Stoker's Dracula: Sucking through the Century, 1897–1997,* edited by Carol M. Davison. Toronto: Dundurn, 1997, pp. 175–194.

Carter, ed. *Dracula: The Vampire and the Critics.* Ann Arbor: UMI, 1988.

Case, Sue-Ellen. "Tasting the Original Apple: Gender and the Struggle for Narrative Authority in *Dracula,*" *Narrative,* 1 (1993): 223–243.

Castle, Gregory. "Ambivalence and Ascendancy in Bram Stoker's *Dracula,*" in *Dracula* by Bram Stoker, edited by J. P. Riquelme. Boston: Bedford/St. Martin's Press, 2002, pp. 518–537.

Coates, Daryl R. "Bram Stoker and the Ambiguity of Identity," *Publication of the Mississippi Philological Association* (1984): 88–105.

Colatrella, Carol. "Fear of Reproduction and Desire for Replication in *Dracula,*" *Journal of Medical Humanities,* 17 (1996): 179–189.

Coppola, Francis Ford, and James V. Hart. *Bram Stoker's Dracula: The Film and the Legend.* New York: Newmarket, 1992.

Craft, Christopher. "'Kiss Me With Those Red Lips': Gender and Inversion in Bram Stoker's *Dracula,*" *Representations,* 8 (1984): 107–133.

Cranny-Francis, Anne. "Sexual Politics and Political Repression in Bram Stoker's *Dracula*," in *Nineteenth Century Suspense: From Poe to Conan Doyle,* edited by Clive Bloom, Brian Docherty, Jane Gibb, and Keith Shand. Basingstoke, U.K.: Macmillan, 1988, pp. 64–79.

Cribb, Susan M. "'If I had to write with a pen': Readership and Bram Stoker's Diary Narrative," *Journal of the Fantastic in the Arts,* 10 (1997): 133–141.

Croley, Laura Sagella. "The Rhetoric of Reform in Stoker's *Dracula:* Depravity, Decline, and the Fin-de-Siècle 'Residuum,'" *Criticism: A Quarterly for Literature and the Arts,* 37 (1995): 85–108.

Dalby, Richard. "The 'Dimitry' from Varna," *Bram Stoker Society Journal,* 2 (1990): 22–23.

Dalby. "*Dracula:* The Working Notes," *Bram Stoker Society Journal,* 9 (1997): 30–31.

Dalby. "Makt Myrkranna-Power of Darkness," *Bram Stoker Society Journal,* 5 (1993): 2–3.

Daly, Nicholas. "Incorporated Bodies: *Dracula* and the Rise of Professionalism," *Texas Studies in Literature and Language,* 39 (Summer 1997): 181–203.

Davies, Bernard. "Bram Stoker's Transylvania: A Critical Reassessment," *Bram Stoker Society Journal,* 10 (1998): 3–16.

Davies. "Inspirations, Imitations and In-Jokes in Stoker's *Dracula,*" in *Dracula: The Shade and the Shadow,* edited by Miller. Westcliff-on-Sea, U.K.: Desert Island Books, 1998, pp. 131–137.

Davison. "Blood Brothers: Dracula and Jack the Ripper," in her *Bram Stoker's Dracula: Sucking through the Century, 1897–1997.* Toronto: Dundurn, 1997, pp. 147–172.

Deane, Seamus. "Landlord and Soil: *Dracula,*" in his *Strange Country: Modernity and Nationhood in Irish Writing since 1790.* Oxford: Clarendon Press, 1997, pp. 89–94.

Demetrakopoulos, Stephanie. "Feminism, Sex Role Exchanges, and Other Subliminal Fantasies in Bram Stoker's *Dracula,*" *Frontiers: A Journal of Women's Studies,* 2 (1977): 104–113.

Dickens, David B. "The German Matrix of Stoker's *Dracula,*" in *Dracula: The Shade and the Shadow,* edited by Miller. Westcliff-on-Sea, U.K.: Desert Island Books, 1998, pp. 31–40.

Dijkstra, Bram. *Idols of Perversity: Fantasies of Feminine Evil in Fin de Siècle Culture.* Oxford: Oxford University Press, 1987.

Dukes, Paul. "*Dracula:* Fact, Legend and Fiction," *History Today,* 32 (July 1982): 44–47.

Dyer, Richard. "Children of the Night: Vampirism as Homosexuality, Homosexuality as Vampirism," in *Sweet Dreams: Sexuality and Gender in Popular Fiction,* edited by Susannah Radstone. London: Lawrence & Wishart, 1988, pp. 47–72.

Eighteen-Bisang, Robert, and J. Gordon Melton. *Dracula: A Century of Editions, Adaptations and Translations,* TSD Occasional Publication #1. Santa Barbara, Cal.: Transylvanian Society of Dracula, 1998.

Ellmann, Maud. Introduction to *Dracula* by Stoker. Oxford: Oxford University Press, 1996.

Eltis, Sos. "Corruption of the Blood and Degeneration of the Race: *Dracula* and Policing the Borders of Gender," in Stoker, *Dracula,* edited by J. P. Riquelme. Boston: Bedford/St. Martin's Press, 2002, pp. 450–465.

Feimer, Joel N. "Bram Stoker's *Dracula:* The Challenge of the Occult to Science, Reason and Psychiatry," in *Contours of the Fantastic,* edited by Michelle Langford. New York: Greenwood Press, 1994, pp. 165–171.

Fernbach, Amanda. "Dracula's Decadent Fetish," in *Dracula: The Shade and the Shadow,* edited by Miller. Westcliff-on-Sea, U.K.: Desert Island Books, 1998, pp. 219–228.

Flood, David Hume. "Blood and Transfusion in Bram Stoker's *Dracula*," *University of Mississippi Studies in English,* 7 (1989): 180–192.

Florescu, Radu, and Raymond T. McNally. *Dracula: Prince of Many Faces.* Boston: Little, Brown, 1989.

Fontana, Ernest. "Lombroso's Criminal Man and Stoker's Dracula," *Victorian Newsletter,* 66 (1984): 25–27.

Foster, Dennis. "'The little children can be bitten': A Hunger for Dracula," in Stoker, *Dracula,* edited by Riquelme. Boston: Bedford/St. Martin's Press, 2002, pp. 483–499.

Frayling, Christopher. *Vampyres: Lord Byron to Count Dracula.* London: Faber & Faber, 1991.

Frost, R. J. "'A Race of Devils': *Frankenstein, Dracula,* and Science Fiction," *Journal of Dracula Studies,* 5 (2003): 1–10.

Fry, Carrol L. "Fictional Conventions and Sexuality in *Dracula*," *Victorian Newsletter,* 42 (Fall 1972): 20–22.

Geary, Robert F. "The Powers of Dracula," *Journal of the Fantastic in the Arts,* 4 (1991): 81–91.

Gelder, Ken. *Reading the Vampire.* London: Routledge, 1994.

Glover, David. *Vampires, Mummies, and Liberals: Bram Stoker and the Politics of Popular Fiction.* Durham, N.C.: Duke University Press, 1996.

Glut, Donald F. *The Dracula Book.* Metuchen, N.J.: Scarecrow Press, 1975.

Gordon, Jan B. "The Transparency of *Dracula*," in *Bram Stoker's Dracula: Sucking through the Century, 1897–1997,* edited by Davison. Toronto: Dundurn, 1997, pp. 95–122.

Greenway, John L. "Seward's Folly: *Dracula* as a Critique of 'Normal Science,'" *Stanford Literature Review,* 3 (1986): 213–230.

Greenway. "'Unconscious Cerebration' and the Happy Ending of *Dracula*," *Journal of Dracula Studies,* 4 (2002): 1–9.

Griffin, Gail B. "'Your Girls That You All Love Are Mine': *Dracula* and the Victorian Male Sexual Imagination," *International Journal of Women's Studies,* 3 (1980): 454–465.

Haining, Peter, and Peter Tremayne. *The Un-Dead: The Legend of Bram Stoker and Dracula.* London: Constable, 1997.

Halberstam, Judith. "Technologies of Monstrosity: Bram Stoker's *Dracula*," *Victorian Studies,* 36 (1993): 333–352.

Harse, Katie. "High Duty and Savage Delight: The Ambiguous Nature of Violence in *Dracula*," *Journal of the Fantastic in the Arts,* 10 (1999): 116–123.

Harse. "Stalwart Manhood: Failed Masculinity in *Dracula*," in *Dracula: The Shade and the Shadow,* edited by Miller. Westcliff-on-Sea, U.K.: Desert Island Books, 1998, pp. 229–238.

Hatlen, Burton. "The Return of the Repressed/Oppressed in Bram Stoker's *Dracula*," *Minnesota Review,* 15 (1980): 80–97.

Hennelly, Mark M. "*Dracula:* The Gnostic Quest and the Victorian Wasteland," *English Literature in Transition,* 20 (1977): 13–26.

Hennelly. "The Victorian Book of the Dead: *Dracula*," *Journal of Evolutionary Psychology*, 13 (1992): 204–211.

Holte, James Craig. *Dracula in the Dark: The Dracula Film Adaptations*. Westport, Conn.: Greenwood Press, 1997.

Howes, Marjorie. "The Mediation of the Feminine: Bisexuality, Homoerotic Desire, and Self-Expression in Bram Stoker's *Dracula*," *Texas Studies in Literature and Language*, 30 (1988): 104–119.

Hughes. *Beyond Dracula: Bram Stoker's Fiction in Its Cultural Context*. New York: St. Martin's Press, 2000.

Hughes. "'For the Blood Is the Life': The Construction of Purity in Bram Stoker's *Dracula*," in *Decadence and Danger: Writing, History and the Fin de Siécle*, edited by Tracey Hill. Bath, U.K.: Sulis, 1997, pp. 128–137.

Hughes. "'So Unlike the Normal Lunatic': Abnormal Psychology in Bram Stoker's *Dracula*," *University of Mississippi Studies in English*, 11 (1993–1995): 1–10.

Hughes. "'Terrors that I dare not think of': Masculinity, Hysteria and Empiricism in Bram Stoker's *Dracula*," in *Dracula: The Shade and the Shadow*, edited by Miller. Westcliff-on-Sea, U.K.: Desert Island Books, 1998, pp. 93–103.

Hughes and Smith, eds. *Bram Stoker: History, Psychoanalysis and the Gothic*. London: Macmillan, 1998.

Jann, Rosemary. "Saved by Science? The Mixed Messages of Stoker's *Dracula*," *Texas Studies in Literature and Language*, 31 (1989): 273–287.

Johnson, Alan P. "Bent and Broken Necks: Signs of Design in Stoker's *Dracula*," *Victorian Newsletter*, 72 (1987): 17–24.

Johnson. "'Dual Life': The Status of Women in Stoker's *Dracula*," *Tennessee Studies in Literature*, 27 (1984): 20–39.

Kirtley, Bacil F. "*Dracula*, The Monastic Chronicles and Slavic Folklore," *Dracula: The Vampire and the Critics*, edited by Carter. Ann Arbor, Mich.: UMI, 1988, pp. 11–17.

Kline, Salli J. *The Degeneration of Women: Bram Stoker's* Dracula *as Allegorical Criticism of the* Fin de Siècle. Rheinbach-Merzbach: CMZ-Verlag, 1992.

Krumm, Pascale. "Metamorphosis as Metaphor in Bram Stoker's *Dracula*," *Victorian Newsletter* (Fall 1995): 5–11.

Langella, Frank. Preface in *Dracula* by Bram Stoker. Parsippany, N.J.: Unicorn, 1985.

Lapin, Daniel. *The Vampire, Dracula and Incest*. San Francisco: Gargoyle Publishers, 1995.

Leatherdale, Clive. *Dracula: The Novel & the Legend, A Study of Bram Stoker's Gothic Masterpiece*, 1985. Revised edition, Westcliff-on-Sea, U.K.: Desert Island Books, 1993, 2001.

Leatherdale. *The Origins of Dracula*. London: William Kimber, 1987.

Leatherdale. "Stoker's Banana Skins: Errors, Illogicalities and Misconceptions in *Dracula*," in *Dracula: The Shade and the Shadow*, edited by Miller. Westcliff-on-Sea, U.K.: Desert Island Books, 1998, pp. 138–154.

Leblanc, Benjamin H. "The Death of *Dracula*: A Darwinian Approach to the Vampire's Evolution," in *Bram Stoker's Dracula: Sucking through the Century, 1897–1997*, edited by Davison. Toronto: Dundurn, 1997, pp. 351–374.

Ludlam, Harry. *My Quest for Bram Stoker*. Chicago: Adams, 2000.

MacGillivray, Royce. "*Dracula*: Bram Stoker's Spoiled Masterpiece," *Queen's Quarterly*, 79 (1972): 518–527.

Marigny, Jean. "Secrecy as Strategy in *Dracula*," *Journal of Dracula Studies,* 2 (2000): 3–7.

Marigny. *Vampires: Restless Creatures of the Night,* translated by Lory Frankel. New York: Abrams, 1994.

McCormack, W. J. "Irish Gothic and After," in *The Field Day Anthology of Irish Writing,* edited by Seamus Deane, volume 2. Derry: Field Day Publications, 1991, pp. 831–854.

McDonald, Beth E. *The Vampire as Luminous Experience.* Jefferson, N.C.: McFarland, 2004.

McDonald. "The Vampire as Trickster Figure in Bram Stoker's *Dracula*," *Extrapolation,* 33 (1992): 128–144.

McGillivray, Anne. "'He Would Have Made a Wonderful Solicitor': Law, Modernity and Professionalism in Bram Stoker's *Dracula*," in *Lawyers and Vampires: Cultural Histories of Legal Professions,* edited by David Sugarman and Wesley Pue. Oxford & Portland: Hart, 2003.

McNally. "Bram Stoker and Irish Gothic," in *The Fantastic Vampire: Studies in the Children of the Night,* edited by James Craig Holte. Westport, Conn.: Greenwood Press, 2002, pp. 11–21.

McNally. *Dracula Was a Woman.* London: Hale, 1984.

McNally and Florescu. *In Search of Dracula.* New York: Graphic Society, 1972. Revised as *In Search of Dracula: History of Dracula and Vampires.* Boston & New York: Houghton Mifflin, 1994.

McWhir, Anne. "Pollution and Redemption in *Dracula*," *Modern Language Studies,* 17 (1987): 31–40.

Melton, J. Gordon. "The Vegetarian Vampire: On Introducing Dracula to Children," *Transylvanian Journal,* 2 (Spring/Summer 1996): 17–23.

Melton and Eighteen-Bisang. "Vampire Fiction for Children and Youth," *Transylvanian Journal,* 2 (Spring/Summer 1996): 24–30.

Mighall, Robert. *A Geography of Victorian Gothic Fiction: Mapping History's Nightmares.* Oxford: Oxford University Press, 1999.

Mighall. "Sex, History and the Vampire," in *Bram Stoker: History, Psychoanalysis and the Gothic,* edited by Hughes and Smith. London: Macmillan, 1998.

Milbank, Alison. "'Powers Old and New': Stoker's Alliances with Anglo-Irish Gothic," in *Bram Stoker: History, Psychoanalysis and the Gothic,* edited by Hughes and Smith. London: Macmillan, 1998, pp. 12–28.

Milburn, Diane. "'For the dead travel fast': *Dracula* in Anglo-German Context," in *Dracula: The Shade and the Shadow,* edited by Miller. Westcliff-on-Sea, U.K.: Desert Island Books, 1998, pp. 41–53.

Miller, Elizabeth. "Back to the Basics: Re-Examining Stoker's Sources for *Dracula*," *Journal of the Fantastic in the Arts,* 10 (1999): 187–196.

Miller. *Dracula: Sense & Nonsense.* Westcliff-on-Sea, U.K.: Desert Island Books, 2000.

Miller. "*Frankenstein* and *Dracula:* The Question of Influence," in *Visions of the Fantastic,* edited by Allienne Becker. Westport, Conn.: Greenwood Press, 1996, pp. 123–130.

Miller. *Reflections on Dracula.* White Rock, B.C.: Transylvania Press, 1997.

Miller. "Worshipping at the Shrine of St. Bram," *Bram Stoker Society Journal,* 12 (2000): 25–32.

Miller, ed. *Dracula: The Shade and the Shadow*. Westcliff-on-Sea, U.K.: Desert Island Books, 1998.

Moretti, Franco. *Signs Taken for Wonders,* translated by Susan Fischer, D. Forgacs, and D. Miller. New York: Verso, 1988.

Morrison, Ronald D. "Reading Barthes and Reading *Dracula:* Between Work and Text," *Kentucky Philological Review,* 9 (1994): 23–28.

Moses, Michael Valdez. "The Irish Vampire: *Dracula,* Parnell, and the Troubled Dreams of Nationhood," *Journal x,* 2 (Autumn 1997): 67–111.

Moss, Stephanie. "Bram Stoker and the London Stage," *Journal of the Fantastic in the Arts,* 10 (1999): 124–132.

Moss. "Bram Stoker and the Society for Psychical Research," in *Dracula: The Shade and the Shadow,* edited by Miller. Westcliff-on-Sea, U.K.: Desert Island Books, 1998, pp. 82–92.

Mulvey-Roberts, Marie. "*Dracula* and the Doctors: Bad Blood, Menstrual Taboo and the New Woman," in *Bram Stoker: History, Psychoanalysis and the Gothic,* edited by Hughes and Smith. London: Macmillan, 1998, pp. 78–95.

Nandris, Grigore. "The Historical Dracula: The Theme of His Legend in the Western and Eastern Literatures of Europe," *Comparative Literature Studies,* 3 (1966): 367–396.

Oinas, Felix. "East European Vampires & Dracula," *Journal of Popular Culture,* 16 (1982): 108–116.

Perry, Dennis. "Whitman's Influence on Stoker's *Dracula,*" *Walt Whitman Quarterly Review,* 3 (1986): 29–35.

Phillips, Robert. "The Agony and the Ecstasy: A Jungian Analysis of Two Vampire Novels: Merideth Ann Pierce's *The Darkangel* and Bram Stoker's *Dracula,*" *West Virginia University Philological Papers,* 31 (1986): 10–19.

Pick, Daniel. "'Terrors of the Night': *Dracula* and 'Degeneration' in the Late Nineteenth Century," *Critical Quarterly,* 30 (1988): 72–87.

Pinkerton, Mark. "Why Westenra?" in *Dracula: Celebrating 100 Years,* edited by Leslie Shepard and Albert Power. Dublin: Mentor Press, 1997, pp. 43–46.

Ploeg, Scott Vander. "Stoker's *Dracula:* A Neo-Gothic Experiment," in *The Fantastic Vampire: Studies in the Children of the Night,* edited by James Craig Holte. Westport, Conn.: Greenwood Press, 2002, pp. 37–44.

Pope, Rebecca A. "Writing and Biting in *Dracula,*" *LIT: Literature Interpretation Theory,* 1 (1990): 199–216.

Raible, Christopher G. "Dracula: Christian Heretic," *Christian Century,* 96 (1979): 103–104.

Rickels, Laurence A. *The Vampire Lectures*. Minneapolis: University of Minnesota Press, 1999.

Riquelme, John Paul. "Toward a History of Gothic and Modernism: Dark Modernity from Bram Stoker to Samuel Beckett," *Modern Fiction Studies,* 46 (Fall 2000): 585–605.

Roberts, Bette. "Victorian Values in the Narration of *Dracula,*" *Studies in Weird Fiction,* 6 (1989): 10–14.

Ronay, Gabriel. *The Dracula Myth*. London: Allen, 1972.

Rosenbach Museum & Library. "Catalogue Description of Bram Stoker's Notes for *Dracula,*" in *Bram Stoker's Dracula: Sucking through the Century, 1897–1997,* edited by Davison. Toronto: Dundurn, 1997, pp. 417–418.

Roth, Phyllis A. *Bram Stoker*. Boston: Twayne, 1982.

Roth. "Suddenly Sexual Women in Bram Stoker's *Dracula*," *Literature and Psychology*, 27 (1977): 113–121.

Ruthner, Clemens. "Bloodsuckers with Teutonic Tongues," in *Dracula: The Shade and the Shadow,* edited by Elizabeth Miller. Westcliff-on-Sea, U.K.: Desert Island Books, 1998, pp. 54–65.

Schaffer, Talia. "'A Wilde Desire Took Me': The Homoerotic History of *Dracula*," *ELH,* 61 (1994): 381–425.

Schmitt, Cannon. "Mother Dracula: Orientalism, Degeneration, and Anglo-Irish National Subjectivity at the Fin de Siècle," *Irishness and (Post)Modernism,* edited by John S. Rickard. London: Associated University Press, 1994, pp. 25–43.

Seed, David. "The Narrative Method of *Dracula*," *Nineteenth Century Fiction,* 40 (1985): 61–75.

Senf, Carol A. *The Critical Response to Bram Stoker*. Westport, Conn.: Greenwood Press, 1993.

Senf. *Dracula: Between Tradition and Modernism*. New York: Twayne, 1998.

Senf. "*Dracula:* Stoker's Response to the New Woman," *Victorian Studies,* 26 (1982): 33–49.

Senf. "*Dracula:* The Unseen Face in the Mirror," *Journal of Narrative Technique,* 9 (1979): 160–170.

Senf. *Science and Social Science in Bram Stoker's Fiction*. Westport, Conn.: Greenwood Press, 2002.

Senf. *The Vampire in Nineteenth-Century English Literature*. Bowling Green, Ohio: Bowling Green State University Popular Press, 1988.

Shepard, Leslie. "Bram Stoker and the Theatre," in *Dracula: Celebrating 100 Years,* edited by Shepard and Power. Dublin: Mentor, 1997, pp. 159–175.

Shepard. "The Writing of Dracula," in *Dracula: Celebrating 100 Years,* edited by Shepard and Power. Dublin: Mentor Press, 1997, pp. 35–42.

Shuster, Seymour. "*Dracula* and Surgically Induced Trauma in Children," *British Journal of Medical Psychology,* 46 (1973): 259–270.

Signoretti, Elizabeth. "Repossessing the Body: Transgressive Desire in 'Carmilla' and *Dracula*," *Criticism,* 38 (Fall 1996): 607–632.

Skal, David J. *Dracula: The Ultimate Illustrated Edition of the World Famous Vampire Play*. New York: St. Martin's Press, 1993.

Skal. "'His Hour Upon the Stage': Theatrical Adaptations of *Dracula*," in *Dracula* by Bram Stoker, edited by Auerbach and Skal. New York: Norton, 1997, pp. 371–381.

Skal. *Hollywood Gothic: The Tangled Web of Dracula from Novel to Stage to Screen*. New York & London: Norton, 1990. Revised edition, New York: Faber & Faber, 2004.

Smart, Robert. "Blood and Money in Bram Stoker's *Dracula:* The Struggle Against Monopoly," in *Money: Lure, Lore, and Literature,* edited by John Louis DiGaetani. Westport, Conn.: Greenwood Press, 1994, pp. 253–260.

Smith, Andrew. *Dracula and the Critics*. Sheffield, U.K.: Pavic, 1996.

Spear, Jeffrey L. "Gender and Dis-Ease in *Dracula*," in *Virginal Sexuality and Textuality in Victorian Literature,* edited by Lloyd Davis. Albany: State University of New York Press, 1993, pp. 179–192.

Spencer, Kathleen L. "Purity and Danger: *Dracula,* the Urban Gothic, and the Late Victorian Degeneracy Crisis," *ELH,* 59 (1992): 197–225.

Stade, George. "Dracula's Women," *Partisan Review,* 53 (1986): 200–215.

Starshine, Sylvia, ed. *Dracula; or The Un-Dead* by Bram Stoker. Nottingham: Pumpkin Books, 1997.

Stevenson, John Allen. "The Vampire in the Mirror: The Sexuality of *Dracula*," *PMLA,* 103 (1988): 139–149.

Stewart, Garrett. "Count Me In: *Dracula,* Hypnotic Participation, and the Late-Victorian Gothic of Reading," *LIT: Literature Interpretation Theory,* 5 (1994): 1–18.

Stoker, Bram. "Author's Preface" in *Makt Myrkranna,* 1901. Republished in *Bram Stoker Society Journal,* 5 (1993): 7–8.

Stoker. "Bram Stoker's Letter to William Gladstone," *Revue roumaine d'histoire,* 31 (1992): 175–178. Reprinted in *Journal of Dracula Studies,* 1 (1999): 48.

Stoker. "Bram Stoker's Original Foundation Notes & Data for his *Dracula.*" Rosenbach Museum & Library, Philadelphia. MS EL3 F.5874D.

Stoker. *Dracula: The Rare Text of 1901,* edited by Eighteen-Bisang. White Rock, B.C.: Transylvania Press, 1994.

Stoker, F. A. L. Bram (Florence). Foreword to *Dracula, Argosy: The World's Best Stories,* 1 (June 1926).

Stoker, Florence Bram. Preface to "Dracula's Guest," in *Bram Stoker's Dracula Omnibus,* edited by Fay Weldon. London: Orion Books, 1992.

Tracy, Robert. "Loving You All Ways: Vamps, Vampires, Necrophiles and Necrofilles in Nineteenth-Century Fiction," in *Sex and Death in Victorian Literature,* edited by Regina Barreca. London: Macmillan, 1990, pp. 32–59.

The Undead: The Book Sail 16th Anniversary Catalogue. Orange, Cal.: McLaughlin Press, 1984.

Valente, Joseph. *Dracula's Crypt: Bram Stoker, Irishness and the Question of Blood.* Urbana: University of Illinois Press, 2002.

Varma, Devendra P. "Dracula's Voyage: From Pontus to Hellespontus," in *Dracula: The Vampire and the Critics,* edited by Carter. Ann Arbor, Mich.: UMI, 1988, pp. 207–214.

Varma. "The Genesis of *Dracula*: A Re-Visit," in *Dracula: The Vampire and the Critics,* edited by Carter. Ann Arbor, Mich.: UMI, 1988, pp. 39–50.

Vrettos, Athena. "Physical Immunity and Racial Destiny: Stoker and Haggard," in his *Somatic Fictions: Imagining Illness in Victorian Culture.* Stanford, Cal.: Stanford University Press, 1995, pp. 154–176.

Walker, Gerald, and Lorraine Wright. "Locating Dracula: Contextualising the Geography of Transylvania," in *Bram Stoker's Dracula: Sucking through the Century, 1897–1997,* edited by Davison. Toronto: Dundurn, 1997, pp. 49–74.

Wall, Geoffrey. "'Different from Writing': *Dracula* in 1897," *Literature and History,* 10 (1984): 15–23.

Walsh, Thomas P. "*Dracula*: Logos and Myth," *Research Studies,* 47 (1979): 229–237.

Waltje, Jorg. "Filming *Dracula*: Vampires, Genre, and Cinematography," *Journal of Dracula Studies,* 2 (2000): 24–33.

Warren, L. S. "Buffalo Bill Meets Dracula: William F. Cody, Bram Stoker and the Frontiers of Racial Decay," *American Historical Review,* 107 (2002): 1124–1157.

Wasson, Richard. "The Politics of *Dracula,*" *English Literature in Transition,* 9 (1966): 24–27.

Waters, Colin. *Whitby and the Dracula Connection.* Whitby, U.K.: Whitby Press, n.d.

Weinstock, J. "Circumcising Dracula," *Journal of the Fantastic in the Arts,* 12 (2001): 90–102.

Weissman, Judith. "Women as Vampires: *Dracula* as a Victorian Novel," *Midwest Quarterly,* 18 (1977): 392–405.

Wicke, Jennifer. "Vampiric Typewriting: *Dracula* and Its Media," *ELH,* 59 (1992): 467–493.

Williams, Anne. "*Dracula:* Si(g)ns of the Fathers," *Texas Studies in Literature and Language,* 33 (1991): 445–463.

Wilson, A. N. Introduction to *Dracula* by Stoker. Oxford: Oxford University Press, 1983.

Winthrop-Young, Geoffrey. "Undead Networks: Information Processing and Media Boundary Conflicts in *Dracula,*" in *Literature and Science,* edited by Donald Bruce and Anthony Purdy. Amsterdam: Rodopi, pp. 107–129.

Witalee, Janet, ed. Twentieth-Century Literary Criticism, volume 144. Farmingham Hills, Mich.: Gale, 2004.

Wixson, Kellie Donovan. "*Dracula:* An Anglo-Irish Gothic Novel," in *Dracula: The Shade and the Shadow,* edited by Miller. Westcliff-on-Sea, U.K.: Desert Island Books, 1998, pp. 247–256.

Wolf, Leonard. *Dracula: The Connoisseur's Guide.* New York: Broadway, 1997.

Wolf. *A Dream of Dracula: In Search of the Living Dead.* New York: Popular Library, 1972.

Wood, Robin. "Burying the Undead: The Use and Obsolescence of Count Dracula," *Mosaic,* 16 (1983): 175–187.

Zanger, Jules. "A Sympathetic Vibration: Dracula and the Jews," *English Literature in Transition 1880–1920,* 34 (1991): 33–44.

Selected Websites

Bram Stoker Organisation (Dublin) <www.bramstokercentre.org>.

The Dracula Library <www.cesnur.org/dracula_library.htm>.

The Dracula Society <www.thedraculasociety.org.uk>.

Dracula's Homepage <www.ucs.mun.ca/~emiller>.

Dracula's Page <www.english.ubc.ca/~gmbaxter/dracula.htm>.

Henry Irving Society <www.theirvingsociety.org.uk>.

Cumulative Index

Dictionary of Literary Biography, Volumes 1-304
Dictionary of Literary Biography Yearbook, 1980-2002
Dictionary of Literary Biography Documentary Series, Volumes 1-19
Concise Dictionary of American Literary Biography, Volumes 1-7
Concise Dictionary of British Literary Biography, Volumes 1-8
Concise Dictionary of World Literary Biography, Volumes 1-4

Cumulative Index

DLB before number: *Dictionary of Literary Biography,* Volumes 1-304
Y before number: *Dictionary of Literary Biography Yearbook,* 1980-2002
DS before number: *Dictionary of Literary Biography Documentary Series,* Volumes 1-19
CDALB before number: *Concise Dictionary of American Literary Biography,* Volumes 1-7
CDBLB before number: *Concise Dictionary of British Literary Biography,* Volumes 1-8
CDWLB before number: *Concise Dictionary of World Literary Biography,* Volumes 1-4

B

E

F

H

Cumulative Index

N

S

U

W

Cumulative Index

ISBN 0-7876-6841-9

90000